D1563858

The NEW ENCYCLOPEDIA *of* SOUTHERN CULTURE

VOLUME 12 : MUSIC

Volumes to appear in

The New Encyclopedia of Southern Culture

are:

The NEW

ENCYCLOPEDIA *of* SOUTHERN CULTURE

CHARLES REAGAN WILSON General Editor

JAMES G. THOMAS JR. Managing Editor

ANN J. ABADIE Associate Editor

VOLUME 12

Music

BILL C. MALONE Volume Editor

Sponsored by

THE CENTER FOR THE STUDY OF SOUTHERN CULTURE

at the University of Mississippi

THE UNIVERSITY OF NORTH CAROLINA PRESS

Chapel Hill

This book was published with the
assistance of the Anniversary Endowment Fund
of the University of North Carolina Press.

Designed by Richard Hendel
Set in Minion types by Tseng Information Systems, Inc.
Manufactured in the United States of America
The paper in this book meets the guidelines for permanence and
durability of the Committee on Production Guidelines for Book
Longevity of the Council on Library Resources.
The University of North Carolina Press has been a member of the
Green Press Initiative since 2003.
Library of Congress Cataloging-in-Publication Data
Music / Bill C. Malone, volume editor.
p. cm. — (The new encyclopedia of Southern culture ; v. 12)
"Sponsored by The Center for the Study of Southern Culture
at the University of Mississippi."
Includes bibliographical references and index.
ISBN 978-0-8078-3239-4 (alk. paper) —
ISBN 978-0-8078-5908-7 (pbk. : alk. paper)
1. Music—Southern States—Encyclopedias. 2. Music—Southern—
History—Encyclopedias. I. Malone, Bill C. II. University of
Mississippi. Center for the Study of Southern Culture. III. Series.
F209 .N47 2006 vol. 12
975.003 s—dc22
2008700086
The *Encyclopedia of Southern Culture*, sponsored by the Center for
the Study of Southern Culture at the University of Mississippi, was
published by the University of North Carolina Press in 1989.
cloth   12 11 10 09 08   5 4 3 2 1
paper   12 11 10 09 08   5 4 3 2 1

Tell about the South. What's it like there.

What do they do there. Why do they live there.

Why do they live at all.

WILLIAM FAULKNER

Absalom, Absalom!

CONTENTS

In 1989 years of planning and hard work came to fruition when the University of North Carolina Press joined the Center for the Study of Southern Culture at the University of Mississippi to publish the *Encyclopedia of Southern Culture*. While all those involved in writing, reviewing, editing, and producing the volume believed it would be received as a vital contribution to our understanding of the American South, no one could have anticipated fully the widespread acclaim it would receive from reviewers and other commentators. But the *Encyclopedia* was indeed celebrated, not only by scholars but also by popular audiences with a deep, abiding interest in the region. At a time when some people talked of the "vanishing South," the book helped remind a national audience that the region was alive and well, and it has continued to shape national perceptions of the South through the work of its many users—journalists, scholars, teachers, students, and general readers.

As the introduction to the *Encyclopedia* noted, its conceptualization and organization reflected a cultural approach to the South. It highlighted such issues as the core zones and margins of southern culture, the boundaries where "the South" overlapped with other cultures, the role of history in contemporary culture, and the centrality of regional consciousness, symbolism, and mythology. By 1989 scholars had moved beyond the idea of cultures as real, tangible entities, viewing them instead as abstractions. The *Encyclopedia*'s editors and contributors thus included a full range of social indicators, trait groupings, literary concepts, and historical evidence typically used in regional studies, carefully working to address the distinctive and characteristic traits that made the American South a particular place. The introduction to the *Encyclopedia* concluded that the fundamental uniqueness of southern culture was reflected in the volume's composite portrait of the South. We asked contributors to consider aspects that were unique to the region but also those that suggested its internal diversity. The volume was not a reference book of southern history, which explained something of the design of entries. There were fewer essays on colonial and antebellum history than on the postbellum and modern periods, befitting our conception of the volume as one trying not only to chart the cultural landscape of the South but also to illuminate the contemporary era.

When C. Vann Woodward reviewed the *Encyclopedia* in the *New York Review of Books*, he concluded his review by noting "the continued liveliness of interest in the South and its seeming inexhaustibility as a field of study." Research on the South, he wrote, furnishes "proof of the value of the *Encyclopedia* as a scholarly undertaking as well as suggesting future needs for revision or supplement to keep up with ongoing scholarship." The two decades since the publication of the *Encyclopedia of Southern Culture* have certainly suggested that Woodward was correct. The American South has undergone significant changes that make for a different context for the study of the region. The South has undergone social, economic, political, intellectual, and literary transformations, creating the need for a new edition of the *Encyclopedia* that will remain relevant to a changing region. Globalization has become a major issue, seen in the South through the appearance of Japanese automobile factories, Hispanic workers who have immigrated from Latin America or Cuba, and a new prominence for Asian and Middle Eastern religions that were hardly present in the 1980s South. The African American return migration to the South, which started in the 1970s, dramatically increased in the 1990s, as countless books simultaneously appeared asserting powerfully the claims of African Americans as formative influences on southern culture. Politically, southerners from both parties have played crucial leadership roles in national politics, and the Republican Party has dominated a near-solid South in national elections. Meanwhile, new forms of music, like hip-hop, have emerged with distinct southern expressions, and the term "dirty South" has taken on new musical meanings not thought of in 1989. New genres of writing by creative southerners, such as gay and lesbian literature and "white trash" writing, extend the southern literary tradition.

Meanwhile, as Woodward foresaw, scholars have continued their engagement with the history and culture of the South since the publication of the *Encyclopedia*, raising new scholarly issues and opening new areas of study. Historians have moved beyond their earlier preoccupation with social history to write new cultural history as well. They have used the categories of race, social class, and gender to illuminate the diversity of the South, rather than a unified "mind of the South." Previously underexplored areas within the field of southern historical studies, such as the colonial era, are now seen as formative periods of the region's character, with the South's positioning within a larger Atlantic world a productive new area of study. Cultural memory has become a major topic in the exploration of how the social construction of "the South" benefited some social groups and exploited others. Scholars in many disciplines have made the southern identity a major topic, and they have used a variety of methodologies to suggest what that identity has meant to different social groups. Literary critics have adapted cultural theories to the South and have raised the issue of postsouthern literature to a major category of concern as well as exploring the links between the literature of the American South and that of the Caribbean. Anthropologists have used different theoretical formulations from literary critics, providing models for their fieldwork in southern communities. In the past 30 years anthropologists have set increasing numbers of their ethnographic studies in the South, with many of them now exploring topics specifically linked to southern cultural issues. Scholars now place the Native American story, from prehistory to the contemporary era, as a central part of southern history. Comparative and interdisciplinary approaches to the South have encouraged scholars to look at such issues as the borders and boundaries of the South, specific places and spaces with distinct identities within the American South, and the global and transnational Souths, linking the American South with many formerly colonial societies around the world.

The first edition of the *Encyclopedia of Southern Culture* anticipated many of these approaches and indeed stimulated the growth of Southern Studies as a distinct interdisciplinary field. The Center for the Study of Southern Culture has worked for more than a quarter century to encourage research and teaching about the American South. Its academic programs have produced graduates who have gone on to write interdisciplinary studies of the South, while others have staffed the cultural institutions of the region and in turn encouraged those institutions to document and present the South's culture to broad public audiences. The center's conferences and publications have continued its long tradition of promoting understanding of the history, literature, and music of the South, with new initiatives focused on southern foodways, the future of the South, and the global Souths, expressing the center's mission to bring the best current scholarship to broad public audiences. Its documentary studies projects build oral and visual archives, and the New Directions in Southern Studies book series, published by the University of North Carolina Press, offers an important venue for innovative scholarship.

Since the *Encyclopedia of Southern Culture* appeared, the field of Southern Studies has dramatically developed, with an extensive network now of academic and research institutions whose projects focus specifically on the interdisciplinary study of the South. The Center for the Study of the American South at the University of North Carolina at Chapel Hill, led by Director Harry Watson and Associate Director and *Encyclopedia* coeditor William Ferris, publishes the lively journal *Southern Cultures* and is now at the organizational center of many other Southern Studies projects. The Institute for Southern Studies at the University of South Carolina, the Southern Intellectual History Circle, the Society for the Study of Southern Literature, the Southern Studies Forum of the European American Studies Association, Emory University's SouthernSpaces.org, and the South Atlantic Humanities Center (at the Virginia Foundation for the Humanities, the University of Virginia, and Virginia Polytechnic Institute and State University) express the recent expansion of interest in regional study.

Observers of the American South have had much to absorb, given the rapid pace of recent change. The institutional framework for studying the South is broader and deeper than ever, yet the relationship between the older verities of regional study and new realities remains unclear. Given the extent of changes in the American South and in Southern Studies since the publication of the *Encyclopedia of Southern Culture*, the need for a new edition of that work is clear. Therefore, the Center for the Study of Southern Culture has once again joined the University of North Carolina Press to produce *The New Encyclopedia of Southern Culture*. As readers of the original edition will quickly see, *The New Encyclopedia* follows many of the scholarly principles and editorial conventions established in the original, but with one key difference; rather than being published in a single hardback volume, *The New Encyclopedia* is presented in a series of shorter individual volumes that build on the 24 original subject categories used in the *Encyclopedia* and adapt them to new scholarly developments. Some earlier *Encyclopedia* categories have been reconceptualized in light of new academic interests. For example, the subject section originally titled "Women's Life" is reconceived as a new volume, *Gender*, and the original "Black Life" section is more broadly interpreted as a volume on race. These changes reflect new analytical concerns that place the study of women and blacks in broader cultural systems, reflecting the emergence of, among other topics, the study of male culture and of whiteness. Both volumes draw as well from the rich recent scholarship on women's life and black life. In addition, topics with some thematic coherence are combined in a volume, such as *Law and Politics* and *Agriculture and Industry*. One new topic, *Foodways*, is the basis of a separate volume, reflecting its new prominence in the interdisciplinary study of southern culture.

Numerous individual topical volumes together make up *The New Encyclopedia of Southern Culture* and extend the reach of the reference work to wider audiences. This approach should enhance the use of the *Encyclopedia* in academic courses and is intended to be convenient for readers with more focused interests within the larger context of southern culture. Readers will have handy access to one-volume, authoritative, and comprehensive scholarly treatments of the major areas of southern culture.

We have been fortunate that, in nearly all cases, subject consultants who offered crucial direction in shaping the topical sections for the original edition have agreed to join us in this new endeavor as volume editors. When new volume editors have been added, we have again looked for respected figures who can provide not only their own expertise but also strong networks of scholars to help develop relevant lists of topics and to serve as contributors in their areas. The reputations of all our volume editors as leading scholars in their areas encouraged the contributions of other scholars and added to *The New Encyclopedia*'s authority as a reference work.

The New Encyclopedia of Southern Culture builds on the strengths of articles in the original edition in several ways. For many existing articles, original authors agreed to update their contributions with new interpretations and theoretical perspectives, current statistics, new bibliographies, or simple factual developments that needed to be included. If the original contributor was unable to update an article, the editorial staff added new material or sent it to another scholar for assessment. In some cases, the general editor and volume editors selected a new contributor if an article seemed particularly dated and new work indicated the need for a fresh perspective. And importantly, where new developments have warranted treatment of topics not addressed in the original edition, volume editors have commissioned entirely new essays and articles that are published here for the first time.

The American South embodies a powerful historical and mythical presence, both a complex environmental and geographic landscape and a place of the imagination. Changes in the region's contemporary socioeconomic realities and new developments in scholarship have been incorporated in the conceptualization and approach of *The New Encyclopedia of Southern Culture*. Anthropologist Clifford Geertz has spoken of culture as context, and this encyclopedia looks at the American South as a complex place that has served as the context for cultural expression. This volume provides information and perspective on the diversity of cultures in a geographic and imaginative place with a long history and distinctive character.

The *Encyclopedia of Southern Culture* was produced through major grants from the Program for Research Tools and Reference Works of the National Endowment for the Humanities, the Ford Foundation, the Atlantic-Richfield Foundation, and the Mary Doyle Trust. We are grateful as well to the College of Liberal Arts at the University of Mississippi for support and to the individual donors to the Center for the Study of Southern Culture who have directly or indirectly supported work on *The New Encyclopedia of Southern Culture*. We thank the volume editors for their ideas in reimagining their subjects and the contributors of articles for their work in extending the usefulness of the book in new ways. We acknowledge the support and contributions of the faculty and staff at the Center for the Study of Southern Culture. Finally, we want especially to honor the work of William Ferris and Mary Hart on the *Encyclopedia of Southern Culture*. Bill, the founding director of the Center for the Study of Southern Culture, was coeditor, and his good work recruiting authors, editing text, selecting images, and publicizing the volume among a wide network of people was, of course, invaluable. Despite the many changes in the new encyclopedia, Bill's influence remains. Mary "Sue" Hart was also an invaluable member of the original encyclopedia team, bringing the careful and precise eye of the librarian, and an iconoclastic spirit, to our work.

Any accounting of the cultural contributions of the American South must rank music near the top of the list. The region had a lively folk music from early on and then in the 20th century produced some of the nation's most acclaimed musical talent. Indeed, much of the most popular American music came out of the South, whether New Orleans jazz, Nashville's country music, the Delta's blues, or Memphis's rock and roll. The two dominant demographic groups, whites from Western Europe and blacks from West Africa, contributed core features to the South's musical culture, but the contributions of other ethnic groups also were part of the mix, sometimes producing such distinctive genres as Cajun music and *música tejana*. Places within the South produced distinctive forms, as seen in Piedmont blues, western Kentucky's bluegrass, or Birmingham's black gospel. H. L. Mencken, the South's sharpest critic in the early 20th century, famously indicted the region for its lack of musical talent as well as lack of poets, but he only mentioned oboe players as an example. Still, his criticism rightly pointed to the difficulties of a poverty-stricken, rural region, like the South of the early 20th century, in fostering the infrastructure to support such "high art" forms as symphonies and dance troupes. The South, nonetheless, has a long tradition in those areas as well, one that has become more accomplished in the contemporary period, all of which is chronicled in this volume.

The music section of the *Encyclopedia of Southern Culture* in 1989 had more entries than any other section, reflecting the recognition of the editors that the region's musical creativity had reached a special level of achievement. Selecting a core group for biographical treatment was difficult, even given the large number of entries we allotted for that subject. The region has produced so many outstanding musicians that picking a core group to study remains a challenge. This volume of *The New Encyclopedia of Southern Culture* includes updated, substantial thematic entries in the major genres of music in the South, including more attention to such African American musical styles as soul music, R&B, and, more recently, hip-hop and rap. Indeed, the latter essay is particularly revealing of how the South continues to nurture a distinctive form of black music that was once thought to be characteristic only of inner-city northern and western urban areas. New topical entries include diverse musical instruments (accordion, mandolin), places (Muscle Shoals Sound, Nashville Sound, New Orleans Sound), and media (*Austin City Limits*, *Hee Haw*).

The editors offer a generous serving of biographical entries, which sometimes recognize figures that were overlooked in the earlier encyclopedia (Johnny Cash, DeFord Bailey), sometimes focus more attention on women performers (Tammy Wynette, "Big Mama" Thornton), sometimes suggest a surprising range of people whose performances were shaped by the South (Alvin Ailey, Dinah Shore), sometimes expand our coverage of key genres (more entries on gospel music), and certainly expand the coverage of contemporary performers, from Arrested Development to R.E.M. to Lucinda Williams.

Music kept the beat as Civil War soldiers marched off to battle, and freedom songs inspired civil rights activists a century later. Music brought economic opportunities to countless poor southerners with few alternatives to sharecropping or grueling factory work, empowering them in the process. Music has brought comfort to people suffering from economic hardship, geographical isolation, and racial injustice. Music has expressed the spiritual outlook for generations of southerners. As new immigrants have come to the South in greater numbers in the last decade, the region is set to become a new crucible for the creation of musical sounds that reflect its people's lives.

MUSIC

For more than a century and a half, the South has fired the imagination of musicians and songwriters. As a land of romance and enchantment and as the home of exotic people—both black and white—the South has inspired a seemingly unending body of songs that speak longingly of old Virginia or the hills of Caroline, while also singing the praises of the region's towns, counties, hills, rivers, bayous, plains, and people. As a source of songs and musical images, the South has inspired a veritable industry of songwriters, from Stephen Foster, Will Hays, and Dan Emmett in the 19th century, to Johnny Mercer, Hoagy Carmichael, Allen Toussaint, Tom T. Hall, Dolly Parton, Hank Williams Jr., Robbie Robertson, and Randy Newman in our own time. Visions of lonesome pines, lazy rivers, snow-white cotton fields, smoky mountains, hanging moss, and eccentric gothic-styled characters have forever ignited the creativity of America's poets and lyricists, while also fulfilling the fantasies of an audience that prefers to believe there is a land where time moves slowly, where life is lived simply and elementally, and whose inhabitants hold clearly defined values and dearly love to make music.

Southerners *have* made music, and many of them have performed it with distinction, thereby contributing immeasurably to the making and enrichment of American music as a whole. Singers, songwriters, musicians, merchandisers (promoters and record producers), folklorists, and others whose lives in some way intersect with music have proliferated in the South. Some performers, of course—like Mary Martin, Kate Smith, and Ann Miller—have carried little of the South in their styles. Nevertheless, like classical pianist Van Cliburn or opera singer Leontyne Price, many have become internationally famous. The success enjoyed by such musicians has been immensely satisfying to the regional pride of southerners, but these entertainers project little regional identity. On the other hand, such singers as Jimmie Rodgers, Bessie Smith, Mahalia Jackson, Elvis Presley, Hank Williams, Ray Charles, James Brown, and Charlie Daniels have exhibited southernness in their dialects and lifestyles. And their music has, for the most part, embodied styles of performance that were indigenous to or deeply rooted in the South. A few performers, such as Charlie Daniels, Hank Williams Jr., and the "southern rock" musicians, have been self-consciously southern in their aggressive "nationalism" or "regionalism." Con-

Squatter's son with a new guitar, Shenandoah Valley, Va., 1935 (Arthur Rothstein, photographer, Library of Congress [LC-USF-33-2184-MS], Washington, D.C.)

sequently, many of the dominant American music styles of the 20th and 21st centuries—from country to jazz—have been southern in origin.

The folk South has given the nation much of its music. America has been blessed by the infusions of many southern-derived styles of music, from blues to Cajun and Tex-Mex, and each has its own special features. Nevertheless, they share an interrelatedness that reflects the pluralism of the culture. The folk South has been basically biracial, that is, its basic components have been Afro-American and Anglo-American, cultures that in turn were never "pure" but were instead composites of Old World and American elements. Blacks and whites have shared music with each other since the colonial era. A "common folk pool" of songs and instruments, strongly audible in the 19th century but still exhibiting strength in our own time, reminds one of the mutual interchange that has long occurred among southerners of all racial and ethnic backgrounds.

Although many scholars have argued convincingly that the African admixture has made southern music distinctive and appealing (syncopation, improvisation, blue notes), other groups have contributed much of importance to the shaping of regional music forms. Pockets of "ethnic" music have existed all over the South (Czech, German, Polish, Tex-Mex, Cajun). The Germans made important contributions to music at the folk, popular, and high-art levels, through shape-note hymnody in the Shenandoah Valley; folk dances such as the "Herr Schmidt," the schottische, and the polka; accordion traditions in Louisiana and south Texas; music publishing houses; music societies; and roles as teachers and classical musicians. Cajuns created a distinctive mélange of country, pop, and blues music in southwest Louisiana and exported it to southeast Texas and the Mississippi-Alabama Gulf Coast. French-speaking black people in Louisiana and Texas, in turn, created their own exciting fusion, a popular style known as zydeco (a mixture of rhythm and blues and Cajun, with "French" lyrics). Since the 1920s, elements of the Cajun and zydeco styles have made their way, via commercial exposure, into the national pop-culture mainstream.

Folk culture was never isolated from the world at large. Music has moved back and forth across the thin and imaginary line that separates folk and popular culture. The folk, in fact, borrowed much from both high-art and popular sources. Some rural dances were of middle- or upper-class origins. The square dance came from the cotillion; the black cakewalk was a burlesque of formal white dancing; the Virginia reel was a variation of the upper-class dance called the Sir Roger de Coverley. Many fiddle tunes that have become hallowed in the folk-rural tradition, such as "Under the Double Eagle" and "Red Wing," came from marches or pop tunes, and many other "folk" songs came from "popular" composers. The blackface minstrel shows of the mid- and late 19th century repeatedly introduced items—such as the five-string banjo, instrumental and vocal styles, songs, dances, comedy—that were preserved in southern rural culture. Some songs collected from black informants in the late 19th century, or from the ex-slave narratives collected by WPA workers in the 1930s, actually began their lives on the minstrel stage. Furthermore, the Chautauqua tents, medicine shows, tent-rep shows, vaudeville, and the popular music industry all introduced styles and songs that became part of the southern folk process.

Many songs that rural southerners cherished and preserved started out on Tin Pan Alley and were published as sheet music designed for urban, middle-class consumers. Songs such as "The Letter Edged in Black," "Little Rosewood Casket," "I'll Be All Smiles Tonight," "The Blind Child," and "Wildwood Flower" celebrated the values of family, home, church, and traditional human relationships or bemoaned their disintegration, and these songs found a welcome reception among rural and small-town southerners. Their descendants still preserve the songs in bluegrass and old-time country music.

Outsiders originally perceived "southern" music as "black" music, and the imagery surrounding the music often projected plantation scenes with happy or doleful "darkies." The presumption that blacks were musical was made very early in American history. Captains of slave ships, slave traders, plantation

Child with phonograph, Transylvania, La., 1939 (Russell Lee, photographer,
Library of Congress [LC-USF-34-31941-D], Washington, D.C.)

masters and overseers, travelers, and others who came in contact with slaves
often commented on black musicality, as did Thomas Jefferson in his *Notes on
the State of Virginia* (1784). Blackface minstrelsy profited greatly from public
perceptions concerning black music, but considerable doubt exists about how
much of the minstrel repertoire really came from black or southern sources
(the minstrel men, who were mostly northern-born entertainers, borrowed
from all kinds of sources, pop and folk, and from cultures outside the South).
Whatever the source, minstrel material moved back into the South and permanently influenced the music made there.

Authentic black musicians eventually profited from an association with minstrelsy. Such black groups as the Georgia Minstrels began flourishing after the
Civil War. As late as the 1920s, many black entertainers still called themselves
"minstrels." Both blessings and burdens obviously accompanied the minstrel
association. Blacks obtained an entrée into the world of show business, but they
also carried with them some of the degrading aspects of minstrelsy—the blacking of their faces with cork or some other substance and the depiction of blacks
as comic characters (practices that carried over into the "coon song" era).

Black musicians made their first real breakthrough into the realm of American popular culture in the late 19th century, a process that flowed through two important channels—high-art cultivation and sponsorship and the "underground" movement of black musicians into new geographical regions. The American fine-arts establishment discovered black music in the famous "spirituals." These songs appeared in print in scattered sources before the 1860s, but their real introduction to the northern literati came through the groundbreaking collection *Slave Songs from the Southern United States* (compiled by three missionaries to the freedmen and published in 1867). Nevertheless, the songs remained known to only a few people until the 1870s, when a small choir of black students from Fisk University in Nashville popularized the spirituals in the North and, eventually, in Europe. By the turn of the century, such songs as "Go Down, Moses" and "Swing Low, Sweet Chariot" were being performed on the concert stage and in symphonic arrangements. In content and style the spirituals represented a major slice of black folk culture, but they did not tell the whole story of black musical life or even of black religious expression.

Meanwhile, black musicians were insinuating themselves into the popular consciousness of American life, well apart from the activities of the high-art establishment (but certainly not apart from the influence of commercial white culture). Emancipation saw the migration of black musicians from the country to town, from town to town, to other parts of the South, and ultimately to cities all over the North. Southerners, of course, heard black musicians everywhere— on street corners, on work gangs, at public gatherings, and in religious settings. But black musicians who hoped to make money at their trade, or to attain some kind of independence, moved into the honky-tonks, saloons, brothels, juke joints, and medicine shows or into minstrelsy or black vaudeville. Often, as in the brothels of New Orleans or in the clubs of St. Louis, the audiences were white or mixed. In areas of high black population density, such as the Mississippi Delta, or in institutions where a white presence was rare, such as the black church, musicians were free to be as expressive as they desired. Presumably, a higher percentage of African traits were preserved in such environments than in regions where blacks and whites mingled freely. Most black musicians, however—whether religious or secular—tended to have different repertoires, and even performing styles, for white and black audiences.

Black musicians demonstrated a mastery of any instrument with which they came in contact. Pianists, though, made the first big musical impact on American life. Barrelhouse pianists roamed through the Southwest and up the rivers, laying the basis for a variety of modern styles such as "fast western" and "boogie-woogie." Piano players proliferated in the "sporting houses" of New Orleans, Kansas City, St. Louis, Sedalia, and other cities, playing a mixture of pop, ragtime, and blues. Some of them, including Ferdinand "Jelly Roll" Morton, one of the creators and pillars of early jazz, became famous.

Black piano styles influenced most musicians who heard them, and they gradually began to make their way into mainstream American music, particularly after World War I, when the nation became jazz crazy. Jazz, though, was preceded by ragtime, another piano-based musical phenomenon that took the country by storm at the end of the 19th century. Itinerant piano players, mostly black, created the style out of folk rhythms. Scott Joplin, who was one of them, put many of these "rags" down on paper and worked to convert them into classical forms. His "Maple Leaf Rag" became a national hit, and by 1900 ragtime was the popular rage. White songwriters and musicians, such as Irving Berlin in "Alexander's Ragtime Band," appropriated the name, if not always the true style, of ragtime. Songwriters, both white and black, who wrote for Broadway or Tin Pan Alley, combined the ragtime style with lyrics about "Negro life." The results were the "coon songs"—songs that perpetuated myths and stereotypes of black people (the myth of a childlike but musical people).

By the beginning of the 1920s, black musical styles had made major inroads into American cultural life at both the "serious" and the "popular" levels. Blues music was also achieving considerable popularity, largely through the work of W. C. Handy and pieces like "St. Louis Blues." Mainstream white performers often did ragtime, jazz, or blues numbers—or songs that were influenced by them. White audiences, then, had considerable exposure to "black" musical expressions, although many people heard such music only through "slumming" (visits to Negro juke joints or to other places of "unrespectable," "naughty," entertainment). Americans associated black music with images of exotic southern life on plantations and in juke joints. Sheet music often reinforced these romantic notions with illustrations of alleged southern scenes, and, in the popular mind, black music and southern music were synonymous.

When the full-scale commercialization of southern music came in the 1920s, most Americans already had strong preconceptions about the South and its music. Southern musical styles could not help but be colored by such images, and the musicians and their commercial promoters responded to these southern-spiced images. Commercialization was made possible by major innovations in media dissemination in the United States. Radio broadcasts and phonograph recordings, above all, made possible the maturation and dissemination of southern-born musical styles. The media exploitation of grassroots music had both positive and negative consequences. Media coverage promoted the standardization and homogenization of styles and weakened local or regional traits. On the other hand, it also presented such styles to a larger audi-

B. B. King with band, c. 1955, photograph on a wall at Club Paradise, Memphis (William R. Ferris
Collection, Southern Folklife Collection, Wilson Library, University of North Carolina at Chapel Hill)

ence, encouraged professionalization, and promoted the cross-fertilization
of musical styles. Musicians learned from each other, and they became more
acutely conscious of audience tastes. Some styles died or remained only locally
rooted; others achieved new life and developed healthy and strong variations.

The 1920s saw the "discovery" and commercialization of a wide variety of
"ethnic" music forms, as well as most of the grassroots genres of the South: jazz,
blues, gospel (black and white), Cajun, German, Czech, Tex-Mex, and hillbilly.
The first significant southern band to be recorded did so more or less by accident. The Dixieland Jazz Band, a group of white boys from New Orleans, was
playing in clubs in Chicago when it made its first recordings in 1917. The band
made the nation jazz conscious, while also popularizing the word "jazz" itself.
Not until 1923 did the first all-black jazz band, that of King Oliver, also playing
in Chicago, make its first recordings. By the middle of the 1920s, jazz was burgeoning, both in the United States and in Europe, and was attracting aficionados and musicians elsewhere. The musical form moved away quickly from its
folk and southern roots, but southerners continued to play invaluable roles in
its development. The first star of this exciting style, for example, was the New
Orleans–born trumpeter Louis Armstrong.

Blues also won great popularity during the 1920s, partly through its alliance

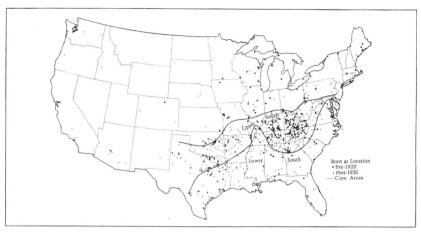

Map 1. *Birthplace of Country Music Performers, 1870–1970. Map by George O. Carney. Source: John F. Rooney Jr., Wilbur Zelinsky, and Dean R. Louder, eds.,* This Remarkable Continent: An Atlas of United States and Canadian Society and Cultures *(1982).*

with jazz. The composer and bandleader W. C. Handy had earlier contributed greatly to the form's popularity, but radio and recording did the most to make Americans conscious of this infectious musical art form. The first blues singers to become highly visible in American popular culture were black women who sang generally to the accompaniment of pianos or jazz bands. These classic blues singers, led principally by the "Empress of the Blues," Bessie Smith, were performers who usually had considerable experience in black vaudeville or on medicine shows. In 1926, however, with the recording of the Texas-born Blind Lemon Jefferson, a guitarist with a supple, wailing vocal style, American entertainment received its first strong infusion of rural black music. This body of musical performance has generally been described as the "country blues"—a predominantly masculine style, usually accompanied by guitars or other string instruments, with rural-folk inflections.

The wide variety of black folk styles that became commercialized in the 1920s came to be subsumed under the rubric of "race music." Not all performers were blues singers. Some were "songsters," that is, entertainers who performed many different styles and songs, usually for both white and black audiences. But they and the jug bands, string bands, pianists, and gospel singers were advertised in the same record catalogs. And of course most of them shared musical traits, because styles flowed freely from entertainer to entertainer. Gospel musicians, for example, might assert their estrangement from the world, but "worldly" musical riffs and phrases constantly intruded into their songs and performances,

LOCATION OF BIRTHPLACES, 1890-1920

MILES

Map 2. Distribution of Blues People. Map by George O. Carney. Source: John F. Rooney Jr.,
Wilbur Zelinsky, and Dean R. Louder, eds., This Remarkable Continent: An Atlas of
United States and Canadian Society and Cultures (1982).

just as musical ideas born in the church have always affected the performances
made by secular black musicians.

Given the reputation for musicianship that white country entertainers enjoy
today, white folk music was discovered remarkably late. When hillbilly music
was first recorded in the 1920s, only 20 years or so had elapsed since the first
faint glimmers of recognition of "mountain music" or "Anglo-American balladry" occurred. White folk music really went unrecognized until the 20th century. Only an occasional traveler, missionary, or local colorist made reference to
frolics, country dances, singing schools, or camp meetings. One receives little
understanding from these accounts of how the music was performed or what
was performed (even though the social context of such performances is sometimes well described).

The discovery of white folk music came in the years before World War I.
The perception that such music was a resource worthy of preservation came
in the context of the rapid industrialization of the nation, the "new" immi-
gration, the rise of cities, and other related factors that seemed to bode ill for
the continued existence of rural, peasant-derived culture. Folklorists and other
interested people sought to preserve folk music before it succumbed to modern
forces. They viewed such music as a static and pure phenomenon, and as the
product of a racially homogeneous, that is, Anglo-Saxon, culture. Some high-

art musicians and composers eagerly utilized folk music for artistic purposes, presenting arrangements of it in concerts and recitals and arguing, as did John Powell of Virginia, that it might make the basis of a national music.

Two famous collectors, John A. Lomax and Cecil Sharp, did the most to demonstrate the wealth of folk music that still existed in the United States. Lomax's *Cowboy Songs and Other Frontier Ballads* (1910) profited from the popular and romantic perception of cowboys as white knights or Anglo-Saxon heroes—even though cowboy culture was racially and ethnically eclectic and the songs themselves came from diverse sources. Cowboy songs soon made their way into the larger society, through the high-art concerts of such musicians as Oscar Fox and David Guion, the phonograph recordings of singers like Bentley Ball and Carl Sprague, and the performances of a multitude of radio and movie cowboys.

Cecil Sharp was primarily a student of folk dance in his native England. Largely through the influence of Olive Dame Campbell, a settlement school-teacher in the Kentucky hills, Sharp traveled through much of southern Appalachia between 1916 and 1918, with his assistant Maud Karpeles, collecting ballads and folk songs. Sharp's expedition came a few years after local color writers and journalists had inspired a vogue for the folkways of the southern mountains. Writers of fiction created images of mountaineers in the 19th century that flowed into American popular culture. With images of a "strange and peculiar people" living in a land where "time stood still," who had preserved "Elizabethan folkways," the local colorists popularized a body of perceptions that influenced the attitudes that surrounded the music. The music was perceived as the product of a dying culture—a body of ballads and folk songs that needed to be collected with great urgency.

Although the local-color literature prompted visions of a static culture, Sharp discovered that singing was common to both young and old in the mountain areas that he visited. He noted that many of the oldest British folk songs still endured in variant forms. Sharp made great contributions to folk music scholarship, but his work nevertheless had serious omissions. He ignored religious songs and instrumental dance tunes, although both traditions were very strong in the southern hills. The scholarship and song performance (by serious recitalists) that he inspired long reflected Sharp's critical judgments. When the first "hillbilly" records were made in the 1920s, the reactions made to them by scholars, collectors, critics, and the recording men themselves were affected by prior perceptions of mountain folk music.

Almost as soon as radio stations opened in the South in the 1920s, they began using live, local talent—string bands, fiddlers, family gospel groups, yodelers,

"Hawaiian" bands. Many of the acts appeared on an irregular, unplanned basis, but some stations, led by WBAP in Fort Worth in 1923, created barn dance formats—regular, weekly performances of down-home entertainment. By the middle of the decade, phonograph companies also began recording such talent, and the resulting "industry" was described by several terms, the most common of which was "hillbilly." The hillbilly music of the 1920s and 1930s reveals a white folk culture far different from that described by Cecil Sharp or by the romantic Anglo-Saxonists. Neither the culture nor the music was ethnically or racially homogeneous, nor were they static. Most crucially, both the music and the culture from which it derived were strongly shaped by commercialization and technology. The music was simultaneously conservative, eclectic, and absorptive; it came from many sources.

All southern musical genres underwent extensive change and experienced some degree of national expansion during the 1930s and 1940s. Expanded radio coverage introduced southern musicians to audiences in every corner of the United States and in Canada. American business often became allied with grassroots music, and the resulting advertising was mutually beneficial to both music and commerce. Radio programming also prompted the expansion of personal appearances, and promoters and booking agents moved to exploit the developing interest. Hollywood played a major role in making musicians visible to the outside world. Musicians of all types—from Louis Armstrong to Roy Acuff—occasionally appeared in short features or sometimes played roles in full-length films. Singing cowboys, of course—led originally by Gene Autry in 1934—constituted a distinct genre of filmmaking up to the early 1950s. Because of this exposure, Autry may very well have been the best-known southern-born musician in the world.

The heightened commercialization of these decades, along with the consequent competition among musicians, encouraged major stylistic innovations that have ever since been part of the nation's music. Performances in nightclubs, bars, and honky-tonks—all of which proliferated after the repeal of Prohibition in 1933—required louder and more percussive sounds. Drums and string basses became common in all kinds of bands, and electric instruments began to make their way into musical organizations by the middle of the 1930s. Pioneering musicians, such as steel guitarist Bob Dunn, experimented with amplifiers and homemade electric pickups, but by the end of the decade guitar manufacturers were merchandising their own lines of electrified instruments. Fledgling musicians everywhere were introduced to electric guitars through the performances of such great southern performers as Dunn, Charlie Christian, and Aaron "T-Bone" Walker.

Guitar on the wall of a house in Tutwiler, Miss., 1968 (William R. Ferris Collection, Southern Folklife Collection, Wilson Library, University of North Carolina at Chapel Hill)

World War II and the years immediately following it saw the nationalization of southern music. The migrations made by civilians and servicemen during those years—to the cities, to the North, and around the world—did much to transport southern-born styles to other areas, while also bringing southerners in direct contact with other forms of music. Black migration to the North and to the West Coast had begun much earlier but was particularly strong during the World War II era. Migration encouraged a new consciousness among young black people, and life in the American ghettoes inspired musical experimentation. Although both black gospel music and the blues had southern rural roots, they achieved new vitality in the segregated neighborhoods of the cities. Georgia-born Tom Dorsey and Louisiana native Mahalia Jackson, for example, contributed greatly to the emergence of modern black gospel music through their work in the churches of Chicago and other cities of the North. Other black migrants in such urban areas as Chicago, Detroit, Los Angeles, and Harlem were far less spiritual than Mahalia, but no less influential and innovative. They created the aggressive, electrified version of blues known as rhythm and blues, as well as its many offshoots, such as rock and roll, soul, and the Motown Sound.

A multitude of small record labels appeared after the war, in and outside the South, which catered to the grassroots music styles of the region. Meanwhile, the big record labels found increasing commercial success with such southern musicians as Hank Williams, Eddy Arnold, Louis Jordan, and Elvis Presley. Although most earlier recordings of southern talent had taken place in cities like New York, Chicago, or Los Angeles, or in makeshift "studios" hastily assembled by traveling record men in southern towns, postwar recording tended increasingly to be in such southern cities as Dallas, Houston, New Orleans, Memphis, Macon, Muscle Shoals, and Nashville. Nashville became one of the three or four leading music centers in the nation, first on the strength of the talent affiliated with the *Grand Ole Opry* and later through the recording of all kinds of music. Memphis did not rival Nashville as a music center, but it was the birthplace of a musical revolution that swept across the world. In 1954, Sam Phillips recorded Elvis Presley for his Sun label and saw that exciting singer become the vanguard of what soon became known as rock and roll. Elvis, Carl Perkins, Jerry Lee Lewis, Johnny Cash, Roy Orbison, and other Sun label "rockabillies" joined with such musicians as Buddy Holly and the Everly Brothers to popularize a fusion of hillbilly and rhythm and blues that was redolent of the working-class South and its musical eclecticism and an element of the social revolution that began to take place in the lives of young people throughout the nation.

Since the 1950s, southern-born music styles have flowered commercially and become popular around the world. None, however, have remained "pure," and each has spawned a variety of offshoots or substylings, which run the gamut from the "traditional" to the "progressive." The Cajun and *música tejana* (Tex-Mex) styles have remained vital in the communities and barrios of southwest Louisiana and south Texas but have also won popularity throughout the United States. Folk festival performances in Newport, Washington, D.C., and other cities, along with exposure on such nationally syndicated television shows as *Austin City Limits*, have permitted entertainers like the Balfa Brothers, Clifton Chenier, and Flaco Jiménez to attract converts from all regions of the nation. Although these styles have mixed with other musical forms that were around them and have both influenced and been influenced by them—the accordion's centrality in Cajun, German, and Mexican *conjunto* bands is illustrative—they nevertheless maintain the imprint of the cultures that gave them birth.

Other southern-born styles have been less successful in maintaining regional identity. Indeed, the promise of national acceptance and prosperity has inspired deliberate efforts by musicians and promoters alike to create products with broad appeal and limited sociocultural identification. The goal is the homogenized mainstream and Grammy nominations, and the vehicles for such exposure are the crossover record or CD, the Top 40 radio music format, and the television special. Many people in country music (the term that has been used since the early 1950s to describe the hillbilly field) have campaigned for

The Soul Stirrers, southern gospel group, c. 1950
(Ray Funk Collection, Fairbanks, Alaska)

the use of the word "American" to designate their music (seemingly oblivious to the existence of *many* American styles of music). Only one musical genre, southern gospel, consciously gives itself a southern label, an effort to distinguish its music from the mélange of modern pop religious sounds known as "Christian contemporary." The gospel quartets clearly have been influenced by other styles of music, but they nevertheless still convey the flavor of singing conventions and old-time evangelism. The Christian contemporary musicians, on the other hand, exude the sounds and flavor of pop radio and soft rock culture, an ambience that has no regional identification.

In all honesty, it has become increasingly difficult to find a regional identification in any form of American music any longer. Ethnic or racial identification, yes, but really nothing that imparts a distinct southern flavor. Many country musicians still sing with the "twang" that detractors use to describe them, and they often inject southern themes or places into their lyrics, but their instrumentation defies a regional identity. Some country musicians, like Hank Williams Jr. and Charlie Daniels, spice their repertoires with songs like "Dixie on My Mind" and "The South's Gonna Do It Again" and adopt aggressive pro-southern postures in their stage shows and publicity. Confederate flags abound at their shows and on the merchandise that they market. Like the southern rock musicians with whom they generally align, Williams and Daniels project a machismo and hedonism that are generally associated with southern masculinity. Their music, on the other hand, while infused with the blues, sounds little different from that made by other rock musicians from other regions.

Country music has prospered as an industry and has won a respect that scarcely seemed possible back in its hillbilly and honky-tonk days. But no field of music has been more torn by debates concerning loss of identity. Nashville is still the commercial capital of country music, but the city periodically encounters some competition from places such as Austin, Tex., where healthy artistic alternatives are presented. Much of the music now bearing the "country" label has little relationship to southern, rural, or working-class life but instead is aimed at middle-class suburban listeners who presumably have little regional or class identification. Nevertheless, tradition-based sounds and styles still prevail—as seen in the enduring popularity of the acoustic-oriented bluegrass field, in the proliferation of festivals such as MerleFest in Wilkesboro, N.C. (a hugely popular event hosted by Doc Watson), that are devoted to "roots" styles or old-time music, and in the commercial success enjoyed periodically by such "neo-traditionalists" as Alan Jackson, Tim O'Brien, Gillian Welch, Patty Loveless, and Brad Paisley. A string band movement, featuring fiddles, banjos, and old-time dance tunes, has also exhibited energy and strength in the early years of the 21st century. Although Nashville and the country music industry paid scant attention to it, the sound track from the movie *O Brother, Where Art Thou?*, an assemblage of bluegrass and old-time songs, sold millions of copies after it was released in 2000. A touring concert called Down from the Mountain, featuring songs and singers heard on the sound track, also won widespread popularity in the two years that followed. Few events have provided such emphatic evidence that the roots music of the South and the romantic imagery that surrounds it are still irresistible to multitudes of people around the world.

We must conclude that southern music is now American music. Southerners have exported their musical treasures to the world and have in turn absorbed much that the larger world has to offer. The resulting syntheses continue to provide enjoyment and enrichment. Southern styles may not be as distinctive as many people would like, and observers might with good reason bemoan their dilution and disappearance, but one can scarcely ignore the fact that the folk cultures that produced them are undergoing similar dissolution. Happily, much of the best of the older traditions—such as old-time fiddling, clog dancing, and sacred harp singing—are being preserved and revitalized by interested groups, and increasing numbers of young people are being won over to the old-time arts. The dominant commercial styles, on the other hand, continue to evolve in ways that reflect the growing homogenization of American life and the immediate awareness of musical styles made possible by modern media technology. Within the realm of commercial music, such musicians as the blues guitarist Stevie Ray Vaughan and the eclectic country stylist Tim O'Brien have proved that it is still possible to create new, exciting, and commercially successful sounds by building on the time-tested musical formulas of the past. Finally, regardless of the directions its musicians may take in the years to come, the South will not soon lose its romantic aura nor its capacity to evoke mythmaking and popular imagery. The South will sing, and it will be sung about.

BILL C. MALONE
Madison, Wisconsin

Lynn Abbott and Doug Seroff, *Ragged but Right: Black Traveling Shows, "Coon Songs," and the Dark Pathway to Blues and Jazz* (2007); Roger Abrahams and George Foss, *Anglo-American Folksong Style* (1968); Bob Artis, *Bluegrass: From the Lonesome Wail of a Mountain Love Song to the Hammering Drive of the Scruggs-Style Banjo; The Story of an American Musical Tradition* (1975); Earl Bargainneer, *Mississippi Quarterly* (Fall 1977); Carl Belz, *The Story of Rock* (1969); Michael T. Bertrand, *Race, Rock, and Elvis* (2000); Lois S. Blackwell, *The Wings of the Dove: The Story of Gospel Music in America* (1978); Rudi Blesh, *Shining Trumpets: A History of Jazz* (1958), with Harriet Janis, *They All Played Ragtime* (1966); John Broven, *Walking to New Orleans: The Story of New Orleans Rhythm and Blues* (1974); Harry O. Brunn, *The Story of the Original Dixieland Jazz Band* (1960); Robert Cantwell, *Bluegrass Breakdown: The Making of the Old Southern Sound* (1984); Samuel Charters, *The Bluesmen: The Story and the Music of the Men Who Made the Blues* (1967), *The Country Blues* (1959); Cecelia Conway, *African Banjo Echoes in Appalachia: A Study of Folk Traditions* (1995); Ronald Davis, *A History of Opera in the American West* (1965); Bill Ellis, *Journal of American Folklore* (April–June 1978); Dena J. Epstein, *Sinful Tunes and Spirituals: Black Folk Music to the Civil War* (1977); Harry Eskew, "Shape-Note Hymnody in the Shenandoah Valley, 1816–1860" (Ph.D. diss., Tulane University, 1966); David Evans, *Big Road Blues: Tradition and Creativity in the Folk Blues* (1981); William Ferris, *Blues from the Delta* (1978); Linnell Gentry, *A History and Encyclopedia of Country, Western, and Gospel Music* (1961); James R. Goff Jr., *Close Harmony: A History of Southern Gospel* (2002); Archie Green, *Only a Miner: Studies in Recorded Coal-Mining Songs* (1972); Douglas B. Green, *Country Roots: The Origins of Country Music* (1976), *Singing in the Saddle: The History of the Singing Cowboy* (2002); John Greenway, *American Folksongs of Protest* (1953); Peter Guralnick, *Careless Love: The Unmaking of Elvis Presley* (1999), *Dream Boogie: The Triumph of Sam Cooke* (2005), *Last Train to Memphis: The Rise of Elvis Presley* (1994), *Lost Highway: Journeys and Arrivals of American Musicians* (1979), *Sweet Soul Music: Rhythm and Blues and the Southern Dream of Freedom* (1986, 1999); Anthony Heilbut, *The Gospel Sound: Good News and Bad Times* (1971); George Pullen Jackson, *White Spirituals in the Southern Uplands* (1933); Paul Kingsbury, ed., *The Encyclopedia of Country Music* (1998); Paul Kingsbury and Alanna Nash, eds., *Will the Circle Be Unbroken: Country Music in America* (2006); Henry Kmen, *Music in New Orleans: The Formative Years, 1791–1841* (1966); Alan Lomax, *Folk Songs of North*

America (1960), *The Land Where the Blues Began* (1992); Bill C. Malone, *Country Music, U.S.A.: A Fifty-Year History* (1968; rev. eds., 1985, 2002), *Don't Get Above Your Raisin': Country Music and the Southern Working Class* (2002), *Southern Music—American Music* (1979, 2003), with Judith McCulloh, eds., *Stars of Country Music: Uncle Dave Macon to Johnny Rodriguez* (1975); Guthrie Meade, *Country Music Sources* (2003); Alan P. Merriam and Robert J. Branford, *A Bibliography of Jazz* (1954); Jim Miller, ed., *The Rolling Stone Illustrated History of Rock and Roll* (1976); Hans Nathan, *Dan Emmett and the Rise of Early Negro Minstrelsy* (1962); Paul Oliver, *Blues Fell This Morning: The Meaning of the Blues* (1960), *Savannah Syncopators: African Retentions in the Blues* (1970), *The Story of the Blues* (1969); Américo Paredes, *A Texas-Mexican Cancionero: Folksongs of the Lower Border* (1975); Nolan Porterfield, *Jimmie Rogers: The Life and Times of America's Blue Yodeler* (1992, 2002), *Last Cavalier: The Life and Times of John A. Lomax, 1867–1948* (1996); Jan Reid, *The Improbable Rise of Redneck Rock* (1974, 2004); Jim Rooney, *Bossmen: Bill Monroe and Muddy Waters* (1971); Neil V. Rosenberg, *Bluegrass: A History* (1985); Tony Russell, *Blacks, Whites, and Blues* (1970), *Country Music Records: A Discography, 1921–1942* (2004); William J. Schafer and Johannes Riedel, *The Art of Ragtime: Form and Meaning of an Original Black American Art* (1973); Arnold Shaw, *Honkers and Shouters: The Golden Years of Rhythm and Blues* (1978); Eileen Southern, *The Music of Black Americans: A History* (1983); Nicholas Spitzer, in *Long Journey Home: Folklife in the South*, ed. Allen Tullos (1977); Marshall Stearns, *The Story of Jazz* (1956); Frank Tirro, *Jazz: A History* (1977); Jeff Todd Titon, *Early Downhome Blues: A Musical and Cultural Analysis* (1977); Robert C. Toll, *Blacking Up: The Minstrel Show in Nineteenth-Century America* (1974); Nick Tosches, *Country: The Biggest Music in America* (1977); Charles R. Townsend, *San Antonio Rose: The Life and Music of Bob Wills* (1976); Barry Ulanov, *A History of Jazz in America* (1955); Elijah Wald, *Escaping the Delta: Robert Johnson and the Invention of the Blues* (2004); D. K. Wilgus, *Anglo-American Folksong Scholarship since 1898* (1959); Mark R. Winchell, *Southern Quarterly* (Spring 1984); Charles K. Wolfe, *A Good-Natured Riot* (1999), *Kentucky Country: Folk and Country Music of Kentucky* (1982), *Tennessee Strings: The Story of Country Music in Tennessee* (1977); Mark Zwonitzer with Charles Hirshberg, *Will You Miss Me When I'm Gone? The Carter Family and Their Legacy in American Music* (2002).

Black Music

Black musical life was never limited to a single style or musical tradition. In the 19th century American popular songs found their way into the repertoire of black folk musicians, European fiddle tunes appeared in medleys performed by itinerant fiddlers, and shape-note singing was adopted by black congregations in imitation of the colonial traditions developed in the North but transplanted to the South in the 1830s. Black musicians were aware of various ethnic musical traditions; and the process of musical acculturation, forced on blacks because of their need to accommodate themselves to a sometimes hostile culture or accepted by them because the other music fitted in so well with their own, led them to learn repertoires acceptable to both races.

Two great periods of musical acculturation have been preserved on records. The first occurred during the pre–World War II era when the radio and phonograph made the quick transmission of personal and regional styles possible; the second occurred immediately following the war when African American music was brought to the attention of a larger audience. Some of the evidence needed for studying black southern music comes from those commercial recordings classified as "blues" and marketed as "race records" in the 1920s and 1930s by producers who sought to profit from the sales of phonographs to black families, more of whom owned a record player than a musical instrument. Because those producers and the major record companies limited their "race" catalogs to those items likely to have strong sales among blacks, the other major recordings come from the fieldwork of folklorists employed by the Library of Congress, the Works Progress Administration (WPA), and a few major universities, evidence that includes examples dating back to the styles of the Civil War era.

Black musicians created in a variety of forms, from art songs to zydeco music (blues-influenced dance music performed by French-speaking Creole blacks). Many black musicians were musically multilingual, capable of absorbing and mastering (1) the Afro-Caribbean rhythms and dance forms brought to the Gulf Coast by emigrants from Haiti, Jamaica, and Cuba; (2) the many ethnic musical styles practiced by Cajun, German, French and Spanish Creole, Mexican, and French performers; and, after Emancipation, (3) the new styles of American and European art and popular music from the North. Studies of the African American style tend to emphasize folk music and jazz, but southern blacks also had a repertoire of material that they shared with whites, a "common heritage" known widely throughout the United States.

The multiethnic character of some antebellum southern cities contributed greatly to the opportunities for musical acculturation. Over 40 percent of the population of New Orleans (116,375 in 1850), 24 percent of Mobile (20,515 in 1850), and 30 percent of Charleston (42,985 in 1840) were foreign born. Each of these cities and its various ethnic groups provided music for urban blacks to learn and, through the "hiring out" practice, opportunities for slaves to join free blacks for performances at dances and other social events.

Following the rage for brass band music that began in Europe and spread to the United States in the late 1830s, brass ensembles, such as the Richmond Light Infantry Blues (c. 1840) and Allen's Brass Band (Wilmington, N.C.), were established in the South. Band books of both the pre–Civil War and postbellum periods reveal a repertoire consisting of everything from transcribed fiddle tunes and popular hymns to selections from European operas and American musical theater. The Negro Philharmonic Society of New Orleans (c. 1838) presented concerts for many years, and one of its directors, Richard Lambert, headed a family that included several generations of famous musicians. Each of the cities of the South seemed to have both slave and free blacks who earned strong vocal reputations for their musicianship. Simeon Gilliat and George Walker were considered the finest musicians in early 19th-century Richmond, and the roster of famous New Orleans musicians at the end of the century features "legends" such as "Klondike," "John the Baptist," Ferdinand "Jelly Roll" Morton, and Anthony Jackson ("the World's Greatest Single-Handed Entertainer").

After 1865 some black artists and composers adopted European aesthetic values and performance traditions. Inspired by the success of the first group of Fisk Jubilee Singers (1871–78), the brilliant career of Mississippi-born Marie Smith Selika, and the many gifted instrumentalists, dancers, and singers who appeared with postbellum minstrel, vaudeville, and tent shows, blacks moved beyond the folk and traditional styles with which they were associated before the war. Trained by such distinguished black educators as John Wesley Work (Fisk University) and Robert Nathaniel Dett (Hampton Institute and Bennett College), many sought professional training for careers as performers or teachers. Few were to realize the dream of international recognition and personal artistic success, but southern-born artists such as Roland Hayes, William Grant Still, W. C. Handy, Leontyne Price, Mahalia Jackson, and many others have made outstanding contributions to the world of music.

The major features of black performance styles are communal singing with call-and-response patterns; polyrhythmic percussive accompaniments to both religious and secular vocal and choral music—foot tapping, hand clapping, and drumming performed in ways similar to known African practices; and the intense, sometimes ecstatic, emotional participation of the audience or congregation in the performance.

A number of vocal techniques distinguish African American singing from the popular, operatic, and theatrical styles of the 19th century. Black performers are described in literary sources as capable of producing a wide variety of vocal effects: ascending or descending glides or runs, frequent use of the head or falsetto voice (especially in quick leaps from low robust tones to high piercing ones), and vocal imitations of natural and animal sounds. Devices that are also commonly found in reports about and recordings of black storytellers include subtle pitch variations that follow the natural inflections of black speech, changes in pitch and dynamics directly related to the emotional content of a musical phrase, and a sometimes completely arrhythmic vocalizing in the manner of an extended free-form sung meditation. Most of these stylistic traits are well known to black and white audiences today, but they were virtually unknown in the popular music of the North prior to the 1920s, even in the minstrel shows, which claimed to be "authentic" imitations of black behavior.

These characteristics can be found in the field cries and hollers, chants, lullabies, ritual songs, ring shouts, and religious songs in which a call-and-response pattern served as a framework for improvising melodies and texts. That ability to spontaneously create texts, tales, and songs has been documented in folklore studies and is a characteristic of almost all African American music such as blues, jazz, and religious song.

Religious institutions, fraternal associations, and traditional seasonal festivals encouraged music making. From the colonial John Canoe or John Conny festivals in North Carolina and Virginia to the regularly scheduled dances in Congo Square in New Orleans; from the corn-shucking parties in Virginia, the Carolinas, and Texas to the cane songs of Mississippi and Louisiana; and from the voodoo ceremonies in Georgia and Florida to the sacred dances of Alabama and Arkansas—music played an important role in black social life. It accompanied dancing and singing and provided a background for an escape from the routines of life.

Three major 20th-century forms of African American music are especially associated with the South: blues, ragtime piano, and New Orleans jazz. Classic ragtime—the syncopated and carefully structured piano and band music of Scott Joplin, James Scott, and Joseph Lamb—evolved from a combination of the rhythmically irregular African American melodic style and the regular background rhythms of postbellum band music, to which should be added the common black folk practice of treating melody, design, and rhythm very flexibly. Ragtime songs and dances were introduced by southern-born blacks, who picked up the techniques of ragging tunes by ear, and the wide distribution of various types of rags in southern folk and popular music suggests that blacks

Othar Turner playing a black folk instrument, a fife, Gravel Springs, Miss., 1971 (Cheryl Thurber, photographer, Memphis)

and whites shared many musical ideas well before ragtime became popular in the North.

The blues, described by Paul Oliver as "arguably the most significant form of folk music to have emerged in this century," is deeply embedded in the black musical experience. Rich in its use of language and poetic imagery, varied in its multiple attraction to the deepest tragedies and most ribald comedies of human existence, and, musically, the source for the chord structures and harmonic patterns used in much American popular music and jazz, the blues is as important to the musical history of the 20th century as black spirituals were to the 19th. Two major blues forms—urban and rural—are widely recognized by blues scholars. The performance of the blues involves very subtle communications processes. The music is a vehicle for sharing complaints, exorcising sorrow, laughing at the world's absurdities, mocking whites, and maintaining the integrity of black culture.

Dixieland jazz is one of the major forms of ensemble jazz. It was not the exclusive possession of blacks or of the South, however, because early New Orleans jazz was played by nearly as many Creoles as blacks, especially after the segregation laws passed by New Orleans in 1894 and 1897 brought African American and Creole cultures together in the uptown section. Still, southern blacks such as Louis Armstrong are inextricably linked with the birth of jazz. The role of black, white, and Creole musicians in creating and developing jazz makes it a classic case of musical amalgamation.

Black southerners, like black Americans elsewhere, adopted many of the same values as whites, but the African American musical style reflects most vividly the inherent dichotomies blacks have faced in being Americans. The tendency to view the style in terms of its various genres—spirituals, blues, ragtime, gospel songs—sometimes obscures the fact that black musicians still treat music as an oral rather than a written art because black culture is still largely an oral culture in both the North and the South. Southern rappers and hip-hop artists have reflected this cultured orientation in the contemporary period. The real strength of southern black music is its diversity, its ability to capture the tensions as well as the achievements of blacks, its indebtedness as well as its contribution to other forms of southern music, and its heritage of preserving older performance practices after the great black exodus from the South. Without southern culture as a stimulant to music acculturation, the African American style would not have produced the unique fusion of traditions that have made it a potent force in this century's popular music.

WILLIAM J. MAHAR
Pennsylvania State University—Capitol Campus

Bruce Bastin, *Red River Blues: The Blues Tradition in the Southeast* (1986); Samuel Charters, *The Blues Makers* (1991); Lawrence Cohn, ed., *Nothing but the Blues: The Music and the Musicians* (1993); Dominique-Rene De Lerma, *Bibliography of Black Music*, 4 vols. (1981–84); Sam Dennison, *Scandalize My Name: Black Imagery in American Popular Music* (1982); Frank Driggs and Chuck Haddix, *Kansas City Jazz: From Ragtime to Bebop: A History* (2006); Dena Epstein, *Sinful Tunes and Spirituals: Black Folk Music to the Civil War* (1977); Ted Gioia, *The History of Jazz* (1998); David Horn, *The Literature of American Music in Books and Folk Music Collections: A Fully Annotated Bibliography* (1981); Gerhard Kubik, *Africa and the Blues* (1999); Bill C. Malone, *Southern Music—American Music* (1979); Paul Oliver, *Songsters and Saints: Vocal Traditions on Race Records* (1984); Tom Sancton, *Song for My Fathers: A New Orleans Story in Black and White* (2006); JoAnn Skowronski, *Black Music in America: A Bibliography* (1981); Eileen Southern, *Biographical Dictionary of Afro-American and African Musicians* (1982), *The Music of Black Americans: A History* (1971; 2d ed., 1983); Jeff Todd Titon, *Early Downhome Blues: A Musical and Cultural Analysis* (1977); Geoffrey C. Ward and Ken Burns, *Jazz: A History of America's Music* (2002).

Bluegrass

Bluegrass took shape as a distinctive style of acoustic southern string band music between 1939 and 1945, dates that are intimately associated with the career of a specific bandleader and his ensemble—Bill Monroe and his Blue Grass Boys. With the possible exception of funk music's association with James Brown, no other American music genre's origins are so singularly traced to one father figure as bluegrass's are to western Kentuckian Bill Monroe. But the classic ensemble sound of bluegrass came into being following crucial contributions from other members of his group. Similarly, while the appellation "bluegrass" suggests origins in western Kentucky, many early exponents of the style came from other southern states, most often from Appalachia and its surrounding regions. Likewise, outsiders to both these regions and even the South have aided in the later spread and stylistic variations of bluegrass, making it a much-admired music in unexpected places all around the world. Yet no matter the distance bluegrass has at times traveled from its roots, it has continued to check its bearings against its southern and Appalachian origins. In recent years, this trend has been best exemplified in the resounding mainstream success of unabashedly traditional and southward-looking albums such as Ricky Skaggs's *Bluegrass Rules*, Dolly Parton's *The Grass Is Blue* and *Little Sparrow*, the sound tracks of *O Brother, Where Art Thou?* and *Songcatcher*, and Patty Loveless's *Mountain Soul*.

Although bluegrass mainly developed out of the Anglo-American string band tradition, popular through much of the South, it also drew upon other music, initially under the supervision of Bill Monroe. Vocally, the strongest influences came from the close-harmony brother duos that had been popular throughout the early decades of commercially recorded country music. Before launching his larger string ensemble, Monroe had partnered with his elder brother Charlie in the harmony duo the Monroe Brothers. Bill Monroe pitched his songs higher and brought a harder nasal edge to the sweet singing styles typical of other 1930s brother duos, such as the Blue Sky Boys and the Delmore Brothers. This high nasal vocalizing had also characterized other traditional singers from Kentucky, such as Roscoe Holcomb, for whom music folklorist John Cohen originally coined the descriptor "the high lonesome sound" but which was later appropriately used to describe bluegrass. To the close harmony of lead and tenor, bluegrass ensembles typically add a baritone part, again usually in close harmony, and on religious songs a bass voice.

Instrumentally, bluegrass ensembles started with the instruments typical of old-time string band music. Fiddle and banjo had been the basis of string bands for a century. Upright acoustic bass, the mandolin, and the steel string flattop guitar were being added to string bands by the end of the 19th century. Early bluegrass ensembles utilized these five instruments. In contrast with old-time ensembles' variable instrumental constitution and loose orchestration, however, in bluegrass the presence of all five instruments soon became de rigueur, and tight, meditated orchestration defined the style. Although Earl Scruggs's three-finger banjo style would become the hallmark of classic bluegrass, many of the characteristics that define the sound of bluegrass as different from its forebears had already coalesced around Monroe's instrument, the mandolin. In 1959 bluegrass would be famously described by Alan Lomax as "folk music in overdrive." In addition to pointing out bluegrass ensembles' proclivity for playing rousing up-tempo tunes, that description partly refers to the forward propulsive drive lent to the music by the prominent muted chopping by the mandolinist on the upbeats; the fiddle, banjo, or Dobro typically take over that function during mandolin solos. Additionally, Monroe brought a strong blues influence into his version of southern string band music, making liberal use of blue notes and blue-note–incorporating dyads; he later acknowledged his debt to the black, west Kentuckian guitarist Arnold Shultz, a sometime collaborator with Monroe's now-famous relative, Pendleton "Uncle Pen" Vandiver. Especially in the instrumental sections, whether on such instrumentals as "Bluegrass Special" and "Bluegrass Boogie" or during instrumental breaks during songs such as "The Road Is Rocky," Monroe and his band members improvised with scalar and often stock licks and riffs strung together to fit the piece. This practice had antecedents in jazz and western swing and departed significantly from the more conservative melodic variations of old-time string band music. As in jazz and swing, they also alternated between lead and accompaniment roles, often switching functions after four or two measures.

Some scholars suggest that when Monroe's band made its debut on the *Grand Ole Opry* in 1939 most elements of the bluegrass sound were already in place. Most, however, agree that it was not until the addition of Lester Flatt and Earl Scruggs in late 1945, and specifically of Scruggs's rolling three-finger banjo playing, that the classic bluegrass sound coalesced. That legendary lineup, which also featured fiddler Chubby Wise and bassist Cedric Rainwater, was together for just over two years, but its influence spread rapidly, and many acoustic string bands updated and tightened up their sound to compete with the rising popularity of the Blue Grass Boys. The most influential of the bands that emerged during this period were the Stanley Brothers, Flatt and Scruggs and the Foggy Mountain Boys, and Reno and Smiley and the Tennessee Cutups. By the early 1950s many other acts, often started by alumni of Monroe's band, joined the fray. Mac Wiseman, Jim and Jesse McReynolds, the

Osborne Brothers, and Jimmy Martin and the Sunny Mountain Boys proved the most enduring. For professional bluegrass bands throughout the late 1940s, the main source of income was live appearances at radio stations, such as WCYB, Bristol, and WSM, Nashville, and touring in the South and in cities with a strong Appalachian migrant population. Record sales supplemented their incomes, and a number of independent labels, such as Rich-R-Tone, Starday, and King, focused on bluegrass. Rebel and County would emerge later as specialist bluegrass labels. In the early 1950s local television shows were added to the list. Still, the majority of bluegrass musicians, then as now, retained semiprofessional or amateur status.

Although it did recognize its debt to bluegrass, as evidenced in Elvis Presley's renditions of a number of Bill Monroe songs during his various Sun Records sessions, early rock and roll was attracting at least the younger section of the bluegrass audiences. In response, the Blue Grass Boys, as well as other traditional bluegrass bands, attempted to slightly rework their sound to appeal to younger tastes. Rock and roll's popularity with youngsters also forced Nashville's country recording industry to focus its attentions on the mainstream adult constituency with a crossover "countrypolitan" sound, which made bluegrass sound even more outmoded by comparison. The folk revival that soon spread across urban America, however, secured bluegrass's future.

Despite the distinctiveness and popularity of the style, bluegrass as a label did not acquire substantial currency until the second half of the 1950s. Early popularizers of that label, urban folklorists and scholars such as Mike Seeger, Alan Lomax, and Ralph Rinzler, were vital agents in folk revivalists' discovery of bluegrass and in the recasting of that music as an "authentic" folk music. For Smithsonian-Folkways Records, Mike Seeger produced and wrote scholarly liner notes for the albums *American Banjo Three-Finger and Scruggs Style* (1957) and *American Music Bluegrass Style* (1959). Lomax and Rinzler wrote important early magazine articles about the music. Rinzler also joined New York's Greenbriar Boys, one of the first bluegrass groups featuring city-bred musicians, and in the liner notes to their 1962 debut album he explained bluegrass to urban audiences. Bluegrass scholarship and readership soon expanded, with theses and dissertations, academic journal issues, and dedicated magazines, such as *Bluegrass Unlimited, Muleskinner News*, and later *Bluegrass Now*, which focused on the genre's new literate audiences. Instrument-specific magazines, such as *Flatpick Guitar* and the *Banjo Newsletter*, and music instruction houses, such as Homespun Tapes, offered alternative manners of learning, contrasting with bluegrass's oral and autodidactic roots.

A wider appreciation for bluegrass music was set in motion with urban folk

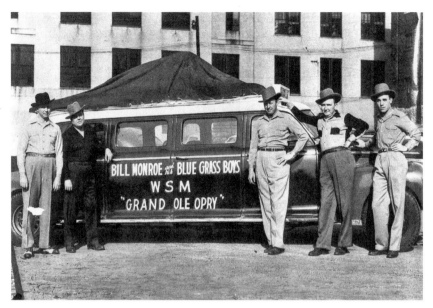

Bill Monroe and the Bluegrass Boys, the classic bluegrass group, c. 1950
(Country Music Foundation, Library and Media Center, Nashville)

festival and college campus appearances by bluegrass groups. The Osborne Brothers took the lead in the crossover, appearing at Antioch College, Ohio, in 1960. Soon other groups, including Bill Monroe and the Blue Grass Boys, now managed by Rinzler, started making regular appearances at festivals and on campuses across the country. Many younger southern bands made self-conscious attempts to meet their new audiences' tastes halfway, at the same time also attempting to reach contemporary country audiences. Monroe, however, as the doyen of an "authentic" American "folk" tradition, succeeded best through a conservative approach. After the first whole-day bluegrass show in 1961 and the first multiday festival dedicated to the genre in 1965, the bluegrass festival appeared as the central structuring event for the expanding bluegrass world.

A number of urban musicians in folk clubs and coffeehouses across America and Canada took up various bluegrass instruments. Initially, mainly from 1961 to 1964, these youngsters attempted to re-create the sound and spirit of original rural roots music, but an imitative eclecticism soon came to characterize this generation's coming-of-age. Youngsters who had learned to play on bluegrass instruments, on bluegrass songs, and in a bluegrass style soon began to experiment with one or all of those variables—instrumentation, lyrical genre, and stylistic approach—leading bluegrass into newer territories, which are still being explored today by artists such as Sam Bush, Tony Rice, Jerry Douglas, Bela Fleck and the Flecktones, Mark O'Connor, and Edgar Meyer.

The results of these experiments were variable, and a number of labels, especially "progressive bluegrass" and "newgrass," were applied as descriptors. In one camp were traditional bluegrass bands, typically from the rural South, which attempted to meet halfway their intended urban audiences' tastes by incorporating elements of commercial styles—whether rock or country—especially drums, electric guitar, and steel guitar. Although the Osborne Brothers and the Dillards achieved commercially successful syntheses, other southern artists fared less well; Lester Flatt, for instance, eventually parted ways with Earl Scruggs over their group's increasingly rock direction. Scruggs, however, believed in bluegrass's new direction and continued undeterred with his family band, the Earl Scruggs Revue. He also championed the ambitious efforts of urban acolytes, most famously the Nitty Gritty Dirt Band's historic all-star 1971 triple album *Will the Circle Be Unbroken.*

In another progressive camp were younger musicians with urban middle- or upper-class backgrounds or southerners with a greater empathy for contemporary tastes. Many of them, after initially playing traditional bluegrass, found popular success with folk-rock or country-rock music, albeit with a strong bluegrass undercurrent. After the commercial heyday of country rock, many such musicians, including Jerry Garcia, Chris Hillman, Herb Pedersen, Bernie Leadon, David Grisman, Bill Keith, and Peter Rowan, returned to record albums even more strongly influenced by bluegrass.

A third forward-looking group, the one most often classified under the "progressive bluegrass" label and also the one most successful and with the least artistic compromise, comprised those musicians who, after tentative dabbling, largely avoided the most overt elements of rock—electric amplification, drums, and loud volume. Still, having grown up with and having shared artistic sensibilities with the softer, more introspective singer-songwriter, folk-rock, and emerging studio-oriented soft-rock genres, these artists led bluegrass into less conspicuously divergent directions. This camp, also called "newgrass," focused its innovations on the choice of lyrical material, nuanced studio recording, and, increasingly, a variable instrumental palette. Bluegrass Alliance, Newgrass Revival, Seldom Scene, J. D. Crowe and the New South, Tony Rice, David Grisman, Dan Crary, Ricky Skaggs, Jerry Douglas, Bill Keith, and Peter Rowan were at the vanguard of this music. Many, most prominently David Grisman and Tony Rice, continued to forge ahead, bringing in strong influences from jazz and sometimes new age and world music, and with new labels, including "Dawg music," "jazzgrass spacegrass," and "new acoustic music."

While much new material continued song structures that were similar to those of early bluegrass and old-time string band music and emphasized country music's traditional themes—religion, sentimental love, home and hearth, and, sometimes, rambling, cheating, and murder—by the early 1960s, like musicians in other genres, the younger progressive urban musicians were reinterpreting contemporary musicians and groups like Bob Dylan and the Beatles into bluegrass. Instrumentally, major updates had occurred in bluegrass by the 1970s. Although the addition of drums and electric instruments was criticized by traditional fans, acoustic instrumental innovation has been welcomed throughout bluegrass's history. Only staunch traditionalists trying to resurrect the classic Blue Grass Boys sound of the 1946–48 period have avoided later instrumental developments. Whereas Monroe's bluesy mandolin and Scruggs's three-finger banjo rolls were innovations integral to the genre, other instrumental innovations have continued to expand the music's sonic palette, and many are well accepted even within the parameters of the "traditional" sound.

The resonator guitar, or Dobro, played in a style emulating three-finger banjo rolls, became a fairly standard element of the bluegrass sound following Josh Graves's tenure with the Foggy Mountain Boys in the 1950s, Mike Auldridge's playing with the Country Gentlemen in the 1960s, and Jerry Douglas's work with a number of supergroups in the 1970s. Major new approaches to the banjo also emerged—especially the melodic style associated with Blue Grass Boys' Bill Keith and styles reflecting more blues, jazz, and chromatic approaches associated with players such as Larry McNeely, Tony Trischka, Tony Furtado, Alison Brown, and especially Bela Fleck. On bluegrass mandolin, Jesse McReynold's cross-picking approach and David Grisman's jazz-informed playing proved widely influential. The flattop, steel string, dreadnought, acoustic guitar, although initially relegated to an accompaniment function with only an occasional bass run, also benefited from the innovations of Don Reno, Doc Watson, Clarence White, Norman Blake, Dan Crary, and Tony Rice, emerging as a lead instrument with a melodic vocabulary matching that of the fiddle and the mandolin. The popularity of the bluegrass flat-pick guitar style among younger bluegrass enthusiasts has ensured that performance on guitar, whether in a solo or a duo setting with a second guitar or mandolin, is enough for the music to be received as bluegrass.

By the end of the 1970s, bluegrass had traveled far from its southern traditional music roots, and, not unexpectedly, a neotraditionalist response was afoot. The two-decade period starting in 1979 is often described by scholars as one of a hard-nosed return to the southern roots of bluegrass. Skaggs and Rice, the Johnson Mountain Boys, bluegrass gospel specialists Doyle Lawson and

Quicksilver, and supergroups Bluegrass Album Band, Dreadful Snakes, and Nashville Bluegrass Band spearheaded this revival. Since then a steadfast contingent of traditional bluegrass musicians and fans has counterbalanced any tendencies of mavericks to drift too far from bluegrass's southern roots. This same period, and continuing into the present, nevertheless, has also seen some of the genre's often southern-born stalwarts make successful inroads into other nontraditional idioms and markets through their individual syntheses of bluegrass with other influences.

In the 1960s and 1970s, young urban-raised rock musicians exposed rock audiences to bluegrass. In the popular music mainstream, their amalgams, by the beginning of the 1980s, had been completely displaced by the more urbane sounds of studio rock, disco, and new wave music. Bluegrass-influenced rock musicians, such as Chris Hillman, Herb Pedersen, Peter Rowan, and the Eagles' Bernie Leadon, then returned to purer bluegrass sounds on albums released on independent labels that had emerged in the 1970s and were dedicated to acoustic Americana, such as Rounder, Sugar Hill, and Flying Fish. In the mainstream country music market, however, following the extended reign of country pop, the time was now ripe for a "neotraditionalist" reply. The studio emphasis of 1970s progressive bluegrass had produced a cadre of versatile musicians who, in the 1980s, brought the sounds of bluegrass to a still-newer audience. Ricky Skaggs, Keith Whitley, Marty Stuart, Vince Gill, and the Desert Rose Band became mainstream country stars but continued to feature bluegrass instrumentation. Instrumental prodigies such as Mark O'Connor, Jerry Douglas, Bela Fleck, and Edgar Meyer, on the other hand, emerged as major session musicians in Nashville and provided bluegrass embellishments on recordings by such artists as Nanci Griffith, Kathy Mattea, Emmylou Harris, Rodney Crowell, Steve Earle, Michelle Shocked, and Mark Knopfler.

In the 1990s and in the new millennium, bluegrass's appeal has continued to spread. Women stars have adapted bluegrass to their voices. Alison Krauss and the Dixie Chicks blended bluegrass with pop and country elements to achieve multiplatinum success with diverse audiences, easily surpassing the sales of the genre's previous top-selling albums by the Nitty Gritty Dirt Band and Old & In the Way. With the rise of the alternative music movement and traveling festivals such as Lollapalooza and H.O.R.D.E., the jam band scene long localized in California now spread and included bluegrass-based bands such as Leftover Salmon and String Cheese Incident. Nickel Creek continues to find success with both of the above constituencies. Alternative country pioneer Steve Earle collaborated on acoustic projects with Norman Blake, Peter Rowan, and the Del McCoury Band. Although set in prebluegrass sub-Appalachian Mississippi, the 2000 Hollywood movie *O Brother, Where Art Thou?* featured a sound track with many bluegrass stalwarts, including Appalachian-born southerners Ralph Stanley, Norman Blake, and Emmylou Harris, and led to great success for the genre. The sound track resulted in the popular music world acknowledging Stanley's stature as a living legend and spawned multiartist tours and album projects. It also proved a shot in the arm for country music artists such as Ricky Skaggs and Dolly Parton, who were attempting to return to their acoustic roots, and encouraged others such as Patty Loveless to follow suit.

Despite these varied progressive and commercial currents, bluegrass, even in the commercial market, has continued to experience traditionalist revivalist trends, which have reminded listeners of the music's regional southern and Appalachian roots. In the 1980s, it was the Johnson Mountain Boys and the Bluegrass Album Band that led the return-to-roots movement. In the 21st century, genre stalwarts Del McCoury, Ricky Skaggs, and a rejuvenated Ralph Stanley have brought back the traditional sounds to the music's now-expanded fan base.

AJAY KALRA
University of Texas at Austin

Thomas Goldsmith, ed., *The Bluegrass Reader* (2004); Paul Kingsbury, ed., *The Encyclopedia of Country Music: The Ultimate Guide to the Music* (1998); Neil Rosenberg, *Bluegrass: A History* (1985).

Blues

In the 1890s several new musical forms arose in the black communities of the southern and border states. Among the most important of these forms were ragtime, jazz, and blues. The generation that created this new music had been born in the years immediately following the Civil War, the first generation of blacks that did not directly experience slavery. As this generation reached maturity in the 1890s, there arose within it a restlessness to try out new ideas and new courses of action. New economic, social, and political institutions were created to provide a network of mutual support within the black community in the face of a hardening of discriminatory patterns of race relations and Jim Crow legislation. Pentecostal denominations with a more emotional style of worship arose to meet the spiritual needs of many who were trying to improve their lot in life and cope with problems of urban migration, industrialism, and unemployment.

These social changes were reflected in new developments in the arts at all levels—formal, popular, and folk—and in none of the arts was the ferment as intense as in music. In border states like Missouri, Kansas, and Kentucky, where blacks had greater opportunities to obtain formal training in music and were exposed to a variety of popular and even classical music forms, they created ragtime. At this same time, the first stirrings of jazz were heard in southern cities along the Atlantic and Gulf coasts, particularly in New Orleans. Blues, on the other hand, was created in the rural areas and small towns of the Deep South, particularly in the areas of large plantations, such as the Mississippi Delta, and in industries that required heavy manual labor—mining, logging, levee and railroad construction, and freight loading. Those who sought work as sharecroppers and harvesters on the plantations and in the other industries were hoping to escape the drudgery and hopelessness of life on tiny plots of worn-out farmland and earn some cash for their labor. With little education or property and no political power in a completely segregated society, they often encountered intolerable working conditions and moved frequently from one plantation or job to another.

Out of this dissatisfaction arose the blues, a music that reflected not only the social isolation and lack of formal training of its creators but also their ability to make do with the most basic of resources and to survive under the most adverse, oppressive circumstances. Blues drew from Western formal music in only the most superficial ways; instead it almost entirely came out of elements taken from the existing black folk music tradition. Until quite recently, blues was not fully accepted by mainstream America as a distinct major musical form. Instead it tended to be viewed as a rather simple and limited, though at times charming and powerfully expressive, type of music, suitable mainly as raw material for jazz and rock and roll or some other more complex popular music. In the history of these other types of music, blues was viewed as one of the "roots."

Blues introduced a number of new elements into the American musical consciousness. The most novel in its initial impact, and now one of the most pervasive elements in American popular music, is the "blue note." Blue notes generally occur at the third and seventh degrees of the scale, though sometimes at other points as well, and can be either flatted notes, neutral pitches, waverings, or sliding tones occurring in the range between the flat and natural of these degrees of the scale. Another primary musical characteristic is the role of the accompanying instrument as a second voice. The musical accompaniment in blues is not simply a rhythmic and harmonic background to the singing. It constantly interacts with, punctuates, and answers the vocal line. Finally, blues introduced a new realism combined with greater individualism into American popular song. During the 1890s most popular songs were either humor-

Dockery Farms, established in 1895, once employed bluesmen Charley Patton, Son House, and Howlin' Wolf and is considered by many to be the place where the Delta blues was born (James G. Thomas Jr., photographer, University of Mississippi)

ous, sentimental, or tragic, dramatizing unusual or exotic situations. The "coon songs," which depicted black life, generally portrayed either nostalgic scenes of the old plantation, romantic love, absurd humor, or stereotypes of black character. Blues, on the other hand, dealt with everyday life and met its subjects head-on in an open-ended celebration of life's ups and downs. Although blues focused on relationships between men and women, it did not avoid commenting on such subjects as working conditions, migration, current events, natural disasters, sickness and death, crime and punishment, alcohol and drugs, sorcery, magic, the supernatural, and racial discrimination. As a secular music, blues generally avoided making religious statements, although it might ridicule preachers and discuss the temptations and powers of the devil, and as a highly individualistic statement it seldom mentioned family and organized community life other than as the immediate context of the dance or party where the music was performed. Blues developed an extraordinary compactness of form and startling poetic imagery in order to make its points on a broad range of subjects.

The basic vocal material for early folk blues came from "hollers," which were sung by workers in the fields and in other occupations requiring manual labor. Hollers were sung solo in freely embellished descending lines employing blue notes and a great variety of vocal timbres. The words tended to be traditional commonplace phrases on the man-woman relationship or the work situation, with successive lines linked to one another through loose thematic associations and contrasts. Hollers appeared to be a direct reflection of the singer's state of mind and feelings poured out in a stream of consciousness. This type of singing had existed long before the 1890s. It was noted by observers during the slavery period and has clear parallels in some singing traditions in Africa and other African American cultures. But it was in the American South that these free, almost formless, vocal expressions were set to instrumental accompaniment and given a musical structure, an expanded range of subject matter, and a new social context. Solo religious expression, such as chanted prayers and sermons, undoubtedly also influenced the vocal component of early blues.

The accompaniment was most often played on instruments that had been rarely used in older forms of black folk music—the piano, the harmonica, and especially the guitar. For the guitar, unorthodox tunings were often used to obtain drone effects. The technique of bending strings helped to achieve blue notes, and sometimes the player would slide a knife, bottleneck, or other hard object along the strings to produce a whining tone, a technique adapted from African stringed instruments. At times, the performer established a simple rhythmic pattern behind the singing and then answered the vocal lines with short repeated melodic or rhythmic figures on the guitar. Blues of this sort is basically an instrumentally accompanied holler, and it allows much of the vocal freedom of the older type of song to be preserved. A few rural blues singers still compose and perform blues in this manner. Other performers, however, saw the need for greater structure in their blues and began to fit the vocal lines taken from hollers to existing harmonic patterns. Usually these patterns accommodated stanzas of 8, 12, or 16 measures, but the blues singers left space at the ends of their lines for the instrument to answer the vocal.

The pattern that emerged by the early 20th century contained three lines of four measures each. The second line repeated the first, and the third line was different but rhymed with the first two. The lines began with harmonies in the tonic, subdominant, and dominant chords, respectively, but always resolved to the tonic. This now-familiar 12-bar AAB pattern was derived from 3-line patterns found in such folk ragtime tunes as "Bully of the Town" and blues ballads like "Stagolee" and "Boll Weevil." Blues singers slowed the tempos of these tunes and left room at the ends of the lines for their instrumental response.

As the blues spread in the early 20th century, local and regional performance traditions developed in different parts of the South. At the local level, performers would share a repertoire of traditional verses and melodic and instrumental phrases, combining and recombining these endlessly and often adding further musical and lyrical elements of their own creation to form blues that sounded original yet familiar at the same time. Within broader geographic regions, the performers generally shared an overall musical stylistic approach and sometimes variants of certain songs in their repertoires. For instance, in the Mississippi Valley and adjacent areas, the folk blues was the most intense rhythmically and emotionally, more modal and less harmonic in conception, often structured upon short repeated melodic or rhythmic phrases, and tending to extract the maximum expression from each note. Variants of tunes like "Catfish Blues" and "Rolling and Tumbling" are familiar to many blues singers throughout this region.

In Texas, the guitarists often set up a constant thumping rhythm in the bass, while treble figures were played in a rather free rhythmic style in response to vocal lines that tended to float over the constant bass rhythm. From Texas guitarists like Aaron "T-Bone" Walker came the contemporary style of electric lead guitar playing, in which the guitar lines often seem to float over a steady rhythm supplied by the other instruments in the band. In Virginia and the Carolinas, as well as in some parts of Georgia and Florida, another style developed, featuring lighter, bouncier rhythms, virtuoso playing, a harmonic rather than modal conception, and a pervasive influence of ragtime music on the blues. In whatever region the early folk blues was performed, the contexts were usually the same. Generally this music was played at house parties; in roadhouses called juke joints; at outdoor picnics for dancing; and for tips from onlookers on sidewalks, at railroad stations, on store porches, and wherever else a crowd might gather.

In the first decade of the 20th century, professional singers in traveling shows began to incorporate blues into their stage repertoires as they worked in the towns and cities of the southern states. W. C. Handy, at that time the leader of a band sponsored by a black fraternal organization in Clarksdale, Miss., encountered folk blues and was so impressed by the music's appeal to both black and white audiences that he began to arrange these tunes for his own group of trained musicians. His success led him to Memphis, and there he published his first blues in sheet-music form in 1912. Other blues songs were published that same year, and soon a flood of new blues compositions appeared from southern songwriters, both black and white, drawing on the resources of folk blues. The songwriters considered folk blues as raw material to be extensively reworked and exploited.

At first the general public perceived blues as a novel type of a ragtime tune with the unusual features of blue notes and three-line stanzas. The professional singers were generally women accompanied by a pianist or a small jazz combo. They performed in both the North and the South in urban cabarets and vaudeville theaters and sometimes in traveling shows that visited smaller southern towns. This professionalized type of blues first appeared on phonograph records by black singers like Ma Rainey, Bessie Smith, Clara Smith, and Ida Cox, beginning in 1920. By 1926 the record companies began to record folk blues artists, mostly male singers playing their own guitar accompaniments, like Blind Lemon Jefferson from Texas, Charley Patton and Tommy Johnson from Mississippi, and Peg Leg Howell and Blind Willie McTell from Georgia. By the end of the 1920s the companies were also recording many boogie-woogie and barrelhouse pianists, such as Pinetop Smith and Roosevelt Sykes.

String bands, brass bands, and vocal quartets had incorporated blues into their repertoires by the first decade of the 20th century, but by the late 1920s there had arisen new types of ensembles created mainly to perform blues. Perhaps the closest to folk blues were the jug bands, which generally consisted of a guitar and harmonica supplemented by other novelty or homemade instruments, such as jugs, kazoos, washboards, and one-stringed basses. Jug bands were recorded in Louisville, Cincinnati, Memphis, Birmingham, and Dallas, and similar kinds of "skiffle" bands existed in many other cities and towns in the South and the North.

The combination of a full-chorded, rhythmic piano and guitar playing melodic lead lines also became popular at this time. The chief exponents of this style of blues were pianist Leroy Carr and guitarist Francis "Scrapper" Blackwell, who were based in Indianapolis. Pianist Georgia Tom (Thomas A. Dorsey) and guitarist Tampa Red (Hudson Whitaker) also made many popular recordings at this time, often performing "hokum" blues, which contained humorous verses and double entendre refrains. Various combinations of stringed instruments, as well as jug bands, also performed hokum blues. By the mid-1930s blues bands not uncommonly consisted of a string section made up of blues musicians and a horn-and-rhythm section made up of artists with a jazz background. One of the most popular of such groups, the Harlem Hamfats, featured trumpet, clarinet, piano, guitar, second guitar or mandolin, string bass, and drums.

The continuing influence of jazz and the rise to prominence of the electric guitar served to reshape the sound of the blues in the years following World War II. Small "jump" bands of jazz-influenced musicians became popular in the late 1940s and 1950s, often performing a mixture of blues and sentimental popular songs. Folk blues guitarists in the rural South became converts to the new electric guitar, and a new type of blues combo appeared, consisting usually of one or two electric guitars, bass, piano or electric organ, drums, and sometimes an amplified harmonica. This type of blues reached its peak of development in Chicago in the 1950s with the bands of artists such as Muddy Waters (McKinley Morganfield) and Howlin' Wolf (Chester Burnett), both originally from Mississippi.

A synthesis of the hard down-home style of blues and the sophisticated jump blues was achieved by Aaron "T-Bone" Walker from Texas and B. B. King, a Mississippian who had moved to Memphis. Both men had strong roots in the folk-blues tradition and had learned to play electric lead guitar fronting a large band of trained musicians. Their vocals were delivered in an impassioned shouting style, showing the influence of gospel singing. This type of blues, developed by Walker in the 1940s and brought to its peak of development by King in the 1950s, remains the most popular blues style.

By the 1960s many white performers in the North and West had begun to identify themselves as blues artists. Southern whites were slower to join this movement, perhaps only because blues already pervaded such established forms as country music and rock and roll. By the 1970s, however, there were plenty of southern white blues performers. Blues clubs and festivals and blues societies, with predominantly white participation, proliferated in the South throughout the rest of the 20th century, reflecting an ongoing national and international blues revival and the institutionalizing of the blues. By the end of the century, there were probably more whites than blacks in the South who identified themselves as blues performers. This development has not resulted in any major new style of blues, but it has led to an exploration and highlighting of older historical as well as more contemporary styles pioneered by black performers.

Blues has had a history of its own, but it has also had a profound influence upon other types of popular music in the 20th century. When popular blues began to be published in 1912 and performed by trained musicians, it was perceived as a new type of ragtime tune with a novel three-line verse form and the exotic element of blue notes. The use of blue notes not only helped to loosen up the formalism of ragtime but also soon paved the way for improvisatory jazz performance. The bulk of the repertoire of the early jazz bands consisted of blues tunes and ragtime tunes incorporating blue notes. The blues form has continued to be a staple for jazz compositions, and whenever jazz has seemed to become overly sophisticated, one usually hears calls for a return to the blues.

In the years before World War I, southern Anglo-American folk musicians began performing blues learned from black musicians. By the 1920s, "hillbilly" artists from all parts of the South were recording the blues. Beginning in 1927, Mississippi singer and guitarist Jimmie Rodgers popularized a distinct type of blues by combining folk blues learned from black artists with a yodeling refrain derived from black field hollers and German-Swiss yodeling that had been popularized on the vaudeville stage. Over the years, blues has given to varieties of country music, such as western swing and honky-tonk, not only the blues form but the qualities of improvisation and greater realism as well.

In the 1950s blues-influenced country music combined with black rhythm and blues to produce a new form of music, which came to be known as rock and roll. The blues form and blues instrumental techniques were very prominent in most rock-and-roll styles through the 1960s and have continued to be important factors in this music's development up to the present. Blues gave rock and roll not only an important verse form but also its basic instrumentation and instrumental technique, as well as a frankness in dealing with themes of love and sex, which proved attractive to an adolescent audience.

Finally, blues could even be said to have influenced gospel music. Thomas A. Dorsey, generally considered the "Father of Gospel Music," was a former blues pianist and songwriter. By the early 1930s he was composing gospel songs that used blue notes and showed a greater individualism and worldliness in their themes. Although gospel has seldom used the blues verse form, it has shown blues influence through its use of blues tonality and emphasis on the individual.

Most Americans today are probably more familiar with blues-influenced music than they are with blues itself. Nevertheless, blues is still a thriving form of music, existing in a variety of styles. In the South there are still excellent solo performers of folk blues, and small combos featuring electric lead guitar perform regularly in black communities in the region, as well as in northern and West Coast cities. Blues can be heard today in forms close to the earliest folk blues, showing that it is still in touch with its roots, and within modern jazz and rock and roll, showing the enormous impact it has had over the last century.

DAVID EVANS
University of Memphis

Bruce Bastin, *Red River Blues: The Blues Tradition in the Southeast* (1986); Samuel Charters, *The Blues Makers* (1991); Lawrence Cohn, ed., *Nothing but the Blues: The Music and the Musicians* (1993); David Honeyboy Edwards, *The World Don't Owe Me Nothing: The Life and Times of Delta Bluesman Honeyboy Edwards* (1997); David Evans, *Big Road Blues: Tradition and Creativity in the Folk Blues* (1982), *Tommy Johnson* (1971); John Fahey, *Charley Patton* (1970); William Ferris, *Blues from the Delta* (1978); Gerhard Kubik, *Africa and the Blues* (1999); Paul Oliver, *Conversation with the Blues* (1965), *The Meaning of the Blues* (1963), *The Story of the Blues* (1969); Harry Oster, *Living Country Blues* (1969); Robert Palmer, *Deep Blues* (1981); Jeff Todd Titon, *Early Downhome Blues: A Musical and Cultural Analysis* (1977).

Cajun Music

Cajun music blends elements of American Indian, Scotch-Irish, Spanish, German, Anglo-American, and Afro-Caribbean music with a rich stock of western French folk traditions. The music traces back to the Acadians, the French colonists who began settling at Port Royal, Acadia, in 1604. The Acadians were eventually deported from their homeland in 1755 by local British authorities after years of political and religious tension. In 1765, after 10 years of wandering, many Acadians began to arrive in Louisiana, determined to re-create their society. Within a generation, these exiles had so firmly reestablished themselves as a people that they became the dominant culture in south Louisiana, absorbing other ethnic groups around them. Most of the French Creoles (descendants of earlier French settlers), Spanish, Germans, and Anglo-Americans in the region eventually adopted the traditions and language of this new society, thus creating the south Louisiana mainstream. The Acadians, in turn, borrowed many traits from these other cultures, and this cross-cultural exchange produced a new Louisiana-based community—the Cajuns.

The Acadians' contact with these various cultures contributed to the development of new musical styles and repertoire. From Indians they learned wailing styles and new dance rhythms; from blacks they learned the blues, percussion techniques, and improvisational singing; from Anglo-Americans they learned new fiddle tunes to accompany Virginia reels, square dances, and hoedowns. The Spanish contributed the guitar and even a few tunes. Refugees and their slaves who arrived from Santo Domingo at the turn of the 19th century brought with them a syncopated West Indian beat. German Jewish immigrants began importing diatonic accordions (invented in Vienna in 1828) toward the end of the 19th century when Acadians and black Creoles began to show an interest in the instruments. The Acadians blended these elements to create a new music just as they were synthesizing the same cultures to create Cajun society.

The turn of the 20th century was a formative period in the development of Louisiana French music. Some of its most influential musicians were the black Creoles, who brought a strong, rural blues element into Cajun music. Simultaneously, blacks influenced the parallel development of zydeco music, later refined by Clifton Chenier. Although fiddlers such as Dennis McGee and Sady Courville still composed tunes, the accordion was rapidly becoming the mainstay of traditional dance bands. Limited in the number of notes and keys it could play in, it simplified Cajun music; songs that could not be played on the accordion faded from the active repertoire. Meanwhile, fiddlers were often relegated to playing a duet accompaniment or a simple percussive second line below the accordion's melodic lead.

By the mid-1930s, Cajuns were reluctantly, though inevitably, becoming Americanized. Their French language was banned from schools throughout south Louisiana, as America, caught in the melting pot ideology, tried to homogenize its diverse ethnic and cultural elements. In south Louisiana, speaking French was not only against the rules. It became increasingly unpopular as Cajuns attempted to escape the stigma attached to their culture. New highways and improved transportation opened this previously isolated area to the rest of the country, and the Cajuns began to imitate their Anglo-American neighbors in earnest.

Social and cultural changes of the 1930s and 1940s were clearly reflected in the music recorded in this period. The slick programming on radio (and later on television) inadvertently forced the comparatively unpolished traditional sounds underground. The accordion faded from the scene, partly because the old-style music had lost popularity and partly because the instruments were unavailable from Germany during the war. As western swing and bluegrass sounds from Texas and Tennessee swept the country, string bands that imitated the music of Bob Wills and the Texas Playboys and copied Bill Monroe's "high lonesome sound" sprouted across south Louisiana. Freed from the limitations imposed by the accordion, string bands readily absorbed various outside influences. Dancers across south Louisiana were shocked in the mid-1930s to hear music that came not only from the bandstand but also from the opposite end of the dance hall, through speakers powered by a Model-T behind the building. The electric steel guitar was added to the standard instrumentation, and drums replaced the triangle as Cajuns continued to experiment with new sounds borrowed from their Anglo-American neighbors. As amplification made it unnecessary for fiddlers to bear down with the bow in order to be audible, they developed a lighter, lilting touch, moving away from the soulful styles of earlier days.

By the late 1940s the music recorded by commercial producers signaled an unmistakable tendency toward Americanization. Yet an undercurrent of traditional music persisted. It resurfaced with the music of Iry Lejeune, who accompanied the Oklahoma Tornadoes in 1948 in recording "La Valse du Pont d'Amour" in the turn-of-the-century Louisiana style and in French. The recording was an unexpected success, presaging a revival of the earlier style, and Iry Lejeune became a pivotal figure in a Cajun music revival. Dance halls providing traditional music flourished. Musicians such as Lawrence Walker, Austin Pitre, and Nathan Abshire brought their accordions out of the closet and once again performed old-style Cajun music, and local companies began recording them. Cajun music, though bearing the marks of Americanization, was making a dramatic comeback, just as interest in the culture and language quickened before the 1955 bicentennial celebration of the Acadian exile.

Alan Lomax, a member of the Newport Folk Festival Foundation who had become interested in Louisiana French folk music during a field trip with his father in the 1930s, encouraged the documentation and preservation of Cajun music. In the late 1950s Harry Oster began recording Cajun music, ranging from unaccompanied ballads to contemporary dance tunes. His collection, which stressed the evolution of the music, attracted the attention of local activists, such as Paul Tate and Revon Reed. The work of Oster and Lomax was noticed by the Newport Foundation, which sent fieldworkers Ralph Rinzler and Mike Seeger to south Louisiana. Cajun dance bands had played at the National Folk Festival as early as 1935, but little echo of these performances had reached Louisiana. Rinzler and Seeger, seeking the real roots of Cajun music, chose Gladius Thibodeaux, Louis "Vinesse" Lejeune, and Dewey Balfa to represent Louisiana at the 1964 Newport Folk Festival. Their "gutsy," unamplified folk music made the Louisiana cultural establishment uneasy, for such "unrefined" sounds embarrassed the upwardly mobile Cajuns, who considered the music chosen for the Newport festival crude—"nothing but chanky-chank."

The instincts of the Newport festival organizers proved well founded, as huge crowds gave the old-time music standing ovations. Dewey Balfa was so moved that he returned to Louisiana determined to bring the message home. He began working on a small scale among his friends and family in Mamou, Basile, and Eunice. The Newport Folk Foundation, under the guidance of Lomax, provided money and fieldworkers to the new Louisiana Folk Foundation "to water the roots." With financial support and outside approval, local activists became involved in preserving the music, language, and culture. Traditional music contests and concerts were organized at events such as the Abbeville Dairy Festival, the Opelousas Yambilee, and the Crowley Rice Festival.

In 1968 the state of Louisiana officially recognized the Cajun cultural revival, which had been brewing under the leadership of the music community and political leaders, such as Dudley LeBlanc and Roy Theriot. In that year it created the Council for the Development of French in Louisiana (CODOFIL), which, under the chairmanship of James Domengeaux, began its efforts on political, psychological, and educational fronts to erase the stigma Louisianans had long attached to the French language and culture. The creation of French classes in elementary schools dramatically reversed the policy that had formerly barred the language from the schools.

Domengeaux's efforts were not limited to the classroom. Influenced by Rinzler and Balfa, CODOFIL organized a first Tribute to Cajun Music festival in 1974 with a concert designed to present a historical overview of Cajun music from its origins to modern styles. The echo had finally reached Louisiana. Dewey Balfa's message of cultural self-esteem was enthusiastically received by an audience of over 12,000.

Because of its success, the festival became an annual celebration of Cajun music and culture, providing exposure for the musicians and even presenting them as cultural heroes. Young performers were attracted to the revalidated Cajun music scene, while local French government officials, realizing the impact of the grass roots, began to stress the native Louisiana French culture. Balfa's dogged pursuit of cultural recognition carried him farther than he had ever expected. In 1977 he received a Folk Artist in the Schools grant from the National Endowment for the Arts to bring his message into elementary school classrooms. Young Cajuns, discovering local models besides country and rock stars, began to perform the music of their heritage. Yet they did not reject modern sounds totally. Performers such as Michael Doucet and Beausoleil are gradually making their presence known in Cajun music, replacing older musicians on the regular weekend dance hall circuit and representing traditional Cajun music at local and national festivals.

Today, festivals such as the annual Mamou Cajun Music Festival in Evangeline Parish, the Festival International de la Louisiane in Lafayette, and the Cajun French Music and Food Festival in Lake Charles are providing Cajuns, as well as everyone else, with opportunities to celebrate Cajun music and folklife and keep those traditions alive.

BARRY JEAN ANCELET
University of Louisiana at Lafayette

Barry Jean Ancelet, *Cajun Music: Its Origins and Development* (1989), *The Makers of Cajun Music / Musiciens Cadiens et Créoles* (1984); Shane K. Bernard, *Swamp Pop: Cajun and Creole Rhythm and Blues* (1996); Glenn R. Conrad, ed., *The Cajuns: Essays on Their History and Culture* (3d ed., 1983); Philip Gould (photographs) and Barry Ancelet (introduction), *Cajun Music and Zydeco* (1992); *J'etais au bal: Music from French Louisiana*, Swallow 6020; *Louisiana Cajun Music*, Old-Timey Records 108, 109, 110, 111, 114, 124, 125; *Louisiana French Cajun Music from the Southwest Prairies*, Rounder Records 6001, 6002; Pat Nyhan, Brian Rollins, and David Babb, *Let the Good Times Roll! A Guide to Cajun and Zydeco Music* (1998); Lauren Post, *Cajun Sketches from the Prairies of Southwest Louisiana* (2d ed., 1974); Irene Therese Whitfield, *Louisiana French Folk Song* (1969).

Classical Music and Opera

By the 18th century, it had become a mark of social distinction for members of the seaboard gentry to demonstrate an appreciation of good music and to perhaps play an instrument. Thomas Jefferson enjoyed the violin and collected a fine music library, consisting of pieces by Corelli, Bach, Handel, and Haydn, and William Byrd's library at Westover included examples of English and Italian opera. Williamsburg emerged as the music center of Virginia, after Peter Pelham began giving recitals there in 1752. Amateur concerts were also held weekly in the drawing room of the Governor's Palace.

Musical life in Charleston became even more sophisticated. The first known concert in that city was presented in April 1732, when John Salter, a local church organist, offered a program in the council chamber. The first ballad opera given in America, *Flora; Or, Hob in the Well*, was staged at the courtroom in Charleston three years later. In 1762 the St. Cecilia Society, the oldest musical society in the United States, was founded by 120 Carolina gentlemen who supported a paid orchestra and a yearly series of concerts. Foreign artists were occasionally imported; Maria Storer, perhaps the finest singer to perform in colonial America, was heard in February 1774. The St. Cecilia Society remained in existence until 1912, although the orchestra was eventually reduced to a quintet.

The Moravian settlements of the colonial South, most notably Salem, N.C., held musical festivals, built organs, and were noted for the quality of their choral singing. Other German and French immigrants brought with them a love of serious music and often scores of musical instruments. By the 19th century, New Orleans had eclipsed Charleston as a music center, especially in the production of French and Italian opera. By the Civil War, violinist Ole Bull and pianist Louis Moreau Gottschalk had played concerts all through the South, while soprano Jenny Lind had been heard in Richmond, Charleston, New Orleans, Natchez, and Memphis.

The first opera known to have been presented in New Orleans was André Grétry's *Sylvain*, given on 22 May 1796, at the St. Peter Street Theater, although there is reason to think earlier productions had been staged there. Later works by Boieldieu, Mehul, Dalayrac, and Monsigny (all stalwarts in Paris) were heard at the St. Peter Street Theater. Throughout the 19th century New Orleans had at least one resident opera company. The Théâtre d'Orléans was built in 1809 and rapidly became the city's cultural center. The theater burned in 1813 but was quickly rebuilt. Artists were recruited each season from the Paris Opera House, making the staging of works by Rossini, Spontini, Mozart, Gluck, Cherubini, and other European masters possible. Meyerbeer's *Les Huguenots* and Doni-

Memphis's Grand Opera House, early 1900s (Ann Rayburn Paper Americana Collection, Archives and Special Collections, University of Mississippi Library, Oxford)

zetti's *Lucia di Lammermoor* (sung in French) were but two of the many operas to receive American premieres at the Théâtre d'Orléans.

In 1835 Meyerbeer's *Robert le Diable* was staged for the first time in the United States at James Caldwell's Anglo-American Theater on Camp Street in New Orleans. The following season an Italian troupe presented the American premiere of Bellini's *Il Pirata* at the St. Charles Theater. After 1859 the French Opera House became the city's major lyric theater. Soprano Adelina Patti was engaged for a series of performances during the theater's second season, and Massenet's *Herodiade*, Lalo's *Le Roi d'Ys*, and Saint-Säens's *Samson and Delilah* all received their initial American stagings there after the Civil War. The well-rehearsed and lavishly mounted productions featured ballet adeptly prepared in the French tradition. Closed during the Civil War, the French Opera House reopened to become "the lyric temple of the South." Not until the close of the century, as New Orleans evolved from a Latin city into a predominantly Anglo-American one, did the theater fall on hard times. The French Opera House burned in 1919, following years of neglect and financial decline.

Although French conductor Antoine Jullien had led concerts in New Orleans before the Civil War, Patrick S. Gilmore rejuvenated a taste for "monster concerts" in 1864 when he assembled a chorus of 5,000 and a band of 500 to perform in Lafayette Square to celebrate Louisiana's return to the Union, a jubilee complete with fife-and-drum corps, church bells, and cannons. Resident orchestras of professional stature were not to return to the South, however, until the 20th century. By 1890, 6 of the 34 symphony orchestras of the United States classified as major orchestras were located in the South. Of those, the Dallas Symphony was the first to achieve that status. An orchestra for Dallas had been conceived in 1900 when Hans Kreissig, a German musician stranded in the city, gathered together what local talent he could and organized the Dallas Symphony Club. Five years later, a more formal attempt was made to establish a symphony by Walter Fried, who had studied conducting in Germany. The modern Dallas Symphony was launched in 1945 with the appointment of Antal Dorati as conductor. Dorati broadened the standard romantic repertoire to include unusual selections by Schumann and Mendelssohn and introduced both classical and modern compositions, not always to the approval of conservative Dallas audiences. When Dorati accepted an offer from the Minneapolis Symphony in 1949, he was replaced by Walter Hendl, formerly associate conductor of the New York Philharmonic, who was with the Dallas Symphony until 1958. Since then, the Dallas Symphony has met with varying success, under the leadership of Paul Kletzki, Georg Solti, Donald Johannos, Anshel Brusilow, and Eduardo Mata. Andrew Litton served as music director from 1994 to 2006.

The Houston Symphony, begun in 1913 under Julian Paul Blitz, reached major status after Efrem Kurtz was made director in 1948. Later a succession of superlative conductors—including Sir Thomas Beecham, Leopold Stokowski, Sir John Barbirolli, and André Previn—honed the Houston Symphony into the finest orchestra in the South. On tour under Barbirolli in 1964, the symphony performed at Philharmonic Hall in New York City, winning a prolonged ovation. Two years later, the orchestra moved into the resplendent Jesse H. Jones Hall for the Performing Arts. Hans Graf assumed leadership of the Houston Symphony in 2001. The symphony holds 170 concerts annually, reaching 350,000 people. It sponsors an exemplary outreach project, which takes volunteer musicians to schools, community centers, hospitals, and retirement homes.

Other major symphony orchestras in the South include the Atlanta Symphony (Robert Shaw directed the symphony for 21 years and Robert Spano now serves as music director); the New Orleans Philharmonic (under Carlos Miguel Prieto); the North Carolina Symphony (under the direction of William Henry Curry); and the San Antonio Symphony (under the direction of Larry Rachleff). Every southern city of importance has received international concert artists on tour: Paderewski, Caruso, Iturbi, Gigli, Rubinstein, and Heifetz. Pianist Van Cliburn, from Kilgore, Tex., who won the International Tchaikovsky Competition in Moscow in 1958, and soprano Leontyne Price, from Laurel, Miss., have each achieved world recognition on the concert stage and through recordings.

The prosperity of the contemporary South has supported a dramatic expansion of a performing arts infrastructure for classical music. Venues such as Dallas's Myerson Symphony Center, Nashville's Schermerhorn Symphony Center, and Birmingham's Alys Stephens Performing Arts Center help attract outstanding conductors and performers and patrons.

During the 1920s the Chicago Civic Opera and later the San Carlo Opera toured the larger southern cities, and New York's Metropolitan Opera Company makes annual visits to Atlanta and Dallas. Resident opera returned to New Orleans in 1943, soon evolving into the New Orleans Opera House Association under the direction of Walter Herbert. Unusual French works have occasionally been revived by the New Orleans Opera, and Verdi's *Attila* was staged by the company in 1969 for the first time in this country since 1850. By 1980, the South supported 14 professional opera companies, 3 of them of major importance. By 2007, there were 44 opera companies in the region.

The Greater Miami Opera Association was begun in 1941 on a limited budget under the management of Arturo Di Filippi. The first opera staged by the Florida company was *Pagliacci*, with Di Filippi himself singing the role of Canio. Under Robert Herman, the company expanded its budget, employing singers like Eileen Farrell, Franco Corelli, Joan Sutherland, and Luciano Pavarotti in his American debut. The Houston Grand Opera was formed in 1956, with Richard Strauss's *Salome* its initial work. A mounting of *Die Walküre* in 1959 gave the South a rare look at Wagner's *Ring* cycle, whereas Massenet's *Don Quichotte* in 1969 and Rossini's *La Donna del Lago* in 1981 were both operas rarely presented anywhere in the United States. The company also revived Scott Joplin's long-forgotten ragtime opera *Treemonisha* and Gershwin's *Porgy and Bess*, productions that were eventually taken to Broadway and the West Coast.

The Dallas Opera, founded in 1957 by Lawrence V. Kelly, has enjoyed solid financial backing and unusual artistic leadership. Soprano Maria Callas launched the company with a series of performances that included a gala concert, Verdi's *La Traviata*, Cherubini's *Medea*, and Donizetti's *Lucia di Lammermoor*. Nicola Rescigno was named musical director, and Italian stage director Franco Zeffirelli did his first work in America with the Dallas company. Alexis Minotis was imported from the Greek national theater to mount the internationally acclaimed production of *Medea*, which eventually traveled to Covent Garden, La Scala, and Epidaurus. Jean Rosenthal and later Tharon Musser came from Broadway to supervise the company's lighting. Joan Sutherland, Montserrat Caballé, Jon Vickers, Teresa Berganza, Gwyneth Jones, Placido Domingo, Helga Dernesch, and the legendary Italian soprano Magda Olivero all made their American debuts with the Dallas Opera, and the company has staged the American premieres of Handel's *Alcina* and Vivaldi's *Orlando Furioso*.

Charleston reemerged as a music center when Gian Carlo Menotti brought the Spoleto Festival to the New World in May 1977. Since then, summer offerings in Charleston have ranged from Tchaikovsky's *The Queen of Spades* (with Olivero as the old Countess) to Haydn's *Creation* to Barber's *Vanessa* to Shostakovich's *Lady Macbeth of the Mtsensk District*. Other southern opera companies include the Charlotte Opera Association, Civic Opera of the Palm Beaches, Fort Worth Opera, Opera Memphis, and Opera/South in Jackson, Miss.

The South has inspired a variety of serious compositions. Bohemian-born Anton Philip Heinrich immigrated to the United States in 1805, publishing *The Dawning of Music in Kentucky* 15 years later. Early in the 20th century, Henry F. Gilbert wrote *Dance in Place Congo* and *Comedy Overture on Negro Themes*, based on black folk melodies. George Gershwin spent several months in South Carolina gathering material for his opera *Porgy and Bess*, and Ferde Grofé, Gershwin's orchestrator on *Rhapsody in Blue*, wrote *Mississippi Suite* in 1925.

John Powell, a native of Richmond, Va., who studied in Vienna, used African American themes in his *Negro Rhapsody* (1918) and Anglo-American folk tunes in his overture *In Old Virginia* (1921). William Grant Still, born on a plantation near Woodville, Miss., developed into a major spokesman for blacks in serious music. His *Afro-American Symphony* was initially performed by the Rochester Philharmonic in 1931, although opera remained the composer's great love. *A Southern Interlude* and especially *A Bayou Legend*, both dating from the 1940s, have solidified Still's reputation among opera enthusiasts. Carlisle Floyd, a native of Latta, S.C., established himself as an American opera composer of the first order with *Susannah* in 1955 and has continued to write prolifically in that field. *Wuthering Heights* was commissioned by the Santa Fe Opera in 1958, and *The Passion of Jonathan Wade*, set in North Carolina during the Civil War, received its premiere four years later at the New York City Opera under a Ford Foundation grant. *Willie Stark*, based on Robert Penn Warren's novel *All the King's Men*, was first staged by Harold Prince in 1981 for the Houston Grand Opera, in a production that combined elements of the operatic and Broadway theater.

Of composers working in a modern idiom, Georgia-born Wallingford Riegger stands at the forefront. Riegger produced a number of dance scores for Martha Graham, then concentrated more on orchestral forms. *His Fourth Symphony* (1959) was performed by the Boston Symphony Orchestra and judged by national critics to have both head and heart appeal. Other southern art composers include William Levi Dawson from Alabama, Lamar Stringfield from North Carolina, and Don Gillis from Texas.

RONALD L. DAVIS
Southern Methodist University

Gavin Campbell, *Music and the Making of a New South* (2004); Ronald L. Davis, *A History of Music in American Life*, 3 vols. (1980–82); Quaintance Eaton, *Opera Caravan* (1957); Robert Bartlett Haas, ed., *William Grant Still and the Fusion of Cultures in American Music* (1972); Henry A. Kmen, *Music in New Orleans: The Formative Years, 1791–1841* (1966); Alex Ross, *New Yorker* (25 June 2007); Hubert Roussel, *The Houston Symphony Orchestra, 1913–1971* (1972); William Schoell, *The Opera of the Twentieth Century* (2006); Beverly Soll, *I Dream a World: The Operas of William Grant Still* (2005); Albert Stoutamire, *Music of the Old South: Colony to Confederacy* (1972); Jack· Sullivan, *New World Symphonies: How American Culture Changed European Music* (1999).

Country Music

Although country music is a powerful cultural presence in the United States and an international export of growing magnitude, it is difficult to define. It is a creation and organic reflection of southern working-class culture, changing as that society has changed, but it is, at the same time, a dynamic element of American popular culture. In the 80 years or so since Texas fiddler Eck Robertson made the first documented phonograph recording by a white rural entertainer, the music has become a massive industry with an appeal that cuts across social, generational, and geographic lines.

Country music had its origins in the folk culture of the South—a diverse culture that drew upon the interrelating resources of Europe and Africa. It was British at its core but eclectic in its borrowing. Long before the decade of the 1920s, when the radio and recording industries made their first exploitations of southern folk talent, fiddlers, banjoists, string bands, balladeers, and gospel singers had proliferated throughout the South. Most of their performances were given at house parties or at other community functions such as house raisings, fish fries, or corn shuckings, but many were able to function on a broader basis, and in a quasi-professional manner, at fiddle contests or in medicine or vaudeville shows. Musicians drew upon their inherited folk resources for songs and performing styles, but they also picked up material that was adaptable to their styles and that fit their community aesthetic standards from black entertainers or from the vast panoply of 19th-century popular music. The establish-

The Gully Jumpers, early country music string band, 1920s
(Country Music Foundation, Library and Media Center, Nashville)

ment of radio stations in the South after 1920 (including wsʙ in Atlanta, wsᴍ in Nashville, and wʙᴀᴘ in Fort Worth) and the recording of rural performers after 1922 encouraged further professionalization, as well as the development of an "industry."

The early entertainers were rural, for the most part, but not exclusively agricultural. Country music has always been a working-class music (although not self-consciously so until the 1960s). The performers of the early period, who were usually part-time musicians, worked as railroad men, coal miners, textile workers, carpenters, wagoners, sawmill workers, and cowboys, and even occasionally as country lawyers, doctors, and preachers. Whatever their occupation, their dialects, speech patterns, and performing styles reflected the rural South. Given the social context of the 1920s, when the rural and socially conservative South seemed greatly out of step with a dynamic nation, and when its rural inhabitants seemed given over to strange oddities and eccentricities, such as snake handling, tenantry, and night riding, it is not surprising that a term such as "hillbilly" should be affixed to the rural music of the region.

The commercialization of southern rural music had both positive and negative consequences. On the one hand, folk styles and folk songs received a wider hearing and, presumably, longer leases on life than they otherwise would have had; on the other hand, folk styles were homogenized and diluted, and traditional songs were gradually replaced with newly composed ones. But too much has been made of this change. Folk styles were never pure; folk songs were drawn from a multitude of sources; and folk musicians were never reluctant to accept or seek some kind of reward for their talents.

The string bands of country music's first decade, including such colorful examples of self-parody as the Skillet Lickers, the Fruit Jar Drinkers, the Possum Hunters, and Dr. Smith's Champion Hoss Hair Pullers, as well as the more conventionally named groups such as the North Carolina Ramblers and the East Texas Serenaders, played hoedown tunes and British dance tunes, but they were also receptive to current popular dance tunes and especially to ragtime, which remained a national passion in the World War I period. Songs originally designed for the parlor piano, such as "Chicken Reel," "Redwing," and "Over the Waves," or for marching bands, such as "Under the Double Eagle," made their way into the repertoires of string band musicians and have become permanently ensconced in the country music repertoire. Singers also ranged far and wide for their songs.

A large percentage of the early hillbilly songs came from 19th-century popular music, the "parlor songs," which had originally been written by professional composers and disseminated as lavishly illustrated sheet music among the nation's urban middle class. Such songs as "The Letter Edged in Black," "Little Rosewood Casket," "Little Old Log Cabin in the Lane," "Listen to the Mockingbird," and "Molly Darling" found a home among rural southerners long after ceasing to be fashionable with their original audience. Many of these sentimental favorites are still performed regularly by bluegrass and old-time country entertainers.

Country entertainers, therefore, were torn between tradition and modernity. They were loyal to their own communities but were eager to build a wider audience. Neither they nor their promoters (radio and recording men, booking agents, advertisers) were quite sure whether the most feasible promotional method would involve a rustic or an urbane approach. Country performers might have preferred conventional suits or even formal attire, but they were encouraged to clothe themselves in rustic or cowboy costumes. The conflict between rusticity and urbanity has been a factor in country music development, in sound as well as in image.

Although string bands and homespun acts predominated on early hillbilly recordings and on radio shows, the star system soon asserted itself and individual talents rose to the top. Vernon Dalhart (born Marion T. Slaughter in Jefferson, Tex.) contributed to the music's commercial acceptance by recording in 1924 such nationally popular songs as "The Prisoner's Song" and "Wreck of the Old 97." Uncle Dave Macon, a comedian, singer, and five-string banjoist from Tennessee, was one of the first stars of the *Grand Ole Opry* and a repository of 19th-century folk and popular songs. Although there were a host of pioneer performers, the most seminal, the ones whose impacts are still felt in the music today, were the Carter Family, from Virginia, and Jimmie Rodgers, from Mississippi, both of whom were first recorded in early August 1927 in Bristol, Tenn. No group better embodied the mood and style of the family parlor and country church than the Carters; their three-part harmony, Maybelle's unique guitar style, and their large collection of vintage songs (such as "Wildwood Flower" and "Will the Circle Be Unbroken") still influence country singers today. In Jimmie Rodgers, the former railroad brakeman from Meridian, Miss., the music found its first superstar. Rodgers personified the rambling man, an image in sharp juxtaposition to that which the Carter Family projected. His "blue yodel," his appealing personal style and tragic early death, plus his eclectic repertoire of blues, hobo, train, rounder, and love songs, made him, posthumously, the "Father of Country Music."

Country music survived the Great Depression and then solidified its position in American popular culture and greatly broadened its market. The 1930s were the heyday of live radio programming, and cowboy singers, duets, string bands, yodelers, and balladeers could be heard everywhere, even in New York City. Radio barn dances—Saturday-night variety shows with a rural or folk flavor—took place in many cities, but none was more important than WLS's *National Barn Dance* (Chicago) or WSM's *Grand Ole Opry* in Nashville. The *Grand Ole Opry*, which first went on the air in 1925, really affirmed its status as a national institution when it gained network affiliation on NBC in 1939. The 50,000-watt, clear-channel stations, such as WSM and KWKH in Shreveport, La., played crucial roles in circulating country music, but no stations had a more profound impact in the national dissemination of country and gospel music than the Mexican-border stations—popularly called X-stations because of their call letters (XERF, XEG, and the like). Their powerful transmission, sometimes surpassing 100,000 watts, blanketed North America with rural music (from the Carter Family to the Stamps Quartet), evangelism, and incessant advertising, which have become part of our national folklore. Radio exposure led to broadened public appearances and the emergence of booking agents and the complex framework of music business promotion.

As the professionalism and commercialization of country music proceeded, the nature of the music also changed. Traditional songs continued to appear with great frequency in the repertoires of such groups as the Blue Sky Boys and Mainer's Mountaineers. Nevertheless, newly composed songs gradually edged the older ones aside, and fledgling performers increasingly sought to find a commercial formula as successful as that of Jimmie Rodgers. Stylistically, the southeastern hoedown-oriented string bands and the "brother duets" (acts such as the Monroe Brothers, who usually featured mandolin and guitar accompaniment) relied heavily on old-time songs and ballads and remained conservative in performance and material. On the other hand, musicians from the southwestern part of the South (Texas, Louisiana, and Oklahoma) were more innovative, producing dynamic styles that would revolutionize country music. Very few observers recognized distinctions within country music before World War II, and performers with widely varying styles and repertoires often appeared together on radio shows or on radio barn dances. Whether cowboy singer, mandolin-and-guitar duet, or hot string band, they all conveyed a homespun or down-home feeling, and hillbilly was the rubric that covered them all. Nevertheless, a modern perspective suggests the great differences among them. In 1934, Gene Autry, a radio hillbilly singer from Texas, went to Hollywood, where he became the first great singing cowboy in film. The romance of the cowboy would have been appealing to country singers in any case, but Autry's Saturday afternoon horse operas, his syndicated Melody Ranch radio show, and his very popular recordings magnified the appeal, while providing country musicians with an identity much more respectable than that of the hillbilly. The popularity of the romantic movie-cowboy songs declined significantly after World War II, but singers wearing cowboy costumes endured long after that.

More strongly reflective of evolving southwestern culture than the movie-cowboy songs was western swing, the jazz-influenced string band music popularized by Milton Brown and his Musical Brownies, the Light Crust Doughboys, and Bob Wills and the Texas Playboys. The western swing bands were eclectic in repertoire and were receptive to new stylistic ideas, including the use of drums, horns, and electrified instruments. Developing alongside western swing, and drawing its inspiration even more directly from the bars and dance halls of the Southwest, was honky-tonk music. Country music's entrance into white roadhouses, which were called generically "honky-tonks," divested the music of much of its pastoral innocence and tone. The result was a realistic musical sound that documented the movement of country people into an urban industrial environment.

World War II was both the major catalyst for change in country music and the chief agent in its nationalization. The country music industry itself lan-

Country star Webb Pierce's guitar-shaped swimming pool at his home on North Curtiswood Lane in Nashville (Charles Reagan Wilson Collection, Center for the Study of Southern Culture, University of Mississippi)

guished under wartime restraints: shellac rationing (which reduced the number of records released), the military drafting of musicians, and the scarcity of gas and tires (which limited personal appearances). On the other hand, jukeboxes became ubiquitous accoutrements in bars, cafés, and penny arcades, and country records began appearing on them in cities like Detroit, Chicago, and Los Angeles (in part, a reflection of the movement of southerners to northern and western industrial centers). The *Grand Ole Opry* gained its reputation as a mecca for country fans during the 1940s, and Tennessean Roy Acuff, who joined the show in 1938, became the unquestioned king of country music during those years, taking his road shows to all parts of the United States and holding down the most important time slots on the Saturday night *Opry*. His versions of "Wabash Cannon Ball" and "The Great Speckled Bird" made both his name and that of the *Opry* famous throughout America. Above all, in the wartime crucible of economic and demographic change and heightened migration, the mood, style, and appeal of country music were destined to change significantly.

Country music's first great commercial boom came in the years immediately following the war, continuing to about 1955. Postwar prosperity and the ending of wartime restraints generated an unprecedented demand for amusement. Record labels proliferated; new barn dances, such as the *Louisiana Hayride*, competed with the *Grand Ole Opry*; and thousands of jukeboxes reverberated with the songs of such country entertainers as Eddy Arnold, Kitty Wells, Lefty Frizzell, and Hank Williams. By the time Williams died, on 1 January 1953, pop singers were "covering" his songs and country music was winning commercial acceptance and respectability that had earlier been scarcely dreamed of. Just a few short years later, country music's "permanent plateau of prosperity" had been shattered by the revolution wrought by Elvis Presley and the rockabillies. All forms of traditional country music suffered temporarily as promoters and recording men began their urgent searches for young and vigorous stylists who could re-create what Elvis had done and who could hold that youthful audience that now dominated American music. One consequence of this quest was the creation of a pop style of country music, known generally as "country pop" or "the Nashville Sound." This form of music was considered to be a compromise that would appeal to both old-time country fans and the newly sought pop audience. By using vocal choruses and a sedate form of instrumentation (vibes, violins, piano, a muted bass), country-pop singers would avoid the extremes of both rockabilly and hillbilly.

Commercially, country music's development since the late 1950s has been one of the great success stories of American popular culture. Country performers now enjoy patronage around the world, and country concerts are regularly presented in the White House and on the Mall near the Smithsonian Institution. Country music's spectacular ascent and expansion have been accompanied by self-doubts and contradictions and by anguished debates among performers and fans concerning the music's alleged dilution or loss of identity. Many adherents fear that the music may lose its soul as it gains the world. Although the quest for crossover records remains a powerful passion in modern country music, revivals of older country forms have periodically taken place since the rock-and-roll era. Honky-tonk music lives in the performances of men like George Jones, Merle Haggard, Moe Bandy, and Alan Jackson. Bill Monroe and his fellow bluegrass practitioners have preserved the acoustic style of instrumentation and the "high lonesome" style of singing; bluegrass festivals are held somewhere almost every weekend from May until November. Doc Watson, a repository of rural styles, continues to revive the older country songs, even dipping occasionally into the song bag of ancient British material.

One of the most remarkable manifestations of interest in older songs and styles has come through the performances of youthful entertainers, or through older musicians who have catered to youth. Emmylou Harris, from Virginia, came to "hard country" through the influence of her friend and mentor, the country-rock singer Gram Parsons. Her fresh, uncluttered style of singing and her choice of material have been considerably more traditional than most of the women singers who grew up in the country music world. Willie Nelson, a veteran honky-tonk singer from Texas and one of country music's greatest writers, has probably done most to bridge the gap between the rock-oriented youth audience and country music. He has done so by being receptive to their music and their heroes and by affecting a lifestyle and mode of dress (beard, earring, jogging shoes) that put them at ease. In the process, he has introduced his young fans to the best of older country and gospel songs. Since the 1980s, although country music has moved inexorably toward a suburban sound (heard in the music of people like Garth Brooks, Kenny Chesney, Faith Hill, Tim Mc-Graw, and Shania Twain) that reflects the new demographics of the South and the United States, the music has nevertheless experienced periodic infusions of music by younger performers who have consciously revived and updated traditional forms of country music. The list includes such people as Ricky Scaggs, Dwight Yoakam, Randy Travis, Steve Earle, Emmylou Harris, Iris DeMent, George Strait, Brad Paisley, Tim O'Brien, Patty Loveless, Joe Nichols, the Dixie Chicks, and Alan Jackson.

Country music, then, endures in many manifestations. Yet it remains as resistant to definition as it did over 80 years ago when it was first gaining an organized commercial identity. It has become a phenomenon with worldwide appeal, but it maintains its southern identification. Nashville remains its financial hub, the center of a multimillion-dollar music business. Country singers still come from southern working-class backgrounds in surprising numbers, and both they and the lyrics of their songs convey the ambivalent impulses that have always been at the center of country music and southern culture: puritanism and hedonism, a reverence for home and a fascination with rambling, the sense of being uniquely different and at the same time more American than anyone else. Country songs convey a down-home approach to life and an elemental view of love, home, and patriotism that are absent from other forms of American music. In an age of computerized complexity, country music owes its appeal to the yearning for simplicity and rootedness that permeates modern American society.

BILL C. MALONE
Madison, Wisconsin

Nicholas Dawidoff, *In the Country of Country: People and Places in American Music* (1997); Curt Ellison, *Country Music Culture: From Hard Times to Heaven* (1995); Bruce Feiler, *Dreaming Out Loud: Garth Brooks, Wynonna Judd, Wade Hayes, and the Changing Face of Nashville* (1998); Douglas B. Green, *Country Roots: The Origins of*

Country Music (1976); Paul Kingsbury, ed., *The Encyclopedia of Country Music* (1998); Paul Kingsbury and Alanna Nash, eds., *Will the Circle Be Unbroken: Country Music in America* (2006); Bill C. Malone, *Country Music, U.S.A.: A Fifty-Year History* (1968; rev. eds., 1985, 2002), *Don't Get above your Raisin': Country Music and the Southern Working Class* (2002); Tony Russell, *Country Music Records: A Discography, 1922–1942* (2004); Ivan Tribe, *Mountaineer Jamboree: Country Music in West Virginia* (1984); Charles K. Wolfe, *A Good-Natured Riot: The Birth of the Grand Ole Opry* (1999), *Kentucky Country: Folk and Country Music of Kentucky* (1982), *Tennessee Strings: The Story of Country Music in Tennessee* (1977).

Dance, Black

An enduring expressiveness, even during the oppression of slavery, marks the history of black dance in America, and through dance many aspects of the African heritage of black Americans thrive. As Lynne Fauley Emery, in her seminal work *Black Dance in the United States from 1619 to 1970* (1972), explains, "A fundamental element of African aesthetic expression was the dance." When slave traders plundered Africa, dance assumed new meaning. Aboard slave ships, the traders frequently forced their captives to dance, either for entertainment for the crew or for exercise (healthy slaves brought higher prices). Even under such conditions the slave ship dances served expressive purposes, too.

A strong African heritage flourished among slaves in the West Indies and spread to plantations of the American South. Among the dances carried over were the Calenda, the Chica, and the Juba or Jumba. The beat of the drum, an integral part of black dance, largely died out in the South after the so-called Stono insurrection in South Carolina in 1739, when escaping slaves beat drums to rally participants. Fearing a secret drum communication system among blacks, slave owners pressed for the banning of slave assemblies and the use of drums. Except in the Georgia Sea Islands and Louisiana, slaves replaced the drum accompaniment to dances by slapping and patting their bodies, stomping their feet, and blowing reed pipes.

On southern plantations, slaves danced both freely and under duress. Plantation owners often brought slaves to "the big house" to entertain through dance and music. Many owners prized slaves who danced well, and they sponsored dancing contests. Some owners allowed slave dances on their own plantations, and some gave written passes for slaves to attend dances on other plantations. Whites held conflicting views about black dance, however. Even those who enjoyed the slave entertainment tended to characterize black dances as heathen, lewd, and wild. Black dances, including ones such as the Ring Shout, which were part of religious services, met with particularly strong disapproval from white Protestants.

Occasions for dancing included funerals, weddings, quiltings, corn shuckings, Saturday evenings, and holidays such as Christmas and St. John's Day (24 June). Funeral dances in particular retained African elements, whereas wedding dances (so-called despite prohibition of legal slave marriages on plantations) showed stronger European influences. Popular dances included the Buck, the Pigeon Wing, the Jig, the Cakewalk, the Ring Dance, the Buzzard Lope, Water Dances, and the Juba. Agnes de Mille notes that the rhythm of such dances infused American dance and music with a new lifeblood through the accent on the offbeat or upbeat, a rhythm completely different from European styles. The cotillions, reels, and quadrilles of whites influenced black dances later in the antebellum period.

Black dance in New Orleans had its own character and importance. New Orleans was one of the river-port cities where the Coonjine, or Counjaille, dance sprang up among the slaves who were hired out by their masters as stevedores or roustabouts. In the late 1700s and early 1800s, quadroon women—those born to a mulatto mother and white father—sought to become the mistresses of upper-class white men and staged elaborate dances in order to form liaisons. The dances, however, represented white American and European trends rather than black ones. The dances of slaves at Congo Square, an open field "northwest of the city limits," contrasted sharply. Seeking to curb the influence of West Indian immigrants in the early 1800s, the New Orleans city council prohibited assemblies of slaves for dancing and other purposes except on Sundays in an open place. Congo Square became that site. Drums were allowed as accompaniment to such popular dances as the Chica, the Babouille, the Cata, the Voudou, and the Congo. New Orleans blacks also witnessed special, frenzied voodoo ceremonial dances incorporating many African elements, and whites saw such dances as cannibalistic rituals. New Orleans's Mardi Gras began as a segregated event, and black participants devised their own festivities and incorporated dances into their parades.

Meanwhile, the minstrelsy tradition spread nationwide. "Even before the Revolutionary War," states Emery, "Americans were being entertained by impersonations of Negroes, and particularly of Negro dancing." In 1828, T. D. Rice, a northern performer, donned blackface and performed as Jim Crow, supposedly mimicking the dance of a crippled, elderly black groom he had seen. Historians generally agree with Emery that "Rice . . . rather than giving audiences a true picture of Negro dance, may have created the first clear-cut, long-lasting caricature of that dance: that grotesque, shuffling, peculiar, eccentric, jumping, loose-limbed, awkward, funny and, of course, rhythmic dance."

One outstanding exception among minstrel performers was the great black dancer William Henry Lane, known as Master Juba, who in his brief lifetime introduced a style that blended Irish and Afro-American dance. In general, though, minstrel shows parodied black life through incorporation of such dances as the Walk-Around and the Cakewalk. Stereotypes of happy, naturally rhythmic, dancing blacks lingered long afterward. Even black minstrel performers of the 1860s felt compelled to wear wigs and paint exaggerated features to conform to white audiences' views of blacks. Among the black minstrel dancers who achieved great fame were Billy Kersands, a member of the Georgia Minstrel troupe and master of the Virginia Essence dance, and Ernest Hogan, a member of the Georgia Graduates minstrel troupe and originator of the Pasmala dance step.

In the 1890s, increasing numbers of black performers entered the stage. In 1891, dancer Bill Robinson, a native of Richmond, Va., joined a traveling show called "The South before the War" and in 1898 settled in New York City. Robinson, later known as "Bojangles" and "The King of Tapology," broke barriers as the first black star of the Ziegfeld Follies but gained more recognition—and criticism—for film roles late in his career as the kindly, shuffling servant in scenes with Shirley Temple. Robinson's ability to create rhythmic sound through dance markedly shaped later tap-dancing trends. Throughout the 1920s, black tap dancers such as Robinson and Clayton "Peg-Leg" Bates, a native of South Carolina, drew applause. Tap became associated with black dancers, despite its origins in Irish and English clogging.

While groundbreaking shows such as Darktown Follies and Shuffle Along enthralled northern audiences with black song and dance, small black minstrel troupes continued to tour the South, eventually forming a vaudeville circuit called the Theatre Owners' Booking Association (TOBA). After the Civil War, blacks in the South turned primarily to the churches as social centers. Many churches strongly disapproved of dance, yet traditions lived on. Emery describes one important trend: "There also developed a peculiar institution called the jook, or juke house. . . . Jook came to mean a Negro pleasure house: either a bawdy house or house for dancing, drinking, and gambling. It is in these jooks that 'the Negro dances circulated over the world' were created. Before being seen on the stage by the outside world, these dances made the rounds of Southern jukes."

Two highly popular dances that had such beginnings were the Black Bottom, which originated in Nashville, Tenn., and the Big Apple, which originated near Columbia, S.C. As masses of southern blacks moved to the North, particularly to Harlem, in the early 1900s, they took or influenced such dances as Charleston, Ballin' the Jack, Shimmy, and Mooche. Other dances with black roots evolved, too, such as Lindy Hop, Jitterbug, Shag, Suzi-Q, Camel Walk, and Truckin'.

Progress came slowly in concert dance and classical ballet. Black dancers were long scorned because of American and European whites' standards of grace, beauty, and aesthetic purity. On an amateur level, however, the Hampton Institute Creative Dance Group (Hampton, Va.) pioneered in exploring black dance traditions in the South. Its student performers toured the country and emphasized dances based on both African and southern plantation traditions. The Hampton Institute programs directly and indirectly influenced black dance trends, and Emery notes that "black concert dance companies were formed throughout the segregated institutions of the South, including Spellman College in Atlanta, Fisk University, Howard University, and Tuskegee Institute." Particularly at the South's predominantly black institutions strong programs in black dance still thrive.

In the realm of professional dance, black southerners have faced limited opportunities, though the black southern dance heritage has definitely influenced nationwide trends. By the 1970s black dancers and choreographers had made many inroads across the country. Alvin Ailey, a native of Texas who moved as a youth to Los Angeles, formed the Alvin Ailey American Dance Theater in 1958, one of the most highly acclaimed and widely known companies in the United States. Various famous productions have focused on themes of black experiences in the South, such as *District Storyville*, focusing on the early black jazz musicians who played in brothels in New Orleans, and Pearl Primus's *Strange Fruit*, dealing with lynchings of blacks in the South. Currently, the South boasts such excellent showcases for dance performance as the Spoleto U.S.A. Festival in Charleston, S.C., and the American Dance Festival in Durham, N.C. Dance companies in the South include some that focus on black dance, such as the African-American Dance Ensemble of North Carolina, and many dance leaders encourage more exploration of forms that uniquely express all realms of black experience.

Blacks continued to influence popular dance styles into the 21st century. Singers such as James Brown often introduced a new dance with an accompanying song. Memphian Rufus Thomas began his musical career on the minstrel circuit and later recorded his "Funky Chicken," the title of both his song and the dance he popularized. Michael Jackson has achieved international fame for his music and accompanying dance step, the "Moon Walk," a "postmodern" example of black dance no longer rooted in southern black culture. Most recently, rap, hip-hop, and crunk music emerged from urban black neighborhoods, including Atlanta, Memphis, and New Orleans, accompanied by the dance styles of break dancing, popping, locking, Gangsta Walking (also known as G-Walking or bucking), and krumping.

SHARON A. SHARP
University of Mississippi

Barbara N. Cohen-Stratymer, *Biographical Dictionary of Dance* (1982); *Dance Magazine* (May 1984, March 1985); Lynne F. Emery, *Black Dance in the United States from 1619 to 1970* (1972); Julia L. Foulkes, *Modern Bodies: Dance and American Modernism from Martha Graham to Alvin Ailey* (2001); Jane Goldberg, *Dance Scope* (Summer 1981); Richard Long, *The Black Tradition in American Dance* (1989); Cobbett Steinberg, ed., *The Dance Anthology* (1980); Ellen Switzer, *Dancers! Horizons in American Dance* (1982); Edward Thorpe, *Black Dance* (1994); Julinda L. Williams, *Dance Scope* (Spring 1980).

Dance, Development of

Ethnic dance traditions and the latest dances dictated by changing fashions in European high culture were not common in the dispersed settlements of the South. Into the mid-20th century, the South's reluctance to adopt popular dance trends and the security afforded it by folk traditions dictated regional dance expressions. No historical studies, however, offer a broad perspective on the development of dance in this region. Folklore studies of dance remain geographically specific and do not deal with issues of time.

Three European nations provided the greatest influences on the development of dance in the Anglo-American South. From the West Indies, Spain penetrated what is now Florida. Spanish court dances such as the *chacona* and *gibao*, as well as peasant dances, have been described in Mexico and the West Indies. England first settled in the Chesapeake Bay area and, after 1713, extended its claim to what would become the 13 American colonies and also parts of the West Indies. France occupied the natural harbor of New Orleans and explored the Mississippi River, north and west. The court and folk traditions of England and France thus entered American life. Among black slaves, rich dance traditions from Africa via the slaves in the West Indies flourished, bringing to America such dances as the Chica and the Juba.

The predominantly Anglican society of the early and mid-18th-century South did not find the amusement of theatrical and fashionable dancing a social disruption like the Calvinists of the Northeast did. Itinerant dancing masters

Women dancing, Birmingham, Ala., 1928 (Woodward Iron Company Collections, Special Collections, University of Alabama Library, Tuscaloosa)

and musicians, like William Dering, Francis Christian, George Brownell, Peter Pelham, and Charles and Mrs. Stagg, connected the upper and middle classes of townships and plantations in a network of teaching circuits. These teachers brought a Western European classical aesthetic, technique, and repertory of essentially baroque court dances—minuet, rigaudon, allemande, gavotte, and others. As the Northeast diversified and expanded its population, these itinerants moved north to cities like Baltimore, Philadelphia, and Boston. Dancing masters filled a social need for the accomplishments of polite company—conducting oneself gracefully at the many military tributes and encampment celebrations, birthnight balls, and festivities for visiting dignitaries. Urban musical societies and clubs, like the St. Cecilia Society of Charleston, S.C. (1762), sanctioned the private performances of music and dance.

Those persons whose daily lives in the South did not allow free time to pursue refinements of high culture retained their traditional dances, which they performed on a seasonal basis and which supported community cohesion. Thus, sailors' competitive jigs, African slaves' tribal dances, and faded variations of 17th-century dances from Western Europe (for example, pavane, allemande, courante, sarabande, galliard, passepied, and minuet) mixed loosely with less intensely performed popular dances like those English country dances modeled on John Playford's *The English Dancing Master* (1651–1726) and, after 1720, informal French contra dances.

The black slave dances served as a mechanism for keeping alive many African traditions, particularly those associated with funerals and festive occasions. Popular dances with distinct African roots included the Buck, the Ring Dance, and the Cakewalk. Although whites frequently described blacks' dances as wild and offensive, slave owners touted their slaves' dancing abilities, had slaves dance as entertainment for guests, and sponsored dancing contests among slaves from various plantations. In New Orleans, many unique black dance traditions developed. Slaves meeting at the city-approved assembly site known as Congo Square enjoyed such popular dances as the Babouille and the Cata, and voodoo traditions from the West Indies also influenced the developing black dance forms in New Orleans.

Economic opportunities presented by the South's climate, fertile land, and raw materials motivated steady trade and settlement. Three centuries of diverse settlement made for a heterogeneous population. However, with the exception of towns like Charleston and New Orleans, whose greater density and economic diversity made them a stage for the display of cultural differences in status and roles, homogeneous communities in which daily life was narrowly focused on agricultural subsistence characterized inland life.

The commitment to an agrarian way of life slowed the development of commerce, manufacturing, and transportation in the South until well into the 20th century. This meant that traditions and styles in physical expression in the South, as in other areas of culture, were generally insular. For example, the conventions of 18th-century public life—dramatized courtesy, elaborate rules of deportment, and formal conduct of events—dominated regional dance. The Northeast and Northwest supported lyceums and established public education in the early 19th century, but the cause of public education was not strongly pursued in the South. Public schools and educational programs typically promoted dance activities. Specifically, physical education programs used dance and helped contribute to the widespread acceptability and appreciation of dance as a useful function of everyday life, something that was lacking in the South except at a few private academies. Furthermore, the emphasis even in private academies was on traditional, 18th-century rationalizations of dance and not on new ideas from physical educators and dancing masters of high fashion. Without a mass communications network afforded by public education and good transportation, the cultural life of the South did not support modern dance.

The growth of southern towns in the late 18th century and of cities in the mid-19th century intensified the contrast between ethnic, social, and theatrical dances and made the nonverbal language of gestures and attitudes in these styles an important aspect of communication. In a city like New Orleans, for example, French, German, Spanish, and English cultures not only met but vied. Dancing cemented participants' and observers' ethnic and national ties. Cajuns, Creoles, mulattoes, and quadroons—representing the infusion of immigrants into the American South—identified performer and observer with dances. Competition and cooperation developed between theaters and opera houses, as well as between those individuals involved in the Mardi Gras and other seasonal festivities.

Theatrical tours helped to knit the South together and give it connections to the mass audience and the fashionable dance activities in the rest of the United States. Theatrical managers brought well-known European and American performers of pantomime, the romantic ballet, and other dance forms into all areas of the South. Charleston, S.C., a haven for expatriates from France and emigrants from the West Indies, had been a theatrical center as far back as the 1790s. French dancer and choreographer Alexandre Placide (c. 1750–1812), a multitalented performer whose pantomime productions were the most popular theatrical dance genre of their day, sent southern touring companies north to Richmond. The Louisiana Purchase of 1803 drew theatrical dancers, itinerant dancing masters, and popular and fashionable dance culture west with the settlers. The Ohio and Mississippi Rivers provided easy travel, and their shore towns had entertainment-starved audiences. Samuel Drake (1769–1854), James H. Caldwell (1793–1863), Noah Ludlow (1795–1886), and Solomon Smith (1801–69) were the most famous theatrical managers to exploit the southern frontier.

Dancers like the black American Willi Henry Lane, "Master Juba" (1825–52), minstrel artists like the blackface Thomas Dartmont Rice, who apparently invented the character of Jim Crow in 1828, and later road companies (1843–1908) that used the minstrel theme romanticized the South to audiences all over the country. Depicting contented, artless slaves, minstrel shows usually only parodied black dance traditions and thus shaped long-held views of black dance as shuffling, rhythmic, and comical. Minstrel shows were popular nationwide during the 1800s. River showboats that presented theatrical dancers, music, and dramatic entertainments were popular from 1836 to 1925.

In the early 20th century the Appalachian and Ozark mountain regions and other protected pockets of culture in the American South remained free from the currents of modern commercial and economic development. These areas attracted adherents of the new scholarly disciplines of folklore and anthropology who felt that early American cultural patterns, including those of music and dance, might still survive in the South untouched by modern times. An early noteworthy researcher in this new fieldwork was British musicologist Cecil Sharp, founder of the English Folk Dance Society, who, in 1916–17, believed he had found vestiges of 17th-century dance in rural Kentucky and Tennessee.

The post–World War II era saw the expansion of professional dance companies in the South. As earlier in the 20th century, southern artists joined national dance companies and made their mark. Alvin Ailey, born in Rogers, Tex., in 1931, founded the Alvin Ailey American Dance Theater. Much of Ailey's choreography reflected African American culture he had grown up with in the South, including blues, jazz, gospel music, and folklore.

The history of dance in the American South offers folklorists and cultural historians a unique challenge. In contrast to recent national trends, the South's historical insularity in ethnic culture, high culture, folk traditions, and styles of performance has contributed to regional distinctiveness in ways yet to be fully explored.

GRETCHEN SCHNEIDER
Arlington, Virginia

Norman Arthur Benson, "The Itinerant Dancing and Music Masters of Eighteenth-Century America" (Ph.D. diss., University of Minnesota, 1963); John W. Blassingame, *The Slave Community: Plantation Life in the Antebellum South* (1972); Thomas A. Burns and Doris Mack, *Southern Folklore Quarterly* (September–December 1978); Jane Carson, *Colonial Virginians at Play* (1965); Thomas F. DeFrantz, ed., *Dancing Many Drums: Excavations in African American Dance* (2002); Lynne F. Emery, *Black Dance in the United States from 1619 to 1970* (1972); Henry A. Kmen, *Music in New Orleans: The Formative Years, 1791–1841* (1966); Douglas McDermott, *Theatre Survey* (May 1978); Nancy Lee Chalfa Ruyter, *Reformers and Visionaries: The Americanization of the Art of Dance* (1979); Marshall Stearns and Jean Stearns, *Jazz Dance: The Story of American Vernacular Dance* (1968).

Festivals, Folk Music

Music festivals have been part of southern cultural experience at least since the fiddlers' contests of the mid-18th century. Prior to 1900, however, most communally shared music was sung and played informally at family reunions, corn shuckings, and barn raisings, on court and election days, at house dances, revivals, and all-day singings at churches, rent parties, school commencements, county fairs, and on a variety of other occasions that brought families, neighbors, and communities together. Festivals modeled partly on these early forms continue in local benefits and fund-raisers (for volunteer fire companies, rescue squads, and the like) in which food and musical performances are the main attractions.

The hundreds of music festivals currently in evidence mirror both the South's cultural diversity and the complex patterns of cultural development and change the region has undergone. Fiddlers' contests, now in their third century, multiplied especially after the mid-1920s, stimulated by both Henry Ford's national promotional efforts and the growth of commercial country music (and especially its radio barn dances). Camp meetings and sacred harp singings still take place annually at Benton, Ky., Tifton, Ga., Etowa, N.C., and elsewhere. The film *Cold Mountain* (2003) highlighted sacred harp singing and brought new popular interest in it. Commercial gospel music of the variety that emanated from the mass revivals of Dwight L. Moody (1837–99) and Billy Sunday (1863–1935) and their many successors and local imitators and the mainly southern-based black and white gospel music industry that grew up in their wake (for example, companies owned by James D. Vaughan and R. E. Winsett in Tennessee) is performed and celebrated weekly—by local congregations, at commemorative anniversary celebrations for gospel quartets, in commercial "all night singings," and at state and regional gospel singing conventions (for example, the Albert E. Brumley sing at Springdale, Ark., and the West Virginia state convention at Nebo). Old-time music festivals such as those at Union Grove, N.C., Galax, Va., and Asheville, N.C., have drawn thousands of visitors annually for many decades. Other older forms, including blues and jazz, are celebrated in festivals such as the Delta Blues and Heritage Festival in Greenville, Miss., and the New Orleans Jazz and Heritage Festival and jazz festivals at Hampton, Va., and Mobile, Ala.

Festivals styled on older social forms and presenting traditional musical idioms to local audiences exist side by side with those that present more recent idioms in festivals that feature more contemporary music and whose audiences assemble from both near and far. Deriving some of their stimulus from the efforts of educational and cultural missionaries who established industrial, settlement, and folk schools among lowland blacks and upland whites at the turn of the century, these more contemporary festivals proliferated after the mid-1920s, and they received further encouragement from supporters such as Allen Eaton and New Deal agencies.

In the post–World War II period, increasing leisure and tourism expanded the market for public cultural presentations, as did the so-called folk revival of the late 1950s and 1960s, some of whose major figures (for example, Pete and Mike Seeger) had learned about southern music partly by attending earlier festivals. Recently, music festivals have been spurred by the post-1965 growth of federal and state funding for cultural activities (and especially by the advent of state, regional, and federal folklife programs). Further impetus has derived from renewed cultural awareness and pride among minority cultural groups (for example, the Cajun festival at Abbeville, La., and related observances among Cherokee and Lumbee Indians in North Carolina).

Since their proliferation in the 1980s, bluegrass festivals have probably multiplied more rapidly than any other type of music festival in the South. The first one was at Luray, Va., in 1962. Scores of them are now held every year, organized by major bluegrass performers (for example, Mac Wiseman, Carter Stanley), bluegrass promoters such as Carlton Haney (Camp Springs, N.C.), and a variety of local individuals and institutions (an annual tribute to the music of Doc and Merle Watson, called MerleFest, is held annually in Wilkesboro, N.C., on the Wilkes Community College campus). Commercial country music is the focus for many other recent festivals, which range from one-time local events headlined by a Nashville star performer, to annual "memorial" festivals (for Hank Williams at Mt. Olive, Ala.; Jimmie Rodgers at Meridian, Miss.; W. C. Handy at Florence, Ala.; and the Carter Family at Hiltons, Va.), to weekly performances at seasonal country music parks (for example, Hiawassee, Ga.). Entrepreneurial development and promotional efforts—frequently with a dual link to tourism and local agriculture (rice, cotton, sugarcane, peaches, and pecans in the lowlands, and apples and tobacco in the uplands)—have produced many music and cultural festivals.

The public "folklife festival," in which music is frequently the most prominent feature, is another important recent form. Drawing distant inspiration from such events as Bascom Lamar Lunsford's Mountain Dance and Folk Festival (Asheville, N.C., 1928), the White Top Folk Festival (White Top, Va., 1931), and the National Folk Festival (1934), but patterned more specifically upon the Smithsonian Institution's Festival of American Folklife (1967), folklife festivals (for example, the North Carolina Folklife Festival and the Blue Ridge Folklife Festival at Ferrum College in Virginia) tend to emphasize precommercial musical idioms.

In their many forms, folk music festivals in the South bespeak both a deep attachment to local and regional tradition and a creative and integrative sensitivity to cultural change. In a few cases, they also reveal a need to invent (for self, local community, or audience) "traditions" whose authenticity is open to question: festivals at Grandfather Mountain and Red Springs, N.C., and Virginia Beach, Va., present a largely fictitious version of Scottish highland music, and the dulcimer festivals at Birmingham, Ala., and Mountain View, Ark., celebrate a romanticized feature of Appalachian music and culture. Music festivals remain, however, one of the most vital contexts in which southerners celebrate their cultural past and interpret their present cultural identity for others.

DAVID E. WHISNANT
Chapel Hill, North Carolina

Robert Cantwell, *Bluegrass Breakdown: The Making of the Old Southern Sound* (1984); Curt Ellison, *Country Music Culture: From Hard Times to Heaven* (1995); Archie Green, *John Edwards Memorial Foundation Quarterly* (Spring 1975); Eric Hobsbawm and Terence Ranger, eds., *The Invention of Tradition* (1983); Paul Kingsbury and Alanna Nash, eds., *Will the Circle Be Unbroken: Country Music in America* (2006); Bill C. Malone, *Southern Music—American Music* (1979); David E. Whisnant, *All That Is Native and Fine: The Politics of Culture in an American Region* (1983), *Folk Festival Issues: Report from a Seminar* (1979); Joe Wilson and Lee Udall, *Folk Festivals: A Handbook of Organization and Management* (1982).

Gospel Music, Black

Despite its immense popularity, widespread appeal, and influence on American popular music, African American gospel music is a comparably recent music phenomenon. Rooted in the religious songs of the late 19th-century urban revival, in shape-note songs, spirituals, blues, and ragtime, gospel emerged early in the 20th century.

The term "gospel music" suggests many things to different people. In its most general application, the word simply refers to any religious music, regardless of the music's age or origin. Congregational songs, ring shouts, quartets, sacred harp choirs, Sanctified groups, and even some work songs would all qualify. Less broadly, the term refers to an innovative, popular style of music combining secular forms, particularly ragtime and blues, with religious texts.

Composed, modern black gospel music became an important style during the 1930s. Thomas A. Dorsey is generally regarded as its "father," although it could be argued that C. A. Tindley should wear that mantle. Tindley was actively composing during the first decade of the 20th century, but his songs did not gain widespread popularity among blacks until the 1920s and 1930s. Dorsey himself was inspired by Tindley's reworkings of older revival songs, blues, and spirituals. Dorsey's own songs, however, made up the first wave of modern gospel music during the Depression.

Thomas A. Dorsey began his career as a blues and gospel singer. He enjoyed an immensely successful stint as a professional blues musician during the 1920s. By the early 1930s he had turned his attention entirely to religious music. During the 1930s and 1940s Dorsey worked with two influential figures, Mahalia Jackson and Sallie Martin. In addition he toured the country as a performer and lecturer and wrote some 500 gospel songs, including "There Will Be Peace in the Valley" and "Precious Lord, Take My Hand."

Rev. W. Herbert Brewster, another important composer from this period, was pastor of the East Trigg Baptist Church in Memphis, Tenn. A contemporary of Dorsey, Brewster composed over 200 gospel songs, beginning in the early 1930s. Many of his compositions were written specifically for his choir, the Brewster Singers, but two of his songs, "Move on up a Little Higher" and "Surely, God Is Able," gained wider popularity.

The music and language of these early gospel songwriters helped to promote an interest in their compositions. Although the compositions of Dorsey and others are formally notated and printed, they almost always undergo a transformation during performance. One of the strong appeals of this music, in fact, is that it encourages participation and improvisation on the part of an audience that feels comfortable with the use of basic chords, standardized chord progression, metaphorical language, and frequent biblical illusions.

By the mid-1930s the appeal of gospel music within black culture was quite evident, and it was soon embraced by commercial record companies wishing to capitalize on its popularity. Radio stations and the major radio networks featured its music on their live broadcasts. These attempts at mass marketing quickly led to a sense of professionalism among the performers. By the onset of World War II, a small but growing cadre of people made their living singing, writing, or promoting black gospel music.

In the decade after 1945 the popularity of groups such as the Spirit of Memphis, Alex Bradford, the Soul Stirrers, Queen C. Anderson, Sallie Martin, and the Famous Blue Jay Singers grew. Dozens of professional and semiprofessional groups appeared on programs throughout the country and recorded for an expanding network of local and regional companies. This interest is well illustrated by Mahalia Jackson's recording of "Move on up a Little Higher" and the Ward Singers' version of "Surely, God Is Able," which both sold a million copies in 1950.

Interest in black gospel music gripped the country, and every city and small town in the South staged gospel music programs in churches and auditoriums. New artists, such as the Dixie Hummingbirds and Shirley Caesar, emerged, initially as second-line acts, then as headliners. Soloists such as Ira Tucker of the Dixie Hummingbirds and Claude Jeter of the Swan Silvertones became well known among devotees. Lavish gospel programs were staged by Joe Bostic of

New York City and Erskine Fausch of New Orleans. With such widespread appeal, groups could afford extravagant costumes and could travel in comfort. Local nonprofessional black gospel groups emulated the dress and singing styles of more popular musicians and even adopted their names. Nearly half a dozen local or semiprofessional groups exploited the "Soul Sisters" name, for instance.

This increasing popularity and professionalism ultimately turned some of the more conservative church members away from contemporary gospel music. By the mid- to late 1950s, there was something of a backlash against "secularization," most clearly manifested in the opulent manner in which some singers lived.

Black gospel music has changed greatly since the mid-1950s. It has become more sophisticated, particularly in terms of marketing and musical diversity. Popular singers such as William Gaither and Andrae Crouch have had formal musical training and education, which has led to more sophisticated arrangements.

These changes are part of a natural musical and cultural evolution. Black gospel music changed as the demands of popular culture increased and as African Americans strove for middle-class status. Black gospel music remains, however, essentially conservative, and its principal mission remains constant—to lift the spirits of its participants and to help them express their religion.

KIP LORNELL
George Washington University

Horace Clarence Boyer, *Black Perspectives in Music* (Spring 1979), *How Sweet the Sound: The Golden Age of Gospel* (1995); Harry Eskew and Paul Oliver, *The New Grove Dictionary of Music and Musicians* (1980); David Evans, *Jazz Forschung/Jazz Research* (1976); Anthony Heilbut, *The Gospel Sound: Good News and Bad Times* (1971); Jerma Jackson, *Singing My Soul: Black Gospel Music in a Secular Age* (2004); Eileen Southern, *The Music of Black Americans: A History* (1983).

Gospel Music, White

For most people, the term "white gospel music" connotes a type of music characterized not so much by style as by content. Although the sound of white southern gospel can range from that of a sedate vocal quartet to an amplified country band, or from a singing convention assembly of 300 voices to the simple brother-duet harmony framed by mandolin and guitar, the message of the music is usually a direct and often optimistic reflection of a working-class Protestant ethos. Since white gospel music emerged as a recognized form in the

1870s and 1880s, it has tended to graft this message onto a rich variety of vernacular musical styles, both folk and pop. This has given white gospel an ambiguous and confusing stylistic identity. To many southerners, though, white gospel is associated with vocal quartets or family groups, singing in three- or four-part harmony, accompanied by a piano, guitar, or other stringed instruments. Also, for many of them, gospel is not a formal church music to be used in regular Sunday services but a brand of Christian entertainment to be enjoyed at special church singings, at concerts, on television and radio, and on records.

The roots of gospel music lie in pre–Civil War southern hymnody traditions such as camp-meeting songs, sacred harp singings, and revival music, but the real beginnings of modern southern gospel can be traced to two events occurring in the 1870s—the emergence of the Reubusch-Kieffer publishing business in the Shenandoah Valley of Virginia and the publication and popularity of a series of books of "general hymns" by two northern-based song leaders, Ira D. Sankey and Phillip P. Bliss. Aldine S. Kieffer, the main force behind the Shenandoah Valley tradition, was a Confederate veteran who happened to be the grandson of Joseph Funk, whose 1851 songbook *Harmonia Sacra* (or "Hominy Soaker," as it was fondly called in the South) was published in a format using seven shapes for different notes—as opposed to the four shapes in the sacred harp tradition. After the war, as the older four-shape systems lost favor, Kieffer began his company in 1866 with an old friend, Ephriam Reubusch, whom he helped free from a Union prison camp, and began a 50-year campaign to popularize the seven-shape note system. He did this by founding the South's first Normal Singing School, at New Market, Va., in 1874; by starting a periodical called the *Musical Million*, to help develop singing conventions and spread news of backwoods singing schools, in 1870; by training and sending across the South singing-school teachers; and by publishing a series of songbooks, such as *The Christian Harp* (1877), a collection of lively, "singable" songs designed for "special singing" rather than for use in regular church services. The seven-shape notation system of the Reubusch-Kieffer Company took root in the South, and the company provided a training ground for hundreds of later writers and singers. The company itself, with its multifaceted operation, became a model for dozens of other gospel publishing companies in the South from 1875 to 1955.

The type of song that filled these new books had its prototype in Sankey and Bliss's 1875 collection, *Gospel Hymns and Sacred Tunes*, published in New York and Cincinnati. Although the term "gospel musick" had been used in print as far back as 1644 in London, the intense popularity of the Sankey-Bliss collection, as well as its use by the popular evangelist Dwight L. Moody from

1875 to 1899, was the real source of the term "gospel music" in American culture. The songs in this collection and in others that followed in the 1880s and 1890s derived from the rise of Sunday school songs in the 1850s, songs that were deliberately designed for younger singers. They were more rhythmical than the older hymns, more sentimental and more optimistic, and were often patterned on popular secular songs. Though popular nationwide, the new gospel hymns were especially successful in the South, where many of them even entered folk tradition: "Bringing in the Sheaves," "What a Friend We Have in Jesus," "Sweeping through the Gates," and "Let the Lower Lights Be Burning." The rise of southern shape-note publishers in the late 19th century provided outlets for hundreds of amateur songwriters to follow in the gospel song tradition. By the turn of the century, graduates of the Reubusch-Kieffer Company had started publishing companies in Georgia (A. J. Showalter, J. B. Vaughan), Texas (Trio Music, Showalter-Patton), Arkansas (Eureka Music Company), and Tennessee (E. T. Hildebrand).

The most successful and influential of these publishers, though, was to be a Giles County, Tenn., native, James D. Vaughan (1864–1941). Early in life, Vaughan studied with Reubusch-Kieffer graduate E. T. Hildebrand and later worked with B. C. Unseld, who had been the first teacher in the Reubusch-Kieffer normal schools. Vaughan became a singing-school teacher and composer and by 1903 had settled in Lawrenceburg, Tenn., where he began publishing songbooks using the seven-shape system. By 1909, he was selling 30,000 books a year, and, by 1912, 85,000 books a year. One or two new books were published each year, often in paperback form and often containing as much as 75 percent new material, with 25 percent old standards or favorites. Some rural churches used Vaughan's books in regular services, but most of the books were used in county or statewide singing conventions and in specialty singing.

Vaughan's business sense, talent, and personality allowed him to build his company into the South's largest and to establish his own singing schools at Lawrenceburg, making it the citadel of modern gospel music. He also, however, used a number of important innovations to publicize his work. Like Reubusch-Kieffer, he started a magazine, *Vaughan's Family Visitor* (1912–present), to announce singing schools, news, and songbooks. In 1922 he began his own record company, Vaughan Records, to help popularize new songs, which became the South's first home-based record company. He bought his own radio station, woan, and encouraged his singers to perform on other commercial stations. Most important of all, though, he used quartets made up of his singing teachers to tour the South, giving free concerts of Vaughan's music. The Vaughan quartets were a spectacular success wherever they went, and soon the company had

16 different quartets on the payroll. Some of these quartets became popular in their own right and soon eclipsed the company they were representing. By the late 1920s groups like the McDonald Quartet, from southern Missouri, were able to travel independently and make a living with their music. The classic southern gospel quartet—four men and a piano—comes from Vaughan's innovations.

The Vaughan Company continued to publish until 1964, but its alumni set up important rival companies that were even more innovative and aggressive. One of Vaughan's editors, V. O. Stamps, joined forces with J. R. Baxter Jr., to form the Stamps-Baxter Music and Printing Company, in 1926. Using as their theme song "Give the World a Smile Each Day," Stamps-Baxter sought out the best of the new, younger songwriters; helped get their quartets record contracts with major labels like RCA Victor, Columbia, and Brunswick; and used radio shows to sell their songbooks. With its effective base of operations in Dallas, the company soon shared the dominance of the market with Vaughan. The company made an important move toward taking gospel music out of the church and into the realm of pure entertainment when it staged an "all-night sing" in the Cotton Bowl Stadium in 1940—thus creating a format that would characterize southern gospel for years.

During the 1930s—when the paperback gospel songbook publishers were at their height—Vaughan claimed cumulative sales of over 5 million books, and some 40 to 50 independent publishers were issuing such books. In addition to Vaughan and Stamps-Baxter, leaders included Hartford (Arkansas), R. E. Winsett (Tennessee), J. M. Henson (Atlanta), and the Stamps Quartet Company (Texas, formed by Frank Stamps, V. O. Stamp's brother). During this decade, too, independent singing groups arose, and, although not formally associated with the companies, they used their songs for their repertoires. The most successful of these was the Texas family known as the Chuck Wagon Gang, which recorded and broadcasted widely, featuring such tunes as "After the Sunrise," "Jesus, Hold My Hand," and "A Beautiful Life."

By the end of World War II the balance of power had shifted away from the song-publishing companies to the quartets and gospel groups. Major country radio shows like the *Grand Ole Opry* had gospel groups as regular members, and in 1946 the Homeland Harmony Quartet of Atlanta saw its "Gospel Boogie" ("Everybody's Gonna Have a Wonderful Time up There") become a nationwide pop hit. In the late 1940s Georgian Wally Fowler left his country band, formed the Oak Ridge Quartet, and began promoting package tours of new gospel stars, often renting an auditorium for a commercialized version of the "all-night sings." A nationwide fad for pop-gospel music in the early

1950s attracted huge audiences for young groups like the Blackwood Brothers, the Statesmen, the Jordanaires, and the Happy Goodman Family. Country artists like the Bailes Brothers, James and Martha Carson, Molly O'Day, and the Louvin Brothers made gospel a major part of their repertoire, while the newly emerging bluegrass bands often borrowed gospel repertoire and quartet singing styles.

By the end of the 1950s, the quartet style no longer dominated southern gospel. Family groups such as the Speer Family and the Rambos injected country and even pop music into their performances, and groups like the Inspirations and the Kingsmen sometimes used five or six singers and a battery of backup instruments. The 1970s saw the rise of smooth, sophisticated "praise music" by singers like Dallas Holm and "contemporary Christian music" by singers like Amy Grant and Texan Cynthia Clawson, who had more in common with Broadway music and even rock than southern gospel. The southern gospel style was, by the mid-1970s, being referred to as "traditional gospel" and, although no longer on the cutting edge of American religious music, remained the most popular form of nonprofessional music across the South, still heard in homes, in churches, and at gatherings from Virginia to Texas.

More recently, Bill Gaither has been an innovator in the renewal of white gospel music. Growing up in southern Indiana, Gaither listened to gospel music radio stations and formed the family Gaither Trio in the early 1960s and the Gaither Vocal Band in 1980. Gaither's 1968 album, *Alleluia*, began a new gospel genre of "praise and inspirational" music, which combines traditional white quartet songs with black gospel songs, as well as drawing from the contemporary Christian music represented by Amy Grant. Gaither staged popular concerts that filled auditoriums across the South and Midwest, and he soon marketed videotapes of his concerts, entitled *Gaither Homecoming*, which are seen on cable and PBS stations. The Southern Gospel Music Association launched its Hall of Fame and Museum at Dollywood in east Tennessee in 1999. Local radio stations, churches, and community centers continue to provide venues for gospel music, while at the same time the Internet has dozens of websites for professional or semiprofessional gospel performers.

CHARLES K. WOLFE
Middle Tennessee State University

Clarice Baxter and Vide Polk, *Gospel Song Writers Biography* (1971); Lois S. Blackwell, *The Wings of the Dove: The Story of Gospel Music in America* (1978); Jesse Burt and Duane Allen, *The History of Gospel Music* (1971); Don Cusic, *The Sound of Light: The History of Gospel and Christian Music* (1990); James R. Goff Jr., *Close Harmony: A*

History of Southern Gospel (2001); Michael P. Graves and David Fillingim, eds., *More Than "Precious Memories": The Rhetoric of Southern Gospel Music* (2004); Ottis J. Knippers, *Who's Who among Southern Singers and Composers* (1937); Bob Terrell, *The Music Men: The Story of Professional Gospel Music Singing* (2000); Charles K. Wolfe, *American Music* (Spring 1983), in *Folk Music and Modern Sound*, ed. William Ferris and Mary L. Hart (1982).

Hip-Hop and Rap

Beginning in the late 1980s, southern hip-hop and rap effectively trumped contemporary R&B as the foremost popular urban music trend. A regional response to the then-burgeoning East and West Coast hip-hop scenes, purveyors of southern rap simultaneously surfaced in cities ranging from Atlanta and Miami to New Orleans, Memphis, and Houston. Although many older music fans downplay the significance and artistic credibility of the genre, southern rap—created by an MC, or rapper, and a DJ, or producer—has emerged as a primary motivator in the youth market, influencing fashion, language, the mass media, and other facets of commercial and popular culture. Similarly, southern rap artists have become the avatars of pop culture in their own right, receiving consistent radio airplay, crossing over to film and television roles, and emerging as popular personalities in the marketing and advertising fields.

A linguistic offspring of blues music, books by "black consciousness" authors (for example, Donald Goines, Eldridge Cleaver, and Iceberg Slim), traditional oral "toasts" (as documented in Bruce Jackson's *Get Your Ass in the Water and Swim Like Me: African-American Narrative Poetry from the Oral Tradition*), and poetry slams, combined with beats and musical samples lifted from soul, rhythm and blues, and pop songs, southern rap is popular with white, black, and Hispanic listeners. Yet, unlike soul music, which was predominantly shaped by whites within the popular music industry, southern rap—and its East and West Coast counterparts—is primarily a black-dominated business, from performing and producing basic tracks to distributing and promoting the finished product. Moreover, southern rap has been largely released on independent record labels, unlike commercial East and West Coast rap music. Emblematically utilitarian photographs and no-frills graphics dominate record and CD cover art, and liner notes are minimal for southern rap albums, which are often self-produced in limited runs.

Southern hip-hop groups such as Arrested Development and OutKast have a reputation for benign, vaguely political- or party-oriented lyrics, but southern rap—also commonly referred to as Dirty South rap—often includes braggadocios and innuendos pertaining to drug use, criminal activity, and sexual conquests. Southern rappers employ a simple, rhythmic delivery propelled by the drum track, which uses quick snare beats and a hi-hat sound, usually created on a drum machine. Archetypal hit songs, such as the Ying Yang Twins' "Salt Shaker" and David Banner's "Like a Pimp," initially gained popularity in strip clubs before receiving radio airplay and crossing over to the dance club scene. Many southern rappers regularly send "shout-outs" to fellow rappers, record labels, and neighborhoods, popularizing urban areas such as Memphis's Orange Mound community or New Orleans's Ninth Ward and advertising additional products via "skits" performed between songs on their CDs.

Miami Bass is one important subgenre of southern rap. The distinctive bass-heavy sound, which combines fast-tempo modern electronic dance music and sustained kick-drum beats and cymbals (produced using a Roland TR-808 programmable drum machine), mixed with samples of funk music as purveyed by musicians such as guitarist Willie "Little Beaver" Hale (a native of Forrest City, Ark., and a Miami resident since the 1960s), is predominant in south Florida cities, including Miami, West Palm Beach, and Fort Lauderdale, particularly in poor urban communities such as Liberty City. 2 Live Crew, led by Luther "Luke Skyywalker" Campbell, brought the Miami Bass or "booty rap" tradition to the national music charts via their 1989 album *Nasty as They Wanna Be* and the song "Me So Horny," which was banned in many urban areas because of its sexual content. According to *All Music Guide* critic Richie Unterberger, James "Maggotron" McCauley is "the father of Miami Bass," although some aficionados argue that Amos Larkins's productions of Double Duce's "Commin' in Fresh" and MC A.D.E.'s "Bass Rock Express," both released in 1985, came first. Other popular Miami Bass–influenced southern rap artists include Disco Rick, TrickDaddy, and Cuban rapper PitBull.

New Orleans Bounce is another formidable southern rap subgenre. Identifiable by its call-and-response choruses, typically laid over samples called either the Triggaman beat or the Brown beat, and influenced by the brass band second-line dances ubiquitous to New Orleans, Bounce surfaced in the late 1980s, when MC TT Tucker, DJ Jubilee, Katey Red, MC Gregory D, and DJ Mannie Fresh began recording tracks like "Monkey on a Stick" and "Buck Jump Time." Many Bounce songs were built off their predecessors, including DJ Jimi's "Bitches (Reply)." Based around the definitive chorus "Suck my pussy for a pork chop," the song was a response to DJ Jimi's own "Where They At," itself a radio-friendly take on MC TT Tucker's "Where Dey At," which included the lyric "Fuck David Duke," a disparaging remark about Louisiana's then-perennial political candidate, a neo-Nazi and proponent of the Ku Klux Klan.

In the 1990s, two dominant New Orleans rap labels emerged: Master P's No

Limit Records and Cash Money Records, co-owned by Ronald "Slim" Williams and his younger brother, Brian "Baby" Williams. Percy "Master P" Miller, a product of the Calliope housing project located in New Orleans's Third Ward, sold 250,000 copies of his first two records, *The Ghetto's Tryin' to Kill Me!* and *99 Ways to Die*, without national distribution, and No Limit went on to earn $400 million by 1999. An entrepreneur who studied business in college, Miller invested his earnings in real estate, fast-food franchises, sports management, magazine publishing, and urban-oriented businesses like car detailing, shaping No Limit into a lifestyle-branding conglomerate. He was also a pioneer within the southern rap industry, signing a contract with Priority Records as an imprint, retaining ownership of his own product, and producing hit records of fellow New Orleans rappers like Mystikal and the late Soulja Slim (gunned down in his mother's yard in the Eighth Ward in November 2003), as well as direct-to-video releases like *I'm 'Bout It*, which sold an unprecedented 500,000 copies. His brother, rapper C-Murder, was indicted on murder charges in 2002 and remains under house arrest. His son, Lil Romeo, is a popular actor with his own show on the Nickelodeon cable television network.

Begun in 1992, Cash Money Records sold hundreds of thousands of records in New Orleans's underground scene under the tutelage of legendary producer Mannie Fresh, before signing a $30 million pressing and distribution deal with the Universal conglomerate in 1998. Home to artists such as Kilo-G and Lil' Slim, the label's most popular group, the Hot Boys, was made up of individual MCs Juvenile, B.G., Lil Wayne, and Turk, all residents of New Orleans's notorious Magnolia housing project. Citing financial mismanagement, B.G. and Juvenile left Cash Money. B.G. formed his own Chopper City Records, but Juvenile returned to the label to release 2003's *Juve the Great*, a triple-platinum selling album. In the aftermath of Hurricane Katrina, which struck New Orleans and the Gulf Coast in 2005, many New Orleans rappers left the city, and, in the months since, many have recorded songs criticizing the federal government's reaction to the crisis, such as Lil Wayne's "Georgia Bush," Juvenile's "Get Ya Hustle On," and Fifth Ward Weebie's Bounce throwback, "Fuck Katrina."

Houston, Tex., is home to rap pioneers the Geto Boys (Scarface, Bushwick Bill, and Willie D), whose self-titled 1990 album, released on Def American Records, was one of the most violent releases of the decade, criticized for its characterizations of rape and necrophilia. Other Houston rappers, such as DJ Screw, Lil' Flip, Lil' Keke, and UGK (short for Underground Kingz), spearheaded the southern rap subgenre Chopped & Screwed, created by mixing multiple copies of the same record, slowed down via the pitch shift control on a manual turntable, causing echo and flanging effects. In the early 1990s, the late DJ Screw (who died of a heart attack following codeine use in 2000) popularized the style via mix tapes sold to fans of "purple drank" (codeine laced with Promethazine, a hypnotic)—fans who liked to listen to Chopped & Screwed versions of hit rap singles as they took drugs. In recent years, southern rappers of all styles, including rapper David Banner, based in Jackson, Miss., and Memphis collective Three 6 Mafia, have released Chopped & Screwed versions of earlier albums, tapping specialist DJs to create slowed-down remixes of their hits. Houston has also provided a launching pad for underground rappers like Memphis's 8Ball & MJG, who moved west in 1992 and came out with *Comin' Out Hard*, which sold more than 100,000 copies for Texas independent Suave House Records, before ultimately signing with Bad Boy, P. Diddy's Warner Music Group subsidiary. Today, the independent Swishahouse label, home to southern rap stars Mike Jones, Chamillionaire, Slim Thug, and Bun B, dominates the Houston scene.

Meanwhile, in Memphis in the late 1980s, rappers such as Pretty Tony, W-Def, Radical T, Al Kapone, Lord Infamous, and 8Ball & MJG, along with the rap collective Three 6 Mafia, which features north Memphis MCs DJ Paul, Juicy J, and Project Pat, initiated a style of southern rap called "buck" or "gangsta" rap. Gangsta Pat, the son of soul music drummer Willie Hall (Stax Records, *The Blues Brothers*), was the first Memphis rapper to sign a major label deal, releasing #1 *Suspect* on Atlantic Records in 1991. A year later, FreakMaster had the first Memphis rap single to make it onto the *Billboard* charts, "Gimme What You Got (for a Pork Chop)." Then and now, the Memphis rap scene has been centered around several hotspots, including Club Memphis and the Pressure World car wash (immortalized on Three 6 Mafia's "Don't Cha Get Mad"), both in the Orange Mound neighborhood, and at locations in north Memphis and the outlying suburb of Frayser, often referred to in local vernacular as "the Bay." At Memphis rap concerts, audience members often buck dance or gangsta walk, a circular dance purportedly invented by a rap collective called the Bovan Family at Club No Name in the late 1980s and still popularized via underground hits like Al Kapone's "Get Crunk, Get Buck" and II Black's "Buck Jumpin."

Despite the success of the made-in-Memphis rap-themed movie *Hustle & Flow*, released in 2005, and its subsequent Golden Globe and Academy Award musical wins (for Kapone's "Whoop That Trick" and Three 6 Mafia's "It's Hard Out Here for a Pimp," respectively), most MCs on the current Memphis rap scene continue to work in the underground, self-releasing CDs and parlaying regional hits into unaccounted-for sales at bodegas and car washes. Memphis's biggest underground rappers, such as Criminal Manne, Mac E, and former Three 6 Mafia cohort Gangsta Boo, have a local cult following in Memphis but remain virtually unknown beyond the city limits. Other Memphis rappers, including 8Ball & MJG and Kinfolk Kia Shine, have traveled to cities like Houston and Atlanta to pursue record deals and fame before returning home as platinum-selling stars. Unlike those urban centers, major labels have made few inroads into the Memphis scene, which is dominated by music distributor Select-O-Hits, a company known for gospel, blues, soul, and now rap. Select-O-Hits also unconsciously influenced the growth of southern rap in Memphis and New Orleans, by distributing "Drag Rap" (alternately called "Triggaman") by New York rappers the Showboys, which was sampled for many Bounce, gangsta walk, and buck jump tunes.

Although the Crunk subgenre has its roots in Memphis, its most popular practitioners, including Lil Jon, Bone Crusher, and the Ying Yang Twins, hail from Atlanta. Coined by combining the words "chronic" (referring to marijuana use) and "drunk," the term "crunk" entered the urban lexicon when Three 6 Mafia released "Tear Da Club Up '97," a Top 50 hit on the national rap charts. Six years later, the trend was still going strong, as evidenced by hits such as Lil Jon's "Get Low," the Ying Yang Twins' "Salt Shaker," and Bone Crusher's "Never Scared." Even nonsoutherners jumped on the bandwagon, via hits like Usher's "Yeah" and Ciara's "Goodies," both produced by Lil Jon. Crunk's hallmarks, which include hoarse vocals, rowdy, crowd-inciting lyrics, and a rhythmic, Bounce-derived four-bar beat, helped make the rap style popular in dance clubs. Although an annual all-star concert called Crunkfest is held in Memphis every summer, Lil Jon, his group the Eastside Boyz, and like-minded followers on the Atlanta scene rule the Crunk genre, with songs like "Crunk Rock," "Kings of Crunk," "Get Crunk," and "Crunk Juice."

Atlanta is also home to many noncrunk artists, such as southern rap pioneers OutKast (featuring Big Boi and Andre 3000), Grammy award–winning girl group TLC, and Goodie Mob, as well as superstars like DJs Jermaine Dupri and Jazze Pha, and Chris "Ludacris" Bridges, who has parlayed his career as a southern rapper into Hollywood fame via his roles in Academy Award–winning movies *Crash* and *Hustle & Flow*. Relative newcomers, such as T. I. and Yung Joc, rap about drug dealing and life in their low-income neighborhoods Bankhead and College Park, both called "the Trap" in street parlance. Popular Atlanta studios include Stankonia and the Dungeon, home to the Dungeon Family Collective, OutKast, Bubba Sparxxx, and Goodie Mob, as well as lesser-known southern rap artists Witchdoctor and Cool Breeze. In 2006 former Goodie Mob vocalist Cee-lo Green partnered with fellow Georgian DJ Danger Mouse to form the popular hip-hop duo Gnarls Barkley. The FBI caused a stir within the Atlanta hip-hop scene in early 2007, when Gangsta Grillz mix-tape creator DJ Drama and members of his collective, the Aphilliates Music Group, were indicted for failing to pay publishing royalties on mix tapes, despite the fact that many major labels were paying the Aphilliates to create underground hits for their artists.

Although there have been no feuds on the level of the West-Coast-versus-East-Coast Tupac Shakur–Biggie Smalls rivalry, the southern rap scene is rife with violence. New Orleans rap artist Soulja Slim was murdered at point-blank range, while T. I., star of the film *ATL*, has been the target of numerous altercations, including a gun battle in Cincinnati, which left his friend Pliant Johnson dead. Drug abuse, ranging from social marijuana use to full-blown cocaine and heroin addictions, also mars the scene, which has popularized the misuse of over-the-counter cough syrup via songs like Three 6 Mafia's "Sippin' on Some Syrup" and Project Pat's "Purple." Many popular southern rappers, including Project Pat, C-Murder, Mystikal, and Turk, have served, or are serving, extended prison terms for felonies, ranging from robbery and drugs and weapons charges to rape, assault, and murder convictions.

In 2007 even hardcore fans began voicing their concerns about the misogyny and violence that plagues the southern rap industry, most notably in the PBS documentary film *Hip-Hop: Beyond Beats and Rhymes*. Nevertheless, the genre continues to dominate, influencing even the automobile industry (via customized wheel rims, car shows, and Donks, urban slang for modified Chevrolet Impalas) and inspiring television advertisements for products like Kentucky Fried Chicken and movies such as *ATL*, *Hustle & Flow*, *Idlewild*, and *Knights of the City*.

ANDRIA LISLE
Memphis, Tennessee

Scott Bedja, *Murder Dog Magazine* (November 2006); Black Dog Bone, *Murder Dog Magazine* 11, no. 1; Vladimir Bogdanov, Chris Woodstra, Stephen Thomas Erlewine, and John Bush, *All Music Guide to Hip-Hop: The Definitive Guide to Rap and Hip-Hop* (2003); Jeff Chang, *Can't Stop, Won't Stop: A History of the Hip-Hop Generation* (2005); Nik Cohn, *Triksta: Life and Death and New Orleans Rap* (2005); Greg Davenport, *Murder Dog Magazine* 13, no. 2; Jim Fricke and Charlie Ahearn, *Yes Yes Y'All: The Experience Music Project Oral History of Hip-Hop's First Decade* (2002); Tony Green, *Vibe Magazine* (August 2003); Bruce Jackson, *Get Your Ass in the Water & Swim Like Me: African-American Narrative Poetry from the Oral Tradition* (2005); Andria Lisle, *Wax Poetics* (December 2006); Tamara Palmer, *Country Fried Soul: Adventures in Dirty South Hip-Hop* (2005); Roni Sarig, *Vibe Magazine* (December 2003); Samantha M. Shapiro, *New York Times Magazine* (February 2007); John "J-Dogg" Shaw, *StreetMasters Magazine* (2006); *Vibe Magazine, The Vibe History of Hip-Hop*

(1999); Carlton Wade, *The Source* (December 2003); Papa Wheelie, *Stylus Magazine* (August 2005).

Honky-Tonk Music

Honky-tonk, also called "hard country" or "beer-drinking music," projects the mood and ambience of its birthplace, the beer joint. Born in the 1930s, honky-tonk became virtually *the* sound of mainstream country music from the late 1940s to about 1955, when rock and roll forced changes in all forms of American popular music. Since then it has endured as a vigorous subgenre of country music, with such important musicians as Ray Price, George Jones, Moe Bandy, and Dale Watson making crucial contributions.

Although conditions that contributed to its development prevailed throughout the South and on the West Coast, honky-tonk music experienced its most significant development in the states of Texas, Louisiana, and Oklahoma. There, in the oil-boom atmosphere of the mid-1930s, the combined forces of Prohibition repeal and increased professionalization in the still-new hillbilly music field led to the movement of musicians into the taverns and beer joints, where their music was welcomed. When country music entered the honky-tonks, its performing styles and thematic content changed significantly. Musicians sought a beat that could be felt even if it could not be heard above the din and merriment of weekend revelers, and they effected instrumental changes that would enhance and diversify their sounds—hence the adoption of electric instruments. Above all, much of the tone of country music changed in this atmosphere of wine, women, and song, where potential danger lurked behind the gay facade and where "honky-tonk angels" lured their men. No force has proved more important in diminishing the pastoral impulse of country music, nor in documenting the transition made by rural southerners to urban industrial culture.

If the 1930s were important as years of nourishment, the war years were absolutely indispensable in both the maturation and the popularization of honky-tonk music. As never before in southern history, people fled agriculture and made their way by the thousands to the towns and industrial centers of the South, as well as to cities in the Midwest and on the West Coast. While civilians changed their locales and occupations, their military sons and daughters moved to training camps both in and out of the South and to combat theaters around the world. For a people in transition, who were urban in residence yet rural in style and outlook, the adjustment was often fraught with frustration and pain. Adjustments were made in diverse ways and with varying degrees of success, but many men sought to reaffirm their identities in a sympathetic setting—over a bottle of beer in a honky-tonk. Servicemen fought the loneliness of enforced separation from loved ones and friends, while their civilian relatives sought relief from the pressures of work and family responsibilities. The music of the honky-tonks, whether performed by live bands or coming from jukeboxes, reflected increasingly the preoccupations of socially and geographically displaced people. Never before had a form of music so effectively mirrored the concerns of the southern working class.

Rustic sounds still thrived in country music during the 1940s—the decade, after all, marked the heyday of Roy Acuff as well as the beginning of the acoustic-based bluegrass style. But sounds introduced and nourished in the honky-tonks of Texas predominated, and names like Bob Wills, Ted Daffan, Cliff Bruner, Moon Mullican, Al Dexter, and Ernest Tubb filled the jukeboxes. Many of their songs described the world of the honky-tonk itself, detailing the pleasures to be found "Down at the Roadside Inn" or confessing the sorrows that might come from overindulgence ("Driving Nails in My Coffin," "Headin' Down the Wrong Highway"). Al Dexter's "Pistol Packin' Mama," the giant country hit of 1943 and a "crossover" of the first magnitude, grew out of its singer-composer's experiences in the oil-town–honky-tonk atmosphere of east Texas in the 1930s. More often, though, the songs concentrated on matters that had little or nothing to do with the honky-tonk. Instead, they commented on the private concerns of listeners. Voicing the cry-in-your-beer side of honky-tonk, almost to the point of suicidal impulse, were such songs as Rex Griffin's "The Last Letter," Ted Daffan's "Born to Lose," and Floyd Tillman's "It Makes No Difference Now," which poured forth from a thousand jukeboxes and were carried around the world by lonely, homesick southern servicemen. When Ernest Tubb moved to the *Grand Ole Opry* in 1943, his Texas-born, beer-joint–shaped style gained a national forum. As he won disciples, his style influenced the music of country entertainers from West Virginia to California.

In the prosperous years that followed World War II, as country music enjoyed its first great period of national expansion, the Texas sounds and styles continued to attract the patronage of country fans everywhere. The honky-tonk style never had a complete monopoly during the period, but, for all practical purposes, it had become the all-pervasive sound of mainstream country music. The typical band was small and featured a fiddle, a steel guitar, a "takeoff" guitar (one that could take the lead in solo passages), a rhythm guitar whose chords were played in closed, percussive fashion, a string bass, and often a piano. The musicians were capable of performing the hot instrumental licks pioneered by the western swing bands of the 1930s, but instrumentation, while crucial and distinctive, was generally subordinated to the needs of a vocalist. A new generation of honky-tonk singers had emerged, men like Hank Thompson, Webb Pierce, and Lefty Frizzell, who were among the most distinctive stylists that the country music field has seen. Surpassing them all, however, was the young singer from Alabama, Hank Williams, whose career marked the greatest commercial flowering of the honky-tonk style.

When Williams died in 1953, few could have anticipated that very soon the honky-tonk style would be driven from recordings and that country music as a whole would be in shambles. As the rock-and-roll wave inundated American music, traditional country music was driven underground, to small record labels and back to the bars, as promoters and recording men began their frantic search for young, vigorous performers who could imitate Elvis Presley. The rock-and-roll invasion proved temporary, but it left in its wake a continuing consciousness of the youth market and a decision by the Nashville music industry to produce a middle-of-the-road product that would be appealing to both country and pop audiences. Honky-tonk music, of course, did not die, but it could not remain dominant in such a social context. In an industry obsessed with "crossovers," the hard honky-tonk sound was unwelcome and even embarrassing. Furthermore, the temptation among performers to cross over to the more lucrative and respectable country-pop field was irresistible.

Honky-tonk music remains a vigorous subgenre of country music, but few entertainers are consistently faithful to it. In the late 1950s and early 1960s, Ray Price, with his band, the Cherokee Cowboys, made crucial contributions to the modern honky-tonk sound, featuring duet harmonies on vocal choruses and a thoroughly electrified sound built around a pedal steel guitar, a heavily bowed fiddle, and walking electric bass patterns (this sound is usually described as the Shuffle Beat and is now best preserved in the music of such Texas musicians as Justin Trevino and Darrell McCall). But after popularizing the sound among a host of disciples, Price abandoned the style for the country-pop field he had earlier resisted. George Jones, the Texas singer whose supple style resembled the moaning, bent notes of the pedal steel guitar (first introduced on Webb Pierce records), remains faithful to the honky-tonk sound, but his producers often smother him under a barrage of string instruments and vocal choruses. Buck Owens, who claimed both Texas and California as home, became country music's leading vocalist in the early 1960s, with an exciting sound that reflected both the honky-tonks of California and the energy of rockabilly music. He too later abandoned the style.

By the beginning of the 1980s, only a few musicians clung to the honky-tonk style, and most of them were seldom heard in mainstream country music. Moe Bandy (born in Meridian, Miss., and reared in San Antonio, Tex.) prospered for a while in the honky-tonk genre, with a clean, crisp articulation of lyrics dealing with those staples of honky-tonk music—drinking, cheating, and heartbreak. Since Bandy's heyday, such singers as Darrell McCall, Justin Trevino, Joe Paul Nichols, and Dale Watson have continued to perform with the accompaniment of fiddle, pedal steel guitar, and walking bass.

Of all country styles, honky-tonk has most closely reflected southern working-class culture and has best marked the evolution of the southern folk from rural to urban industrial life. Although intimately associated with the urban adjustment of southern plain folk, honky-tonk music has been ignored by folklorists because it is not pastoral and because it does not protest. It is dismissed by many, perhaps, because it is too real. Honky-tonk instrumentation both attracts and repels: to many, the whine of the pedal steel guitar and bounce of the shuffle beat evoke elemental impulses and emotions. Honky-tonk music conjures up distasteful, seedy images. The lyrics and instrumentation of honky-tonk music evoke emotional pain, isolation, and human weakness, which everyone has shared. The songs can be so full of trite self-pity that they drown listeners in their sentimentality. But, at its best, honky-tonk music speaks to loneliness and the need for human empathy felt by each person.

BILL C. MALONE
Madison, Wisconsin

Bill C. Malone, *Country Music, U.S.A.: A Fifty-Year History* (1968; rev. ed., 2002), *Don't Get above Your Raisin': Country Music and the Southern Working Class* (2002), with Judith McCulloh, eds., *Stars of Country Music: Uncle Dave Macon to Johnny Rodriguez* (1975).

Jazz

"Jazz started in New Orleans," Ferdinand La Menthe "Jelly Roll" Morton pronounced confidently to Alan Lomax in 1938. Morton's magisterial oral autobiography-history resounds with invaluable insights into the story of jazz, New Orleans in the 1890s, and southern life and culture. But, like many great insights, this is a mythic truth.

Jazz was an agglomeration of black and white folk music, a rich synthesis that occurred in southern, southwestern, midwestern, and eastern urban centers in the last decade of the 19th century. Jazz began in New Orleans as well— but ragtime and blues musicians wandered the Gulf Coast, the Mississippi Delta, and the red-light districts of Washington, D.C., Baltimore, Kansas City, New York City, and St. Louis. Early black folk music became widely identified as southern, in its associations with vaudeville, theater, and circuses, as part of a vast cultural myth of the Old South plantation days, and as building on Stephen Foster's songs, on the spirituals of the Fisk Jubilee Singers, and on the traditions of blackface minstrelsy.

New Orleans, the most cosmopolitan and urbane center in the South before and after the Civil War, provided a hospitable climate for local and itinerant musicians and had a long tradition of musical culture, high and low. In the second half of the 19th century, New Orleans mixed a vivid combination of music—brass band marches, parlor music, Creole and Cajun folk songs, Caribbean music, church music—and produced a style known as "ragtime," after the spicy, syncopated piano music of the Mississippi River Valley. By about 1915, this new music was often called "jass" or "jazz." Other musical centers flourished at the same time: Memphis, with its bawdy Beale Street district featuring W. C. Handy's dance orchestra; Kansas City, with legions of ragtime writers and publishers; and St. Louis, a repository for even more intense ragtime playing, composing, and publishing.

Jazz drew on local scenes and traditions, indigenous southern sensibilities and languages. Handy captured blues songs from the Delta, with resonant lines like "I'm going where the Southern cross the Dog," a near-mystical reference to a Mississippi railroad junction of the Southern and the Yazoo-Delta lines ("Yellow Dog Blues"). Or Jelly Roll Morton could sing, "Michigan water tastes like sherry wine, Mississippi water tastes like turpentine" ("Michigan Water Blues"). Local customs and scenes were paid homage by southern musicians, as Morton hailed the Lake Pontchartrain resort area in "Milenberg Joys" or Louis Armstrong recalled a Basin Street brothel in "Mahogany Hall Stomp."

Jazz in the South was created and exported by blacks and whites, by musicians of every ethnic background—Irish, Italian, French-Spanish-Creole, Jamaican, German, Greek, Protestant, Catholic, and Jewish. This diversity of backgrounds guaranteed variety within the music. Place-name blues celebrated the region: "Atlanta Blues," "Vicksburg Blues," "Memphis Blues," "New Orleans Blues." Other kinds of jazz registered local color: "Beale Street Blues," "South Rampart Street Parade," "Bogalusa Strut," "Chattanooga Stomp," "Ole Miss," "Chef Menteur Joys." Jazz drew from church music—"Sing On," "When the Saints Come Marching In," "Down by the Riverside"—and from popular exotica—"Big Chief Battle-Ax," "Hindustan," "Lena from Palesteena," "The Sheik of Araby," "Chinatown." The music consciously echoed opera, military bands, call-and-response church singing, ethnic dance music, country blues singing, genteel parlor songs, light classics, and Tin Pan Alley productions.

Southern music absorbed cosmopolitan influences easily and converged with a wide world of vaudeville and minstrel shows, road companies of musicals and

Jazz performer Bunk Johnson (left) and folk-blues musician Leadbelly (right), late 1940s
(Hogan Jazz Archive, Tulane University, New Orleans)

operettas, and the long-established French opera in New Orleans's *Vieux Carré*.
The most local and original of New Orleans traditions, Mardi Gras, adopted as
its musical theme "If Ever I Cease to Love," a ditty from a New York musical.
And another "jazz standard" was created from a New York publisher's arrangement of a novelty march by Yale student Porter Steele—"High Society."

The turn of the century witnessed an explosion of popular music creation
and dissemination. Phonograph records, piano rolls, and sheet music made
possible a nationwide popular musical culture on a large scale. Scott Joplin's
"Maple Leaf Rag" (1899) probably sold a million copies in sheet music form,
published first in Sedalia, Mo. Local publishers and artists sprang up everywhere, with important centers in southern and midwestern cities: St. Louis,
New Orleans, Kansas City, Indianapolis, and Chicago. Southern music was exported on a grand scale, and local fairs and exhibitions held in Atlanta and
New Orleans, the Chicago Columbian Exposition of 1893, and the St. Louis
World's Fair of 1904 brought Americans into direct contact with the new southern music.

In New Orleans, instrumental music was in constant demand for parties
and formal dances and in neighborhood dance halls, cabarets, and social clubs.

Popular social dances like the waltz, mazurka, schottische, quadrilles, and reels, along with black vernacular dances, created a need for a wide range of highly rhythmic accompaniment. By the 1890s strongly syncopated dance music of the sort echoed in piano ragtime was provided by various instrumental combinations. In the regulated red-light district (sardonically nicknamed "Storyville" after the alderman who proposed its legislation), ragtime and blues piano players worked in bordellos. In the rest of the city, bandsmen played for dances and parties.

Charles "Buddy" Bolden, a black cornetist, was the best-known leader of a rough-and-ready early jazz band of the 1890s. "Papa" Jack Laine, a white drummer-entrepreneur, organized many dance and marching bands around 1900. John Robichaux formed a long-lived "society" orchestra that played popular music scores. Freddie Keppard, another cornet virtuoso, led a group called That Creole Band on extensive vaudeville tours from New Orleans after 1910. But the New Orleans band that created a nationwide (ultimately worldwide) consciousness for a new popular music was the Original Dixieland Jazz Band—five white New Orleanians from Jack Laine's stable who went to Chicago and New York, and then to London, making in 1917 and 1918 the first New Orleans jazz records and achieving a monumental success in vaudeville and cabaret appearances.

The repertoire of the Original Dixieland Jazz Band was that of New Orleans jazz as it had developed for some 20 years: "Tiger Rag," "Livery Stable Blues," "Clarinet Marmalade," "Ostrich Walk," "Bluin' the Blues," and others became jazz staples and were drawn from the shared traditions of black and white musicians. The Original Dixieland Jazz Band Americanized jazz and jazzified America. Imitations of their music were heard everywhere, and "jazz" passed from the argot of the demimonde (where it meant either sexual intercourse or sexual fluids) into the vocabulary of middle America as the name of this new physical, sensual music. The Original Dixieland Jazz Band was followed by a continuous out-migration of southern musicians to Chicago, New York, the West Coast, and Europe. What had been a provincial oddity, a local delicacy like hog's maw, grits, or pralines, a purely regional music, became a significant force in world culture.

A "second generation" of musicians who grew up in the earliest days of New Orleans jazz disseminated it as a complex and sophisticated musical form, a form based on individual improvisational styles blended into an intuitive whole: Jelly Roll Morton (piano-composer); Joseph "King" Oliver (cornet), who took young Louis Armstrong to Chicago in 1922; Sidney Bechet (clarinet, soprano sax), who took jazz genius to Europe in 1919 with the Southern Syncopated

Orchestra; Johnny Dodds (clarinet); Edward "Kid" Ory (trombone); Warren "Baby" Dodds (drums). The New Orleans Rhythm Kings, Clarence Williams's bands, and many other New Orleans bands recorded and brought live jazz to the speakeasies of 1920s America.

The impact of the new jazz recordings was huge. Jazz was absorbed and imitated by society dance bands everywhere by 1920, with great financial success realized by white bandleaders like Art Hickman, Paul Specht, and Paul Whiteman. "Jazz" to most Americans of the mid-1920s was simply synonymous with "pop music" of any description, and novelist F. Scott Fitzgerald could create the idea of a "Jazz Age." Jazz was identified with youth, excess, exuberance, sin, and license, with gin mills and crime, and with some of the old red-light-district stigma.

In the 1920s and 1930s jazz was established in Chicago and New York, with luminaries like Fletcher Henderson (from Birmingham), Edward "Duke" Ellington (from Washington, D.C.), Jack Teagarden (from Texas), and others rising to the top of the jazz world. Jazz also flourished in the South, especially in so-called territory bands that succeeded regionally. Top-flight big bands created their own versions of jazz (now known more frequently as "swing") in Kansas City (Bennie Moten, Harlan Leonard, Walter Page), Missouri (Charlie Creath, Jesse Stone, the Missourians), Memphis (Jimmie Lunceford), Texas (Don Albert, Alphonso Trent), and New Orleans (Sam Morgan, Fate Marable, Armand J. Piron). Some of these groups made the national scene: Bennie Moten's band became the great Count Basie Orchestra of the 1930s; the Missourians became Cab Calloway's band; and Jimmie Lunceford created one of the most innovative bands of the era.

Other southern jazz stars became nationally known: blues singers like Gertrude "Ma" Rainey, Bessie Smith, and Ethel Waters rose from backgrounds in minstrelsy and vaudeville to great fame. Jazz virtuosi like Louis Armstrong, Jimmie Noone, Sidney Bechet, and others established exalted standards for playing. Itinerant blues pianists like Pinetop Smith, Jimmy Yancey, Eurreal "Little Brother" Montgomery, Crippled Clarence Lofton, Albert Ammons, Meade Lux Lewis, and Pete Johnson popularized a form of Deep South keyboard style most commonly called "barrelhouse" or "boogie-woogie" piano, which enjoyed a wild vogue in the late 1930s. A rough, powerful form of piano blues, the music was familiar in turpentine camps and rural juke joints a generation before it reached the nation's radios and phonographs.

The South supplied vernacular dances to America after jazz became a national phenomenon in 1918. The brisk one-step "animal dances" of 1910—the Grizzly Bear, Bunny Hug, Turkey Trot, Cubanola Glide—were superseded by the Charleston, Black Bottom, Varsity Drag, tangos, Lindy Hop, Suzie-Q, and dozens of variants based on old black social dance patterns. Formalized versions of such dances could be seen at big dance halls, in revues like the famous Cotton Club extravaganzas in Harlem, and in vaudeville routines by such stars as Bill "Bojangles" Robinson, Florence Mills, Snakehips Tucker, and John Bubbles. Jazz was music for dancing, and long before aficionados made it intellectually respectable, America voted with its feet for the new music.

By the 1930s radio had joined with the phonograph to popularize jazz. Radio promotion helped establish bands like those of Duke Ellington and Benny Goodman, while jazz-oriented dance bands like the Coon-Sanders Orchestra, the Casa Loma Orchestra, Paul Whiteman's band, and others brought jazz into the nation's parlors nearly every day over network radio. What started as a provincial cultural phenomenon in one generation became the best-known trademark of America, a symbol for the nation's youthful vitality and melting-pot variety. In Europe, jazz was studied, imitated, and admired by young students and musicians.

The movements of modern jazz after the 1930s have been nationwide, with important centers of activity on the East and West coasts. The South, however, has continued to contribute major jazz artists, such as pianist-composer Thelonious Monk, the Adderly brothers Nat and Julian ("Cannonball"), and trumpet virtuoso Wynton Marsalis. Jazz of every variety flourishes in southern cities, from "revivalist" centers like New Orleans's French Quarter, Memphis's Beale Street area, and St. Louis's Gaslight Square, to cabarets and concert-hall performances in every major city. Since the 1950s jazz has moved from the center of popular musical culture to become a kind of "alternative culture" of great vigor and variety.

Jazz was woven into the fabric of southern life. An urban synthesis of rural music, it reflected the development of the modern South after the turn of the 20th century. Created by black musicians from a multiethnic culture, jazz unified the nation's sensibility. Jazz radically altered its listeners through its feelings about freedom, equality, imagination, joy, and physical vitality.

WILLIAM J. SCHAFER
Berea College

Joachim Ernst Berendt, *The Jazz Book: From Ragtime to Fusion and Beyond* (1982); Rudi Blesh, *Shining Trumpets: A History of Jazz* (1976); Leonard G. Feather, *The Book of Jazz: From Then till Now* (1965); Ted Gioia, *The History of Jazz* (1998); Mark C. Gridley, *Jazz Styles: History and Analysis* (1985); Rex Harris, *The Story of Jazz* (1960); Nat Hentoff, *Jazz Is* (1976); Tom Sancton, *Song for My Fathers: A New Orleans Story in Black and White* (2006); Gunther Schuller, *The History of Jazz* (1968); Marshall Stearns, *The Story of Jazz* (1956); Frank Tirro, *Jazz: A History* (1977); Barry Ulanov, *A History of Jazz in America* (1972); Geoffrey C. Ward and Ken Burns, *Jazz: A History of America's Music* (2002); Otto Werner, *The Origin and Development of Jazz* (1984).

Minstrelsy

It is something of a historical paradox that the popular desire for an autonomous cultural tradition in the South—one separating it from the perceived imperfections of the industrial North and of European civilization—should induce the region's white citizenry to turn to the enslaved African Americans for their music, dance, and humor. Blackface minstrelsy is the clearest antebellum example of this contradictory cultural pattern. In the 1820s individual white thespians began doing imitations of African American song and dance in urban theaters. Their performances presented caricatures of black slaves, portraying them as superstitious, happy-go-lucky "dancing darkies." The actors blackened their faces with burnt cork to accent these portrayals. The most renowned of the early blackface performers were George Washington Dixon, who created a sensation with his "Zip Coon" character, and Thomas D. Rice, who popularized the song and dance "Jump Jim Crow." Rice copied his famous act from an elderly, crippled, African American stable hand—and even borrowed his suit of ragged clothing for the initial stage performance. His comic rendition of "Jump Jim Crow" was an overwhelming success, catapulting him into a much-heralded tour of the major entertainment halls in the United States and then in England. By the 1840s blackface minstrelsy in the South had evolved into a stylized entertainment formula based on the music, dance, and comedy of African Americans and featuring an entire troupe of actors for the show.

From its inception, minstrelsy's characterization of black people was stereotyped. Plantation slaves were depicted as contented, comical, and childlike, while urban house servants were portrayed as dandies and dummies who aped white mannerisms and longed to be white themselves. Most of the popular figures in antebellum minstrel entertainment were from the South and had some knowledge of African American folklore prior to putting on burnt cork. The best known among these performers were Dixon, Rice, Dan Emmett, E. P. Christy, and Stephen Foster. Although its performers reinforced the prevailing racism of the era, in both the South and the North, southern minstrelsy presented a more complex and even varied caricature of African slaves to the American public than had been attempted in previous decades. And even though the characters were terribly distorted, one important effect of the antebellum minstrel tradition was to help force the issues of slavery and emancipation to the forefront of the nation's political agenda. Moreover, the song and dance performed by the white minstrels laid the groundwork for a better appreciation of authentic African American music and humor by white Americans. This trend became more evident in the postbellum era.

After the Civil War, black entertainers joined the ranks of minstrelsy, and by the 1870s they dominated the minstrel scene. The more popular and profitable of these troupes, however, were still owned and operated by such white entrepreneurs as Charles Callender, owner of the famous Georgia Minstrels, and W. A. Mahara, owner of the popular Mahara's Minstrels. This select group of white owners and managers, and those who followed in their footsteps, insisted that the material and the format of the shows remain faithful to the content and formulas of early blackface minstrelsy. They required the black entertainers they hired to reproduce the outdated routines of the antebellum minstrel tradition. In essence, they functioned as guardians of the old-culture order, and their collective endeavors resulted in the perpetuation of demeaning racial stereotypes in American show business well into the 20th century. Talented black entertainers who joined the white-owned minstrel troupes often found themselves between the hammer and the anvil with respect to their cultural identity and their artistic integrity. The white entrepreneurs dominated the business; they determined who could work in the most prestigious companies and offered limited fame and fortune in exchange for the African American performers' compliance with the blackface minstrel legacy. Although there was some latitude in negotiating these arrangements, even the most popular—and, therefore, potentially the most powerful—of the black performers in these shows sacrificed their artistic independence in return for stardom and financial gain.

The careers of minstrelsy's most acclaimed African American performers—James Bland, Billy Kersands, and Bert Williams—offer a clear, if disheartening, illustration of the dilemmas of black minstrel entertainers. Bland, known as the "Negro Stephen Foster," was an accomplished musician and composer who wrote over 700 songs in his lifetime, among them "Oh Dem Golden Slippers" and "Carry Me Back to Old Virginny." Although his material included some authentic black folklore, it was overshadowed by a permeating nostalgia for the Old South and slavery. The characters in his songs and his stage performances were replicas of the antebellum minstrel stereotypes—contented plantation slaves, faithful servants, and comic urban dandies being the most prominent. Only during an extended tour of Europe was he able to perform without the customary blackface makeup and routines.

Likewise, Billy Kersands, the most popular African American minstrel entertainer of the postbellum period, based his comedy routines on demeaning racial caricatures of his own people. He portrayed black males as dull-witted and gullible, while burlesquing black women as matronly and unattractive. To his credit, Kersands also made good use of authentic African American folk humor, and he was an excellent dancer who pioneered the use of soft-shoe dancing routines on the minstrel stage. These aspects of his performances may have offset his more self-abasing comedy routines and may help to explain his widespread popularity among black people in the South. Billy Kersands's successor in minstrel comedy was Bert Williams, the last major African American entertainer to perform in blackface. His career began in the 1890s and peaked in the 1910–20 period, when he became the first African American to perform with the Ziegfeld Follies. He was a brilliant humorist, but he was also stuck in the role of a hapless, antebellum darky, in spite of criticism from his own race. This situation led fellow comic W. C. Fields to comment that "Bert Williams is the funniest man I ever saw, and the saddest man I ever knew."

With the advent of the 20th century, minstrelsy in the South went into a slow but steady decline. Some of the more popular troupes, like F. S. Wolcott's Rabbit Foot Minstrels, based in Port Gibson, Miss., and the black-owned Silas Green's Minstrels from New Orleans, La., continued to perform for segregated southern audiences, bolstered by an influx of talented female blues singers such as Ma Rainey and Bessie Smith. But the heyday of southern minstrelsy was over, eventually replaced by other forms of entertainment like vaudeville and motion pictures. The minstrel tradition left behind a conflicting legacy: it was the training ground for many gifted African American entertainers who would not have had the opportunity to develop their talents otherwise, but it was also the spawning ground for many degrading racial stereotypes that found their way into the popular culture of 20th-century America.

BILL BARLOW
Howard University

Gary D. Engle, ed., *This Grotesque Essence: Plays from the American Minstrel Stage* (1978); Eric Lott, *Love and Theft: Blackface Minstrelsy and the American Working Class* (1993); Sarah Meer, *Uncle Tom Mania: Slavery, Minstrelsy, and Transatlantic Culture in the 1850s* (2005); Hans Nathan, *Dan Emmett and the Rise of Early Negro Minstrelsy* (1962); Ike Simond, *Old Slack's Reminiscence and Pocket History of the Colored Profession from 1865 to 1891* (1974); Robert C. Toll, *Blacking Up: The Minstrel Show in Nineteenth-Century America* (1974).

Música Tejana

Música tejana, or "Tex-Mex music" as it is sometimes called, is the music of the Texas-Mexicans, or Tejanos. Inhabiting the same geographic area of south Texas, the Tejanos have successively been citizens of a Spanish colony, an independent Mexico, the Republic of Texas, the Confederate states, and the United States of America. The development of *música tejana* is interwoven with the history of the Tejanos from the 1700s to the present.

In a cultural sense, from the 1700s until the early 1900s the Tejanos were basically a Mexican provincial people, living in an isolated frontier area of the southern United States. In the past 80 years there has been a steady migration of Tejanos from the farms and ranchos of south Texas to the urban industrial centers of Texas and throughout the United States. Tejanos have incorporated aspects of Anglo-American culture, but overall they have resisted becoming a colonized and absorbed people. They have developed a unique regional Texas-Mexican culture, which is one of the most distinctive subcultures in the South and one that is reflected in the Tejanos' own musical styles. Over the course of two centuries, *música tejana* has resulted from a blending of early Spanish and Mexican music, French-European styles filtered through Mexico, Latin-Caribbean music, and now Mexican and American popular music. *Música tejana* is thus an especially revealing indicator of the subregion of south Texas and the role of music in reflecting broader ethnic patterns within the South.

Little is known about the beginnings of *música tejana*. Paintings and diaries depict fandangos, or dances, being held in San Antonio and south Texas through the 1800s, but they give little descriptive information about the sound of the music, other than to call it "Spanish" or "Mexican." Violins and *pitos* (wind instruments of various types) usually provided the melody, with a guitar for harmonic accompaniment. Sometimes a rustic drum, a *tambora ranchera*, was used to accentuate the rhythm.

By the mid- to late 1800s, Tejano musicians were playing the Spanish and Mexican dance music less and were adopting a new European style, which was trickling in from central Mexico. In the 1860s, Maximilian, backed by his French army, ruled in Mexico. In his court in Mexico City and in garrisons throughout the country, the European salon music and dances of the time, such as the polka, waltz, mazurka, and schottische, were popular. These styles were enthusiastically embraced in south Texas by the Tejanos. The Tejanos' musical culture was also influenced by the Germans, who began immigrating to the central Texas area in the 1840s. These German Texans also favored the European salon music and dances. At times they would hire local Tejano musicians to play for their own celebrations. By the late 1800s, the informal Tejano bands of violins, *pitos*, and guitars were almost exclusively playing European salon music for the local dances. Taking root in this frontier area, far from its European and central Mexican sources, this music was being thoroughly adapted to the Tejano aesthetic. With French and German styles layered over the base of Spanish and Mexican music, the modern development of *música tejana* began.

Between 1900 and the 1930s, three important Tejano styles began to distinguish themselves—the *guitarrero* tradition, *música norteña*, and *orquesta tejana*.

The tradition of singing troubadours has a long history in Spain and Mexico. The *guitarrero* tradition in Texas represented a continuation of that tradition and was the first to become solidified and commercially popular in *música tejana*. By the late 1800s and early 1900s, many professional *guitarreros* sang in the plazas and cantinas of south Texas towns. Their repertoire consisted of romantic, lyrical songs spawned by the popularity of the operatic style in Mexico and local ballads called *corridos*, which developed from the transplanted Spanish romance ballad tradition. When singing topical *corridos* of local or national events, the *guitarreros* were often the only source of news for the local population.

La Plaza del Zacate (Haymarket Square) in San Antonio was a favorite gathering place for many of these singers through the 1930s. In the 1920s American recording companies, such as Vocalion, RCA, Okeh, Bluebird, and Decca, came to San Antonio. Setting up makeshift studios in hotels, they made "ethnic records" of local groups to sell to the growing Tejano market. The *guitarreros* that performed in Haymarket Square were some of the first to be commercially recorded. Duets such as Pedro Rocha and Lupe Martínez, Juan Gaytán and Timoteo Cantú, and "Los hermanos Chavarría" (the Chavarria Brothers) were well known in the plazas, as well as on recordings, by the early 1930s. Although the *guitarrero* style was mostly a male tradition, one of the most famous of these singers was a young girl with a beautiful quavering voice—Lydia Mendoza, "La Alondra de la Frontera" (The Lark of the Borderlands). She began recording at an early age with her musical family but later enjoyed a solo career with her famed recordings of songs such as "Mal Hombre" (Bad Man) and "Pero Ay Que Triste" (But Oh How Sad).

The commercial heyday of the *guitarreros* was short-lived, however. The same factors of urbanization that prompted the recording companies to see a commercial value in the style ultimately wrought irrevocable changes in the singing tradition. English- and Spanish-language radio and other mass media were taking over the *guitarrero*'s role as the major source of news and information. Also, by the 1940s, in the urban environment, attitudes about the separate functions of the singing and dance music traditions had become blurred. The working-class *conjuntos* (groups) performing *música norteña* in the cities gravitated toward performing in the cantinas, which had been the domain of the *guitarreros*. Previously performers of a strictly instrumental dance music, the *conjuntos* could add romantic song lyrics and duet harmonies to their polkas and waltzes in the more permissive urban atmosphere without alienating their audience. The *guitarreros* then slowly faded from commercial popularity as their function was usurped by the media and the dance music tradition. Although singing guitarists, or "mariachis"—named for the famous central Mexican musical groups—are prevalent today in Texas, their repertoire and style are part of a more general Mexican musical tradition made popular by Mexican movies and recordings of the past 60 years. Few of the old-style *guitarreros* remain.

From the informal ensembles of musicians of the late 1800s, two styles of instrumental dance music emerged as the Tejanos entered the 20th century. A new German instrument, the diatonic button accordion, which was perfectly suited to playing polkas and waltzes, was gaining great popularity among rural Tejanos engaged in agricultural labor. Shopkeepers and skilled Tejanos working in the small towns, however, were hiring small bands of musicians called *orquestas típicas*. The style of these bands was similar to that of the earlier violin, *pito*, and guitar dance ensembles, but they had become more organized and sophisticated over time.

From the 1920s to the 1940s, lured by the economic promises of the urban American way of life, many Tejanos moved to the cities of south Texas—San Antonio, Corpus Christi, Brownsville, and Laredo. The rural agricultural workers had few skills to advance themselves in their new environment and became employed in low-paying, working-class jobs. The shopkeepers and skilled Tejanos from the towns moved into more upwardly mobile, middle-class positions in business and trades. In the cities, the difference between the aspirations and cultural values of the working-class Tejanos, on the one hand, and the emerging middle-class Tejanos, on the other, became more pronounced. The working class, which suffered from discrimination and received few economic benefits from contact with Anglo-American culture, sought refuge within its own traditional culture. The middle class, encouraged by economic gains, however, saw the adoption of some American culture and values as a passport to greater opportunity and a release from Anglo-American prejudice. Working-class musical groups, or *conjuntos*, developed one distinctive musical tradition, and the middle-class bands, renamed *orquestas tejanas*, developed another.

By the 1940s and 1950s these two dance music styles were intrinsically tied to the identities of these different segments of the Tejano community. Over the basic foundation of the traditional Tejano music of 1900, the conservatism and resistance to acculturation of the *conjuntos* and the incorporation of Anglo-American stylistic traits in the *orquestas tejanas* created two unique Texas-Mexican styles.

Música norteña, meaning "music of the North" (from the point of view of Mexico), played by *conjuntos*, is synonymous with the sound of the German diatonic button accordion. The instrument may have been brought and popularized by the Germans and Bohemians settling in central Texas or by the Germans working in the mining and brewing industries in northern Mexico. Newspaper accounts nonetheless show that by 1898 Tejanos in rural areas of the south Texas chaparral country were playing their Texas-Mexican polkas, waltzes, and schottisches on a one-row, one-key button accordion.

Norteña accordion music began as a solo tradition. The accordion gradually replaced the violins and *pitos* as the preferred instrument for dance music in the rural areas, but because it was played in the rural areas of the ranchos for the laboring people, the button accordion became associated early on with working-class Tejanos. As more of these Tejanos moved from the ranchos to the cities, the instrument was heard in the houses and cantinas of the barrios (Tejano neighborhoods). By the 1930s the popularity of the *norteña* style was such that accordionists, paired with guitarists or *bajo sexto* (a type of 12-string guitar, originally from central Mexico) players, began recording their own ranch-style Tejano polkas. Following the lead of the *guitarreros* in making "ethnic records" for American companies, the developing *conjuntos* were commercializing their style and bringing the nostalgia for the rancho to the city.

Although accordion dance music had been popular for some 30 years in rural areas, two men, Santiago Jiménez, from San Antonio, and Narciso Martínez, from the lower Rio Grande Valley, were responsible for pioneering the *norteña* style on recording and radio broadcasts in the 1930s. Because of their popularity and exposure on recordings, their individual accordion styles became models for a generation of musicians. Jiménez had a smooth, fluid style of playing the polkas and waltzes he composed, and he emphasized the bass notes and chords of his instrument. Expanding his *conjunto*, he utilized a guitarist for harmonic accompaniment and added a *tololoche*, or upright string bass, for a stronger bass line. Martínez meanwhile had a faster, more ornamented style than Jiménez and emphasized the treble buttons of his accordion. Rarely using the bass notes or chords of his instrument, Martínez delegated the harmonic accompaniment and bass line completely to his accompanying guitarist or *bajo sexto* player. Both musicians used the newer two-row, two-key model

Lydia Mendoza, Tejana singer, from the Les Blank film Chulas Fronteras *(1976)*
(Brazos Films/Arhoolie Records, El Cerrito, Calif.)

of accordion. In the 1940s, taking over the singing tradition of the *guitarreros*, these pioneer accordionists began to add song lyrics with duet harmonies to their previously instrumental dance music. The typical lyrics of lost love, often framed in a rural setting, seemed to reflect the working-class Tejanos' ties with the past on the rancho and their resistance to adopting urban American culture.

By the 1950s *música norteña* was crystallizing into a mature style, as a second generation of accordionists came to popularity in the working-class cantinas, clubs, and dance halls. Tony de la Rosa, from Kingsville, Tex., became an extremely popular performer in that decade. He used amplification for the four instruments that by this time had become standard in the *conjuntos*—the three-row, three-key button accordion, the *bajo sexto*, the electric bass-guitar, and drums. De la Rosa's *conjunto* was also one of the first of a score of groups to perform on what became known as the migrant trail. Areas like Fresno, Calif., and Chicago accumulated large communities of transplanted Tejanos, who paid well to have *conjuntos* from Texas play for their weekend dances.

From the late 1950s to the early 21st century, the four-member amplified *conjunto* has changed little. *Música norteña* has continued its conservative stance toward Anglo-American culture by reflecting and reinforcing the identity and values of the working-class Tejano public. Because of his decades of crossing over into Anglo-American musical styles, Flaco Jiménez, son of the pioneer accordionist Santiago Jiménez, has been the exception to most of the *música norteña* musicians of the past 20 years. Although some younger Tejano audiences appreciate a more progressive *conjunto* sound that has added other American musical elements, most *conjuntos* have continued in the traditional style, such as Ramon Ayala y los Bravos del Norte, a constant favorite and recent Grammy winner in the *música norteña* category.

In the late 1800s, *orquestas típicas* (small, genteel orchestras of violins, flutes, clarinets, mandolins, and guitars) formed in south Texas from the earlier informal Tejano ensembles. Their audience was primarily a middle class one, made up of small-town shop owners and skilled employees descended from those tenacious Tejanos who had held their land in the face of the Anglo-American economic advance. With more continuous income from their clientele, these bands playing *música tejana* became better trained and more professional than ever before. When these small-town Tejano patrons moved to the cities in the 20th century, the *orquestas* followed.

Orquestas tejanas developed in an urban environment among those Tejanos seeking to balance their traditional culture and the trappings of middle-class American culture. Striving to play in a smoother, more orchestrated style, blending Tejano, Latin, and American music, the *orquestas tejanas* took over in the cities where the *orquestas típicas* had left off. Paralleling the rise of the *conjuntos*, by the 1930s and 1940s the *orquestas tejanas* were solidifying their style on recordings and were a necessity for the dances of the more upwardly mobile segment of Tejano society.

Beto Villa, a saxophone player from south Texas, is recognized as the father of the *orquesta tejana* style. Patterning his *orquesta* after American dance bands, like that of Glenn Miller, he used a full horn section, trained musicians, and written musical arrangements. Thus, the flutes and violins of the *orquestas típicas* were replaced by trumpets, saxophones, and trombones. The new *orquestas tejanas'* choice of repertoire was American fox-trots and swing music and Latin-Caribbean dances popularized in the United States by the orchestras of musicians such as Desi Arnaz and Xavier Cugat. But never straying too far from their ties to Tejano culture, they also played highly arranged versions of the same Tejano polkas and waltzes played by the *conjuntos*.

In the 1950s the *orquesta tejana* style crystallized into a well-developed form, adding sound reinforcement, complex vocal arrangements, and some new instruments—the electric guitar, the electric bass, and the electric organ. By the 1960s and 1970s two groups, "Little Joe y la Familia" and "Sunny Ozuna and the Sunliners," were at the height of popularity. A new generation of *orquestas tejanas* was playing for a younger, more educated, and more affluent Tejano audience. The groups still played American and Latin dance music, but fox-trots were replaced by rock and soul music, and earlier Latin dances like the mambo and rumba were replaced by New York–Cuban salsa music and Caribbean *cumbias* from the *música tropical* style. But refusing to lose touch completely with their Texas-Mexican traditions, the polkas continued to constitute the core of the *orquesta tejana* style. By the early 1990s, a young female vocalist from the Corpus Christi area named Selena Quintanilla Pérez, with her group Los Dinos, had become very popular in Texas and was poised to cross over into the mainstream American music market. Although she did use various musical styles, such as *cumbias* and rock, in her recordings, before her tragic death in 1995, Selena owed most of her local popularity in Texas and Mexico to her recordings of *orquesta tejana*–style polkas.

Today within the Tejano community one can find an audience for almost any style of Tejano, Mexican, or Anglo-American music. Country-and-western music sung in English or Spanish, Tejano rock and jazz, *música tropical* from the Caribbean, mariachi music, rap music in Spanish, and the traditional Tejano styles can all be heard on radio stations and in dance halls all over south Texas. Tejano working-class and middle-class perspectives and identities have begun to change in the past years with Tejanos' greater numbers, visibility, and economic and political impact. Although diversity within the Tejano community has become more pronounced, *música norteña* and the *orquestas tejanas* continue to appeal to the largest segments of the Tejano community.

DAN W. DICKEY
Austin, Texas

Ramero Burr, *The Billboard Guide to Tejano and Regional Mexican Music* (1999); Kay Council, *Exploratory Documentation of Texas Norteño-Conjunto Music* (M.A. thesis, University of Texas at Austin, 1978); Dan Dickey, *The Kennedy "Corridos": A Study of the Ballads of a Mexican American Hero* (1978); Américo Paredes, *A Texas-Mexican Cancionero: Folksongs of the Lower Border* (1976), *With His Pistol in His Hand: A Border Ballad and Its Hero* (1958); Manuel Peña, in *And Other Neighborly Names: Social Process and Cultural Image in Texas Folklore*, ed. Richard Bauman and Roger D. Abrahams (1981), *The Texas-Mexican Conjunto: History of a Working Class Music* (1985); Chris Strachwitz, *Texas-Mexican Border Music* (1974).

Music Industry

The development of commercial popular music in the South has paralleled trends in other industries. The region has served as a source of musical raw materials—styles, performers, and creative talents—for the nation as a whole.

Until World War II, however, nonsoutherners controlled most of the institutions vital to marketing popular music, including publishing houses, recording companies, and theater chains. Professional musicians in the South pursued the American goal of material advancement, but profits tended to flow toward New York, Chicago, and Hollywood, the three major music centers of the United States before World War II. Of course, there were exceptions to this generalization, chiefly in the form of southern publishers, who were beginning to tap a market for spiritual music by the mid-19th century. Between the Civil War and World War I, minstrelsy and ragtime music offered opportunities for both black and white southern musicians.

Northern executives also held sway in the pop market, the mainstream of American commercial music centering on Broadway shows, New York's Tin Pan Alley music-publishing district, and, later, Hollywood film musicals. This pattern continued as the music industry turned to country music (then called "hillbilly") and jazz in the 1920s. Both genres were southern based, but their markets were not strictly regional. In that decade, the phenomenal growth of commercial radio frightened many recording executives, who saw radio as a competing source of popular entertainment. Northern record companies, eager to reach new markets, had ready access to the southern-born jazz musicians of both races who had left their native region for the thriving jazz centers of Chicago and New York. Record firms also sent white hillbilly singers north, or sent agents to Atlanta, New Orleans, Memphis, Charlotte, and other southern cities to record dozens of local musicians in the hillbilly and jazz fields. These musicians frequently received only flat fees (as opposed to long-term royalties) for their work. Northern businessmen and their southern allies (typically retailers in some other line who carried recordings as an adjunct product) often secured control of musical copyrights or stole them outright from relatively unsophisticated performers.

Some southerners were more industry-wise, and they began to sell their own songbooks. A handful moved north and set up publishing houses. The most successful southern entrepreneurs in music-related endeavors prior to World War II were those who organized radio stations, in many cases companion operations to insurance companies, newspapers, or retail stores. Stations like Nashville's wsm originated programs for network broadcast and served as proving grounds for pop singers and big bands.

The modern southern music industry took shape during the two decades after 1940. Prosperity revived popular music markets, which had been blighted by a decade of economic depression. Urbanization and interregional migration advanced the nationalization of country music, rhythm and blues, and rock and roll, all styles with solid southern foundations. The formation of the performance-rights society Broadcast Music, Incorporated (BMI) in 1940 paved the way for a decentralization of music institutions. Set up by radio networks to rival the older, exclusive, and pop-oriented American Society of Composers, Authors, and Publishers (ASCAP), BMI allowed songwriters and publishers in all fields to join, and it monitored local as well as network programming. By collecting and distributing performance royalties on a wide range of music, it assisted fledgling publishing operations, which sprang up across the South and Midwest, including firms that soon captured significant shares of the pop, country, and rhythm-and-blues markets. After 1945 record manufacturers and recording studios complemented broadcasting and publishing in emerging music centers like Nashville, Atlanta, and Dallas. Southern music entrepreneurs extended a long tradition of urban boosterism through shrewd promotion and publicity, formed national trade organizations like the Country Music Association, and enhanced urban growth by investing in banking, real estate, and other ventures. Southern businessmen now sit on the boards of most national music organizations.

Today, southern musicians and their business allies operate in a commercial world more complex than ever before. New media, including cable television, satellite radio, and the Internet, together with changing business structures, have brought both challenges and opportunities. On the one hand, consolidation in the recording industry and advances in multitrack recording have driven up both recording costs and sales expectations, making it difficult for newly emerging talent to find sustained record label support. Similarly, consolidation in radio broadcasting, the fragmentation of the radio market into stations aiming at specific demographic groups, and the reliance on consultants to program entire chains of stations has tightened stations' playlists, thus limiting exposure for both rising talent and older, established stars seeking continued airplay. On the other hand, the development of relatively inexpensive digital recording equipment has allowed artists to make their own records, and the Internet provides a platform for record sales.

In the processes of commercialization and nationalization, southern music entrepreneurs have helped to transform the social settings that originally spawned folk-derived styles like country music and jazz and to dilute these music forms to the point that they have lost many of their qualities as southern-based idioms. To be sure, southern executives, after the fashion of their northern counterparts, have helped to perpetuate images of the region as a land of folksy and sometimes backward characters, such as the unlettered white hillbilly or the exotic, sensual black. More often, southern businessmen have prompted the adoption of the cowboy or western image, a nonsouthern image more palatable to a national audience.

Some scholars believe that in country music, at least, such images have helped to dilute the music to the point that western attire and stock allusions to rural life have become clichés, mere symbols unconnected to an authentic culture underlying southern-based popular music. Others insist that country music maintains genuine connections to regional culture and also reflects the adoption of southern sounds, musical styles, and images on a national basis. However one strikes the balance between these opposing views, all of these images have furthered the purposes of southern entrepreneurs and musicians, who continue to assert their own interests within the now-international world of commercial music.

JOHN W. RUMBLE
Country Music Foundation
Nashville, Tennessee

Bill C. Malone, *Southern Music—American Music* (1979); John W. Rumble, "Fred Rose and the Development of the Nashville Music Industry, 1942–1954" (Ph.D. diss., Vanderbilt University, 1980); D. K. Wilgus, *Journal of American Folklore* (April–June 1970).

Protest Music

Despite the South's reputation as a conservative region, protest activities and protest music have flourished at various times in its history. Indeed, southerners played vital roles in the shaping of the protest genre in the 20th century.

Protest has never been absent from American music. America's revolution against the British was waged in song as well as on the battlefield, and antebellum reformers fought slavery and alcohol in scores of militant songs. In the years surrounding World War I, the famous Industrial Workers of the World (IWW) made music an integral part of their struggle with capitalism, and their *Little Red Songbook* continues to be a source of anthems for anyone concerned with labor rights or social justice.

Protest music as a distinct genre, though, developed in the 1930s in the context of the Great Depression and was linked directly to southern workers' struggles for economic dignity. Long presumed to be docile and fatalistic, the southern folk made themselves known in a number of dramatic ways during that period—through their presence in relief offices and hobo jungles, through their migrations (as in the case of the Okies), and, above all, in the wave of strikes that made such names as Gastonia and Marion, N.C., and Harlan County,

Ky., well known throughout the United States. The traditional southern habit of ballad making was put to the service of topical songs, which commented on a wide range of social grievances. Such songs even appeared in the repertoires of professional country and blues performers, as exemplified by Frank Welling and John McGhee's "The Marion Massacre" (about the shooting of unarmed strikers in North Carolina), the Monroe Brothers' "The Forgotten Soldier Boy" (about the Bonus Marchers of 1932), and Billie Holiday's "Strange Fruit" (about lynching). Even cowboy singer Gene Autry recorded a song of tribute for a radical labor leader—"The Death of Mother Jones."

Most socially conscious songs, however, emerged from areas of worker discontent that dotted the southern landscape. There, "conservative" southern workers often came in contact with ideologically radical labor organizers and political activists, many of whom came from the North, who further fueled the impulse toward song making. In the Mississippi River Delta area of Arkansas, a black sharecropper and preacher named John Handcox supplied songs like "Raggedy" and "There Are Mean Things Happening in This Land" for his fellow farmers and members of the Southern Tenant Farmers' Union, who had organized to protect themselves from landlords. At least one of his songs, "Roll the Union On," came into the possession of union members in other parts of the country.

In Gastonia, N.C., a young mother and millworker named Ella May Wiggins emerged as a spokesperson for the striking cotton-mill workers, who walked out of their plants in protest against low pay and the dehumanizing "stretch out" system (a requirement that workers operate additional machines at the same pay). The Gastonia strike attained national notoriety when the Communist-dominated National Textile Workers Union appeared with its policy of "dual unionism," which challenged both the conservative American Federation of Labor and the local power structure. Wiggins's songs lifted the morale of the workers and presented their case to a larger public. They also gave her the reputation of "labor agitator," and when she was shot to death on 14 September 1929, while riding in the back of a truck with other strikers, many people felt that she had been singled out for execution. She became a martyr in the American labor community, and her songs were printed in such liberal and radical journals as the *Nation* and *New Masses* and were sung at northern labor rallies by such activists as Margaret Larkin.

Strikes in the coal-mining district of Harlan and Bell Counties, in Kentucky, inspired a similar wave of topical ballad making. One of the most famous labor songs in American history, "Which Side Are You On?," appeared when Florence Reece, the wife of a Harlan County organizer, voiced her anger at the brutality of the company-paid deputy sheriffs. The most famous trio of balladeers, though, to come out of the Kentucky coalfields was Aunt Molly Jackson and her brother and half-sister, Jim Garland and Sara Ogan. Before they were blacklisted and forced to leave Kentucky, each of them turned out a steady stream of songs that graphically portrayed the grim lives of coal miners, while also championing their rights. These included Aunt Molly's "Dreadful Memories" and "I Am a Union Woman," Garland's "I Don't Want Your Millions Mister" and "Ballad of Harry Simms" (about a young Communist organizer who was killed by company "gun thugs"), and Ogan's "I Hate the Capitalist System."

These and other songs like them moved north to become the nucleus of an incipient urban folk music movement. They were received by northern radicals, who recognized their organizing potential, and, of course, by such southern singers as Aunt Molly Jackson, Jim Garland, and Woodrow Wilson "Woody" Guthrie. Until he moved to New York in 1940, where he became part of the labor-radical community, Guthrie had been identified as a hillbilly singer with a storehouse of traditional songs and a guitar style roughly modeled on that of Maybelle Carter. The Okemah, Okla., native, though, had been a champion of his fellow Okie migrants ever since he began singing over KFVD in Los Angeles in 1937. With such songs as "Talking Dust Bowl Blues," "Dust Bowl Refugee," and "Do-Re-Mi," Guthrie established his reputation as a champion of the poor and dispossessed. In New York he was welcomed as "the new Joe Hill" and very quickly became the center of a coterie of musicians, which included such fellow expatriate southerners as Aunt Molly Jackson, Brownie McGhee, Sonny Terry, Josh White, Sis Cunningham, Lee Hays, and Huddie "Leadbelly" Ledbetter. He also inspired a host of disciples within his northern audiences, including, most notably, Cisco Houston, Jack Elliott, and Pete Seeger, who carried on Guthrie's commitment to the use of the folk song as a weapon in the struggle for social justice.

The protest song movement of the 1930s and 1940s was confined to a narrow segment of Americans—labor activists, radical intellectuals, and some college students. That of the late 1950s and early 1960s, on the other hand, was of a much broader scope and was in fact introduced to virtually every American home through national television and stereophonic sound reproduction. Again, southerners played direct and vital roles in the development of a body of protest material. Although modern protest song making was clearly linked to the traditions and singers of the 1930s, especially through the continued presence of such activists as Pete Seeger, the phenomenon gained most of its inspiration from the civil rights movement. In the aftermath of the Montgomery Bus Boycott in 1956, black people began resurrecting older religious songs to provide moral strength and spiritual sustenance in their marches and demonstrations, and, in the time-tested folk fashion, they attached new words to old folk and religious melodies. Such songs as "Oh Freedom" and "We Shall Not Be Moved" filled the air in places like Selma and Birmingham, where black people battled against the entrenched forces of segregation and racial bigotry.

The most famous and stirring song of the civil rights movement, "We Shall Overcome," came from a still-surviving center of 1930s radicalism, the Highlander Folk School, in Grundy County, Tenn. Apparently based on a gospel song written by Charles Tindley in 1901, "I'll Overcome Some Day," the song was taken to the folk school by black workers, who had sung fragments of it during a 1946 strike. Zilphia Horton, wife of the school's director, Myles Horton, added some verses to it and taught them to the other students. White folksinger Guy Carawan introduced the song to the civil rights movement when he sang it during sit-in workshops at Nashville in 1960. During the first half of the decade, students sponsored by the Student Nonviolent Coordinating Committee (SNCC), such as Bernice Reagon and Julius Lester, took the song to every section of the South. By the time President Lyndon B. Johnson quoted the phrase in a speech endorsing the 1964 Civil Rights Act, "We Shall Overcome" had become known, in at least fragmentary form, to most Americans. Indeed, the whole grassroots phase of protest singing was followed by the absorption of such songs into American popular culture. Civil rights songs, antiwar songs, and ballads protesting against a wide range of social evils became vital ingredients of a major urban folk music revival that swept the United States in the early 1960s. Southern singers continued to play distinctive roles, but usually on phonograph recordings, in coffeehouses and college folk music clubs, in auditorium concerts, or on radio and television broadcasts. Sis Cunningham, an Arkansas-born veteran of 1930s labor struggles, provided a forum for new songwriters with her journal, *Broadside*. Another Arkansas singer and radical, and an alumnus of both the Almanac Singers and the Weavers, Lee Hays, functioned as an elder statesman for the new protest musicians. In conservative Dallas, a most unlikely milieu for radical music, singer-writer Lu Mitchell lent encouragement to singers of all kinds and acted as a kind of mentor-patron for the small folk music community there. Among the singers who were active throughout the nation were such southern-born musicians as Odetta Felious (Alabama), Hedy West (Georgia), Carolyn Hester (Texas), Tom Paxton (Oklahoma), and Phil Ochs (Texas). Of course, a very large contingent of singers and musicians received their introduction to music through their participation in the urban folk revival. Among the more important who went on to successful careers in other forms of music were Gram Parsons, from Georgia, and Michael Murphey and Janis Joplin, both from Texas.

Protest music faded during the 1970s, as national polarization subsided in the aftermath of the Vietnam War. Adult Americans exhibited a growing conservative impulse, and younger people were increasingly won over to the more aggressive, electronic sounds of rock music. Nevertheless, some singers and writers have remained faithful to the cause of human rights and social justice and have never wavered in their use of music for such purposes. Guy and Candie Carawan and Jane Sapp still promote local folk music resources at the Highlander Education and Research Center in Tennessee; Si and Kathy Kahn sing and write songs as part of their work as community organizers in the north Georgia mountains; Art and Margo Rosenbaum, working in the same area of Georgia, have documented the lives of poor black and white people through sketches, photographs, and traditional songs. In 1966 Anne Romaine and Bernice Reagon, fine singers in their own right, organized the Southern Folk Festival Tour, which provided wider exposure for native folksingers. In the annual tours that followed, audiences saw and heard such powerful singers as Hazel Dickens from West Virginia. Strongly reminiscent of earlier singers such as Aunt Molly Jackson, Dickens sang older material and her own compositions, which dealt with contemporary problems of poverty and social and sexual inequality.

Protest music appears occasionally in the repertoires of professional musicians, and listeners to country music in the late 1960s and early 1970s discovered that protest does not always have an explicit ideological reference. A spate of country songs during those years defended the Vietnam War, protested against protesters and counterculture lifestyles, attacked welfare programs, and identified with establishment values, while others criticized small-town hypocrisy, documented worker alienation and exploitation, commented on environmental waste and pollution, and indicted the mistreatment of Indians and migrant workers.

BILL C. MALONE
Madison, Wisconsin

Ed Cray, *Ramblin' Man: The Life and Times of Woody Guthrie* (2004); R. Serge Denisoff, *Great Day Coming: Folk Music and the American Left* (1971), *Journal of American Folklore* (January–March 1969); Lawrence Gellert, *Negro Songs of Protest, Rounder 4004*; Archie Green, *Only a Miner: Studies in Recorded Coal-Mining Songs* (1972); John Greenway, *American Folksongs of Protest* (1953); John W. Hevener, *Which*

Side Are You On? The Harlan County Coal Miners, 1931–39 (1979); Joe Klein, *Woody Guthrie* (1980); Shelly Romalis, *Pistol Packin' Mama: Aunt Molly Jackson and the Politics of Folksong* (1999), *Sing Out* (July 1966), *Textile Labor* (April 1961).

R&B

R&B (rhythm and blues) is a term that is understood in a number of different ways. In the broadest sense, it covers most low- to middle-brow African American popular music from the World War II era to the present. In the narrow sense, it refers to the buoyant music of the 1940s and 1950s that echoed the upbeat mood of blacks migrating from the rural South to the promise held out by the city, a promise of alleviation of racial inequities and of economic opportunity spurred by the war after a decade spent in the throes of the Depression. As an industry label, however, the category "rhythm and blues" emerged only in 1949, when *Billboard* magazine, at the behest of editor Jerry Wexler, adopted the term to replace such racially marked categories as "race music" and such prefixes as "sepia." These terms had been used to designate recorded African American music but were increasingly being seen as derogatory. As a trade term, "rhythm and blues" did not designate a genre but rather included all commercially recorded African American music—gospel records that sold in significant numbers, for instance, appeared on the R&B sales charts. Yet those concerned with jazz, "folk" blues, and religious African American music strongly dissociated themselves and the music of their interests from the stylistic category of rhythm and blues—a usually catchy, up-tempo populist music, typically played by electrified combos of five to eight instruments and serving primarily the tastes of working-class blacks recently migrated from the South and living in the expanding urban ghettos. New York, Los Angeles, Chicago, and Detroit were the major centers that drew southern working-class blacks, and these became the hubs of rhythm-and-blues recording activity. Many urban centers in the South, such as Dallas, Houston, New Orleans, Memphis, Atlanta, and Birmingham, and in the neighboring midwestern states, especially Kansas City and St. Louis, also featured vibrant live rhythm-and-blues scenes, and some, like Houston and Memphis, increasingly developed into important recording centers. Often these regional centers served as training grounds for southern musicians before they sensed greater opportunity in outside centers with burgeoning recording activity. The majority of early rhythm-and-blues musicians, nevertheless, were born in the South.

Although the name came into use only in 1949, the music itself had more or less coalesced a decade earlier, although it is difficult to delineate the precise moment at which precursor forms such as boogie-woogie, hokum and urban blues, and combo swing jazz through cross-pollination morphed into R&B. And as soon as the R&B designation became accepted, subtle changes moved much of the music of its performers into the stylistic territories that would foreshadow and overlap with music later designated rock and roll and soul music. A focus on crossing over to the emerging white teen market, adjustments in lyrical content, rhythmic characteristics, and instrumental constitution, and the introduction of electric distortion made a number of R&B recordings by black artists between 1949 and 1953 contenders for the retrospectively applied label of "the first rock and roll record." Meanwhile, in music directed at adult and African American markets, a stronger influence from gospel, which had itself continuously been influenced by developments in secular music, infused into R&B a new emotive charge that could range from a seething undercurrent to devotional fervor. African American musicians soon started to describe this new amalgam as "soul," although again it was not admitted as a category by trade magazines until much later. R&B's ebullience had reflected the hopeful outlook of the recently migrated southern blacks, and soul's gravity resulted from the quashing of their initial dream by continuing inequities and ghettoization. Yet strains of R&B continued into the soul era and beyond. Although several subsequent stylistic developments from the late 1960s onward led to the development of fairly distinctive named styles of urban African American music, such as funk, disco, and hip-hop, within African American communities, which have always constituted the core audience of these styles, the overall descriptive category of R&B has continued to hold sway. Mainstream media also increasingly returned to using the term for most urban contemporary African American music that is not exclusively hip-hop.

The term "rhythm and blues" essentially designates blues-based music with an emphasis on rhythmic aspects, which make it particularly suitable for dancing. Although the biggest migration of southern blacks to northern industrial centers would come only on the eve of World War II, many had already moved during the years prior, and cities such as Chicago had become major locales where blacks infused their rural blues with elements of sophisticated pop. Other piano-based styles served as stepping stones in the transition to rhythm and blues, especially the urbane piano-and-guitar-duo styles of Nashville-born Leroy Carr and Scrapper Blackwell and of Thomas A. "Georgia Tom" Dorsey and Hudson "Tampa Red" Whittaker. Although, in the narrow sense, classic rhythm and blues of the 1940s and 1950s is associated with the up-tempo, upbeat dance and novelty numbers of the likes of Louis Jordan, Big Joe Turner, Wynonie Harris, and Little Richard, on the R&B charts these performers' success was matched by that of balladeers such as Alabaman Nat King Cole, Tennessean Pvt. Cecil Gant, Texans Charles Brown and Ivory Joe Hunter, Louisianan Percy Mayfield, Arkansan Little Willie John, and Tennessean Johnny Ace. Pianist Dorsey and guitarist Tampa Red popularized the double-entendre, up-tempo, novelty blues style known as hokum blues that was a forerunner of the up-tempo rhythm and blues, whose similarly adult lyrics often had to be bowdlerized when covered by white singers for the white teen market in the 1950s.

Stylistically, the last elements of rhythm and blues, and to a great extent even of rock and roll, coalesced sometime around 1938, a year marked by the boogie-woogie revival set off from the Carnegie Hall stage by Kansas City pianist Pete Johnson and vocalist Big Joe Turner and the sounds of a septet formed by the saxophonist in Chick Webb's swing band, Arkansan Louis Jordan. Many other black swing bands increasingly featured similar male "blues shouters," made upbeat music directed at the black urban audience, and served as incubators of stylistic traits later continued by jump blues and R&B combos. Most prominent among them were Cab Calloway with his orchestra, Oklahoman Jimmy Rushing with the Count Basie Orchestra, Wynonie Harris with Alabaman Lucky Millinder's band, and Texan Walter Brown and Arkansan Jimmy Witherspoon with Oklahoman Jay McShann's band. Big bands also were the first to feature the energetic, repetitive, abrasive, and powerful style of saxophone playing called "honking," which provided a deliberately lowbrow antithesis to the florid lines of the emerging bebop style. Although Illinois Jacquet, from Texas, playing with Lionel Hampton, sparked the new expressive style, Oklahomans Earl Bostic and Hal Singer, North Carolinians Tab Smith and Red Prysock, Texans Wild Bill Moore and King Curtis, Georgia's Eddie Chamblee, Florida's Willis "Gator" Jackson, Mississippi's J. T. Brown, and Tennessee's Sam "the Man" Taylor made it an integral part of rhythm and blues over the next two decades. Still, it was Arkansas-born alto saxophonist Louis Jordan, in his role as singer and bandleader, who proved the most influential of the era's horn blowers. His "jump blues" combo sound combined blues structures with boogie-woogie bass lines, triplet rhythms that fell between swing and shuffle, depending upon the tempo, and short riffs played by three horns—alto and tenor saxophone and trumpet. Compared to swing, the music was less complex structurally and less elaborately arranged and orchestrated, used improvised saxophone solos, and had rhythmic emphasis rather than elaborate melody. This was not the polite swing music of the ensconced northern urban middle class, white or black. Hilarious novelty lyrics repeatedly invoked southern rural imagery most familiar to recent immigrants and reflected in the song titles—"Ain't Nobody Here but Us Chickens," "Choo Choo Ch'Boogie," and "Saturday Night Fish Fry." Jordan's "Let the Good Times Roll" (1946) was especially successful across racial lines, because its timing captured the mood of a jubilant nation, and it made him the most successful black crossover artist playing music with an uncompromised black aesthetic.

In many ways, rhythm and blues was the first widely popular African American–based music made by African American musicians. Ragtime, published Tin Pan Alley blues, and jazz had achieved wide popularity largely through versions by whites for white audiences. Parallel developments in media, especially the jukebox, the radio, and the record, were central to rhythm and blues' nationwide spread. War economics resulted in the channeling of resources to that effort—large dance halls closed down, and many smaller venues switched from live entertainment to the jukebox. Efforts to curb juvenile delinquency in the swelling cities also contributed to the rise of jukebox parlors. Shellac rationing disproportionately slowed "race" and "hillbilly" record production by major record labels, and independent labels—"indies"—emerged in response to the demand. ASCAP's monopoly and increased royalty demands had already led many radio stations to form the rival publishing company BMI, which turned its attention to songwriters and musicians excluded by the Tin Pan Alley–based ASCAP—the hillbilly and race artists. Also, although the major labels considered radio to be competition to their record sales, the indies were more experimental, and, to pitch their records, they increasingly turned to the black "personality DJ," initially on black music time slots on white-owned stations and later on black radio stations. With increasing wattages, stations such as WDIA Memphis turned on more than just the black audience to the latest sounds in urban black music and set the stage for the advent of the rock-and-roll phenomenon.

Connections to specific regions within the South were often reflected in the specific stylistic amalgams. For instance, the West Coast urban-blues and rhythm-and-blues sound benefited from connections with Texas blues and New Orleans's Caribbean-inflected rhythms. Texas's distinctive blues tradition, epitomized in Blind Lemon Jefferson's style, and its jazz guitar tradition, embodied in Eddie Durham's and Charlie Christian's work, informed the developments of the jazz blues of Oak Cliff's T-Bone Walker, the "cocktail jazz" of Austin's Oscar Moore with the Nat King Cole Trio, and the blues ballad stylings of Austin's Johnnie Moore with his Three Blazers featuring Charles Brown. New Orleans's Caribbean-influenced rhythms and distinctive R&B sounds, likewise, were brought to bear upon the widely influential recordings of Los Angeles–based independent labels Imperial and Specialty, by Dave Bartholomew, a composer, arranger, bandleader, producer, and talent scout, who recorded Fats Domino, Lloyd Price, and Shirley & Lee. Similarly, Chicago received the bulk of its musical immigrants from the Mississippi Delta region, and the rhythm-and-blues combo sound associated with that city was an amplified, ensemble-based descendant of the gritty rural Delta blues sound. Because of its distinctiveness and closeness to its southern rural forebear, postwar Chicago blues in retrospect has often been separated from the rhythm-and-blues category under which it was originally marketed.

Postwar Chicago blues and the earlier jump blues genres both served an adult working-class audience that had ambivalent feelings about its southern past, and they sometimes offered contrasting takes on that relationship. Many in the next generation of black immigrants to the North, however, were unsentimentally willing to leave behind rural southern associations, just as the Mills Brothers, the Ink Spots, and the Nat King Cole Trio had done during the 1930s and 1940s. The first two of these vocal harmony groups, which had had significant crossover success with white audiences, by the end of the 1940s had inspired numerous a cappella harmony groups practicing on street corners and in school gyms and city parks, mostly in northern cities, but also in southern urban centers. Within the rhythm-and-blues market, the vocal artistry of such artists on recordings, like other northern black vocal harmony groups, was typically enhanced with R&B combo backing. Gospel and jubilee quartet influences were particularly strong in the raisings of southern vocal harmony groups and vocalists, such as Don Covay, Clyde McPhatter, Jimmy Ross of the Ravens, the Five Royales, and the Five Keys, and guided some artists' later maturation into deep soul music.

Rhythm-and-blues influences continued in up-tempo soul in the 1960s, but, especially on slower songs, soul music introduced new elements into African American secular music. With the wartime dream of civil equality crushed, African Americans needed more than a music that was always jumping. Gospel's powerful style emotionally offered deliverance while sociopolitically conscious lyrics intellectually demanded it. R&B artists who had initially succeeded in crossing over to rock-and-roll audiences did continue offering their original styles at rock festivals, while older rhythm-and-blues artists continued with theirs on the southern chitlin' circuit. In the 1970s, funk, a development within soul music, increasingly informed more urbane soul styles, which, by the mid-1970s, spawned disco. The rhythm-and-blues category by this point had lost its mainstream usefulness with regard to contemporary music, although with black musicians and audiences the contraction "R&B" retained some currency as an overarching term for their secular music. In the 1980s, as black artists sought and found unprecedented success in the larger international pop market, with Michael Jackson, Prince, Diana Ross, Georgia-native Lionel Ritchie, and Tennessean Tina Turner emerging as megastars, the music industry curtailed the use of labels such as "R&B" for music with clear crossover appeal. Significantly, it was in the rock and pop categories that these artists swept the Grammy awards. *Billboard*, meanwhile, relabeled its "Soul Singles" chart as the "Black Singles" chart in 1982, the "R&B Singles" chart in 1990, and the "R&B/Hip-Hop Singles" chart in 1999.

In the last two decades, African American popular music has proved at least as influential on international audiences as the original rhythm-and-blues sounds were in the 1940s and 1950s. In the 1990s, an unprecedented 18 black music acts were featured on *Billboard*'s Top 25 singles artists list. The aforementioned specialist charts, in addition to reflecting the success of artists whose appeal is more limited to African American audiences, continue to serve as barometers of upcoming hot trends and hits, which are still understood under the umbrella of R&B, especially until individual ones cross over to the wider mainstream. Although contemporary trends in African American music do not show as strong a regional flavor as during the initial advent of rhythm and blues, a number of urban centers in the South, for instance, Atlanta and Houston, have yielded R&B and hip-hop scenes and styles that evince strong regionalisms.

AJAY KALRA
University of Texas at Austin

Mellonee V. Burnim and Portia K. Maultsby, eds., *African American Music: An Introduction* (2006); Richard J. Ripani, *The New Blue Music: Changes in Rhythm & Blues, 1950–1999* (2006); Arnold Shaw, *Honkers and Shouters: The Golden Years of Rhythm and Blues* (1978).

Radio

Radio was a key institution in the popularization of many forms of music in the American South. Broadcasting stations beamed traditional forms of southern music to listeners throughout the region and the nation. Disc jockeys became important personalities associated with southern culture, and performers made use of radio to expand their commercial opportunities through selling records and promoting performance appearances.

The earliest radio stations in the South appeared in the early 1920s, including two destined to be mainstays among the region's broadcasters—WWL in New Orleans, licensed to Loyola University, and WSB, operated by the *Atlanta Journal*, both of which have long broadcast music as part of their programming. The southern states were slower to develop substantial radio facilities than the nation as a whole. Indeed, a continuing complaint of Dixie's politicians during the middle 1920s was the supposed discrimination being suffered by a South saddled with inadequate radio service.

From its earliest days, southern broadcasting developed a close association with country and gospel music. With the coming of radio, southern folksingers found an important new outlet for their talents. Probably the first station to feature country music was WSB in Atlanta. Within a few months after going on the air in 1922, WSB was presenting several folk performers, including the Rev. Andrew Jenkins, a blind gospel singer, and Fiddlin' John Carson. With WSB leading the way, radio stations all over the South—and the Midwest, as well—began showcasing country and gospel musicians and singers. Radio enabled white gospel performers to gain independence from the song-publishing companies that had once sponsored their performances. Radio provided direct access for performers, who gained increasing control of their careers because of it. Border radio stations, beginning with XERA, established in 1932 by John R. Brinkley in Del Rio, Tex., provided a unique forum for performers, whose high-powered transmitters, located across the border in Mexico, enabled them to broadcast to the far reaches of the United States.

No discussion of southern country music and its relationship to radio would be complete without recognizing the impact of Nashville's *Grand Ole Opry*. The vehicle by which it gained attention was WSM, a station owned by the National Life and Accident Insurance Company. In November 1925, just a month after WSM first went on the air, it broadcast a program initially known as the WSM *Barn Dance*. A year later the country music show acquired the new name of *Grand Ole Opry* (to contrast it with the Grand Opera concerts being broadcast by the networks). Agents of National Life often took advantage of the connection by introducing themselves to potential clients as being from the *Grand Ole Opry* Insurance Company. By World War II the program had become the most important country music show on the air, especially after 1939, when NBC began carrying a 30-minute segment on the network every Saturday night. Shreveport's *Louisiana Hayride* was another important radio venue for country music performers, broadcast over KWKH. The *Hayride* served as a regional institution that attracted young rockabilly performers like Elvis Presley in the 1950s, as well as country musicians.

Stations such as Memphis's WDIA and Nashville's WLAC were key institutions in the spread of black music in the 1940s and 1950s. WDIA popularized the blues of the Mississippi Delta and Beale Street, and Gatemouth Moore became a popular radio personality, playing the black gospel music that thrived in

Memphis. WLAC was typical of other stations in broadcasting news and popular music during the day but switching to blues, gospel, and rhythm and blues at night. The station's 50,000-watt signal reached 20 states, and its format made celebrities of disc jockeys such as William T. "Hoss" Allen and John R. (Richbourg).

Radio stations in rural areas, small towns, and isolated parts of Appalachia are true community institutions that have long used daily live musical performances as essential parts of their programming. The line between evangelical preaching and musical performance was a thin one on such stations, with religious songs a key part of the musical repertoire of country singers as well as of gospel entertainers. Sanctified and Pentecostal faiths produced some of the liveliest music on such stations, and the spontaneity of live broadcasts gave listeners an early morning or midday boost, placed between the farm reports and the news of the sick and shut-ins.

Today southern musical genres of all types can be found on radio stations, but, except for country music, they rarely can compete for the largest audiences with pop music. Still, local stations often feature segments on blues, rhythm and blues, jazz, gospel, or other musical forms as part of their weekly programming. Mississippi Public Broadcasting features *Highway 61*, a weekly blues broadcast; New Orleans public radio has much jazz; and North Carolina public stations carry the bluegrass that comes out of the nearby hills. Traveling through the South today, one hears *norteña* music, which is popular among the new Latino immigrants in the region. Internet radio makes it possible to hear one's favorite form of southern music 24 hours a day, 7 days a week.

C. JOSEPH PUSATERI
University of San Diego

Bill Barlow, *Voice Over: The Making of Black Radio* (1999); Louis Cantor, *Wheelin' on Beale: How WDIA-Memphis Became the Nation's First All-Black Radio Station and Created the Sound That Changed America* (1992); Howard Dorgan, *The Airwaves of Zion: Radio and Religion in Appalachia* (1993); Robert Gordon, *It Came from Memphis* (1995); C. Joseph Pusateri, *Enterprise in Radio: WWL and the Business of Broadcasting in America* (1980).

Ragtime

In the generation following the Civil War, various elements of southern folk music, especially black-evolved styles from the Mississippi Valley, coalesced to form a piano music known by the 1890s as "ragtime." Marked by an idiomatic syncopation in the treble (right-hand) part against a steady, marchlike bass (left-hand) part, the piano rag developed as a highly formalized music in 2/4 time, built of three or more contrasting strains.

In its origins ragtime drew from blackface minstrel sources, string band music, sentimental parlor music, brass band music, and many other sources. Called "jig-piano" or "ragged time" by early practitioners, it was transformed at the turn of the century by black composers in the Missouri-Kansas region into a serious, carefully notated musical genre. Among the principal pioneers of piano ragtime were Thomas Turpin (c. 1873–1922), James Scott (1886–1938), Artie Matthews (1888–1958), and, most centrally, Scott Joplin (1868–1917) and his protégés—Arthur Marshall (1881–1968) and Scott Hayden (1882–1915).

In 1897 the first score entitled a "rag" appeared in print—white bandleader-arranger William H. Krell's "Mississippi Rag." Within weeks this was followed by Thomas Turpin's "Harlem Rag." Scott Joplin entered the scene in 1899 with "Original Rags" and "Maple Leaf Rag," the single composition that most epitomized and defined the genre for the public. Other popular artists like Benjamin Harney (1873–1938), Hubert "Eubie" Blake (1883–1983), and James P. Johnson (1894–1954) worked on the East Coast with songs, blues, and other musical materials related to ragtime. Between 1895 and 1905 ragtime spread across the United States via itinerant pianists, mechanical player-piano rolls, gramophone records, published sheet-music scores, and adaptations of the music to bands, orchestras, and every other musical medium. The two decades between 1895 and 1915 can justifiably be called the "ragtime age."

Ragtime became the basis for the whole modern popular music industry. Its infusion of fresh African American musical styles and practices turned the nation away from European models and provided a basic matrix of syncopated, contrapuntally voiced, rhythmically sophisticated music from which followed jazz and rock and roll. It was identified in the public mind with black southern culture, especially through widely popular ragtime songs, which continued the old minstrelsy imagery of the idyllic South of carefree easy living on magnolia-scented plantations. Ragtime also transformed popular social dancing, especially in the years after 1910. One early ragtime song, written by Roberts and Jefferson in 1900, summarized (and satirized) the wild enthusiasm for the new music:

> I got a ragtime dog and a ragtime cat
> A ragtime piano in my ragtime flat;
> Wear ragtime clothes, from hat to shoes,
> I read a paper called the "Ragtime News."

Got ragtime habits and I talk that way,
I sleep in ragtime and I rag all day;
Got ragtime troubles with my ragtime wife,
I'm certainly living a ragtime life.

The impact must have seemed revolutionary to a generation hitherto unexposed to popular musical fads disseminated by mass media.

The "classic" piano rag developed by Joplin, Turpin, Scott, and others evolved into a simple but effective form: a bisectional construction connecting strains of 16 bars, typically in an arrangement or sequence of (for example) AA BB A // CC DD. The first section of the rag (AA BB A) always featured a cyclical return of the first strain. The second section (CC DD) featured two (or more) strains in varied sequences. There are two primary variations in the form: (1) a linear construction (for example, AA BB A // CC DD) or (2) a rounded construction, which returns to material from the rag's first section, the A or B strains (for example, AA BB A // CC DD A or AA BB A // CC A DD). The multirhythmic nature of the classic piano rag (so-called by Scott Joplin and his publisher, John Stilwell Stark [1841–1927], of Sedalia, Mo.) challenged composers to use a broad variety of compositional creativity.

In the mid-1890s Ben Harney dazzled New York City with ragtime songs like "You've Been a Good Old Wagon" (1895) and "Mr. Johnson, Turn Me Loose" (1896), replete with forceful syncopations, exuberant melody, and racy colloquial lyrics. At the same time, the cakewalk was popularized via vaudeville and minstrelsy. The cakewalk was a stylized "walk-around" dance performed to syncopated march music, livelier and more extroverted than the fast two-step popular since the mid-1880s. Frederick "Kerry" Mills composed "At a Georgia Camp Meeting" (1896) and "Whistlin' Rufus" (1899); Sadie Koninsky had one popular hit in "Eli Green's Cakewalk" (1896); J. Bodewalt Lampe published "Creole Belles" (1899); and ragtimer Charles L. Johnson of Kansas City wrote "Doc Brown's Cakewalk" (1899).

From popular songs and dances ragtime evolved also to purely instrumental music—a highly idiomatic and "pianistic" form invented by the itinerant Mississippi Valley entertainers. Composers like Turpin, Joplin, and Scott served their apprenticeships as pianists in saloons, bordellos, or small theaters with traveling minstrel shows or aboard riverboats. Their music was lively, loud, and percussive, designed to make a piano sound like a band, to convey the sounds of high conviviality. The new music was derived from familiar folk styles and practices, echoing banjo and guitar music, hoedown dance rhythms, and the sentimental strains of popular song.

Traces of the folk origins in the pastiche construction of early piano rags occur in Joplin's "Original Rags" (1899) and Seymour and Roberts's "St. Louis Tickle" (1904). Joplin's title indicates that he had composed a set of original themes (little "rags"), which were then assembled in a linear, suitelike form of one highly inventive strain after the other. The Seymour and Roberts rag commemorated the St. Louis World's Fair and the "ticklers" (pianists) who lined the "pike" or midway, and it included a very old river-culture folk tune, which "Jelly Roll" Morton later played and sang as "Buddy Bolden's Blues." The piano rag form allowed for maximum inventiveness and borrowing from the folk culture.

After 1899 the nationwide popularity of Joplin's "Maple Leaf Rag" opened a lucrative market for piano rags, piano rolls, and ragtime "professors" as entertainers. Joplin created dozens of unique, carefully crafted rags—"The Easy Winners" (1901), "The Chrysanthemum" (1904), "The Ragtime Dance" (1906), and "Magnetic Rag" (1914). James Scott, from Neosho, Kans., entered the scene with works like "Sunburst Rag" (1909) and "Climax Rag" (1914). The impact of this new force was so great that a young white composer growing up in New Jersey, Joseph Lamb (1887–1960), could become a major composer in the wake of Joplin and Scott, studying the Stark scores and beginning his own publication in 1908 with "Sensation Rag." He produced a series of deeply felt, black-inspired rags, like "Excelsior Rag" (1909), "American Beauty Rag" (1913), "The Ragtime Nightingale" (1915), and "Bohemia Rag" (1919). In a curious postlude to the ragtime era, Lamb would be rediscovered and resume his composing career in the late 1950s, after a 40-year hiatus.

John S. Stark was the disseminator of classic ragtime, printing Joplin, Scott, Lamb, Matthews, Marshall, and other ragtime giants. When he saw the magnitude of his ragtime publishing success, Stark became a champion of "high-class" or "quality" ragtime, which he and Joplin differentiated from popular songs, improvisational folk rags, or ephemeral mass-produced ditties. Stark insisted that rags should be played carefully, at moderate tempos, as written. Stark and Joplin viewed ragtime as a genuine African American art form, and Stark was for his day a remarkably tolerant and fair-minded collaborator with the black composers he sponsored. His large, handsome piano scores are aesthetic prizes of the epoch.

Ragtime became a genuinely national music, composed and published in towns and cities all across the United States, and it also achieved international fame, becoming for Europe an indication of America's lively genius. Its roots in the Mississippi Valley remained firm, and Ferdinand "Jelly Roll" Morton (1885–1941), from New Orleans, recalled the large numbers of itinerant pianists and composers traveling from New Orleans through Memphis and St. Louis on up to Chicago in the years around 1900. As the music was published and distributed, other "schools" of non-notated ragtime flourished, including an important East Coast or "stride" piano group, which included James P. Johnson, Eubie Blake, Charles Luckeyth Roberts (1887–1968), and, later, Thomas "Fats" Waller (1904–43). Ragtime artists like Joe Jordan (1882–1971), New Orleans's Tony Jackson (1876–1921), and many others made Chicago a jazz center.

Ragtime was not a wholly southern phenomenon, but its taproots were in the Deep South and Southwest, and it reflected an authentic musical culture of the Mississippi Valley and environs. It was a powerful influence on a new instrumental music, later called "jass" or "jazz," which grew up in the region in the years around 1900. Early jazz musicians uniformly referred to their music as "ragtime," though it was largely an improvised, non-notated form of syncopated dance music.

The impact of ragtime on America—and world—culture is hard to overstate. The imaginative brilliance, emotional depth, and sheer joie de vivre of the music shaped all subsequent popular music. It introduced the black musical imagination and sensibility to a receptive general audience and established high standards for popular composition. When commercial songwriters and arrangers in New York City, in the area dubbed "Tin Pan Alley," took up the thrust of ragtime, around 1910, they were simply passing on a dense, complex, and culturally significant body of musical information and practices. George and Ira Gershwin in 1918 memorialized the ragtime era with "The Real American Folk Song (Is a Rag)." The music that had begun as nobody's music had become everybody's music.

Although the ragtime era seemed dead and gone by 1920, swept away during World War I by the advent of jazz and the new one-step and fox-trot dances, its basic themes and patterns profoundly influenced American music. The lyrics added to Joplin's "Maple Leaf Rag" promised that it would "shake de earth's foundation," and indeed it did.

WILLIAM J. SCHAFER
Berea College

Edward A. Berlin, *Ragtime: A Musical and Cultural History* (1980); Rudi Blesh and Harriet Janis, *They All Played Ragtime* (1966); Frank Driggs and Chuck Haddix, *Kansas City Jazz: From Ragtime to Bebop: A History* (2006); David A. Jasen and Trebor Jay Tichenor, *Rags and Ragtime: A Musical History* (1978); William J. Schafer and Johannes Riedel, *The Art of Ragtime: Form and Meaning of an Original Black American Art* (1973); Terry Waldo, *This Is Ragtime* (1976).

Rockabilly

Memphis, December 1954. In a 30-by-18-foot recording studio, which had earlier served as a radiator shop, three musicians unfamiliar with such surroundings just a few months before were attempting to recapture lightning in a bottle. Specifically, they were hoping to replicate the surprising success that had greeted their first two commercial recordings. Along with a former radio-engineer-turned producer, the three, all of whom had recently quit their day jobs, were pinning their hopes on a 20-year-old blues song that had become a staple within western swing. At first, it seemed like their version of "Milkcow Blues" would differ little from previous ones performed by Kokomo Arnold, Robert Johnson, Johnny Lee Wills, and the Maddox Brothers and Rose. Indeed, the group sleepily started out as if in a melodic malaise: "Oh well, I woke up this-a morning, and I looked out the door. I can tell that old milkcow by the way she's low." Suddenly the meandering music came to a premature halt. Employing slang then prevalent in bebop and jazz circles, the 19-year-old vocalist in control of the session, feigning spontaneity, enjoined his bandmates: "Hold it fellas! That don't *move* me. Let's get real, real gone for a change." Ratcheting up the tempo, the trio then soared full speed into a rendition that resembled a runaway freight train raring to jump its tracks. After much preparation yet seemingly without effort, the group had gotten really gone. Filled with slurs, falsettos, growls, breathless hiccups, and other vocal gymnastics that merged with a slap-happy bass and steady rail-riding lead guitar, the song that resonated from the playback speakers satisfied the studio's four listeners. It was different, and although it clearly referenced all three genres, it could not be classified as country, rhythm and blues, or pop. In applying the kinetic energy of working-class gospel to a successful fusion of rocking black R&B and white hillbilly music, Elvis Presley, Bill Black, Scotty Moore, and Sam Phillips had again hit upon a winning commercial formula. In negotiating a significant racial divide, they had created a music without boundaries. Only later would others call it "rockabilly."

Presley, Black, Moore, and Phillips, of course, were not the only southern white natives of the post–World War II era experimenting in musical forms that explored new racial frontiers. Nonetheless, they were the first to gain commercial prominence from doing so. The breakthrough, however, did not happen overnight. Since the late 1940s, "race music" had been slowly and surreptitiously infiltrating the listening habits of a growing number of listeners in the South, particularly through the spread of African American radio programming. Phillips had been profitably recording blues and rhythm-and-blues artists like Howlin' Wolf, Rufus Thomas, and Little Junior Parker for the African American market since 1950 and believed that such music also appealed to Dixie's white teenagers. Yet he understood that the racial intolerance and segregated circumstances inherent within popular music and the South would prevent a black rhythm-and-blues act from gaining the broad exposure needed to achieve large-scale commercial and crossover success. He faced a dilemma but also possessed a solution. Influenced by popular music trends occurring inside and outside of the region, as well as his own business instincts, the Sun Records owner relentlessly sought a white man who could perform rhythm-and-blues material with the same feeling and authenticity he had observed while recording African American vocalists. Phillips believed that if he could find such an artist, he could make a million dollars.

Phillips, of course, found Elvis (only after his earlier "discovery," the eccentric 43-year-old white itinerant Harmonica Frank, failed to catch on). In the summer of 1954, Presley, along with guitarist Moore and bass player Black (dubbed the Blue Moon Boys), created a commercially successful working-class and biracial synthesis. Phillips would release five Presley recordings before the year 1955 concluded, as Elvis rapidly built a youthful following throughout the South and Southwest. After 18 months the young singer left Sun (where he had been marketed as a country singer), signed an exclusive contract with industry giant RCA Victor (which promised to promote him in the pop, R&B, and country fields), appeared on national network television, and began making motion pictures in Hollywood. He was destined to become the "King of Rock 'n' Roll." His subsequent career would prove that Presley was an eclectic vocalist whose style could not be easily classified, but his success as a country singer who performed rhythm and blues convincingly nevertheless opened the door for others crafting similar musical mergers. That there were many regional artists whose musical tastes, talents, and proclivities followed a trajectory comparable to that of Elvis suggests strongly that the postwar southern world they inhabited was in the midst of significant economic, social, and racial transformation.

Phillips certainly did not have to look very far to find rockabilly aspirants seeking to replace the hip-swiveling "Hillbilly Cat." Young musicians from throughout the South who performed in a similar style traveled to Memphis to record for Phillips, including such performers as Carl Perkins, Jerry Lee Lewis, Johnny Cash, Roy Orbison, Charlie Rich, and Conway Twitty. Phillips and Sun, however, did not enjoy a monopoly on rockabilly. By the middle to late 1950s, other record labels had signed Buddy Holly, the Everly Brothers, Bob Luman, Johnny and Dorsey Burnette, Paul Burlison, and Gene Vincent, young adults who were as influenced by R&B shouter Roy Brown as they were by Smokey Mountain Boy Roy Acuff. The rockabilly club also included Wanda Jackson,

Janis Martin (the "Female Elvis"), and Brenda Lee, women whose dynamic on-stage demeanor not only resisted what country music demanded of its female performers but also challenged prevailing postwar models of domestic femininity. For a time, it appeared that rockabilly would alter forever the influence of Nashville and country music. Virtually all of the region's talented (and not so talented) young white working-class singers, both women and men, seemed intent on becoming the next Elvis, not the next Hank Williams or Kitty Wells.

Ironically, despite the Nashville music establishment's initial fear of and opposition to rockabilly, the music itself and the performers who sang it were steeped deeply in country traditions. For many, rockabilly simply represented a youthful version of "hillbilly" music transplanted to an urban environment and played with a rocking beat that borrowed from black gospel and rhythm and blues. The fact that many of the southern white performers associated with rockabilly returned to country music once their popularity as pop idols began to fade indicated that they had never completely abandoned their more rural time-honored roots. The same held true for their audiences. As listeners grew older, they too tended to move back toward the commercial country music emanating from Nashville and Bakersfield, Calif. Yet their explorations into rockabilly had expanded the boundaries of the genre, giving it a more modern, urban, and national character.

Presley and his fellow rockabilly performers, however, were not the first southern white songsters to dabble in musical styles associated with their black neighbors. Vernacular music of the pre-1920s rural South, for instance, cannot be designated as either black or white. It was a complex composite made up of British and West African sources. Such traditions flowed, although not always unimpeded, into the commercial era. Jimmie Rodgers, the eclectic "Father of Country Music" and its first recording star, had apparently absorbed much of his style from African Americans. Nor was he the last "hillbilly" singer to reflect the influence of black bluesmen; others of note would include Bill Monroe, the Delmore Brothers, Red Foley, Tennessee Ernie Ford, Moon Mullican, and Hank Williams. They and a slew of lesser-known local and regional country boogie practitioners borrowed heavily from contemporary black music. Their sound, style, and appearance, however, generally remained conventional within country music. More important, perhaps, their public demeanor and attitudes toward race stayed within the restrictive bounds established by the region's adherence to Jim Crow segregation.

What distinguished the rockabilly rebels from their predecessors was their willingness to identify completely with the rhythm-and-blues singers they emulated. Through their performing styles, dress, speech, and behavior, they were attempting to relate on some level to their black counterparts. In this manner they forced their way out of the intricate and rigid southern folk and country music traditions they were born into. Accordingly, rockabilly performers and audiences in the South engaged in a degree of public interchange and acceptance of black music and culture that separated them from the region's past.

Indeed, the complex and contradictory relationships between place and past and between race and class in the South were nowhere more evident than in the rockabilly phenomenon. Historically labeled as lazy, dependent, and biologically inferior, the music's white performers consisted primarily of truck drivers, dishwashers, tenant farmers, sharecroppers, and sundry blue-collar laborers. And they emerged from the same alienated audiences they entertained. In this light, rockabilly significantly revealed that although law, etiquette, and custom may have kept the region's blacks and whites legally and physically apart, they could not keep them culturally separate. Because of their traditionally low position within the socioeconomic structure and their customary emphasis on preindustrial nonmarket values and personal style (rockabilly would amplify impulses seemingly inherent to the rural, bottom-rail South: excessive hedonism, arrogant masculinity, overt aggressiveness, and, paradoxically, a deep-seated emotionalism and sensitivity that defied conventional gendered behavior), working-class southerners of both races were predisposed to the merging of black and white along cultural lines. To be sure, the merger was not always a welcome one, particularly among marginalized working whites, whose social and economic impotence openly challenged the logic of white supremacy. Certainly no group consistently had worked harder to escape or prevent interaction with their African American counterparts.

It is within this heritage of working-class animosity toward the biracial nature of southern culture that the origins of rockabilly should be placed. This is not to suggest that the music appealed only to the region's proletarian base. Neither is it to imply that all southern "hipsters" who tuned into the rockabilly explosion suddenly became more appreciative of African American culture or that popular music magically cured the South's racial ills. Nor does it overlook or trivialize the many people whose heroic efforts and sacrifices ensured the success of the black freedom struggle. It does, however, raise questions concerning our understanding of the relationship between popular culture and social change.

For rockabilly was not simply a southern or country version of rock and roll, a meaningless fad to be resurrected periodically. It was tied to a particular era, a time when the volatile issues of class, race, gender, and generation shook the postwar South to its foundations. Rockabilly undoubtedly embodied the conflicts and tensions indicative of a southern world in transition. Consequently, it was in its relationship to race that rockabilly, as well as the southern culture that produced it, proved most innovative and enigmatic. Heeding the sentiment to "get real, real gone for a change," artists and audiences across the region had created and adopted a music without boundaries.

MICHAEL T. BERTRAND
Tennessee State University

Michael T. Bertrand, *Race, Rock, and Elvis* (2005); B. Lee Cooper and Wayne S. Haney, *Rockabilly: A Bibliographic Resource Guide* (1990); Colin Escott with Martin Hawkins, *Good Rockin' Tonight: Sun Records and the Birth of Rock 'n' Roll* (1991); Greil Marcus, *Mystery Train: Images of America in Rock 'n' Roll Music* (1981); Craig Morrison, *Go Cat Go! Rockabilly Music and Its Makers* (1998); Billy Poore, *Rockabilly: A Forty Year Journey* (1998).

Rock and Roll

Emerging in the 1950s as a genre that blended various strains of southern music, rock and roll incorporated influences from such older musical genres as blues, rhythm and blues, boogie-woogie, jazz, gospel, folk, and country. Although rock (as the genre is presently known) is an internationally popular music genre today with a relatively limited presence in the South, most of the musicians, producers, and promoters responsible for the initial popularity of rock and roll were southerners. Entering the national consciousness through trend-setting mid-1950s hit recordings by such white southerners as Elvis Presley, the genre was first associated with black musicians. The term "rock and roll," in fact, was originally coined by blacks as a triple-entendre expression that conjoined black slang for three physical actions: spiritual ecstasy through bodily contortions, secular dancing, and sexual intercourse. As early as 1916 and continuing into the 1950s, black singers incorporated that coinage—sometimes with overtly religious connotations and sometimes with secular implications—into the lyrics of songs released as gospel or as blues recordings. In the 1940s and the early 1950s certain singles from rhythm-and-blues performers foreshadowed rock and roll, including two influential songs from southern-born black musicians—"Good Rocking Tonight" (by Roy Brown in 1947) and "Rocket 88" (a 1951 single that was performed by Ike Turner's band but credited to that band's singer, Jackie Brenston). Some white southerners who made records during that same period likewise anticipated rock and roll—notable examples being Hardrock Gunter's 1949 "Birmingham Bounce" and Tennes-

Album cover of Bill Haley's Shake, Rattle, and Roll (Charles Reagan Wilson Collection, Center for the Study of Southern Culture, University of Mississippi)

see Ernie Ford's 1950 "Shotgun Boogie." Many of the rhythm-and-blues songs originally recorded by black musicians during the late 1940s and early 1950s were subsequently "covered" in the mid-1950s by white performers, who reinterpreted those songs with a pronounced backbeat, a rhythmic technique that characterized early rock and roll. The earliest rock-and-roll recordings tended to feature relatively small configurations of instruments, including some combination of electric guitar and/or saxophone for instrumental solos, and, for rhythm, acoustic guitar, bass, piano, and drums. Indeed, those would remain the integral core instruments within the genre (with the exception of the saxophone) even after the incorporation of numerous other instruments into rock-and-roll recordings beginning in the 1960s.

Many music scholars cite Presley's cover version of bluesman Arthur "Big Boy" Crudup's song "That's All Right (Mama)," recorded on 5 July 1954 and released by the Memphis-based Sun label, as the earliest single to feature a determinably rock-and-roll sound. Presley's record quickly became a local hit. Sun Records owner and producer Sam Phillips, who had previously recorded blues and rhythm-and-blues acts but had expressed his intention of finding "a white man who had the negro sound and the negro feel," capitalized on the rapidly growing popularity of rock and roll by recording and releasing additional singles by Presley. The first rock-and-roll recording to rise to No. 1 on the national pop record charts was by a white musician not from the South: Bill Haley's "Rock around the Clock" (which was recorded on 12 April 1954, though it did not become a major hit until the summer of 1955). But Presley commanded the most attention among all the musicians in the first generation of rock and rollers. In addition to "discovering" Presley, Phillips recorded for his Sun label such other white performers as Johnny Cash, Jerry Lee Lewis, Carl Perkins, Roy Orbison, and Charlie Rich. Collectively, these Sun singles featured a distinctive version of rock and roll shaped by both black (that is, blues and rhythm and blues) and white (that is, country) musical influences. The "rockabilly" sound of these Sun recordings was characterized by energetic vocals (featuring such stylistic embellishments as hiccuping, stuttering, and yelping) over a small band arrangement (including lead electric guitar over a background of acoustic rhythm guitar and upright bass and, sometimes, drums). All the aforementioned acts soon left Sun Records for various major labels and began recording more polished and heavily produced singles—for instance, Presley (signing with the RCA label in 1955) and Orbison (with Monument Records in 1960) became major stars in pop music, and Cash (joining Columbia Records in 1958) became a leading figure in country music.

Memphis may have been most closely associated with rock and roll during its early years, but other southern cities were significant in the rise of the genre. New Orleans had several independent recording companies and studios that yielded influential records by such early rock-and-roll acts as Fats Domino, Little Richard, and Lloyd Price. Nashville, as the center for the country music industry, possessed several studios primarily operated for the recording of country music, but those same studios served, from the mid-1950s onward, as the recording sites for numerous important rock-and-roll releases (for example, Presley's breakout RCA hit "Heartbreak Hotel" was recorded on 10 January 1956 at an independent studio on Nashville's McGavock Street). By the early 1960s, however, new music scenes had developed in other American cities, yielding a wider range of local and regional rock styles. By the mid-1960s, rock and roll was in decline in the South but had become an international phenomenon. In Great Britain, members of such "British Invasion" rock groups as the Beatles and the Rolling Stones—who as teenagers had idolized commercial recordings from southern performers—reinterpreted 1950s- and early 1960s-era rock and roll by re-creating the energy and sense of social rebellion initially associated with that genre and by employing a heightened degree of craftsmanship and sophistication. British rockers also composed original rock songs modeled on older recordings by southern musicians.

In the late 1960s and early 1970s, the South was again significant in the shaping of rock music. During those years, several southern cities—Memphis; Muscle Shoals, Ala.; Macon, Ga.; and Miami—emerged as centers for the production of distinctive rock recordings. Each of those cities could claim at least one internationally renowned recording studio (American and Ardent in Memphis, FAME and Muscle Shoals Sound in Muscle Shoals, Capricorn in Macon, and Criteria in Miami). Such studios generally employed backup bands made up of leading musicians who assisted local, regional, national, and international performers with the making of recordings, and, as a result, records made at a particular studio tended to bear the distinctive sound associated with that studio. Although many records made at such studios (whether of the rock, rhythm-and-blues, or soul genres) were intended for local or regional distribution, some records produced at independent southern studios during this time became major national—and, in numerous instances, international—hits. For example, Percy Sledge's 1966 No. 1 pop hit, "When a Man Loves a Woman," was recorded at the small Norala (later, Quinvy) Recording Studio in Sheffield, Ala.

Also emerging during the late 1960s and early 1970s were two rock subgenres with distinctly southern influences—country rock and southern rock. The former subgenre evolved on the late-1960s southern California music scene, as several musicians of the counterculture—notably such southerners as Gram Parsons, Steve Young, Vern Gosdin, and Doug Dillard—fused rock and country musical elements into their own music. Flourishing by the mid-1970s, southern rock employed distinctively southern thematic and stylistic musical elements and gradually built a broad-based audience across the United States. Most of the musicians associated with the latter genre were southerners, including members of such first-wave southern rock groups as the Allman Brothers Band, Lynyrd Skynyrd, the Marshall Tucker Band, Wet Willie, Black Oak Arkansas, the Ozark Mountain Daredevils, Grinderswitch, Cowboy, and Barefoot Jerry. "The South's Gonna Do It Again," a 1975 hit song written and performed by another practitioner of southern rock, Charlie Daniels, not only chronicled that subgenre by naming its practitioners but also celebrated southern regional identity and encouraged young southerners to resist the national trend toward homogenization. Additionally, in the mid-1970s, Daniels founded the Volunteer Jam, a concert held annually in Tennessee that showcased the music of various southern rock groups.

By the late 1970s, new southern rock groups were becoming popular regionally and nationally, including the Amazing Rhythm Aces, the Rossington-Collins Band, Molly Hatchet, .38 Special, Blackfoot, Sea Level, the Elvin Bishop Band, the Dixie Dregs, and the Outlaws (the name of the last group reflected the influence upon southern rock of country music's mid-1970s outlaw movement). Images historically associated with the South—including the Confederate flag—were incorporated into the lyrical content of southern rock songs and into that subgenre's visual imagery (for example, album cover art and T-shirt designs). Some critics nationally accused southern rock of perpetuating "redneck" attitudes, but certain southern rock groups were culturally progressive and politically liberal (the Allman Brothers Band, for example, claimed two black musicians as key group members, and several southern rock groups participated in Jimmy Carter's 1976 campaign for president).

Hundreds of musicians born and/or reared in the South and not mentioned previously were also influential within the genre of rock and roll. Noteworthy among those musicians were the 1940s-era rhythm-and-blues innovator, Louis Jordan, as well as numerous 1950s-era rhythm-and-blues and early rock-and-roll acts, including Chuck Willis, Professor Longhair, Big Mama Thornton, Larry Williams, Billy Lee Riley, Charlie Feathers, Bo Diddley, Wilbert Harrison, Billy Burnette, Johnny Burnette, Pat Boone, Ronnie Hawkins, Smiley Lewis, Junior Parker, Link Wray, Gene Vincent, "the Big Bopper" (J. P. Richardson), Huey "Piano" Smith, the Everly Brothers, Buddy Holly and the Crickets, and the Bill Black Combo.

Throughout its history, rock music has been profoundly shaped by the blues, and most of the major blues musicians have been from the South, including Skip James, Robert Johnson, Leadbelly, Muddy Waters, Howlin' Wolf, Aaron "T-Bone" Walker, John Lee Hooker, B. B. King, Slim Harpo, Odetta, Rev. Gary Davis, Johnny "Guitar" Watson, Buddy Guy, Johnny Winter, and Stevie Ray Vaughan. Similarly, rock has been strongly influenced by country music. Aficionados of rock music have particularly appreciated such southern-affiliated country performers as Johnny Cash, the Carter Family, Jimmie Rodgers, Bob Wills, Hank Williams Sr., George Jones, Willie Nelson, Waylon Jennings, Don Williams, Dwight Yoakam, and Emmylou Harris.

Many soul musicians who landed hits on the national pop charts during the 1960s and early 1970s—and who have inspired countless rock musicians since that time—had southern connections, including Garnet Mimms, Otis Redding, Ernie K-Doe, Chris Kenner, Sam Cooke, Bar-Kays, James Brown, Isaac Hayes, Aretha Franklin, Jerry Butler, Ray Charles, Sam & Dave, Nina Simone, Gladys Knight and the Pips, Swamp Dogg, Rufus Thomas, Betty Wright, Johnnie Taylor, Bill Withers, and Billy Preston. Southern-born and/or -reared musicians active in rock during the 1960s include such individual acts as Chubby Checker, Tommy Roe, Gary "U.S." Bonds, Jackie DeShannon, Johnny Rivers, Janis Joplin, Joe South, and Glen Campbell, as well as members of such rock groups as Booker T. & the MG's, the Box Tops, the Classics IV, the 13th Floor Elevators, the Chambers Brothers, Blues Image, Sam the Sham and the Pharaohs, Delaney and Bonnie, and the Sir Douglas Quintet.

From the 1970s to the first years of the 21st century, numerous rock groups entirely or largely made up of musicians from the South had national followings, including Big Star, Seals and Crofts, the Edgar Winter Group, the Atlanta Rhythm Section, Z. Z. Top, K. C. and the Sunshine Band, the Meters, the Neville

Brothers, the B-52s, R.E.M., the Georgia Satellites, the Black Crowes, the Fabulous Thunderbirds, the Indigo Girls, the Butthole Surfers, Collective Soul, Let's Active, Tom Petty and the Heartbreakers, Widespread Panic, Government Mule, Jason and the Scorchers, Sister Hazel, Blind Melon, and the Drive-By Truckers. Also hailing from the South were numerous solo acts that composed their own songs (this type of performer is often referred to as a "singer-songwriter"), including Tony Joe White, Jimmy Buffett, Dr. John, Alex Chilton, Jesse Winchester, Steve Forbert, Bruce Hornsby, Steve Earle, Mojo Nixon, Delbert McClinton, Townes Van Zandt, Allen Toussaint, Van Dyke Parks, Freddy Fender, Meat Loaf, Lucinda Williams, Charlie Sexton, James Taylor, Vic Chesnutt, Michelle Shocked, and Ryan Adams. Other individual rock musicians from the South are not known for original songwriting but have nonetheless distinguished themselves through their singing (such as Rita Coolidge) and/or their instrumental prowess (such as Levon Helm). Also from the South were key members of several prominent contemporary black music groups (including the Commodores, the Crusaders, the SOS Band, Kris Kross, Arrested Development, 2 Live Crew, Take 6, and OutKast) that attracted attention from many rock fans.

Granted the enormous early influence of southerners in the creation of rock and roll, numerous acts not from the South have composed rock songs that comment on southern politics (such as Bob Dylan's "Only a Pawn in Their Game" and Neil Young's "Southern Man"), or celebrate the southern landscape (John Denver's "Country Roads, Take Me Home"), or characterize southern identity (Creedence Clearwater Revival's "Born on the Bayou"), or reinterpret southern cultural imagery (the Grateful Dead's "Sugar Magnolia" and Little Feat's "Dixie Chicken"), or acknowledge the complexity of southern history ("The Night They Drove Old Dixie Down," by The Band, a group composed of four Canadians and one southerner).

TED OLSON
East Tennessee State University

Stanley Booth, *Rythm Oil: A Journey through the Music of the American South* (1991); Marley Brant, *Southern Rockers: The Roots and Legacy of Southern Rock* (1999); John Einarson, *Desperados: The Roots of Country Rock* (2001); Colin Escott, with Martin Hawkins, *Good Rockin' Tonight: Sun Records and the Birth of Rock 'n' Roll* (1992); Holly George-Warren, Patricia Romanowski, and Jon Pareles, *The Rolling Stone Encyclopedia of Rock & Roll* (2001); Charlie Gillett, *The Sound of the City: The Rise of Rock and Roll* (1996); Peter Guralnick, *Feel Like Going Home: Portraits in Blues and Rock 'n' Roll* (1971), *Last Train to Memphis: The Rise of Elvis Presley* (1994); Mark Kemp, *Dixie Lullaby: A Story of Music, Race, and New Beginnings in a New South* (2004);

Rick Kennedy and Randy McNutt, *Little Labels—Big Sound: Small Record Companies and the Rise of American Music* (1999); Jan Reid, *The Improbable Rise of Redneck Rock* (1977); James M. Salem, *The Late Great Johnny Ace and the Transition from R & B to Rock 'n' Roll* (2001); Nick Tosches, *Unsung Heroes of Rock 'n' Roll: The Birth of Rock in the Wild Years before Elvis* (1999).

Sacred Harp

On most weekends somewhere in the Deep South (and in many areas outside the South since the last quarter of the 20th century), one can find a gathering of amateurs singing from *The Sacred Harp*, a tunebook first published in Georgia (but printed in Philadelphia) in 1844. *The Sacred Harp*, one of many tunebooks of the 19th-century South, is the most popular of several that have survived, the others being Joseph Funk's *Genuine Church Music* (Harrisonburg, Va., 1832, now entitled *New Harmonia Sacra*); William Walker's *Southern Harmony* (Spartanburg, S.C., printed in New Haven, Conn., 1835, with later editions printed in Philadelphia), used for over a century in an annual singing in Benton, Ky.; Walker's *Christian Harmony* (Spartanburg, S.C., printed in Philadelphia, 1866), used in Alabama, western North Carolina, Georgia, and Mississippi; and W. H. and M. L. Swan's *New Harp of Columbia* (Knoxville, Tenn., 1848), used in eastern Tennessee. In contrast to the limited geographical spread of these other tunebooks, *The Sacred Harp*, in addition to being used in regularly scheduled singings in the Deep South, by the turn of the 21st century was in use in singings in almost every state in the United States and in the Canadian province of Quebec.

The Sacred Harp is a product of the American singing-school movement, which flourished in New England in the late 18th century and spread to the rural South and Midwest in the early 19th century. As is typical of other tunebooks of its kind, *The Sacred Harp* is oblong in shape and contains an opening summary of the rudiments of music for use in singing schools, followed by an anthology of harmonized music.

The invention of shape notes around 1800 facilitated the learning of music reading and proved so popular in the South and Midwest that practically every singing-school book, including *The Sacred Harp*, used the four-shape notation of William Little and William Smith's *The Easy Instructor* (Philadelphia, 1802), which became standard in the pre–Civil War period. The major scale was notated as follows:

fa	sol	la	fa	sol	la	mi	fa
1	2	3	4	5	6	7	8

In sacred harp singing it has become standard practice to sing through a song first using the fa-sol-la solmization syllables before singing the words, hence the designation "fasola" singing.

The music in *The Sacred Harp* and other shape-note tunebooks, although primarily intended for singing-school use, is predominantly set to religious texts, primarily those of 18th-century English hymn writers and especially those of Isaac Watts (1674–1748). The texts were compiled from the collections of Watts and of numerous other words-only hymnals known in the early 19th-century South, such as South Carolinian Staunton S. Burdett's *Baptist Harmony* (1834) and Georgian Jesse Mercer's *The Cluster* (5th ed., 1835).

The texts found in *The Sacred Harp* are strongly Calvinistic in theology, with their emphasis on the sovereignty of God and the depravity of humankind. They are also otherworldly, with much emphasis on the vanity of this world and a longing for death and the afterlife, as in Charles Wesley's text for "Animation."

> And let this feeble body fail
> And let it faint or die;
> My soul shall quit this mournful vale,
> And soar to worlds on high.

Broadly speaking, the music in *The Sacred Harp* may be divided into three categories:

1. Psalm or hymn tunes—ranging from those of metrical psalmody and other 18th-century American hymnody to folk hymnody of the early 19th century and even later 19th- and 20th-century tunes essentially in the same earlier styles.
2. Fuging tunes—tunes in which all voices move together in the opening phrases, followed by a second section in which the voices enter separately in imitation and then move together once again to approach the final cadence. The second section is normally repeated, making a compact A B B form.
3. Longer pieces—normally designated odes or anthems. These pieces, often with prose texts such as Bible passages, are multisectional and are generally regarded as the most challenging to the singers.

The music of *The Sacred Harp* is printed in open-score format in three (later four) voice parts, with the melody in the tenor. In practice, the treble and tenor parts are doubled by men and women, creating a richer, fuller sound.

The type of music most commonly associated with *The Sacred Harp* is folk hymnody, in which melodies, and sometimes texts as well, first appeared in oral tradition. These folk hymns are related melodically to Anglo-American secular folk song and are characterized by such traits as the use of gapped scales and the modes. The frontier camp meetings from the early 1800s simplified the corpus of folk hymns with a type that George Pullen Jackson termed "revival spirituals," characterized by repeated phrases and often the addition of a refrain. To "On Jordan's Stormy Banks I Stand" was added the following refrain:

I am bound for the promised land,
I am bound for the promised land,
O who will come and go with me?
I am bound for the promised land.

The Sacred Harp was compiled by two Georgia Baptist singing-school teachers, Benjamin Franklin White (1800–1879) and Elisha J. King (c. 1821–44). Little is known of King, listed as the composer of more songs in the first edition of *The Sacred Harp* than any other person, for he died in the same year it was published. Much is known about White, who lived for more than three decades after its publication and was greatly influential in its acceptance. A native of Spartanburg County, S.C., White moved to Harris County, Ga., around 1840. He served as mayor of Hamilton, as clerk of the inferior county court, and as a major in the militia before the Civil War. In addition to composing, compiling, and teaching in singing schools, in 1847 White founded (and led for more than two decades) the Southern Musical Convention, an important organization in promoting sacred harp singing.

During White's lifetime, *The Sacred Harp* was revised and enlarged under the auspices of the Southern Musical Convention, in 1850, 1859, and 1869, increasing the original 263 pages of 1844, respectively, to 366, 429, and 477 pages. With the 1859 and especially the 1869 editions, the fuging tunes received a more prominent place. Indeed, so prominent are fuging tunes in this tradition that they constitute a large portion of the favorites in current sacred harp singings. Another change was the increasing number of tunes in four voice parts rather than three, even though White himself composed in three parts only.

Without attempting to treat all editions of *The Sacred Harp*, which are described in detail by Buell E. Cobb, mention will be made of those that remain in current or recent use:

1. The Cooper revisions, made under the supervision of W. M. Cooper of Dothan, Ala., in 1902, with subsequent editions in 1907, 1919, 1927, 1950,

1960, and 1992. The Cooper revision is used mainly in southern Alabama, northern Florida, southern Mississippi, and eastern Texas.

2. The James revision, called *The Original Sacred Harp*, revised by a committee of 23, with Joe S. James of Douglasville, Ga., as chairman, published in 1911. This revision was used for singings in central and south Georgia through 1975, when these singers changed to the Denson revision.

3. The J. L. White revisions, the fifth edition of *The Sacred Harp*, brought out in 1909 in Atlanta by the son of B. F. White. It was rejected for its concessions to modernity, but White brought out another revision in 1911, omitting objectionable aspects of his earlier edition. Although used at one time in several states, today the White book is mainly in use in north Georgia.

4. The Denson revision, published by the Sacred Harp Publishing Company in 1936, with later editions in 1960, 1967, 1971, and 1991. Although appearing later than the editions of Cooper and White, the Denson revisions are more traditional. In 1933 Thomas Denson organized the Sacred Harp Publishing Company and purchased all legal rights to *The Sacred Harp* from the James family. The Denson revision is the edition of *The Sacred Harp* most widely used today.

In 1930 there appeared a small collection, *The Colored Sacred Harp*, compiled by Judge Jackson of Ozark, Ala. This volume of 77 songs has functioned as a supplement to *The Sacred Harp* in the southeast corner of Alabama and northwestern Florida. The main tunebook blacks use, however, is the Cooper revision. The Cooper edition is also used in African American singings in Texas. African American singers in Mississippi use the Denson revision.

A sacred harp singing is an informal gathering that emphasizes fellowship and group singing. A typical day's singing begins about mid-morning. Singers are seated facing each other in a square grouped by the four voice parts: tenor (melody), treble, alto, and bass. Each person who wishes to do so leads one or two songs (a turn at leading is called a "lesson," in traditional singing-school terminology). The song is first vocalized by the shape-note syllables and then sung to its words. At the close of the morning the singers adjourn for the traditional dinner on the grounds, a feast of home-cooked food set out on tables. After lunch the singing continues, normally through at least the middle of the afternoon. When the time comes to close, the final song is often "Parting Hand."

Sacred harp singing reflects traditional southern culture, in terms of its music, its religious outlook, and its sense of community. The sacred harp tra-

Ethel Mohamed stitchery depicting sacred harp singing, photographed in 1977 (William R. Ferris Collection, Southern Folklife Collection, Wilson Library, University of North Carolina at Chapel Hill)

dition has preserved styles of music prominent in the pre–Civil War South through the institution of the singing school and many of the rural churches. In addition to the corpus of music from early America, sacred harp singing reflects a traditional southern manner of performance. For example, the tone color of sacred harp singing with its bite and edge contrasts with the sweeter styles of singing found outside the South.

Although sacred harp singings are not church services, they commonly take place in churches. The religious outlook of sacred harp singing is reflected in the piety that is manifested at these gatherings. For example, singings normally open and close with prayer, and personal testimonies are often given. Southern religion is also exemplified in the sacred harp singers' use of the parliamentary procedures found in the democratic church business meetings of rural congregations. The music is from the singing-school tradition, yet it includes the church music sung by Baptists, Methodists, and others in the Upland South before the Civil War. Although these mainline denominations in large measure moved away from the sacred harp tradition, an increasing number of hymn tunes from its pages have appeared in their recent hymnals. The theological perspective of the main denomination to support sacred harp singing—Primitive Baptist—is expressed in many of the texts of the songs, with its stern Calvinism, its willingness to face death, and its emphasis on the hereafter.

Especially strong in sacred harp singing is the southern sense of community with its focus on the family. The annual reunions of sacred harp singers can be compared to the annual southern family reunions. Furthermore, certain families, such as the Denson family, have played crucial roles in preserving sacred harp singing. These singings are a time for remembering. Some gatherings are memorial singings named after a prominent sacred harp singer. An important feature of many sacred harp singings is the memorial lesson, in which the recently deceased are remembered in word and in song. Thus, the conservative values that sacred harp singing embraces and preserves are representative of traditional southern culture.

HARRY ESKEW
New Orleans Baptist Theological Seminary

John Bealle, *Public Worship, Private Faith: Sacred Harp and American Folksong* (1997); Joe Dan Boyd, *Judge Jackson and "The Colored Sacred Harp"* (2002); Buell E. Cobb Jr., *The Sacred Harp: A Tradition and Its Music* (1978, 1989); D. J. Dyen, "The Role of Shape-Note Singing in the Musical Culture of Black Communities in Southeast Alabama" (Ph.D. diss., University of Illinois, 1977); Charles Linwood Ellington, "The Sacred Harp Tradition: Its Origin and Evolution" (Ph.D. diss., Florida State University, 1969): Harry Eskew and James C. Downey, "Shape-Note Hymnody," in *New Grove Dictionary of American Music*, ed. H. Wiley Hitchcock and Stanley Sadie, vol. 4 (1986); Dorothy D. Horn, *Sing to Me of Heaven: A Study of Folk and Early American Materials in Three Old Harp Books* (1970); George Pullen Jackson, *The Story of "The Sacred Harp," 1844–1944* (1944), *White and Negro Spirituals: Their Life Span and Kinship* (1943), *White Spirituals in the Southern Uplands* (1933).

Soul Music

A genre of commercial American music that emerged in the mid-1950s, soul music gained its widest popularity during the mid-1960s and was later subsumed by other music genres (funk, disco, pop, urban, contemporary R&B, rap, hip-hop) during the 1970s and 1980s. Even after ceasing to be a factor in the commercial music business, "classic" soul recordings continued to be heard and appreciated in the South, as well as across the nation and around the world. Recordings by the leading performers of soul have received consistent airplay on radio and have been prominently featured on best-selling film sound tracks (such as *The Blues Brothers* and *The Big Chill*). Accordingly, the genre has attracted new fans and has continued to influence younger musicians working in multiple music genres.

Closely associated with the civil rights movement of the 1950s and 1960s, soul music often reflected the aspirations and frustrations of that movement's participants. Evolving out of the genre of black music known as "rhythm and blues" (the latter term—coined by Atlantic Records producer Jerry Wexler, who subsequently played a leading role in promoting soul music—was meant to acknowledge the equal influence of jazz and blues on R&B), soul music by the mid-1960s had expanded its fan base to encompass countless white listeners. Although soul emerged from the black community and black singers were its major "stars," whites—session musicians, recording engineers, producers, and executives—played integral roles in shaping the genre.

Numerous soul acts hailed from the South (including such luminaries as Ray Charles, James Brown, Sam Cooke, Aretha Franklin, Otis Redding, Wilson Pickett, and Al Green), and many of the most influential soul recordings were made in the South. Both factors led to the emergence of a subgenre of soul music known as "southern soul." The sound of that subgenre was generally characterized by highly emotive singing, a driving beat, and instrumental accompaniment that featured syncopated rhythm guitar strumming, prominent bass lines, and horn parts that served as a kind of choral response to the lead vocals.

Major soul music scenes emerged far from the South, in such cities as Chicago, Detroit, and Philadelphia. Indeed, some significant soul performers associated with southern soul, such as Aretha Franklin, lived much of their lives outside the region. Regardless of soul performers' personal connections to the South, the soul genre blended musical elements of several southern music genres (primarily gospel, blues, and rhythm and blues, but also rock and roll and country). Additionally, the studios that generated many of the most important soul recordings—including Stax (in Memphis) and FAME (in Florence, Ala.)—were located in the South.

Soul developed after several singers originally from the South—most notably Ray Charles, James Brown, and Sam Cooke—began to incorporate into their live performances and their recorded performances of rhythm-and-blues songs pronounced musical and thematic elements associated with gospel music. Whereas rhythm and blues tended to feature improvised instrumental solos and larger combinations of instruments (a carryover from its stylistic predecessor, jazz), soul music was characterized by the emotive interpretation of lyrics, generally emphasizing vocals over instrumental soloing (the role of a band in soul music was primarily to accompany singing). In the performance of soul songs, singers employed vocal elements associated with gospel singing, such as call-and-response, verbal banter, melisma, and a sense of emotional release. The lyrics of soul songs usually focused on the vagaries of love (albeit soul blurred the line between secular and sacred lyrical sentiments by featuring expressions of human love that could also be interpreted as devotional paeans to God). In live performances, soul singers echoed gospel style by heightening the pitch of emotion in their interactions with audiences.

One of the most influential early soul singles was Ray Charles's 1954 recording of the song "I Got a Woman," a hit on the R&B singles chart. That recording prompted bluesman Big Bill Broonzy to comment of Charles, "He's mixing the blues with the spirituals. He should be singing in a church." Reflecting the attitude of many blacks toward soul music in the 1950s, Broonzy was expressing a belief that the mixing of secular and sacred music was a sacrilege. A southerner (having grown up in south Georgia and north Florida), Charles began his music career in the late 1940s performing jazz and pop in Seattle, Wash. But, by the early 1950s, he was performing rhythm and blues on the so-called southern chitlin' circuit (that is, performing exclusively for black audiences across the South). In his 1950s-era recordings released on the Atlantic label (most notably, the singles "Hallelujah, I Love Her So," "Drown in My Own Tears," and "What'd I Say"), Charles established a template for subsequent soul releases by other acts—namely, the overlaying of an emotionally charged, individualistic singing style on rhythmically simple yet infectious, gospel-influenced instrumentation.

Another pioneer of soul music was James Brown, a native of Augusta, Ga. Unlike Ray Charles, Brown was first affiliated with gospel—as a singer with the group the Gospel Starlighters. By 1956 that group, now called the Famous Flames and fronted by Brown, had ventured into secular music, having released Brown's breakthrough hit "Please, Please, Please," which peaked at No. 2 on the R&B chart. Scoring several additional hits on that chart during the late 1950s and early 1960s, Brown became a factor on the pop music chart after the release of the best-selling and critically acclaimed 1963 album *Live at the Apollo*. Two of the most enduring soul recordings are Brown's 1965 singles "Papa's Got a Brand New Bag" and "I Got You (I Feel Good)," both of which were "crossover" hits (that is, singles that became significant hits on both the pop and the R&B charts). Brown's career continued after the decline of soul music, when, in the late 1960s and early 1970s, he became a leading figure in the rise of funk music.

A native of Clarksdale, Miss., Sam Cooke first gained notice in the black community as the charismatic lead singer for the gospel group the Soul Stirrers. When his first solo soul hit, the self-composed 1957 single "You Send Me," rose to No. 1 on both the R&B and the pop charts, he was accused by many blacks of succumbing to worldly ways. More than any other performer, Cooke popularized soul music by writing and recording a string of crossover singles (including "Chain Gang," "Bring It on Home to Me," and "Shake"). He also established a successful recording company (SAR Records) and music publishing company (Kags Music), becoming one of the first blacks in the music industry to do so. One of the final singles Cooke recorded shortly before his untimely death in 1964, his self-penned soul classic "A Change Is Gonna Come," helped transform southern society by becoming an unofficial anthem of the civil rights movement.

The most influential soul singers to emerge in the 1960s were Aretha Franklin and Otis Redding. Franklin, born in Memphis but reared in Detroit, recorded her first important soul single—the crossover hit "I Never Loved a Man (The Way I Love You)"—at FAME Studio. Her subsequent singles, recorded in studios outside the South, consistently featured instrumental support by the Muscle Shoals Sound Rhythm Section. Redding, from Macon, Ga., composed Franklin's biggest crossover hit, the 1967 single "Respect." Redding's best-selling recording was "(Sittin' on) the Dock of the Bay," which was released shortly after the singer's tragic 1967 death, becoming a No. 1 hit on both the pop and the R&B charts.

Redding was one of several major southern soul performers to record primarily in Memphis for the two record labels owned by Jim Stewart and Estelle Axton (Stax Records and the Stax subsidiary label Volt Records)—the other acts being Wilson Pickett, Rufus Thomas, Carla Thomas, Eddie Floyd, Johnnie Taylor, Sam & Dave (Sam Moore and Dave Prater), and Isaac Hayes. The recordings produced for the Stax/Volt labels were distributed by Atlantic Records through May 1968, when the distribution arrangement was curtailed. Stax continued to release soul recordings in various distribution arrangements through the mid-1970s, when the company went bankrupt. Other Memphis studios that recorded soul singers were American Sound Studio (founded by producer-songwriter Chips Moman) and Royal Recording (operated by soul musician Willie Mitchell). Soul recordings from the latter studios—including singles by important soul acts O. V. Wright and James Carr—were often released on the Memphis-based Goldwax Records (owned by Quinton Claunch). Royal Recording hosted significant late 1960s and early 1970s soul sessions (by such acts as Al Green, Ann Peebles, Otis Clay, and Syl Johnson) for another important Memphis label, Hi Records (founded by Ray Harris and managed by Willie Mitchell).

Soul performers who recorded at FAME (an acronym for the company name, Florence Alabama Music Enterprises) Studios (founded by producer Rick Hall) included Pickett, Joe Tex, Jimmy Hughes, Clarence Carter, Arthur Conley, and Etta James. Recordings made at FAME—many of which were licensed to Atlantic Records—featured instrumental support from a roster of studio musicians that included Barry Beckett, Roger Hawkins, David Hood, Jimmy Johnson, and Spooner Oldham. These musicians, dubbed collectively the Muscle Shoals Rhythm Section, left FAME in 1969 to establish the Muscle Shoals Sound Studio in Sheffield, Ala. This studio subsequently produced numerous internationally acclaimed soul and rock recordings. Two other soul acts associated with the Florence-Sheffield–Muscle Shoals music scene were Arthur Alexander (whose songs were covered by such rock acts as the Beatles, the Rolling Stones, and Bob Dylan) and Percy Sledge (whose 1966 No. 1 crossover single, "When a Man Loves a Woman," recorded at a small Sheffield studio owned by Quin Ivy and Marlin Greene, has become a classic American popular song perennially played on radio and on movie sound tracks).

Nationally respected soul music scenes were present during the 1960s and 1970s in such southern cities as New Orleans (which boasted important soul acts like Allen Toussaint, Lee Dorsey, Irma Thomas, Johnny Adams, the Meters, and the Neville Brothers) and Miami (the home of Sam & Dave, Betty Wright, Gwen McCrae, and Latimore). Local soul music scenes were active in Atlanta, Birmingham, and Shreveport. Outside the South, the most significant soul music centers were in Chicago, Detroit, Philadelphia, New York City, Washington, D.C., and Los Angeles, and the southern musical and cultural roots of soul influenced the soul music emanating from all those cities.

Initially, soul music was popular primarily among black audiences. But by the mid-1960s black soul performers had attracted large followings of white fans. For instance, three soul acts (Otis Redding, Booker T. & the MG's, and Lou Rawls) starred at the 1967 Monterey Pop Festival, which otherwise featured popular rock music acts. Also, several mid-1960s groups composed of white musicians began to perform their own interpretations of soul, creating a subgenre known as "Blue-Eyed Soul." The best-known such groups of the 1960s were the Righteous Brothers, the Box Tops, the Rascals, Mitch Ryder and the Detroit Wheels, and Rare Earth. During the late 1960s and early 1970s, other white performers were releasing their own interpretations of soul, including Elvis Presley, Dusty Springfield, Van Morrison, Rod Stewart, Boz Scaggs, Tony Joe White, Roy Head, and Eddie Hinton. In the 1980s and 1990s, new rock and pop acts—including Hall and Oates, Paul Jones, Paul Carrack, Culture Club, Simply Red, George Michael, Michael Bolton, and Bonnie Raitt—were making recordings that echoed the sound and sensibility of soul. From the 1960s through the 1990s, a number of country singers—notably Charlie Rich, Conway Twitty, George Jones, Tammy Wynette, Joe Stampley, Ronnie Milsap, Willie Nelson, Kenny Rogers, and Wynonna Judd—made recordings that revealed the strong interrelationship between southern soul music and country music. More illustrative of soul's power to ameliorate racial tensions was the fact that the key studios to make soul recordings during the final, turbulent years of the civil rights movement—Stax and FAME—showcased black singers performing over backup instrumentation provided by white musicians. Additionally, one of the most popular instrumental groups in the history of soul music was Booker T. & the MG's, a racially integrated band featuring two black musicians (Booker T. Jones and Al Jackson) and two white musicians (Steve Cropper and Donald "Duck" Dunn).

Since the mid-1990s, soul music has been revived and reinterpreted by a new generation of musicians, some black (Lauryn Hill, Alicia Keyes, and Jill Scott) and some white (Joss Stone, Norah Jones, and James Hunter). The music by these acts has been collectively labeled by critics "neo soul," and such performers have drawn the attention of their younger fans to "classic" soul music. In the first years of the new millennium, a number of singers from the South who originally recorded during the heyday of soul music—such as Aaron Neville, Irma Thomas, Wilson Pickett, Percy Sledge, and Howard Tate—continued to perform and record music deeply rooted in southern soul.

TED OLSON
East Tennessee State University

Rob Bowman, *Soulsville U.S.A.: The Story of Stax Records* (2006); James Brown, with Bruce Tucker, *The Godfather of Soul: An Autobiography* (2003); Matt Dobkin, *I Never Loved a Man the Way I Love You: Aretha Franklin, Respect, and the Making of a Soul Music Masterpiece* (2004); Scott Freeman, *Otis! The Otis Redding Story* (2002); Peter Guralnick, *Dream Boogie: The Triumph of Sam Cooke* (2005), *Sweet Soul Music: Rhythm and Blues and the Southern Dream of Freedom* (1986); Gerri Hirshey, *Nowhere to Run: The Story of Soul Music* (1994); Michael Lydon, *Ray Charles: Man and Music* (2004); Craig Werner, *A Change Is Gonna Come: Music, Race, and the Soul of America* (2006); Jerry Wexler, with David Ritz, *Rhythm and the Blues: A Life in American Music* (1993).

Southern Rock

Southern rock is difficult to define. After all, rock and roll itself is a product of southern influences. Elvis Presley, Little Richard, Jerry Lee Lewis, and many others melded different sorts of southern music together to make something brand new. Yet many people think of something more unified than the very different sounds turned out by 1950s rockers. Almost immediately one thinks of the late 1960s and early 1970s, when a new kind of sound was emanating from the most embattled region of the nation, the American South. But what was so distinctive about it?

It has been said that rock music in the late 1960s was suffering from a sense of laid-back ennui, but a few groups such as Credence Clearwater Revival (from California) and the Band (Levon Helm was from Arkansas, but most members were from Canada) were creating music that evoked a passion for rural life— music that longed for the good times past and bemoaned the hard times of Tom Joad. These groups are similar to those of the southern rock movement and are sometimes grouped among them. They have an analogous sound because of the similarity in influences: country, blues, gospel, rockabilly, and folk can all be heard in their tunes. Also, with songs like "Born on the Bayou" and "The Night They Drove Ole Dixie Down," many southerners assumed that the bands that played them were southern groups.

What sets southern rockers apart comes from a defiance, more pronounced in some bands than in others, in the face of overwhelming disdain from the rest of the nation for the South and its culture. The musical groups who would be- come the founders of southern rock sang about being southerners unapologeti- cally, and, as one might expect, most Americans in the late 1960s either were not prepared to hear songs like that or, maybe more important, had no way of hearing them.

Phil Walden helped with the latter of the two problems in 1969 when he founded Capricorn Records in his hometown of Macon, Ga. The first band he signed to the label was the Allman Brothers Band, led by slide guitarist Duane Allman. Duane's guitar talents had already been featured on albums by Aretha Franklin and Wilson Pickett, produced in Muscle Shoals, Ala., but his fame came when he teamed with his brother Gregg's bluesy vocals and gospel-style organ. Their sound was made even more distinctive because they used two drummers and two lead guitars. Dickey Betts and Duane Allman mastered the art of playing two different lead guitar riffs at the same time. Some people call it playing in counterpoint. Their musical interplay is what many recognize as the unique sound of the Allman Brothers Band. After touring the country and releasing two albums with little commercial success, the Allman Brothers hit it big with their live two-record album *At Fillmore East* in 1971. Many still regard it as one of the greatest live albums ever recorded.

Duane Allman was killed in a motorcycle wreck near Macon, Ga., in the fall of 1971, and, just over one year later, the bassist, Barry Oakley, died, ironi- cally, in a similar motorcycle accident very near Duane's crash site. The All- man Brothers continued to tour and succeed commercially with tunes such as

"Ramblin' Man," written and sung by Dickey Betts, but the loss of Duane's creative genius was too much to recover from. Their heyday was over by the mid-1970s.

But groups like the Marshall Tucker Band and the Charlie Daniels Band continued to fuse a rock attitude and style with more traditional forms of southern music. The Marshall Tucker Band, from South Carolina, carried on the Allman Brothers' laid-back, breezy style by adding a flute player. This seemed to lessen some of the aggressiveness heard in the music of other southern rock bands.

Not so with Charlie Daniels. His song "The South's Gonna Do It Again" is a very country-sounding anthem about the rise of southern rock and the hope that the South as a whole will "rise again" with it. The lyrics seem to cry out: "Be proud of southern rock; be proud to be from the South." Daniels's lyrics could be playful, but there was an attitude of "we're here. Deal with it." Aggressiveness, though, was not his hallmark. It was Lynyrd Skynyrd's.

Led by lead singer Ronnie Van Zant, Lynyrd Skynyrd emerged from the Florida swamps with a sound that almost slapped listeners in the face. The group was influenced by country, the blues, and the Rolling Stones, who had earlier created a sound from country and blues music. But Skynyrd brought something new that no other southern rock band, or rock band in general, had: a screw-you attitude that applied to both musicians and politicians. The musicians singled out Neil Young in their first album for what they considered disparaging remarks toward the South in his song "Southern Man": "A southern man don't need him around anyhow!" They also defended George Wallace in "Sweet Home Alabama." Interestingly, Gary Rossington, one of the three lead guitar players in the band, has related that Ronnie Van Zant, who wrote the lyrics, was not necessarily a fan of Wallace's politics, but only of his attitude, his moxie. Ronnie had plenty of that to spare. As anyone can see in footage of Lynyrd Skynyrd in concert, Ronnie Van Zant prowled around the stage as he sang song after song about whiskey, other men's women, guns, and raisin' hell. With his glare alone, he seems to be challenging anyone in the crowd to a fight. Many feel that Lynyrd Skynyrd is the quintessential southern rock band, and its string of hits and fulfillment of many southern stereotypes seems to back this up. The members were a rough bunch, and like most who live hard, they died young.

In 1977 their private plane crashed in a swampy field near McComb, Miss. Ronnie Van Zant, lead guitarist Steve Gaines, and Steve's sister and background singer Cassie Gaines were killed in the crash. With the death of Steve and Ronnie, Lynyrd Skynyrd lost its two creative geniuses. The group still tours and has a loyal fan base, but it has not been able to recapture past glory.

Other bands in the 1970s tried to follow the lead of the Marshall Tucker Band, Charlie Daniels, the Allman Brothers, and Lynyrd Skynyrd, but they never reached such heights of commercial success and musical mastery—Grinderswitch, Molly Hatchet, and .38 Special continued in the same vein, but the nation had lost interest. Southern rock, by the early 1980s, was even being parodied. Only ZZ Top had real success during the Reagan era.

Some say that southern rock died with Ronnie Van Zant in that plane crash, but in fact the South has seen a revival in this music scene. Bands like Widespread Panic, the Kudzu Kings, Beanland, Blue Mountain, the Drive-By Truckers, the Grapes, and others have continued to thrive on long, improvised jams made popular by southern rock bands in the 1970s. They are heavily influenced by bands like the Grateful Dead and Phish, but they are also influenced by the same artists that influenced their southern rock predecessors. These so-called Jam Bands are proud of where they are from—the Deep South—but not defiantly so. Instead of menacing stares, one gets hippie friendliness. However, as Jeff Mosier of the Aquarium Rescue Unit once said, these guys "unashamedly play blues and southern rock. They were baptized on southern rock." Maybe these new bands are the true carriers of this legacy of the 1970s southern rocker—and not of the washed-up southern stereotype.

RANKIN SHERLING
University of Mississippi

Marley Brant, *Freebirds: The Lynyrd Skynyrd Story* (2002), *Southern Rockers: The Roots and Legacy of Southern Rock* (1999); Scott Freeman, *Midnight Riders: The Story of the Allman Brothers Band* (1996); Martin Kemp, *Dixie Lullaby: A Story of Music, Race, and New Beginnings in a New South* (2004); Jim Miller, ed., *The Rolling Stone Illustrated History of Rock 'n' Roll* (1980); Martin Popoff, *Southern Rock Review* (2001).

Spirituals

Spirituals are African American sacred folk songs, sometimes also called anthems, hymns, spiritual songs, jubilees, or gospel songs. Distinctions among these terms have not been precise, different terms being used in different communities at different times. The term "spiritual song" was widely used in English and American hymnals and tunebooks during and after the 18th century, but "spiritual" was not found in print before the Civil War. Descriptions of the songs that came to be known by that name appeared at least 20 years earlier, and African American religious singing that was recognized as distinct from white psalms and hymns was described as early as 1819.

The musical elements that distinguished African American songs from European folk song were described by travelers and traders in Africa in the early 17th century. The elements that appeared exotic and unfamiliar to these Europeans included strong rhythms—accompanied by bodily movement, stamping, hand clapping, and other percussive devices to accent rhythm—gapped scales, general group participation, improvised texts (frequently derisive or satiric in nature), and the call-and-response form in which leader and responding chorus overlapped. To European observers, the music seemed wholly strange, although later analysts would find elements common to European music. The performance style of African music was one of its unique aspects, one that has survived in many forms of African American music.

In Africa, song played a prominent role in religion, public ceremonies, and work, in which it was used to regulate the pace. Though scholars do not agree about whether harmony was present, the simultaneous sounding of more than one pitch was common. Vocal embellishments were widely used, and a strong, rasping voice quality was admired. These musical elements continued among the Africans transported to the New World and were reported by numerous witnesses of slave singing throughout the West Indies and the North American mainland during the mid-17th century. Songs to accompany dancing were most frequently reported, with work songs a close second. Not enough is yet known about the transmission of African religions to North America, making the relationship of spirituals to African religious song largely a matter of conjecture.

The conversion of Africans to Christianity, considered a prerequisite to the development of the spiritual, proceeded slowly. In the 17th century, individual slaves were often converted by the families with whom they lived on Lowcountry plantations, although in the southern colonies some planters opposed the baptism of their slaves in the belief that baptism might disrupt the master-slave relationship. Where planters permitted religious instruction, Africans responded with enthusiasm, but the few missionaries sent from England were kept too busy ministering to the widely separated white population to permit much attention to the blacks or the Indians. By the mid-18th century, a few Presbyterian ministers, led by Samuel Davies, of Hanover, Va., made special efforts to convert blacks within their neighborhoods, using Isaac Watts's hymnbooks shipped from England. The style of singing European hymns may have been influenced by African musical patterns, but scholars have no concrete information about the singing of African songs during this period.

Toward the end of the 18th century, Methodist itinerants, such as Bishop Francis Avery, assisted by the black exhorter Harry Hosier, began to hold meetings lasting several days. Large crowds overflowed the meeting rooms, and

Gospel music singer, Centerville, Miss., 1972
(William R. Ferris Collection, Southern Folklife
Collection, Wilson Library, University of North
Carolina at Chapel Hill)

blacks and whites attended these meetings together. On the frontier, where the population was very widely scattered and organized churches were few, the camp meeting developed, beginning with the Cane Ridge, Ky., meeting in August 1801. Black worshippers attended this meeting, and they participated in white camp meetings throughout the antebellum period. As blacks and whites worshipped and sang together in an atmosphere highly charged with emotion, mutual influences were inescapable. The call-and-response style of singing was ideally suited to this kind of participatory service, where vast numbers of people required musical responses they could learn on the spot. The practice of "lining out," in which a leader sang or read two lines of a hymn to the congregation, which then repeated them, was widely used in churches with illiterate members or with too few books to go around. The camp meeting provided an introduction for both groups to the sound and style of each other's singing.

The first documented reports of distinctive black religious singing date from the early 19th century, somewhat earlier than the first organized missions to plantation slaves. Spirituals were not transcribed in musical notation until the Civil War, and, when they were, conventional musical notation was inadequate to convey the distinctive features of the music as it was performed. Whatever degree of acculturation may have existed, certain elements in the music could not be represented in a notation developed for European music. The more sensitive transcribers explicitly stated that their transcriptions could not capture all they heard—notes outside the scale system—"blue" notes, swoops, glissandos, growls, rhythmic complexities, and the overlapping of leader and chorus in the call-and-response style.

In the South, during the antebellum period, spirituals were sung widely and were discussed in letters, diaries, and the periodical press, but they were largely unknown in the North. When wartime conditions brought plantation slaves into contact with northern whites, the songs became known to a wider public. Individual songs were published as sheet music or in magazine articles, and a comprehensive collection was published in 1867, *Slave Songs of the United States*, edited by William Francis Allen, Charles Pickard Ware, and Lucy Mc-Kim Garrison. Although the transcriptions had to omit many of the characteristic and distinctive features of the music because of notational limitations, the collection was an attempt to preserve songs that otherwise might have been lost. The collection set a pattern for transcribing the songs in conventional musical notation (despite its shortcomings) that was followed in more influential collections of songs as sung by the Fisk Jubilee Singers, the Hampton Singers, and other touring groups from predominantly black schools in the South. The college groups had been trained in European music and were conscious of their mission to herald the emerging black population. After northern and European audiences heard spirituals, their popularity became firmly established. Songs were modified in arrangements for concert performance, although the extent of this modification has not been determined.

As spirituals grew more popular, elaborate arrangements that departed still more widely from the folk originals were made, for both solo singers and for choirs. Beginning in 1892, a theory was developed that spirituals were based on European folk hymns and other forms of white popular music, a theory based solely on the examination of the published transcriptions. The elements of improvisation and the performance style were not considered. Only with the advent of sound recording has it been possible to study the performance itself. Current performances cannot fully replicate antebellum ones, but they can capture much of the excitement described by 19th-century listeners. Ethnomusicologists may be able to reconstruct the music as it was performed in earlier eras by utilizing field recordings and contemporary descriptions.

DENA J. EPSTEIN
University of Chicago

Afro-American Spirituals, Work Songs, and Ballads, Library of Congress Recording AAFSL3; James H. Cone, *The Spirituals and the Blues: An Interpretation* (1972); Dena J. Epstein, *Sinful Tunes and Spirituals: Black Folk Music to the Civil War* (1977);

Miles Mark Fisher, *Negro Slave Songs in the United States* (1953); George Pullen Jackson, *Spiritual Folk Songs of Early America* (1964), *White Spirituals in the Southern Uplands* (1933); Lawrence Levine, *Black Culture and Black Consciousness: Afro-American Folk Thought from Slavery to Freedom* (1977); A. E. Perkins, *Journal of American Folklore* (July–September 1922); Andrew Ward, *Dark Midnight When I Rise: The Story of the Jubilee Singers Who Introduced the World to the Music of Black America* (2000); John W. Work, *American Negro Songs: 230 Folk Songs and Spirituals, Religious and Secular* (1998).

Square Dancing and Clogging

Square dance in the South has traditionally provided a means to exercise the virtually universal human tendency to move to the accompaniment of music. It is best to think of "square dance" as a generic term for a variety of related dance forms, styles, and occasions. In familiar stereotypes, traditional square dancing is often associated with the South, although it has not been an exclusively southern form; in its assorted revivalistic forms the square dance has become a national phenomenon.

Cecil Sharp, the English collector and scholar of folk music and dance, helped bring the southern square dance to national—and even international—attention after encountering it in Kentucky. In 1918 Sharp wrote, "In the course of our travels in the Southern Appalachian Mountains in search of traditional songs and ballads, we often heard of a dance, called the Running Set, but as our informants had invariably led us to believe that it was a rough, uncouth dance, remarkable only as an exhibition of agility and physical endurance, we had made no special effort to see it." When Sharp and his colleague Maud Karpeles finally did encounter the dance at the Pine Mountain Settlement School in eastern Kentucky, they were captivated by it, and Sharp felt certain that they had found a relic of English dance traditions older than any on record. Actually, they had "discovered" a dance that, although rooted in English and French dance forms, is generally thought to be a 19th-century American development—the southern square dance.

Dancing to the chanted instructions of a caller—one of the major identifying features of square dancing—emerged about the time of the War of 1812. The other common square dance features—the couple as the basic unit, danced interactions between couples in a bounded group, the group arranged in a simple geometric formation—may be found in any number of British and French antecedent dance forms, folk, popular, and elite. The calling distinguishes the dance.

In the South, couples generally arrange themselves in squares consisting of four male-female couples or in circles made up of as many couples as can be accommodated. Less frequently, the dance may take the form of two parallel lines, one for men, one for women, with couples facing each other. In some communities, the dance is based in a circle formation of couples. The caller may dance, or he or she may stand nearby.

Traditionally, the music is provided by a fiddle or by fiddle and banjo or by any of the typical string band ensemble forms. The fiddle repertoire in the South is, in fact, dominated by square dance tunes. Although no distributional studies of the square dance in the South exist, the dance tune repertoire has been played by fiddlers all through the region. It seems reasonable to conclude from this that square dancing may be, or might formerly have been, found wherever there has been an active dance tune tradition—virtually everywhere in the South.

Square dancing has traditionally been a part of the community life in the South. Moreover, it has often provided one of the major settings for community interaction. Until the World War II era, people commonly danced in the homes of their neighbors, particularly in farming areas. Such events were essentially parties for the neighbors, and all were invited. Other community events have also been occasions for dancing. These include communal work activities (corn shuckings and log rollings), picnics and barbecues, holiday observances, and other festivals. A rise in commercially motivated dances in local armories and other halls has, in many instances, kept people dancing despite the declining significance of some of the older community social events. The dance associations themselves seem to encourage friendly interactions among community members, young and old, male and female, and the dancing itself seems to involve the enactment, at some deep level, of community norms and expectations, such as the notion of the couple as a basic social unit.

Each dance typically involves a number of formulaic movements in response to the caller's instructions. Many dance calls, such as "Ocean Wave" and "Cage the Bird," are known widely across the South; others may be limited to subregions. Dance movements will sometimes vary in their execution (in response to the formulaic calls) according to local and regional preferences.

Square dancing is also traditionally a part of southern African American culture, despite its dominant association with Anglo-Americans. Slave narratives describe square dancing among slaves, and recent interviews with black musicians and dancers suggest that square dancing was often a feature of rural life in southern black communities through perhaps the 1930s.

A number of 20th-century revivalistic movements have added to the complexity of the square dance in the South. These range from dance schools and festivals under the sponsorship of southern Appalachian cultural and educational institutions to the efforts of various national square dance organizations. The latter have tended to emphasize new dance styles based on traditional dances but showing the touch of the choreographer. Typically identified as western dancing, this is generally bound up in a large network of local clubs, whose members dress in stylized cowboy-cowgirl garb and dance to records rather than to live music. A number of publications and supply houses, regional and national, cater to revivalist dancers. As a result of the various dance revivals, many communities in the South typically have a range of square dance activities, from regionally traditional forms done perhaps weekly at a VFW or sportsman's club, and done occasionally at festivals, to square dance groups practicing precision dance forms derived from regional models, to clubs that are part of the western square dance movement. There may well be more people square dancing in the South today than ever before.

Clog dancing is a group dance, synthesizing the older square dance and the solo "buck and wing" or "buck dance." Buck dancers traditionally danced on bare earth, front porches, or parlor floors, their arms hanging loose at their sides and their feet close to the floor. The origin of the term "buck and wing" is unclear, but it was used in Lancashire, England, in the early part of the 20th century to describe dancing in wooden shoes. Buck dancing, which has other local names such as "flatfoot dancing," likely has roots in the dancing of Scottish, Irish, and English immigrants to the Appalachian Mountains, but African Americans, who had developed various step dance traditions, also influenced its development through minstrel performers and traveling medicine shows.

Clog dancing as public performance probably originated in western North Carolina in the 1920s or 1930s, associated with the Asheville Mountain Dance and Folk Festival. A landmark was a 1939 performance in Washington, D.C., by the Soco Gap Dancers for President Franklin Roosevelt and British king George VI. This was apparently the first time cloggers used costumes, and publicity from the performance helped popularize this dance style in the 1940s. Taps were added and costumes became more prominent as the folk dance became increasingly oriented toward public performance. James Kesterson, of Henderson County, N.C., introduced precision clogging—complex choreographed exhibition dancing—in the late 1950s, and his popular Blue Ridge Mountain Dancers won awards at the Asheville Festival five times in the 1960s.

Precision clogging groups like Kesterson's dance to patterned footwork in unison in set routines. They frequently emphasize colorful costumes and choreography, using both old-time mountain music and popular tunes. The other main type of exhibition clogging is freestyle, or traditional. Here the dancers keep time to the music, but each performer uses spontaneous footwork, improvising steps as the team moves about the floor. Freestyle clogging is especially associated with older mountain folk culture, but clogging in general remains a not-uncommon practice in mountain areas of the South.

BURT FEINTUCH
University of New Hampshire

S. Foster Damon, *The History of Square Dancing* (1957); Lynne F. Emery, *Black Dance in the United States from 1619 to 1970* (1972); Burt Feintuch, *Journal of the Folklore Institute* (January–April 1981); Cecil J. Sharp and Maud Karpeles, *The Country Dance Book*, part 5 (1918, 1946); Susan Eike Spaulding and Jane Harris Woodside, eds., *Communities in Motion: Dance, Community, and Tradition in America's Southeast and Beyond* (1995); Ann Elise Thomas, *Western Folklore* 60 (2001).

Western Swing

Like so many other forms of American music, western swing is a cultural product of the South. The founders of the music borrowed from other southern styles—ragtime, New Orleans jazz, folk, frontier fiddle music, pop, Tex-Mex, and country and classic blues. In one stage of development, they borrowed heavily from big-band swing. Despite its eclecticism, western swing has remained one of the most distinctive genres in southern musical history. Western swing brought a new vitality and sophistication to the country music of the South. All three periods in the development of western swing were inextricably interwoven with the career of Bob Wills. The first of these eras was the formative period in Texas; the second was the years of experimentation and maturity in Oklahoma; and finally came the years of national recognition and musical influence.

James Robert Wills was born into a family of fiddle players near Kosse, in east Texas. He eventually combined folk fiddle music with the blues, jazz, and ragtime from the Black Belt of east Texas. This was the nucleus from which western swing grew. When he was 10, Bob Wills played his first dance as a fiddler at a ranch in west Texas. For the rest of his career, he played dance music. The most obvious characteristic of western swing is that the music "swings," or is danceable.

The early fiddle bands often had only a fiddle and an accompanying guitar or mandolin. When Bob Wills moved to Fort Worth in 1929, he started the Wills Fiddle Band, which featured only his fiddle and Herman Arnspiger's guitar. In

1929, Wills and Arnspiger recorded on the Brunswick label what may have been the first western swing ever put on record, "Wills Breakdown" and "Gulf Coast Blues." Wills soon added Milton Brown as vocalist and his brother Durwood Brown on guitar. The Wills Fiddle Band became the Light Crust Doughboys in 1930 and eventually played on the Texas Quality Network, originating at WBAP in Fort Worth and broadcasting on the network in Waco, Houston, and Oklahoma City. The Wills group was, if not the first, among the first to play western swing and to perform it on radio.

Between 1929 and 1933, Bob Wills revolutionized popular music in Texas. His success and fame spread throughout the state and inspired the formation of numerous fiddle bands that played his type of swinging dance music. The first and most successful in terms of first-rate western swing was Wills's protégé, Milton Brown, who came into the Wills Fiddle Band with little or no musical experience. He learned quickly from Wills and left the Light Crust Doughboys in 1932 to form a group called Milton Brown and His Musical Brownies. Outside of Wills himself, Brown was the most important figure in the formative years of western swing. The Wills-Brown style could soon be heard in many western swing bands, in the Light Crust Doughboys, W. Lee O'Daniel's Hillbilly Boys, Cliff Bruner's Texas Wanderers, the True Wranglers, Bill Boyd and His Cowboy Ramblers, the Hi-Flyers, Jimmy Revard and His Oklahoma Playboys, Adolph Hofner and His Texans, Bob Dunn's Vagabonds, Roy Newman and His Boys, the Sons of the Pioneers, the Prairie Ramblers with Patsy Montana, and Shelly Lee Alley and the Alley Cats, to name a few of the better-known recorded groups.

By the time Bob Wills moved with his band, the Texas Playboys, from Waco, Tex., to Oklahoma in 1934, the formative years of western swing were over. East and west Texas gave birth to his music; Fort Worth was the nursery; and it reached full maturity in Tulsa, Okla., between 1934 and 1942. There the music moved out of its southwestern provincialism to a much broader audience. Wills's experimental spirit led him to take the music far beyond its fiddle band origins. Shortly after he arrived in Oklahoma, he added enough horns to give him a second front line, made up of trumpet, saxophone, and trombone. The reeds and brass played more modern, uptown music and therefore appealed to a broader audience. Wills added drums and began to lay down a solid jazz beat heretofore unheard of in the fiddle band tradition. In short, he was moving further from his rural roots to jazz, blues, race music, and popular music. Wisely, he kept his front line of fiddles and added more guitars, both amplified and acoustic. By 1938 he could play anything from folk and breakdown fiddle music to a George Gershwin composition, giving them a swinging rhythm and solid beat. The recordings from his first session in 1935, for Vocalion (later Columbia), outsold every other artist in the Vocalion catalog.

In April 1940, with an orchestra of 18 members, Wills recorded the song that took the nation by musical storm and introduced western swing to hundreds of thousands of people who otherwise would never have heard it. The song itself revealed much of the evolution and history of western swing. It was originally a breakdown fiddle selection recorded with Wills's heavy 2/4 jazz beat and was called "San Antonio Rose." In 1940 he recorded it with his horn band without the use of any fiddles. It was recorded in the big-band style of the period and was entitled "New San Antonio Rose." Wills sold 3 million recordings of it, and Bing Crosby brought it to a new audience when his recording sold over 1.5 million discs. Crosby had his second gold record, and Bob Wills was soon in Hollywood making movies. With his hollering and "ah haas," western swing was assured of a place in Americana and in the history of American music.

During World War II and in the postwar years, western swing underwent its final stage of development. From the early 1940s to the early 1950s, the music enjoyed its most successful years. As a style, it was so popular that western swing bands performed in movies, over radio, and on the earliest television shows. At that time the term "western swing" was first used, although historians cannot pinpoint its first usage. Before World War II, the bands that performed in the style were labeled everything from "hot dance," "hillbilly," "hot string," "country dance," and "old time" to "novelty hot dance." The musical establishment simply did not know what to call this new hybrid sound, and recording companies listed Wills, the Light Crust Doughboys, and others in the so-called race catalogs with black artists. Wayne Johnson, who played in the saxophone section on the recording of "New San Antonio Rose," explained in an interview how the terms "western" and "swing" were brought together in the 1930s to describe the Bob Wills style: "That was the swing era, and people were swing dancing. . . . In the Bob Wills band, we did exactly the same thing with a western flavor. We were still playing the same kind of beat, the same kind of arrangements and everything else." But Johnson added: "Bob also had the western flavor, because of the fiddles, the steel guitars, the costumes."

Some authorities believe the term was first used in reference to Spade Cooley and his band on the West Coast. Cooley grew up in Oklahoma and was a fan of Bob Wills and His Texas Playboys. When Cooley organized his band in California in the 1940s, the Wills sound was obvious, but Cooley's band played from written arrangements and produced a clean, rehearsed sound, a sound that was distinctive and very popular. Spade Cooley appeared in films and made many successful recordings. His ability as a musician, bandleader, and showman helped gain new audiences and national acceptance for western swing.

In the postwar years many other musical groups got on the western swing bandwagon. Bob Wills's brother, Johnnie Lee, formed Johnnie Lee Wills and the Boys and was successful from the war years to 1958. Leon McAuliffe organized the Cimarron Boys, one of the most popular of all western swing bands. Luther J. Wills, another of Bob Wills's brothers, had minor success with an excellent band called the Rhythm Busters. In the early 1950s Bob Wills's youngest brother formed Billy Jack Wills and His Western Swing Band in northern California; the band leaned toward rhythm and blues and anticipated the rockabilly style. On the West Coast, Tex Williams performed in a western swing style and recorded big-selling novelty songs. Hank Penny spread western swing from Alabama to Nashville. Pee Wee King was successful both as a bandleader and as the composer of "Tennessee Waltz." Bob Wills's great singer, Tommy Duncan, left the Texas Playboys in 1948 and hired some of the best musicians in the field for his Western All Stars.

World War II was a watershed in the history of American music. The age of the big bands began to close about the time the war ended. Television soon cut into the audiences that had kept the dance floors hot before and during the war. Dance audiences, though quite large until the late 1940s, began to dwindle and no longer supported the big bands. Western swing groups, such as Wills's Texas Playboys, took fewer musicians on the road. Stringed instruments dominated western swing as never before. Styles did not change; bands continued to play dance music and to produce jazz and swing. Fiddles in particular became more important after the war. There were generally more of them in the bands, and they were used to a greater extent, particularly as an ensemble. The "take off fiddlers" still took jazz choruses. The guitarists, especially in the Cooley, McAuliffe, and Bob Wills bands, continued to use their guitars like traditional jazz or swing instruments. They took choruses and improvised as jazzmen do with trumpets and clarinets. When the western swing bands no longer had enough reeds and brass to provide the sound of the big-swing bands, they relied on guitars to simulate it. They often combined guitars, steel guitars, and amplified mandolins into a string ensemble to simulate a big-band horn section.

After 1950 television and new entertainment habits shifted popular tastes away from western swing bands. Young people of that affluent decade, who for the first time dominated record buying and determined the direction of much of American entertainment, began to dance to different drummers. Western swing went into a decline and might well have ended like the big bands in the early 1950s had it not been for the lasting popularity of Bob Wills and the use of so many stringed instruments by Wills and other western swing bands. Wills and others in his field influenced rockabillies like Bill Haley, Buddy Holly, and Elvis Presley. The influence of western swing on country music was even greater and continues to this day.

When Bob Wills's health forced him to retire in the mid-1960s, an era ended. Three groups discovered western swing in the 1970s and attempted to keep its sound and history alive. Country-and-western performers have claimed it as part of their musical heritage, and Merle Haggard, Alvin Crow, Red Steagall, Asleep at the Wheel, Waylon Jennings, Willie Nelson, and Ray Price either play it in a pure form or draw from its repertoire. Some rock artists such as Commander Cody, Charlie Daniels, and others perform in the swing style. Finally, many jazz artists performing on strings are continuing what western swing did years ago.

CHARLES R. TOWNSEND
West Texas State University

Jean Ann Boyd, *Jazz of the Southwest: An Oral History of Western Swing* (1998); Cary Ginell, *Milton Brown and the Founding of Western Swing* (1994); Rich Kienzle, *Southwest Shuffle: Pioneers of Honky Tonk, Western Swing, and Country Jazz* (2003); Bill C. Malone, *Country Music, U.S.A.: A Fifty-Year History* (1968; rev. eds., 1985, 2002), *Southern Music—American Music* (1979); John Morthland, liner notes, *Okeh Western Swing*, Epic EG 37324; Tony Russell, *Blacks, Whites, and Blues* (1970); Chris Strachwitz and Bob Pinson, *Western Swing*, Old Timey T 105; Charles R. Townsend, brochure notes to *For the Last Time*, United Artists UA-LA216-J2, *San Antonio Rose: The Life and Music of Bob Wills* (1976).

Zydeco

Zydeco is a fast, syncopated dance music of Louisiana's black Creole population. Played in urban and rural dance halls from St. Martinville and Lafayette to Houston's black French Fifth Ward, it has evolved in Louisiana over the last 150 years, influenced by Cajun, African American, and Afro-Caribbean cultures. Some zydeco musicians may prefer a more Cajun sound; other musicians, especially in urban settings, mix blues and soul into the music, reflecting the increasing impact of African American mainstream culture. But nearly all zydeco groups maintain a rhythmic complexity in their music that harks back to their Afro-Caribbean inheritance, an inheritance also found in the early informal bands of New Orleans jazz and the great "second-line" rhythm-and-blues pianists like Huey "Piano" Smith, Professor Longhair, and Fats Domino.

Zydeco reflects the multicultural and multiracial background of the Creole population on the French Gulf Coast from southern Louisiana into southeast Texas. In French Louisiana and the French Caribbean, the term "Creole" originally referred both to descendants of the French and Spanish colonists from the Old World and to African slaves born in the New World. This original meaning of Creole, which refers to the planter class as well as to people from New Orleans and southeastern Louisiana, still persists. The other meaning of the term (the one used here) developed later. It refers to the French-speaking people whose mixed ancestry may include black slaves from the Caribbean and American South, *gens libres de couleur* (free people of color), and Spanish, French, and German planters and merchants, local Indian tribes, Anglo-Americans, and Cajuns.

Many persons in southwestern French Louisiana who identify themselves as Creole or "noir" have some parentage from the Cajuns or Acadians—the peasant farming, fishing, and trapping people who entered the area over a 30-year period (1760s to 1800), following their expulsion from what is now Nova Scotia. The cultural ties between Creoles and Cajuns are more significant thàn the genetic ties: the two cultures share, in part, essential features of life, including religion, festivals, foods, language, and music.

The largest numbers of black and *mulâtre* ("mulatto") French-speaking people came to Louisiana either as slaves for French planters in the second half of the 18th century or as *gens libres de couleur* both before and after the Haitian revolution of 1791–1803. In general, to be of "mixed" blood or *mulâtre* carried greater social status. The shift in the use of the term "Creole" may have come from its use by such persons of "mixed" blood claiming their European ancestry and from an attempt to distinguish the descendants of French culture from the English-speaking *Américains* (Americans), who acquired the territory in 1803.

The word "zydeco" is thought to be a creolized form of the French *les haricots* (snap beans). Zydeco music is said to take its name from a dance tune in both the Cajun and Creole traditions called *Les Haricots Sont Pas Salés* (The Snap Beans Are Not Salted). The spelling of "zydeco" used here is one found on posters advertising dances and promoting bands in south Louisiana and southeast Texas. Alternate spellings are "zodico," "zordico," and "zologo." All of these are English spellings used to represent the Creole pronunciation. A closer phonetic spelling would be "zarico" (stress on the last syllable), which preserves the French a and r.

Zydeco refers not only to the fast, syncopated dance numbers in a Creole band's repertoire, but also to the dance event itself. Old-time musician Bébé Carrière of the Louisiana prairie town of Lawtell says that in the old days word of a dance would be left at the general store, or someone would ride around the countryside on horseback yelling, "Zydeco au soir . . . chez Carrière!" (Zydeco tonight at the Carrière's place!) Similarly, in urban Houston, the lyrics of *Bon Ton Roulet*, by Clarence Garlow, describe people going "way out in the country to the zydeco."

Because of the cultural interchange between Cajuns and Creoles in southwest Louisiana, there has been a tendency to overlook the differences between Cajun music and zydeco. Cajun music places more emphasis on developing the melodic line; zydeco melodies are played much faster and consist of Acadian or African American blues tunes placed in an Afro-Caribbean rhythmic framework. The rhythms are highly syncopated, with accents often shifting to various beats.

Whether the original Cajun tune is a one-step—a "la-la"—or a two-step dance, it can be transformed into a zydeco by the Creole musician, with faster tempo, melodic simplification, and increased syncopation. The rhythm may also change when a Cajun two-step—which accents the first and third beats—is played with the accents on the second and fourth beats. The melody, although simplified to a repeated figure, remains unrecognizable.

Even genres from outside the Afro-Caribbean and Acadian cultural sources, such as African American blues and the Central European polka and mazurka, may be performed in a zydeco style. This is also true of the waltz, which the Creoles probably inherited from Cajun and other traditions.

The repertoire and style of individual zydeco musicians may be more Cajun, more African American, or more Afro-Caribbean. For example, Creole musicians such as Fremont Fontenot of Basile and the Carrière brothers of Lawtell often play in a Cajun style because of their strong European cultural affiliations (though these performers do play zydeco and blues). On the other hand, the Lawtell Playboys of Frilot Cove and Sampy and the Bad Habits of Carencro show more Afro-Caribbean and African American inclinations (though they also play waltzes and enjoy "French music"). As young accordionist Clinton Broussard says, "Zydeco bands, they all plays the same tunes, but everybody got their own style to do it."

Although West Indian influences on Louisiana culture can be traced in language, foods, folk beliefs, and music, a musical form called zydeco or sounding like zydeco did not exist in the French West Indies. This suggests the importance of contact between Cajuns and black Creoles in generating a music form unique to Louisiana.

One item that does survive more directly from the Afro-French West Indian inheritance (although in modified form) is the dance *Calinda*. A dance called

Calinda, Kolenda, Kolinda, and other names is mentioned in travelers' accounts as appearing in the French West Indies—Martinique, Guadeloupe, and St. Domingue—as well as in Trinidad from the late 18th century onward. Recent anthropological studies also note the presence of the dance in contemporary French West Indies in the contexts of *vodoun* (voodoo) worship and social dancing, Mardi Gras, and *Rara* (a form of Haitian festival music) festivities. The *Calinda* may involve such diverse activities as mock stick fighting and erotic courtship gestures.

Slaves gathering in New Orleans's Congo Square in the early 19th century were said to have danced the West Indian–style *Calinda.* In rural French Louisiana, the *Calinda* was transformed by Cajuns into a two-step and by Creoles into a zydeco. It has become part of the dance band repertoire, and hints of eroticism or extraordinary behavior exist in the lyrics, which refer to dancing the old dances in a way that will make old women mad. Thus, *Calinda* becomes the name of a young woman enticed by her beau to dance too close while her mother is not looking. That the *Calinda* may still have Afro-Caribbean influences is indicated by its heavily syncopated beat and by accordionist Delton Broussard's comment that "back toward New Iberia (in the area with more French West Indies influence), they want *Calinda* to dance wild to. You get to Lake Charles, and they want that French waltz." Removed from its West Indies source, the *Calinda* is now a part of most Cajun and zydeco bands' repertoires.

At dances in the Creole community today, zydeco musicians usually choose fewer waltzes and more blues and fast two-steps than do Cajun musicians. Although Cajun bands make wide use of the violin (an Acadian inheritance), they rarely play the vest *frottoir* (a metal rubbing board worn as a vest and played with spoons, can openers, or thimbles). Played by old-time and rural zydeco groups, the vest *frottoir* has its antecedents in Africa and the Caribbean as a scraped animal jaw, notched stick, and, later, a washboard. The current model, made in Louisiana by tinsmiths, became popular in the 1930s when sheet metal was introduced to the area for roofing and barn siding. Also popular is the Cajun *bas trang* or *'tite fer* (triangle).

The accordion, used in both zydeco and Cajun music, was probably introduced to the area by German immigrants in the 1870s. The traditional model, and the one made by a number of local accordion makers, is the *une rangée* (one row) diatonic push-pull instrument. It is used by Cajuns and most rural and old-time zydeco musicians. Urban performers have also experimented with the two- and three-row button accordion and the chromatic piano accordion.

Cajun music and zydeco are meant for dancing. Indeed, the choice of dance halls and musical style often marks the boundaries of Cajun and Creole communities. Performance of both of these types of Louisiana French music in a club setting is usually highly amplified for dancing, and the lyrics are difficult to hear above the music or noise of the club. In general, lyrics to the dance tunes are not as elaborate as those of the home singing traditions. They are often fragmentary and tend to convey a "feeling" rather than a story.

Cajun music has been influenced by country and western music in style and instrumentation (the steel guitar); zydeco has been affected more by rhythm-and-blues and soul music. Urban bands, such as Sampy and the Bad Habits and Mike and the Soul Accordion Band, have dropped the *frottoir* and violin, switching to two- and three-row accordions and sometimes adding a lead guitar. Though these bands play relatively slower zydeco numbers at a dance, the continued impact of the Creole and Cajun repertoire in urban areas is retained, as both bands still play waltzes and highly syncopated numbers.

African American traditions have long existed side by side with the Afro-Caribbean and Cajun traditions in south Louisiana's Creole community. But since World War II they have become heavily integrated with Creole traditions and lifestyles. These changes in zydeco music reflect the assimilation of the Creole population into English-speaking African American culture.

Creole culture remains strongest in the countryside, and here the dance hall is an essential social institution. Men and women come to dances well dressed in sport coats and ties, pantsuits, carefully set hair, and jewelry. At a rural dance hall, like the Ardoins' Club Morris in Duralde, entire families, from children to grandparents, come to dance. Zydeco is also performed at church dances, barbecue picnics, occasional *fais-do-do* (house dances), and in a variety of urban clubs that alternate bookings with disc jockey and soul bands. The new popularity of such bands as Terrence Semiens and the Mallet Playboys, Buckwheat Zydeco, and Fernest Arceneaux reflects this change. On the other hand, more traditional groups such as Delton Broussard and the Lawtell Playboys, the Lawrence Ardoin Band, and John Delafose and the Eunice Playboys perform in a more French-influenced style. The new broader range of zydeco styles as projected in films and television programs, on records, on the radio, and at the Southwest Louisiana Zydeco Festival in Opelousas suggests that Creole music is increasingly a symbol for cultural emergence of the Afro-French people of rural and urban south Louisiana.

NICHOLAS R. SPITZER
University of New Orleans

Shane K. Bernard, *Swamp Pop: Cajun and Creole Rhythm and Blues* (1996); Philip Gould (photographs) and Barry Ancelet (introduction), *Cajun Music and Zydeco*

(1992); Rick Koster, *Louisiana Music: A Journey from R&B to Zydeco, Jazz to Country, Blues to Gospel, Cajun Music to Swamp Pop to Carnival Music and Beyond* (2002); Pat Nyhan, Brian Rollins, and David Babb, *Let the Good Times Roll! A Guide to Cajun & Zydeco Music* (1998); Nicholas R. Spitzer, "Zydeco and Mardi Gras: Creole Identity and Performance Genres in Rural French Louisiana" (Ph.D. diss., University of Texas at Austin, 1986), *Zydeco: Creole Music and Culture in Rural Louisiana*, film, Center for Gulf South History and Culture, Abita Springs, La., 1984; Michael Tisserand, *The Kingdom of Zydeco* (1999).

Accordion

The accordion is a key instrument in two forms of southern music—Cajun music from south Louisiana and *música norteña* from the Texas borderland. It is a bellows-driven, handheld, free-reed instrument, played by compression and expansion of a bellows, which generates airflow across the reeds. A keyboard, with buttons, levers, or keys, controls which reeds receive air and what tones occur. The accordion appeared first in Germany in the early 19th century, and German immigrants to Louisiana and Texas likely introduced it into the American South.

The accordion is the traditional lead instrument for much of Cajun music, producing an infectious beat. In early Cajun bands, the fiddle and guitar combined with the accordion for lead sounds, with a metal triangle in the background. In 1926, accordionist Joseph Falcon and his wife, Cléoma Breaux, recorded "Allons à Lafayette," one of the earliest songs that showed the accordion's role. Ambrose Thibodeaux and Nathan Abshire were among the legendary Cajun accordionists. In the 1930s, the new string sounds of western swing, from nearby Texas, pushed the accordion into the background of Cajun music, but after World War II the instrument emerged once again as the central one. "Dancehall Cajun" bands included the bass or steel guitar and drums, but the accordion was the lead instrument. Cajun, and related zydeco, have recently reflected rock and other influences, but the accordion remains central to the distinctive sounds.

The lower Rio Grande Valley of south Texas was the other location for the accordion's prominent musical role in southern places. *Música norteña* has long been a popular form of Latino music there, an ensemble form in which the accordion paired with the guitar or *bajo sexta* (a Mexican 12-string guitar). In the 1950s, the saxophone, drums, and bass guitar were added to *norteña* bands. Closely related to another Mexican border musical genre, mariachi music, *música norteña* differs from it by the prominent role of the accordion, which produces a rhythmic beat from adapted polka or waltz forms. Narciso Martínez was one of the most popular early *norteña* accordionists, and Ramon Ayala has been an influential performer of modern *norteña* music, with a distinctive accordion playing style and the addition of the electric guitar to his band. Accordionist-singer Flaco Jiménez has helped to popularize accordion-driven *norteña* music into folk and country worlds in Texas and beyond.

CHARLES REAGAN WILSON
University of Mississippi

Barry Jean Ancelet, *Cajun and Creole Music Makers—Musiciens cadiens et creoles* (1999); Bill C. Malone, *Country Music, U.S.A.* (2002); Guadalupe San Miguel, *Tejano Proud: Tex-Mex Music in the Twentieth Century* (2002).

Acuff, Roy

(1903–1992) COUNTRY MUSIC SINGER.

Roy Acuff was the dominant country singer of the World War II years and the first living person to be elected to the Country Music Hall of Fame, in 1962. Generally described as "the

King of Country Music," a title first given to him by baseball player Dizzy Dean, Roy Claxton Acuff was born in Maynardville, Tenn., on 15 September 1903. Acuff was a star athlete at Central High School in Knoxville (winning 12 athletic letters), but after suffering heat-stroke in 1929 during a Florida fishing trip, he abandoned a promising baseball career and began perfecting his skills as a fiddler and singer. He joined a medicine show in 1932 as a musician and comedian, and in the following year he began performing with a string band, the Tennessee Crackerjacks, on WROL in Knoxville. From 1934 to 1938, Acuff and his band played, at various times, on both WROL and WNOX in Knoxville and were part of the cast of the *Mid-Day Merry Go Round* at WNOX. In 1936, Acuff recorded for the Okeh label one of his most famous songs, "The Great Speckled Bird." The performance of this song during an audition at the *Grand Ole Opry* on 19 February 1938 probably did the most to win him a permanent position on that famous show.

Acuff's rise to fame in country music paralleled that of the *Grand Ole Opry* in American entertainment. He was the first host of the show after it attained network status on NBC in 1939. During the war, such Acuff songs as "The Great Speckled Bird," "Wabash Cannon Ball," and "Precious Jewel" appeared on juke-boxes all over the nation, and Acuff and his band, the Smoky Mountain Boys, drew larger crowds than any other act in country music. Polls indicated that Acuff enjoyed great popularity among American military personnel, and he even outpolled pop vocalist Frank

Roy Acuff, the "King of Country Music," 1930s (Country Music Foundation, Library and Media Center, Nashville)

Sinatra in a two-week contest sponsored by the Armed Forces Network. Acuff's earnest, emotional singing style and his preference for religious, sentimental, and old-time songs seemed to make him a fitting symbol of bedrock American values. According to legend, a Japanese banzai charge on Okinawa hurled these taunts at American troops: "To hell with Roosevelt; to hell with Babe Ruth; to hell with Roy Acuff!"

Although his record sales declined significantly after World War II and his style became increasingly anachronistic amid the rock, pop, and swing sounds that inundated country music, Acuff maintained a high public visibility. He enjoyed considerable economic affluence as the co-owner, along with Fred Rose, of Acuff-Rose Publishing Company, and he ran strongly, though unsuccessfully, as the Republican candidate for governor of Tennessee in 1948. He continued to appear each Saturday night at the *Grand Ole Opry*, established a souvenir and gift shop at Opryland, remained active in Tennessee Republican politics, and often acted as a spokesperson for country music. When the Nitty Gritty Dirt Band made Acuff a central focus of their best-selling album, *Will the Circle Be Unbroken*, in 1972, the young country-rock musicians demonstrated just how far the Smoky Mountain Boys' name and influence had extended into American popular culture.

BILL C. MALONE
Madison, Wisconsin

Roy Acuff and William Neely, *Roy Acuff's Nashville: The Life and Good Times of Country Music* (1984); Elizabeth Schlappi, *Roy Acuff* (1978); Charles K. Wolfe, *A Good-Natured Riot: The Birth of the Grand Ole Opry* (1999).

Ailey, Alvin

(1931–1989) DANCER AND CHOREOGRAPHER.

Alvin Ailey was born on 5 July 1931, in Rogers, Tex., in the southeastern county of Bell. He was a central figure in the creation of modern dance, with an estimated 15 million people in 48 states and 45 countries having viewed the works of his Alvin Ailey American Dance Company. Ailey's work drew on what he called "blood memories, blood memories about Texas, the blues, spirituals, gospel, work songs, all those things going on in Texas in the 1930s during the depression."

Ailey's childhood reflected the complexities of African American experience in the mid-20th-century American South. Economic deprivation, incidents of racial oppression, and feelings of abandonment because of his father's desertion of his family alternated with small-town family and community nurturing. Ailey was unusually close to his mother, Lula. She picked cotton, did laundry, and was a domestic worker. She was raped while working in a white household, and at times young Ailey saw Klansmen riding in their white robes. He grew up in a world of cotton fields and of snakes, which lived under his house and became his pets.

Ailey and his mother lived in other Texas towns, including Navasota and Cameron. He peeped in the windows of a juke joint called the Dew Drop Inn, where his mother went to dance and hear the blues on Saturday night. He attended the True Vine Baptist Church, where he heard gospel music on Sunday morning. He remembered his home being "full of the heady smells of cornbread, biscuits, collard greens, pies, pork chops, fried chicken, and black-eyed peas." He also heard music from the Silas Green traveling show, which toured southern small towns with vaudeville-style entertainment, and he attended house parties with itinerant blues performers.

Ailey and his mother moved to Los Angeles when he was 12, and he first saw performance dance while in junior high school. He studied under choreographer Lester Horton, who had the nation's first integrated dance company and whose use of Native American dance and Japanese theater influenced

Ailey's later work. When Horton died in 1953, Ailey became director of Horton's company, although he was only 22 years old. Ailey first danced on Broadway in the 1954 production of Truman Capote's *House of Flowers*. He remained in New York City after that, studying ballet, acting, and modern dance with Martha Graham. He continued to appear in Broadway musicals and acted in the film *Carmen Jones*. In March 1958, his choreographed *Blues Suite* became a success in New York and led to the formation of his own dance company. From 1962, Ailey's troupe toured the world in trips sponsored by the U.S. Department of State, helping to popularize modern dance internationally.

Ailey used his "blood memories" in constructing a distinctive body of choreography rooted in the southern black culture in which he grew up. He noted in his autobiography that *Blues Suite* came out of the Dew Drop Inn. His ballet *Cry* reflected his memory of "seeing my mother on her hands and knees scrubbing these white folks' rooms and halls." His masterpiece, *Revelations*, uses slave spirituals to evoke the southern world that long haunted him.

CHARLES REAGAN WILSON
University of Mississippi

Alvin Ailey, with A. Peter Bailey, *Revelations: The Autobiography of Alvin Ailey* (1995); Thomas F. DeFrantz, *Dancing Revelations: Alvin Ailey's Embodiment of African American Culture* (2004).

All-Day Singings

All-day singing has long been one of the most cherished social institutions of the rural South. The term has been applied to a wide range of musical affairs and even has its counterpart in the all-night singings of modern gospel quartet music, but it is most closely associated with the shape-note singing convention.

Singing conventions are events that feature the performance of shape-note music, of both the four-shape and seven-shape varieties. The four-shape conventions have always been the most conservative in that they adhere to the use of one songbook, usually the venerable *Sacred Harp*, first published by Benjamin F. White in 1844, and they tend to resist newer songs and innovative styles of performing them (they instead preserve the fasola style of singing). In short, the four-shape singers try to remain faithful to the music and, in some respects, to the way of life of their ancestors. The seven-shape conventions, which are by far the most numerous of these events, were originally marked by their acceptance of the do-re-mi system of singing, and they have generally been receptive to innovations in songs and singing style. The singers at such conventions sing not from one book but from a wide variety of paperback shape-note hymnals generally published twice a year by such companies as Vaughan, Winsett, and Stamps-Baxter. The song repertoire therefore includes both the older, familiar religious material and the newest songs "hot off the press." Although everyone in attendance is encouraged to sing, performances are also made by soloists, duets, and trios and often by visiting professional quartets. People clearly attend these conventions not merely to sing but also to be entertained.

Whatever the style of singing, the singing conventions meet regularly throughout the rural and small-town South, often on a monthly basis, in the case of the seven-shape singers, and much more infrequently in the case of the fasola people. (Sacred harp singings actually occur all over the United States, particularly after being shown in the popular movie *Cold Mountain*.) Singers gather at a church or at the county courthouse, renew old acquaintances, sing for several hours under the guidance of experienced song leaders, and then sit down at long tables for a sumptuous feast of fried chicken, ham, potato salad, assorted pastries, and other delectables brought by the guests and participants. The practice of combining food and religious music long ago gave rise to the phrase "all-day singing with dinner on the grounds," which describes one of the most common events in the rural South.

BILL C. MALONE
Madison, Wisconsin

Alan Lomax, Commentary on All Day Singing, from *The Sacred Harp*, Prestige Records 25007.

Allison, Mose

(b. 1927) JAZZ AND BLUES MUSICIAN. Mississippi musician Mose Allison has enjoyed a prolific and critically acclaimed musical career, eschewing easy definitions or labels. He has charted his own course, blending a unique sound reflecting his Delta roots and introspective nature. Accumulating a legion of followers and influencing a range of artists, from the groundbreaking punk band the Clash to such venerated acts as the Rolling Stones and Hot Tuna, Allison's music continues to evolve in scope but retains the blues aesthetic that evokes the unique region of Mose's childhood.

Mose Allison was born on 11 November 1927, in the small Mississippi Delta town of Tippo. The Allison family was close knit and well respected in the community. Mose's father, Allison Sr., became an early advocate of land rights for African Americans in the racially segregated Delta. His efforts to promote reform prompted the town of Tippo to build a monument in his honor. Allison's mother, Maxine Collins, was born in Booneville, Miss., in 1905. She arrived in Tippo and soon caught the eye of Allison Sr. Possessing a sharp wit and a gift for storytelling, Maxine played the ukulele and traveled the world. Similarly, Allison Sr. was an accomplished stride piano player. Mose can recall early childhood memories of sawdusted floors and rollicking ragtime music in the family home.

The blues genre particular to the Delta region of Mississippi profoundly influenced Allison's approach to the blues-based sound that typifies his music. Interpreting the blues of his childhood as an artistic aesthetic, Allison renders the blues in his own unique signature style, one that is heartily embraced overseas. Allison's music has always enjoyed a particular popularity in England, achieving a cult status, with his mood-mellow, blues-inflected jazz. Evidence of the esteem with which he is held is seen by the legion of Allison cover songs emerging from British artists.

Allison began formal piano lessons at the age of five, and by grade school he was an accomplished songwriter and piano and trumpet player. After graduating from high school, he enrolled as a chemical engineering major at the University of Mississippi. His passion remained music, and he joined the popular Ole Miss jazz band, the Mississippians. Following a brief stint in the army, Allison briefly returned to Ole Miss, before heading to Louisiana State University to earn a degree in philosophy and literature.

Following graduation, Allison married Audre Mae Schwartz, a native of St. Louis, before embarking on an extended tour of the South. In the fall of 1956, Allison moved to New York to try his hand in America's premier jazz city. New York offered him the opportunity to associate with legendary jazz artists such as Stan Getz and tenor saxophone player Lester Young. While in New York, Allison found an artistic home in the legendary jam sessions in a 34th Street apartment, honing his skills among a loose affiliation of provocative jazz musicians such as Zoot Sims and Buddy Jones. The 34th Street apartment served as an oasis of artistic freedom for southern expatriates, helping Allison establish his stellar reputation as an artist with a southern-inflected style.

Allison's career spans several decades. He recorded with several significant music labels, including Prestige, Columbia, and Atlantic Records. His debut recording session with Prestige Records in 1957, *Back Country Suite*, harks back to his roots, evoking the warm pastoral setting of his youth. Alli-

son's lyric capabilities match his prowess on the piano; he sings in a candid and conversational idiom, lacing his lyrics with biting wit and introspective observation. Allison, refusing to compromise his music for a mass market audience, remains true to his vision and philosophy of music making. Nevertheless, his accolades include a 1987 Grammy nomination in the Best Jazz Vocalist category and a 2002 nomination for *Mose Chronicles, Live in London, Vol. 1*. He also appears in the major motion picture *The Score*, starring Robert De Niro. Allison adheres to a strict touring schedule; he opts for smaller venues and local musicians, to the delight of fans and musicians. When not on tour, Allison lives with his family in New York. The Allisons have four children.

CAT RIGGS
University of Mississippi

Wayne Enstice and Paul Ruban, *Jazz Spoken Here: Conversations with Twenty-two Musicians* (1992); Patti Jones, *One Man's Blues* (1995); Paul Zollo, *Songwriters on Songwriting* (1997).

Allman Brothers Band

SOUTHERN ROCK BAND.
In the late 1960s and early 1970s, the Allman Brothers Band created a new kind of southern music, one that embraced and acknowledged influences from both the white and the black sides of the South. The band itself, though all men, was integrated and embodied a new kind of vision for southern society that was rooted in brotherhood across racial lines. The members represented a more peaceful alternative to the image of the violent, racist southern white

men who opposed the civil rights movement in the 1960s. The Allman Brothers Band even played a few benefit concerts in the mid-1970s for that other emblem of progressive, post–civil rights southern politics, Jimmy Carter. The band started the southern rock movement of the 1970s, and bands like Lynyrd Skynyrd, Charlie Daniels, and Marshall Tucker followed in its footsteps. Though the Allman Brothers Band has seen its musical fortunes wax and wane over the years, it continues to bring its music to a new audience in the new millennium.

Duane and Gregg Allman were born in Nashville, Tenn., in 1946 and 1947, respectively. They grew up in a single-parent household after their father was killed in the late 1940s. When the boys were about 10, the family moved to Daytona Beach, Fla., where they both became interested in music, through listening to artists like Little Milton, B. B. King, Muddy Waters, John Lee Hooker, Ray Charles, Howlin' Wolf, Otis Redding, Jimmy Reed, Sonny Boy Williamson, Bobby "Blue" Bland, and many others, often on the rhythm-and-blues radio station WLAC, from Nashville. The two brothers played with a series of bands during their high school years at bars and frat parties around the Southeast. A Los Angeles record label showed some interest in the band, then called Hour Glass, and brought it to the West Coast. It became popular in the burgeoning California psychedelic rock scene but had little success in the studio. Eventually the band became discouraged and moved back to Florida, but not before it had cut a few songs at FAME Studios in Muscle Shoals, Ala.

Gregg remained in California to honor the record contract.

Duane started jamming with bassist Berry Oakley and guitarist Dickey Betts, two veterans of the Florida music scene. Duane was also called back to Muscle Shoals to play on several recording sessions, playing guitar on Wilson Pickett's version of "Hey Jude," as well as with Aretha Franklin, Clarence Carter, and King Curtis. Meanwhile, Phil Walden, Otis Redding's ex-manager, heard Duane playing and offered to manage him. Walden also introduced Duane to Jai Johnny Johnson, otherwise known as "Jaimoe," a drummer from Gulfport, Miss., who had played with Percy Sledge and Otis Redding. Walden started Capricorn Records in Macon, Ga., with help from Jerry Wexler of Atlantic Records, and Duane moved the band to Macon to start practicing. The band still did not have a singer or a songwriter, so Duane called his little brother in California, who returned to the South.

The band combined its collective roots in blues, soul, R&B, jazz, country, and psychedelic rock to create its first album, titled *The Allman Brothers Band*, released in 1969. Though the album originally did not sell well, it received stellar reviews from major rock publications. The band toured the Southeast in 1970 while recording its second album, *Idlewild South*, with producer Tom Dowd. Duane also continued to do studio work, including recording with Delaney and Bonnie, where he met Eric Clapton and collaborated with the guitarist on his album *Layla and Other Love Songs*. The Allman Brothers played at Bill Graham's Fillmore East in New

York City several times, and the resulting live album from the venue went gold. Duane Allman died shortly afterward in a motorcycle crash back home in Macon. He was 24.

The band, devastated, decided to carry on with the tour and released another album, *Eat a Peach*, containing some songs with Duane and some new songs without him. After several personnel changes, it released another album, *Brothers and Sisters*, in 1973 and hit the No. 1 spot on the billboard charts, largely thanks to "Ramblin' Man," a tune penned and sung by Dickey Betts.

After a string of successful and critically acclaimed albums in the early 1970s, the latter part of the decade found the band members suffering a series of personal and professional difficulties, often exacerbated by their problems with drugs and alcohol. The band split into three groups but got back together in 1978 and recorded *Enlightened Rogues*, which hit the Top 10 and went platinum, but Capricorn Records folded later that year amid a series of lawsuits. Southern rock was no longer a popular genre, and though the band signed with Arista Records, the few albums it recorded in the early 1980s did not sell well. It broke up again in 1982. In the late 1980s, "classic rock" bands experienced a resurgence in popularity, fueled by reunion tours, greatest hits releases, and new radio formats. PolyGram records, which had acquired Capricorn's back catalog, released *Dreams*, a four-disc retrospective of the Allman Brothers Band's career. Buoyed by the success of the boxed set, the band re-formed, signed with Epic Records, went on tour, and recorded *Seven Turns*, released in 1990 and widely heralded as a return to form.

Tensions resurfaced within the Allman Brothers Band as Dickey Betts left in 2000. As of 2008, the Allman Brothers Band lineup included Gregg Allman, Butch Trucks, Jaimoe Johanson, Warren Haynes, Derek Trucks, Marc Quinones on percussion, and Oteil Burbridge on bass. The Allman Brothers Band has continued to tour and release a series of albums, which have been well received by critics and fans. It has also had several Grammy nominations.

ELLIE CAMPBELL
University of Mississippi

Marley Brant, *Southern Rockers* (1999); Scott Freedman, *Midnight Riders: The Story of the Allman Brothers Band* (1995); *Rolling Stone Rock and Roll Encyclopedia* (2001).

Armstrong, Louis

(1900–1971) JAZZ MUSICIAN AND ENTERTAINER.

Born 4 July 1900 in New Orleans, Daniel Louis "Satchmo" Armstrong achieved acclaim as a jazz emissary to the world. Duke Ellington once called him "the epitome of jazz." As a child, Armstrong played music on the streets of New Orleans and received musical training in the public schools and at the Coloured Waif's Home (1913–14). He heard and was influenced by such early jazz performers as Charles "Buddy" Bolden, William "Bunk" Johnson, and Joseph "King" Oliver, who became his mentor. Armstrong performed briefly in a New Orleans nightclub at age 15 but did not become a full-time professional until he was 17. He joined Edward "Kid" Ory's band in 1918 and thereafter played with other jazz greats and led his own groups, especially the Hot Five and the Hot Seven, in the 1920s. His recording debut was with Oliver in 1923. Recordings made him a celebrity, and he toured widely in the 1930s, including a trip to Europe in 1932. He acquired his nickname, "Satchmo," in England from the editor of a music magazine. Armstrong made a historic recording with Jimmie Rodgers, the "Father of Country Music," on 16 July 1930. Rodgers sang his "Blue Yodel No. 9" with accompaniment by Armstrong on the trumpet and with his wife, Lillian Hardin Armstrong, on piano.

Louis Armstrong, premier jazz musician, c. 1931 (Hogan Jazz Archive, Tulane University, New Orleans)

Armstrong was a popular international figure by the 1940s and thereafter performed around the world. He played at major jazz festivals; recorded frequently; performed in Broadway musicals, on radio, and later on television; and appeared in 60 films, including *Cabin in the Sky* (1943), *New Orleans* (1947), *High Society* (1956), *Satchmo the Great* (1956), *Jazz, the Intimate Art* (1968), and *Hello, Dolly* (1969). He died in New York City on 6 July 1971.

Armstrong's powerful trumpet and soulful, gravelly singing voice, as well as his infectious smile and effusive good humor, helped to establish the image of the archetypal jazzman. "Satchmo" communicated to everyone the irrepressible message that jazz was "good-time" music. His nickname, as well as his use of street vernacular for expressions of endearment and cordiality, reflected the communal New Orleans roots of the music.

The jazz personality that Armstrong helped create grew out of the southern urban underclass found most clearly in New Orleans. Armstrong's demeanor was as a loose-mannered, self-assertive (that is, "bad"), somewhat "hip," good-time person, whose music was a refuge from the external world. The jazz personality that emerged through Armstrong from the southern urban world included a bold and flirtatious manner, a zany sense of humor, a familiarity bordering on impertinence in interpersonal contact, a flashy, fancy code of dress, and an open and adventurous attitude toward life. Certainly, all jazz musicians have not fit this personality mold, but Armstrong—the most influential role model available to early jazz performers—did much to implant that abiding notion in the public mind.

Armstrong's jazz personality reflected certain aspects of the black culture in the South. He found his niche through music entertainment, a common pattern among blacks in southern urban areas. He drew on the vernacular tradition of black street and saloon life. His loose manner reflected an easygoing tolerance essential to the southern black underclass and fit squarely into the laid-back folk tradition. The hip mentality infusing the jazz personality is also a form of pride, validating the jazzman's self-assertiveness ("badness") in musical activities.

CURTIS D. JERDE
W. R. Hogan Jazz Archive
Tulane University

Louis Armstrong, *Louis Armstrong, in His Own Words: Selected Writings*, ed. Thomas Brothers (2001), *Satchmo* (1954), *Swing That Music* (1936); Laurence Bergreen, *Louis Armstrong: An Extravagant Life* (1997); Gary Giddins, *Satchmo: The Genius of Louis Armstrong* (2001); Robert Goffin, *Horn of Plenty: The Story of Louis Armstrong* (1947); Max Jones and John Chilton, *Louis: The Louis Armstrong Story, 1900–1971* (1971).

Arrested Development

HIP-HOP GROUP.

From the very beginning, the Atlanta-based hip-hop group Arrested Development sounded off like a veritable pastiche of southern music. Though the brainchild of a Milwaukee transplant—Speech, the group's artistic and spiritual leader—Arrested Development's music drew heavily from the distinctly southern traditions of blues, gospel, old-world African rhythms, and call-and-response song structures, while focusing on themes of southern rural life and respect for black women and traditional family values. Dressed in African garb and pouring libations to ancestors before every show, Arrested Development made a name for itself as one of the few hip-hop groups that could hold its own on a stage as well as in a recording studio.

The group's breakthrough single, "Tennessee," from its 1992 album, *3 Years, 5 Months, and 2 Days in the Life of . . .* (the length of time it took the group to land a record deal), marked a stark departure from the gangster-rap that dominated the industry at the time, while simultaneously bringing a southern aesthetic to hip-hop. The song, written by Speech on the occasion of his grandmother's passing, faced the darkness of African American history in the South ("walk the roads my forefathers walked. Climb the trees my forefathers hung from") while pleading for divine guidance in a voice that could have easily seeped out from under the doors of any one of a number of historically black churches.

The album featured other mainstream hits, such as "Mr. Wendal" and "People Everyday." Arrested Development found its particular brand of southern hip-hop (termed "life music" by the group itself), landing squarely at the top of the charts, selling 5 million copies of its debut worldwide, and winning Grammy awards for Best New Artist and Best Rap Single. Though *3 Years, 5 Months, and 2 Days in the Life of . . .* was a major commercial success, the group's follow-up album was much less well received, and by 1996 the members of the group had gone their separate ways.

In the years before the group disbanded (it has recently reunited with a new album, *Since the Last Time*), Arrested Development forged new ground in hip-hop, covering songs by Buddy Guy and Junior Wells, while speaking to the shameful issue of slavery and promoting self-determination for the African American community. Speech sees his work with Arrested Development as a direct continuation of that of his grandmother and his mother. His grandmother was a precinct committeewoman known as the "Fannie Lou Hamer" of Henning, Tenn., who worked tirelessly to encourage southern African Americans to vote. His mother was owner and operator of the *Milwaukee Community Journal*, which for the last 31 years has covered the issues and concerns of the black community.

On 16 April 2007, the city of Atlanta issued a proclamation, recognizing and honoring Speech's (and, by proxy, Arrested Development's) commitment to bettering the world through music.

MITCH COHEN
Oxford, Mississippi

Maurice Weaver, *Ebony* (November 1993).

Austin City Limits

Austin City Limits is a PBS program that has been a key presenter of American musical talent in concert performances since the mid-1970s. Program director Bill Arhos, at KLRN (later KLRU-TV) in Austin, Tex., developed the program to showcase southwestern musical talent, and he attracted national attention through the support of the PBS network. The pilot for the show featured Willie Nelson, who had recently moved from Nashville to Austin, and the first broadcast show, in 1976, was a reunion of Bob Wills's Original Texas Playboys.

The early years of *Austin City Limits* highlighted "progressive country," a popular musical genre that had emerged in Austin and combined country music, folk influences, and soft rock sounds. Filmed on the University of Texas at Austin campus, the program tapped into the burgeoning Austin musical scene of the 1970s, which included clubs, recording studios, and performers moving to central Texas, and it helped showcase the city's claim as an emerging musical center, even challenging the preeminence of Nashville in regional musical culture. The Lone Star Brewing Company was an early sponsor, providing an iconic Texas connection and funding support and also kegs of beer for the audience members getting ready for the taping of the show.

As the seasons went on, the program moved well beyond progressive country and traditional country, to feature jazz, blues, folk, bluegrass, zydeco, Cajun, and Tejano music. Entertainers who appeared, all of whom were paid union scale, included such prominent figures as Ray Charles, B. B. King, Emmylou Harris, Johnny Cash, Neil Young, and Roy Orbison. The show produced tributes to Texas musical legends Stevie Ray Vaughan in 1995 and Townes Van Zandt in 1997. "Songwriters Specials" gave an acoustic forum for a range of respected lyricists.

Today, *Austin City Limits* is television's longest-running musical concert show. Producer Terry Lickona has been with the program almost since its beginning and continues to oversee its development. It increasingly highlights songwriters and folk performers, but it still presents an eclectic mix of entertainers, both established and emerging. The skyline of Austin—the "Live Music Capital of the World"—and images from central Texas continue to establish the show's anchoring in that state.

CHARLES REAGAN WILSON

University of Mississippi

John T. Davis, *Austin City Limits: 25 Years of American Music* (2000); Clifford Endres, *Austin City Limits* (1987).

Autry, Gene

(1907–1998) COUNTRY AND WESTERN SINGER.
Though he became known throughout the world as a symbol of the West, Gene Autry's music remained firmly rooted in the southern soil from which it came. Orvon Gene Autry was born on a ranch near Tioga, Tex., on 29 September 1907, and moved to a ranch near Achille, Okla., as a youth. He was interested in a career in entertainment from an early age and even joined a medicine show in his teens; but it was as a guitar-strumming blue yodeler—under the influence of the enormously popular Jimmie Rodgers—that Autry achieved his first success as an entertainer in the late 1920s.

Although he continued to perform blue yodels as late as his 15th film (*The Old Corral* [1936]), he abandoned his imitation of Rodgers to adopt a gentler country sound, best exemplified by his first major record success, *That Silver Haired Daddy of Mine* (1931). A pure cowboy period followed, with popular records like *The Last Roundup* and *Tumbling Tumbleweeds* in the early 1930s, followed by standards like *Mexicali Rose, South of the Border*, and *There's a Gold Mine in the Sky*, among many others. By the late 1930s, his recordings were predominantly country love songs, and he had settled into an immediately recognizable style: swelling violins and muted trumpet for mainstream appeal, yet with a trademark steel guitar and with Autry's straightforward, homespun, laconic voice most prominent. Like all great country singers, he possessed the ability to convey honesty, sincerity, and lack of affectation in his delivery; he sang as though he were speaking with each listener on a one-to-one basis. His recording career reached its apex in the late 1940s, with the multimillion-selling children's records *Here Comes Santa Claus* and *Rudolph the Red-Nosed Reindeer*.

The first singer-actor to popularize the singing cowboy in film, Autry fostered a new musical and film genre of worldwide popularity in a film career that included some 93 films and 91 television programs. He was a country songwriter of consequence; a record-seller seldom matched in recording history, with major hits spanning many years (1930–51) and styles; an enormously successful businessman and owner of the California Angels baseball club; and a cultural icon who brought an image of the West and western music to the world.

Of primary significance, however, was Gene Autry's adherence to an unabashedly sincere country singing style throughout his career. His stature as a major entertainer in the 1930s and 1940s gave country music a badly needed dignity and respectability, and though he is not often given credit for such a pioneering role, it was largely Autry and the singing cowboys who followed in his footsteps who made millions aware of the sincerity and emotion inherent in the music of the hills and ranges.

DOUGLAS B. GREEN
Nashville, Tennessee

Gene Autry, with Mickey Herskowitz, *Back in the Saddle Again* (1978); Douglas B. Green, *Journal of Country Music* (May 1978), *Singing in the Saddle: The History of the Singing Cowboy* (2002); Bill C. Malone, *Country Music, U.S.A.: A Fifty-Year History* (1968; rev. ed., 1985).

Bailey, DeFord

(1899–1982) COUNTRY MUSIC SINGER.

Country Music Hall of Fame member DeFord Bailey was born near Bellwood, Tenn., on 14 December 1899 and is quoted as saying, "My folks didn't give me no rattler, they gave me a harp." By all accounts true, this exposure to the harmonica while in infancy was augmented by his contracting polio at age three. Unable to move for a year, he cultivated his ability to listen: to dogs, to birds, and, most importantly, to trains. (His signature song would become "Pan American Blues.") Following the early death of his mother, Bailey was raised

by his aunt Barbara Lou, whose highly musical family further inundated the child with what he termed "black hillbilly music." Perhaps in part because of his unusually small stature and slight hunch, the result of his polio infection, DeFord's teenage years included jobs as a "house boy" for prominent white families. It was in such a setting that, following a move to Nashville in 1918, his talent on the Hohner Marine Band harmonica was first employed as social entertainment, and in lieu of what he termed "good work."

Bailey's growing reputation would bring him ever closer to professional musicians over the next few years, and in 1926 he was invited to join Dr. Humphrey Bate and his "Possum Hunters" on the newly established *Barn Dance* radio program, on radio station WSM in Nashville. Program host (and celebrity founder of Chicago's *National Barn Dance*) George "Judge" Hay invited Bailey to become a regular on the show and soon after dubbed the rising star the "Harmonica Wizard." Though never identified by ethnicity on air, his "black hillbilly music" captivated radio audiences and made Bailey one of the *Opry*'s most beloved and showcased performers—a designation that would last for 15 years. His music even indirectly inspired Judge Hay to change the very name of the program. Upon conclusion of a train-themed installment of the classical music broadcast that proceeded *Barn Dance* (and whose pretension Hay wished to publicly deflate), DeFord opened *Barn Dance* with his signature "Pan American Blues," prompting the host to proclaim, "For the past hour, we have been listening to music largely from Grand Opera, but from now on, we will present Grand Ole Opry." Bailey married Ida Lee Jones, and the couple would have three children: DeFord Junior, Dezoral Lee, and Christine Lamb.

Though costars such as the Delmore Brothers would openly "stick by me through thick and thin," Bailey spent many nights, while touring the Jim Crow South, seeking out kitchens that would serve him or sleeping in cars instead of in hotel rooms. With respect to his overall *Opry* experience, biographers give a mixed interpretation of peer acceptance and paternalism, of Bailey's fondness for the experience, and of his dislike for being typecast.

What is certain is that his dismissal from the *Opry* in 1941 remains one of the most controversial moments in the program's history. Despite Judge Hay's public explanation that "our mascot" was "lazy" and refused to learn new material, biographers claim that besides being African American, Bailey fell victim to the publishing dispute between wSM radio and the American Society of Composers, Authors, and Publishers (ASCAP). Following wSM's disputation of ASCAP licensing fees, Bailey was ordered by Judge Hay to quit performing the very songs for which he was celebrated, those that his audiences came to expect. Dismissing the warning, DeFord continued to perform his biggest hits, ultimately resulting in his dismissal.

Expelled from professional music, Bailey went on to open an extremely successful shoe shine business in Nashville, an unusual, fully integrated enterprise, which he would manage for decades. Despite his talent, his celebrity, and his early impact upon the success of the *Grand Ole Opry*—and thus the genre as a whole—DeFord Bailey was not inducted into the Country Music Hall of Fame until 2005, 23 years after his death. His recorded music, originally captured on a handful of 78 and LP recordings from Columbia, Brunswick-Balke-Collander, and Victor, was anthologized on Revenant Records' 1998 collection, *The Legendary DeFord Bailey: Country Music's First Black Star.*

ODIE LINDSEY
University of Mississippi

Jessica Janice Jones, *Black Music Research Journal* (Spring 1990); David C. Morton and Charles K. Wolfe, *DeFord Bailey: A Black Star in Early Country Music* (1991); John W. Rumble, "DeFord Bailey," Country Music Hall of Fame and Museum.

Baker, Etta

(1913–2006) BLUES SINGER.
Born 31 March 1913 and raised in a family of farming musicians in the foothills of North Carolina, legendary Piedmont blues guitar and banjo picker Etta Baker played music since age three. Picking up both guitar and banjo from her father, Baker first recorded in 1956, when she was featured on the highly influential Tradition Records compilation *Instrumental Music of the Southern Appalachians*. Of the songs on that album, Baker's version of "One Dime Blues" was considered by many to be a definitive performance—so much so

that those who could imitate it were said to be "one diming it."

For much of her life, Baker worked in a textile mill in Morganton, N.C., and raised nine children. Only at age 60 did she decide to quit her job in order to pursue a career in music full time. She quickly found fame on the international folk festival circuit and performed live well into her eighties, garnering a Folk Heritage Fellowship from the National Endowment for the Arts in 1991. Baker's first full-length album on a major label also came in 1991, with Rounder Records' *One Dime Blues*. In the mid-1990s, Baker joined with North Carolina–based Music Maker Relief Foundation, which led to the 1999 album *Railroad Bill*. In 2005, Music Maker also released the album *Carolina Breakdown*, featuring Baker and her older sister, Cora Phillips, both picking away at guitar and banjo. The album was taken from field recordings made in the late 1980s by North Carolina folklorists Wayne Martin and Lesley Williams. Baker also recorded with blues hero Taj Mahal on the 2004 release *Etta Baker with Taj Mahal*.

A largely forgotten entry in Baker's discography is a long out-of-print and rare recording Stephan Michelson had made of Baker in the mid-1970s, called *Music from the Hills of Caldwell County*. Released in 1975 on Physical Records, the album features field recordings Michelson made during a yearlong stay with the Baker family. Baker also appeared on the critically acclaimed Kenny Wayne Shepherd recording *10 Days Out: Blues from the Backroads* (2007).

Etta Baker's unique talent was silenced on 23 September 2006 when she died at age 93 in Fairfax, Va. She had made the trip to Fairfax from her home in Morganton, N.C., to visit a daughter who had recently suffered from a stroke.

MARK COLTRAIN
Hillsborough, North Carolina

Balfa, Dewey

(1927–1992) CAJUN FOLK MUSICIAN. Dewey Balfa was one of the nation's most widely respected folk musicians and Cajun cultural activists. His calm, homespun eloquence and sincerity made him a spokesman for traditional cultures in general, but most of his battles to save his Cajun French culture were fought with a fiddle in south Louisiana, his home.

Balfa's musical heritage was a family affair. "My father, grandfather, great-grandfather, they all played the fiddle, and, you see, through my music, I feel they are all still alive." Balfa's father, Charles, was a sharecropper on Bayou Grand Louis in rural Evangeline Parish near Mamou. He instilled a love of life and music in his children, and Dewey and his four brothers grew up making music for their own entertainment. Born 20 March 1927, Dewey Balfa began playing the fiddle when he was about 13. Dewey had many models to follow, some outside the family, some even outside the culture. "You know, I was influenced by J. B. Fusilier, Leo Soileau, Harry Choates, and I think Bob Wills and the Texas Playboys had a little effect on my fiddling."

Dewey and his brothers soon were

playing together for family gatherings and house dances. In the 1940s, when dance halls were at the height of their popularity, the Balfa Brothers band stayed busy, sometimes playing eight dances a week. String bands dominated Cajun music in the 1940s. The traditional music of Balfa's French Louisiana became increasingly Americanized as it was influenced by western swing, bluegrass, and country music. In the years following World War II, musicians such as Iry Lejeune, Nathan Abshire, Alph Bergeron, and Lawrence Walker dusted off their long-abandoned accordions to perform again and to record traditional Louisiana Cajun French music. Many people were then convinced of the need for deliberate efforts to encourage the maintenance of the music's traditional form.

In 1964 Balfa played as a last-minute replacement on guitar at the Newport Folk Festival, and after that national and local interest was focused on traditional south Louisiana music. Balfa was involved in Louisiana contests sponsored by the Newport Folk Festival to discover talented musicians, and in 1967 the Balfa Brothers band performed at the Newport Folk Festival. South Louisiana itself was soon providing greater encouragement to its traditional artists, such as Balfa. As a result of the overwhelming response to Lafayette's 1974 "Tribute to Cajun Music," the music festival became an annual outdoor event. Dewey Balfa viewed the festival as a way to attract young musicians to Cajun music. Two of Balfa's brothers died in a 1978 automobile accident, but Dewey Balfa and other family members

continued to perform and to carry on the spirit of the Balfa Brothers. Dewey Balfa died of cancer in June 1992.

BARRY JEAN ANCELET
University of Louisiana at Lafayette

Barry Jean Ancelet, *Louisiana Life* (September–October 1981), *The Makers of Cajun Music / Musiciens Cadiens et Créoles* (1984); John Broven, *South to Louisiana: The Music of the Cajun Bayous* (1983).

Banjo

The five-string banjo is a distinctive feature of the indigenous rural music of the South; it is generally not indigenous to rural music elsewhere. But while the banjo has been commonly associated with rural white southern culture, urban and black influences have significantly shaped its history.

The banjo originated in black culture, proto-banjos having been brought by slaves from Africa. Until recently, legend honored Joel Sweeney as the inventor of the five-string banjo. This Virginian, around 1830, allegedly improved the slave instrument by adding a short, high-pitched fifth (or thumb) string to its original four. However, reliable illustrations show that some slave banjos in the Americas had short thumb strings well before Sweeney was born.

Until the 1830s the banjo was strictly a black instrument. The first whites to play it became, like Sweeney, minstrel performers, and it was an essential element in the minstrel show, born in the urban North in 1843 and the most popular entertainment form of the century. Minstrel banjo playing, a down-stroking style undoubtedly reflecting preexisting black performance, also became the

An 1850s fretless banjo (Robert Winans, photographer, Gettysburg College, Gettysburg, Pa.)

early style of white rural performers, who called it "frailing" or "clawhammer." By the 1870s the banjo was being played widely by southern rural whites, who probably learned from both black musicians and minstrel players who toured the South with minstrel shows, circuses, and medicine shows. Blacks continued to play the banjo, and until recently musical exchange between white and black players was active; now, however, only a few blacks play.

The first major group of styles, frailing, continues to be used in the South and, through the impetus of Pete Seeger and other figures in the folk song revival of the 1960s and 1970s, has also spread elsewhere. The second major group of styles, finger-picking, entered rural tradition around the turn of the

20th century, apparently in imitation of "classical" banjo, which developed in the 1870s and 1880s as the successor to the minstrel style on the stage and in urban areas. The early, two-finger styles are still used, but in the 1940s Earl Scruggs and other southerners transformed them into the more driving, syncopated, three-finger style known as bluegrass banjo, the most widely heard style at present, as bluegrass gains popularity in rural and urban areas far from the South.

Despite the spread of revivalist "old-time" players and bluegrass, the five-string banjo remains a symbol of the rural South.

ROBERT B. WINANS
Wayne State University

Cecelia Conway, *African Banjo Echoes in Appalachia: A Study of Folk Traditions* (1995); Dena J. Epstein, *Ethnomusicology* (September 1975); Scott Odell, in *New Grove Dictionary of Music and Musicians*, vol. 2, ed. Stanley Sadie (1980); Robert B. Winans, *Folklore and Folklife in Virginia* (1979), *Journal of American Folklore* (October–December 1976).

Beach Music

A treasure of popular culture in the Carolinas, beach music is not historically indigenous to Carolinas' beaches, where it now finds its greatest popularity, and does not traditionally celebrate beach culture. The origins of beach music lie in both the blues of the mid-20th-century South and the harmonious rhythm and blues of urban black street-corner singing groups like the Clovers, who enjoyed national success in the 1950s. Visitors to the Carolinas often find familiar oldies sanctified as classic "beach music."

The development of beach music as a cultural phenomenon began in the post–World War II era, as whites became attracted to the previously taboo music and dance of blacks. With the expansion of modern roadways and the mass availability of automobiles, this music became accessible in city concert halls and in the developing beach towns.

Beach music prospered in the late 1950s and early 1960s, but died down somewhat in the Vietnam era, as both musically and thematically it had become traditional and therefore suspect in the social and political climate of the time. Amid the frenzy of hard rock and the earnestness of "message music," rhythm and blues was by no means hip, cool, or relevant for many young people. In this period, "beach music" emerged as a cover term for an eclectic assortment of rhythm-and-blues songs. Some people claim the term always existed, but many insist that it did not appear until around 1970 or later. Though the temptation is to credit the Drifters' "Under the Boardwalk" from 1964 with popularizing the term, beach music more likely arose from a nostalgic looking back toward happier times, symbolized by the music that permeated them.

With the advent of disco music in the late 1970s, beach music revitalized and prospered. The return of "touch dancing" at this time contributed to the popularity of the "shag," beach music's dance ritual. Essentially a sophisticated, more refined cousin of the jitterbug (and not related to the shag of the Northeast in the 1940s), the shag be-

came the focal point of beach music. The shag was named the state dance by the South Carolina Legislature in 1985, and beach music has become a cultural icon in the Carolinas. Purists seek to preserve it in its earliest, most intricate forms, and a circuit of dance competitions has developed, with support from a growing number of teaching professionals.

With the resurgence of beach music in the late 1970s and early 1980s, the beach music scene became self-conscious and lyrically self-glorifying, celebrating itself and the beer-drinking, love-making side of beach culture, in regional, independently produced songs such as the Embers' 1979 "I Love Beach Music." Performers now are mostly white, reside principally in the Carolinas, and stress the horns in their rhythm sections.

The resurgence of beach music reached its peak in the early part of the 1980s with two Beach Music Awards shows filmed in 1982 and 1983 in Myrtle Beach, S.C., a capital for the music. A Society of Stranders (from "The Grand Strand," the popular name for the northeast South Carolina coastal area) meets each year in North Myrtle Beach and brings thousands of beach music fans together for several days of festivities. Some predicted that it would "go national," but this has not occurred. Beach music's true value lies in the regional bonding it inspires in the Carolinas.

STEPHEN J. NAGLE
University of South Carolina,
Coastal Campus

Orin Anderson, *Sandlapper* (June 1981); Bill King, *Atlanta Constitution* (6 June 1981); Steven Levy, *Rolling Stone* (30 September 1982); Stephen J. Nagle, *On the Beach* (Summer 1983).

Beale Street

Beale Street, one of the most celebrated streets in the South, was the black main street of Memphis and of the surrounding rural region, comparable in its heyday to Auburn Avenue in Atlanta and Maxwell Street in Chicago. Beginning at the Mississippi riverfront and extending eastward a mile and a half, the street was lined with commercial buildings, churches, theaters, parks, elegant mansions, everyday dwellings, and apartment houses. The diversity of its built environment showed that Beale Street was a mosaic of southern cultures. For more than a century, indigenous white and black southerners, Italian Americans, Greek Americans, Chinese Americans, and Jews lived or worked on Beale.

Unlike its northern counterparts, Beale Street never became a black ghetto. But it was Beale's black culture that gave the street its fame, and it stood as testimony to the decision of black people to strive to achieve the American Dream in their American homeland, the South, rather than to move North. From the 1830s, when the street was laid out, to the Civil War, black people were present on Beale Street, either as slaves living in quarters behind their masters' homes or as free blacks, some of whom owned Beale Street property. After Emancipation, thousands of freed slaves left the declining farms and small towns of the rural South and came to Memphis and to Beale Street in particular, seeking to fulfill the promises of freedom. Alongside white-owned establishments, they founded banks, insurance companies, retail shops, newspapers, schools, churches, fraternal institutions, nightclubs, and political and civil rights organizations. From the 1880s to the 1920s, Beale was one of the South's most prosperous black communities. On weekends, thousands of blacks from Memphis and the surrounding countryside came to Beale for shopping and entertainment, crowding the sidewalks so thickly "you had to walk in the street to pass by."

As the urban center of black nightlife for north Mississippi, east Arkansas, and west Tennessee, Beale attracted hundreds of musicians and became one of the nation's most influential centers of African American music. Variety was its hallmark—vaudeville orchestras, marching bands, ragtime, jug bands, blues, jazz, big bands, and rhythm and blues. A meeting place for urban and rural styles, Beale served as a school where young talent was nurtured, and it produced musicians who shaped the course of American music. In 1909, W. C. Handy was the first person to pen the blues, a form of music he had first heard in the Mississippi Delta town of Clarksdale, thus enabling it to be played around the world.

Since the 1920s, Beale Street has produced a succession of outstanding jazz musicians, such as Jimmy Lunceford, a principal creator of the big-band sound. In the 1940s and 1950s, Beale Street musicians like B. B. King and Bobby "Blue" Bland blended traditional blues with jazz arrangements to help produce the new form of music known as rhythm and blues. In the 1950s, young white musicians from the region, like Elvis Presley, were attracted to the music, dance, and dress styles of Beale Street and merged these with their country music traditions to shape a new type of music—rockabilly—and to lay the foundations for rock and roll.

But if Beale Street was a cultural sanctuary, it was a precarious one. Segregation denied blacks effective access to political and economic power beyond their own communities, and they were therefore unable to protect their Beale Street haven when hard times came. After World War II, downtown Memphis, like other American inner cities, began to change radically in character; the two most dramatic responses, the civil rights movement and urban renewal, transformed Beale. Although the civil rights movement achieved integration of Memphis's public facilities, it ironically damaged Beale by enabling blacks to do business throughout the city. The assassination of Martin Luther King Jr. near Beale and the turbulent aftermath accelerated the street's decline. Urban renewal then claimed most of the old buildings.

Since the late 1970s, however, Beale Street, like other historic areas in the South, has received new recognition as a cultural resource, and governmental, nonprofit, and private organizations have substantially revitalized the street. The resulting preservation of original landmarks, together with new nightclubs, restaurants, retail stores, an in-terpretive center, and Memphis in May, a monthlong event, which includes the Beale Street Music Festival and the World Championship Barbecue Cooking Contest, has produced a significant blend of old and new, and the future development of the street will no doubt continue to reflect major trends of urban southern culture.

GEORGE MCDANIEL
Charleston, South Carolina

Margaret McKee and Fred Chisenhall, *Beale Black and Blue: Life and Music on Black America's Main Street* (1981); David Stuart and Ryan Sheeler, *From Bakersfield to Beale Street: A Regional History of American Rock 'n' Roll* (2006).

Bechet, Sidney

(1897–1959) JAZZ MUSICIAN AND COMPOSER.

Like Jelly Roll Morton, Sidney Joseph Bechet, who was born 14 May 1897 in New Orleans, was a black Creole, a member of the group that played a pivotal part in the genesis of jazz. He grew up in the rich musical environment of New Orleans, taught himself clarinet, and later studied intermittently with George Bacquet, "Big Eye" Louis Nelson, and Lorenzo Tio Jr. By about 1910, he was performing with established New Orleans bands such as Bunk Johnson's. In 1914, he began to tour, settling in Chicago in 1917.

He performed in Europe from 1919 to 1921. He was among the first jazzmen to be critically praised; in 1919, Swiss conductor Ernest Ansermet called him "an artist of genius." Also in 1919 Bechet began playing the soprano saxophone, making it his primary instrument for the rest of his life. In the mid-1920s he recorded with Clarence Williams and Louis Armstrong and worked briefly with Duke Ellington. From 1925 to 1928 he toured Germany, France, and the Soviet Union. He returned to the United States with Noble Sissle's band and performed intermittently with it through 1938. During the revival of traditional jazz, beginning about 1939, he was praised as one of the master jazz pioneers, and his career rebounded. From 1951 on he lived in France, where he became a celebrity as the dominant figure in traditional jazz. He composed both short works (*Petite Fleur*) and longer works (*Nouvelles Orléans*) and appeared in a number of films.

Bechet was one of many jazz pioneers who moved from New Orleans to Chicago during the 1910s and 1920s and, making records there, spread jazz from its southern beginnings to the nation and beyond. Like Armstrong, Bechet had a melodic voice that was so strong and original that he came to dominate his ensembles; both musicians helped transform early jazz from an ensemble music to a soloist's art. Bechet made the soprano saxophone into a jazz instrument and set the standard by which all subsequent players have been measured. He developed a strong, individual jazz voice, distinctive for its rhythmic freedom, flowing expressiveness, rich tone, and wide vibrato. He greatly influenced Duke Ellington's saxophonist Jimmy Hodges, who in turn perpetuated Bechet's legacy. Bechet was also notable for the longevity of his musical career,

which spanned nearly 60 years, and for maintaining his beautiful style almost until his death, in Paris, on 14 May 1959.

JOHN EDWARD HASSE
Smithsonian Institution

Sidney Bechet, *Treat It Gentle* (1960); John Chilton, *Sidney Bechet: The Wizard of Jazz* (1996); Raymond Horricks, *Profiles in Jazz: From Sidney Bechet to John Coltrane* (1991); Hans J. Mauerer, *A Discography of Sidney Bechet* (1969); Raymond Mouly, *Sidney Bechet: Notre Ami* (1959); Martin Williams, *Jazz Masters of New Orleans* (1967).

Blackwood Brothers

GOSPEL MUSIC SINGERS.
Perhaps the most popular group in southern gospel music history, the Blackwood Brothers parlayed their rural Mississippi sharecropping background into a million-dollar entertainment empire. For many fans in both the South and the Midwest the Blackwoods defined the singing quartet style that is the backbone of classic southern gospel music and engineered many of the musical and promotional innovations that permitted gospel singers to professionalize their music. They were among the first to issue their own phonograph records, to break from the songbook publishers that had dominated gospel music for the first four decades of the century, to begin their own radio transcription service, to consciously seek out and adapt new or original songs, to travel by air, and to adapt harmonies and accompaniment for appeal to a nationwide popular audience.

The original quartet was formed in 1934 at Ackerman, Miss., by three

The Blackwood Brothers, gospel music group, 1950s (Skylite Records photograph, Cheryl Thurber Collection, Memphis)

brothers, Roy, Doyle, and James, sons of a Delta sharecropper and his wife, who sang casually in church; the fourth member was Roy's young son, R. W. By 1937, the group found itself broadcasting on radio at Jackson, Miss., doing not only gospel but pop and country tunes, and after April 1939 they performed on a 50,000-watt station recently opened in Shreveport, La., KWKH. Here they began an affiliation with the songbook publisher V. O. Stamps, who provided them with a car, contracts, a stipend, and a piano player, thus casting them into the format of "four men and a piano" that had become characteristic of earlier gospel quartets. In 1940, Stamps sent them to Shenandoah, Iowa, where they began a decade's stay at KMA that saw them develop their unique style and build a huge following in the Midwest.

In Iowa, the quartet began to experiment with modern harmonies (built on sixth and ninth chords), developing their precise enunciation and diction and borrowing verve, dynamics, and

solo breaks from pop and black gospel music. In 1946 they began to make records, first on the White Church label and then on their own Blackwood label, recording some 49 singles between 1946 and 1951. A move back to Memphis in August 1950 put them in the center of the then-burgeoning gospel movement, where black and white groups vied for airtime and for places at "all-night sings." From their broadcasting base at WMPS, the Blackwoods—now with only two of the original four still singing— became one of the first postwar gospel groups to sign with a major label when they began recording for RCA Victor on 4 January 1952. Hit records and a win on the nationally broadcast *Arthur Godfrey Talent Scouts* show in 1954 followed, but barely two weeks after the Godfrey show, two members of the group, R. W. and bass singer Bill Lyles, were killed in a plane crash.

Within a month, the Blackwoods had recovered and regrouped and were back on the concert circuit—another Blackwood, Cecil, the brother of R. W., stepped in, as did bass singer J. D. Sumner, who was to play an important role in the group's sound throughout the 1950s. A string of national television appearances and successful record albums followed in the mid-1950s, and the group's promotional activities reached new heights through their founding of the National Quartet Convention in 1957 and of a new all-gospel record company, Skylite, in 1960, as well as through the purchase of several of the old gospel songbook companies, which had fallen on hard times. From 1967 to 1977 the group won numerous Grammy awards and as late as the mid-1970s still featured James Blackwood, his son Jimmy, and his nephew Cecil.

The Blackwood Brothers discography is voluminous. In addition to hundreds of singles, it includes at least 58 LP albums on RCA Victor recorded from 1956 to 1973 and at least 42 albums on the Skylite label recorded from 1961 to 1981. Probably 20 albums exist on various other labels. Songs the Blackwoods have been most associated with include "Have You Talked to the Man Upstairs" (their first RCA hit and the winning song on the Godfrey show), "Swing Down Chariot," "My Journey to the Sky," "Paradise Island," "In Times Like These," "Looking for a City," and "The Old Country Church."

CHARLES K. WOLFE
Middle Tennessee State University

James Blackwood, with Don Martin, *The James Blackwood Story* (1975); Paul Davis, *Legacy of the Blackwood Brothers* (2000); Allen Dennis, ed., *James Blackwood Memories* (1997); Kree Jack Racine, *Above All: The Fascinating and True Story of the Lives and Careers of the Famous Blackwood Brothers Quartet* (1967).

Bland, Bobby "Blue"

(b. 1930) BLUES SINGER.
Born Robert Calvin Bland on 27 January 1930 in Rosemark, Tenn., Bobby "Blue" Bland has had a looming influence on R&B, blues, and southern soul that is still being felt more than 60 years after he began singing in local Memphis groups in the late 1940s.

Bland's family moved to Memphis from rural Rosemark in 1947 in search of better financial opportunities. Not long after arriving there, Bland started singing spirituals with a local group that was modeled after the Pilgrim Travelers, a popular gospel group of the day. Shortly after starting to hang around on Beale Street, though, Bland fell in with a set of local amateur musicians called the Beale Streeters, who performed in a park near the Palace Theater. This group of locals included at one time or another legends such as Johnny Ace, Roscoe Gordon, and B. B. King.

Despite being surrounded by such talent, Bland did not get his career off the ground for some time. One of the few 1950s blues musicians who did not play an instrument, Bland was still honing his unique vocal style. Singles in 1951 for the Chess, Modern, and Duke labels were unsuccessful, but after Bland's two-and-a-half-year stint in the army, his vocal style had matured. Still under contract with Duke Records (which recently had been sold to Houston-based nightclub owner and record producer Don Robey), Bland started to enjoy success almost immediately. Initially modeling his vocal style after the soaring falsetto of B. B. King, Bland soon fell under the spell of the guttural gospel squall of Rev. C. L. Franklin (Aretha's father) and decided to combine both styles into his own singular voice.

Bland's "Farther On up the Road" in 1957 and "Little Boy Blue" in 1958 did well on the R&B charts, and his hits "Cry, Cry, Cry," "I Pity the Fool," and "Turn on Your Love Light" in the early 1960s led to the release of his 1961 album on Duke, *Two Steps from the Blues*. It would prove to be one of the most influential and pivotal blues and soul-blues albums of all time because of the seamless and powerful blend of juke joint blues, gospel, and southern soul.

Most of the 1960s saw Bland with a busy schedule on the road, touring all over the world. However, the touring did not stop Bland from recording several hit albums during these years, scoring a staggering 45 songs on the R&B charts. After a few years out of the spotlight in the late 1960s, Bland resurfaced after Don Robey sold Duke to ABC Records. Still under contract, Bland was part of the package, and several moderately popular albums like *His California Album* (1973) and *Dreamer* (1974) came out of the deal. A couple of mid-1970s albums with former Memphian B. B. King also followed, to moderate success. Several hit-or-miss albums and a moderate touring schedule sprinkled the late 1970s and early 1980s, until Bland signed with the southern soul label Malaco Records, based in Jackson, Miss., in 1985. Since then, Bland has enjoyed veteran blues superstar status.

Garnering numerous awards during his career, including the National Academy of Recording Arts and Sciences Lifetime Achievement Award and the Blues Foundation's Lifetime Achievement Award, Bland continues to enjoy a successful career on southern soul and blues circuits, dazzling crowds, especially women, with live shows and consistently strong albums.

MARK COLTRAIN
Hillsborough, North Carolina

Peter Guralnick, *Living Blues* (July/August 1978); Jim O'Neal and Amy O'Neal, *Living Blues* (Winter 1970/1971).

Blues-Singing Women

In his classic collection of essays, *The Souls of Black Folk* (1903), W. E. B. Du Bois expressed the meaning of "sorrow songs" to black people: "They that walked in darkness sang songs in the olden days—sorrow songs—for they were weary at heart. They came out of the South unknown to me, and yet I knew them as of me and mine." In the sorrow songs, Du Bois heard "the voices of the past," preserved from generation to generation through oral tradition.

The origins of the blues are in the sorrow songs of the slaves. Both musical forms describe the daily experience of human oppression, while also maintaining a breath of hope that someday, somewhere, human beings will be judged by their souls, their minds, and their acts, rather than their racial backgrounds. At the same time, the blues express personal themes and dilemmas that are practically universal. Women who sing the blues sing primarily about love, infidelity, sex, and passion, as they occur in everyday situations and as they are altered by death, liquor, superstition, migration, natural disasters, and loneliness.

Unlike the sorrow songs, which portray the shared oppression of the slave community, the blues portray idiosyncratic and specific experiences in the lives of individuals. This thematic change reflects the social history of southern blacks. In antebellum times, slaves sang of their despair, hope, and protest primarily in their work songs and spirituals. After Emancipation, black sharecroppers who worked small plots of land sang about the trials and hardships of their individual lives. Early blues developed in the late 19th-century South as a form of leisure entertainment, a way of communication, and a form of autobiography. In the early blues or "country blues," an individual lament combined with an affirmation of self, representing the black experience in general through an individual life.

By the turn of the century, the rural blues were familiar to southerners, black and white, but until a number of black women recorded the "classic blues" during the 1920s most Americans were unfamiliar with the music. The most successful classic blues singers were southern black women, and their themes are written predominantly from a woman's point of view. In their study *Negro Workaday Songs* (1926), Howard W. Odum and Guy B. Johnson noted that "among the blues singers who have gained more or less national recognition, there is scarcely a man's name to be found." Among the more famous women who recorded classic blues are Ma Hunter, Bertha "Chippie" Hill, and Memphis Minnie. Lesser-known recording artists include Sara Martin, Lizzie Miles, Trixie Smith, Ada Brown, Eliza Brown, Cleo Gibson, Edmonia and Catherine Henderson, Mary Mack, Ann Cook, Mary Johnson, Lottie Beamon, Lucille Bogan, Georgia White, and Lillian Glinn. These blues-singing women were extremely popular during the 1920s and early 1930s, until the Depression ended the era of classic blues. Born in the late 19th century or the early 20th, a majority of them enjoyed a decade of success and afterward were sadly forgotten. They died poor and unrecognized.

According to historian Bill C. Malone, Americans were gradually introduced to the blues between 1914 and 1920, a period when numerous southern blacks were migrating to the North. Many blues lyrics are a direct response to northern urban life, and blues women who moved to the North were also likely to alter the instrumental style of their music. The blues were not recorded until Mamie Smith (a northern cabaret singer who was probably the first black singer to record a solo performance) sang "Crazy Blues" for Okeh Records in 1920. The record sold well, demonstrating that there was a market for blues music, particularly among black listeners. Following this, Lucille Hegamin ("The Georgia Peach"), Rosa Henderson, and Edith Wilson recorded smooth, refined, professionalized versions of the blues (including "St. Louis Blues" and "He May Be Your Man, but He Comes to See Me Sometimes") in a style influenced by both vaudeville and ragtime.

Ma Rainey and Bessie Smith are primarily responsible for recording and popularizing more authentic southern blues and for inspiring the numerous southern women who recorded "classic blues" during the 1920s. Rainey, often called the "Mother of the Blues," provided the link between country and classic blues. Like traditional male blues artists, she spent most of her career on the road, attracting large audiences across the South and, less frequently, among southerners who had migrated to the North, particularly in Chicago. According to author and music critic Le Roi Jones (Amiri Baraka), "Ma Rainey's singing can be placed squarely between the harsher, more spontaneous country styles and the smoother, theatrical styles of later blues singers." Born and raised in Columbus, Ga., she retained a rapport with southern audiences. Accompanied by a traditional jug band, she sang country blues, including "Counting the Blues," "Jelly Bean Blues," "See See Rider," "Corn Field Blues," "Moonshine Blues," and "Bo-Weevil Blues."

The influence of Ma Rainey upon Bessie Smith is well documented. Often called the "Empress of the Blues" or the "Queen of the Blues," Smith is probably the best of the recorded classic blues singers. Her life story has become a legend. Born in Chattanooga, Tenn., in 1898 to a large, poor family, Smith enjoyed a decade of success and affluence beginning in 1923. At first she recorded a number of songs previously sung by others, including "Gulf Coast Blues," "Aggravatin' Papa," and "T'Aint Nobody's Business If I Do." During her career, she recorded over 180 songs, among them "Mama's Got the Blues," "Lady Luck Blues," "See If I'll Care," "Kitchen Man," "Black Mountain Blues," "Nobody Knows You When You're Down and Out," "Nashville Woman Blues," "I Ain't Gonna Play No Second Fiddle," and "Safety Mama." Backed by professional jazz musicians, Smith enjoyed brief success performing for northern urban audiences, but she was most popular among southerners, black and white. Like other classic blues artists, her success ended during the Depression. She died a tragic and unnecessary death in an automobile accident in 1937.

Although numerous southern women sang and recorded the blues during the 1920s, few are remembered today. A small number continued to record during the 1940s and 1950s, but blues-singing women were never again as popular as they had been during the classic era. A contemporary blues style is exhibited in the recordings of Big Mama Thornton. Backed by electric guitar, she projects a strong, vibrant voice in a style influenced by rock and roll and rhythm and blues. Born and raised in Alabama, Thornton recorded during the early 1950s and 1960s, appealing to audiences in the United States and Europe. At the same time, countless women who had once sung and performed the traditional or classic blues remained unrecognized. For example, Mary McClain Smith, who is Bessie Smith's half sister and who sings in the classic blues style, was known as "Diamond Teeth Mary" in her heyday. She had performed mostly on the road, traveling by train or bus, spending her money as soon as she earned it. After a career spanning 32 years, performing with Nat King Cole, Duke Ellington, Billie Holiday, and Fats Waller, among others, she retired poor and was never recorded. She lived in obscurity, depending upon social security alone for income, until recently, when she was rediscovered by the Florida Folklife Center.

Whether or not they were recorded, blues-singing women have greatly influenced southern and American music. In the South, blues and white folk music have influenced and enriched one another. Blues themes about love, infidelity, sex, and passion have frequently appeared in the lyrics of female country stars such as Loretta Lynn, Dolly Parton, and Tammy Wynette, as well as lesser-known country artists Alice Gerrard and Hazel Dickens. In addition to influencing country lyrics, women who sang classic blues have influenced the lyrics and recording styles of rock singers Janis Joplin and Bonnie Raitt. Blues-singing women are also a major influence upon jazz, particularly represented in the delicate voices and music of Jackson, Miss., native Cassandra Wilson and of Billie Holiday. Holiday's recording of "Strange Fruit," for example, clearly illustrates her kinship to the classic blues. By describing the brutality of a lynching, this haunting tune protests the inhumanity of a racist society, as did the sorrow songs of the slaves. An idiosyncratic response to an isolated event becomes representative of the black experience in general.

RUTH A. BANES
University of South Florida

Chris Albertson, *Bessie* (1972), liner notes for *Bessie Smith: The World's Greatest Blues Singer*, Columbia Records GP33CV1040; *Blues Classics by Memphis Minnie*, Blues Classics 1, Arhoolie Records BC-1; Angela Y. Davis, *Blues Legacies and Black Feminism: Gertrude "Ma" Rainey, Bessie Smith, and Billie Holiday* (1998); W. E. B. Du Bois, *The Souls of Black Folk* (1903); Peter B. Gallager, *St. Petersburg Times* (6 August 1982); Alberta Hunter, *Amtrak Blues*, Columbia Records JC36430; Buzzy Jackson, *A Bad Woman Feeling Good: Blues and the Women Who Sing Them* (2005); Le Roi Jones, *Blues People* (1963); *Memphis Minnie*, vol. 2, *Early Recordings with "Kansas Joe" McCoy*, Blues Classics 13, Arhoolie Records BC-13; Bill C. Malone, *Southern Music—American Music* (1979); Paul Oliver, *Bessie Smith* (1971), *The Story of the Blues* (1969); Harry Oster, *Living Country Blues* (1969); Tony Russell, *Blacks, Whites, and Blues* (1970); *Sippie: Sippie Wallace with Jim Dapogny's Chicago Blues Band*, Arhoolie Records F-1032; Derrick Stewart-Baxter, *Ma Rainey and the Classic Blues Singers* (1970); Chris Strachwitz, liner notes for *Big Mama Thornton in Europe*, Arhoolie Records F-1028, liner notes for *When Women Sang the Blues*, Blues Classics, 26 Arhoolie Records BC-26; *Big Mama Thornton*, vol. 2, with the Chicago Blues Band, Arhoolie Records F-1032.

Bolden, Buddy

(1877–1931) JAZZ MUSICIAN.

The story of Charles "Buddy" Bolden is part of the earliest history of New Orleans jazz. Bolden was an accomplished cornetist and one of the first musicians to mix ragtime and blues into a sound that would later be called "jazz." He was born in New Orleans on 6 September 1877. His father, a drayman, died of pneumonia when Bolden was six years old. His mother worked to support the family, and Bolden and his sister did not have to work as children. No other members of the Bolden family were interested in music; Bolden learned from religious music and from various types of street music that were heard in New Orleans in the late 19th century. His natural musical ability showed itself when he began to play the cornet at age 17.

Bolden played in small string bands for dances and parties and in parades in New Orleans between 1895 and 1900. He achieved citywide fame around 1900 as the leader of his own band. Until 1906 Bolden continued to improvise his music, attracting a considerable following of admirers and being dubbed the "King" of New Orleans jazz. He and his band played in parks and at picnics, in city music halls, at lawn parties, and in bars. Sometimes they traveled outside New Orleans, playing at train stops along the way. Bolden was immersed in his music, enjoyed drinking, and was said to have hypnotic powers over women.

In the spring of 1906 Bolden began to have severe headaches and reportedly suffered from delusions. He attacked his mother in a fit and was taken into police custody. Once released, Bolden continued to play, but friends said he became increasingly depressed and easily angered. His erratic behavior led to another arrest in September 1906. His condition deteriorated quickly after his release, and in June 1907 Bolden was committed to the Insane Asylum of Louisiana, where he spent the last 24 years of his life. The official cause of his insanity was listed as alcoholism.

Bolden achieved his status as the legendary ancestor of jazz after his death. Jazz fans repeat fictional stories, such as the one in which Bolden supposedly blew his cornet so hard that the tuning slide flew out and landed 20 feet away. Most of the stories suggest the remarkable power of Bolden's playing. Even the *New Orleans Times-Picayune* in 1940 reported that Bolden "played with such volume that it is said he could often be heard while playing across the river in Gretna." "King" Bolden's increasing notoriety as a musician is underscored by the tragic nature of his short but inspired career.

KAREN M. MCDEARMAN
University of Mississippi

Danny Barker and Alyn Shipton, eds., *Buddy Bolden and the Last Days of Storyville* (2001); Ole Brask, *Jazz People* (1976); Daniel Hardie, *The Loudest Trumpet: Buddy Bolden and the Early History of Jazz* (2000); Donald M. Marquis, *In Search of Buddy Bolden: First Man of Jazz* (1978).

Brooks, Garth

(b. 1962) COUNTRY MUSIC SINGER. Although he does not equal their stature as a songwriter, Garth Brooks probably won more adherents to country music than Hank Williams and Willie Nelson combined. During the early 1990s he was the best-selling recording and concert artist in American popular music. So astounding was his artistic and financial impact that he was featured on the cover of *Time* and *Forbes* magazines. In country music, he became the highest-achieving member of the fabled "Class of '89," a group of artists who charted their first songs that year and which included Clint Black, Alan Jackson, Travis Tritt, and Mary Chapin Carpenter.

Troyal Garth Brooks was born 7 February 1962 in Tulsa, Okla. He grew up in Yukon, a suburb of Oklahoma City, in a family that included children from his father's and his mother's former marriages. During the 1950s his mother, Colleen, had performed briefly on Red Foley's *Ozark Jubilee* television show and recorded a few songs for Capitol Records, the label to which Brooks would eventually sign.

Although Brooks had dabbled in music while still in high school, it was not until he enrolled at Oklahoma State University in Stillwater that he heard a George Strait record and was moved to cast his lot with country music. He began performing regularly in clubs in and around Stillwater. Following his graduation, in 1984, with a degree in marketing, he made his first pilgrimage to Nashville. Nothing came of it, so he returned to Stillwater to enroll for graduate studies. In 1987 he returned to Nashville. By this time he was married to Sandy Mahl. He supported himself by singing "demos" (demonstration records for music publishing companies) and clerking in a boot store. After being rejected by every major recording label in Nashville, Brooks finally signed to Capitol in 1988. Capitol released his first album, *Garth Brooks*, in 1989.

A series of hit singles followed (many accompanied by music videos), which included "If Tomorrow Never Comes," "The Dance," "Friends in Low Places," and "The Thunder Rolls." As John Denver had done in the 1970s, Brooks appealed to young people with songs that alternated between a seize-the-day enthusiasm and a grim awareness of impending mortality. They offered profundity with complexity. During this period, "The Dance" became a high school prom staple, and yearbook editors besieged Brooks's publicists with requests for the singer's photos.

Moreover, Brooks earned goodwill by making himself approachable. At one Nashville event, he signed autographs and posed for pictures with fans for an uninterrupted 23 hours. He used his increasing economic power with concert promoters to insist that tickets to his shows be sold at the lowest possible price. He even waged a war briefly—and unsuccessfully—to support songwriter royalties by halting the sale of used CDs. All these efforts paid off. In addition to starring in his own TV specials, he made guest appearances on the most popular network programs. His concerts routinely sold out, sometimes necessitating repeat appearances. In 1993 he attracted sell-out crowds to the 65,000-seat Texas Stadium in Dallas for three consecutive nights. His free concert for an HBO special in 1997 filled New York's Central Park. By 2000, when he announced that he was leaving the music business to help raise his three daughters, he had sold more than 100 million albums.

In 2001 Brooks emerged from his self-imposed retirement to promote a new album. He did so in a typically grand Brooksian manner—performing three live television concerts across the country in three consecutive weeks. Brooks and Mahl divorced after 12 years of marriage, and in 2005 he married fellow country singer Trisha Yearwood. That same year Brooks signed a contract with Wal-Mart that gave the giant retail chain exclusive rights to sell his recordings.

EDWARD MORRIS
Former country music editor of
Billboard

Bruce S. Feiler, *Dreaming Out Loud: Garth Brooks, Wynonna Judd, Wade Hayes, and the Changing Face of Nashville* (1998); Edward Morris, *Garth Brooks: Platinum Cowboy* (1993); Joel Whitburn, *Top Country Songs: 1944 to 2005* (2006).

Brown, James

(1933–2006) SOUL MUSIC SINGER. "Soul Brother No. 1," "The Godfather of Soul," and "Mr. Dynamite" are all names given to the only black rhythm-and-blues artist of the 1950s to successfully bridge the gap to soul artist in the 1960s and funk artist in the 1970s. Maintaining his popularity through 30 years, James Brown single-handedly anticipated and shaped 1970s funk and, to a slightly lesser degree, disco music. The repercussions of his aesthetic conceptualizations are heard everywhere on black radio. His influence can be detected in European new wave music, West African Afro-beat, and West Indian reggae.

Brown was born on 3 May 1933 near Augusta, Ga., in abject poverty. Twenty-one years later, he formed the first version of his Famous Flames. Initially, the Flames sang only gospel music. They soon adapted their highly emotional repertoire to secular subjects and started working regularly in and around Macon, Ga. A demo tape of the secularized gospel song "Please, Please, Please" was sent to King Records in Cincinnati (at the time, one of the leading independent record labels specializing in black music), and in February 1956 James Brown and the Famous Flames recut the song and attained their first Top 10 rhythm-and-blues hit. It would be four years before Brown would cross over to the pop charts and nine years before "Papa's Got a Brand New Bag (Part I)" would go Top 10 on the pop charts.

In that nine-year period, Brown developed his legendary show-stopping revue with supporting singers, comedians, and dancers. His bands rehearsed meticulously, achieving a professionalism virtually unknown in rhythm and blues or rock and roll, and Brown exuded nonstop energy, replete with dancing, splits, knee drops, microphone acrobatics, and his fabled simulated collapse. The whole package was captured on vinyl in *Live at the Apollo*, a 1962 album, which, although a hardcore rhythm-and-blues album, reached the No. 2 spot on *Billboard*'s album charts and stayed on the charts for a total of 66 weeks.

Brown began with a style based on gospel intensity and interaction. His early records consist largely of call and response between himself and the Famous Flames. The Flames would echo, shadow, double, and respond to Brown's every nuance. The instrumentalists on these early records largely played a 12/8 triplet feel over a pronounced backbeat. By 1959, Brown, originally a drummer, started to change his style, opting for increasingly complex, out-front, crack, rhythmic arrangements, usually consisting of extended one-chord vamps featuring repetitive "groove" vocal figures,

James Brown, soul singer, 1960s (Solid Smoke Records photograph,
Living Blues *Archival Collection, University of Mississippi Blues Archive, Oxford*)

choked rhythm guitar, staccato horn bursts, and broken two- and three-note bass patterns. In both styles, Brown's singing was marked by a complete lack of inhibition, extensively utilizing gospel devices, such as falsetto cries, grunts, hoarse screams, and gasps.

Brown was always completely in control of his own career. He wrote lyrics, produced records, and made all executive decisions, eventually man-

aging himself and forming his own record production company. He also put himself in the vanguard of the black consciousness movement through records such as "Say It Loud, I'm Black and I'm Proud." As a classic example of the rags-to-riches American dream, Brown's meaning as a symbol to black youth cannot be overestimated. Forty-million-selling records and over one hundred chart entries later, James

Brown remained "The Hardest Working Man in Show Business" until his death in Atlanta at age 73 on Christmas morning, 2006. As evidence of his drive to perform and love of the stage, James Brown was scheduled to play at B. B. King's nightclub in New York City on New Year's Eve. Although he had been hospitalized just two days before his death, for pneumonia, he was quoted as saying, "I'm the hardest working man in show business, and I'm not going to let them down."

ROBERT BOWMAN
Memphis, Tennessee

Geoff Brown, *James Brown: A Biography: Doin' It to Death* (1996); James Brown, Bruce Tucker, and Al Sharpton, *James Brown: The Godfather of Soul* (2003); Tony Cummings, in *The Soul Book*, ed. Ian Hoare (1975); Gerri Hirshey, *Nowhere to Run: The Story of Soul Music* (1984); Robert Palmer, in *The Rolling Stone Illustrated History of Rock 'n' Roll*, ed. Jim Miller (1980); Jon Pareles, *New York Times* (26 December 2006); Cynthia Rose, *Living in America: The Soul Saga of James Brown* (1991).

Brumley, Albert

(1905–1977) GOSPEL MUSIC
SONGWRITER.

Albert Brumley was one of the premier composers of gospel songs and was intimately associated with the rise and expansion of the southern gospel quartet business. Many songs from his repertoire still command the allegiance of musicians in both the gospel and country fields (and particularly in bluegrass music, where his songs are frequently played).

Brumley was born near Spiro, Le-Flore County, Okla., on 29 October 1905, into a tenant farm family that provided inspiration for many of his most popular songs. He began writing songs shortly after attending his first singing school in 1922 at the Rock Island community in eastern Oklahoma, but none were published until 1927, when "I Can Hear Them Singing Over There" appeared in *Gates of Glory*, a convention songbook issued by the Hartford Music Company of Hartford, Ark. Brumley was intimately associated with the Hartford Company from 1926 to 1937, first as a student in its Musical Institute and then as a traveling teacher at many of its shape-note singing schools, as a bass singer in some of the Hartford quartets, and as a staff writer. Above all, Brumley profited from the guidance and counsel of Eugene M. Bartlett, the owner of the Hartford Company and the writer of such songs as "Victory in Jesus," "Everybody Will Be Happy Over There," and "Take an Old Cold Tater and Wait."

In January 1932, Brumley's most famous song, "I'll Fly Away," was published by the Hartford Company in one if its many paperback songbooks, *Wonderful Message*. Reminiscent of 19th-century camp meeting songs, with its catchy rhythm and repeated chorus, "I'll Fly Away" has since been recorded over 500 times in virtually every field of music and has become one of the standards of white gospel music. It may have reached its largest audience, however, in the huge-selling sound track of the movie *O Brother, Where Art Thou?* Brumley eventually composed over 600 songs, first for the Hartford Company up to 1937, then for the Stamps-Baxter

Company from 1937 to 1945, and finally for the Stamps Quartet Publishing Company after 1945. Such songs as "Jesus Hold My Hand," "I'll Meet You in the Morning," "I Found a Hiding Place," "Camping in Canaan's Land" (cowritten with Eugene M. Bartlett), and "If We Never Meet Again" won a wide circulation in homes and churches all over the South through the performances of the quartets. Radio was a prime medium through which his songs were popularized, and Brumley wrote a very popular song, "Turn Your Radio On," which paid tribute to that powerful commercial force while advising listeners to "get in touch with God" by tuning in "the Master's radio."

Although Brumley said that he never consciously wrote a country song, several of his songs (in addition to the purely gospel numbers mentioned previously) have become standards in the country and bluegrass fields. These include "By the Side of the Road," "Dreaming of a Little Cabin," "Did You Ever Go Sailin'," "Nobody Answered Me," and "Rank Strangers to Me." These sentimental and nostalgic songs, which juxtapose memories of a cherished but decaying rural past with visions of a reconciliation with loved ones in heaven, have struck sensitive chords among many southerners who have been conscious of their region's disquieting transition from ruralism and agriculture to urban industrialism. Indeed, all Brumley's songs, both religious and secular, spoke directly to people who often felt discouraged in a world of disappointment and bewildering change. Consequently, his songs were particularly cherished during the Depression, when people needed the comfort and assurance of a personal, caring Savior.

Brumley wrote few songs after World War II, but he remained in the music business as the owner of the Hartford Company and Albert Brumley and Sons and was the promoter of two music festivals, the Sunup to Sundown Sing in Springdale, Ark., and the Hill and Hollow Folk Festival in Powell, Mo. Before his death, on 15 November 1977, Brumley was named to the Gospel Music Hall of Fame and the Nashville Song Writers Hall of Fame. He is buried near Powell, Mo., where he had resided since 1931.

BILL C. MALONE
Madison, Wisconsin

Clarence Baxter and Vide Polk, *Gospel Song Writers Biography* (1971); Kay Hively and Albert E. Brumley Jr., *I'll Fly Away: The Life Story of Albert E. Brumley* (1990); Ottis J. Knippers, *Who's Who among Southern Singers and Composers* (1937); Bill C. Malone, *Bluegrass Unlimited* (July 1986); *Music City News* (July 1965).

Buffett, Jimmy

(b. 1946) SINGER, WRITER, AND BUSINESSMAN.

James William "Jimmy" Buffett was born on 25 December 1946, in Pascagoula, Miss., and grew up in Mobile, Ala. His South is the Gulf Coast, and he has used its musical rhythms, especially the Coast's ties to the Caribbean Islands, to establish a unique cultural identity, which he has marketed to legions of fans. Buffett expresses American musical interest in the Caribbean, and he is particularly significant in introducing the islands' sounds into country music.

The son of a naval architect, James Delaney Buffett Jr., and Mary Loraine "Peets" Buffett, young Jimmy Buffett often went sailing with his father and stayed close to the Gulf Coast while attending college at Auburn University and the University of Southern Mississippi, from which he received a bachelor's degree in 1969. He played guitar in local bands while in college and became a *Billboard* magazine correspondent in Nashville after graduation. Buffett recorded a country music album, *Down to Earth*, in 1970, followed by *White Sport Coat and a Pink Crustacean* (1973) and *Living and Dying in 3/4 Time* (1974). After moving to Key West, Fla., in the early 1970s, Buffett formed the Coral Reefer Band in 1975, and his *Changes in Latitudes, Changes in Attitudes* (1977) gave him a pop hit, including its million-selling single, "Margaritaville."

Margaritaville became a larger-than-life mythic place, with Buffett the easygoing beach bum luxuriating in a tropical lifestyle. This image rests at the foundation of Buffett's creative work. His tours have been extremely successful, with such names as the Cheeseburger in Paradise Tour (1978), Coconut Telegraph Tour (1980), Last Mango in Paris Tour (1985), A Pirate Looks at Forty Tour (1987), Off to See the Lizard Tour (1989), Havana Daydreamin' Tour (1997), and the Beach House on the Moon Tour (1999). His fans, known at Parrotheads, bring a Carnival-like spirit to the concerts, often dressed in the Margaritaville clothing that Buffett markets. He is financially involved with two restaurant chains, the Margaritaville

cafes and the Cheeseburger in Paradise restaurants.

Buffett, a fan of William Faulkner and other southern writers, published his first book, *Tales from Margaritaville*, in 1989. It spent over seven months on the *New York Times* best-seller fiction list, as did his *Where Is Joe Merchant* (1992). His memoir, *A Pirate Looks at Fifty* (1998), reached No. 1 on the *Times'* nonfiction best-seller list. He also co-wrote with his daughter, Savannah Jane Buffett, two children's books, *The Jolly Mon* (1988) and *Trouble Dolls* (1991). Buffett's *A Salty Piece of Land* was published in 2004.

Buffett's business enterprises have ranked him consistently in *Fortune* magazine's list of highest-earning performers. He has also long been active in charity work, including founding the Save the Manatee Club in 1981, establishing the "Singing for Change" Foundation in 1995 (which makes grants to local charities), and raising more than $3 million in a 23 November 2004 concert to benefit hurricane victims that year. In the summer of 2007 Buffett the entrepreneur partnered with Harrah's Entertainment to build the Margaritaville Casino and Resort in Biloxi, Miss., near his birthplace.

Jimmy Buffett has continued to record both pop-rock and country songs. In 2003 his duet "It's Five O'clock Somewhere," with country singer Alan Jackson, became a No. 1 hit on the country charts. His *License to Chill* album in 2004 became his first chart-topping album. His box set *Boats, Beaches, Bars, and Ballads* contains 72 tracks of music and the *Parrothead Handbook*. It is one of the best-selling box sets on the market. Buffett's extensive creative exploration of the relationship between the South and the Caribbean makes him a prime musical talent of the Global South.

CHARLES REAGAN WILSON
University of Mississippi

Steve Eng, *Jimmy Buffett: The Man from Margaritaville Revealed* (1991).

Burnett, Chester Arthur (Howlin' Wolf)

(1910–1976) BLUES SINGER.
Howlin' Wolf, alongside Muddy Waters, remains the most legendary of the postwar Chicago bluesmen. Among blues musicians, only Robert Johnson, Waters, and B. B. King have wielded a comparable influence on subsequent popular music in the Western Hemisphere, whether in blues or in rock. Among urban blues giants, Wolf was the one who provided the link to the first generation of acoustic rural Delta bluesmen to record, having played with Charley Patton, Son House, Willie Brown, Sonny Boy Williamson II, and Robert Johnson. Among electric urban blues musicians, Wolf was also the one whose music stayed closest to its rustic Delta origins in the South, in sound and in lyrical imagery. Although relatively late in coming to wider attention, in his forties Wolf quickly became and remained one of Chicago-based Chess Records' most successful urban blues artists through the 1950s. In the 1960s he was discovered by a younger set of white acolytes

Howlin' Wolf, bluesman, 1970s (Diane Allmen, photographer, Living Blues Archival Collection, University of Mississippi Blues Archive, Oxford)

in Britain and the United States, and he had incalculable influence on their blues rock, and later hard rock and heavy metal, music. Hard rock and heavy metal singers' menacing macho braggadocio, many of their vocal stylings, and their stage theatrics are descended from Howlin' Wolf—the man, his voice, his music, his lived persona.

Born Chester Arthur Burnett, on 10 June 1910, at the edge of the Mississippi hill country in White Station just outside West Point, Burnett had an extremely trying childhood at the hands of his ruthless uncle Will Young; his escape from Young's tyranny later fed the imagery of Wolf's signature song and 1956 hit "Smokestack Lightnin'." Burnett's teenage years with his father were a reprieve from the brutality he had suffered in his childhood, which haunted him throughout his life. In January 1928, he received his first guitar and harmonica, a gift from his father, a farmer with whom Wolf continued to work off and on through the 1930s. Burnett received some pointers on guitar from Charley Patton and on the harmonica from the legendary Sonny Boy Williamson II. Unlike those of most other legendary Mississippi bluesmen, though, Wolf's reputation rests largely on his unmistakable voice and not on his instrumental talents. The spectacle at a Howlin' Wolf performance was the man himself.

The young Burnett was particularly impressed by Charley Patton's rough growling vocals. To that influence Wolf added a high falsetto inspired by Tommy Johnson and, surprisingly, the yodeling of hillbilly singer Jimmie Rodgers, born in nearby Meridian, Miss. The final effect had a menace and an ominous potency quite its own, one that made the sobriquet Howlin' Wolf, previously also used by bluesman John T. "Funny Papa" Smith, sit particularly well on Burnett, whose imposing six-foot-three, 275-pound frame only made the bestial associations more credible. Although he actually howled on some of his trademark songs, such as "Smokestack Lightnin'," Wolf's regular singing voice was as attention grabbing—a menacing, brassy rasp, not unlike the sound of a muted trumpet, riding over a deep resonance emanating from the throat. It has been compared to the sounds of throat singing found in some other cultures, but Wolf's voice was unlike any other heard in American popular music. Many subsequent singers in rock, espe-

cially Captain Beefheart, John Fogerty, and Tom Waits, would continue to find inspiration in it.

Through the 1930s Burnett continued to work on his father's farm seasonally, while also traveling around the Delta playing on plantations and at juke joints, at times associating with the aforementioned Delta blues legends. After a harrowing stint in the army during World War II and a brief return to farming, Wolf decided, at age 38, to take a shot at a career as a full-time musician. Moving to West Memphis, Ark., Wolf quickly put together a band that came to be regarded as the best on that side of the state line. A half-hour slot on KWEM in West Memphis brought him to the notice of teenaged talent scout Ike Turner, who brought him to Sam Phillips's attention. Phillips recorded Wolf's earliest sides at his Memphis Recording Service studio in 1951; when Chess acquired Howlin' Wolf's contract, he moved to Chicago, in 1951.

Wolf put together a new band there and launched a rivalry with the already-established doyen of Chicago blues, Muddy Waters, that would continue to Wolf's death. Wolf continued to rival Waters's performance on the regional and national rhythm-and-blues charts through the decade with such classics as "Rockin' Daddy," "Evil," "Smokestack Lightnin'," "Who's Been Talking?," "Sittin' on Top of the World," and "I'm Leavin' You." Although authorship of some songs was credited to Burnett and others reportedly had been part of his Delta repertoire in different forms, the majority were ascribed to the pen of Chess bass player, producer, and songwriter Willie Dixon. Dramatic live performance remained Wolf's forte and distinguished him from the studied reserve of his closest rival, Muddy Waters. Riding a broom in his overalls, licking or mouthing his harmonica, going bug-eyed, crawling and pounding on the floor, and even climbing up the curtains were all part of Wolf's repertoire.

At the turn of the decade, as soul music started displacing urban blues from the African American market, Wolf found a new audience with urban white youth. His music was released in the album format for the first time in January 1959, and, along with many other electric blues artists, Wolf was pitched as a "folk blues" artist. But, unlike many others, he never stripped down to a largely acoustic format. Although a number of musicians, especially guitarists Jody Williams and Willie Johnson, had helped shape the sound of Wolf's band, through the last decade and a half of Wolf's life guitarist Hubert Sumlin's playing became most integral to it. Wolf continued to record even-stronger performances of songs, which would become classics and later standards of blues rock. Between 1960 and 1966 these included "Wang Dang Doodle," "Back Door Man," "Spoonful," "The Red Rooster," "I Ain't Superstitious," "Tail Dragger," "May I Have a Talk with You," "Love Me Darlin'," "Killing Floor," and "Commit a Crime."

During this phase Wolf also traveled to Western and Eastern Europe and Britain as part of the stellar lineup of the 1964 American Folk Blues Festival and appeared on BBC and British TV, followed in May 1965 by a legendary performance on ABC's *Shindig* with the Rolling Stones. Leonard Chess's son Marshall tried to focus Wolf's appeal on the counterculture market in the late 1960s, with variable results. Wolf's 1971 album with his white British blues rock devotees, *The London Howlin' Wolf Sessions*, however, received popular and critical acclaim. Numerous rock bands covered songs written or made famous by Wolf, including the Rolling Stones, the Animals, the Doors, Cream, Jeff Beck Group, Electric Flag, Jimi Hendrix, the Grateful Dead, and, later, Stevie Ray Vaughan. Led Zeppelin had to pay a large sum to Wolf's publishers, ARC, for the inspiration they drew for their "Lemon Song" from Wolf's "Killing Floor."

Despite two heart attacks and failing kidneys from renovascular hypertension, Wolf continued to give his all in each performance until his last one in November 1975. He was diagnosed with metastatic brain carcinoma days before his death. During the ensuing brain surgery, his heart failed. Howlin' Wolf passed away on 10 January 1976. His influence, however, continues to be felt in newer genres—from the grunge of Soundgarden, to the Americana of Lucinda Williams, to the punk blues of Jon Spencer Blues Explosion.

AJAY KALRA
University of Texas at Austin

Peter Guralnick, *Feel Like Going Home: Portraits in Blues and Rock 'n' Roll* (1971), *Lost Highway: Journeys & Arrivals of American Musicians* (1979); James Segrest and Mark Hoffman, *Moanin' at Midnight: The Life and Times of Howlin' Wolf* (2004).

Burnside, R. L.

(1926–2005) BLUES SINGER.

In the early 1990s, R. L. Burnside became an unlikely star of the blues world, largely the result of a unique marketing strategy employed by his label, Fat Possum Records, based in Oxford, Miss. He was born on 23 November 1926 in Harmontown, Miss., north of Oxford, and from ages 7 to 17 lived in Coldwater with his mother and maternal grandparents. His given name appears to have been R. L. His friends often called him "Rule" or "Rural." He began playing guitar as a young man after receiving an instrument from his brother-in-law. His major influence was the Como-based bluesman Mississippi Fred McDowell, who popularized the distinctive north Mississippi style of blues during the 1960s blues revival. Other local influences were Ranie Burnette and Son Hibler.

Shortly after World War II Burnside moved to Chicago, where he often saw performances by Muddy Waters, whose slide guitar technique Burnside adopted. He found Chicago to be too rough for his taste and soon moved back to Mississippi, where he met his wife, Alice Mae, to whom he was married for over 50 years. For much of his adult life, Burnside worked as a cotton sharecropper, drove farm machinery, and worked with commercial fishing, playing music mostly on the weekends.

During the 1950s he served briefly at the Parchman Penitentiary. In a 1994 account, he suggested it was associated with transporting stolen goods. He later said it was for manslaughter committed in self-defense and often joked, "I didn't mean to kill him. I just shot him in the head. His dying was between him and his God." Burnside was famously good-natured and a master storyteller; several of his "toasts" were captured on record.

In 1967 and 1968, folklorist George Mitchell, who was documenting the distinctive musical styles of north Mississippi, recorded Burnside, as well other local artists, including Jessie Mae (Hemphill) Brooks, Joe Callicot, and Othar Turner. Six of Mitchell's recordings of Burnside, including repertoire staples "Poor Black Mattie," "Goin' Down South," and "Long Haired Doney," appeared on the 1969 Arhoolie compilation album *Mississippi Delta Blues, Volume 2*. In 2003 the Fat Possum label issued 14 Burnside recordings made by Mitchell on the CD *First Recordings*.

In the wake of the Arhoolie release, Burnside began appearing at music festivals, including one in Montreal where he met Lightnin' Hopkins and John Lee Hooker, who were both major influences. Over the next several decades, Burnside received relatively little attention in blues circles and, aside from occasional small tours, performed mostly locally, often at juke joints run by fellow Marshall County bluesman David "Junior" Kimbrough and in the company of guitarist and Nesbit native Kenny Brown.

In the late 1970s and early 1980s, Burnside recorded two acoustic albums for the Dutch Swingmaster label and a single with the electric Sound Machine band—which included his sons Joseph and Daniel and son-in-law Calvin Jackson—for folklorist David Evans's

High Water label. Two full CDs of the High Water recordings, *Sound Machine Groove* and *Raw Electric*, were issued many years later.

In the early 1990s, Peter Lee, former editor of *Living Blues* magazine, and Mathew Johnson formed the Oxford-based Fat Possum Records, whose first release was the 1992 Burnside CD *Bad Luck City*. Burnside's live band sound was more accurately captured on the 1994 Fat Possum CD *Too Bad Jim*, which was recorded at Junior Kimbrough's juke joint in Chulahoma. Music scholar and critic Robert Palmer produced both CDs and also narrated the 1993 documentary *Deep Blues*, directed by Robert Mugge, which helped bring broader attention to Burnside, Kimbrough, and other north Mississippi musicians.

Burnside's first two Fat Possum CDs were well received by critics but sold poorly. On the 1996 CD *A Ass Pocket of Whiskey*, Fat Possum embarked on a new marketing strategy by teaming Burnside with the alternative band Jon Spencer and the Blues Explosion and various outside producers who used modern technologies such as sampling and looping. The album—and Fat Possum's marketing of Burnside and other acts as primitives with chaotic lifestyles—was successful in introducing Burnside to alternative rock circles. At the same time he began appearing as a headliner at blues festivals internationally, performing with Kenny Brown on second guitar and his young grandson, Cedric Burnside, on drums.

Fat Possum also used the remix approach on the CDs *Mr. Wizard* (1997) and *Come on In* (1998). A remixed version of the blues standard *Rollin' and Tumblin'* from the latter was featured often in the opening credits of *The Sopranos*. The various studio innovations were not reflected in Burnside's live sound, which was captured on the Fat Possum CD *Burnside on Burnside* (2001). *Wish I Was in Heaven Sitting Down* (2000) and *Bothered Mind* (2004) mixed Burnside's "regular" sound and the remixes of outside producers, and they demonstrated the limitations of creating numerous records based around Burnside's relatively limited repertoire.

In the early 2000s Burnside began suffering from various health problems, which kept him from touring regularly. He died on 1 September 2005 and was buried in Harmontown. Many family members, including sons Duwayne and Garry, grandson Cedric, and his "adopted" son Kenny Brown, have carried on his legacy through recordings and live performances.

SCOTT BARRETTA
Oxford, Mississippi

David Evans, *Sound Machine Groove*, High Water/HMG (1997); Tom Freeland, *Living Blues* (November/December 2005); Michael Pettengell, *Living Blues* (October 1994).

Byrd, Henry (Professor Longhair)

(1918–1980) RHYTHM-AND-BLUES MUSICIAN.

Professor Longhair was a pioneer of the post–World War II New Orleans rhythm-and-blues idiom. Although he made the transition to rock and roll with only modest commercial results, his artistic influence on popular music in the Crescent City was immense.

Professor Longhair, New Orleans rhythm-and-blues musician, 1978 (Hogan Jazz Archive, Tulane University, New Orleans)

Pianist-composer Allen Toussaint dubbed him "the Bach of Rock."

Born in Bogalusa, La., a rural saw-mill town, Henry Roeland Byrd moved to New Orleans as a child. He grew up near Rampart Street, then a musical strip connecting black central-city wards to the downtown neighborhoods. His early exposure to music came in church, which he attended with his mother, who played guitar and piano. For the most part, though, Byrd was self-taught, inspired by blues pianists like Kid "Stormy" Weather, Champion Jack Dupree, and Isidore "Tuts" Washington. As a teenager, Byrd acquired his sense of rhythm by tap dancing. In time, he took the drum-infused movements of his feet and translated them to piano, adding layers of melody to intricate rhythm patterns. Chief among them was boogie-woogie. Another important influence was Sullivan Rock, an obscure honky-tonk pianist about whom little is known.

Byrd—or Fess as fans called him—played with a sizzling left hand, and to this percussive flavor he added "a mixture of mambo, rhumba, and calypso." This fusion resonates in "Go to the Mardi Gras," an anthem that is now a classic and is played on hundreds of jukeboxes during Carnival. His stage name came in 1947 at the Caldonia Inn. The white proprietor announced, "We'll call you Professor Longhair and the Four Hairs Combo." In the early 1950s, recording with Atlantic Records, he cut the memorable "Tipitina." By the late 1960s he had sunk into obscurity, but the following decade saw a gallant comeback. In 1977 friends opened Tipitina's, a club that served as Byrd's home base in New Orleans.

Byrd's albums include *New Orleans Piano, Mardi Gras in New Orleans, The Last Mardi Gras*, and *Crawfish Fiesta*, which was being shipped to record stores when he died on 30 January 1980. The jazz funeral in his honor was one of the largest and most exciting in decades. An excellent video documentary, *Piano Players Seldom Play Together*, features Toussaint, Tuts Washington, and Professor Longhair and includes moving scenes at Byrd's funeral.

JASON BERRY
New Orleans, Louisiana

Jason Berry, Jonathan Foose, and Tad Jones, *Up from the Cradle of Jazz: New Orleans Music since World War II* (1987); John Broven, *Rhythm and Blues in New Orleans* (1978); Jeff Hannusch, *I Hear You Knockin'* (1985); Hal Leonard, ed., *New Orleans Piano Legends* (2000); Robert Palmer, *A Tale of*

Two Cities: Memphis Rock and New Orleans Roll (1979).

Carter Family

COUNTRY ENTERTAINERS.
The Carter Family was one of country music's most influential groups and a valuable link to the music's folk origins. The family was composed of Alvin Pleasant (A. P.) Carter, who was born in Scott County, Va., in 1891; his wife, Sara Dougherty Carter, who was born in Wise County, Va., in 1898; and A. P.'s sister-in-law, Maybelle Addington Carter, who was born at Nickelsville, Va., in 1909. After their marriage, on 18 June 1915, A. P. and Sara began singing for friends and relatives who gathered at their home at Maces Spring in the Clinch Mountains of Virginia. After Maybelle married A. P.'s brother Ezra in 1926, she joined the duo, bringing an exceptional talent for the autoharp, banjo, and guitar.

The trio made their first records for the famous talent scout Ralph Peer and the Victor Company in Bristol, Tenn., on 1 and 2 August 1927. Recording at the same session at which Jimmie Rodgers made his debut, the Carter Family introduced a style of performing that remained recognizable and appealing for many years, and they began circulating a body of songs that still endure in the repertory of modern country musicians. From 1927 to 1943 the Carters popularized their large catalog of gospel, sentimental, and traditional songs at personal appearances, on live radio broadcasts, and on recordings made until 1941 for the Victor, American Record, Decca, and Columbia compa-

nies. Most country and folk music fans still know such Carter Family songs as "Wildwood Flower," "Keep on the Sunny Side," "Worried Man Blues," "I'm Thinking Tonight of My Blue Eyes," and "Will the Circle Be Unbroken."

Vocally, the Carter Family featured Sara's strong soprano lead, Maybelle's alto harmony, and A. P.'s baritone. Instrumentally, the family's distinctive sound was centered around Maybelle's much-copied guitar style, which was often supported by rhythm chords produced by Sara on the autoharp. Although she sometimes played other styles, Maybelle generally used a thumb-brush technique in which the thumb picked the melody on the bass strings while the fingers provided rhythm with a downward stroke of the treble strings. This style was immensely appealing to other guitarists, and her version of "Wildwood Flower" was the model used by most fledgling guitarists when they did their first solo guitar pieces.

Although their records circulated widely, the Carter Family was best known to millions of Americans through their performances over the Mexican border station XERA from 1938 to 1941. During these years the Carter children also began performing, and after 1943, when the original trio officially disbanded, new versions of "the Carter Family" began to emerge. Maybelle began performing with her daughters Helen, June, and Anita (as Mother Maybelle and the Carter Sisters), and by 1950 the group had begun a *Grand Ole Opry* career that would last for 17 years. The Carter Family became more dramatically linked to mainstream country music in 1968 when June Carter married Johnny Cash. Mother Maybelle and her daughters were regular members of Cash's road show until 1973. Neither A. P. nor Sara remained active in music after 1943 (and in fact had separated in 1933), but they did join with their children, Joe and Janette, to make records in 1952 and 1956 for the Acme label.

The Carter Family won renewed respect and recognition during the urban folk revival of the early 1960s from a legion of new fans, who knew them only through their old records and radio transcriptions. Maybelle, however, became an active participant in the folk scene, and in 1967 she and Sara made one album for Columbia called *An Historic Reunion*. A. P. died in 1960, and Maybelle and Sara died within two and a half months of each other in late 1979. The country music industry paid tribute to the trio in 1970 by naming them to the Hall of Fame.

BILL C. MALONE
Madison, Wisconsin

Charles Hirshberg and Mark Zwonitzer, *Will You Miss Me When I'm Gone? The Carter Family and Their Legacy in American Music* (2002); Bill C. Malone, *Country Music, U.S.A.: A Fifty-Year History* (1968; rev. eds., 1985, 2002); Irwin Stambler and Grellin Landon, *The Encyclopedia of Folk, Country, and Western Music* (2d ed., 1983); Charles K. Wolfe, *Tennessee Strings: The Story of Country Music in Tennessee* (1977).

Cash, Johnny

(1932–2003) COUNTRY, FOLK, AND GOSPEL MUSICIAN.
J. R. Cash was born in the small town of Kingsland in the hill country of southern Arkansas. Born to Southern Baptist sharecropping parents, Ray and Carrie Rivers Cash, Johnny spent his youth farming alongside his father and siblings. By the time he was three, the Great Depression had destroyed what little prosperity there was in farming in southern Arkansas, and life for the family there was a struggle. But in 1935 Franklin D. Roosevelt's New Deal administration developed the Dyess Colony Scheme, a project created to give land in northeastern Arkansas bordering the Mississippi River to suffering farm families. In 1936 Cash's family was one of 600 chosen to participate in that program. They moved to Dyess Colony and, working as a family, cleared 20 acres of fertile land in order to grow cotton.

In 1937, when the banks of the Mississippi flooded the area, the Cashes were evacuated, an event that Cash recalled in his 1959 country hit "Five Foot High and Risin.'" "Pickin' Time," "Christmas as I Knew It," and "Look at Them Beans" were among songs Cash later wrote that were inspired by his early years on the farm. In the evenings of his youth, when all the farm chores were done, Cash would sit with his family on the front porch and listen to his mother play guitar and sing hymns and traditional tunes. This was Cash's earliest exposure to music, along with listening in rapt attention to country and gospel singers on his uncle's battery-powered radio.

Cash graduated from high school in 1950, and he set off to Detroit in search of work. He landed in Pontiac, Mich., and began a job at an automotive plant.

His time spent in the North was short-lived, however. He joined the air force, eventually ending up in Landsberg, Germany. It was there that he joined his first band, the Landsberg Barbarians.

In 1954, Cash was discharged from the air force, returned to the United States, and married Vivian Liberto. The newlyweds settled in Memphis, where Cash worked at several jobs—one being as a door-to-door appliance salesman—while trying to break into the music business. It was in that year that he auditioned as a solo gospel artist for Sam Phillips, owner of Sun Records, a label that primarily recorded young men from the Mississippi Delta area. Phillips rejected Cash's gospel music, but the following year found Cash recording his first single for the label, "Hey Porter." Although this was an impressive start to an illustrious career, it was his second single, "Cry, Cry, Cry," that first won national recognition for him. The single topped out on *Billboard*'s Top 20 list at No. 14 and sold over 100,000 copies in the southern states alone. Cash and his sidemen, the Tennessee Two, started touring with Elvis Presley and other Sun Records artists. Soon a string of hit singles, such as "Folsom Prison Blues" and "I Walk the Line," propelled him to become considered the top artist in his field.

By 1958 Cash had published 50 songs. He had sold over six million records for Sun Records by the time he transferred to New York–based Columbia Records and moved his family out to California. Cash's hectic touring and recording schedule in the 1960s took its toll on him, however, and he even-

tually developed a severe addiction to tranquilizers and amphetamines. Spinning out of control, Cash gave up his marriage and life in California and relocated to Hendersonville, Tenn., near Nashville. With the help of his singing partner, June Carter, Cash was able to overcome his addictions. The couple eventually married—a marriage that lasted for 35 years, until her death in 2003.

Over the course of Cash's career, he recorded some of country music's most memorable songs, such as "Ring of Fire," "I Still Love Someone," "Big River," and "Don't Take Your Guns to Town." His imposing figure and trademark of wearing black—thus the nickname, "Man in Black"—made him one of country music's most recognizable figures.

Throughout his career, Cash helped to raise the social awareness of causes such as the plight of Native Americans, prison reform, and the conflict in Vietnam. His 1975 autobiography, *Man in Black*, sold 1.3 million copies. In 1980, at the age of 48, Johnny Cash became the youngest musician ever to be inducted into the Country Music Hall of Fame, and in 1995 he was inducted into the Rock and Roll Hall of Fame, becoming one of the few country musicians to reside within each organization. He died of complications from diabetes at Baptist Hospital in Nashville, Tenn., four short months after the passing of his wife, June.

JAMES G. THOMAS JR.
University of Mississippi

Ken Burke, *Country Music Changed My Life: Tales of Tough Times and Triumph from Country's Legends* (2004); Johnny Cash, *Cash: The Autobiography* (1997); Rosanne Cash, *Cash* (2004); Michael Streissguth, ed., *Ring of Fire: The Johnny Cash Reader* (2002); Dave Urbanski, *The Man Comes Around: The Spiritual Journey of Johnny Cash* (2003); Charles Wolfe, *Classic Country: Legends of Country Music* (2000).

Charles, Ray

(1930–2004) RHYTHM-AND-BLUES MUSICIAN.

Ray Charles's recording career spanned almost 40 years, yet his fame and influence lie with a series of recordings made for Atlantic and ABC-Paramount from 1955 to 1962. These recordings exhibited unprecedented versatility—Charles recorded jazz, blues, gospel, show tunes, and, finally, country and western music. His significance rests primarily on his fusing of gospel with pop and blues styles and, secondarily, his liberation of country and western as a white-only music.

Born 23 September 1930 in Albany, Ga., as Ray Charles Robinson, he and his family moved to Greenville, Fla., where, at the age of six, he developed glaucoma and became blind. His father died when he was young, and when his mother passed away in 1945, Charles turned to music full time to provide a living for himself. Wanting to get away from Florida, he moved to Seattle, Wash., in 1947. There, he dropped his surname to avoid confusion with the boxer Sugar Ray Robinson. In 1948 he made his first records for Bob Geddins's Swingtime label. These first record-

ings were done with a trio made up of Charles's piano plus guitar and bass.

His recordings for Atlantic Records in the early 1970s gradually exhibited less polish and more blues and gospel influence. In late 1953 Charles arranged and played piano on New Orleans guitarist Guitar Slim's monumental "The Things That I Used to Do." Slim's impassioned, gospel-influenced vocal must have set Charles's mind whirring, as his very next sessions were cut in New Orleans without session musicians, and they exhibited a marked gospel feel.

In 1955, in Atlanta, Charles hit his stride. Recording at a local radio station, he cut "I Got a Woman." Featuring horns and a churchy piano rather than the "tasteful" jazz guitar heard on the majority of his earlier cuttings and featuring an unrestrained vocal track replete with falsetto shrieks, the record became a No. 2 rhythm-and-blues hit. Several similar gospel-pop records followed, some written by Charles and many others adapted from extant gospel songs. The Pilgrim Traveler's "I've Got a New Home" became "Lonely Avenue"; Clara Ward's "This Little Light of Mine" became "This Little Girl of Mine"; and the Caravan's "What Kind of a Man Is This, Nobody but You Lord" became simply "Nobody but You."

Charles had effectively created a whole new type of black pop music, which became the basis for the unrestrained soul vocalists of the 1960s. This period of his recording career culminated in the 1959 recording of his self-penned "What I Say." The record opens with a blues gospel electric piano hammering out a Latin-feeling rhythm and builds through a series of fragmentary choruses to extended call and response between Charles and his three-piece female backup vocalists, the Raelets. The record sounds like the re-creation of a revival meeting and was seen, by many at the time, as blasphemy. It nonetheless became a No. 6 pop hit and brought a huge white audience to Charles.

"What I Say" prompted ABC-Paramount Records to entice him away from Atlantic. For the first few years at ABC, Charles continued to record similar material, although gradually the Ralph Burns Orchestra increasingly made its presence felt. "Georgia on My Mind," Charles's 1960 version of Hoagy Carmichael's "Georgia," was his biggest hit in this period.

The year 1962 saw the release of a revolutionary album entitled *Modern Sounds in Country and Western Music*, with several ensuing hit singles, including "I Can't Stop Loving You" and "You Don't Know Me." At the time, the idea of a black jazz-blues-soul artist recording white country music was extremely daring. Nevertheless, the album went on to sell 3 million copies and further established Charles with a middle-of-the-road white audience.

After Charles's early 1960s' successes, his output was steady but somewhat less original, a pastiche of contemporary pop hits, nostalgic sentimental tunes, Broadway standards, and the odd blues. In 1968 he formed his label, Tangerine Records, which was distributed by ABC-Paramount, and in 1973 he formed the independent Crossover Records (an apt name), which was later distributed by Atlantic. On 24 April 1979, Charles's

version of "Georgia on My Mind" was proclaimed the state song of Georgia.

During Charles's lengthy career, he starred on over 250 records and appeared in the hit film *The Blues Brothers* (1980) and several television commercials. He received numerous honorary awards, was one of the original inductees into the Rock and Roll Hall of Fame, and was also inducted into the Jazz Hall of Fame and the Rhythm and Blues Hall of Fame.

Ray Charles died on 10 June 2004 from complications of liver disease. "We lost a genius and we lost my brother," James Brown said. "You've lost a cornerstone of good, and that hurts real bad." The film *Ray*, based on his life story and starring Jamie Foxx as Charles, opened in October 2004.

ROBERT BOWMAN
Memphis, Tennessee

Ray Charles, *Ray Charles: A Man and His Soul* (1999), with David Ritz, *Brother Ray: Ray Charles' Own Story* (1978); Tony Cummings, in *The Soul Book*, ed. Ian Hoare (1975); Gerri Hershey, *Nowhere to Run: The Story of Soul Music* (1984); Susan Sloate, *Ray Charles: Find Another Way!* (2006).

Chenier, Clifton

(1925–1988) ZYDECO MUSICIAN.
Born 25 June 1925 near Opelousas in Saint Landry Parish, La., Clifton Chenier became the nation's premier zydeco performer. His father, Joseph, played the accordion, and he took his sons Clifton and Cleveland to local parties where he performed. The two boys themselves started playing at a young age—Clifton the accordion his father gave him, and Cleveland his

mother's rub board. In the early 1940s they performed with Clarence Garlow's group in clubs around Lake Charles, La., and in 1947 Clifton left home and joined his brother in Lake Charles. The two worked at the oil refineries in Port Arthur, Tex., and formed the Hot Sizzling Band, which played along the Texas-Louisiana Gulf Coast in the late 1940s and early 1950s.

J. R. Fulbright, a talent scout for Elko Records in California, met Chenier in 1954 and made the first recording of his music. During the middle and late 1950s, Chenier recorded for the Imperial, Specialty, Chess, Argo, Checker, and Zynn labels, and he and his band toured not only in the Southwest but on the West Coast and in Chicago.

Known mostly as a rhythm-and-blues artist in the early 1960s, Chenier returned to his south Louisiana roots after signing with Chris Strachwitz's Arhoolie Records in 1964 and recording zydeco music on such albums as *Louisiana Blues and Zydeco*, *Bon Ton Roulet*, *King of the Bayous*, and *Bogalusa Boogie*. He recorded the classic zydeco song "Oh! Lucille" in 1966 for Crazy Cajun Records in Pasadena, Tex. In the late 1960s Chenier toured widely, including appearances at the Berkeley Blues Festival (1966), the Newport Folk Festival (1969), and in Europe (1967–69). In the 1970s his name became synonymous with the best in zydeco, and he remained a popular performer in rhythm-and-blues clubs as well.

Known as the "Black King of the South" and the "King of Zydeco," Chenier performed wearing a crown and leading his sometimes-raucous group, the Louisiana Hot Band. Poor health from a kidney infection plagued him in 1979, but he returned to better health in the early 1980s. He continued to play east Texas–southern Louisiana clubs and performed nationally as well until his death. Les Blank's *Dry Wood and Hot Peppers* (Flower Films, 1973) captured Chenier in performance and in his off-stage lifestyle.

CHARLES REAGAN WILSON
University of Mississippi

Barry Jean Ancelet, *The Makers of Cajun Music / Musiciens Cadiens et Créoles* (1984); Shane K. Bernard, *Swamp Pop: Cajun and Creole Rhythm and Blues* (1996); John Broven, *South to Louisiana: The Music of the Cajun Bayous* (1983); Sheldon Harris, *Blues Who's Who: A Biographical Dictionary of Blues Singers* (1979).

Cline, Patsy

(1932–1963) COUNTRY SINGER.
Patsy Cline, born Virginia Patterson Hensley on 8 September 1932, was one of the first country-and-western entertainers to become successful on both the country and popular music charts. Her first big success was winning the *Arthur Godfrey Talent Scouts* contest in January 1957 with her hit song, "Walkin' after Midnight." Over the next six years, Cline became the highest-ranked female singer with the *Grand Ole Opry* and achieved such popular success that Bill C. Malone has called her "the first woman to dethrone Kitty Wells from her position as 'queen of country music.'"

Virginia Hensley grew up in Winchester, Va., where she displayed a talent for music early in life. She played the

Patsy Cline, country music star, 1957 (Country Music Foundation, Library and Media Center, Nashville)

guitars with background voices and smooth instrumentation. Among Cline's biggest hits were "I Fall to Pieces" (1960), "Crazy" (1961), and "She's Got You" (1961). She received numerous awards, including *Billboard* magazine's Favorite Female Artist and Cash Box's Most Programmed Album in 1962. She was elected to the Country Music Hall of Fame in 1973.

Cline's career was cut short tragically in March of 1963 with her death in a plane crash. She remains a popular country music figure, and her records have continued to be released and are sold worldwide. She was a prominent character in Loretta Lynn's autobiography, *Coal Miner's Daughter*, the successful screen version of which premiered in 1980. Patsy Cline's own life was portrayed in *Sweet Dreams* (1985), starring Jessica Lange as the legendary vocalist.

KAREN M. MCDEARMAN
University of Mississippi

Stuart E. Brown Jr., *Patsy Cline, Singing Girl from the Shenandoah Valley* (1996); Doug Hall, *The Real Patsy Cline* (1998); Margaret Jones, *Patsy: The Life and Times of Patsy Cline* (1999); Bill C. Malone, *Country Music, U.S.A.: A Fifty-Year History* (1968; rev. eds., 1985, 2002); Brian Mansfield, *Remembering Patsy* (2003); Ellis Nassour, *Honky Tonk Angel: The Intimate Story of Patsy Cline* (1994), *Patsy Cline* (1981).

piano and cultivated an intense interest in country music, dedicating herself to becoming a serious singer when she was a young teenager. Bill Peer, a disc jockey and musician with ties in Nashville, has been credited with giving Patsy Cline her first professional break as well as her first stage name, in 1952. In the spring of 1953 Patsy Hensley married Gerald Cline, a contractor she met during one of her performances. Though they divorced in January 1957 and she married Charlie Dick in September of the same year, Cline kept the name under which she had had her first commercial success.

Cline's music was characteristic of the traditional style in country music and was also a part of the "Nashville Sound," a calculated attempt by the country music industry to attract new listeners from the pop market while retaining the older ones. Innovations included replacing fiddles and steel

Coltrane, John

(1926–1967) JAZZ MUSICIAN.
Jazz saxophonist John Coltrane is one of the most significant and controversial figures in the history of jazz. Although his formal career spanned only 12 years (1955–1967), he recorded prolifically in

his lifetime, leaving much material for posthumous release. The trajectory of Coltrane's career moved from his earlier, more conventional (although still intensely creative) approach to jazz, to his later, highly experimental style. Critics debate the supremacy of these two phases, with each mode finding staunch adherents.

Born in Hamlet, N.C., in 1926, Coltrane was the son of John R. Coltrane, a tailor and amateur musician, and Alice (Blair) Coltrane. When he was two months old, his maternal grandfather was promoted to presiding elder at the AME Zion church and moved the family to High Point, N.C. Coltrane spent his childhood in High Point, enjoying comparative privilege as part of the black middle class during an era of racial segregation. During his seventh-grade year, in 1939, the Blair-Coltrane family suffered the deaths of maternal grandparents, Coltrane's father, and an uncle, who had also brought in income to support the family. These tragedies brought financial crisis, forcing Coltrane's mother and aunt to find domestic service work in white households. During this difficult period Coltrane learned to play music and began the vigorous practice regimen that he would be known for in later years. He initially joined a community band where he learned to play the E-flat alto horn and then the clarinet. Around age 15, Coltrane joined his high school band, where he took up the alto saxophone, and also sang in the boys chorus.

Coltrane's southern middle-class upbringing profoundly affected his artistic and personal development in several key ways. First, Coltrane was raised in the church and by church elders, and he grew up understanding spirituality as the centerpiece of individual life and connection to the universe. This emphasis on spirituality would serve Coltrane as he coped with addiction and experimented with other religions and the manifestation of the spiritual in his musical compositions. Second, Coltrane was exposed in school chorus and band to complex arrangements and modes of Western music, a training that helped him cultivate a level of musical sophistication that allowed him to examine, incorporate, and challenge these forms. Coltrane also heard jazz for the first time in High Point, on the radio, at the movies, and on jukeboxes.

During World War II, Coltrane's mother and aunt traveled north, in the midst of the Great Migration, to New Jersey, in search of better employment opportunities, leaving Coltrane in the care of family friends in High Point. After graduating from high school in 1943, Coltrane also headed north to Philadelphia, where he was eventually reunited with his family. While working odd jobs, he briefly attended the Ornstein School of Music and studied at Granoff Studios. During this period, he also began playing in local clubs. In 1945 he was drafted into the navy and was stationed in Hawaii, where he played in the navy band and made his first recording with a quartet of other sailors. Coltrane returned to Philadelphia in 1946 and played with several bands, including both a big band and a septet with Dizzy Gillespie from 1949 to 1951. He switched during this period from alto to tenor saxophone, possibly because of the instrumental configurations of the bands that he was in, and became addicted to heroin, which made him difficult to employ.

In the early 1950s, Coltrane would continue to struggle to keep work because of his drug problem. It was his association with Miles Davis, a former heroin addict, that altered the course of his career and established him as an important jazz musician. His work with Davis also initiated a period during which he began to record as a sideman. Although Davis and Coltrane recorded a number of albums, Davis fired Coltrane several times for reasons related to his drugs. One of these firings may ultimately have been the impetus for Coltrane's efforts to quit taking heroin, which he successfully accomplished in 1957. At this time, he also recorded for the first time as band leader and began to play with the Thelonious Monk Quartet. In a review of his performances with Davis and Monk in 1958, critic Ira Gitler coined the phrase "sheets of sound" to describe Coltrane's unique playing—a phrase often invoked by Coltrane critics and listeners since. In 1959, Coltrane played on the Davis album *Kind of Blue*, one of the best-selling and most acclaimed albums in jazz history. Soon after, he began recording his Atlantic Records debut, *Giant Steps*, which consisted entirely of his own compositions. After its release in early 1960, Coltrane recorded a series of sessions for Atlantic that would produce several albums, including the critically praised *My Favorite Things* (1961).

Signing as the flagship artist of the new Impulse! label, Coltrane became increasingly experimental in the early 1960s, with formless, extended solos evident in famous recordings like *Live at the Village Vanguard* (1961). His controversial experiments attracted large audiences and led him on a constant quest for new sounds. His increasing dedication to spirituality can be seen in *A Love Supreme* (1964), an expression of faith in and love for higher powers. Coltrane's philosophy of jazz was a spiritual inspiration to his fans, as he experimented with music as a representation of the entire self and a mode of spiritual connection to the many world faiths. He was known for his support of younger avant-garde musicians, his passionate religious convictions, and his obsessive striving for musical ideals. John Coltrane died in 1967 at age 40 of liver disease.

FRANCES ABBOTT
Emory University

Ashley Khan, *A Love Supreme: The Story of John Coltrane's Signature Album* (2002); Eric Nisenson, *Ascension: John Coltrane and His Quest* (1993); Lewis Porter, *John Coltrane: His Life and Music* (1998); J. C. Thomas, *Chasin' the Trane* (1975); Carl Woideck, ed., *The John Coltrane Companion* (1998).

Cooke, Sam

(1931–1964) SOUL SINGER.
Sam Cooke is widely credited with having played a major role in the invention and popularization of soul music. After an early-1950s stint as lead vocalist for the Soul Stirrers, an acclaimed African American gospel singing group, Cooke, during the late 1950s and early 1960s, became not only one of the best-

selling black performers in secular popular music but also a successful and widely respected songwriter, music publisher, and record company owner.

Samuel (nicknamed "Sam") Cook (the "e" was added to his last name at the beginning of his solo music career) was born on 22 January 1931, in Clarksdale, Miss., the fourth of seven children, to Rev. Charles and Annie May Cook. Cooke spent his first few years immersed in the diverse musical traditions associated with Clarksdale, a small city that was more economically prosperous and socially diverse than most other communities in the Mississippi Delta. Cooke's earliest memories included joining the congregation at his father's Church of Christ Holiness services in the singing of traditional and newer sacred songs, as well as listening to blues performers on Clarksdale's streets.

In 1933, the Cooks moved to "Bronzeville," a section of south Chicago with a dense concentration of African American migrants from the South (an estimated 300,000 blacks had settled in "Bronzeville" by 1945). Rev. Cook worked in Chicago's stockyards to sustain his family economically and was named pastor of a Holiness church in the Chicago Heights neighborhood. Young Sam sang African American gospel songs in church—often with his siblings in a vocal group called the Singing Children. He eventually performed popular songs of that era on nearby streets for tips, and he became familiar with jazz.

While traveling during the 1940s with their preacher father, the Singing Children gained experience performing gospel songs for audiences across the United States. When the family group disbanded, Sam Cooke began to sing with neighborhood friends, imitating such popular vocal groups as the Ink Spots. Cooke joined the Teenage Highway QCs (later shortened to The Highway QCs), an a cappella vocal gospel group that became associated with the Soul Stirrers.

In 1949, after graduating from high school, Cooke began touring with the QCs. Eventually settling in Memphis, the group performed frequently on radio station WDIA and gave concerts in local churches and other venues. In 1950 the 19-year-old Cooke became the lead vocalist of the Soul Stirrers. In his first recording session for specialty Records, his lead singing on "Jesus Gave Me Water" helped it become a national gospel hit. Cooke became a gospel star with the Soul Stirrers and was widely admired for his exciting, smooth voice and his charisma. He left the group in 1956, after recording his first solo single (featuring a secular song "Loveable").

Cooke also knew that whites across the country were discovering African American music. Recordings by some rhythm-and-blues acts had been selling well among whites since the early 1950s. By the mid-1950s white singers were having major hits with songs written by blacks. By 1957 white performers had co-opted African American musical genres and styles to such an extent that relatively few black musicians were successfully competing with white rock-and-roll and pop acts on the national Top 40 pop music chart. Cooke became the musical figure most responsible for the full integration of blacks into mainstream American popular music through the early 1960s.

By 1956, feeling artistically and financially constrained by gospel music, Cooke sought to make recordings that appealed equally to blacks and whites. Accordingly, in late spring 1957, he entered a Los Angeles studio and recorded a secular single featuring Sam's cover of the classic Gershwin-Heyward song "Summertime" and "You Send Me," his own song composition. The latter caught the public's attention, becoming a major national hit, first on the rhythm-and-blues chart and then on the pop chart (ultimately reaching No. 1 on both charts). Cooke subsequently recorded a string of crossover hits for Keen Records, including such songs as "For Sentimental Reasons" (1957), "Only Sixteen" (1959), and "(What a) Wonderful World" (1960). In 1960 he signed with a major label—RCA—and recorded several more significant hits (most of which he had written), including "Chain Gang" (1960), "Cupid" (1961), "Twistin' the Night Away" (1962), "Bring It On Home to Me" (1962), "Another Saturday Night" (1963), and "Shake" (1964). In addition to being a major black singer and songwriter, Cooke was the first African American to establish his own music publishing company (Kags Music) and recording label (Sar Records), both founded in 1959.

Sam Cooke died on 11 December 1964, under mysterious circumstances, after being shot at a Los Angeles motel. His final hit, the self-penned "A Change Is Gonna Come," became an unofficial anthem of the civil rights movement.

Cooke was one of the initial inductees into the Rock and Roll Hall of Fame, in 1986. In 1987 he was inducted into the Songwriters Hall of Fame, and in 1999 he was honored as the recipient of the Rhythm and Blues Foundation's first Legacy Tribute Award.

TED OLSON
East Tennessee State University

Peter Guralnick, *Dream Boogie: The Triumph of Sam Cooke* (2005); Daniel Wolff, with S. R. Crain, Clifton White, and G. David Tenenbaum, *You Send Me: The Life and Times of Sam Cooke* (1995).

Daniels, Charlie

(b. 1936) COUNTRY-ROCK SINGER. Charlie Daniels, a native of Wilmington, N.C., became one of the leading exponents of southern rock music in the 1970s. In 1967, after more than a decade as an obscure veteran of the southern club circuit, Daniels began working as a studio-session musician in Nashville. His most notable session work occurred in the period from 1969 to 1971, when he backed rock star Bob Dylan on a series of albums.

In 1971 Daniels formed his own band, and a year later he experienced substantial record sales with a satirical single release, "Uneasy Rider." The song and the album on which it appeared helped introduce Daniels to rock audiences, though he continued to live and record in Nashville. Daniels was a versatile performer who most often played guitar or fiddle. His dynamic work on the fiddle reinforced his identification as a country artist. From 1973 to 1977 Daniels gained little recognition as a recording artist, due undoubtedly to his position in between rock and country. In 1975 he reemerged as a successful recording artist, with a best-selling album, *Fire on the Mountain*, and a hit single, "The South's Gonna Do It Again." By the mid-1970s country rock had become a potent commercial subgenre within country music, and Daniels had established himself as an exemplar of the sound. In addition, "The South's Gonna Do It Again" became a veritable anthem of the southern rock movement. Daniels was perhaps the preeminent musical spokesman of the region.

Daniels's albums include *Night Rider* (1975), *High Lonesome* (1976), and *Saddle Tramp* (1976). In 1979 Daniels released *Million Mile Reflections*, an album that rapidly gained platinum status (over 1 million units sold) and also yielded one of the most popular single recordings of the decade, "The Devil Went Down to Georgia." A quintessential Daniels number, it reflected the southern folk tradition in both content and style but tapped the contemporary rock idiom for most of its rhythmic impetus. The single won a Grammy and three Country Music Award trophies, became a staple of the *Urban Cowboy* movie sound track, and pushed *Million Mile Reflections* album sales to triple-platinum status.

The title for the album marked a milestone in Daniels's touring career. His band made legendary coast-to-coast tours, regularly spending 250 days of the year on the road, and by the time of the album's release the band had logged more than one million miles of touring.

By 1981 the Charlie Daniels Band had been twice voted the Academy of Country Music's touring band of the year.

Full Moon, issued in 1980, became Daniels's third Platinum album, followed by *Simple Man* (1989), which is also platinum. He earned a Dove Award from the Gospel Music Association in 1994 for *The Door* and a 1997 Country Music Award nomination for his remake of "Long Haired Country Boy," featuring John Berry and Hal Ketchum. *Amazing Grace: A Country Salute to Gospel*, a compilation album, which includes Daniels's "Kneel at the Cross," garnered a 1995 Grammy award. In 1998 he was honored with the Pioneer Award by the Academy of Country Music.

Daniels often generated controversy, for his outspoken political views—he was one of the few Nashville artists to openly oppose the Vietnam War and campaigned ardently for Jimmy Carter in 1976 and 1980—and for his spirited defense of country music against such critics as jazz musician Stan Kenton. In 2003 Daniels published an *Open Letter to the Hollywood Bunch* in defense of George W. Bush's Iraq policy. His 2003 book *Ain't No Rag: Freedom, Family, and the Flag* includes this letter, along with other personal statements. He performed for U.S. military troops at a USO concert at Camp Victory in Iraq on 10 April 2005.

Perhaps Daniels's most impressive contribution to southern music has been the Volunteer Jams, a popular series of concerts held annually in Murfreesboro, Tenn. This musical extravaganza has served as the prototype for contemporary daylong music marathons featuring current and heritage stars across the South and the nation. Few individuals have symbolized the South in popular culture as directly and indelibly as Charlie Daniels. Daniels now resides in Mount Juliet, Tenn., where the city has named a park after him.

STEPHEN R. TUCKER
Tulane University

Bob Allen, *Country Music* (April 1980); Charlie Daniels, *Ain't No Rag: Freedom, Family, and the Flag* (2003), *Open Letter to the Hollywood Bunch* (2003); Russell Shaw, *Country Music* (March 1977).

Dawson, William Levi

(1899–1990) COMPOSER AND EDUCATOR.
Born 26 September 1899 in Anniston, Ala., William Levi Dawson became interested in music at an early age, particularly the rhythms and music of his African American heritage. He ran away from home at the age of 13 to attend the Tuskegee Institute, where Booker T. Washington was headmaster. At Tuskegee, Dawson learned to appreciate hard work, joining the band and the choir, in addition to his academic lessons and shifts in the fields surrounding the school.

After graduating from Tuskegee in 1921, Dawson taught band at Kansas Vocational College for a year, before becoming the choir director at Lincoln High School in Kansas City. He met artist Aaron Douglass, another teacher at Lincoln High School, who would become a lifelong friend. Although teaching full time, Dawson continued his education at the Horner Institute of Fine Arts. The institute's policies on segregation forced him to study privately with professors at night and excluded him from his own graduation ceremony in 1925.

William Levi Dawson began composing and arranging while he was a teenager. In 1921, he published his first piece, "Forever Thine," and sold it door-to-door. In order to persuade potential buyers, he sang the piece himself. Dawson also arranged African American spirituals for his high school choir, leading to the publication of "King Jesus Is A-Listening" in 1925.

Dawson moved to Chicago to continue his studies in music. He earned a master of music in composition at the American Conservatory of Music in 1927. He joined the Civic Orchestra of Chicago as its first chair trombonist and only African American member. He also participated in the thriving jazz scene, playing in Charlie "Doc" Cook's dance band, Doctors of Syncopation.

In 1928, Dawson began work on a symphony. Inspired by Antonín Dvořák's *New World Symphony*, he wanted to produce a work that gave voice to the music of his ancestors, friends, and neighbors in rural Alabama. Dawson titled the piece the *Negro Folk Symphony*. It premiered on 20 November 1934 under the baton of renowned conductor Leopold Stokowski. Dawson produced another version of the symphony in 1956. The new symphony incorporated the rhythms and sounds he had heard during a trip to West Africa.

Although Dawson was a successful composer, he remained committed to education. In 1930 he returned to the Tuskegee Institute to organize a formal school of music. Dawson established a program that reflected both Tuskegee's heritage as a vocational school and its future as a center for higher learning, hiring faculty members with impressive credentials yet remaining committed to a strong music education program. Shortly thereafter, on 21 September 1935, he married Cecile Demae Nicholson in Atlanta, in the home of artist Hale Woodruff.

Under Dawson's direction, the Tuskegee Institute Choir became one of the most popular choirs of its generation. The 100-voice choir appeared at the opening of Radio City Music Hall in New York in 1932, sang for both Herbert Hoover and Franklin D. Roosevelt, and was the first African American performing organization to appear at Constitution Hall in Washington, D.C., in 1946, breaking a long-standing race barrier. Dawson arranged a number of African American spirituals for his choir. These spirituals are possibly Dawson's greatest legacy and remain perennial favorites of audiences and choirs around the world.

Dawson retired from the Tuskegee Institute in 1956. He continued to publish and conduct after his retirement. Committed to educating audiences about African American music, he led seminars and guest-conducted high school and college choirs. William Levi Dawson died on 2 May 1990, in Montgomery, Ala., at the age of 90.

ELIZABETH RUSSEY
Emory University

William Levi Dawson Papers, Emory University, Manuscript, Archives, and Rare Book Library, Atlanta, Ga.; Mark Hugh Malone, "William Levi Dawson: American Music Educator" (Ph.D. diss., Florida State University, 1981).

Diddley, Bo

(1928–2008) BLUES AND R&B SINGER. Combining R&B and blues with an eccentric onstage performance, Bo Diddley is often considered one of the pioneers of rock-and-roll music. Diddley was named Otha Ellas Bates at birth on 30 December 1928, in McComb, Miss. He never knew his father, Eugene Bates. His mother, Ethel Wilson, was only 15 or 16 years old when Ellas was born. Ethel's first cousin Gussie McDaniel raised Ellas while the family tried to make a living as sharecroppers. In 1934, in the midst of the Great Depression, the family moved to Chicago, where Ellas started to develop an interest in music. His first instrument was a violin, and he took lessons with classical teacher O. W. Frederick. He also taught himself to play other instruments, such as the drums and the trombone.

At age 12 Ellas received his first guitar, a Christmas present from his stepsister Lucille. John Lee Hooker had already become one his heroes, and Ellas wanted to play just like him. But he had trouble strumming the guitar in a regular way. "I couldn't play the guitar like everyone else," Diddley later said in an interview. "Guitarists have skinny fingers. I didn't. I play drum licks on the guitar." This music style would evolve into the distinctive "shave-and-a-haircut-six-bits" rhythm that would characterize most of Bo Diddley's repertoire.

Ellas probably started to use the name "Bo Diddley" around 1940. Where this moniker originated is uncertain—it might have been Ellas's nickname during his brief boxing career or it may refer to a harmonica player he saw in Mississippi or to the southern folk instrument, the diddley bow. Not even Bo Diddley himself knows the origins of his stage name. "I don't know," he said. "The kids gave me that name when I was in grammar school in Chicago."

While he was still in high school, Diddley formed his first band, named the Hipsters. The group, which later changed its name to the Langley Avenue Jive Cats, performed on the street corners and in clubs in Chicago. Jerome Green played the maraca and Billy Boy Arnold joined the band as harmonica player. In 1955, Diddley cut a demo of two songs, "Uncle John" and "I'm a Man," and took it to the Chess Records studio, one of Chicago's preeminent blues labels. Leonard and Phillip Chess liked the music, but they could not really appreciate the lyrics of "Uncle John," which they viewed as derogatory to blacks. They suggested that Diddley change the words, which he did. The song "Bo Diddley" was born, and it reached the top of the R&B charts when it was released as a single in 1955. The rumba-like beat was trademark Bo Diddley. "When I used to walk from spot to spot looking for work, everybody played like T-Bone Walker and those cats, so I tried something different," Diddley explained. This innovative music style would launch his music career.

After the success of "Bo Diddley," other hits followed, such as "Diddley Daddy" and "You Can't Judge a Book by Its Cover." Diddley rocked the stage with his peculiar moves, flamboyant suits, and his square guitars, which he made himself. British bands like the Beatles and the Rolling Stones were influenced by his music, and the Animals celebrated him in their song "The Story of Bo Diddley," calling him "the rock 'n' roll senior general." Later artists, such as Bruce Springsteen and U2, also found inspiration in Diddley's songs, but by the time these latter artists became popular Bo Diddley's fame had waned considerably. He reached the zenith of his career during the 1950s and early 1960s, when he was one of the founding fathers of rock-and-roll music.

Diddley himself believed that the impact he had on the development of rock and roll is underestimated. "What gets me is when white brothers started playing guitars and sounding like us, and folks said that Elvis started rock 'n' roll," he said in an interview. "Well, let me tell you Elvis ain't started a damn thing. I love what he did. But he came three years after me. I was already breaking records at the Apollo Theater."

During the 1970s, when his career was on a downhill slope, Diddley went to New Mexico, where he served as a deputy sheriff. In 1987, the same year he was inducted into the Rock and Roll Hall of Fame, he moved to the Gainesville area in Florida. Around that time his popularity again started to rise. Diddley performed at the inaugurations of Presidents George H. W. Bush and Bill Clinton, and his 1996 album *A Man amongst Men*, which featured renowned musicians such as Jimmie Vaughan and Keith Richards, received a nomination for a Grammy award. But the bitterness remained. "When kids hear me play now they say, 'Hey, you sound like so-and-so.' Wow, that's an insult; it's degrading. They don't know I started the sound and the so-and-so's copied me," Diddley explained. "When I hear that, it's a bad feeling, a hurting feeling. I ask myself why I'm still out here performing when all that has happened is that I've been forgotten."

MAARTEN ZWIERS
University of Mississippi

Richard Weinraub, *New York Times* (16 February 2003); George R. White, *Bo Diddley: Living Legend* (1995).

"Dixie"

The word "Dixie" has been a part of the American vocabulary ever since it appeared in the song "Dixie's Land." The song, though closely associated with the history of the South, is not of southern origin. Both tune and text were written by Ohio native Daniel D. Emmett in 1859, shortly before the outbreak of the Civil War. The song immediately gained popularity, first in the North, then as a "battle hymn" in the secessionist Confederate states. The word "Dixie" even became a synonym for the South.

What was compelling about the tune was its blend of incisiveness and exhilaration, giving force to such sentences as "Den I wish I was in Dixie, Hooray! Hooray! In Dixie Land, I'll took my stand, To lib an die in Dixie." The song was commissioned by Bryant's Minstrel Troupe, a highly successful company, and was performed for the first time in New York on Broadway on 4 April 1859 under the title "Plantation Song and Dance, / Dixie's Land / Introducing the whole Troupe in the Festival Dance." The scene involved voices (solo and group alternating), with instrumental accompaniment, and steps and gestures in imitation of black plantation dances. It was pure entertainment, amply supported by the comedy style of all six stanzas. The protagonist was a black, who, following a minstrel tradition, expressed his yearning for the never-never land of the southern plantation, a view with special appeal to a white audience.

After the theatrical event came a swift transformation of "Dixie's Land." With the accents and tempo of a quick-step, it became a fierce military statement. Confederate soldiers used new words, such as "Southrons, hear your country call you," but sections of the original were retained.

The origin of the word "Dixie" has not yet been determined; there is no evidence of its existence as a name on southern plantations. Yet it was known to entertainers, for a playbill of 1850 listed a play (probably blackface) "The United States Mail and Dixie [a post-boy] in Difficulty." Continuing a trend of early black minstrel music, the tune of "Dixie's Land" includes elements of British folk song, with an Irish hornpipe pattern at the beginning and traces of Scotch tunes in the second part.

HANS NATHAN
Arlington Heights, Massachusetts

Hans Nathan, *Dan Emmett and the Rise of Early Negro Minstrelsy* (1962; 2d ed., 1977); Howard L. Sacks and Judith Rose Sacks, *Way Up North in Dixie: A Black Family's Claim to the Confederate Anthem* (1993); John A. Simpson, *Southern Folklore Quarterly* (1981); Cheryl Thurber, "'Dixie': The Cultural History of a Song and Place" (Ph.D. diss., University of Mississippi, 1993).

Dixie Chicks

COUNTRY MUSIC GROUP.
The Dixie Chicks will likely be remembered more for an intemperate but prophetic remark one of their members made than for the quality of their music. The core and cofounders of the Chicks are sisters Martha "Martie" Erwin Maguire (born 12 October 1969 in York, Penn.) and Emily Erwin Robison (born 16 August 1972 in Pittsfield, Mass.). The final and newest member of the trio is lead vocalist Natalie Maines Pasdar (born 14 October 1974 in Lubbock, Tex.).

Formed in 1989 in Dallas, the Chicks initially included two members besides the Erwin sisters: bass player Laura Lynch and guitarist Robin Macy. All four sang. Working as street musicians, they became fairly popular even before they chose a name for themselves. At first, they dubbed themselves the Dixie Chickens (after the Little Feat song) but soon shortened it to Dixie Chicks. Their music made them a favorite of the family of Texas senator John Tower and his daughter, Penny Cook, who, according to biographer James L. Dickerson, loaned them the money to make their first album, *Thank Heavens for Dale Evans*, in 1991.

The women made two more albums on their own, *Little Ol' Cowgirl* (1992) and *Shouldn't a Told You That* (1993), before they succeeded in signing with a major country label. Macy left the group in 1992 over artistic and personality differences. Their growing popularity landed the trio a deal with Monument Records (a division of Sony Music) in 1995, and they immediately began working up material for their debut album. Lloyd Maines, the highly regarded Texas musician and producer, had been working with the Chicks, and through him they first heard his daughter Natalie sing. Four months after they signed the Monument contract, the Erwin sisters informed Lynch they wanted to buy out her share in the group and replace her as lead vocalist with Natalie Maines.

Wide Open Spaces, the Chicks' first album for Monument, came out in 1998. Almost immediately, they became a media sensation. Three singles from the album went No. 1, beginning with "There's Your Trouble," and two others reached Top 10. The album also won a Grammy for Best Country Album. *Fly*, the next collection, also earned a Grammy for Best Country Album, as did the succeeding ones, *Home* and *Taking the Long Way*.

In 2001 the Dixie Chicks sued Sony, alleging underpayment of royalties and asking to be released from their contract with the label. Sony countersued, and eventually an agreement was reached in which the Chicks would continue to record for the label but sever their ties with its Nashville division and assume artistic control over subsequent albums.

At a concert in London in March

2003, just before the United States invaded Iraq, Maines made the off-the-cuff remark that she was ashamed that President George W. Bush was from her home state of Texas. The comment caused a furor among conservative country music fans. Their resentment was fuelled and magnified by hostile remarks from disc jockeys. Many radio stations—including entire chains—refused to play the Chicks' records, and there were even public burnings of their albums. (In fact, the Chicks had played for Bush's inauguration as governor of Texas in 1995, although before Maines became a member.)

The backlash was so strong that the Chicks' record sales plummeted and concerts had to be cancelled. As the war dragged on, however, and American casualties mounted, the Chicks' opposition to the war, mild as it was, appeared justified. Ultimately, if polls and elections are to be believed, it became the prevailing opinion among Americans.

Barbara Kopple and Cecilia Peck's 2006 documentary *Shut Up and Sing* tells the story of the backlash and of the creation of *Taking the Long Way*. In a move interpreted by many as a slap against Bush and the Iraq war, Grammy voters named *Taking the Long Way* not just the country album of the year but the album of the year among all popular music genres.

EDWARD MORRIS
Former country music editor of
Billboard

James L. Dickerson, *Dixie Chicks: Down-Home and Backstage* (2000); Joel Whitburn, *Top Country Songs: 1944 to 2005* (2006).

Dixie Hummingbirds

GOSPEL MUSIC GROUP.

The Dixie Hummingbirds, a gospel "quartet," most of whose members were from South Carolina, began their long recording career in the late 1930s with the selection "When the Gates Swing Open" (Decca 7645). Ira Tucker, their famous lead singer, joined the group in 1940, soon followed by Willie Bobo, their well-known bass singer. The Birds, as they came to be known, consisted by 1945 of James Walker, Ira Tucker, William Bobo, Beachey Thompson, and James Davis, the original leader. Guitarist Howard Carroll joined the quartet in the early 1950s. (Male groups were usually referred to as "quartets," even though most of them consisted of five or six members.)

The recording of black quartets singing spirituals and gospel songs began with the Dinwiddie Colored Quartet's 1902 Victor recording of "Down on the Old Camp Ground." The performing style, musical structure, and vocal literature of quartets changed in the 1930s, and the Birds arrived toward the end of the transitional period, so that they, together with the Blind Boys of Mississippi, the Soul Stirrers of Tyler, Tex., the Blue Jays of Alabama, the Pilgrim Travelers, and the Spirit of Memphis, became the first of the more modern gospel quartets.

Other than the Golden Gate Quartet, a very popular transitional group, the Birds were the only gospel quartet to achieve a measure of success with white listeners. They have always been regarded as among the foremost of the quartets by black audiences. Their first

The Dixie Hummingbirds, gospel music quartet, c. 1950 (Ray Funk Collection, Fairbanks, Alaska)

discs: *An Introduction to Gospel Song* (Folkways RF5), *Brighten the Corner Where You Are* (New World Records NW 224), *Birmingham Quartet Anthology* (Clanka Lanka CL 144,001/002 [the American distributor is Douglas Seroff, Box 506, Rt. 3, Goodlettsville, Tenn.]), and *Jubilee to Gospel* (John Edwards Memorial Foundation JEMF 108).

WILLIAM H. TALLMADGE
Berea College

Barbara Baker, "Black Gospel Music Styles—1942–75" (Ph.D. diss., University of Maryland, 1978); J. Jerome Zolten, *The Dixie Hummingbirds: Great God A'Mighty! The Dixie Hummingbirds Celebrating the Rise of Soul Gospel Music* (2003).

interracial success came during 1942 at Café Society Downtown, in New York City, where they received a standing ovation. Their second such success came in 1966, at the Newport Folk Festival. Finally, a million or more young white listeners became acquainted with them in 1973 when they were included on Paul Simon's "Loves Me Like a Rock," on his successful album *There Goes Rhymin' Simon.*

Tony Heilbut devotes an entire chapter of his book *The Gospel Sound: Good News and Bad Times* (1971) to the Birds, mentioning "Trouble in My Way," "Let's Go Out to the Program," and "In the Morning" as perhaps their best recorded performances. To that trio might be added "The Devil Can't Harm a Praying Man," which is on the album *A Christian Testimonial* (Peacock PLP 100).

Information about the music and early history and development of the gospel quartet is given on the following

Dr. John

(b. 1941) NEW ORLEANS MUSICIAN. Malcolm "Mac" John Rebennack Jr., the pianist, composer, singer, and producer now widely known as Dr. John, is one of the best-known New Orleans–based artists and has had a career that spans four decades and a wide range of musical styles. He cut his teeth during one of the most exciting periods in New Orleans's rhythm-and-blues scene at the side of legends like Huey "Piano" Smith, Allen Toussaint, and Earl King. During an era when segregation still ruled in the South, he was one of the only white session musicians and arrangers to contribute in any significant way to the New Orleans R&B scene in the 1950s and early 1960s. Through the last three decades, he has cultivated the mystical persona of "the Night Tripper," which fuses elements from New Orleans's Carnival and voodoo traditions into a mysterious, shamanlike figure.

Rebennack became involved with the New Orleans R&B scene at an early age. By the age of 16, the prodigious youngster was working as a session guitarist in Cosimo Matassa's studio, backing up legends Professor Longhair, Frankie Ford, and Joe Tex, among others. He soon demonstrated his substantial talents at songwriting, arranging, and producing, helping to shape Allen Toussaint's production of teen idol Jimmy Clanton's 1958 song "Just a Dream," which spent 17 weeks at the top of the *Billboard* charts. He also wrote and produced Johnny Adams's first national record, "Losing Battle," which spent five weeks on the R&B charts. Under his own name, he produced a single for the Ace subsidiary Rex Records featuring the instrumental song "Storm Warning."

The early 1960s saw several setbacks in Rebennack's life. While touring in Florida in 1960, a portion of one of his fingers was shot off in a barroom gunfight, resulting in a switch from guitar to keyboards as his primary instrument. In 1963, he was arrested on narcotics charges and served two years in prison. Upon release, he headed to Los Angeles, joining the ranks of other New Orleans musical expatriates like producer-arranger Harold Battiste and singers Jessie Hill and Shirley Goodman.

In Los Angeles, Battiste helped him find work backing a variety of big-name artists, including Sam Cooke, Aretha Franklin, and Sonny and Cher. He played on the Rolling Stones' *Exile on Main Street* and John Lennon's *Rock 'n' Roll*. He signed with Atco Records and released his first album, *Gris-Gris*, in 1968. The record introduced the Night Tripper character, as well as Rebennack's psychedelic take on the classic rhythm-and-blues sound of New Orleans. The name "Dr. John" is a reference to a 19th-century voodoo practitioner who claimed to be descended from West African royalty. His 1971 release *The Sun, Moon, and Herbs* featured guest appearances by Mick Jagger and Eric Clapton.

Rebennack pursued a variety of explorations on his successive albums for Atco but returned to his New Orleans roots with his fifth album, 1972's *Gumbo*, which featured songs by the likes of Professor Longhair, Earl King, and Archibald. Backed by the Meters, he had his biggest hit to date in 1973 with "Right Place, Wrong Time," produced by Allen Toussaint.

Since the mid-1970s he has continued to release a variety of material, ranging from traditional New Orleans music, to pop standards, to solo piano outings. He wrote an autobiography, *Under a Hoodoo Moon*, which was published in 1994. After the devastation of Hurricane Katrina, he recorded and released a four-song CD called *Sippiana Hericane*.

MATT MILLER
Emory University

John Broven, *Rhythm & Blues in New Orleans* (1988); Dr. John, *Under a Hoodoo Moon* (1994).

Domino, Fats

(b. 1928) ROCK AND R&B MUSICIAN. Antoine "Fats" Domino is to his home city, New Orleans, what Elvis Presley and B. B. King are to Memphis and what Roy Acuff is to Nashville—the personification of musical values closely associated with those cities. His popular recordings for Lew Chubb's Imperial label—many of which were produced with Dave Bartholomew and engineered by Cosimo Matassa—represent a distillation of the New Orleans sound: piano virtuosity featuring right-hand triplets and a dominant bass line; heavy second-line rhythms from Domino's left hand or from the shuffle of a drummer; and harsh but powerful horn riffs, often featuring tenor saxophone solos from Herb Hardesty or Lee Allen. Domino's mellow, agreeable vocals find a comfortable home within this instrumental context. Taken together, these elements define the sound of New Orleans during the 1950s.

Born in New Orleans on 26 February 1928, Domino inherited the musical sensibility that shaped his music. His father was an accomplished violinist. His older brother-in-law, Harrison Verrett, had played guitar and banjo with Dixieland jazz ensembles led by Kid Ory and Papa Celestin. Verrett tutored young Domino and later served as his adviser and as a member of his band. In New Orleans, Domino was surrounded by master pianists like Henry Byrd ("Professor Longhair"), Cousin Joe, Walter "Fats" Pichon, and Leon T. Gross ("Archibald"). He absorbed these local influences, as well as the influences of non–New Orleans pianists like Meade Lux Lewis, Albert Ammons, and Pete Johnson. To his piano, Domino added a gentle and easy vocal style, complete with exotic Creole accent, which stood in contrast to the rawer, darker voices of the gutbucket country blues singers of the Deep South.

Domino has had more commercial success than any other New Orleans musician, and his biggest hits came from 1950 to 1963, when he recorded on the Imperial record label. Twenty of Domino's records have sold over a million copies (the number keeps growing as his records continue to sell), among them such classics as "The Fat Man" (his first record), "Ain't It a Shame," "I'm in Love Again," "Blueberry Hill," "Blue Monday," "I'm Walkin'," and "Walking to New Orleans." White audiences enthusiastically bought his records, and white artists such as Pat Boone, Ricky Nelson, Elvis Presley, and the Beatles either covered his hits or imitated his sound.

Domino made successful transitions from rhythm and blues to rock and roll and now does occasional Las Vegas lounge acts. He continues to play throughout the world to audiences who appreciate his music for its contemporary appeal rather than for its nostalgic value. In 1986, Domino became one of only 10 charter inductees into the Rock and Roll Hall of Fame, an institution established by members of the recording industry to honor achievement in that field. That same year, he was also featured in a nationally televised special entitled *Fats Domino and Friends.* He received Hall of Fame and Lifetime Achievement Awards at the 1987 Grammy awards.

In the 1980s, Fats Domino decided to settle permanently in New Orleans, making yearly appearances at its Jazz and Heritage Festival. He moved into a mansion in the predominantly working-class Lower Ninth Ward neighborhood, where his bright pink Cadillac became a familiar sight to neighborhood residents. Since 1995, Domino and his manager (since the 1980s), Robert Vernon, have been partners in the Bobkat Music Trust. Bobkat Music is an entertainment company that manages the careers of many notable artists, some posthumously, including Elvis Presley, Jerry Lee Lewis, and Paul Shaffer.

When Hurricane Katrina hit New Orleans in August 2005, Domino decided to stay at home with his family, because of his wife's poor health. His home was located in the Lower Ninth Ward, an area that was heavily flooded, and many feared that Domino was a casualty of the storm. On 1 September 2005, CNN aired footage of Domino being rescued from his home by a Coast Guard helicopter and taken to a shelter in Baton Rouge. His daughter, gospel singer Karen Domino White, identified him from photos shown on CNN. His home and office were lost in the flooding. Plans to gut and rebuild the home began in January 2006. Fats Domino was the first artist to be announced to perform as scheduled at the 2006 Jazz and Heritage Festival in his beloved "Big Easy."

JAY ORR
Country Music Foundation
Nashville, Tennessee

John Broven, *Rhythm and Blues in New Orleans* (1978); Rick Coleman, *Blue Monday: Fats Domino and the Lost Dawn of Rock 'n' Roll* (2006); Peter Guralnick, in *The Rolling Stone Illustrated History of Rock 'n' Roll*, ed. Jim Miller (1980); Robert Palmer, *A Tale of Two Cities: Memphis Rock and New Orleans Roll* (1979).

Donaldson, Lou

(b. 1926) JAZZ MUSICIAN.
The recording career of bop alto saxophonist Lou Donaldson evinces both the singular influence of jazz legend Charlie Parker and the consistent development of Donaldson's own unique blues-based style. A key member of the hard-bop movement of the mid-1950s, he helped establish the popularity of saxophone and organ combos during the late 1950s and early 1960s.

Born and raised in Badin, N.C., Donaldson opted to learn the clarinet around age 15 instead of studying under his mother, a piano teacher. He attended college at North Carolina A&T College in Greensboro, where he played in the marching band until enlisting in the navy in 1945. Looking to play the clarinet in the navy marching band, Donaldson auditioned but was referred to the navy dance band after promising that he could also play the alto saxophone, although he had never even picked one up before. After furious practicing in his barracks, he picked up the alto sax well enough to fit into the dance band.

After navy service, Donaldson returned to A&T to get a degree in political science and continued to play both clarinet and alto saxophone. He made the permanent switch to alto sax after sustaining a baseball injury to his little finger, which made the clarinet difficult to play. After the injury, Donaldson gave up baseball to concentrate on music. During this period, he began to play with a show band in Greensboro clubs, where he sat in with touring musicians like Dizzy Gillespie, who encouraged him to come to New York. He relocated there in 1950 to live in Harlem and play in local clubs, using the connections that he had made in Greensboro.

Influenced by the playing of Charlie Parker, Donaldson was noticed for his Parkeresque style and signed to Blue Note Records, first recording with the Milt Jackson quintet in 1952. In the same year, he made his recording debut as a leader, recorded with Thelonious Monk, and worked briefly with Charles Mingus. In 1954, Donaldson participated in a notable gig with Art Blakey, Clifford Brown, Horace Silver, and Tommy Potter, which was extensively documented by Blue Note on the albums *A Night at Birdland, Volumes I and II* and which directly predated the Jazz Messengers. However, Donaldson was never a member of the Messengers, and although he recorded as a sideman in the 1950s and occasionally afterward, he has been a bandleader from the mid-1950s up until the present.

Donaldson's early recordings expressed the classic motifs of the bop genre. In 1958 he began often using a conga player, and starting in 1961 his bands incorporated an organist rather than a pianist. Donaldson's bluesy style was easily transferable to soul-jazz, and this context brought out his unique style. His association with Blue Note (1952–63) was succeeded by sets for Cadet and Argo (1963–66). He returned to Blue Note in 1967 and soon became caught up in the increasingly commercial leanings of the label. For a time, he played an electronic Varitone sax. The success of "Alligator Boogaloo" in 1967 led to a series of funk recordings.

After he was off records a few years, Lou Donaldson's artistic return in 1981 and subsequent soul-jazz and hard-bop dates for Muse, Timeless, and Milestone show him interacting with both organists and pianists. Donaldson continues to tour and record in Europe, as well as to play several significant dates, such as 1989s Chicago Jazz Festival, in the United States.

When asked to explain the popularity of his music, Donaldson told one interviewer: "It's really groove music that's made for people to dance to. That's what jazz used to be about. But what's also essential is that my music has blues flavor, because when you get down to it, that's what jazz is. And that's the problem with a lot of music today . . . there's no blues feeling. Blues is the backbone, and if you don't have it in jazz it's like taking sugar out of a cake. So I think that's why my old music still sells, because it has blues feeling and it swings."

FRANCES ABBOTT
Emory University

Ken Franckling, *Jazz Times* (June 1995); Les Tomkins, *Crescendo International* 19, no. 11 (1981); Stan Woolley, *Jazz Journal International* (January 1997).

Dorsey, Thomas

(1899–1993) BLUES AND GOSPEL MUSICIAN AND COMPOSER.
Thomas A. Dorsey, the acknowledged father of modern African American gospel music, remains its most influential figure. Dorsey was born in Villa Rica, Ga., on 1 July 1899, and was raised in the Atlanta area. During his youth he

Thomas Dorsey, gospel music songwriter and performer, 1975 (Amy Van Singel, photographer, Living Blues Archival Collection, University of Mississippi Blues Archive, Oxford)

absorbed a variety of influences, from the traditional Dr. Watts hymns to the emerging early blues and jazz. A versatile composer who began writing both blues and gospel songs in the 1920s, Dorsey initially authored blues tunes but eventually penned many of the best-known songs in the gospel canon, including "Take My Hand, Precious Lord" and "Peace in the Valley." In the early 1930s Dorsey also founded the National Convention of Gospel Choirs and Choruses (NCGCC) in Chicago, where he helped launch the careers of such distinguished singers as Mahalia Jackson and Sallie Martin.

Dorsey joined the Great Migration from the South, settling in Chicago in 1918, where he briefly enrolled at the city's College of Composition and Arranging. He began playing with area jazz bands, but in less than a year Dorsey formed his own group, the Wildcats Jazz Band, which eventually accompanied vaudeville blues shouter Ma Rainey. He later successfully collaborated in a duo with blues guitarist and singer Tampa Red, but in 1928 he decided to move away from the blues scene and into sacred music.

His first attempt at writing a gospel song, in 1921, "If I Don't Get There," met with little success, but after several years of struggle Dorsey's decision to work in the gospel world began to bear fruit. In 1932, the year he organized one of the first gospel choirs at Chicago's Pilgrim Baptist Church, Dorsey and his pianist, Roberta Martin, quickly emerged as one of the top talents in African American gospel music. That same year Dorsey also hired a powerful and charismatic singer named Sallie Martin to join his group at the Ebenezer Baptist Church. The next year Dorsey and Sallie Martin were among the principal organizers of the annual NCGCC, where they introduced new songs to choir directors from across the nation.

The fateful year of 1932 also brought Dorsey's great personal tragedy. While Dorsey was in St. Louis on gospel business, his wife died giving birth to their son, who himself died two days later. Dorsey locked himself away for several days, emerging with a completed draft of "Take My Hand, Precious Lord," a song whose popularity in the gospel community is rivaled perhaps only by "Amazing Grace." Setting his loss behind him, he had his most prolific period in the years that followed, composing dozens of songs with a distinctively optimistic sensibility for audiences held in the grip of the Depression.

By the mid-1930s, Dorsey's songs gained enormous popularity among both black churchgoers and white southerners. By the beginning of World War II, even the leading white gospel publishers were anthologizing his music. That year, he composed "Peace in the Valley," with Mahalia Jackson, his demo singer at the time, in mind. But this song enjoyed its greatest success in the white market—both Elvis Presley and Red Foley, among others, scored major hits with the song following World War II.

After successfully establishing the Chicago-based Singers Convention, Dorsey, along with Sallie and Roberta Martin, hit the so-called gospel highway. Between the early 1930s and mid-1940s, he toured the nation under the banner "Evenings with Dorsey," during which time he trained young singers to perform his material. Perhaps his greatest popular successes came during World War II, when he added Mahalia Jackson to his tour, raising his visibility to even greater levels among both black and white gospel fans.

By the early 1950s, with the rise of hard gospel music and shouters such as Brother Joe May gaining audience share, Dorsey's influence began to slip. The popularity of his greatest material remained, and, during the middle of the decade, with the rise of R&B, his melodies began to resurface in many of the era's secular hits by artists as diverse as James Brown and the Coasters. As James Cleveland emerged as the undisputed king of contemporary gospel in the 1960s, Dorsey's age forced him to slowly curtail his writing and traveling. However, he remained active, spearheading the annual NCGCC event and other conferences. In the late 1980s, he was the focus of a well-received documentary film, *Say Amen, Somebody*, and remained one of the most revered figures in spiritual music until his death, on 23 January 1993.

KIP LORNELL
George Washington University

Michael Harris, *The Rise of Gospel Blues: The Music of Thomas Andrew Dorsey in the Urban Church* (1992).

Dulcimer

The plucked dulcimer, often called the Appalachian dulcimer, is a southern mountain folk instrument. Its sound is soft and restrained, with a gentle charm and a slight touch of melancholy. Its diatonic scale and heavy drones make it sound like a gentler version of bagpipes. The most common shapes are the "teardrop" and the "figure-eight," but other shapes are sometimes made. Dulcimers usually have three or four strings (although they may have as many as eight) running over a fret board. The diatonic scale of the fret board makes the dulcimer an ideal instrument to accompany songs in the various modes. Mountain people have used them for generations to accompany the tragic English and Scots ballads, as well as to play sprightly instrumental pieces.

The dulcimer is a lap instrument, played with the tuning pegs to the left (for right-handed musicians). In the traditional style, the melody is played on the string nearest the player while the other strings drone. The earliest dulcimers had frets under the first string only. The left hand stops the strings, often with the aid of a "noter" (a small cylinder of very hard wood), while the right hand strums the strings with a quill or plectrum or plucks the strings as though playing a banjo or guitar.

Although the dulcimer first appeared in its American form in the Appalachian South, it is structurally related to the German *Scheitholt*, the Swedish *hummel*, and the Norwegian *langeleik*. It may have been introduced to the Appalachians by Pennsylvania Germans.

The folk music revival of the 1960s brought the dulcimer to the attention of urban audiences, especially through the playing of two artists from the southern highlands, Jean Ritchie of Kentucky and Frank Proffitt of North Carolina. A new demand for the instrument created markets for traditional mountain craftspeople and sparked interest in the craft of dulcimer making on the part of disaffected young urbanites. A number of southern craftspeople, such as A. W. Jeffreys of Virginia, Homer Ledford of Kentucky, Jean Schilling of Tennessee, Lynn McSpadden of Arkansas, and Stanley Hicks, Edsel Martin, and Edd Presnell of North Carolina, earned national reputations for their artistry as dulcimer makers.

CHARLES JOYNER
University of South Carolina, Coastal Campus

R. Gerald Alvey, *Dulcimer Maker: The Craft of Homer Ledford* (1984); Charles Faulkner Bryan, *Tennessee Folklore Society Bulletin* (March 1952, December 1954); Gene DuBey, *Sourwood Mountain Dulcimers* (Appalshop film, 1976); Charles Joyner, *Southern Folklore Quarterly* (December 1975); Jean Ritchie, *The Dulcimer Book* (1963); Charles Seeger, *Journal of American Folklore* (January–March 1958); L. Allen Smith, *A Catalogue of Pre-Revival Appalachian Dulcimers* (1983); Ralph Lee Smith, *Appalachian Dulcimer Traditions* (1997).

Engel, Lehman

(1910–1982) COMPOSER AND CONDUCTOR.

Time magazine called Lehman Engel "one of the nation's busiest and most versatile men-about-music." He was a composer, conductor, author, and teacher. *A Streetcar Named Desire*, *The Consul*, *Murder in the Cathedral*, and *Li'l Abner* are a few of the many, diverse Broadway shows with which he was associated as a composer or pit conductor. His efforts brought widespread recognition, including two Antoinette Perry ("Tony") awards: one in 1950 for conducting the Menotti opera *The Consul* and one in 1953 for conducting Gilbert and Sullivan operettas and *Wonderful Town*.

Born to Jewish parents in Jackson, Miss., Engel played the piano "by ear" until age 10, when his parents were able to afford piano lessons for him. He wrote that his first piano teacher was an "aristocratic southern lady" whose lessons, like those of his subsequent teachers, he quickly outgrew. He completed his first composition, *The Scotch Highlander*, shortly after he began taking piano lessons, and musical composition for the theater became one of his primary interests. A Jackson movie house, the Majestic Theater, with its small orchestra accompanying the silent movies, impressed the young boy greatly and provided some of his most memorable early experiences.

Although not an extremely talented pianist, Engel entered the Cincinnati Conservatory of Music upon graduation from high school. When he discovered that he had been eligible for a partial scholarship for piano lessons but was the only student not on scholarship, he became angry that his parents had spent so much money unnecessarily and transferred immediately to the Cincinnati College of Music. Two years later, he turned down a faculty position at Cincinnati and moved to New York. With a graduate scholarship to the Julliard School, Engel took courses in composition from Rubin Goldmark and studied privately with Roger Sessions.

In New York, Engel worked diligently to make contacts and establish his career. He persisted for several months in an attempt to meet Martha Graham, who encouraged him to write compositions for her dance company and for other concert dancers as well. *Within the Gates* provided his first Broadway credit. When he heard the music already written for the play, he expressed his dislike to director Melvyn Douglas, offering to write a new version by the next morning. Even though the play itself was unsuccessful, Engel's music was praised.

A group of madrigal singers was organized by the Federal Music Project, a subsidiary of the Works Progress Administration (WPA), and Engel was the group's conductor from 1935 to 1939. He composed music for the Federal Theater Project and the WPA Children's Theater before he began working with Orson Welles and John Houseman at their Mercury Theater. During World War II he joined the U.S. Navy, conducted a military orchestra at the Great Lakes Naval Training Station, and later served as chief composer of the navy's film division in Washington, D.C. His other pursuits included founding (with Aaron Copland, Marc Blitzstein, and Virgil Thompson) the Arrow Music Press, Inc., to publish the work of American composers; conducting on more than 60 recordings for major record companies such as Columbia, Decca, and RCA Victor; composing four operas and music for radio, film, and television; writing books about musical theater; and teaching workshops in musical lyrics.

Nicknamed by some the "Poor Man's Lenny Bernstein," Engel became one of the most respected and sought-after musicians on Broadway. He never returned to the South to live but did return to Jackson to conduct the premier performances of two of his operas. Engel died of cancer in 1982, but his life's accomplishments and honors had been many. With regard to the demands of writing music for the theater, Engel had often spoken of Mozart: "That genius had to write on order. He had no time for the muse to belt him." It seems that the same had been true for Engel himself.

JESSICA FOY
Cooperstown Graduate Program
Cooperstown, New York

Josh Barbanel, *New York Times* (30 August 1982); Lehman Engel, *This Bright Day: An Autobiography* (1974), *Words with Music: Creating the Broadway Musical Libretto* (rev. ed., 2006); Walter Rigdon, ed., *The Biographical Encyclopedia and Who's Who of the American Theatre* (1966); Nicolas Slonimsky, *Baker's Biographical Dictionary of Musicians* (7th ed., 1984); *Time* (8 December 1958).

Estefan, Gloria

(b. 1957) LATIN POPULAR SINGER. Born in Havana, Cuba, on 1 September 1957, as Gloria Maria Fajardo, Gloria Estefan is one of the best-selling popular singers in the world and a leading exemplar of the Latin music that took root in south Florida and now ties the American South to the broader Global South. Estefan's music is rooted in her native Cuba. Her father was a bodyguard to Cuban dictator Fulgencio Batista. He was imprisoned and expelled from Cuba when Fidel Castro overthrew the Batista regime in 1959, and he fought at the Bay of Pigs invasion. Miami became home to his family, as it did to tens of thousands of exiled Cubans, who soon formed a dynamic Cuban American community and a distinctive culture in the South.

Gloria Fajardo married bandleader Emilio Estefan in 1978, and they made their group, the Miami Sound Machine, into a leading band of the 1980s, combining rhythm and blues, disco, and funk with Afro-Cuban percussion. In 1979 the band produced its first Spanish-language album, which helped secure its Latino constituency. Soon Gloria Estefan was receiving star billing with the band, which was producing numerous Top 10 hits through the 1980s. In 1989, while touring, a bus accident left her with a broken vertebra and led to a year in which she did not perform or record. Estefan returned as a solo performer in the early 1990s, and *Mi Tierra*, a Spanish-language recording of songs coming out of her Cuban roots, earned a Grammy award for Best Tropical Latin Album. The songs were not traditional Cuban tunes but were songs written to evoke Cuban styles. This album sold over eight million copies worldwide, becoming Spain's best-selling international album of all time.

Estefan produced platinum-selling albums through the 1990s and Top 10 dance hits. Combining disco and salsa sounds, Estefan's song "Reach" was the official theme song of the 1996 Summer Olympics in Atlanta, and she sang the song in the closing ceremonies. Estefan has received five Grammy awards, including the first Latin Grammy for Best Music Video (for "No Me Dejes de Querer"). A legendary figure now in south Florida, she performed at the 2003 World Series and the 2007 Super Bowl, both of which were played in Miami.

Estefan is an international celebrity who has sold more than 90 million albums and has been dubbed the "Queen of Latin Pop." She represents a distinctive form of "roots rock," with pop stylings that draw from Cuban sources and the musical creativity of south Florida's displaced Cubans over the past half century.

CHARLES REAGAN WILSON
University of Mississippi

Fiddler, Tutwiler, Miss., 1967 (William R. Ferris Collection, Southern Folklife Collection, Wilson Library, University of North Carolina at Chapel Hill)

Fiddle and Fiddlers' Conventions

The fiddle is a four-string, bowed instrument—most often a violin, though resourceful musicians have fashioned facsimiles from cigar boxes and tin cans—upon which are played a variety of folk melodies, primarily for dancing. Some people argue that the fiddle has one string more than the violin—the one used to hang it on the wall. Because of its portability, its common use as dance accompaniment, and its folk heritage extending back to the 18th century in the British Isles and Western Europe, the fiddle quickly assumed a role as the primary folk musical instrument of settlers in the New World. In the 19th and early 20th centuries, southern fiddlers exhibited subregional variation according to such characteristics as bowing patterns, bowing method, fiddle placement, tunings, repertoire, tune titles, tune texts, tune structure, and instrumental accompaniment. The predominant tune forms in southern fiddling are variously referred to as reels, breakdowns, or hoedowns and are played in double meter to accompany dancing. Southern fiddlers also perform rags, waltzes, blues, and hornpipes, though these forms are less common.

By the early 21st century, improved travel conditions, the radio, the phonograph, and the proliferation of fiddle contests whose judges adhere to rigid aesthetic standards had blunted the more pronounced regional distinctions that once characterized southern fiddling. However, the broad stylistic designations of Appalachian or Blue Ridge (further subdivided into Galax, North Georgia, and others), Deep South (including the unique Mississippi fiddle bands, which show an apparent black influence), Ozark, Cajun, and Southwestern (sometimes referred to as "contest"-style fiddling for its emphasis on ornate improvisation and precise execution) still have relevance.

Fiddlers' conventions, at which the central event is usually a competition or "contest," have become a primary performance outlet for contemporary fiddlers. As early as 1736, in Hanover County, Va., southern fiddlers competed against one another for prizes and prestige. The most famous contests were held in Atlanta, Union Grove, N.C., and Knoxville. In the early part of the 20th century, Henry Ford sponsored a series of competitions to determine a national champion through his automobile dealerships. Ford felt that fiddlers and fiddle music embodied the moral, conservative values he wanted his contests to inspire in those who attended them. Today, every fiddler in the South lives within easy distance of several of the numerous conventions sponsored by communities, civic groups, state agencies, local businesses, and regional and local fiddlers' associations.

JAY ORR
Country Music Foundation
Nashville, Tennessee

Linda C. Burman-Hall, "Southern American Folk Fiddling: Context and Style" (Ph.D. diss., Princeton University, 1973); Gavin James Campbell, *Music and the Making of the New South* (2004); Alan Jabbour, *American Fiddle Tunes from the Archive of Folk Song* (record and accompanying booklet) (1971); Earl V. Spielman, "Traditional North American Fiddling" (Ph.D. diss., University of Wisconsin at Madison, 1975); Charles K. Wolfe, *The Devil's Box: Masters of Southern Fiddling* (1997).

Fisk Jubilee Singers

SPIRITUAL SINGING GROUP.
The Fisk Jubilee Singers originally consisted of a black American group of eight singers and a pianist, all students

at Fisk University in Nashville, Tenn. This double quartet, together with musical director George L. White, chaperone Miss Well, the pianist, and two other students to help with the packing and moving, set off on a tour in 1871 to raise money for their university. By 1880, when the university ended official sponsorship of the group, it had toured the northern United States, England, and Europe and had sung at the White House and for Queen Victoria. From the singing of this organization, the world at large first became aware of a body of black music called "spirituals" (they were called "slave songs" in those days).

The term "jubilee" has a number of different meanings. It has been used to designate those black spirituals whose texts refer to freedom—freedom in death from the hardships of life, followed by the attainment of heavenly bliss, and freedom from slavery. The term has also been used to specify those spirituals having a joyous character, and it has been used to refer to the entire body of black spirituals. It has also been used in reference to special celebrations or annual events, such as the Pinkster Jubilee, a celebration of Pentecost Sunday in certain areas of New York, Pennsylvania, and Maryland during the colonial period. It was at Columbus, Ohio, after the singers had been on the road for several weeks, that White came up with the idea that the name "Jubilee Singers" would be a good one for the group. He had recalled the Old Testament "year of jubilee," a year provided by ancient Hebrew law when slaves were emancipated, and thinking of the students at the university, most of whom had been former slaves, he felt that their year of jubilee had come—"this little band of singers was a witness to it, an outgrowth of it."

Two years after the success of the Fisk choir, the Hampton Institute also sent a choir on tour, followed by groups from Tuskegee and Utica Institutes, but it was the name of the Fisk Jubilee Singers that remained in the public's memory.

WILLIAM H. TALLMADGE
Berea College

Alain Locke, *The Negro and His Music* (1936); J. B. T. Marsh, *The Story of the Jubilee Singers; with Their Songs* (1877); G. D. Pike, *The Jubilee Singers, and Their Campaign for Twenty Thousand Dollars* (1873); Thomas Rutling, *Tom: An Autobiography* (1907); Andrew Ward, *Dark Midnight When I Rise: The Story of the Jubilee Singers Who Introduced the World to the Music of Black America* (2000).

Foster, Stephen

(1826–1864) COMPOSER AND SONGWRITER.

Born in Lawrenceville, Penn., and raised in comfortable circumstances in a suburb of Pittsburgh, Stephen Collins Foster began composing for the blackface minstrel theater, where "Oh! Susanna," "Nelly Bly," and "Camptown Races" were popularized by the troupe of E. P. Christy. His ambition, however, was to be a composer of sentimental parlor songs on themes of romantic love and nostalgic yearning. Among his songs of this type are "Old Dog Tray," "Jeanie with the Light Brown Hair," and "Beautiful Dreamer." Although some of his songs achieved commercial success, Foster failed to capitalize on his successes and died in poverty.

In his minstrel songs, Foster made no attempt to present realistically the song and speech of southern plantation slaves. In "Oh! Susanna," for example, the dialect, the deadpan irony, and the references to southern places and foods are merely conventions of the minstrel stage. The melody is no more African American than it is English or Irish, and the rhythm is that of the European polka. From about 1850 Foster began to modify the conventions of minstrelsy in the direction of middle-class sentimentality. Songs like "Old Folks at Home" and "Old Black Joe" attribute more delicate and varied sentiments to the stage black than had previously been the stereotype. In a few songs, like "My Old Kentucky Home," he omitted the dialect. Many of these less-typical minstrel songs were popularized in dramatizations of *Uncle Tom's Cabin*. Indeed, Foster's notebooks reveal that "My Old Kentucky Home" was originally written as "Poor Uncle Tom, Good Night." Ironically, Foster's songs are, with the exception of Dan Emmett's "Dixie's Land," the best-known representatives of minstrelsy today.

Since the late 19th century, Foster's songs have been widely accepted as genuine American folk songs. Although Foster never lived in the South, popular myth has associated him with the region. Florida and Kentucky have adopted "Old Folks at Home" and "My Old Kentucky Home," respectively, as official state songs. Bardstown, Ky., and White Springs, Fla., boast shrines to Foster's memory and music—the latter, on the Suwannee River, serves as the home of the state's folklife program. Though black critic Alain Locke has observed that "Foster's ballads did more to crystallize the romance of the plantation tradition than all the Southern colonels and novelists put together," adaptations of Foster songs by Ray Charles and Taj Mahal have been sincere portrayals of African American culture and experience. Sung in widely varying arrangements, often with bowdlerized texts, Stephen Foster's songs continue to form part of the musical experience of nearly every American.

DAVID WARREN STEEL
University of Mississippi

William W. Austin, *"Susanna," "Jeanie," and "The Old Folks at Home": The Songs of Stephen C. Foster from His Time to Ours* (1975); Ken Emerson, *Doo-Dah: Stephen Foster and the Rise of American Popular Culture* (1998); John T. Howard, *Stephen Foster: America's Troubadour* (1953; rev. ed., 1962); Richard Jackson, ed., *The Stephen Foster Song Book* (1974).

Fountain, Pete

(b. 1930) JAZZ MUSICIAN.
Peter Dewey Fountain Jr. was born on 3 July 1930 in New Orleans, La. His father was a drummer and violinist who played in local jazz bands in Biloxi, Miss., when Pete was young. Fountain's own musical interest began early, and he played the clarinet in the school band. While still very young, Fountain played with the Junior Dixieland Band, Phil Zito's International Dixieland Express, and the Basin Street Six.

Already an accomplished musician at 16, Fountain replaced Irving Fazola at the Opera House Burlesque Theater. At 19, Fountain joined the Dukes of Dixieland band in Chicago in 1949 and played with them until 1954. Fountain was a member of Lawrence Welk's orchestra from 1957 through 1960. In 1960, he opened his own club, the French Quarter, on Bourbon Street in New Orleans. He played at the club frequently, in addition to appearing on such television programs as the *Ed Sullivan Show* and *Kraft Music Hall* and on specials with Bob Hope and Bing Crosby. He was an occasional guest on Johnny Carson's *The Tonight Show*, where he played with Doc Severinsen's orchestra. Through television, he became a prime symbol for Americans of modern New Orleans jazz.

In the early 1980s, Fountain relocated his club, now called Pete's Place, to the New Orleans Riverside Hilton, where he was involved until his retirement in early 2003. He makes frequent appearances at the annual New Orleans Jazz and Heritage Festival and is the founder and most prominent member of the Half-Fast Walking Club, one of the best-known marching Krewes that parade in New Orleans during Mardi Gras. He has recorded nearly 50 records on the Coral label, including *South Rampart Street Parade*, *New Orleans at Midnight*, *Plenty of Pete*, and *Both Sides Now*. In 1997 he was inducted into the Big Band and Jazz Hall of Fame.

KAREN M. MCDEARMAN
University of Mississippi

Pete Fountain, with Bill Neely, *A Closer Walk: The Pete Fountain Story* (1972);

Howard Mandel, *Down Beat* (January 1985); Nicolas Slonimsky, *Baker's Biographical Dictionary of Musicians* (7th ed., 1984).

Franklin, Aretha

(b. 1942) GOSPEL, SOUL, JAZZ, R&B, AND POP SINGER.

"Queen of Soul" Aretha Franklin was born the daughter of a Baptist preacher in Memphis, Tenn., on 25 March 1942. After her mother's death, when Aretha was only 10, her minister father moved Aretha and her four siblings to Buffalo, N.Y. Soon after, the family moved again to Detroit, where Aretha's father became the preacher at New Bethel Baptist Church, a position that led to Aretha becoming acquainted with and influenced by gospel singers Clara Ward and Mahalia Jackson. "I guess I was about nine when I decided to sing," Aretha said. "The best, the greatest gospel singers passed though our home in Detroit. Sometimes they stayed with us. James Cleveland lived with us for a time and it was James who taught me how to play the piano by ear. But the ladies. How I loved my gospel ladies!" By the time Aretha turned 14 she was recording gospel songs on the Checker Records label, and in 1956 she released *The Gospel Soul of Aretha Franklin*.

Aretha's singing career was interrupted by the births of her first two sons in 1955 and 1957. When she returned to recording, she ventured into the secular world of pop, jazz, blues, and soul music, although her gospel background was always the foundation of her style. She signed a recording contract with Columbia Records in New York in 1960, and although she had a handful of hits with the label, including "Today I Sing the Blues" and "Won't Be Long," her early recording career was slow to catch fire. By late 1966, Aretha decided to move to a label that reached a larger R&B audience. She signed a new contract with Atlantic Records, a label that was producing new and exciting music by R&B heavyweights such as Otis Redding, Carla Thomas, Sam & Dave, and Wilson Pickett. The move was the beginning of an unprecedented music career. Between the years 1968 and 1975, Aretha won eight consecutive Grammy awards for Best Female R&B Vocal Performance (an award that came to be nicknamed the Aretha Award) for songs such as "Respect," "Chain of Fools," and the album *Young, Gifted and Black*. To date, Aretha holds the record for the award, having won it 11 times and been nominated 23.

Besides beginning her impressive run of Grammy award wins, the year 1968 was a particularly important year for Aretha. In April of that year Aretha sang at the funeral of Martin Luther King Jr., who was a friend of Aretha's father and who had visited the Franklin home in Detroit often during Aretha's youth. Two months later, on 28 June 1968, Aretha became the first black woman to appear on the cover of *Time* magazine.

In 1972, Aretha returned to her gospel roots, recording her live gospel album *Amazing Grace* at New Bethel Baptist Church in Los Angeles with James Cleveland and the Southern California Community Choir—her first gospel album in 15 years. The album sold over 2 million copies in the United States and became the biggest-selling gospel recording of all time.

Aretha's career stalled in the 1970s as a result of the rising popularity of disco, but in 1980 Aretha appeared in the movie *The Blues Brothers*, where she performed a soul-stirring rendition of her song "Think." Later that same year Aretha signed a contract with Arista records and went on to record gold and platinum albums with the label, such as *Jump to It* (1982), *Who's Zoomin' Who?* (1985), *Aretha* (1986), and *A Rose Is Still a Rose* (1998).

Shortly after releasing the album *So Damn Happy* in 2003, Aretha left Arista Records and began her own recording company, Aretha Records, the following year. She has since been awarded a number of honors, including, in 2004, being named ninth out of the 100 greatest artists of all time by *Rolling Stone* magazine (followed by Ray Charles in the 10th spot). She was awarded the Presidential Medal of Honor by George W. Bush in 2005.

JAMES G. THOMAS JR.
University of Mississippi

Mark Bego, *Aretha Franklin: The Queen of Soul* (1989); Matt Dobkin, *I Never Loved a Man the Way I Loved You: Aretha Franklin, Respect, and the Making of a Soul Music Masterpiece* (2004); Gerri Hirshey, *Nowhere to Run: The Story of Soul Music* (1984).

Gillespie, Dizzy

(1917–1993) JAZZ MUSICIAN.
John Birks "Dizzy" Gillespie was born on 21 October 1917 in Cheraw, S.C. Gillespie showed his musical talent at an early age, and he began to play the trumpet when he was 15. He attended

Laurinburg Institute in North Carolina, and when he was 18 Gillespie went to Philadelphia, where he joined a local jazz band. He played with the Cab Calloway and Earl Hines bands, and in 1944, when Hines's lead singer, Billy Eckstine, formed his own band, Gillespie joined the group.

Gillespie, along with his friend Charlie "Bird" Parker, who also played with the Eckstine band, was an innovator in the jazz style known as bebop (or bop) beginning in the late 1940s. Bebop introduced revolutionary changes in the traditional rhythmic and harmonic jazz patterns. Gillespie and Parker made a few recordings after leaving Eckstine's band but had difficulty finding club owners willing to let them play the new style. Club patrons preferred the blues and older-style tunes that were danceable. Gillespie continued to play in a style directly related to bebop, which eventually came to be heralded as a remarkable and original development in jazz.

Gillespie was given the nickname "Dizzy" because of his playing style, which incorporated wild gesturing and grimacing. He was a trumpet virtuoso and has been credited with extending the upper ranges of the instrument. He was also known for improvising long passages at breakneck speed. A brilliant showman, Gillespie entertained thousands with his stage antics and superior instrumentals. His creativity is demonstrated on albums such as *In the Beginning* and *Oscar Peterson and Dizzy Gillespie.*

KAREN M. MCDEARMAN
University of Mississippi

Ole Brask, *Jazz People* (1976); Ira Gitler, *Jazz Masters of the Forties* (1974); Barry McRae, *Dizzy Gillespie: His Life and Times* (1988); Alyn Shipton, *Groovin' High: The Life of Dizzy Gillespie* (2001); Marshall Stearns, *The Story of Jazz* (1956).

Golden Gate Quartet

GOSPEL MUSIC GROUP.

The Golden Gate Quartet came out of the musical culture of southern Virginia's Tidewater and went on to become one of the most prominent and influential black gospel quartets. The quartet began in a barbershop in Berkeley, Va., in 1930, when Booker T. Washington's schoolmates Willie Johnson and Henry Owens joined with barber A. C. "Eddie" Griffin and one-legged bass singer Robert "Peg" Ford. They performed around Norfolk, Va., and then at churches in North Carolina, and by June 1936 they were singing over radio station WIS in Columbia, S.C. By then, Griffin had returned to his barbershop, replaced by tenor William "Highpockets" Langford. In 1936, a teenage singer named Orlandus Wilson replaced Ford. The group began recording in 1937, cutting 14 songs for Victor Records, and these recordings soon led to increased demand for live performances, not only in churches but at clubs.

The Golden Gate Quartet recorded in New York in the late 1930s and appeared at the landmark "Spirituals to Swing" concert at Carnegie Hall. This led to a long-term engagement at the Café Society in New York and national popularity. The group had a prime-time radio program on CBS, recorded a series of records with Huddie "Leadbelly"

Ledbetter, and appeared on the 1941 Franklin D. Roosevelt inaugural program. During the war years the quartet performed on popular radio shows and in several films, including *Star-Spangled Rhythm*, *Hit Parade of 1943*, *Hollywood Canteen*, and *Bring on the Girls*. Clyde Reddick replaced Highpockets Langford in 1940, and other singers filled in for Jackson and Wilson when they were drafted. After the war, the quartet lost popularity to newer black gospel groups like the Dixie Hummingbirds, but the quartet toured Europe in the 1950s and opened a new area of influence.

In the early 1950s the Golden Gate Quartet performed in variety shows in the South with such white gospel groups as the Blackwood Brothers. It influenced many white groups and subsequently drew from those groups' repertoires for its recordings. This important example of biracial musical cross-pollination ended with the white South's increased resistance to desegregation in the mid-1950s. Nonetheless, the Gates influenced early southern rock performers, including Elvis Presley, who, while in the army in Europe, went to Paris to see them perform and to visit with them about their shared interest in gospel music. As a result of the Gates' several trips to South Africa, an a cappella male gospel quartet movement began there in the 1970s and continues today, preserving the black quartet sounds of the 1930s and 1940s.

Black male gospel groups had emerged from the 1910s, first with essentially folk performers who built on the late 19th-century style of the Fisk Jubilee Singers. The Golden Gate Quartet dominated the "Jubilee" period (1930–45), adopting vocal mannerisms from Holiness congregations and borrowing melodic and rhythmic aspects from jazz. The Gates also borrowed the instrumental imitations from pop music's Mills Brothers and added jazz syncopation to traditional plantation hymns and folk songs. Willie Johnson defined their style as "vocal percussion," as it was "like a drum but had notes to it, it had lyrics to it you see." The quartet retold biblical stories, as in "Jezebel," "Joshua Fit the Battle of Jericho," "Shadrack," and "Moses Smote the Water." "No Restricted Signs" affirms racial equality, and "Atom and Evil" tells of the need to return to an old-time faith in the face of the threat of nuclear weapons. Songs of inspiration, such as "High, Low, and Wide" and "Hold the Water," were also typical of this highly stylized group.

CHARLES REAGAN WILSON
University of Mississippi

Ray Allen, *Singing in the Spirit: African American Sacred Quartets in New York City* (1991); Horace C. Boyd, *How Sweet the Sound: The Golden Age of Gospel* (1995); Peter A. Grendysa, liner notes to *The Golden Gate Quartet: Swing Down, Chariot*, Columbia 47131.

Gottschalk, Louis Moreau

(1829–1869) CLASSICAL MUSIC COMPOSER.

The most renowned American composer of the early 19th century, Louis Moreau Gottschalk blended the European romantic tradition with the black rhythms and Creole melodies he had experienced as a child in New Orleans.

Gottschalk's works possess an individual charm and a spontaneity and verve that draw listeners inside the music. The son of a wealthy English Jew and a titled French Creole, the musician grew up in cultured surroundings and was recognized by age four as a prodigy. Seven years later, his teacher declared that the boy must be sent to Paris to study further. In 1842, Gottschalk sailed for France, and a great-aunt introduced him to Parisian society.

Having heard French and Italian opera in New Orleans, the youth preferred operatic transcriptions for piano over the German classics. In France, he studied both piano and composition. During the revolutionary turmoil of 1848 he was forced to flee Paris, and during that absence he wrote the two piano pieces for which he is best remembered, *La Bamboula* and *La Savanne*. Both were drawn from folk music he had known as a child, and Parisian listeners were enchanted by their rhythmic virtuosity and exotic themes.

In 1849 the composer made his debut as a professional pianist at the Salle Pleyel. While in France he performed for Hugo, Chopin, Bizet, and Berlioz, all of whom praised his work. He continued writing and enjoyed special success with *Le Bananier* and *Le Banjo*. He toured Switzerland and Spain, and then in 1853 decided to return to the United States. His first New York concert, given in Niblo's Garden, was a triumph that he repeated all over the United States. His flamboyant style met sharp criticism, although audiences were attracted by his personality and European reputation.

As Gottschalk became more the entertainer, his compositions grew increasingly sentimental; *The Dying Poet* and *The Last Hope* stand among the more saccharine. He spent six years giving concerts in the West Indies and writing orchestral works like his *Grand Tarantelle* and *A Night in the Tropics*. He returned to the United States, making the most of the fiction that surrounded his life, performing concerts in the thick of the Civil War, and touring the goldfields of California and Nevada. He also staged "monster concerts" in Latin America, but he grew despondent. In Rio de Janeiro, he collapsed during a concert and died shortly afterward. His body was eventually moved to Greenwood Cemetery, Brooklyn.

RONALD L. DAVIS
Southern Methodist University

Ronald L. Davis, *A History of Music in American Life: The Formative Years* (1982); John G. Doyle, *Louis Moreau Gottschalk, 1829–1869: A Bibliographical Study and Catalog of His Works* (1983); Louis Moreau Gottschalk, *Notes of a Pianist* (1964); Vernon Loggins, *Where the Word Ends: The Life of Louis Moreau Gottschalk* (1958); James E. Perone, *Louis Moreau Gottschalk: A Bio-Bibliography* (2002); S. Frederick Starr, *Louis Moreau Gottschalk* (2000).

Grand Ole Opry

The *Grand Ole Opry* is America's longest-running radio program. It began in 1925, soon after Nashville station WSM first began broadcasts as the voice of the National Life and Accident Insurance Company. This Nashville-based firm was then expanding rapidly, moving beyond its initial base of sickness and accident policies into the more profitable life insurance field. Along with classical ensembles and pop dance bands, country musicians like Dr. Humphrey Bate's Augmented Orchestra supplied early WSM programming and helped attract prospective policyholders.

The father of the *Opry* was WSM program director George D. Hay, who came to the station in November 1925, a few weeks after Bate's group arrived. Earlier, Hay had helped announce Chicago's WLS *Barn Dance*, a program that inspired country radio jamborees nationwide. By the year's end, he had organized WSM talent into a regular Saturday-night show known simply as "the barn dance." Early performers included Hawaiian groups, minstrel acts, and military bands, but old-time string bands like Bate's soon prevailed.

Using strategies typical of the genre, Hay shaped the *Opry* into a folksy but highly commercial production that appealed to a broad-based audience of rural and small-town listeners scattered throughout the nation. He gave string bands names such as "Possum Hunters" or "Fruit Jar Drinkers" and urged them to wear countrified costumes. As master of ceremonies, Hay himself became the Solemn Old Judge, a stage persona with deep roots in American vaudeville and minstrelsy. In short, he made the *Opry* a variety show with a rural southern accent.

About 1927, Hay named the program the *Grand Ole Opry*, in an impromptu parody of classical music programs broadcast over WSM as an NBC network affiliate. "For the past hour," he announced, "we have been listening to music taken largely from the Grand Opera, but from now on we will present the Grand Ole Opry." Hay then introduced harmonica player DeFord Bailey, a black man whose musical portrait of a speeding locomotive symbolized the *Opry*'s homespun realism, reminiscent of an authentic rural barn dance or husking bee.

Fan letters, commercial sponsors, and rising insurance income convinced National Life to continue the *Opry* despite opposition from proper Nashvillians, who saw it as a threat to the city's genteel reputation. As WSM's power climbed from 1,000 watts in 1925 to 50,000 in 1932, the program's radio audience expanded dramatically, and the *Opry*'s position became secure. WSM's clear-channel signal, broadcast through a new, superbly engineered tower built in 1932, blanketed most of the nation, and the show steadily gained supporters in almost every state. By 1936, the *Opry* was generating as much as 80 percent of the station's weekly mail. Southerners were the mainstay of the *Opry* audience, and WSM naturally played up southern themes in *Opry* costumes, band names, radio dialogue, and publicity. But the program's national audience increased pressures for variety: within a decade, cowboys, western swing bands, and honky-tonk singers surpassed old-time string bands as the dominant acts on the *Opry* roster.

The *Opry*'s listenership widened further after 1939, when the R. J. Reynolds Tobacco Company, makers of Prince Albert smoking tobacco, began sponsoring a half hour of the show on

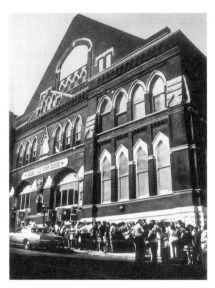

Ryman Auditorium, Nashville, early home of the Grand Ole Opry (Country Music Foundation, Library and Media Center, Nashville)

a 26-station NBC network. By 1952, this web had expanded to a coast-to-coast chain of 176 stations boasting a weekly audience of 10 million. Although WSM originated many other country and pop programs for network broadcast, the *Prince Albert Show* was by far the most visible and the longest running, lasting until 1961. Network airtime was especially important in sustaining the *Opry* through the late 1950s, a period in which most other radio barn dances withered in the face of competition from network television and the conversion of country radio stations to rock programming.

Along with the program's network connections, aggressive promotion, stylistic diversification, and the cultivation of a star system, television also helped the *Opry* thrive. Since the mid-1950s, *Opry* performers have appeared on

numerous network TV specials, as well as on syndicated programs produced by WSM or by independent firms. In 1978, PBS aired portions of the *Opry* itself for the first time, and in 1985, the Nashville Network began carrying a live, half-hour segment to cable-television viewers across the nation.

Early in the *Opry*'s evolution, a live audience became vital to the broadcast, and a popular stage show developed around the radio program. To gain ever-greater seating space, the show moved from WSM's studios (located in the National Life Building in downtown Nashville) to a succession of local halls, before settling in the Ryman Auditorium in 1943. The Ryman, which was originally called the Gospel Tabernacle, was built in 1892 with funds raised by riverboat captain Thomas G. Ryman. After a 31-year run there, the *Opry* shifted to the magnificent new *Opry* House at Nashville's Opryland theme park, opened in the early 1970s by NLT Corporation, successor to National Life. Although subsequent owner Gaylord Entertainment Company closed the theme park in 1997—while also buying and selling the cable operations of CMT (Country Music Television) and The Nashville Network (TNN)—the entertainment complex now embraces a large hotel and convention center, the General Jackson, a Cumberland River showboat, and WSM-AM. Gaylord has also bought and renovated the historic Ryman Auditorium, where the *Opry* is staged during winter months and diverse entertainers perform year-round, and the nearby Wildhorse Saloon club. In 2004, the *Opry* made a presenting sponsorship deal with Cracker Barrel Old Country Store. Even in its now-elegant surroundings, however, the *Opry* has remained refreshingly informal, belying the planning each show requires. Announcers reading commercials, artists waiting to be introduced, and stagehands moving props all create a complex and entertaining spectacle.

In addition to drawing millions of tourists, the *Opry* has nurtured Nashville's music industry. About 1934, WSM organized its Artists Service, which booked *Opry* stars into schoolhouses and theaters, at first mostly in the Southeast. Before long, independent promoters were working with *Opry* officials to broaden the range of *Opry* tours throughout the United States and abroad. After World War II, as the *Opry* began to recruit country music's leading stars, national recording companies began to center their country recording operations in Nashville. Independent recording studios built by WSM engineers or musicians helped produce hits that further established Nashville's reputation as Music City, U.S.A., a name coined by WSM announcer David Cobb about 1950. Capitalizing on the *Opry*'s popularity, Nashville-based music publishers furnished song material for stage shows and recording sessions and helped promote *Opry* artists' careers.

For more than 60 years, the *Grand Ole Opry* has survived not only changes in media and corporate ownership but also transformations in sounds, styles, and repertoires, reflecting the adaptation of a rural-based music to an increasingly urban society. In Octo-ber 2005 the *Opry* celebrated its 80th birthday with a week of performances by artists such as Garth Brooks, Travis Tritt, and Ralph Stanley. Today, the *Opry* is a showcase for almost every type of country music, including honky-tonk, bluegrass, old-time, cowboy, Cajun, and country-pop, all of which continue to enjoy widespread popular favor. As art and as enterprise, the *Opry* remains country music's most enduring institution and one of the most significant in the history of American popular entertainment.

JOHN W. RUMBLE
Country Music Foundation
Nashville, Tennessee

Jack Hurst, *Grand Ole Opry* (1975); John W. Rumble, notes to *Radio Barn Dances*, Franklin Mint Record Society CW 095/096; Charles K. Wolfe, *A Good-Natured Riot: The Birth of the Grand Ole Opry* (1998).

Green, Al

(b. 1946) SOUL AND GOSPEL SINGER. Part preacher, part soul singer, and full-time performer, the Rev. Al Green is an anomaly of artists. Lauded for his silky voice and sexy tunes, Green is celebrated as one of the foremost soul singers in R&B. His uncanny ability to wed powerful falsetto with guttural moans creates a signature style often thought of as a bridge between the sound of Memphis's Stax Studio and that of Detroit's Motown Records.

Born Albert Greene on 13 April 1946 in Forrest City, Ark., this celebrated soul star was kicked out of the family gospel quartet when his father found him covertly listening to Jackie Wilson. The

Greenes moved to Grand Rapids, Mich., in the mid-1950s, putting young Albert closer to the Motown revolution that was taking place in nearby Detroit. By age 16 he was the lead singer in a high school soul band called Al Greene and the Creations. The band later renamed themselves Al Greene and the Soul Mates and recorded "Back Up Train," the group's only R&B hit. Green would soon drop the "e" from his last name and begin the journey to becoming a solo artist.

A chance meeting in Midland, Tex., with bandleader and talent scout Willie Mitchell got Green on the Hi Records label and into the charts. The two began their first collaboration in 1969, working to hone Green's voice for his debut album, *Green Is Blues*. He was greatly influenced by Jackie Wilson, James Brown, and Sam Cooke, but Mitchell helped Green break away from mimicking his idols and emerge with an intensely passionate sound all his own. The signature Al Green sound could be heard on *Green Is Blues*, but it was the 1970 release of *Al Green Gets Next to You* that fully immersed fans in the sweet strains, passionate wails, and seductive allure of his voice. Backed by energetic horns, sumptuous grooves, and tight beats, Green's sound still remains one of the most distinctive among American musicians.

Green's first hit single, "Tired of Being Alone," sparked a string of four consecutive solid gold singles. Three of those singles would emerge from his 1972 release *Let's Stay Together*, including title track "Let's Stay Together," "I'm Still in Love with You," and "Look What You Done for Me." Green continued to wow fans with the 1973 release of *Call Me*, establishing himself as a staple in the 1970s smooth soul genre. Over the next two years, Green's singles would continue to mark the charts. "Call Me," "Here I Am," and "Sha-La-La (Make Me Happy)" all became Top 10 hits.

However, in October 1974, at the height of his stardom, Green was attacked by then-girlfriend Mary Woodson. Woodson broke into Green's home and threw boiling grits on the artist as he was bathing. She then walked into the next room and killed herself with Green's gun. The singer suffered second-degree burns on his back, stomach, and arm, and took the event as a sign from God to clean up his life.

In 1976 Green bought the Full Gospel Tabernacle in Memphis and became an ordained minister. Even though Green's life was becoming progressively more religious, he did collaborate on three more secular albums with Mitchell in the late 1970s. From 1969 to 1976 Green produced eight albums with Mitchell, selling over 20 million copies worldwide.

Green stopped working with Mitchell in 1977 and self-produced *The Belle Album*, a sincere and partly acoustic record that received much acclaim but low sales. Two years later, Green fell off the stage during a performance and again saw the accident as a sign from God. The singer then completely retired from secular music and devoted himself fully to the ministry.

Green worked solely as a minister and gospel singer, songwriter, and performer in the 1980s. He produced a number of gospel albums on Myrrh records and appeared alongside Patti LaBelle in the 1982 musical *Your Arms Too Short to Box with God*. His messages from the pulpit were as highly praised and moving as his stage performances, and many from his congregation and among his followers began to see Green as an exemplary model for living righteously in a secular world. During the late 1980s Green released two widely recognized gospel albums, *Soul Survivor* and *I Get Joy*. In 1987 he and Mitchell cowrote and coproduced an autobiographical documentary, *The Gospel according to Al Green*.

By the 1990s Green was once again recording secular music but still devoting time and energy to the Full Gospel Tabernacle and the ministry. He collaborated with the likes of Lyle Lovett and Annie Lennox for two separate film sound tracks and found himself drawing new interest when "Let's Stay Together" was featured in the 1994 film *Pulp Fiction*. Green was inducted into the Rock and Roll Hall of Fame in 1994.

Mitchell and Green got back to their roots in 2003 when they collaborated on the 2003 release *I Can't Stop* on the Hi Records label. Green's most recent release with Mitchell, *Everything's OK*, proved successful, and Green embarked upon a worldwide tour promoting the part-secular, part-religious album.

Green was inducted into both the Songwriters Hall of Fame and the Gospel Hall of Fame in 2004. He is the recipient of eight Soul Gospel Perfor-

mance Grammy awards and has produced over 37 albums and 10 Top 10 hits.

MARY MARGARET MILLER
University of Mississippi

Al Green, *Take Me to the River* (2001).

Guthrie, Woody

(1912–1967) FOLK SINGER.
Woodrow Wilson Guthrie was born on 14 July 1912, in the small frontier town of Okemah, Okla. Born to politically liberal parents (as evidenced by his given name), Charles and Nora, Guthrie grew up relatively poor. His father played in cowboy bands and owned and ran a trading post. His father's business failed when Guthrie was still young, and shortly thereafter tragedy revisited the family two more times. Woody's sister died in a fire, and his mother died from Huntington's disease. When his father decided to return to his native Texas—a place Guthrie had visited often growing up and where he had learned the guitar, banjo, and fiddle—Guthrie struck out on his own. Okemah's boomtown period was long past, and Guthrie went in search of a better life. He was 19 years old.

Guthrie soon settled in the Texas panhandle. He met and married Mary Jennings in 1933, and they quickly had three children, Gwen, Sue, and Bill. With brother-in-law Matt Jennings and Cluster Baker, Guthrie formed his first band, the Corn Cob Trio. Riding on the heels of the Great Depression, however, was the Great Dust Storm, which hit the Great Plains in 1935. If it was hard to make a living during the Depression, the Dust Storm made it impossible. The band broke up, and Guthrie set out for California and the prosperity he hoped he would find there.

En route to California, Guthrie joined the mass migration west of "dust bowl refugees," called "Okies." Some of these people were from Oklahoma, but there were also farm families from Kansas, Tennessee, and Georgia who had lost their homes and land and were traveling west in search of opportunity. Guthrie used whatever means he could to get to California: hitchhiking, hopping freight trains, even walking much of the way. When he arrived, he experienced a great deal of scorn and hatred from the residents of California who were opposed to the influx of immigrants. Guthrie worked as a migrant worker while penning songs about the hardship and unfair working conditions he and those around him were experiencing. Some songs to come out of his experiences were "Dust Bowl Blues," "I Ain't Got No Home," "Goin' down the Road Feelin' Bad," and "This Land Is Your Land." These songs came to be known as "Dust Bowl Ballads."

In 1937, Guthrie began doing radio shows on KFVD in Los Angeles and XELO just over the Mexican border. It was through radio that he found a large audience for his political and social commentary and criticism. Not one to rest on success, or in any one place, for long, Guthrie divorced his wife and soon headed east to New York City. He began collaborating on projects with other "folkies" such as Leadbelly and

Pete Seeger and worked for a short time on a radio show for CBS.

Guthrie moved back to California and then to Oregon, where he recorded *The Columbia River Songs* for a documentary project about the building of the Grand Coulee Dam. Among the songs included in this collection were "Roll on Columbia" and "Grand Coulee Dam." When the project was over, Guthrie moved back to New York and married dancer Marjorie Mazia. He and Marjorie had one daughter and several sons, including his future singer/songwriter son, Arlo. In New York, Guthrie penned several songs about the war in Europe (first opposing the war on principal, then supporting the war against Nazi fascism). In 1943, he wrote his autobiography, *Bound for Glory*.

After serving brief tours in the Merchant Marines and the U.S. Army, Guthrie returned to New York and to tragedy. His daughter Cathy was killed in an apartment fire. Guthrie became severely depressed and all but quit songwriting. In 1948, he wrote his last great ballad, "Deportees," a song about the crash of a plane carrying Mexican immigrants.

Guthrie's health mysteriously declined over the following few years, and in the mid-1950s he was diagnosed with Huntington's disease—the disease which had taken his mother's life. After many years of poor health, Woody Guthrie passed away in October 1967—one of the most influential folk musicians of his or any generation. His "people's songs" reflected the struggles and hardships Americans faced in the 1930s,

1940s, and 1950s and are a history in verse about what it means to endure adversity. He was posthumously inducted into the Rock and Roll Hall of Fame in 1988.

JAMES G. THOMAS JR.
University of Mississippi

Ed Cray, *Ramblin' Man: The Life and Times of Woody Guthrie* (2004); Woody Guthrie, *Bound for Glory* (1943); Joe Klein, *Woody Guthrie: A Life* (1999).

Handy, W. C.

(1873–1958) BLUES COMPOSER AND PERFORMER.

In 1909, W. C. Handy's band was engaged by E. H. Crump's forces to deliver the black vote to their man. In his campaign for mayor of Memphis, Crump promised to clean up the city, particularly Beale Street. Though hired by Crump to promote his campaign, Handy wrote a piece called "The Memphis Blues," which mocked this idea:

Mister Crump won't 'low no easy
riders here.
Mister Crump won't 'low no easy
riders here.
I don't care what Mister Crump don't
'low.
I'm gwine bar'l-house anyhow—
Mister Crump can go an' catch
hisself some air!

This was the first time the blues came out of the backwoods and the cotton fields, off the levees, and out of the work camps and the lonesome roads to land on main street. Called "Mister Crump" at the time, the piece was an immediate hit, launched W. C. Handy as a

local celebrity, and helped elect Crump mayor of Memphis.

Born William Christopher Handy in Florence, Ala., eight years after the Civil War, Handy said he received no musical talent from his parents, nor did he have any encouragement from them when he showed promise in music. In fact, his father, a Methodist minister, hinted that he would rather see him dead than pursuing a career in music. But his teacher knew music and taught his pupils to sing. By the age of 10, young Handy could "catalogue almost any sound that came to [his] ears, using the sol-fa system."

Handy's inspiration for the blues grew out of his personal experiences and the life around him. But his conscious decision to make the blues his forte was formed in Clarksdale, Miss. One night, while playing a dance, he was asked to play some of his native music. He tried to comply. The request then came for a local group to be permitted to play. Three rather ragged young black men began to play, as he recalled in his autobiography, "one of those over-and-over strains that seemed to have no very clear beginning and . . . no ending at all. The strumming attained a disturbing monotony, but on-and-on it went, a kind of stuff that has long been associated with cane rows and levee camps." Before long, "a rain of silver dollars began to fall around the outlandish, stomping feet. The dancers went wild." After it was over, Handy strained his neck and saw that "there before the boys lay more money than my nine musicians were being paid for the entire engagement. Then I saw the beauty of primitive music." Seeing that folks would pay money for this unpolished music, Handy concluded, "There was no virtue in being blind when you had good eyes."

Handy was cheated out of his profits on the "Memphis Blues" when he published it in 1912. However, he lived long enough to have the copyright revert to him 28 years later. In 1914, Handy wrote "St. Louis Blues," which became a national anthem and established Handy in the forefront of American composers. He proudly wore the title "Father of the Blues." In 1931, Memphis honored W. C. Handy by naming a park for him, and in 1949 he was named one of the 10 outstanding older men in the world.

Handy died of natural causes in 1958. Today the Handy Awards are presented in his honor each year at the Orpheum Theater, on Beale Street in Memphis, by the Blues Foundation, to recognize the nation's outstanding blues musicians.

LEANDER C. JONES
Western Michigan University

W. C. Handy, *Father of the Blues: An Autobiography*, ed. Arna Bontemps (1941), ed., *A Treasury of the Blues* (1926).

Harris, Emmylou

(b. 1947) MUSICIAN.

Emmylou Harris has been an important voice of southern music for over 30 years, winning countless awards, including 12 Grammy awards, and selling over 15 million records worldwide. Primarily a country musician, Harris has been successful in a wide variety of other music genres, including folk, country rock, bluegrass, rock, pop, and alt-country. She has performed and recorded with such talents as Gram Parsons, Willie Nelson, Bob Dylan, Neil Young, Roy Orbison, Dolly Parton, Linda Ronstadt, and Johnny Cash.

Harris was born in 1947 in Birmingham, Ala., but spent her childhood in North Carolina and Virginia. Following high school, she enrolled at the University of North Carolina at Greensboro, where she studied music and sang with a local folk duo. Before graduating, Harris moved to the folk music mecca of mid-1960s Greenwich Village in New York City to wait tables and perform in coffeehouses. In 1969, Harris married Tom Slocum, and in 1970 she recorded her first album, *Gliding Bird*. Within the next year, she and Slocum divorced, after the birth of a daughter, Hallie, and Harris went to live with her parents, now in Washington, D.C.

After hearing Harris sing at a nightclub in Washington, D.C., the one-time front man of the country-rock group the Flying Burrito Brothers, Gram Parsons, recruited Harris to work with him on his first solo album, *GP*. During 1973, Harris toured with Parsons's group, the Fallen Angels, and worked with Parsons recording his second solo effort, *Grievous Angel*. Following Parsons's fatal overdose in a California hotel room, Harris returned to Washington, D.C., and formed her own country band. *Grievous Angel* was released posthumously in 1974.

In 1975 Harris released her second solo album, *Pieces of the Sky*, with her legendary Hot Band, which included a rotating roster of world-class musicians, such as James Burton, Glen Hardin (both of whom had played with Elvis Presley), Albert Lee, Rodney Crowell, Hank DeVito, and Ricky Scaggs. Her following albums, *Elite Hotel* (1975), *Luxury Liner* (1977), and *Quarter Moon in a Ten Cent Town* (1978), appealed to both country and rock audiences, but her next album, *Blue Kentucky Girl* (1979), consisted of straight-ahead country and bluegrass tunes. *Blue Kentucky Girl* and the following album, *Roses in the Snow* (1980), yet another collection of purely country and bluegrass songs, both went gold. The albums included songs written by some of the biggest names in country and bluegrass, including Willie Nelson, Flatt and Scruggs, Jean Ritchie, the Carter Family, Johnny Cash, and Loretta Lynn. Dolly Parton and Linda Ronstadt sang harmony on both albums.

The early 1980s found Harris experimenting with pop recordings, as evidenced on her *Evangeline* (1981) and *White Shoes* (1983) albums. Her 1985 album, *The Ballad of Sally Rose*, marked a shift in Harris's approach toward record making, as it was the first album for which she had written two or more songs since her *Gliding Bird*. Harris and her husband, Paul Kennerley (married from 1985 to 1993), cowrote all the songs, and Harris described the album as a "conceptual album," based on her relationship with Gram Parsons. In 1987, Harris, Dolly Parton, and Linda Ronstadt teamed up again for the album *Trio*, which earned a Grammy for Best Country Vocal Performance—Duo or Group.

In 1995, Harris released the acclaimed album *Wrecking Ball*, which contained songs by artists such as Jimi Hendrix, Neil Young, Gillian Welch, and Steve Earle. Although the album got little airplay on country music stations, it did bring her to the attention of a younger, more rock-oriented audience. Harris followed *Wrecking Ball* with the live album *Spyboy* (1998) and with *Trio 2* (1999), teaming up again with Parton and Ronstadt on the latter album.

In 2000, Harris performed on the *O Brother, Where Art Thou?* sound track, a movie and American-roots sound track that culminated in a nationwide Down from the Mountain Tour and a documentary-concert film, *Down from the Mountain*. Harris was involved in both. The sound track won a Grammy for Best Album of the Year in 2001 and brought American roots music, and the artists who recorded for the album, into the American mainstream.

JAMES G. THOMAS JR.
University of Mississippi

Jim Brown, *Emmylou Harris: Angel in Disguise* (2004); Ben Fong-Torres, *Hickory Wind: The Life and Times of Gram Parsons* (1991); Jessica Hundley, *Grievous Angel: An Intimate Biography of Gram Parsons* (2005); David Meyer, *Twenty Thousand Roads: The Ballad of Gram Parsons and His Cosmic American Music* (2007).

Hayes, Isaac

(1942–2008) SOUL SINGER, SONGWRITER, MUSIC PRODUCER, ACTOR.

Described by Stax Records founder Jim Stewart as one of the main roots of the Memphis Sound, Isaac Hayes cowrote some 200 compositions for Stax artists, including Sam & Dave's "Hold On, I'm

Comin'" and Carla Thomas's "Let Me Be Good to You." With the exception of Booker T. & the MG's, Isaac Hayes worked on more Stax sessions and tracks than any other musician.

Born into rural poverty, as the son of a sharecropper, on 20 August 1942, in Covington, Tenn., Isaac Hayes was singing in church by the age of five. During adolescence, he quit singing because his voice cracked, but a high school guidance counselor convinced him to sing again in a talent competition. His rendition of "Looking Back," Nat King Cole's 1958 hit, brought the Manassas High School crowd to its feet. He went on to join the school band as a saxophonist and played in various short-lived gospel, doo-wop, and jazz bands on the Memphis club circuit.

After graduating in 1962 at the age of 21, Hayes rejected seven college scholarships for vocal music. Instead, he landed playing gigs as a pianist with Stax sessionist Floyd Newman. Within two years, he was playing paid sessions with Otis Redding and soon after began collaborating as a songwriter with David Porter. As writers, arrangers, and producers, the Hayes-Porter duo, known as the "Soul Children," became Stax's hottest commodity.

From an anonymous session keyboardist to a hit songwriter, Isaac Hayes began to emerge as a top-selling soul and funk innovator with his 1968 debut release *Presenting Isaac Hayes*. A year later, the landmark *Hot Buttered Soul* album was released, staying on the pop chart for an amazing 81 weeks, forcing the music industry to conceive of soul music as an album art form for the first

Isaac Hayes, soul singer (Courtesy Stax Museum of American Soul Music, Memphis)

time. Over the next five years, Hayes delivered a record-setting seven No. 1 R&B albums for the new Stax subsidiary label Enterprise, creating more No. 1 albums than any other artist of the period.

The arrival of the movie *Shaft* sound track double LP and theme-song single in the summer of 1971 was a career-defining moment. The album became the first in history by a solo African American artist to hit No. 1 on both the pop and the R&B charts. The work also led to the first African American composer to win an Oscar for Best Musical Score at the Academy Awards. In addition, the motion picture music garnered him three Grammy awards, a Golden Globe, the NAACP Image Award, and Europe's highest music honor, the prestigious Edison award.

After the success of *Shaft*, Hayes quickly released the double LP *Black Moses*, a nickname that he reluctantly carried for years. A tour throughout Europe and the United States followed, introducing many audiences to Hayes for the first time—an imposing persona in shades and gold chains. It was Isaac Hayes, incidentally, who turned chains, a symbol of slavery, into ornaments, decades before hip-hop artists.

By 1975 Hayes had left Stax Records and formed his own label, Hot Buttered Soul Records. A series of unsuccessful albums eventually led to bankruptcy in 1976, but he bounced back with the release of "A Man and a Woman" with Dionne Warwick in 1977. He released more than 25 albums throughout his career, and today his music still lives, with many hip-hop artists, such as Eric B. & Rakim and Dr. Dre, sampling his music an estimated 200 times.

Although his calling card was an extended, orchestrated approach to both ballads and up-tempo funk, Hayes's low-key vocal style approach influenced various musicians, including Marvin Gaye, Curtis Mayfield, and the Ohio Players. Yet he also forged a career as an actor, accepting roles in approximately 40 feature films, including Mel Brooks's *Robin Hood: Men in Tights* and the 2000 version of *Shaft*, starring Samuel L. Jackson. He also made numerous television appearances in such shows as *The Rockford Files* and the *A-Team*, but his most famous was as the voice of Chef on Comedy Central's over-the-top cartoon *South Park*.

After being inducted into the Rock and Roll Hall of Fame in 2002, Isaac Hayes returned to Memphis, living across from some of the same cotton fields he once worked in as a child. He was an active humanitarian, helping to fund an after-school program at the Central Library in Memphis, the renovation of the Elmina slave castles on Africa's western coastline, and the construction of an 8,000-square-foot school in Ghana. His devotion to helping others obtain an education led to his being tapped as the international spokesperson for the Applied Scholastics' World Literacy Crusade. He was even made a king. Given the royal name Nene Katey Ocansey, he was crowned "King of Development" in Ghana in 1992.

TOBIE BAKER
University of Mississippi

Rob Bowman, *Soulsville U.S.A.: The Story of Stax Records* (1997).

Hays, Will

(1837–1907) SONGWRITER.

Will Hays was one of America's most popular songwriters in the 19th century. Many of his songs still endure today. William Shakespeare Hays was born in Louisville, Ky., in 1837. Although most of the details of his early life remain undocumented, he is known to have been the captain of the *Grey Eagle*, a Mississippi River steamboat, and was an authority on the lore and life of the country's great interior river system. He was the river editor of the *Louisville Democrat* at the age of 19 and was later a columnist for many years on the *Louisville Courier-Journal* and the *Cincinnati Enquirer*. He served briefly during the Civil War as a war correspondent in the South. He was also a poet of popular, sentimental verse, and the writer of over 500 songs.

His first successful song was "The Drummer Boy of Shiloh" (1862), which was popular in both the North and the South. Before his death in 1907 Hays achieved remarkable popularity as a songwriter. Like most popular songwriters of the mid-19th century, Hays was much influenced by the repertoire and style of blackface minstrelsy, and he wrote both lighthearted and pathetic lyrics, some of which were couched in black dialect. His chief forte lay in the composition of nostalgic laments or tender love songs that breathed Victorian morality and imagery. Some of his popular compositions include "We Parted by the River Side" (1866), "I'll Remember You, Love, in My Prayers" (1869), "Mollie Darling" (1871), "Nobody's Darling on Earth" (1870), and "The Little Old Cabin in the Lane" (1871). He also wrote a poem, "The Faithful Engineer," on which the popular gospel song "Life's Railway to Heaven" was based.

Although music critics and historians have paid little attention to Hays and have never ranked him in the same class with Stephen Foster, in some ways his songs have been more popular than those of the great Pennsylvania composer. Hays never profited from high-art patronage as Foster did (Foster's songs, for example, were warmly endorsed by the Czech composer Antonín Dvořák), and his compositions were never anthologized in the songbooks given to America's schoolchildren. Nevertheless, Hays's songs endured among the folk and have been collected often "in the field" by folklorists. His "Little Old Cabin in the Lane" inspired the creation of other well-known songs such as "Little Old Sod Shanty," "Little

Joe the Wrangler," and "Little Red Caboose behind the Train." Hays's songs also received renewed life and demonstrated their down-home appeal in the commercial country music field, where they were often performed. "Little Old Cabin" (recorded as "Little Old Log Cabin in the Lane") was one side of Fiddlin' John Carson's historic recording of 1923, the disc that marked the beginning of the country music industry. As late as 1948 the commercial power of Hays's songs was demonstrated when superstar Eddy Arnold recorded a best-selling version of "Mollie Darling" (spelled "Molly" on the label). As is often true of older musical material, Hays's songs have found acceptance today among bluegrass musicians.

BILL C. MALONE
Madison, Wisconsin

Bill C. Malone, *Register of the Kentucky Historical Society* (Summer 1995), *Southern Music—American Music* (1979).

Hee Haw

The impact of *Hee Haw* on southern culture is undeniable. First broadcast on 15 June 1969 on CBS, the Nashville-based hillbilly variety show ultimately became one of the most popular syndicated television programs of all time. Appropriately named for the braying of a donkey, the show is best recognized for down-home, cornball humor set in fictitious Cornfield County. Based on Rowan and Martin's successful comedy variety show, *Laugh-In*, *Hee Haw* combined humorous skits, fast one-liners, rusticated vaudeville, and both country and gospel music to create one of the longest-running and most Emmy award–winning syndicated series in television history. During *Hee Haw*'s heyday in the 1970s and early to mid-1980s, between 20 and 30 million viewers tuned in each week.

The format of *Hee Haw* suggested a casual gathering of friends, similar to the atmosphere featured on popular barn dance–style radio programs of the early 20th century. Ensemble skits and musical numbers reminiscent of old-fashioned hoedowns and barn raisings promoted fellowship through song and appreciation of clean country living. Set designs included hay bales and make-shift barns, while costumes primarily consisted of revealing gingham frocks for female cast members and denim overalls for males. Adding to the pastoral feel of *Hee Haw* were cornfields, Burma Shave signs, wagon wheels, and musical instruments that adorned the sets. Most of the skits during the hour-long show took place in a cornfield, general store, barber shop, the KORN newsroom, or other typically "southern" venues. Animation also served as a key component of *Hee Haw*. Throughout the course of each episode, a menagerie of cartoon barnyard animals appeared, adding to the rural flavor and introducing an innovative element to the country variety show.

Hee Haw reinforced traditional southern stereotypes: backwoods moonshiners, crooked small-town judges, illiterate bumpkins, egotistical belles, and buxom beauties introduced an entire generation of viewers to the already-established character types associated with the region. The impact

of these exaggerated drawls and pickled moonshiners on perceptions of southerners was twofold. In the short term, it provided comedic fodder, as outlandish characters took their "southernness" to a ridiculous level. In the long term it had a much more profound effect. Over a 25-year period, *Hee Haw* introduced a new national audience to the Old South while also reminding older viewers of that same South. The show projected an innocent, lighthearted, peace-loving image of southerners, an image much different from the violent racists captured on network news programs of the period.

On average, approximately 40 people made up the cast of *Hee Haw*, including the show's hosts, country musicians Roy Clark and Buck Owens. Other widely recognized cast members included Minnie Pearl, Grandpa Jones, Stringbean, and Junior Samples. In addition to show regulars, *Hee Haw* also featured special guest stars each week. Although the guests were usually established country musicians such as Loretta Lynn, Charley Pride, or Johnny Cash, celebrities of both television and film donned straw hats and overalls for their appearances on the series. However, for the most part, *Hee Haw* capitalized on the emerging and continued success of country music stars to bolster its ratings. Traditional country and gospel music served as the backbone of the program and took up most of the time of the hour-long show. A typical episode featured the ensemble cast pickin' and grinnin' to some old school country tunes and the *Hee Haw* Gospel Quartet singing Christian (and southern) staples such as

"Amazing Grace." The "SA-LOOT" segment also enhanced the down-home flavor of *Hee Haw*. Reflecting the regional pride and sense of place typically shared by southerners, each special guest star stood in the cornfield while wearing a straw hat and overalls and, with a flourish of his or her hat, saluted his or her hometown.

Ultimately, *Hee Haw* made the South a recognized venue for nationally televised entertainment and placed many little-known southerners in the national spotlight. The show's combination of country and gospel music, country comedy, and hillbilly characters provided southern audiences with an opportunity to both enjoy their unique culture and parody it in a lighthearted, nonconfrontational manner.

SALLY HODO WALBURN
Jackson, Mississippi

Marc Eliot and Roy Clark, *My Life in Spite of Myself* (1994); Marc Eliot and Sam Lovullo, *Life in the Kornfield: My 25 Years at Hee Haw* (1996); Jack Gould, *New York Times* (16 June 1969); Neil Hickey, *TV Guide* (7 March 1970); R. Douglas Hurt, ed., *The Rural South since World War II* (1998); Joli Jensen, *The Nashville Sound* (1998); Jack Temple Kirby, *Media-Made Dixie* (1978); Bill C. Malone, *Don't Get above Your Raisin': Country Music and the Southern Working Class* (2002); Alex McNeil, *Total Television: A Comprehensive Guide to Programming from 1948 to the Present* (1984); Richard A. Peterson, *Creating Country Music: Fabricating Authenticity* (1997).

Hill, Faith

(b. 1967) COUNTRY MUSIC SINGER.
Faith Hill's career blossomed during the 1990s, which some observers regard as the golden age of modern country music. This was the period of Garth Brooks's ascendance, when the Nashville Network showcased country music around the clock to America's growing cable audience and when it was commonplace for country artists to sell a million or more copies of each new album. With her striking physical beauty and strong expressive voice, Hill was a natural for stardom.

Born 21 September 1967 in Jackson, Miss., the future singer and actress was adopted within a week of her birth and named Audrey Faith Perry. She grew up in the small town of Star, Miss. As she sang in church, family and neighbors took note of her vocal talent, and before long she was performing wherever the town afforded her the opportunity. By the time she was in high school, she knew she wanted a career singing country music.

Perry moved to Nashville in 1987 when she was 19 years old. She soon discovered that people who were already in the music business were reluctant to hire aspiring singers and songwriters because they feared—and with good reason—that such employees would neglect their assigned duties to focus on their careers. That being the situation, Perry hid her ambitions. She got a job as a receptionist at singer Gary Morris's company by telling him she was in Nashville to attend school. About a year later a songwriter overheard her singing along with the radio and concluded she had something to offer show business. Her big break came when songwriter Gary Burr asked her to sing with him at Nashville's fabled Bluebird Café. During these early years, Perry married music publisher Daniel Hill, whose name she kept after they were divorced.

Hill's work as a "demo" (demonstration record) singer and her growing network of music business acquaintances ultimately helped secure her a recording contract with Warner Brothers Records. Her first album, *Take Me as I Am*, in 1993, yielded her the No. 1 hits "Wild One" and "Piece of My Heart." Both these songs were supported by music videos that emphasized Hill's high spirits and girl-next-door good looks.

Hill continued to score No. 1 songs throughout the ensuing decade—among them "It Matters to Me," "This Kiss," "Let Me Let Go," "Breathe," "The Way You Love Me," and "Mississippi Girl." Each of her albums routinely sold multiple millions of copies. By 2007, her worldwide album sales exceeded 25 million units.

In 1996, Hill teamed with Tim McGraw for a concert tour. During the tour they fell in love, and they married on 6 October of that year. The next year Hill and McGraw topped the country charts with their duet "It's Your Love," the first of several vocal collaborations. As of 2007 Hill had won a total of five Grammy awards, including those she shared with McGraw.

Hill has also dabbled in acting. She performed in the television series *Promised Land* and *Touched by an Angel* and played a supporting role in the 2004 movie *The Stepford Wives*.

Hill and McGraw have usually toured separately. But in 2006 they united for the "Soul2Soul" tour. It became the best-selling country music tour up to that time, grossing $88.6 million and surpassing concurrent tours by Madonna and the Rolling Stones. Hill and McGraw toured together again in 2007.

EDWARD MORRIS
Former country music editor of Billboard

James L. Dickenson, *Faith Hill, Piece of My Heart* (2001); Joel Whitburn, *Top Country Songs: 1944 to 2005* (2006).

Holly, Buddy

(1936–1959) ROCK-AND-ROLL SINGER, SONGWRITER, GUITARIST, PRODUCER.

West Texas–born Buddy Holly was perhaps the most multifaceted and creative individual among the first wave of white rock-and-roll stars in the 1950s. A singer, guitarist, songwriter, and innovative force in the studio, the young Holly also was the most influential early rock-and-roll singer to work with his own self-contained band, a format that soon became standard in the idiom. Like the Everly Brothers, Holly brought a sweet pop and country harmony duo sensibility to rockabilly, somewhat restoring the balance between white and African American influences in rock and roll, which in its early stages had been decidedly closer to rhythm and blues. His bespectacled, everyman look inspired generations of youngsters not bestowed with Elvis Presley's spectacular looks— for instance, Elvis Costello, Marshall Crenshaw, and members of Weezer— to dream of careers in rock music. Yet it was in his early death at age 22 that Holly became immortalized as one of the most prominent of 20th-century popular culture icons.

Buddy Holly was born Charles Hardin Holley on 7 September 1936, in Lubbock, Tex., into a musical family. At age five, he accompanied his two elder brothers to a singing competition and wound up with a $5 prize. By November 1953 Holly was performing on Lubbock's country-and-western radio station, KDAV. Then, with Bob Montgomery, Holly formed the duo Buddy and Bob, performing a mix of country and bluegrass songs but increasingly gravitating toward the rhythm and blues he heard on the radio. Although some sources suggest that he might have predated Elvis Presley in synthesizing white and black music, the Lubbock native's efforts were certainly galvanized following the success of Presley's Sun Records sides and the Mississippian's stops in Holly's hometown in 1955, when Buddy and Bob, accompanied by bassist Larry Welborn, opened for him.

Holly made some studio recordings in Wichita Falls, Tex., and soon received a recording contract with Decca. The ensuing 1956 sessions were held at the legendary Bradley's Barn and were produced by "Nashville Sound" architect Owen Bradley. Holly wrestled the Nashville bigwigs for creative control. The resulting singles had many flashes of what would become Holly's trademark mannerisms—stutters, stammers, hiccups—but a clash in artistic direction led Decca to can most of them and later drop Holly's contract.

Through 1956 Holly had been honing his performing and recording skills at Norman Petty's studios in Clovis, N.Mex. He and drummer Jerry Allison recorded for Petty a version of "That'll Be the Day," a song also recorded previously in Nashville that Bradley had refused to release. Petty believed in the song and used his connections to gain its release on Brunswick under the band name the Crickets. The single zoomed to No. 1, and, in the wake of its success, Holly was signed independently to Coral Records.

In the next year and a half, Holly, recording under his name for Coral and under the Crickets' moniker for Brunswick, had one of the most influential runs in the history of popular music, yielding 11 charting singles and many more that have since become pop staples, including "Peggy Sue," "Words of Love," "Not Fade Away," "Everyday," "Maybe Baby," "Rave On," "Well, All Right," "Think It Over," "Heartbeat," "It's So Easy," "Love's Made a Fool of You," and "True Love Ways."

Holly toured as part of stellar rock and soul revues when he was not recording and, after his December 1958 split with the Crickets and move to New York, embarked on what would become his last album, the *Winter Dance Party*, also featuring Richie Valens, J. P. "The Big Bopper" Richardson, and Dion and the Belmonts. On the morning of 3 February 1959, a four-seat private plane carrying Holly, Valens, and Richardson crashed soon after taking off from Clear Lake, Iowa, killing all on board. The commemoration of Holly's death as "the day the music died" in the 1971 Don McLean chart topper "American Pie" ensured posthumous renown for one of rock's originals.

AJAY KALRA

University of Texas at Austin

Ellis Amburn, *Buddy Holly: A Biography* (1995); John Goldrosen, *The Buddy Holly Story* (1979); John Goldrosen and John Beecher, *Remembering Buddy: The Definitive Biography* (1975); Philip Norman, *Rave On: The Biography of Buddy Holly* (1996).

Hooker, John Lee

(1917–2001) BLUES SINGER.

John Lee Hooker, bluesman, 1986 (Michael Stachnik, photographer, Living Blues Archival Collection, University of Mississippi Blues Archive, Oxford)

"The King of the Boogie" began life near the city that spawned so many seminal blues musicians, Clarksdale, Miss. Born one of 11 children into a sharecropping family, he followed a familiar pattern of early exposure to both sacred and secular music, experimentation with homemade instruments, and migration first to Memphis and then farther north. Arriving in Detroit in 1943, he recorded his first impressions in a song that would be among his most famous, "Boogie Chillen." "I was walking down Hastings Street / I saw a little place called Henry's Swing Club / Decided I'd stop in there that night / And I got down." Other well-known Hooker compositions include "Boom Boom" and "House Rent Boogie."

An extremely individual stylist, Hooker spoke with a slight speech impediment that brought a jarring intensity to his vocal phrasing when he sang. He combined this with a guitar technique that was paradoxically repetitious and yet utterly unpredictable. His radically syncopated playing, not constrained by the tyranny of bar lines, complemented his own sense of meter. "Word by word, lyric by lyric music— that's from the book: that ain't the way I feel. If I feel some way, I'm gonna let it come out. . . . It might rhyme and it might not. I don't care."

At the height of its popularity among post–World War II black audiences, Hooker's work contained another paradox, that of a southern phenomenon flourishing unabated and unmodified in the North. Where other rural southern musicians yielded to the standardizing, homogenizing forces of the commercial music business, Hooker continued to improvise material freely and pursue a rhythmic and metrical style so unique as to make him difficult to accompany or imitate. Hooker steadfastly maintained the idiosyncrasies of a unique regional and individual stylist, and his success was a testament to the deeply affecting power of this most personal approach. In 1989 Hooker recorded his Grammy-winning album, *The Healer.* He was inducted into the Rock and Roll Hall of Fame in 1991.

WILLIAM A. COCHRANE
University of Mississippi

Sheldon Harris, *Blues Who's Who: A Biographical Dictionary of Blues Singers* (1979); John Lee Hooker, *John Lee Hooker: A Blues Legend* (1991); Charles Murray, *Boogie Man: The Adventures of John Lee Hooker in the American Twentieth Century* (2002); Robert Neff and Anthony Connor, *Blues* (1975); Paul Oliver, *Blues Off the Record* (1984); Jim O'Neil and Amy O'Neil, *Living Blues* (Autumn 1979).

Hopkins, Lightnin'

(1912–1982) BLUES SINGER.
Born 15 March 1912 in Centerville, Leon County, Tex., Sam "Lightnin'" Hopkins learned to play a homemade cigar-box instrument when he was eight, picked up a little about playing the guitar later from his brother Joel, sang in the church choir as a youth, and absorbed musical materials from fellow farmworkers and in nearby bars. He was a hobo and traveled throughout Texas in the 1920s doing farmwork and playing for small pay in clubs and bars and at dances and parties. He moved to Houston in the 1930s but was unable to find steady work as a musician and soon moved back to near Centerville.

In the mid-1940s Hopkins was living in rural east Texas, surviving as a farm laborer and playing music in his free time. He went back to Houston and became a fixture in the blues scene on Dowling Street. A California talent scout arranged a recording session for Hopkins and Wilson Smith, his piano accompanist, in Los Angeles, and in 1946 Hopkins made his first recordings for Aladdin Records. In promoting the release, an Aladdin executive came up with the names of Lightnin' Hopkins and Thunder Smith. Hopkins returned to Houston after spending some time in California. He recorded across the nation during the late 1940s and early 1950s, but he performed mostly at clubs around Houston.

Folklorist Mack McCormick met Hopkins in 1959 and promoted him on the folk music circuit of the early 1960s. In 1960 alone, Hopkins played a hootenanny at the Alley Theater in Houston, performed at the California Blues Festival in Berkeley, and debuted at Carnegie Hall on a bill with Bob Dylan and Joan Baez. Television shows were soon being made about him, many of them on PBS. Throughout the 1960s and 1970s, Hopkins continued recording, and record companies released many of his earlier titles. He recorded in this period on, among others, the Bluesville, Arhoolie, Prestige, and Verve labels, and he appeared throughout the 1960s and the 1970s at major folk festivals, on college campuses, and in clubs. The 1972 film *Sounder* used songs by Hopkins, and Les Blank's documentary film *The Blues accordin' to Lightnin' Hopkins* appeared in 1968. Hopkins died in February 1982 in Houston.

CHARLES REAGAN WILSON
University of Mississippi

Dan Bowden, *Lightnin' Hopkins: The Gold Star Years* (1998); Samuel Charters, *The Country Blues* (1959); Sheldon Harris, *Blues Who's Who: A Biographical Dictionary of Blues Singers* (1979); Lightnin' Hopkins and Dan Bowden, *Lightnin' Hopkins: Blues Guitar Legend* (1995); Irwin Stambler and Grellin Landon, *The Encyclopedia of Folk, Country, and Western Music* (2d ed., 1983).

Howell, Peg Leg

(1888–1966) BLUES SINGER.
Joshua Barnes Howell was born in Eatonton, Ga., on 5 March 1888. He was one of the leaders of the East Coast Piedmont Blues. Howell worked on a farm, where he would have heard the field hollers and other plantation work songs of former slaves, and at the age of 21 he taught himself to play the guitar. Allegedly shot in the leg by his brother-in-law in 1916, Howell had the leg amputated and fitted with a prosthesis, and soon he became known as "Peg Leg." No longer fit for farmwork, he relocated to Atlanta. There he played music for change and sold bootleg whiskey to make a living. He spent a year in jail after a 1925 conviction for bootlegging. He likely spent time on a chain gang, referred to in his "Ball and Chain Blues" and "New Prison Blues."

Columbia Record's field recording unit swung through Atlanta every spring and fall from 1927 through 1931 to record Howell and other artists, secular and sacred, such as Tampa Joe, Macon Ed, and Barbecue Bob. His early recordings were solo efforts, but soon he recorded with a group known as his "gang." The gang's two mainstays were fiddler Eddie Anthony and guitarist Henry Williams. He recorded everything from ballads to dance music.

His songs such as "Monkey Man Blues," "Chittlin' Supper," and "Broke and Hungry Blues" bridge the gap between preblues African American field hollers and work songs and the later conventional 12-bar styles. He also recorded songs in the 16-bar blues ("Turtle Dove") and 8-bar blues ("Rolling Mill"), which had strong links to traditional white blues.

Columbia dropped Howell after his April 1929 session, but he continued to play until his good friend Anthony died in 1934. Howell then returned to bootlegging and other occupations. He lost his other leg to diabetes in 1955. In 1963 Document Records located Howell strapped to a wheelchair and living on welfare in Atlanta government housing. There he recorded for the first time in 34 years, though his hard life had taken its toll on his singing ability. Howell died in 1966 and is buried in Chestnut Hill Cemetery in Atlanta.

WILLIAM S. BURDELL III
St. Simons Island, Georgia

Bruce Bastin, *Red River Blues: The Blues Tradition in the Southeast* (1986); Samuel Barclay Charters, *Country Blues* (1975), *Sweet as the Showers of Rain* (1977); Paul Oliver, *The Story of the Blues* (1969).

Hurt, Mississippi John

(1893–1966) BLUES SINGER.
Born in Teoc, Miss., Hurt was a self-taught guitarist who performed for many years in Avalon, Miss. He made his first recording in 1928. His most

noted recorded selections, including "Candy Man," "Avalon Blues," "Spike Driver Blues," and "Stagger Lee Blues," were produced by the Okeh Recording Company. He seldom appeared in public performance between 1929 and the early 1960s, but he gained popularity in 1963 through his appearance at the Newport Folk Festival. In 1963 he recorded the album *Mississippi John Hurt: Folk Songs and Blues* for Piedmont Records. This album served as an incentive for the recording of "Worried Blues" in 1964. He toured extensively throughout the United States until his death on 2 November 1966 in Grenada, Miss. Two of his most noted concert appearances were at Carnegie Hall and Town Hall in New York City. He became one of the most beloved of Mississippi Delta bluesmen, with an almost lyrical musical style.

LEMUEL BERRY JR.
Alabama State University

Samuel Charters, *The Bluesmen: The Story and the Music of the Men Who Made the Blues* (1967); Richard K. Spottswood, *Blues Unlimited* (August 1963).

Jackson, Mahalia

(1911–1972) GOSPEL SINGER.
Born in New Orleans on 26 October 1911, Mahalia Jackson grew up in the Baptist church, but she was heavily influenced by the music of Holiness congregations and such blues singers as Bessie Smith and Ma Rainey. She moved to Chicago in 1927, joined the choir of Greater Salem Baptist Church, and then in 1928 became a member of the Johnson Gospel Singers, composed of

Mahalia Jackson, gospel singer, as portrayed on a paper fan produced by the Dillon Funeral Homes and Burial Association, Leland, Vicksburg, Greenville, Indianola, and Cleveland, Miss., 1968 (William R. Ferris Collection, Southern Folklife Collection, Wilson Library, University of North Carolina at Chapel Hill)

three Johnson brothers—Robert, Prince, and Wilbur—and Louise Lemon, who together were one of the first professional gospel singing groups. The group toured the Midwest, and their concerts featured religious plays written by the director, Robert Johnson, and starring Johnson and Mahalia. Jackson met Thomas A. Dorsey in the mid-1930s and began a 14-year association with him, first as one of the singers he accompanied and later as the performer of his songs. Through his connection, she secured a recording contract with Decca Records in 1937 and cut four sides for the label, none of which attracted much attention.

Jackson's reputation as a soloist with the National Baptist Convention gained her a wide following, and with her 1947 recording of W. Herbert Brewster's "Move on Up a Little Higher," she was catapulted into the limelight as a gospel star, becoming the "Queen of Gospel Singers" by 1950. She had her own radio program in Chicago, appeared on the Ed Sullivan and Dinah Shore television shows, and began a series of concert tours of Europe in 1952. She was invited to perform at one of the inaugural parties of President John F. Kennedy, and she sang at the March on Washington in 1963 and at the funeral of Martin Luther King Jr. She appeared in several films, including *Imitation of Life* (1959) and *The Best Man* (1964). Jackson was offered huge sums to appear in nightclubs or to switch to a secular repertoire, but she rejected such offers. She did, however, record Duke Ellington's "Come Sunday" with his orchestra in 1958. Her dark, deep, and powerful contralto inspired many singers, including Aretha Franklin, Linda Hopkins, and Brother Joe May. Her best-known recordings include "Just over the Hill," "In the Upper Room," and "He's Got the Whole World in His Hands."

HORACE CLARENCE BOYER
University of Massachusetts, Amherst

Horace Clarence Boyer, *The Gospel Song: An Historical and Analytical Study* (M.A. thesis, Eastman School of Music, University of Rochester, 1964); Darlene Donloe, *Mahalia Jackson* (1992); Laurraine Goreau, *Just Mahalia, Baby* (1975); Leslie Gourse, *Mahalia Jackson: Queen of Gospel Song* (1996); Marleen Hengelaar-Rookmaaker, *New Orleans Jazz, Mahalia Jackson and the Philosophy of Art* (2002); Mahalia Jackson and Evan Wylie, *Movin' on Up* (1966); Barbara Kramer, *Mahalia Jackson: The Voice of Gospel and Civil Rights* (2003); Roxane Orgill, *Mahalia: A Life in Gospel Music* (2002); William H. Tallmadge, *Ethnomusicology* (May 1961); Charles K. Wolfe, *Mahalia Jackson* (2003).

Jefferson, Blind Lemon

(1897–1929) BLUES SINGER.
Blind Lemon Jefferson was the South's most renowned country blues oracle in the 1920s. He was born blind into a poor sharecropping family on a farm about 50 miles east of Dallas in 1897. Like other blind bluesmen, such as Blind Blake, Blind Willie McTell, and Gary Davis, he turned to music at an early age because it was the only way he could make a living. Early in his career Jefferson became a popular bluesman in the east Texas farming communities around his birthplace. Then he took to the road, and throughout the 1920s he made frequent trips outside of Texas to Oklahoma, the Mississippi Delta, Georgia, Virginia, and eventually Chicago, where he recorded for Paramount Records. In the late 1920s Jefferson recorded over 90 songs. He proved to be the most commercially viable of all the rural blues musicians who made records during this period. His high-pitched voice and eclectic guitar style were especially popular among blacks in the South.

The blues repertoire that he recorded in Chicago reflected the range of themes prevalent in the black oral tradition in the South at the turn of the century.

They included travel, work, sexual relationships, poverty, and prison life. His sympathies were always with the downtrodden. The blues he recorded were a mixture of traditional numbers such as "See See Rider" or "Boll Weevil Blues" and his own compositions like "Matchbox Blues"—which ultimately became one of his best-known signature pieces. Taken all together, Jefferson's blues lyrics represent a firsthand account of African American life in the South during the early 1900s. They are humorous and painful, ripe with sexual metaphor and fantasy, skeptical about love, and strikingly blunt in their portrayal of the society from the perspective of those at the bottom.

Blind Lemon Jefferson was in Chicago for a recording session in December 1929 when he was found dead in a snowdrift. Apparently he lost his way after playing at a house party late one night and froze to death. His body was taken back to Texas for burial. Although he died young, he left an impressive blues legacy through the recordings he made in his lifetime. He is still known and respected as one of the greatest rural bluesmen of his era.

BILL BARLOW
Howard University

Blind Lemon Jefferson, Milestone Records M-47022; Samuel Charters, *The Bluesmen: The Story and the Music of the Men Who Made the Blues* (1967); Bob Groom, *Blind Lemon Jefferson* (1970); Sheldon Harris, *Blues Who's Who: A Biographical Dictionary of Blues Singers* (1979); Robert L. Uzzel, *Blind Lemon Jefferson: His Life, His Death, and His Legacy* (2002).

Jennings, Waylon

(1937–2002) COUNTRY MUSIC SINGER.

Texas-born guitarist, singer, and songwriter Waylon Jennings enjoyed a prolific career that spanned over four decades. Building on an early career as a rock-and-roll performer in the late 1950s, he became a country superstar in the 1970s and introduced "outlaw country," which represented a new approach to performance, composition, and imagery revolving around a rejection of Nashville pop-country slickness and the move toward a more personalized and reflective lyrical voice.

Born in Littlefield, Tex., Jennings started playing guitar at age 8, and by age 12, he had become a radio dj. Shortly afterward he formed his first band. He left school at 14, worked picking cotton for several years, and ended up in nearby Lubbock. He secured a job as a DJ at station KLLL and developed a mentor relationship with Buddy Holly. He began his recording career with the cover of the Cajun waltz "Jole Blon" in 1958. Jennings filled in as the bass player on Holly's final tour with the Crickets and narrowly missed being in the tragic plane crash in February 1959 that ended Holly's career, as well as those of Ritchie Valens and J. P. "Big Bopper" Richardson.

After Holly's death, Jennings returned to Lubbock, and for a couple of years he drifted around the Southwest with his wife and three young children in tow. After settling in Phoenix, Ariz., he put together a backup band called the Waylors, which developed a local following with a wide variety of material—pop, country, folk, blues, and rock and roll—for the late-night bar crowd and were hired as the house band at a new club called J.D.'s. At this time his marriage was dissolving but his career was taking off. He came to the attention of Herb Alpert, who signed him to the newly formed A&M Records. But Jennings's country leanings did not fit well with Alpert's vision of him as a pop artist, and the A&M material attracted little attention.

In 1965 Jennings left A&M and signed with RCA, relocating to Nashville to work with producer Chet Atkins. Having brought the Waylors along with him, he released his RCA debut album *Folk Country* in 1966. The same year he was cast in the lead role in the film *Nashville Rebel* and released an album by the same title. In Nashville he developed friendships with Johnny Cash, Willie Nelson, and Kris Kristofferson, among others, relationships that had a significant impact upon his future musical career. In 1969 he married his fourth wife, country singer Jessi Colter; the pair would remain together until his death in 2002.

In 1970, after a string of moderately successful folk-country records for RCA, he began his transition from the typical Nashville arrangements and production to a more spare and stripped-down aesthetic. He took control of the production of his albums when he renegotiated his contract with RCA in 1972. *Honky Tonk Heroes*, released in 1973, represented a new level of creative independence for Jennings and signaled the rise of outlaw country.

While his fellow outlaw Willie

Nelson set up shop in Texas, Jennings stayed in Nashville. In 1976, he enjoyed huge crossover success with the album *Wanted! The Outlaws*, an album of previously released songs that also featured Jessi Colter, Willie Nelson, and Tompall Glaser. The album reached the No. 1 spot on the *Billboard* pop charts, and he achieved a level of stardom that few country musicians have been able to top, before or since. His success continued into the 1980s and included a successful collaboration with Willie Nelson, 1978's *Waylon and Willie*, which included the No. 1 single "Mammas, Don't Let Your Babies Grow Up to Be Cowboys."

The late 1970s and early 1980s represent a high point in Jennings's career, and during this period he enjoyed 10 No. 1 hits, including among others "Luckenbach, Texas (Back to the Basics of Love)," "Theme from *The Dukes of Hazzard* (Good Ol' Boys)," as well as several duets with Willie Nelson. Jennings also worked as the narrator for the television show *The Dukes of Hazzard* between 1979 and 1985. Jennings's career slowed after this period, largely because of health problems related to years of drug abuse and diabetes. He died in 2002.

MATT MILLER
Emory University

Waylon Jennings with Lenny Kaye, *Waylon: An Autobiography* (1996).

Jiménez, Flaco

(b. 1939) CONJUNTO MUSICIAN.
The Jiménez family has established a musical dynasty in the field of *música*

norteña, a south Texas contribution to music in the South. It began with Patricio Jiménez, who worked in San Antonio's Brackenridge stone quarry and learned the button accordion from local German-Texans in the early 1900s. His son, Santiago Jiménez, pioneered the Texas *norteña* accordion style in San Antonio by performing on a one-row, one-key, button accordion on radio broadcasts and recordings beginning in the early 1930s. Since the 1950s Santiago's son, Leonardo "Flaco" (Skinny) Jiménez, now the third generation of the musical family, has brought *música norteña* to heights of artistic virtuosity and gained international renown.

Flaco Jiménez grew up in an environment enriched by his grandfather's musical status in the community and his father's professional music career. Between the 1940s and early 1950s Santiago and his *conjunto* (group), Los Valedores, played most Saturday nights at the Gaucho nightclub in "el Westside" of San Antonio. On occasion, Flaco accompanied his father to the club, and sometimes, when Don Santiago took a break to drink a beer, he would let Flaco play a tune or two on the accordion with the band.

Flaco's professional career started in 1955 when, at the age of 16, he began playing the now-standard three-row, three-key, button accordion with an established *conjunto*, Mike Garza y los Caminantes. By the late 1950s Flaco was traveling with his own *conjunto* to play at dances in Dallas and other Texas towns and cities.

In the early 1960s Flaco also began recording, as his father had done 30 years before. The records were produced by new local San Antonio record companies that specialized in *norteña* music. Some of his first hit songs with his *conjunto*, Los Caporales, such as "Hasta la Vista" (Until I See You), "Los Amores del Flaco" (The Loves of the Skinny One), and "Virgencita de mi Vida" (Little Virgin of My Life), were recorded in these years. In the same years, Flaco, like many other *conjunto* musicians, began to travel farther afield and carried *norteña* music along what was referred to as "the migrant trail." Flaco and his *conjunto* traveled to Fresno, Calif., Chicago, and through the Midwest, as well as in Texas, following the trail of Texas migrant farmworkers.

Although a recognized artist on the button accordion among Mexican Americans throughout the United States, until the early 1970s Flaco remained unknown to the larger American public. This situation changed, however, when he became friends with rock, blues, and folk music innovators who were interested in *norteña* music, such as Doug Sahm of San Antonio and Ry Cooder and Peter Rowan of California. All three musicians recorded on national record labels and helped open the door to Flaco's recognition in Anglo-American society. Since the 1970s, when Flaco was introduced to a larger American and world audience, he has recorded with these and many other nationally known artists, made several national television appearances, recorded parts of the sound tracks of several major motion pictures, and toured extensively in the Americas, Europe, and Africa. In the 1990s Flaco performed in the "super groups"—the Texas Tornadoes, with Freddy Fender and Doug Sahm, and in Los Super Seven, also with Freddy Fender, members of Los Lobos, and others. Over the years, Flaco has received five Grammy awards for his recordings and has been inducted into the National Hispanic Hall of Fame and the International Latin Music Hall of Fame. Most recently Flaco has done crossover work into blues, rock, ballads, and country music, on recordings with Dwight Yoakam and Buck Owens, and has recorded traditional *norteña*-style songs with lyrics in Spanish and English. Now in his sixties, Flaco is still actively touring, recording, and taking the *música norteña* sound of his button accordion in many directions.

Flaco's brother, Santiago Jr., is also a well-known accordionist in San Antonio and performs in folk music festivals around the United States, and Flaco's son David has made some recordings, extending the Jiménez tradition into the fourth generation.

DAN W. DICKEY
Austin, Texas

Manuel Peña, *The Texas-Mexican Conjunto: History of a Working Class Music* (1985).

Johnson, Bunk

(1879–1949) JAZZ MUSICIAN.
One of the earliest black jazz cornetists, Willie Geary "Bunk" Johnson, who was born in New Orleans, began to study on that instrument at the age of eight and in 1894 joined his first band, the Adam Olivier Orchestra. From 1896 to 1898, he may have played second cornet with Buddy Bolden's band, the first in New Orleans renowned for improvising in a "hot" syncopated style. From 1900 to 1910 he toured in minstrel and circus bands and in ocean-liner orchestras. Returning to New Orleans in the 1910s, Johnson became locally famous as lead cornetist with the Eagle Band, a parade and dance band re-formed from the earlier Bolden band, and with the formal society orchestra of John Robichaux. Johnson resumed touring in the 1920s, but his career rapidly declined with the onset of the Depression. In 1931 he moved to New Iberia, where he worked as a WPA public-school music teacher, a sugarcane field hand, and a Tabasco pepper sauce factory worker. By 1934 dental problems forced him to quit playing altogether, and his career seemed at an end.

In 1938, however, he was rediscovered by jazz critics William Russell and Frederic Ramsey Jr., who had been directed to him by Louis Armstrong as a source for their book, *Jazzmen* (1939). This renewed attention spurred Johnson to resume playing, and in 1942 he made his first recordings in New Orleans with George Lewis and Jim Robinson. These records generated widespread enthusiasm among jazz critics and listeners, made Johnson a cult figure, and spawned a full-scale revival of "classic" New Orleans jazz, as distinct from later Dixieland styles. As the spearhead of this revival, Johnson's performances and recordings increased during his last years, including appearances in San Francisco with Mutt Carey and Kid Ory (1943) and in New York with Sidney Bechet (1945).

Although Johnson's revival revealed much about the schooled proficiency of early black jazz instrumentalists, it also obscured his own contribution to early jazz. Faulty memory and self-aggrandizement have compromised many statements in his recorded interviews, and stylistic accretions in his belated recordings make them an undependable reflection of his early cornet style. One of the oldest of the technically skilled black brassmen in New Orleans, Johnson was a primary participant in the shaping of jazz, whereby vocal devices of rural blues and gospel songs were adapted to the forms, techniques, and rhythms of instrumental band music.

JOHN JOYCE
Tulane University

M. Berger, in *Frontiers of Jazz*, ed. Ralph De Toledano (1947); Mike Hazeldine and Barry Martyn, *Bunk Johnson: Song of the Wanderer* (2000); Christopher Hillman, *Bunk Johnson: His Life and Times* (1989); William Russell and S. W. Smith, in *Jazzmen*, ed. Frederic Ramsey Jr. and Charles E. Smith (1939); Martin Williams, *Jazz Masters of New Orleans* (1967).

Johnson, Robert

(1912–1938) BLUES SINGER.
Robert Johnson was the most celebrated and legendary of the blues artists who emerged from the Mississippi Delta prior to World War II. He was born near Hazelhurst, Miss., in 1912 and was raised at a sharecroppers' settlement called Commerce. While still a youngster, he was drawn to the blues he heard around him, learning to play the music on a harmonica and then on a guitar.

Still in his teens, he left home to become an itinerant bluesman, traveling throughout the Delta and then up the Mississippi River to Helena, Ark., Saint Louis, and finally Chicago. In the mid-1930s, he also traveled to Dallas and San Antonio, where he made a series of 29 blues recordings, which were his legacy to the blues.

Johnson's blues repertoire has proved to be one of the most provocative in the entire history of the music. He was not only a gifted musician but also a visionary poet. His vision of African American life in the Delta is a haunting one. Songs like "Hellhound on My Trail" and "Me and the Devil Blues" point to his fatalistic assessment of the human condition and the supernatural powers in control of that condition. He saw no way out for blues musicians like himself. Such a choice of vocations necessitated making a pact with the forces of darkness because blues was the Devil's music.

The themes that dominated the landscape of Robert Johnson's blues were erotic, unrequited love, the urge to constantly move and explore new places, and the omnipotent powers of the supernatural. "Love in Vain" was his masterpiece on unrequited love; it was a theme he was obsessed with, appearing in about one-third of his songs. Erotic love was his counterpoint to heartbreak, and in songs like "Traveling Riverside Blues" he portrayed it with graphic and savory delight. Among his best-known travel songs were "Dust My Broom," "Rambling on My Mind," and "Walkin' Blues." The recurring message in these pieces was epitomized in the line

"Travel on poor Bob, just can't turn you 'round."

Robert Johnson's restless spirit reflected the changing social consciousness of the times, especially among the rural black population living in the South. Paradoxically, he was always drawn back to the Delta region he was so obsessed with leaving, until, as fate would have it, he was tragically poisoned to death in a Greenwood, Miss., juke joint in 1938. He was in his twenties when he died, and with his passing the legend of Robert Johnson was born. Today, he is considered one of the most popular and mysterious bluesmen of the century. According to blues legends, there are three possible graves, but he is likely buried at the Little Zion Missionary Baptist Church north of Greenwood, where the Mississippi Blues Commission honored him with one of its first Blues Trail markers in May 2007.

BILL BARLOW
Howard University

Samuel Charters, *Robert Johnson* (1973); Alan Greenburg, *Love in Vain: The Life and Legend of Robert Johnson* (1983); Peter Guralnick, *Searching for Robert Johnson* (1989); Robert Johnson, *King of the Delta Blues*, vol. 1, Columbia Records CL 1654, and vol. 2, Columbia Records C30034; Robert Palmer, *Deep Blues* (1981); Barry Lee Pearson and Bill McCulloch, *Robert Johnson: Lost and Found* (203); Patricia R. Schroder, *Robert Johnson: Mythmaking and Contemporary American Culture* (2004); Elijah Wald, *Escaping the Delta: Robert Johnson and the Inventing of the Blues* (2004).

Johnson, Tommy

(1896–1956) BLUES SINGER.

Tommy Johnson helped create the Delta blues, and thus the blues itself and its accompanying mythology. Born on George Miller's Plantation in Terry, Miss., in 1896, Johnson was one of 13 children. His uncles and brothers all played guitar, while other family members played various instruments in a brass band. After his family relocated to Crystal Springs, Miss., around 1910, Johnson's brother LeDell taught him the basics of the guitar, and by the time Johnson turned 18 he and his brothers were playing parties and gigs in Copiah County and beyond. In 1916, Johnson moved to Webb Jennings's plantation near Drew, Miss., with his first wife, Maggie Bidwell, where he fell under the artistic influence of the Mississippi Delta's first blues superstar, Charley Patton, who lived on the nearby Dockery Plantation. Although he was greatly influenced by Patton, Johnson developed his own particularly unique sound, complete with syncopated bass notes and unmistakable falsetto voice. After a year of playing in the Delta with Patton, Dick Bankston, and Willie Brown, Johnson began playing juke joints across Mississippi, Arkansas, and Louisiana. Johnson moved back home to Crystal Springs in 1920 and resumed sharecropping, traveling to the Delta to play with Patton once the season's crops were in.

By the time Johnson moved back to Crystal Springs, he had developed an alcohol addiction that would itself eventually become both famous and infamous. Although he was also a notorious gambler and womanizer, it was his drinking addiction that was his ultimate downfall and the subject of one of his most well-known songs, "Canned Heat Blues." Johnson recorded the side at a session for the Victor label in Memphis, in February 1928. In the song, he laments his habit of drinking Sterno, an often-lethal denatured and jellied alcohol used as an artificial heat source and often mixed with water and drunk when store-bought alcohol was unavailable or too expensive: "Crying, canned heat, canned heat, mama, crying, sure, Lord, killing me. / Crying, canned heat, mama, sure, Lord, killing me. / Takes alcorub to take these canned heat blues." Johnson's alcoholism appears once again in his song "Alcohol and Jake Blues": "I woke up, up this morning, crying, alcohol on my mind. / Woke up this morning, alcohol was on my mind. / I got them alcohol blues and I can't rest easy here."

In 1930 Johnson traveled to Grafton, Wis., for his last recording session, for Paramount. Once the economic hardships of the Great Depression set in, limiting the record-buying public's expendable income, Johnson's short recording career was abruptly ended. Between the two recording sessions for Victor and Paramount, only 17 tracks exist as evidence of his talent. Among them are "Big Road Blues," "Maggie Campbell Blues," "Slidin' Delta," and "Cool Drink of Water Blues."

Until his alcoholism-related death on 1 November 1956, in Crystal Springs, Johnson continued playing the blues in his signature style (he was well known for playing the guitar between his legs and behind his head), mainly at local dances, juke joints, and fish fries around south Mississippi. Although demand for his records had waned, demand to see and hear his dynamic performances had not. The self-propagated rumor that he had sold his soul to the devil did much to mystify the man and enhance his reputation, much in the way that the unrelated Robert Johnson's rumored deal with the devil did. Years later, filmmakers Joel and Ethan Cohen would revive the legend of deal-making Tommy Johnson, played by contemporary musician Chris Thomas King, in their 2000 film *O Brother, Where Art Thou?* His music was a powerful influence on other bluesmen of his day, including Robert Nighthawk, Houston Stackhouse, Howlin' Wolf, Floyd Jones, and Otis Spann, and it continues to shape the sound of the blues today.

JAMES G. THOMAS JR.
University of Mississippi

David Evans, *Big Road Blues: Tradition and Creativity in Folk Blues* (1982), "The Blues of Tommy Johnson: A Study of a Tradition" (Ph.D. diss., University of California at Los Angeles, 1967), *The Legacy of Tommy Johnson* (1972); Stefan Grossman, *Delta Blues Guitar* (1969); Gérard Herzhaft, *Encyclopedia of the Blues* (1997); Robert Palmer, *Deep Blues: A Musical and Cultural History of the Mississippi Delta* (1982); Jeff Todd Titon, *Early Downhome Blues: A Musical and Cultural Analysis* (1977); Gayle Dean Wardlow and Edward M. Komara, *Chasin' that Devil Music: Searching for the Blues* (1998).

Jones, George

(b. 1931) COUNTRY SINGER.
George Glenn Jones was born on 12 September 1931, in a Saratoga, Tex.,

cabin situated within the oil-rich rural area of east Texas known as the Big Thicket. Moving with his family into government housing in Beaumont, Tex., Jones coped with his difficult childhood (partly caused by his father's alcoholism) by embracing music, initially through listening to country music on the radio and singing gospel songs in church. By age nine, he was performing as a street singer in downtown Beaumont, singing for tips to his own guitar accompaniment. At age 16, in Jasper, Tex., Jones sang for the first time on radio and was soon regularly appearing on his own country music show on Beaumont radio station KRIC.

In 1950 Jones married Dorothy Bonvillion. Jones enlisted in the Marines by late 1951. Stationed in California, he took advantage of every opportunity to perform country music near his base—including the songs of Roy Acuff, Hank Williams Sr., and Lefty Frizzell, Jones's three main musical influences during that period in his career. In early 1954, after being divorced and discharged from the military, Jones returned to Texas, married Shirley Ann Corley, and resumed full-time performing in Houston. Producer Harold W. "Pappy" Daily heard Jones and signed him to the label he owned, Starday Records. In 1955 the Jones composition "Why, Baby, Why" became his first hit, rising to No. 4 on the national country charts, and he was soon performing on two popular radio barn dance programs, at the *Grand Ole Opry* and the *Louisiana Hayride.*

In 1957 Jones began recording in Nashville for Mercury Records, and while with that label he recorded the No. 1 smashes "White Lightning" (1959) and "Tender Years" (1961). In 1962, Jones began recording for United Artists Records, which soon released his third No. 1 single, "She Thinks I Still Care." The next year he recorded the first of a series of influential vocal duets with Melba Montgomery. In 1964, Jones's classic single "The Race Is On" was a No. 3 country hit. In 1965, Jones began a productive five-year stint with the Musicor label, recording nearly 300 songs during that time, 17 of which became Top 10 hits.

Jones and his second wife divorced in 1968, and the next year Jones married fellow country singer Tammy Wynette. Wishing to record with Wynette, Jones in late 1971 signed with Epic Records, and the couple began to record duets and to tour together. For Epic, Jones recorded under the supervision of acclaimed producer Billy Sherrill, a leading proponent of the sophisticated "Countrypolitan Sound" popular on country music recordings produced during the early 1970s. Jones's solo records for Epic, bearing Sherrill's unique, lush production, became major hits, including two No. 1 hits in 1974, "The Grand Tour" and "The Door." Jones's material from this period often reflected the singer's personal travails—his own self-destructive behavior and a troubled marriage to Wynette. In 1975, Jones and Wynette divorced, though they continued to record as a duo. In 1976, two of their duet singles, "Golden Ring" and "Near You," rose to No. 1 on the country chart. The last years of the 1970s were difficult for Jones, whose abuse of alcohol and drugs was taking its toll.

In 1980, Jones experienced a major comeback, as his single "He Stopped Loving Her Today" became the biggest hit of his career and his album *I Am What I Am* became his best-selling album. Those recordings brought Jones new attention and several prestigious industry awards, including a 1980 Grammy award, as well as the Country Music Association's Male Vocalist of the Year awards for 1980 and 1981.

In 1988, Jones severed his association with Epic Records and Billy Sherrill and eventually signed with MCA Records. Given the changed (that is, younger and increasingly female) demographic for country music by the early 1990s, Jones's singles and albums for the latter label were less commercially successful than his output for Epic had been, yet critics praised Jones's MCA releases for remaining true to the spirit of "traditional" country music.

In 1992, Jones was inducted into the Country Music Hall of Fame. In March 1999, having recently signed with Elektra/Asylum and having nearly completed a new album for that label, Jones was seriously injured in a car crash (he was charged with driving under the influence of alcohol). The singer made a full recovery, and his Elektra/Asylum album—released later in 1999, entitled *The Cold Hard Truth* and featuring a "hard country" sound—was widely judged to be his best work in years. The first single from that album, "Choices," won Jones his second Grammy award.

TED OLSON
East Tennessee State University

Bob Allen, *George Jones: The Life and Times of a Honky Tonk Legend* (1996); George Jones, *I Lived to Tell It All* (1997).

Joplin, Janis

(1943–1970) BLUES SINGER.
Born on 19 January 1943, in Port Arthur, Tex., Janis Joplin began singing folk music around her hometown while still in high school. An outcast in her hometown, she moved to the more liberal environment of the University of Texas at Austin and sang in various cafés around the city. Joplin hitchhiked to California in 1963 with her friend Chet Helms, who later became the manager of the Avalon Ballroom in San Francisco. Helms convinced Joplin to return to California in 1966 to front a local rock band, Big Brother and the Holding Company, which was popular among the nascent hippie movement. The psychedelic rock band gained a wide following after performing at the Monterey Pop Festival in San Francisco in 1967. Its album, *Cheap Thrills*, was released soon after and reached No. 1 on the *Billboard* charts. The single "Piece of My Heart," originally recorded by Erma Franklin, became a Top 40 hit.

Joplin left Big Brother and the Holding Company and formed her own group, the Kozmic Blues Band, in order to explore a more rhythm-and-blues-based sound by adding a brass section. Though they were not well received by the press nor by Joplin's audience, that group released *I Got Them Ol' Kozmic Blues Again, Mama* and backed Joplin at Woodstock in 1969. She formed another group, Full Tilt Boogie, in 1970. Joplin passed away from an overdose of heroin during the recording sessions for her last, posthumously released, album, *Pearl*. That album featured her biggest hit, "Me and Bobby McGee," written by singer-songwriter Kris Kristofferson, a friend of Joplin's, as well as "Mercedes Benz," a spoken-word piece demonstrating Joplin's wry sense of humor.

After her death Joplin exerted a huge influence on rock and roll, particularly for women. Not content to remain a quiet backup singer, through her impassioned performances, brazen stage presence, liberated beliefs, and outrageous costumes, she helped create a new role for women in rock music. Joplin also, along with many other white rock performers in the 1960s, helped introduce the blues to a new audience. She was influenced by many female blues singers, especially Bessie Smith, and she showed her gratitude by buying a headstone for Smith's previously unmarked grave.

ELLIE CAMPBELL
University of Mississippi

Alice Echols, *Scars of Sweet Paradise* (1999); Laura Joplin, *Love, Janis* (1992).

Joplin, Scott

(1868–1917) RAGTIME COMPOSER. At the peak of his fame (1900–1905), Scott Joplin was billed in vaudeville as the "King of Ragtime." His fame rested on the publication in 1899 of "Maple Leaf Rag," a brilliant piano solo in a new popular style called "ragtime." Born in 1868 near Texarkana, Tex., Joplin was a skilled itinerant musician who studied piano and composition in Sedalia, Mo., at George R. Smith College (1896) to expand his musical horizons. Playing

in saloons and bordellos from Texas to St. Louis, Joplin teamed with other black ragtime composers such as Otis Saunders and Louis Chauvin, helping them notate and sell their compositions. A farsighted publisher, John S. Stark of Sedalia, aided Joplin in his first steps to ragtime, and both men were enriched by this composer-publisher collaboration. Stark expanded his small venture into a fountainhead of "classic" piano ragtime, and Joplin wrote dozens of brilliant rags in the wake of "Maple Leaf Rag."

Joplin experimented with popular songs in a sentimental parlor vein in the mid-1890s, but his ability to compose and notate piano rags led him to ambitious works: "Original Rags" (1899), "The Easy Winners" (1901), "Elite Syncopations" (1902), "The Entertainer" (1902), "Pine Apple Rag" (1908), "Scott Joplin's New Rag" (1912), and some two dozen other published rags. Driven by a desire to make ragtime a respectable musical form, he and Stark admonished sheet-music buyers: "Do not play fast," "It is never right to play ragtime fast," "Do not fake" (that is, improvise). Joplin experimented with ragtime in a ballet, "The Ragtime Dance" (1900, published 1906), and a ragtime opera, *A Guest of Honor* (1903), now lost. He tried syncopated waltzes ("Bethena" [1905] and "Pleasant Moments" [1909]) and a habanera ("Solace" [1909]) and enlarged ragtime's vocabulary in advanced rags like "Euphonic Sounds" (1909) and "Magnetic Rag" (1914).

After traveling from Sedalia to St. Louis and then to New York City on vaudeville circuits, Joplin settled in

Harlem. He never matched the fame and fortune of "Maple Leaf Rag," though his works were lauded for their consistent gentle genius. From about 1905 Joplin became consumed with ideas for "elevating" ragtime, via symphonic or operatic forms. In 1910 he completed an ambitious and unique folk-oriented opera, *Treemonisha*, which he only performed once in public, as a piano read-through. Failure to achieve support for *Treemonisha* may have contributed to Joplin's collapse. He died on 1 April 1917 in New York City.

Joplin's peers in ragtime composition were Thomas M. Turpin, Charles H. Hunter, Charles L. Johnson, James Scott, and Artie Matthews. His collaborators included Louis Chauvin, Scott Hayden, and Arthur Marshall. He assisted the careers of S. Brunson "Brun" Campbell and Joseph F. Lamb and scores of other ragtime players who did not leave compositions. Joplin's version of ragtime derived from the playing of Mississippi Valley itinerant composers and from rich late 19th-century folk reservoirs. His contribution to African American music lay in his skill as a composer: he created fluid, lyrical themes, organized them into the coherent multipart form of the piano rag, and forged an individualized, easily recognizable style. His works are marked by a delicacy and grace achieved by few of his contemporaries. Within the form of the piano rag as a serious composition (or "classic," the term he and Stark favored), Joplin fused the vigor of banjo tunes, the swing of country dances, and the limpidity of song. His mark on American popular music is deep and indelible, and inter-

est in his work revived in the 1970s. *Treemonisha* was performed in Atlanta in 1972, and Joplin's compositions were chosen for the sound track of the popular 1973 motion picture *The Sting*.

WILLIAM J. SCHAFER
Berea College

Edward A. Berlin, *King of Ragtime: Scott Joplin and His Era* (1996); Rudi Blesh and Harriet Janis, *They All Played Ragtime* (1966); Susan Curtis, *Dancing to a Black Man's Tune: A Life of Scott Joplin* (1994); James Haskins and Kathleen Benson, *Scott Joplin* (1978); Vera Brodsky Lawrence, ed., *The Collected Works of Scott Joplin* (1971); Carol Lems-Dworkin, *Africa in Scott Joplin's Music* (1996); Steven Otfinoski, *Scott Joplin: A Life in Ragtime* (1995); C. Ogbu Sabir, *Scott Joplin: The King of Ragtime* (2000); William J. Schafer and Johannes Riedel, *The Art of Ragtime: Form and Meaning of an Original Black American Art* (1973).

Jordan, Louis

(1908–1975) JAZZ AND BLUES MUSICIAN.

Louis "King of the Jukebox" Jordan was a music pioneer who inspired generations of American blues, jazz, and rhythm-and-blues musicians with his performances and songwriting abilities. Born in Brinkley, Ark., on 8 July 1908, Jordan was drawn to a career in music from a young age, singularly influenced by his father, James Jordan. James was a local music teacher and bandleader for the local Brinkley Brass Band and a member of the touring Rabbit Foot Minstrels, a famous black variety troupe that toured in the South in the first half of the 20th century and counted blueswomen Ma Rainey, Bessie Smith, and

Ida Cox as part of its lineup. James exposed his son to music and pushed him toward a career in entertainment, which would allow him to leave the racially restrictive world of segregation-era Arkansas. Jordan first learned the clarinet and continued with the piano in the early years of his career, but it was the alto saxophone that would become his main instrument. He played and toured with James Jordan's group, the Brinkley Brass Band and later, after attending Baptist College and majoring in music, the Rabbit Foot Minstrels.

Although Jordan left Arkansas for Philadelphia and then New York in the early 1930s, he would remember Brinkley fondly in interviews throughout his career. The strong influence of the musicians, musical genres, and audiences to which he was exposed during his youth would provide a strong foundation for his most famous work as a vocalist, songwriter, and performer. In 1932 Jordan began playing with a band led by Clarence Williams, and in 1936 he was invited to join the famous orchestra led by drummer Chick Webb based at New York's Savoy Ballroom. In Webb's ensemble Jordan began to introduce songs and sing leads, honing his skills as a magnetic performer. He also sang duets with Ella Fitzgerald, the rising star lead female vocalist of the group.

Jordan left the Webb band in 1938 and began his first ensemble, a sextet in residence at the Elks Rendezvous club in Harlem. The group recorded for Decca Records, under the name the Elks Rendezvous Band before Jordan changed the name to the Tympani Five. The band enjoyed many lineups, and Jordan played alto, baritone, and tenor saxophone and sang lead on most numbers. In 1941 Jordan signed with the General Artists Corporation agency, and his group won breakthrough engagements at Chicago's Capitol Lounge and the Fox Head Tavern in Cedar Rapids, Iowa. Jordan would later remember the Iowa stint as the turning point in his career, as the group began to develop the novelty aspect of their repertoire and performance.

In 1941, Decca launched the Sepia Series, a line that featured artists considered to have crossover potential to sell in both black and white markets, and Jordan's band was transferred from Decca's "race" label to the Sepia Series, along with other soon-to-be-famous groups, including the Nat King Cole Trio. Sessions for the Sepia Series produced a series of hits for Jordan that ranked on *Billboard*'s Harlem Hit Parade, including "Five Guys Named Moe," which introduced the fast-paced, swinging rhythm-and-blues style that became Jordan's signature sound. Returning to the studio in 1943, Jordan recorded "Ration Blues," a song from his Fox Head Tavern days that had new significance in the context of wartime rationing and that found crossover success on white and black charts.

In the 1940s Jordan's career peaked, as he made dozens of "crossover" records, including the fantastical narrative hit, "Saturday Night Fish Fry" (considered a contender for the first rock-and-roll song) and the raucous "Caldonia (What Makes Your Big Head So Hard?)." On these records Jordan continued to develop his unique style, introducing elements of spoken vocals, humor, and intense musical energy into songs that celebrated black life. His songs were featured in films and on television shows, and the success of his work during this period contributed to his lingering status as top-selling black artist of all time in terms of weeks at No. 1 on the *Billboard* charts.

Jordan's career began to decline in 1951 when he organized a short-lived big band, just as the big band sound was on the way out. After the early 1950s Jordan never regained the commercial success he had once enjoyed, and during the 1960s he seldom recorded. Jordan died of a heart attack on 4 February 1975 in Los Angeles and is buried in St. Louis. His music influenced a new wave of black artists, including Chuck Berry and Little Richard—both practitioners of his "jump blues" style—and James Brown. His music is considered an important precursor to both rock and roll and rap music, and in 2004 *Rolling Stone* magazine ranked him number 59 in their lineup of the *100 Greatest Artists of All Time*.

FRANCES ABBOTT
Emory University

John Chilton, *Let the Good Times Roll: The Story of Louis Jordan and His Music* (1997).

Kimbrough, David "Junior"

(1930–1998) BLUES SINGER.
Rockabilly pioneer Charlie Feathers referred to his friend, fellow musician, and teacher, Junior Kimbrough, as "the beginning and end of music." Feathers (1932–1998), a native of the Holly Springs, Miss., area, was famous for his idiosyncratic theories about music, but his assessment of Kimbrough highlighted the fact that the bluesman's music was almost a genre unto itself.

David Kimbrough Jr. was born in Hudsonville, Miss., just north of Holly Springs, on 28 July 1930. His father, three older brothers, and a sister were blues musicians. At age eight he learned guitar from his father, whom he cited as his most important influence, and he was soon playing and singing for friends and family. He recalled to researcher Sylvester Oliver that musicians who visited the family home included Fred McDowell, Eli Green, Johnny Woods, and early blues pioneer Gus Cannon.

As a teenager Kimbrough sang in a gospel group, and by the late 1950s Kimbrough had formed the first incarnation of the Soul Blues Boys, which played at weekend functions in the area. Kimbrough was unusual among traditional north Mississippi blues artists in leading an electric band so early on, and performing in this format served to differentiate his music from locals, who played largely solo or in duos, such as R. L. Burnside or Fred McDowell. Feathers, who farmed on the same Hudsonville plantation as Kimbrough, called Kimbrough's music "cottonpatch blues."

In 1968 Kimbrough recorded a session for the Memphis-based Philwood label; a single was issued under the name of "Junior Kimbell," which included a cover of Lowell Fulson's "Tramp." The following year Charlie Feathers, who had recorded at Philwood around the same time, recorded with Kimbrough at Kimbrough's juke joint. The song "Feel Good Again" appeared in 1986 on a limited-issued 78-rpm single on the Perfect imprint; it later appeared on the Revenant Charlie Feathers CD *Get with It*.

Kimbrough was otherwise not recorded during the great wave of field recordings in the 1960s and early 1970s. In the 1970s his song "Meet Me in the City" appeared on a British LP of demos played on Charlie Gillet's influential BBC radio show *Honky Tonk*. In 1982 he was recorded by Sylvester Oliver of Rust College in Holly Springs, resulting in a single on the Highwater label. In the wake of its issue, Kimbrough gained recognition in blues circles and began appearing at festivals. Several of his songs from a festival appearance in Georgia in 1984 appeared on the LP *National Downhome Blues Festival*, vol. 2, in 1986 (later issued on CD as *National Downhome Blues Festival*, vol. 1).

In 1984 Kimbrough began hosting Sunday afternoon house parties, which soon became a popular local institution, and in 1991 he opened a juke joint in Holly Springs. Robert Mugge filmed Kimbrough at the Chewalla Rib Shack that same year for the documentary *Deep Blues*. Kimbrough gained more exposure in 1992 when Oxford's Fat Possum label recorded his debut CD, *All Night Long*, at Kimbrough's new juke joint in Chulahoma, located on Route 4 about 10 miles southwest of Holly Springs.

Kimbrough and R. L. Burnside, who also recorded a CD for Fat Possum at the juke joint, played at Junior's Place every Sunday evening, often accompanied by their offspring. Kimbrough usually played in a trio, accompanied by his son Kinney Malone on drums and Burnside's son Garry on bass. Rock stars made pilgrimages to the club, which was oddly shaped and adorned with folk art, and it eventually became a popular destination for University of Mississippi undergraduates.

Kimbrough typically performed his mostly original songs for over 10 minutes apiece, and writer and critic Robert Palmer, who produced *All Night Long* and Kimbrough's second Fat Possum CD *Sad Days, Lonely Nights*, emphasized their droning and hypnotic qualities on his barebones productions. Kimbrough's music didn't sell very well, but it was embraced by critics and many fans of alternative music, who appreciated his music's unorthodox qualities and bought into Fat Possum's "Not the same old blues crap" marketing strategy.

In the wake of this attention, Kimbrough did some national touring, including serving as an opening act for proto-punk icon Iggy Pop, but was otherwise not very interested in traveling outside the area. He continued to host his Sunday evening gatherings and made two more CDs for Fat Possum but slowed down for health reasons in the mid-1990s. He died of a heart attack on 17 January 1998.

Posthumously, Fat Possum issued a greatest hits package and organized a tribute record, consisting of alternative rock bands covering Kimbrough's songs. Kimbrough's son David Malone (aka David Kimbrough Jr.) has recorded several CDs and consciously pays tribute to his father's music, and his son Kinney (Malone), a drummer, usually sings his father's signature "All Night Long" when performing.

SCOTT BARRETTA
Oxford, Mississippi

Anthony DeCurtis, liner notes to *You Better Run: The Essential Junior Kimbrough*, Fat Possum (2002); Sylvester Oliver, with David Evans, liner notes to *Do the Rump!*, HMG/ Highwater (1997).

King, B. B.

(b. 1925) BLUES SINGER.
Riley "B. B." King was born on a plantation between Itta Bena and Indianola, Miss. One of five children, he often sang in local churches as a young child. When his parents separated, King moved with his mother to Kilmichael, Miss., where he sang in a school spiritual quartet from 1929 to 1934. After his mother's death, he returned to Indianola and continued to develop his music while working as a farmhand.

B. B. King, 1960s, photograph on a wall at Club Paradise, Memphis (William R. Ferris Collection, Southern Folklife Collection, Wilson Library, University of North Carolina at Chapel Hill)

In 1946 King hitched a ride to Memphis and for 10 months lived with noted bluesman Bukka White, his mother's cousin. He returned to the Delta briefly at the end of 1947 and in early 1948, and he harvested a cotton crop. Later that year he returned to Memphis and worked amateur shows at the W. C. Handy Theater/Palace Theater. He frequently performed with Bobby Bland, Johnny Ace, and Earl Forrest in a group called "the Beale Streeters" and appeared regularly on his own *Pepticon Boy* show on WDIA radio in Memphis. His nickname, the "Beale Street Blues Boy," was shortened to "Blues Boy," then to "B. B." In 1950 his "Three O'Clock Blues" climbed to the top of the rhythm-and-blues charts and

stayed there for four months. Its success launched his musical career, and he gave up his disc jockey job to go on the road with his own group, scarcely two years since he had made his last cotton crop in the Delta. For nearly 20 years he performed some 300 one-night stands a year in black night spots known as the chitlin' circuit. Once a year he played weeklong engagements in large urban black theaters, such as the Howard in Washington, D.C., the Regal in Chicago, and the Apollo in New York.

In the early 1960s King's career was in a slump, with blacks finding his music uncomfortably close to their "down-home" roots and folk enthusiasts considering him too commercialized. King's return to fame came when the Rolling Stones, Paul Butterfield's Blues

Band, and other British and American groups acknowledged him as their idol. After his first European tour in 1968 he was finally recognized by American critics, and since that time his career has steadily grown, with frequent television and film appearances.

King's guitar style is influenced by blues guitarists Lonnie Johnson and T-Bone Walker and by jazz guitarists Django Reinhardt and Charlie Christian. He has always played with an electric guitar, which he nicknamed "Lucille." His delicate "bent" notes and powerful vocals echo the blues style of the Mississippi Delta where King first learned his music.

From his early years in rural Mississippi to his international acclaim, B. B. King's blues career is a rare success story. He has issued over 700 recordings and continues to produce and perform at a pace younger musicians would find exhausting. His achievements as a blues performer, composer, and spokesman were recognized in 1977 when Yale president Kingman Brewster awarded him an honorary doctorate of music with the accolade, "In your rendition of the blues you have always taken us beyond entertainment to the deeper message of suffering and endurance that gave rise to the form."

In "Why I Sing the Blues," King explains the meaning of his music:

> When I first got the blues, they
>   brought me over on a ship,
> Man was standing over me, and a lot
>   more with a whip,
> Now everybody want to know why I
>   sing the blues,

> Well I've been around a long time,
>   I've really paid my dues.

King was inducted into the Blues Foundation Hall of Fame in 1984 and into the Rock and Roll Hall of Fame in 1987. He received the Lifetime Achievement Grammy award in 1987 and has been given honorary doctorates by a number of institutions, including Tougaloo College (1973), Berklee College of Music (1982), Rhodes College of Memphis (1990), and Mississippi Valley State University (2002). He received the National Award of Distinction from the University of Mississippi in 1992. He has received 14 Grammy awards, most recently in February 2006 for his album *80*, a collaborative record with friends honoring his 80th birthday.

In 1991 B. B. King's Blues Club opened on Beale Street in Memphis, and in 1994 a second club launched at Universal City Walk in Los Angeles. New York's Times Square became home to a third club, opened in June 2000, and two more followed at Foxwoods Casino in Connecticut in January 2002. In 1996 King's autobiography, *Blues All around Me*, was released, written with David Ritz.

Until 2006 King continued to tour extensively, averaging 250 concerts per year around the world. Every June, King continues to return to his hometown of Indianola, Miss., for the B. B. King Homecoming Festival, a blues concert featuring performances from local and national blues talents, including King, and an after-show at local juke joint Club Ebony. In 2002 the City of Indianola donated 2.3 acres of land to the

B. B. King Museum Foundation. In June 2005 during Homecoming Festival, King broke ground for the museum. The vision statement for the space is simple but profound: "Through its authentic presentation and interactive exhibits, performance venues, and educational programming, the B. B. King Museum and Delta Interpretive Center seeks to honor international Bluesman B. B. King's life, celebrate Delta Blues heritage, encourage and inspire young artists and musicians, and use the arts to enrich the lives of Delta youth and all those who visit the museum campus."

WILLIAM FERRIS
University of North Carolina at Chapel Hill

Lawrence Cohn, ed., *Nothing but the Blues: The Music and the Musicians* (1999); Sheldon Harris, *Blues Who's Who: A Biographical Dictionary of Blues Singers* (1979); B. B. King, with David Ritz, *Blues All around Me* (1996); Paul Oliver, *The Story of the Blues* (1969); Charles Sawyer, *The Arrival of B. B. King: The Authorized Biography* (1980); David Shirley, *Everyday I Sing the Blues: Story of B. B. King* (1999).

Ledbetter, Huddie (Leadbelly)

(1885–1949) BLUES SINGER.
A singer and composer, Ledbetter was born on 21 January 1885, two miles from Mooringsport, La., in the Caddo Lake area near the Texas border, where his parents, Wess Ledbetter and Sallie (Pugh) Ledbetter, owned 65 acres of farmland. Wess Ledbetter's parents had both been slain by the Ku Klux Klan in Mississippi. Huddie Ledbetter's maternal grandmother was a Cherokee, a fact he often mentioned. Huddie Led-

better was first exposed to music by his mother, who led her church choir. Two songster uncles, Bob and Terrell Ledbetter, encouraged him to become a musician. Huddie Ledbetter was soon known as the best guitar picker and songster in his part of Louisiana. At 16 he started visiting Fannin Street, the red-light district of nearby Shreveport. Here he heard accomplished blues musicians and learned their style and verses. He recalls these early experiences in his song "Fannin Street." Bud Coleman and Jim Fagin were two musicians with whom he worked closely.

Ledbetter soon moved away from Mooringsport. He married a girl named Lethe, and they worked together during summers on farms near New Boston, Tex., in the blackland counties east of Dallas. In the winter they moved to Dallas, where he played his guitar and sang in the red-light district. There he met the Texas bluesman Blind Lemon Jefferson and learned many songs from him. Ledbetter received the nickname "Lead Belly" (or "Leadbelly") because his voice was a powerful bass. A handsome, strongly built young man, he had early learned that he was attractive to women. In Marshall, Tex., he attacked a woman who rejected his advances, was sentenced to a year on a chain gang, and escaped from prison three days later. In late 1917 Leadbelly became involved in another fracas over a woman. He was convicted on two counts, murder and assault to murder, on 24 May 1918. Once more he escaped from his cell, but on 7 June 1918, under the alias of Walter Boyd, he entered Shaw State Prison Farm, sentenced to 30 years at hard

Leadbelly album cover (Charles Reagan Wilson Collection, Center for the Study of Southern Culture, University of Mississippi)

labor. For the third time he escaped. He was soon recaptured, and in 1920 he was transferred to the Central State Farm near Houston. He worked on labor gangs for 12 to 14 hours a day cutting logs and hoeing cotton, and through his strength and endurance he became the lead man on the fastest work gang.

Leadbelly was also known for his skill as a musician and was asked to sing when visitors came to the prison. When the governor of Texas, Pat M. Neff, came to visit, Leadbelly sang a plea for mercy to him:

> [If I] had you, Governor Neff, like
>   you got me,
> I'd wake up in the mornin', and I'd set
>   you free.

The governor was impressed with the man and his song, and on 15 January 1925 he pardoned Leadbelly, who had then served about six and a half years. After working for a Buick agency in Houston, Leadbelly returned to his home near Mooringsport in 1926. He

worked for the Gulf Refining Company, and he continued to develop as a blues singer. In 1930 he was accosted by a group of men who wanted whiskey. Leadbelly wounded five of them with his knife and was sentenced to 10 years at hard labor for assault with intent to murder.

On 28 February 1930 he entered Angola Penitentiary in Louisiana and became the lead man on prison gangs, as he had been in Texas. He composed another plea for mercy to Gov. O. K. Allen of Louisiana. It was recorded (along with a song that was to become even more famous, "Irene, Good Night") by folklorists John and Alan Lomax in 1934. The Lomaxes played the record for the governor in his office and obtained a reprieve for Leadbelly on 7 August 1934.

The next month Leadbelly joined John Lomax in a journey that helped make both men famous. Lomax recorded folk songs in southern prisons, and Leadbelly accompanied him, telling of his own experiences and singing to encourage the inmates to record for Lomax. Lomax's tapes of Leadbelly's songs were eventually deposited in the Library of Congress. After 6,000 miles of travel, performances, and recording, the duo arrived in New York City. Leadbelly was given an enthusiastic reception by the New York intellectual and literary scene, which embraced him as the embodiment of the "bad nigger," a traditional figure from black folklore.

Leadbelly's repertoire included traditional folk and children's songs, blues, and topical numbers, all of which are an important part of American folklore. His best-known songs include

"Boll Weevil," "Rock Island Line," "Old Cottonfields at Home," "Take This Hammer," "Pick a Bale of Cotton," and "Midnight Special." Few other blues musicians have been so studied and appreciated. He died of myotrophic lateral sclerosis on 6 December 1949 at Bellevue Hospital in New York.

WILLIAM FERRIS
University of North Carolina at Chapel Hill

Richard M. Garvin and Edmond G. Addeo, *The Midnight Special: The Legend of Leadbelly* (1971); John Lomax and Alan Lomax, *The Leadbelly Legend* (1965), *Negro Folk Songs as Sung by Lead Belly* (1936), Recordings of interviews and music made with Leadbelly, listed in Recording Division of the Library of Congress; Kip Lornell and Charles K. Wolfe, *The Life and Legend of Leadbelly* (1999); Frederick Ramsey, *Last Sessions* (record), Folkways FA-2941 and FA-2942.

Lewis, Furry

(1893–1981) BLUES SINGER.
Walter "Furry" Lewis was born into a Greenwood, Miss., sharecropping family in 1893. His father left around the time he was born, but Furry, his mother, and his siblings remained in the Greenwood area until Furry was about six, when they all moved north to Memphis in the hope of a better life. Memphis would be the city that Furry would call home the rest of his life. This was the result, in part, of a train-hopping accident in his late teens that left Furry with one leg and a prosthetic.

Lewis's first guitar was homemade, and it was one he played with skill at fish fries, picnics, medicine shows, and on street corners. Furry's repertoire was vast and his style all his own: loose, eclectic, and full of bottleneck slide. It was on one of those Memphis street corners that W. C. Handy discovered a young Furry, bought him a proper guitar—a Martin six-string—and offered him a few opportunities playing with the Handy band.

Furry's recording career began in April 1927 with a trip to Chicago to record for Vocalion, which resulted in five sides. Later that year, in October, Furry traveled back to Chicago to record six more sides. In 1928 and 1929 Furry recorded 13 more sides in Memphis for Victor and again for Vocalion. These later sessions resulted in signature tunes such as "I Will Turn Your Money Green" and influential recordings of the standards "John Henry" and "Kassie Jones."

The Depression stifled Furry's career as a recording artist, and he subsequently put the guitar down and picked up the broom. From the beginning of the Depression on into the 1960s, Furry worked as a laborer and street cleaner for the city of Memphis. Blues scholar Sam Charters's rediscovery of Lewis in the late 1950s brought him back into the spotlight for an entirely different set of fans. Charters persuaded Lewis to resume his recording career with a 1959 Folkways LP, giving way to two Prestige/Bluesville studio albums, *Back on My Feet Again* and *Done Changed My Mind*. Both were recorded in 1961 and were reissued on one compact disc by Fantasy Records in 1992.

Amid all the rediscovered prewar blues performers of the 1960s blues boom, Furry Lewis was always one of the most respected and well loved. Lewis's popularity never waned but only increased into the 1970s, after an April 1970 interview in *Playboy*. He appeared in two films, *W. W. and the Dixie Dance Kings* (1975) and *This Is Elvis* (1981); opened for the Rolling Stones at one of their Memphis concerts; and was the subject of the Joni Mitchell song "Furry Plays the Blues" (1976)—a song that, according to some sources, Lewis immensely disliked. Furry even appeared once on *The Tonight Show*, trading quips with Johnny Carson.

As was the case with most of his peers, Furry Lewis never made any money off his music, though his influence on the scores of musicians who listened to his recordings and followed his lead was and still is beyond any amount of money. Memphis lost one of the last links to its unique and rich past on 14 September 1981, when Furry Lewis died in a Memphis hospital after a period of quickly declining health.

MARK COLTRAIN
Hillsborough, North Carolina

Stanley Booth, *Playboy* (April 1970); Edward Komara, ed., *Encyclopedia of the Blues* (2006).

Lewis, Jerry Lee

(b. 1935) ROCK AND COUNTRY SINGER.
Jerry Lee Lewis, of Ferriday, La., one of the most charismatic and controversial musicians of his generation, has long exemplified many of the most profound tensions in southern history. He was born on 29 September 1935 into an extremely talented yet volatile family—two of his cousins are television evangelist Jimmy Swaggart and country musician Mickey Gilley. He was profoundly influenced by Pentecostal religion as a child. But he was also attracted to secular sources, such as a black Ferriday juke joint called Haney's Big House. Lewis has cited Al Jolson, Jimmie Rodgers, Gene Autry, and Hank Williams as vocal influences, but his highly personalized boogie-woogie piano style reflects indigenous black folk sources from his immediate region.

By adolescence Lewis was a skilled entertainer, performing at numerous political rallies, religious services, talent contests, and nightclubs and on radio in Natchez, Miss. In 1956 he began recording for Sun Records in Memphis and achieved national popularity and notoriety as perhaps the wildest of all rock-and-roll performers. To many observers, Lewis was a public menace, but from 1956 to 1958 he had numerous hit recordings, including "Whole Lotta Shakin' Goin' On" and "Great Balls of Fire," and he made several appearances on national television and in movies. Lewis generated copious public criticism in 1958 after marrying his 13-year-old second cousin, Myra Brown. Although he defended his marriage as customary in his native South, Lewis's recording career declined precipitously. Touring unceasingly (primarily in the South) for over a decade, he subsequently deepened his already-vast repertoire and enhanced his reputation as an unrivaled live performer.

In 1968 Lewis staged a remarkable comeback in the country field, and

Jerry Lee Lewis, rockabilly and country singer, 1970s (Country Music Foundation, Library and Media Center, Nashville)

more than a score of country hits ensued. Despite his success as a country artist, Lewis continued to perform predominantly in the rockabilly style that had brought him his initial success. He remained a successful recording artist well into the 1980s despite a strange series of financial, physical, and emotional crises.

Lewis found new opportunities in the mid-1980s with the movie *Great Balls of Fire*, a biopic about his life. Lewis was tapped to record songs for the sound track, and his songs received attention from a new generation of fans. In 1986 he was in the first group to be inducted into the Rock and Roll Hall of Fame. Lewis published an autobiography, *Killer*, in 1993. In February 2005 he was given the Lifetime Achievement Award by the Recording Academy. Lewis released a new album, *The Last Man Standing: Duets with Twenty-two*

Great Performers, in 2006. He currently resides on his ranch in Nesbit, Miss., which is open to tours for visitors.

Jerry Lee Lewis has been widely hailed by both popular journalists and scholars as one of the most creative and important figures in American popular culture. His peculiar resonance as a southern cultural symbol is matched only by Elvis Presley. No one has demonstrated a more thorough command of the South's musical heritage, from minstrelsy and blues to hymns and hillbilly music. His career has operated as a paradigm of the southern experience, dramatizing many of the region's fundamental tensions.

STEPHEN R. TUCKER
Tulane University

Jimmy Guterman, *Rockin' My Life Away: Listening to Jerry Lee Lewis* (1991); Jerry Lee Lewis and Charles White, *Killer! The Baddest Rock Memoir Ever* (1995), *Whole Lot of Shakin' Going On: The Life and Times of Jerry Lee Lewis* (1994); Linda Gail Lewis with Les Pendleton, *The Devil, Me, and Jerry Lee* (1998); Myra Lewis with Murray Silver, *Great Balls of Fire: The Uncensored Story of Jerry Lee Lewis* (1982); Robert Palmer, *Jerry Lee Lewis Rocks!* (1981); Nick Tosches, *Hellfire: The Jerry Lee Lewis Story* (1998).

Lomax, John A.

(1867–1948) FOLK SONG COLLECTOR.
Born in Goodman, Miss., on 23 September 1867, John Avery Lomax was one of five sons of natives of Georgia. They always worked their own land, but Lomax described his family as belonging to the "upper crust of the po' white trash." In 1869 the family moved to a farm on the Bosque River near Me-

ridian, Tex. From his country childhood Lomax acquired a love for and appreciation of the rural folklore he later captured on record. He absorbed the popular hymns he heard at the Methodist camp meetings his family attended.

In 1895, at age 28, he entered the University of Texas, where he took courses with feverish enthusiasm and received his B.A. degree in two years. From 1897 to 1903, Lomax served the university simultaneously as registrar, secretary to the president, and steward of men's dormitories, for $75 a month. Subsequently, he became instructor and then associate professor of English at Texas Agricultural and Mechanical College (1903–10). Meanwhile, he doggedly pursued graduate studies, despite financial constraints. He received the M.A. in literature in 1906 from the University of Texas and an M.A. in English from Harvard the following year.

Since childhood, Lomax had been writing down the cowboy songs he heard. His English professors at Texas had scorned such frontier literature as unworthy, but at Harvard, Barrett Wendell and George Lyman Kittredge strongly encouraged Lomax to continue his collecting. After his return to Texas, Lomax secured three successive fellowships, which enabled him to travel through the cattle country with a notebook and a primitive recording machine. Around campfires and in saloon back rooms, he persuaded cowboys to sing their songs. Among his findings were the well-known "Git Along Little Dogies" and "Home on the Range," the latter sung to him in San Antonio by a black saloonkeeper who had been a

trail cook. The result was Lomax's first published collection, *Cowboy Songs and Other Frontier Ballads* (1910), which he dedicated to Theodore Roosevelt, a firm supporter of his efforts. The book is a landmark in the study of American folklore.

Later, in 1932, with a contract from the Macmillan Company for a book of American folk songs and with support from the Library of Congress and the American Council of Learned Societies, he set out on the first of a series of collecting trips that were to occupy the rest of his life. He concentrated on recording songs of the southern black— blues, spirituals, and work chants. Often accompanied by his son, Alan, he visited remote rural black communities, lumber camps, and penitentiaries, where blacks were isolated and where singing softened the pain of prison life. The quality and number of the songs he recorded for the Library of Congress Archive of American Folk Song—more than 10,000 in all—reflect Lomax's unusual skill as a fieldworker. In the Arkansas Penitentiary he came upon two important songs, "Rock Island Line" and "John Henry," the rhythmic ballad of a "steel drivin' man."

Lomax's two collections, *American Ballads and Folk Songs* (1934) and *Our Singing Country* (1941), opened an entirely new area of American folk music to the public and were largely responsible for the folk song movement that developed in New York City and spread throughout the country. One of Lomax's discoveries was an influential figure in that movement: Huddie Ledbetter, nicknamed "Leadbelly" because of his deep bass voice. Lomax and his son found Leadbelly in a Louisiana penitentiary in 1933, arranged for his freedom, brought him to Greenwich Village in New York, and published *Negro Folk Songs as Sung by Lead Belly* (1936).

Lomax died on 26 January 1948 at the age of 80 of a cerebral hemorrhage while visiting in Greenville, Miss., and was buried in Austin, Tex.

WILLIAM FERRIS
University of North Carolina at Chapel Hill

John A. Lomax, *Adventures of a Ballad Hunter* (1947), *American Ballads and Folk Songs* (1934), "The Ballad Hunter: John A. Lomax" (record), AAFS L53, *Cowboy Songs* (1922), *Cowboy Songs and Other Frontier Ballads* (1910), *Negro Folk Songs as Sung by Lead Belly* (1936), *Our Singing Country* (1941), Recordings at the University of Texas, Harvard University, and the Archive of American Folk Song at the Library of Congress; D. K. Wilgus, *Anglo-American Folksong Scholarship since 1898* (1959).

Louisiana Hayride

The *Louisiana Hayride* was a north Louisiana musical institution from 1948 to 1960. It was one of several radio barn dances that helped popularize country music in the 20th century, broadcasting over 50,000-watt station KWKH from Shreveport's Municipal Auditorium to 28 states. The radio show was second only to Nashville's *Grand Ole Opry* in broadcasting significance. The show also sponsored touring performers associated with the program.

The *Louisiana Hayride* grew out of a distinctive north Louisiana musical culture. Shreveport had the easy mo-

bility of a river town—it was located on the Red River—which brought musical performers of all sorts to the clubs and bars in its red-light district in the early 20th century. The city seemed poised between a southern culture to the east and a more open rural frontier society to the west. KWKH broadcast the music of the Old Time Fiddlers Club of North Louisiana as early as 1925, followed by showcasing other local performers and then broadcasting the *Hillbilly Amateur Hour* beginning in 1939.

Shreveport became the focus for a musical interchange between whites and blacks, nurturing for a time both blues singer Huddie "Leadbelly" Ledbetter and Jimmie Davis, the "singing governor" of Louisiana who wrote "You Are My Sunshine." By the mid-20th century, Shreveport was a center for gospel, blues, country, and rock and roll.

The producers of the *Louisiana Hayride* appreciated diverse talents and often took chances on unknown performers, providing an important venue for emerging stars, who often did not fit easily into record label categories. Horace "Hoss" Logan produced the *Louisiana Hayride* and nurtured its reputation as the "Cradle of the Stars." The country music performers who were regulars on the show included Slim Whitman, the Maddox Brothers, Sister Rose, Claude King, Jim Reeves, Kitty Wells, Floyd Cramer, Sonny James, Faron Young, Tex Ritter, Billy Walker, and Lefty Frizzell. Hank Williams, who had been rejected by the *Grand Ole Opry* producers, performed on the *Hayride* in 1948, an untried artist whose

"Lovesick Blues" wowed the audience and led to 10 months on the show. Williams left to become a member of the *Opry* but returned to the *Hayride* near the end of his brief career. West Monroe, La., native Webb Pierce, "King of the Honky-Tonk," succeeded Williams as country music's best-selling performer, and he too was a *Hayride* performer. A 19-year-old Elvis Presley sang his early rockabilly mix of country and blues on the *Hayride* on 16 October 1954 and then signed a one-year contract with *Hayride* producers. Other rockabilly stars such as Johnny Cash and Johnny Horton also used the *Hayride* to help launch their careers. South Louisiana Cajun music talents, including Jimmie C. Newman, Doug Kershaw, and Thibodeaux "Tibby" Edwards, also performed on the *Hayride*.

The last *Louisiana Hayride* show performance was on 27 August 1960, although Shreveport has hosted concerts since then under the *Hayride* name.

CHARLES REAGAN WILSON
University of Mississippi

Tracey E. W. Laird, *Louisiana Hayride: Radio and Roots Music along the Red River* (2004); Horace Logan and Bill Sloan, *Louisiana Hayride Years: Making Musical History in Country's Golden Age* (1998).

Lunsford, Bascom Lamar

(1882–1973) MUSIC COLLECTOR, PERFORMER, AND PROMOTER.
Born on South Turkey Creek in Buncombe County, N.C., and trained as a lawyer, Lunsford worked in a variety of occupations (college teacher, lawyer, newspaperman, seller of fruit trees and war bonds) but achieved local and na-

tional renown as a collector, performer, promoter, and interpreter of the old-time music and dance of western North Carolina. During the late 1920s, when mountain music and culture were being stereotyped and exploited for commercial (mainly media and tourism) purposes, Lunsford—who called himself "the squire of South Turkey Creek"—championed their dignity and worth.

In 1928 Lunsford began his Mountain Dance and Folk Festival in Asheville, first as a segment of the Chamber of Commerce–sponsored and booster-oriented Rhododendron Festival, but later as an independent event. During the next half century the festival became a major showcase for traditional Appalachian music and dance. It developed its own traditions, opening each year the first weekend in August, "along about sundown," with the fiddle tune "Grey Eagle." Some of the outstanding performers who made appearances at the festival were banjo players Aunt Samantha Bumgarner and George Pegram, harmonica player Walter "Red" Parham, and the Soco Gap clog team led by Sam Queen.

Lunsford has been criticized for his somewhat idiosyncratic selectivity in presenting mountain music. During his lifetime, for example, no blacks ever performed at the festival, despite the existence of a substantial black population in the area. Nevertheless, as fellow festival promoter Sarah Gertrude Knott observed, Lunsford succeeded better than virtually all of his peers at "finding a way between the old and the new"—uncovering and nurturing the oldest levels of tradition; presenting and interpreting traditional music and dance in a dignified manner; respecting the tastes, styles, and choices of the performers themselves; and honoring traditional values and idioms while remaining sensitive to the dynamic quality of tradition.

As a performer and collector, Lunsford recorded both for commercial record companies (Okeh, Brunswick, Columbia, Folkways) and for folklore archives at Columbia University and the Library of Congress. Some of his personal papers and memorabilia are on deposit at Mars Hill College in North Carolina.

DAVID E. WHISNANT
Chapel Hill, North Carolina

Bill Finger, *Southern Exposure* (Spring 1974); Loyal Jones, *Minstrel of the Appalachians: The Story of Bascom Lamar Lunsford* (2002); Harold H. Martin, *Saturday Evening Post* (22 May 1948); David E. Whisnant, *Appalachian Journal* (Autumn–Winter 1979–80).

Lynn, Loretta

(b. 1937) ENTERTAINER.
Country music is an essential accompaniment to contemporary images of the South and is the source for a resonant regional mythology. Loretta Lynn is a rural southerner who celebrates the traditional values of the South through her original compositions and her authentic folk style. She created and portrayed the "coal miner's daughter," a popular myth of the working-class southern woman, which may become as pervasive as the myth of the antebellum southern belle, Scarlett O'Hara.

Loretta Lynn was born in the small community of Butcher Holler, Ky., on 14 April 1937, the second of eight children of Clara Butcher and Ted Webb. When she was 13, she married Mooney Lynn, a soldier who had recently returned from World War II. The first of her six children was born when she was 14, and she was a grandmother by 28. Loretta Lynn had been married over 10 years before she began singing for audiences other than her family. She was successful almost immediately after the release of her first record, "I'm a Honky Tonk Girl" (1960), which was her own composition. Neither the small recording company, Zero, nor the Lynns could finance promotion of "I'm a Honky Tonk Girl," so Loretta and Mooney mailed copies of the record, along with a short letter of explanation, to disc jockeys across the nation. When they realized that the record was a hit, the Lynns sold their home in Washington state and drove to Nashville in a 1955 Ford to sign a contract.

From 1963 to 2004 Loretta Lynn released over 60 albums for Decca and MCA, including many of her own compositions. Based upon *Billboard*'s year-end charts of hit songs, her most successful singles have been "Success" (1962), "Wine, Women, and Song" (1964), "Blue Kentucky Girl" (1965), "Happy Birthday" (1965), "You Ain't Woman Enough" (1966), "Dear Uncle Sam" (1966), "If You're Not Gone Too Long" (1967), "Fist City" (1968), "You've Just Stepped In (From Stepping Out on Me)" (1968), "Woman of the World—Leave My World Alone" (1969), "That's a No, No" (1969), "You Want to Give Me a Lift" (1970), "I Know How" (1970), "I Wanna Be Free" (1971), "You're Look-

Loretta Lynn, country music singer (Courtesy John Edwards Memorial Collection of the University of North Carolina at Chapel Hill)

ing at Country" (1971), "One's on the Way" (1972), "Rated X" (1973), "Hey, Loretta" (1974), "She's Got You" (1977), and "Out of My Head and into My Bed" (1978). Loretta Lynn has won a number of awards, including a Grammy, twelve nominations and three awards from the Country Music Association for top female artist, two awards from Record World, three from *Billboard*, and four from Cash Box. In 1961 she received an award as the Most Promising Female Artist, and by 1972 she had become the first woman to be honored as the Country Music Association's Entertainer of the Year. In 1980 the album sound track of the film *Coal Miner's Daughter*, which featured Loretta's hit songs sung by actress Sissy Spacek, was named Album of the Year by the Country Music Association. The movie was based on Lynn's autobiography of the same title. She has since published another memoir, *Still Woman Enough*.

In 1993 Lynn teamed up with fellow country legends Dolly Parton and Tammy Wynette for the album *Honky Tonk Angels*. Lynn was a recipient of Kennedy Center Honors in 2003 and was named Artist of the Decade for the 1970s by the Academy of Country Music. In 2004 she made a comeback with the critically acclaimed album *Van Lear Rose*, produced by and featuring the guitar playing of Jack White, of the rock band the White Stripes. The album reached new generational audiences and garnered airplay on rock radio. At the end of 2004, she was nominated for five Grammy awards, including Best Country Song, Best Country Album, Best Country Collaboration with Vocals, and Best Female Country Vocal Performance. At the 2005 Grammy awards, she won for Best Country Album and Best Country Collaboration with Vocals.

Loretta Lynn is popular regionally, nationally, and internationally. She received an honorable mention in the 1973 Gallup Poll list of the world's 10 most admired women. In addition to creating southern regional mythology, Loretta Lynn's lyrics and life history reflect the social history of working-class southern women and reinforce the American values of individualism, patriotism, and freedom. She embodies the American "rags to riches" story within a southern setting.

RUTH A. BANES
University of South Florida

Ruth A. Banes, *Canadian Review of American Studies* (Fall 1985); Dorothy A. Horstman, in *Stars of Country Music*, ed. Bill C.

Malone and Judith McCulloh (1975); Loretta Lynn and Patsi Bale Cox, *Still Woman Enough: A Memoir* (2002); Loretta Lynn with George Vecsey, *Coal Miner's Daughter* (2001); Vertical file on "Loretta Lynn," Country Music Foundation Library and Media Center, Nashville, Tenn.

Lynyrd Skynyrd

SOUTHERN ROCK BAND.

Lynyrd Skynyrd is a southern rock band that reached the height of its popularity in the 1970s. The driving force behind Skynyrd was singer Ronnie Van Zant, who was born on 15 January 1948 in Jacksonville, Fla. He formed his first band in 1964, together with drummer Bob Burns, guitarists Gary Rossington and Allen Collins, and bass player Larry Junstrom. During these early years, Van Zant's group used different names, such as the Noble Five, My Backyard, and the One Percent. The band members eventually decided to name their band Lynyrd Skynyrd, a mocking tribute to Robert E. Lee High School gym teacher Leonard Skinner. Van Zant, Rossington, and Burns all went to Lee High, and they were frequently reprimanded because their long hair violated the school's dress code. Coach Skinner in particular rigidly enforced these regulations, and he became the symbol of authoritarianism for Ronnie and his friends. The name Lynyrd Skynyrd thus signifies rebellion against school rules and, more generally, mainstream values. This defiant attitude would become a trademark of the band in the following years.

Lynyrd Skynyrd's first album, *Pronounced Leh-Nerd Skin-Nerd*, was released in 1973 by MCA Records. Producer Al Kooper had noticed the band during a performance at a club in Atlanta, and he was impressed by Skynyrd's straightforward rock-and-roll music. By then, the band had already gone through a number of personnel changes. Ed King had become the new bassist, and Billy Powell was added to the band as keyboard player. *Pronounced Leh-Nerd Skin-nerd* contained a couple of numbers that would quickly be considered signature Skynyrd songs, such as "Simple Man," "Gimme Three Steps," and "Freebird." *Sounds* magazine described the band's first album as "a raw blend of blues, hillbilly country, and British boogie packed with typically Southern flavor: moaning slide guitar, country pickin' mandolin, aggressive guitars, driving rhythm section in straight 4/4, and dry, thirst-parched vocals. Van Zant's lyrics completed the geographical picture with tales of disapproving daddies, guns, trains, rides, ghettos, the Lord, and getting high on dope and booze."

Skynyrd's real breakthrough came in 1974 with the release of the album *Second Helping*. Leon Wilkeson had joined the band on bass and King switched to guitars, thus forming Lynyrd Skynyrd's first three-guitar army, together with Rossington and Collins. *Second Helping* featured the number "Sweet Home Alabama," which was a response to Neil Young's "Southern Man" and "Alabama." In both songs, Young criticized the racist legacy of the South and in particular the state of Alabama. The guys from Lynyrd Skynyrd believed that the folksinger from Canada had constructed a bloated caricature of their homeland, and "Sweet Home Alabama" was supposed to set things right. The writing of the song had started off as a joke and it was recorded in no time, but the track would become the band's biggest hit, reaching a Top 10 position in August 1974. "Freebird" was rereleased as a single the following year. It received notable national airplay and eventually hit the Top 20 in the national charts.

The band's lineup again changed when Bob Burns and Ed King decided to leave the group. Artimus Pyle was selected as the new drummer, and Steve Gaines replaced King. The Honkettes were added to the band as background singers in 1975, during the recording of the album *Nuthin' Fancy*. In the meantime, the popularity of Lynyrd Skynyrd continued to grow. By 1977 it was one of the most successful rock groups from the South, with a devoted fan base in the United States and across the world. The band had scored four gold records in a row, and the live LP *One More for the Road* went platinum. But then tragedy struck. On 20 October 1977, three days after the release of the album *Street Survivors*, Skynyrd's rented airplane crashed into a swamp near Gillsburg, Miss., while en route to a concert at Louisiana State University. Ronnie Van Zant, Steve Gaines, backup singer Cassie Gaines, and road manager Dean Kilpatrick did not survive the crash, and other band members were injured, some very seriously. The plane accident seemed to mark the end of Skynyrd, but the band made a surprising comeback in 1987, with Johnny Van Zant replacing his brother on vocals. Lynyrd Skynyrd was inducted into the Rock and Roll Hall of Fame in 2006.

Lynyrd Skynyrd was one of the most prominent representatives of the so-called southern rock movement, which became popular in the 1970s. Southern rock was not so much a unified musical style as a label that denoted the regional background of a number of bands. Although these groups all adopted and adapted particular southern music traditions, such as blues and country, each of them had a distinct character. Lynyrd Skynyrd epitomized the hard rock side of the movement, with its triple guitar attack and songs such as "Freebird" and "Gimme Three Steps." Country legend Merle Haggard was an important source of inspiration for Ronnie Van Zant, and Skynyrd's repertoire likewise expressed a close connection with the southern white working class. Besides its reputation as a rowdy bunch of hard-drinking, long-haired rebels, the band was sometimes branded as racist. This was mainly caused by the band's strong identification with the South. Every time Skynyrd played "Sweet Home Alabama" on stage, an enormous Confederate battle flag would unfurl behind them, and in the spring of 1975 they were declared honorary lieutenant colonels in the Alabama state militia by Gov. George Wallace himself. The band members claimed that the rebel flag was part of an MCA marketing campaign to promote Skynyrd as a genuine southern rock group, and Ronnie Van Zant described their new position in Wallace's militia as a "bullshit gimmick thing." In spite of the neo-Confederate sentiments that were attached to the band, Lynyrd Skynyrd remained extremely popular across the nation until the fatal plane crash. Its popularity was perhaps an indication of how the times were changing in the seventies.

MAARTEN ZWIERS
University of Mississippi

Lee Ballinger, *Lynyrd Skynyrd: An Oral History* (1999); Marley Brant, *Freebirds: The Lynyrd Skynyrd Story* (2002), *Southern Rockers: The Roots and Legacy of Southern Rock* (1999); Mark Kemp, *Dixie Lullaby: A Story of Music, Race, and New Beginnings in a New South* (2004); Gene Odom, *Lynyrd Skynyrd: Remembering the Free Birds of Southern Rock* (2002); Ted Ownby, in *Haunted Bodies: Gender and Southern Texts*, ed. Anne Goodwyn Jones and Susan V. Donaldson (1997).

Macon, Uncle Dave

(1870–1952) BANJO PLAYER
AND EARLY COUNTRY MUSIC
ENTERTAINER.

Not the first on-air performer, but certainly the first celebrity of WSM's *Grand Ole Opry*, Uncle Dave Macon did not begin his historic career in entertainment until the gold-toothed banjo player was 50 years old. Born David Harrison Macon in Warren County, Tenn., Uncle Dave spent a good part of his teens living at the Broadway Hotel, a boardinghouse that his parents operated in downtown Nashville. Vaudeville and circus performers often stayed at the Broadway, and young Macon observed rehearsals that materialized in the basement of his parents' establishment. After

Macon's mother gave him the money for his first banjo, he began learning some of the musical stunts he had witnessed in the Broadway Hotel's basement.

Macon's father was killed during a fight at the Broadway, and his family moved back to the country, east of Nashville. Dave Macon then started a mule-driven freight line called the Macon Midway Mule and Wagon Transportation Company, which ran between Woodbury and Murfreesboro, Tenn. In those more rural parts of Tennessee, he was exposed to the work songs and blues music of both black and white folks. Often Macon could be heard singing improvised songs about the wares he delivered as he drove the pack trains. In 1920, after a lengthy career in freight hauling via mule, Macon opted not to compete with a motorized truck company that emerged and threatened his business. At age 50 he retired from one career and set out on a new path.

Family in Arkansas pushed Macon to try his hand at performing, and the banjo player started playing benefit shows around middle Tennessee. Word of his energetic performances spread quickly, and Macon became a popular live draw in his region of the South. In 1924 Macon hit New York City alongside fiddler Sid Harkreader, and the two made their first recording for Vocalion Records. "Chewing Gum," Macon's first release from the Vocalion recording session, incorporates a humorous dose of onomatopoeia—Macon uses both instrumental and vocal repetition to imitate the elastic quality of gum in a chewer's mouth. After this initial hit, the artist continued to tour and record successfully, with Harkreader on fiddle and Sam McGee on guitar.

By the time Macon made his 1926 debut on the WSM *Barn Dance* (which soon became the *Grand Ole Opry*) radio show, he was already a celebrity. Journalist Rufus Jarman remembers that first Saturday evening: "We had one of the two radio sets in the community, and we were afraid that everybody in that end of the county would swarm into our house to hear Uncle Dave and trample us."

After initially wowing the *Opry* audience, Macon only intermittently appeared on the show, preferring to tour and play live concerts rather than commit to WSM. In 1930, after four years of trying to make a living on the road during the Great Depression, he sought a regular gig at the *Opry*. It was during his time there that he began to collaborate with the Delmore Brothers and other *Opry* stars. The wild popularity of the weekly Saturday night show and its ensemble cast led to a Hollywood film based on the *Opry*. Uncle Dave both acted and performed music in the 1940 movie, *Grand Ole Opry*. The film contains the only known footage of Uncle Dave Macon in action. He plays the role of a constable in a small town and pulls off several banjo tricks, including playing the instrument while swinging it between his legs.

Macon, by this time nicknamed "The Dixie Dewdrop" by *Opry* director George D. Hay, continued to please *Opry* fans with his quick wit, political humor, suggestive songs, and polished banjo-picking style until two weeks before his death at age 81. Macon was elected posthumously into the Country Music Hall of Fame in 1966.

His life's work bridged the gap between the medicine show music of the 19th-century South and the more modern recorded and broadcast music of the early 20th century. Through records, radio, and touring, Macon managed to bring his mix of southern music to audiences both within and outside the South.

Macon's legacy lives on through an annual music festival in Murfreesboro, Tenn. Through music competitions and dance contests, Uncle Dave Macon Days both honors Uncle Dave's contribution to old-time country music and ensures that the music Uncle Dave so passionately performed goes on.

CAROLINE KEYS
Missoula, Montana

Robert Cantwell, *Bluegrass Breakdown: The Making of the Old Southern Sound* (1992); Charles K. Wolfe, *A Good-Natured Riot: The Birth of the Grand Ole Opry* (1999).

Malaco Records

The roots of Malaco Records, based in Jackson, Miss., stretch back to 1961, when cofounder Tommy Couch Sr. began booking R&B bands at the University of Mississippi while serving as social chairman of his fraternity, Pi Kappa Alpha. After graduation, Couch moved to Jackson to work as a pharmacist and formed the booking agency Malaco Productions with his brother-in-law, Mitchell Malouf. The operation moved into recording in 1966, by which time Couch's fraternity brother Gerald "Wolf" Stephenson had joined as a partner.

In its first years, Malaco released few recordings, concentrating instead on leasing masters to other labels. One of the most notable—if untypical—sessions resulted in the 1970 Capitol LP *I Do Not Play No Rock 'n' Roll* by down-home bluesman Mississippi Fred McDowell. The label gained momentum the same year via productions by New Orleans arranger Wardell Quezergue that yielded two major hits: Jean Knight's "Mr. Big Stuff" on Stax Records and King Floyd's "Groove Me" on Malaco's own Chimneyville label. "Groove Me" marked the beginning of a distribution and production arrangement with Atlantic Records, but the relationship ultimately did little for Malaco's shaky finances. Salvation came in the form of Dorothy Moore, whose ballad "Misty Blue," released on Malaco, was in the Top 5 on both the R&B and pop charts in early 1976; she subsequently scored many other hits for the label.

The company finally found its niche in the early 1980s following the signing of Texan Z. Z. Hill, whose 1982 smash hit "Down Home Blues," penned by Memphis/Muscle Shoals songwriter George Jackson, alerted the record industry to a seemingly untapped, mostly southern market for "soul-blues." Malaco's eventual conquest of this market can be attributed to a number of factors: the hiring of legendary veteran record promotion man Dave Clark; the development of a distinctive studio "sound," aided by Malaco's purchase of Muscle Shoals Sound in the mid-1980s; and a pool of talented songwriters, including George Jackson, Larry Addison, Rich Cason, and Frederick Knight.

Upon the rise of disco and the "urban contemporary" radio format, veteran soul stars, including Denise LaSalle, Little Milton, Johnnie Taylor, Latimore, and Bobby "Blue" Bland, lost major label contracts, and Dave Clark helped bring them to Malaco. With these artists Malaco subsequently became the major force on the largely southern chitlin' circuit, garnering impressive record sales but relatively little national attention. During the 1990s Malaco added veterans, including Shirley Brown and Tyrone Davis, and Tommy Couch Jr., a University of Mississippi graduate and booking agent like his father, started the Waldoxy subsidiary, bringing aboard artists that included Artie "Blues Boy" White, Carl Sims, Mel Waiters, Bobby Rush, and blues comedian Poonanny. More recently the label has signed many younger stars of "southern soul."

Less well known but of great importance to Malaco's prosperity is its gospel catalog. The label ventured into the gospel market in the mid-1970s with the Jackson Southernaires and subsequently signed artists that include the Soul Stirrers, the Sensational Nightingales, the Williams Brothers, and the Angelic Gospel Singers. After purchasing the catalog of pioneer gospel label Savoy Records in 1986, Malaco became the leading gospel label and has scored many hits with artists such as the Mississippi Mass Choir, the Rev. Clay Evans, Dorothy Norwood, and the Rev. James Cleveland.

SCOTT BARRETTA
Oxford, Mississippi

Peter Guralnick, *Living Blues* (January–February 1989); Jeff Hannusch, *Rolling Stone* (2 June 1988).

Mandolin

The mandolin is widely used in bluegrass music. It has a wooden hollow body, with a carved top and a flat back. The instrument, which in effect is a miniature lute, came to the United States from Italy and was used in the 19th century in Italian American folk music and by concert performers. In the late 19th century it became a Victorian era parlor instrument, along with such novelty instruments as the zither, the mandola, and the ukuleles, all designed to amuse a new middle class. The mandolin that was associated with bluegrass was designed in this era by Orville Gibson, a furniture maker, who gave the instrument a striking ornamentation through extensive use of the scroll, carved not only on the body of the mandolin but also on bridges, pegheads, tailpieces, and sound holes. Lloyd Loar, working for the Gibson Company, designed the slim, finely engineered F5 mandolin in 1919, and it would become the popular model for string bands and, later, country and bluegrass musicians.

The mandolin entered the South more widely in the early 20th century through mail order catalogs. Blues performers used the instrument for a time, but it took deeper root in white mountain music, often played by the youngest child in the family, as a smaller, more manageable musical instrument than larger stringed instruments. It had its greatest influence in country music in the 1930s, as duets such as the Blue Sky Boys and Charlie and Bill Monroe made especially prominent use of it. With the introduction of electrical amplification into country music in the 1940s, though, bands abandoned the gentler mandolin sounds.

Bill Monroe, who grew up in western Kentucky, would fashion a new musical genre, bluegrass, in the late 1940s, and he accompanied his high-pitched singing with the sounds of the mandolin. What had been a rather soft, lyrical sound became in Monroe's hands percussive, providing a fast-paced drive for this energetic music. Bluegrass bands in this era were acoustic ensembles that included the fiddle, five-string banjo, guitars, and double bass, as well as the mandolin. Monroe used the mandolin for jazzy improvisations.

Monroe became especially identified with the mandolin, but the South produced other accomplished musicians on the instrument as well. Knoxville's Kenneth Burns (who would perform as Jethro in the duo Homer and Jethro) developed the jazz possibilities of the mandolin; Jesse McReynolds (of Jim and Jesse) devised a distinctive crosspicking style of playing the instrument; and Bobby Osborne was the inventor of a fluent, embellished approach to melody. Tennessee's Frank Wakefield developed a complex mandolin chord progression and unusual tunings, which in turn influenced David Grisman, who since the 1980s has been an innovator in acoustic music that features the mandolin in his fusion of jazz, classical, and bluegrass styles into "dawg music."

CHARLES REAGAN WILSON
University of Mississippi

Robert Cantwell, *Bluegrass Breakdown: The Making of the Old Southern Sound* (1984); R. C. Hartman, *Guitars and Mandolins in America* (1984); Bill C. Malone, *Country Music, U.S.A.* (2002).

Marsalis, Wynton

(b. 1961) JAZZ MUSICIAN.

Wynton Marsalis is one of the most prominent contemporary jazz performers and the leader of a neoclassical postbop return to jazz roots, an approach that has highlighted New Orleans's—and the South's—role as of central importance in music history.

Marsalis is from a musical family. His father, Ellis, is a well-known New Orleans figure, and his three brothers, including saxophonist Branford Marsalis, are all accomplished musicians. Born on 18 October 1961, Wynton Marsalis studied jazz and classical music as a boy and marched at age eight in Danny Barker's children's band, performing at the New Orleans Jazz and Heritage Festival. As a teenager he played his instrument of choice, the trumpet, in jazz bands, funk groups, and the New Orleans Symphony. He studied at the Berkshire Music Center and the Julliard School, and in 1980, he joined Art Blakely's Jazz Messengers.

Marsalis's first recordings, such as *Wynton Marsalis* (1981) and *Black Codes (from the Underground)* (1985), reflected a postbop rhythmic sensibility and tonal-harmonic style associated with the post–World War II era, as well as the fusion of free jazz styles. In 1984 he won Grammy awards for both jazz and classical recordings, becoming the first musician to do so. Since then he has become one of the best-known American musicians. His recordings, including 16 classical and more than 30 jazz albums, have sold close to eight million copies, and he has performed in over 30 countries, averaging 120 concerts per year. He was coproducer of the Ken Burns documentary *Jazz*, which aired on PBS nationwide and affirmed the key role of classic jazz performers like Louis Armstrong and Duke Ellington.

Marsalis has been influential through his position as artistic director for the Jazz at Lincoln Center program, which he helped establish in 1987. Marsalis's own compositions for the program have earned much acclaim, including his winning the 1997 Pulitzer Prize for music for his oratorio *Blood on the Fields*, a meditation on slavery. He was the first jazz musician to win the Pulitzer. Marsalis has composed notable works for dance, including ballets for Peter Martins and Twyla Tharp and his 1996 *Sweet Release*, a collaboration with the Alvin Ailey American Dance Theater. Marsalis has been influential as an energetic advocate for jazz education, especially through the "Jazz for Young People" programs at Lincoln Center, his master classes in jazz schools across the nation, and his countless workshops and lectures.

Marsalis has explored African American and southern culture through his work. *At the Octoroon Balls* featured

Marsalis's first string quartet, and one version was prepared for John Singleton's film *Rosewood*, about horrific racial violence in Florida. A recent Marsalis work, *From the Plantation to the Penitentiary* (2007), suggests a sharpened social conscience. The albums *Thick in the South: Soul Gestures in Southern Blue*, vol. 1; *Uptown Ruler: Soul Gestures in Southern Blue*, vol. 2; *Levee Low Moan: Soul Gestures in Southern Blue*, vol. 3; and *Standard Time*, vol. 2: *Intimacy Calling* were all evocative works that explicitly attached jazz to a southern sensibility.

Marsalis became one of the most prominent celebrities in promoting the recovery of his hometown of New Orleans after Hurricane Katrina in 2005. He organized a major benefit performance at Lincoln Center for the city's musicians. He appeared in numerous television commercials and made countless speeches nationwide urging tourists to return to Louisiana.

CHARLES REAGAN WILSON
University of Mississippi

F. Davis, *Outcasts: Jazz Composers, Instrumentalists, and Singers* (1990); Wynton Marsalis, *Marsalis on Music* (1995); Tom Sherman, *American Heritage* (October 1995).

Mercer, Johnny

(1909–1976) SONGWRITER.
John Herndon Mercer was born in Savannah, Ga., on 18 November 1909, to George A. Mercer and Lillian Ciucevich Mercer. His mother's family came to the United States from Croatia in the 19th century; the Mercers had lived in Savannah since the colonial era. After completing his education at Wood-

berry Forest School in Virginia, Mercer moved to New York and obtained roles in traveling variety shows. He began writing music and lyrics for these performances, including the *Garrick Gaieties of 1930*, which resulted in his first published lyric, "Out of Breath (and Scared to Death of You)." While working for the show, he met and married Ginger Meehan.

Continuing to write in New York, Mercer began collaborating with popular jazz and big band composers, including Harold Arlen ("Accentuate the Positive," "One for My Baby (And One More for the Road)"), Jerome Kern ("I'm Old Fashioned"), Duke Ellington ("Satin Doll"), Hoagy Carmichael ("Lazybones"), and Henry Mancini ("Moon River"). Prominent singers, including Frank Sinatra and Ella Fitzgerald, gave voice to his words in songs like "Summer Wind" and "Something's Gotta Give."

In 1942, with Buddy DeSylva and Glen Wallichs, Mercer cofounded Capitol Records, in California, which was the first major West Coast label. Early artists signed to the label were Peggy Lee, Nat "King" Cole, Bing Crosby, and Les Paul. By the 1950s such stars as Frank Sinatra, Andy Griffith, Judy Garland, the Andrews Sisters, Dean Martin, and Nancy Wilson were staples on the label. In 1955, EMI bought Capitol for $8.5 million.

Mercer often drew on his southern upbringing for lyrical inspiration. "Blues in the Night (My Mama Done Tol' Me)," written with Harold Arlen and sung by Ella Fitzgerald, uses African American vernacular to express being double-crossed by a woman. "Jubilation T. Cornpone," from the show *Li'l Abner*, describes a southern Civil War figure who advocated retreating rather than fighting. In the most notable of these songs, "Pardon My Southern Accent," a lover is advised to just kiss the protagonist if she does not like the way he speaks.

Mercer remained in California for the rest of his life, dying from a brain tumor on 25 June 1976. The Mercer catalog holds over 1,000 songs, the royalties of which support the Johnny Mercer Foundation, an organization that promotes the work of great American songwriters to children. The Georgia State University Special Collections Department holds Mercer's papers. In 1995 the Georgia legislature voted to make 19 April Johnny Mercer Day, in light of his contribution to American music.

RENNA TUTAN
University of Mississippi

Bob Bach and Ginger Mercer, *Our Huckleberry Friend: The Life, Times, and Lyrics of Johnny Mercer* (1982); Philip Furia, *Skylark: The Life and Times of Johnny Mercer* (2003).

Meters

NEW ORLEANS SOUL AND FUNK MUSICIANS.
The Meters are a soul and funk group from New Orleans consisting of keyboardist Art Neville, guitarist Leo Nocentelli, bassist George Porter Jr., and drummer Joseph "Zigaboo" Modeliste, who were joined by percussionist Cyril Neville in 1974. With a string of albums for Josie and Reprise, the group brought a mixture of funky instrumental grooves and the irrepressible spirit of

a New Orleans street party to national audiences for a decade, beginning in the late 1960s. It represents one of the core groups that came to define funk in the 1970s, a fact that is underscored by its status as one of the most heavily sampled groups within rap music production.

Neville put the group together in 1967, stripping down his larger band, Art Neville and the Neville Sounds, to a Hammond B3 organ backed up by a tight rhythm section of bass, drums, and guitar. The group was the house band at the Ivanhoe bar on Bourbon Street and became known for extended, sparse, percussive grooves. It also worked as a studio band at Cosimo Matassa's studio, backing up local artists like Betty Harris and Lee Dorsey for producers Allen Toussaint and Marshall Sehorn.

The musicians signed with Josie Records and began calling themselves the Meters, a reference to their precise rhythmic sensibility. Outstripping the expectations for an all-instrumental group, their first four singles charted on *Billboard*'s Hot 100 in 1969. Their debut outing, "Sophisticated Cissy," went to No. 7 on the R&B charts. Not long afterward the group hit again with "Cissy Strut," which spent 12 weeks on the charts, peaking at No. 4. All told, the group had 10 singles on the *Billboard* R&B charts between 1969 and 1971. Its first three albums for Josie Records— *The Meters*, *Look-Ka Py Py*, and *Struttin'*—were mainly instrumental, infusing gritty New Orleans funk into a mixture of originals and cover versions of popular songs, reminiscent of the early work of Memphis-based group Booker T. & the MG's.

In 1972 the Meters moved to Reprise Records, where they released *Cabbage Alley*, in which the musicians continued to move away from the all-instrumental format by utilizing Art Neville's vocal talents. They followed up with *Rejuvenation* in 1974. An offer to open for the Rolling Stones in 1975 and 1976 led to the addition of Cyril Neville as a permanent member of the band, contributing percussion and vocals to the group's efforts. With his help, the Meters produced several more albums for Reprise, including *Fire on the Bayou* and *Trick Bag*. The group continued to mine the local musical culture for inspiration, releasing songs that related to the Mardi Gras Indian subculture and its music, like "Hey Pocky Way," as well as covers of hits from previous eras such as "Mardi Gras Mambo" and Earl King's "Trick Bag."

Throughout the 1970s the group continued to work backing up other artists as well as recording its own material. It helped fellow New Orleans native Dr. John score a hit in 1973 with "Right Place, Right Time," and in 1975 it backed Labelle on the track "Lady Marmalade." These were not all positive experiences, however. The Meters provided much of the music for Robert Palmer's 1974 album *Sneakin' Sally through the Alley*, but these contributions went unacknowledged when the album was released. Various disputes have led to the dissolution of the group's relationship with Toussaint, who produced all of its material through 1977. The group

recorded *New Directions* in 1977 before disbanding, after which Art joined his brothers in the Neville Brothers band. In recent decades the group has reunited occasionally and with various of the members, with the exception of drummer Joseph "Zigaboo" Modeliste.

MATT MILLER
Emory University

John Broven, *Rhythm & Blues in New Orleans* (1988); Art Neville, Aaron Neville, Cyril Neville, and Charles Neville, *The Brothers: An Autobiography* (2000).

Mexican Border Stations

Popularly known as X-stations because of their call letters, the Mexican border radio stations in the 1930s and afterward were powerful disseminators of music and other forms of popular culture throughout North America. Their programming techniques and advertising practices became part of the nation's folklore, and they did much to make the world at large conscious of southern rural folkways.

With transmitters located on the Mexican side of the border and operating with wattage generally far in excess of that permitted in the United States, X-station broadcasts could be heard clearly in this country and Canada. The era of border radio began in 1932 when John R. Brinkley, "the goat-gland doctor" who promoted a cure for male sexual impotence, established XER (later XERA), with offices in Del Rio, Tex., and transmitter in Villa Acuna, Mexico. Station XER claimed power of 500,000 watts, and Brinkley advertised his medical ideas and Del Rio hospital on it and also leased time to other American businessmen to sell patent medicines and other products. Additional stations, such as XEPN, XEAW, XENT, and XEG, soon followed, with each of them pursuing a pattern of radio programming similar to that pioneered by Brinkley.

Late-night listeners were introduced to an unforgettable deluge of Americana on the border radio shows. Long-winded announcers incessantly promoted such products as baby chicks, songbooks, records, photographs, prayer cloths, Resurrection plants, Bibles, "genuine simulated" diamonds, laxatives, hair dyes, forms of patent medicines (such as Crazy Water Crystals), and "autographed pictures of Jesus Christ." Listeners were constantly solicited for money, asked to send in box tops and labels, and told to get their orders in the mail immediately for once-in-a-lifetime offers that were due to go off the air forever at midnight.

Border radio advertising was accompanied also by strong doses of southern popular culture: fundamentalist religion, populist politics, and grassroots music of various kinds. Country musicians such as the Carter Family, the Pickard Family, the Callahan Brothers, and the Herrington Trio, cowboy singers like Cowboy Slim Rinehart, Jesse Rodgers, and the Utah Cowboy (J. R. Hall), and gospel singers such as the Chuck Wagon Gang and the Stamps Quartet performed on the border stations either on live broadcasts or on transcriptions. They sold their sponsors' products, hawked their own records and picture-songbooks, and disseminated their particular versions of southern music to audiences in the most remote corners of North America. The radio stations still broadcast their southern-influenced programs.

BILL C. MALONE
Madison, Wisconsin

Gerald Carson, *The Roguish World of Dr. Brinkley* (1960); Gene Fowler and Bill Crawford, *Border Radio: Quacks, Yodelers, Pitchmen, Psychics, and Other Amazing Broadcasters of the American Airwaves* (2002); Bill C. Malone, *Country Music, U.S.A.: A Fifty-Year History* (1968; rev. ed., 1985).

Minnie, Memphis

(1897–1973) BLUES SINGER.
Born Lizzie Douglas, in Algiers, La., in 1897, Memphis Minnie was one of the most influential and prolific female blues artists of the 20th century. Her talent as a guitar player, singer, and lyricist combined with her Louisiana roots and experience in Memphis to create a unique sound that was extremely popular in the 1930s and 1940s. In 1904 she moved to Walls, Miss., and within the next few years received a guitar that she quickly learned to play. Faced with a life of being either a domestic servant or a fieldworker, Douglas chose the alternative of playing and singing for house parties and traveling shows and on the streets of Delta towns like Walls and in Memphis, Tenn. These performances soon led her to play with such notables as Casey Bill Weldon (to whom it is commonly thought she was married), Willie Brown, and Joe McCoy (to whom she was wed by common

law). Her musical partnership with Mc-Coy was noticed, and the couple was recorded together by Columbia Records in 1929, yielding "Bumble Bee," which was later recorded by Muddy Waters as "Honey Bee," as well as "When the Levee Breaks," further popularized by Led Zeppelin.

Memphis Minnie and McCoy made Chicago their base in the early 1930s, steadily adding to their repertoire such songs as "What's the Matter with the Mill?," encountering other blues artists like Big Bill Broonzy, Tampa Red, and Sleepy John Estes, and influencing a younger generation of Chicago blues-men. After her relationship with McCoy ended, Minnie married Ernest "Little Son Joe" Lawlars and entered a pros-perous time in her career. Touring and recording with and without Lawlars, Minnie embraced the electric guitar and expanded her recordings to include a wider range of instrumentation. Langs-ton Hughes chronicled one of her Chi-cago performances on New Year's Eve 1942 in the piece "Memphis Minnie on the Icebox." He described the rhythm and power of her electric sound, pic-tured her legs as "musical pistons," and referred to her music as harder than the coins crossing the counter to enter the pockets of the white men who owned the club.

Minnie and Lawlars continued to tour into the 1950s, although changing audience tastes limited their popularity. In 1957, Minnie suffered a heart attack that left her incapacitated, and Lawlars became ill, forcing the couple to return to Memphis and their family. Lawlars died in 1961, and Minnie entered a nurs-ing home, passing away in 1973. She is buried in New Hope Cemetery in Walls, Miss.

RENNA TUTEN
University of Georgia

Anna Stong Bourgeois, *Blueswomen: Profiles of 37 Early Performers, with an Anthology of Lyrics, 1920–1945* (1996); Paul Garon and Beth Garon, *Woman with Guitar: Memphis Minnie's Blues* (1992).

Monk, Thelonious

(1917–1982) JAZZ MUSICIAN.
Jazz pianist and composer Thelonious Monk invented a musical style both steeped in tradition and uniquely his own. Showcasing the influence of many moments of jazz tradition, from stride piano to avant-garde, Monk emerged as a creative, eccentric genius of American music and a performer impossible to imitate. His work reinvented jazz and changed the course of American music.

Monk was born on 17 October 1917 in Rocky Mount, N.C., to Thelonious Monk Sr., a day laborer, and Barbara Batts Monk, a domestic worker. Frus-trated with the limited opportunities available to her family in Jim Crow North Carolina, Barbara packed her three children and boarded a train to New York City in 1922, along with scores of other southern black migrants of her day. Barbara found a job working at a nursery in Manhattan and became the family breadwinner, earning enough money to buy a radio, a Victrola, and an upright piano—sources of Monk's early exposure to a wide variety of musical styles. Thelonious Sr. had remained in North Carolina because of health prob-lems but visited the family in New York

294 MONK, THELONIOUS

for periods of time, bringing his love of the harmonica and the piano into the home. Monk studied both the trumpet and the piano and began to take some lessons at the age of nine, quickly establishing himself as a musical prodigy. By his early teen years, he was playing at rent parties and the local Baptist church and winning competitions, possibly including those held for amateurs at Harlem's Apollo Theater.

Although Monk did well in school and was admitted to one of the city's best high schools, Stuyvesant, he dropped out to pursue music. After traveling for several years with an evangelist, Monk formed his own band and played in small clubs until he was hired as the house pianist at Minton's Playhouse in Harlem. Minton's was an important site of musical exchange and collaboration during bebop's flowering, and Monk encountered other emerging jazz artists there, including Charlie Parker and Dizzy Gillespie. While Monk explored and created this new music alongside his contemporaries, he charted his own musical course, particularly in the equal activity of both hands engaging the entire piano keyboard. His contemporaries made their marks with long, complex solos, but Monk was known for his use of silences. His compositions evinced a unique preference for working with the structure of melody and harmony and rhythm, instead of the more popular penning of melody atop familiar chords.

Despite Monk's innovations, he did not achieve wide recognition outside of the world of jazz performers. He played with several ensembles and was finally signed to Blue Note in 1947 when he was 30 years old. Monk made his first recordings for Blue Note, bringing in musicians that he had met and respected. These early recordings are now considered some of the best of his career, but at the time of their release they were commercial failures and received harsh reviews from music critics of the day. Such criticism made it difficult for Monk to find work. Refusing to compromise his musical vision, he played in clubs and at random concerts, composed new music, and recorded for the Prestige label. In 1954 he traveled to perform in the Paris Jazz Festival. While there, he recorded his first solo album for Vogue—an album that would begin to establish him as a formidable musical talent worthy of widespread recognition and acclaim.

In 1955 Monk signed with a new label, Riverside, and recorded several albums that received critical praise, including *Thelonious Monk Plays Duke Ellington*, *Brilliant Corners*, and *Thelonious Monk Alone*. He enjoyed a long engagement at the Five Spot Café beginning in 1957, playing with an ensemble that included John Coltrane. During this period, Monk received acclaim and success, and his career finally peaked. Throughout the 1960s, Monk performed in prestigious venues, signed and recorded with Columbia Records, and received media attention. This attention included endless stories of Monk's eccentricities, and accounts of his behavior often overshadowed analysis of his music and recognition of his talent.

Monk's success continued into the 1960s with albums like *Straight, No*

Chaser, but Columbia/CBS records began to favor rock music over jazz, and he recorded for the last time with Columbia in 1968. In failing health, he toured and recorded less often in the early 1970s, and his band members began to move in different professional directions. Monk made his final public appearance in 1976 and passed away from a stroke in 1982. His music continues to inspire jazz enthusiasts and American musicians alike, who cover his work across a variety of genres and pay tribute to his unique, inventive piano style and compositions.

FRANCES ABBOTT
Emory University

Thomas Fitterling, *Thelonious Monk: His Life and Music* (1997); Leslie Gourse, *Straight, No Chaser: The Life and Genius of Thelonious Monk* (1998); Rob van der Bliek, ed., *The Thelonious Monk Reader* (2001).

Monroe, Bill

(1911–1996) BLUEGRASS MUSICIAN. William Smith "Bill" Monroe was born 13 September 1911 on a farm near the small town of Rosine, Ohio County, in western Kentucky. The youngest of eight children, Monroe had extremely poor sight. He was a shy lad, for whom his family's musical traditions afforded comfort and identity. His mother died when he was 10 and his father when he was 16. He lived for several years with his Uncle Pen (Pendleton Vandiver), a fiddler who strongly influenced his music and who was later immortalized in song by Monroe. He also learned much from a black guitarist and fiddler, Arnold Shultz, with whom he played

at dances. In 1929 he joined two older brothers at industrial jobs near Chicago. In 1932 the three became part of an exhibition square dance team for the *National Barn Dance* on Chicago radio station WLS. In 1934 Bill and his brother Charlie became professional "hillbilly" radio singers. By 1938 their duets had become popular throughout the Southeast through their radio broadcasts in Iowa and the Carolinas, their personal appearances, and their Victor Bluebird recordings (1936–38).

In 1938 the brothers parted, and Bill formed his own group, the Blue Grass Boys. In October 1939 he joined the cast of the *Grand Ole Opry* on WSM and remained in Nashville after that. His recordings for Victor (1940–41), Columbia (1945–49), and Decca/MCA (since 1950) sold consistently over long periods—many are still in print. His compositions include instrumentals, religious songs, and secular songs on a variety of topics.

During the 1940s, Monroe, who played mandolin and sang in a distinctive high tenor voice, developed an innovative ensemble-band style based on the instrumental and vocal styles of earlier southeastern fiddle-band music. His band's sound, which included the five-string banjo of Earl Scruggs, was copied by a number of groups during the late 1940s. By the mid-1950s it was considered a style and had acquired· the name "bluegrass"—taken from his band's name. In the late 1960s Monroe was the central figure in the emergence of bluegrass festivals. Monroe's reputation came not just from his musical ability and his skill as a composer but also from his role as a bandleader and teacher. In his early years he was as an older brother to his band members. Later in life he became a patriarch.

His contributions to country music were recognized in 1971 when he was elected to the Country Music Hall of Fame in Nashville. His national prominence was underscored in July 1982 when he was among the first recipients of the Annual National Heritage Fellowship Awards made by the Folk Arts Program of the National Endowment for the Arts. His award described him as "one of the few living American musicians who can justly claim to have created an entirely new musical style."

In 1988 the state of Kentucky named Monroe's signature song, "Blue Moon of Kentucky," an official state song, and in 1991 Monroe was inducted into the International Bluegrass Music Hall of Honor. In 1995 he was presented with the National Medal of the Arts by President Clinton. *Grand Ole Opry* president Hal Durham called Monroe "the epitome of the stately, Southern gentleman, a shy and generous man who was justly proud of the acceptance of bluegrass music."

NEIL V. ROSENBERG
Memorial University
St. Johns, Newfoundland

Tom Ewing, ed., *The Bill Monroe Reader* (2000); Ralph Rinzler, in *Stars of Country Music: Uncle Dave Macon to Johnny Rodriguez*, ed. Bill Malone and Judith McCullough (1975); Jim Rooney, *Bossmen: Bill Monroe and Muddy Waters* (1971); Neil V. Rosenberg, *Bill Monroe and His Blue Grass Boys: An Illustrated Discography* (1974), *Bluegrass: A History* (1985); Richard D. Smith, *Can't You Hear Me Callin': The Life of Bill Monroe, Father of Bluegrass* (2000).

Morganfield, McKinley (Muddy Waters)

(1915–1983) BLUES SINGER.
Muddy Waters was born in Rolling Fork, Miss., and at an early age taught himself to perform on both the guitar and the harmonica. His skills as a young bluesman were widely advertised in north Mississippi and in the Memphis area. During the early 1940s he recorded blues selections for folklorists Alan Lomax and John Work. Shortly after his recording session, he joined the Silas Green Tent Show. Through his employment with Silas Green, he formed a professional association with William Lee Conley (Big Bill Broonzy). He made his first professional recording in 1946. Two of the musicians with whom he recorded were Andrew Luandrew (Sunnyland Slim) and Leroy Foster.

Morganfield formed his own band, which performed in Chicago for several years and included such noted Chicago bluesmen as Willie Dixon, Otis Spann, Pat Hare, James Cotton, and Little Walter Jacobs. From 1942 to his death he recorded extensively. Among his most celebrated recorded selections are "Caledonia," "Hoochie Koochie Man," "Rolling Stone," "Baby, Please Don't Go," and "Mannish Boy." He also toured throughout the United States and in several foreign countries. His foreign tours included appearances in England, Australia, New Zealand, Germany,

Muddy Waters, bluesman, 1960s (Ray Flerlage, photographer, Living Blues Archival Collection, University of Mississippi Blues Archive, Oxford)

and France. His peers nicknamed him "Godfather of the Blues."

Muddy Waters bought his first electric guitar in 1944, and he was especially significant for introducing electrified instruments to the blues, which helped make the blues into ensemble music. The electric blues was a major influence on rock and roll. Waters was a leader in the transformation of Delta blues from southern folk music into a nationally and internationally popular music.

LEMUEL BERRY JR.
Alabama State University

Robert Gordon, *Can't Be Satisfied: The Life and Times of Muddy Waters* (2002); *Living Blues* (Autumn 1983, March–April 1985); Bob Margolin, *Muddy Waters* (2002); Robert Palmer, *Deep Blues* (1981); James Rooney, *Bossmen: Bill Monroe and Muddy Waters* (1971); Sandra B. Tooze, *Muddy Waters: The Mojo Man* (1997).

Morton, Jelly Roll (Ferdinand Le Menthe)

(1885–1941) JAZZ MUSICIAN.
Self-proclaimed inventor of jazz, Ferdinand Le Menthe was among the earliest and most prominent of New Orleans jazzmen. Better known on the streets and among the world's musical fraternity as "Jelly Roll" Morton, he was born in 1885 on the Gulf Coast near New Orleans. His African-Mediterranean-Caribbean ancestry placed him among that city's Creoles of color, and he drew from their musical traditions. Morton's family moved to New Orleans while the young Ferdinand was quite small, and he grew to manhood there within a community that enjoyed frequent contacts with Mexico and the Caribbean. The young Morton learned on his own to play various musical instruments and was playing on street corners in a band by age eight. He studied piano at age ten, learning from the resident pianist of the local French opera. Much of the European form and attitude long prevalent in jazz has its source in this kind of training received by Creole musicians such as Morton. By age 15 he was regarded as one of New Orleans's leading ragtime-blues pianists.

Morton grew up on the margin of the New Orleans marketplace, struggling to survive within the urban underclass. The street-and-saloon environment fostered the proliferation of flesh parlors and honky-tonk dance halls where musicians of color often worked. Prevented from performing in formal musical circles, the city's schooled black musicians turned out of necessity to

Jelly Roll Morton, jazz musician, early 1920s
(Hogan Jazz Archive, Tulane University, New Orleans)

the honky-tonks, cabarets, and sporting houses in places like Storyville.

The honky-tonk culture of the urban underclass in the early 20th century formed a national network, which permitted artists like Morton to take their music to other cities. Between 1910 and 1925, Jelly Roll Morton performed in St. Louis, Los Angeles, San Francisco, Chicago, and New York, in addition to New Orleans. He toured with vaudeville shows operating out of Memphis and later Georgia. From 1917 to 1923, he performed mainly on the West Coast. In these and in subsequent years, Morton composed and recorded a host of songs on the piano, including such jazz classics as "The Pearls," "The Chant," "The Fingerbreaker," "New Orleans Joys," and "Buddy Bolden's Blues."

By the early 1920s, Morton's interest, along with that of the rest of the nation, had shifted to jazz bands. He moved to Chicago, where he recorded and performed frequently. There he organized and produced the Red Hot Peppers, a seven-piece classic jazz ensemble for which he composed and orchestrated such immortal jazz pieces as "Jungle Blues," "London Blues," "Hello Central, Give Me Doctor Jazz," "Sidewalk Blues," and "Georgia Swing." He moved to New York City in 1928, performing there in nightclubs and ballrooms, recording, working with musical revues, and touring out of town. In 1938 Alan Lomax extensively recorded Morton for the Library of Congress Archive of American Folk Song.

CURTIS D. JERDE
W. R. Hogan Jazz Archive
Tulane University

Ray Bisso, *Jelly Roll Morton and King Oliver* (2001); Samuel Barclay Charters, *Jelly Roll Morton's Last Night at the Jungle Inn* (1994); Alan Lomax, *Mister Jelly Roll: The Fortunes of Jelly Roll Morton, New Orleans Creole and "Inventor of Jazz"* (2001); Philip Pastras, *Dead Man Blues: Jelly Roll Morton Way Out West* (2003); Howard Reich and William Gaines, *Jelly's Blues: The Life, Music, and Redemption of Jelly Roll Morton* (2003); Martin Williams, *Jelly Roll Morton* (1963).

Muscle Shoals Sound

Perhaps no other area in rural or small-town America has been as significant a wellspring of internationally influential music as the northwest Alabama quad-town area of Florence, Muscle Shoals, Sheffield, and Tuscumbia, often referred to as the Muscle Shoals area. For over two decades, from the mid-1960s to the 1980s, this diminutive area in rural

Appalachian Alabama challenged the major urban popular music recording centers for the title of "hit recording capital of the world." Initially emerging alongside Memphis as the second main southern recording center for soul music, with Rick Hall's FAME studios in the town of Muscle Shoals, the region's laid-back sounds and recording aesthetics crossed over to the broader rock and pop arenas in the 1970s, especially with the success of the offshoot Muscle Shoals Sound (MSS) Studios, established in Sheffield by erstwhile FAME rhythm section musicians. In the wake of the area's skyrocketing industry reputation, many musicians from near and far relocated to the area, and a bustling scene of studios and publishing firms with staffs of musicians and songwriters blossomed. Whether playing on their home turf or being shuttled to studios elsewhere, the region's musicians contributed to the success of hundreds of chart-topping singles and multitudes of gold and platinum albums by some of the most famous 20th-century recording artists, including Percy Sledge, Wilson Pickett, the Rolling Stones, Lynyrd Skynyrd, Willie Nelson, Traffic, Paul Simon, Cat Stevens, Joe Cocker, Rod Stewart, Bob Seger, Bob Dylan, Dire Straits, Paul Anka, and the Osmonds. With competition from slicker styles of studio rock and such ascendant genres as disco, punk, and new wave, and with soul and rock petering out, Muscle Shoals reinvented itself as a song-publishing center, especially for the country music industry.

Although the "Muscle Shoals Sound" refers to the specific hybrid of rhythm-and-blues, country, gospel, and rock music elements that emanated from the region's studios in this roughly two-decade period, the area had long been a hotbed of musical talent, much of which, however, relocated to one of the two already-established southern regional musical centers, Memphis and Nashville.

Early area music-industry landmarks include Bobby Denton's 1956 recording of the regional hit "A Fallen Star" at James Joiner and Kelso Herston's Tune Records and Publishing in Florence, Joiner and Tom Stafford's establishment of Spar Music studio and publishing, and Joiner's publishing of Tuscumbian Earl Green and Carl Montgomery's perennial trucking anthem "Six Days on the Road." Stafford then partnered with Hamilton-based country music songwriters Rick Hall and Billy Sherrill to launch Florence Alabama Musical Enterprises (FAME). Keyboardists Donnie Fritts of Florence, Spooner Oldham from Center Star, and David Briggs from Killen; bassist Norbert Putnam from Muscle Shoals; drummer Jerry Carrigan from Florence; and singer-songwriter Dan Penn from Vernon, Ala., were participants in this early scene, whose main success came through demos pitched in Nashville and which ended when Stafford and Sherrill, tired of Hall's domineering ways in the sessions, decided to let him go, along with the copyright to the FAME name. Sherrill would move to Nashville in 1962 and later become a chief architect of a lusher "Nashville Sound."

The Muscle Shoals area's next significant success as a recording center came in 1962, with ex-bellhop Arthur Alexander's self-penned "You Better Move On." The song was released by Hollywood-based Dot Records, peaked at No. 24 on the national pop charts, and was later famously covered by the Rolling Stones on their 1964 debut album. The Beatles, Elvis Presley, Bob Dylan, and Otis Redding were likewise inspired to cover Alexander's songs. Hall used the returns from FAME's success to construct a new studio at 603 East Avalon Avenue, Muscle Shoals, which would accrue exceptional legend and continue into the new millennium.

A second rhythm section proved to be the one that would finally establish the Muscle Shoals area as not mere breeding grounds of musical talent but also as a recording mecca. Local band Del-Rays' guitarist Jimmy Johnson and drummer Roger Hawkins and rival local band Mystics' bassist David Hood finally became the core of the second section, although Junior Lowe played bass initially. Spooner Oldham continued on keyboards until 1967, when he moved to Chip Moman's American Records in Memphis and was replaced by Birmingham-born Barry Beckett. A succession of exceptional lead guitarists, including Merlin Greene, Duane Allman, Wayne Perkins, Eddie Hinton, and Pete Carr, would play with this section during its heyday.

Southern soul's first national pop No. 1 hit emerged in 1965 with Percy Sledge's "When a Man Loves a Woman," released by New York's Atlantic Records, thus forging a famously productive association between Muscle Shoals music and national soul superstars on Atlantic's roster. Atlantic president Jerry Wexler had been experiencing some problems with the Stax Records establishment in Memphis and started bringing his singers to the Muscle Shoals area, initially to FAME studios, to record. Classic singles from this period included Wilson Pickett's "Mustang Sally," "Land of 1000 Dances," "Hey Jude," and "Funky Broadway," Otis Redding's production of his protégé Arthur Conley's "Sweet Soul Music," Aretha Franklin's first two recordings for Atlantic, "I Never Loved a Man (the Way I love You)" and "Do Right Woman (Do Right Man)," Bobby Purify's "I'm Your Puppet," and Clarence Carter's "Patches."

Following their recordings with Aretha Franklin in New York, FAME's second rhythm section started freelancing for Wexler and, in 1968—rechristening themselves the Muscle Shoals Rhythm Section (MSRS)—established the Muscle Shoals Sound (MSS) studio at 3614 Jackson Highway in Sheffield, one of the hallowed studios of American recording history. Cher's *3614 Jackson Highway* album cover famously announced the launch, and R. B. Greaves's Top 10 pop hit "Take a Letter, Maria" provided the first hit. The Rolling Stones' recording of their classics "Brown Sugar" and "Wild Horses" solidified in the wider popular music world Muscle Shoals' reputation for versatility. Paul Simon's Grammy-nominated *There Goes Rhymin' Simon* album opened the floodgates for almost around-the-clock recording activity. Through that decade, a nonstop cavalcade of international-level artists that were signed to Stax, Atlantic, CBS, and Capitol rolled through the sleepy Appalachian area. More than 400 albums were recorded in the legendary Jackson Highway facility in less than a decade, 50 of them earning gold or platinum sales.

In 1978 MSRS relocated the MSS studio to a 31,000-square-foot former Navy Reserve Guard building at 1000 Alabama Avenue in Sheffield. In this facility the studio recorded with luminaries such as Bob Dylan, Dire Straits, Levon Helm, John Prine, and Carlos Santana. For Malaco records, based in Jackson, Miss., they recorded with a number of black R&B artists, including Johnnie Taylor, Z. Z. Hill, Little Milton, and Bobbie Bland. In 1985 Malaco bought the whole operation and hired the rhythm section to run it. Malaco's African American artist roster brought the MSRS back full circle to its initial R&B emphasis, but the studio also continued to record with rock musicians, including Gregg Allman and Jimmy Buffett, and with country stars, including the Oak Ridge Boys and Johnnie Paycheck.

Because of the increasing centralization of the recording industry, Muscle Shoals' stature no longer compares to that from its glory days, but the Muscle Shoals area remains a rare regional music recording center that continues to thrive in new guises. Both native and transplanted musicians in the area since the 1980s have increasingly focused on publishing and found consistent success, especially with Nashville artists. Although the Malaco-run MSS studio closed its doors in February 2005, FAME studio continues operation, and the cinderblock building at 3614 Jackson Highway has been admitted into the National Register of Historic Places and restored as a functioning living history museum.

AJAY KALRA
University of Texas at Austin

Dan Forte, *Guitar Player* (April 1982); Peter Guralnick, *Sweet Soul Music: Rhythm and Blues and the Southern Dream of Freedom* (1999); Leon Topar, *Musician* (April 1981).

Nashville Sound

Most popular and scholarly accounts of country music history describe the Nashville Sound—a conscious sophistication of country music's traditional rusticity—as a low point. Deliberately forged in the late 1950s and early 1960s when rock and roll captured the country's audience for the rough and ready, the Nashville Sound echoed some of the stylistic traits of mainstream popular music—that is to say, of music more popular than country music. Hank Williams, arguably country music's first superstar, died in 1953. That same year, Bill Haley and the Comets turned from country to rock and roll, with their recordings "Crazy, Man, Crazy" and "Rock around the Clock." In 1954 Elvis Presley, then also known as the "Hillbilly Cat," released his first Sun Records single; by 1956 he was a star in a different galaxy, gyrating on *The Ed Sullivan Show* and dividing teenagers and adults into separate music markets.

It has been argued that all of country music history can be told as a conflict between the desire for profitable popularity and the desire to stay true to country's supposedly less popular but more populist roots; the Nashville Sound may be the clearest example of this dynamic, since it was formulated as a deliberate business strategy. At first, the country music industry reacted to the new market configuration by trying to appeal to both teenagers and adults. Many well-known country artists experimented with rock or rockabilly sounds. George Jones, then in the early years of his career, recorded a few singles, such as the transparently named "Rock It," as Thumper Jones. Similarly, Buck Owens recorded as Corky Jones. Already practically an elder statesman, Eddy Arnold sang "Hep Cat Baby" in 1954. Marty Robbins, also an established country star, covered a few rock hits, such as Elvis Presley's debut "That's All Right" (itself a cover of blues artist Arthur Crudup's original) and Chuck Berry's "Maybellene." His "A White Sport Coat (and a Pink Carnation)," about a prom trauma, topped the pop charts in 1957. The cover of Chet Atkins's 1960 album, entitled *Teensville*, depicted clean-cut teenagers at a dance.

Attempts to capture the adult market met more sustained success. Some scholars name Ferlin Husky's 1957 hit "Gone" as the first record with the "Nashville Sound." The ironies of this landmark articulate clearly how market oriented the sound was. Husky first recorded the song in 1952 under the uncountry-sounding name "Terry Preston" but had little success with it. In 1956, working with Los Angeles–based Ken Nelson, his smoother version reached No. 1 on both the country and pop charts in 1957. As the fan-oriented

magazine *Country Song Roundup* put it in the August 1957 issue, "Husky broke through the 'sound barrier' with the beautiful 'Gone.'" After this turning point, top Nashville producers, particularly Owen Bradley at Decca Records and Chet Atkins at RCA, created a formula for repeating the sound by toning down the nasal twang and southern accents of country voices with smoother backup vocals and adding swelling string sections to soften (or replace) steel guitars and raspy fiddles. While songs about heartbreak still dominated, Nashville Sound hits stayed away from the hangovers and home wreckers that Hank Williams and Kitty Wells sang about.

Jim Reeves, who was also consistently crossing over to the pop charts by 1957, produced by Atkins, and Patsy Cline, produced by Bradley, were the major stars of the Nashville Sound. Reeves, nicknamed "Gentleman Jim," started his recording career singing in the hard country style, but under Atkins's guidance the Texan began to croon like a Crosby and traded his cowboy suits for dinner jackets and sport coats. By 1957 he, like Husky, achieved significant crossover success with songs like "Am I Losing You" and "Four Walls."

Patsy Cline also achieved her first crossover success in 1957 with "Walkin' after Midnight." Dressed in cocktail dresses and pearls rather than the western wear she preferred, Cline clashed with Owen Bradley over many aspects of her performance persona. A native of Winchester, Va., she wanted to yodel and sing Hank Williams songs but achieved her greatest sales with songs she didn't want to record, such as her 1961 singles "I Fall to Pieces" and "Crazy."

Nashville Sound producers had a reliable stable of virtuoso musicians who could efficiently create the "Sound": the Anita Kerr Singers or the Jordanaires for vocals; Harold Bradley (Owen's brother), Hank Garland, and Grady Martin on guitar; Jerry Byrd and Lloyd Green on steel guitar; and Floyd Cramer and Hargus Robbins on piano. In short, studio musicians, rather than the artist's band, created the Nashville Sound. In an interview with John Rumble, historian at the Country Music Foundation, Harold Bradley named specific sonic features that these musicians relied upon, citing Patsy Cline's "Crazy" (1961) as a "classic" example. He mentioned in particular the "guitar chink" that worked with the rhythm section, announcing to listeners that "it's not going to be hardcore country." The muted percussion in general, along with the tinkling piano, similarly mark a place that is neither barn dance nor sock hop. As Bradley notes, "We've used that formula so many times. . . . That was money in the bank for many, many years." In 1981 Bradley and Atkins joined forces to electronically pair Jim Reeves's and Patsy Cline's voices to create a best-selling duet, "Have You Ever Been Lonely." Owen Bradley also used the formula to produce Canadian k.d. lang's 1988 gold record *Shadowland*.

Patsy Cline and Jim Reeves both died in airplane crashes—Cline in 1963 and Reeves in 1964. By then, the American popular music landscape had also changed dramatically. No longer dominating the rock world, Elvis Presley was starring in a string of Hollywood movies. Beatlemania took hold in early 1964, and Buck Owens's Bakersfield sound (produced by Ferlin Husky's Ken Nelson) brought honky-tonk sounds and rocking electric guitars to the top of the country charts.

The sales figures achieved by Husky, Robbins, Reeves, Cline, and other country singers such as Don Gibson and Sonny James may have helped Nashville's music industry survive through the first of many downturns in its fortunes. Atkins is even said to have defined the Nashville Sound by jingling a fistful of coins. The need (or greed) for commercial success continues to shape business decisions made by country music executives and artists, a situation that gives rise to ongoing debate about where the soul of country music lies and whether success in Nashville sells that soul. Moreover, when placed in the context of southern cultural history, the Nashville Sound period of country music opens an interesting perspective on the place of the South in the nation's cultural hierarchies. Nashville, after all, is a southern *city*, so any attempt to characterize a sound named after it must consider the opposed relationships between the country and the city, the rustic and the refined, and, in the case of a music genre with such strong ties to the South, the relationship between the North and the South. Harold Bradley told Rumble that Decca Record executives had directed Owen to "make us a record we can get played in New York" when he went into the studio with Patsy Cline. The dialect used in *Country Song*

Roundup also reveals an "us" against "them" dynamic in the Nashville Sound. In a short article on Jim Reeves's success with "He'll Have to Go," the headline promises that Reeves himself "will never leave." The text, however, suggests that reaching pop success presents an opportunity to move uptown: "Why is it that ev'ry time one of our Country artists gets a song swingin' high and mighty in the pop music field as well as our own, rumors start flyin' about that artists deserting Folk music?"

The rumors still fly, and after the Nashville Sound country musicians frequently locate the soul of country music in other, more southern and more countrified places. In 1978, for example, Waylon Jennings and Willie Nelson sang the praises of "Lukenbach, Texas," and many "alternative country" artists from the 1990s on similarly praise the towns around Austin, Tex., as they denigrate Nashville's still-thriving production studios and record companies.

BARBARA CHING
University of Memphis

Joli Jensen, *Nashville Sound: Authenticity, Commercialization, and Country Music* (1998); Bill C. Malone, *Country Music, U.S.A.* (1968; rev. eds., 1985, 2002); Richard A. Peterson, *Creating Country Music: Fabricating Authenticity* (1997); John W. Rumble, "Country Music Foundation Oral History Project, Interview with Harold Bradley," Country Music Hall of Fame and Museum (1991).

Nelson, Willie

(b. 1933) COUNTRY MUSIC SINGER. Willie Hugh Nelson was born in Fort Worth, Tex., on 30 April 1933 and was reared in the little central Texas town of Abbott, where he was exposed to a wide variety of musical influences. He grew up singing gospel songs in the Baptist church but also played in honky-tonks all over the state. Before he was a teenager, he began playing guitar in the German-Czech polka bands in the "Bohemian" communities of central Texas; he listened to the country music of Bob Wills, Lefty Frizzell, and Floyd Tillman, but he was also an avid fan of jazz and vintage pop music. All of these forms clearly influence the music he plays today.

Despite his skills as a guitarist and unorthodox singer (with his blues inflections and off-the-beat phrasing), Nelson's ticket to Nashville came through his songwriting. In 1960 he moved to Nashville, where he became part of an important coterie of writers, which included Hank Cochran, Harlan Howard, and Roger Miller. Nelson made a major contribution to country music's post–rock-and-roll revival with such songs as "Funny How Time Slips Away," "Hello, Walls," "Night Life," and "Crazy," all of which were successfully recorded by other singers.

Recording for RCA Victor in the mid-1960s, Nelson became widely admired by his colleagues as a "singer's singer," but he did not achieve the stardom that he sought. In 1972 he relocated to Austin, Tex., where he became part of an already-thriving music scene that was strongly oriented toward youth who had grown up listening to rock and urban folk music. Nelson made a calculated attempt to appeal to this audience by changing his physical image: he let

*Willie Nelson, country music singer, 1980s
(Columbia Records, New York)*

his hair grow long, grew a beard, and began wearing a headband, an earring, jeans, and jogging shoes (a striking contrast to the well-groomed, middle-class appearance he had affected during his Nashville years). He also publicized himself with his huge annual "picnics," first held in Dripping Springs, Tex., in 1972 and 1973 and later staged in a variety of Texas communities, usually on the Fourth of July. These festivals were intended to bridge the gap between youth and adults, while bringing together varied lifestyles and musical forms. The picnics, however, soon lost their appeal to older people or to traditional country fans and instead became havens for uninhibited youth and for musicians who seemed most comfortable with a country-rock perspective.

After winning the youth audience, Nelson then captured the adult market. In 1975 he recorded a best-selling album called *The Red Headed Stranger*, and one song from the album, Fred Rose's

"Blue Eyes Crying in the Rain," became the No. 1 country song of the year (it is ironic that the first superhit recorded by this master songwriter was a song written by someone else). Nelson's ascent to superstardom and his building of a large and diverse audience were accomplished without significant departures from his traditional style. Indeed, his repertoire became even more traditional as he reached back to the performance of older gospel, country, and pop songs. No one in American music performed a more eclectic sampling of songs. He also preserved his unorthodox style of singing and sang over a rather spare and uncluttered scheme of instrumentation, which was dominated by his own inventive, single-string style of guitar playing.

Nelson has won many country music awards since the mid-1970s, including the Country Music Association's Entertainer of the Year award in 1979, but his appeal has extended far beyond the country music world. Nelson has collaborated with a diverse array of stars from various genres of music, including Toby Keith, Johnny Cash, Bob Dylan, Bonnie Raitt, Merle Haggard, and Paul Simon.

Nelson has received favorable reviews for his roles in several movies, such as *The Electric Horseman* (1979) and *Wag the Dog* (1997). Nelson also played Uncle Jesse in the 2005 cinematic remake of *The Dukes of Hazzard*. He has been feted constantly by the American media, and he has entertained often at political events, including the Democratic National Convention in 1980, during the Carter presidency. Few country singers have enjoyed such broad exposure. In addition to performance, Nelson has invested his energies in charity work, such as establishing the Farm Aid concert in 1985 and organizing a concert in 2005 for the victims of the Indian Ocean earthquake with UNICEF. Nelson continues to tour, and during breaks from touring he spends time at his Pedernales estate outside of Austin, Tex.

BILL C. MALONE
Madison, Wisconsin

Willie Nelson, *The Facts of Life and Other Dirty Jokes* (2002), *Willie Nelson: Teatro* (2001); Willie Nelson and Bud Shrake, *Willie: An Autobiography* (1992); Jan Reid, *The Improbable Rise of Redneck Rock* (1974); Al Reinert, *New York Times Magazine* (26 March 1978); Clint Richmond, *Willie Nelson: Behind the Music* (2000); Lola Scobey, *Willie Nelson* (1982).

Neville Brothers

RHYTHM-AND-BLUES, SOUL, AND FUNK SINGERS.

The Neville brothers—Art, Aaron, Charles, and Cyril—are likely the best-known musical family to come out of New Orleans in recent decades. Both as individuals and as a group, they have made crucial contributions to several genres of popular music. Building on early careers in the fields of R&B and soul, the brothers were instrumental in defining the funk sound of the 1970s by reconnecting New Orleans music with its Caribbean and Afro-diasporic roots.

Art, Charles, and Aaron were born in 1937, 1938, and 1941, respectively. Music and dance were central in their upbringing. Although not a musician, their father, Arthur, was close to

singer-guitarist Smiley Lewis, and their mother, Amelia, had performed in a dance team with her younger brother, George Landry. Known to his nephews by the nickname "Uncle Jolly," Landry was a gifted piano player who, like their father, traveled the world as a merchant seaman.

As they grew up, Art learned to play barrelhouse-style piano, Aaron built his skills as a vocalist by singing gospel music, and Charles studied the saxophone. The brothers played in various groups, and by the time Cyril was born in 1948, Art was well on his way to making a name for himself in the local music scene. His group, the Hawketts, recorded a song called "Mardi Gras Mambo" for radio dj Ken "Jack the Cat" Elliot. The record, released by Chess in 1954, was widely popular and quickly became an enduring staple of the Carnival season, although the performers saw none of the profits.

Charles, who also played with the Hawketts, dropped out of school at age 15 to tour as a tenor saxophone player with Gene Franklin's House Rockers. R&B star Larry Williams took several of the brothers under his wing and, along with producer Harold Battiste (who ran the New Orleans office of L.A.-based Specialty Records), helped Art develop as a solo artist. He cut several sides for Specialty, including "Cha-Dooky-Doo" and "Ooh-Whee Baby," before moving to the Instant label in 1962, where he had a local hit with the ballad "All These Things."

Aaron began recording songs for local label Minit in 1960 and was working as a longshoreman when he had a hit record with the Allen Toussaint–produced ballad "Tell It Like It Is" in late 1966. The song showcased his impressive falsetto range and spent 17 weeks on the *Billboard* R&B charts, peaking at No. 1 and earning him a gold record in the early part of 1967. Unfortunately, this success overwhelmed the start-up independent Par-Lo record label, which soon folded. With few royalties arriving, Aaron went on the road, backed by his brother Art's group, to exploit his hit record.

Art Neville and the Neville Sounds was a large group, which included, among others, Art, Aaron, and Cyril Neville on percussion and vocals. The group played regularly at the Nite Cap until 1967, when Art Neville and the rhythm section departed, forming a new four-piece group, which would become known as the Meters, releasing a string of albums in the late 1960s and early 1970s. Aaron, Cyril, and other remaining members formed another group, called the Soul Machine. Charles, meanwhile, had his musical career interrupted by a three-and-a-half-year stint in the state prison at Angola, after being arrested on minor drug charges. Upon release, he moved to New York City, where he found work playing with a white soul group, Tony Ferrar and the Band of Gold.

By 1976 George "Chief Jolly" Landry had become centrally involved in the city's Mardi Gras Indian scene and teamed up with the four brothers in 1976 to record the *Wild Tchoupitoulas* album for Island Records. The effort marked the beginning of a new era in the brothers' careers, with New Orleans Carnival and parade music becoming even more central than before. Soon afterward, they formed the Neville Brothers, which has been their musical home ever since.

After building their local reputation, the brothers secured a record deal with Capitol, releasing their eponymous debut in 1978. The eclectic album was poorly promoted, and the brothers soon moved to A&M Records, where they released *Fiyo on the Bayou* in 1981. They documented one of their frequent appearances at New Orleans bar Tipitina's on 1984's *Live Nevillization* and won a Grammy for their song "Healing Chant" from their 1989 album *Yellow Moon*. Through most of the 1990s, they continued to record for A&M, moving to Columbia late in the decade, where they released *Valence Street* in 1999.

MATT MILLER
Emory University

Jason Berry, Jonathan Foose, and Tad Jones, *Up from the Cradle of Jazz: New Orleans Music since World War II* (1986); Art Neville, Aaron Neville, Cyril Neville, and Charles Neville, *The Brothers: An Autobiography* (2000).

New Orleans Sound

New Orleans has played a central role in the development of American—and especially African American—popular music and dance styles. Although jazz remains its most famous product, the city has made key contributions to rhythm and blues, rock and roll, soul, funk, and rap. Within the context of the United States, New Orleans's uniquely diverse and layered history of cultural intermixture has helped the city to maintain a central presence in the national popular music culture, even as it remains on the margins of the corporate music industry.

Settled by the French in 1718, Louisiana depended heavily upon enslaved black labor, which in its early decades was extracted largely from the Senegambia region. A high level of cultural cohesion and continuity among these slaves, combined with the relatively tolerant attitude of the French, contributed to the continuation and adaptation of West African–originated cultural practices in musical and other contexts, which in turn significantly influenced the development of a creolized culture in the colony generally.

The numbers of slaves and free blacks grew under a brief period of Spanish control and were augmented by refugees from the revolutions in San Domingo and Cuba. After the Louisiana Purchase in 1803 and the beginning of American control, the city became an important commercial center heavily invested in the slave trade. Throughout the first half of the 19th century, large numbers of enslaved and free blacks from New Orleans and its hinterlands regularly gathered in city markets to buy and sell produce and to engage in a variety of leisure activities, including music and dance. The most famous of these was a large field off of Rampart Street, which became known as Congo Square. The gatherings there had largely ended by the Civil War, but their mythic reputation as a manifestation of African-originated cultural practices has persisted.

The assumption of control by the United States introduced several important changes. The full implementation of a more restrictive Anglo-Protestant approach to race and social control would take more than a century, but an influx of English-speaking Americans began to alter the character of the city almost immediately. Blacks from the surrounding Delta region flowed into the city, their numbers surging after the Civil War and Emancipation. These migrants generally settled in the less desirable parts of the Uptown area, upriver from the French Quarter; French-speaking blacks remained tied to an area downriver called Downtown, which included neighborhoods like Faubourg Tremé. The French-speaking blacks enjoyed traditions of education, mutual aid, and formal musical instruction, but the American blacks brought with them a more rural musical sensibility rooted in blues and string band music. The interaction of these two distinct but compatible musical traditions formed the basis for the emergence of jazz in the final decades of the 19th century.

Charles "Buddy" Bolden, a black barber, cornetist, and bandleader from Uptown, is widely credited with the introduction of jazz as it is generally understood—highly syncopated ensemble dance music in which improvisation plays a central role. Bolden failed to reap the full rewards of what he had introduced in the 1890s—he never recorded and retired from playing relatively early—but his efforts laid the groundwork for the development of a new direction in New Orleans music. Like many of his contemporaries, Bolden was able to draw from a rich array of environmental musical influences that existed in New Orleans, which ranged from military bands to the cries of street vendors hawking their wares.

Jazz developed in diverse forms and contexts. Building upon the ragtime genre, piano players like Tony Jackson and Jelly Roll Morton entertained patrons with propulsive dance music in various establishments of the Storyville tenderloin district, which operated legally between 1897 and 1917. Other venues—including barrooms, ballrooms, steamboat excursion rides, dances of all kinds, and outdoor gatherings—called for larger and louder music, and the city soon saw the proliferation of the five- to seven-piece ensemble groups playing "hot" jazz music characterized by chaotic-seeming collective improvisation.

By the time the secretary of the navy ordered the closing of Storyville in 1917, jazz was already being disseminated throughout the country. River towns like Memphis, St. Louis, Kansas City, and Chicago were a natural destination for New Orleans musicians, and several established themselves in New York. Some players, like the early cornet innovator Bunk Johnson, remained in the Gulf South, while others, like Joseph "King" Oliver and, later, his young protégé Louis Armstrong, struck out for greener pastures upriver. Chicago became a home away from home for many New Orleans musicians, who by leaving their native city avoided some of the effects of Jim Crow segregation.

In the closing decades of the 1800s, large numbers of Italians and Irish had immigrated to New Orleans, and these groups also contributed to the ranks of early jazz artists and audiences. The first band to make a jazz recording was the white Nick LaRocca's Original Dixieland Jazz band in 1917, which produced the first million-seller for RCA Victor. Other important figures in the development of New Orleans jazz in the 1910s and 1920s include cornetist Freddie Keppard, clarinetist Sidney Bechet, and bandleader George Vital "Papa Jack" Laine.

The combined effects of the Depression and World War II severely curtailed the ability of New Orleans musicians to record, although a vital vernacular music culture persisted. The city's Carnival (the largest in the United States) has helped to foster a collective musical sensibility and has presented opportunities for celebration, self-expression, and the occupation of public spaces, which blacks rarely failed to exploit. So-called Social Aid and Pleasure Clubs and Carnival societies like the Zulus hire brass bands for members' funerals, which often feature the now-familiar mixture of somber music on the way to the graveyard followed by celebratory and expressive dance music after interment. In a tradition that dates back to the 19th century, parades with brass bands are usually accompanied by a "second line," an informal contingent of spectator-participants who dance and accompany the band on percussion instruments, including tambourines, glass bottles, and other improvised materials. Musical techniques derived from street parade music have formed a crucial component of the city's distinctive musical sensibility over the last century.

The music of the Mardi Gras Indians—groups of working-class blacks organized along neighborhood lines who parade in elaborate Native American–inspired costumes during Carnival season—has also exercised significant influence over popular music forms emanating from New Orleans in the last century. The rehearsals and public appearances of these groups are characterized by music making that relies heavily upon percussion ensemble and the collective performance of chanted lyrics in a call-and-response format.

During the postwar years, a thriving music scene developed again in New Orleans, now based around a genre known as rhythm and blues, or R&B. Bands led by Roy Brown and Dave Bartholomew were among the top acts in the city during the late 1940s and early 1950s. Working with California-based Imperial Records in the 1950s, Bartholomew produced a string of national hits for the amiable piano player and singer Antoine "Fats" Domino, who remains one of the most popular artists to emerge from New Orleans in any time period. A host of other talented R&B artists came out of the city in these years, including Smiley Lewis, Jewel King, Lloyd Price, and the teen piano sensation James Booker, among others. In the 1950s, L.A.-based labels like Imperial and Specialty Records mined the New Orleans scene for marketable talent and also sent performers there to record with expert musicians and arrangers.

The city's relationship with the emerging rock-and-roll genre was relatively brief but crucial in terms of the influence that New Orleans–based studio musicians, like drummer Earl Palmer and saxophone player Alvin "Red" Tyler, exercised over the developing rhythmic sensibility of the genre. With artists like Huey "Piano" Smith, Jimmy Clanton, and others, Ace Records released many pioneers of the style and drew "Little" Richard Penniman to the city, where he made his early recordings in 1955 and 1956 and hired the band the Upsetters to back him on the road.

The Dew Drop Inn, a combination bar and hotel where the city's top black performers and sidemen shared the stage with female impersonators and burlesque dancers, was a musical hot spot during these years, along with other clubs like the TiaJuana and the Caldonia. Among the many talented performers from this period, Roy "Professor Longhair" Byrd is one of the most celebrated, although he was only moderately successful during his peak of recording activity in the 1950s. Longhair flavored his barrelhouse piano style with Caribbean accents and bouncing left-hand rhythms, producing a style that, for many, would come to represent the city's musical identity.

During the 1960s New Orleans was the home of a thriving independent music scene, with producers like Wardell Quezergue and Allen Toussaint frequently using Cosimo Matassa's recording facilities and studio band. Nothing can quite match the success of

Fats Domino in the 1950s, but the 1960s saw a string of national hits emerge from the city by the likes of Chris Kenner, Robert Parker, the Dixie Cups, Johnny Adams, and Irma Thomas, among others. The city's musical reputation attracted international stars like Paul McCartney and Robert Palmer, who both recorded there during the mid-1970s.

During the late 1960s and early 1970s, New Orleans–based artists like the Meters and Dr. John increasingly began to draw inspiration from the parade and Carnival traditions of the city. Aided by the inauguration of the annual Jazz and Heritage Festival, the city experienced an R&B revival of sorts in the 1970s, reviving the career of Professor Longhair, among others. Other dimensions of the city's musical heritage also reached wider audiences: several Mardi Gras Indian groups released albums during the 1970s, and the brass band form began a revival, with groups like the Dirty Dozen, which broke new ground by infusing the form with a swinging funkiness. Groups like Re-Birth, the Hot 8, and others continue to produce some of the most compelling and propulsive brass band music to be heard anywhere in the United States.

The city's musical distinctiveness continued into the rap era. A dance-oriented style called "bounce" took over the local market in the early 1990s and by the end of that decade had helped to propel artists like Juvenile into the national spotlight. However, the Katrina disaster of 2005 severely disrupted the deeply rooted traditions and cultural practices of working-class and poor black communities, a loss that will doubtlessly affect the ability of New Orleans to produce innovative forms of dance music in the future.

MATT MILLER
Emory University

Danny Barker, *Buddy Bolden and the Last Days of Storyville*, ed. Alyn Shipton (1998); John Broven, *Rhythm & Blues in New Orleans* (1988); Court Carney, *Popular Music in Society* (2006); Jeff Hannusch, *I Hear You Knockin': The Sound of New Orleans Rhythm and Blues* (1985); Curtis D. Jerde, *Black Music Research Journal* (Spring 1990); Jerah Johnson, *Louisiana History* (Spring 1991), *Popular Music* (April 2000; Frederic Ramsey Jr. and Charles Edward Smith, eds., *Jazzmen* (1939); Michael P. Smith, *Black Music Research Journal* (Spring 1994); Alexander Stewart, *Popular Music* (October 2000).

Oliver, King

(1885–1938) JAZZ MUSICIAN.
Joseph "King" Oliver was born in or near New Orleans and became an early black jazz cornetist and bandleader. By 1900 he was playing cornet in a youthful parade band. From 1905 to 1915 Oliver became a prominent figure in various brass and dance bands and with small groups in bars and cafés. He soon gained the title "King" in competition with other leading local cornetists. In 1918 he joined a New Orleans band playing in Chicago, and by 1920 he was leading his own group there. He toured with this band in California in 1921 and, returning to Chicago the next year, enlarged it as King Oliver's Creole Jazz Band. This handpicked ensemble boasted some of New Orleans's

best black instrumentalists, including Johnny and "Baby" Dodds (clarinet and drums, respectively) and Oliver's brilliant young protégé, Louis Armstrong (second cornet). The Creole Band's beautifully drilled performances at Chicago's Lincoln Gardens and its tour through the Midwest created a sensation among northern musicians, and in 1923 it made the most extensive series of recordings (some three dozen) of any early jazz band.

When several members, including Armstrong, left the band in late 1924, Oliver formed a new, larger dance orchestra with saxophones, called the Dixie Syncopators. This sporadically successful orchestra, with changing personnel, played in Chicago from 1925 to 1927 and at New York's Savoy Ballroom in 1927. Between 1926 and 1928 the orchestra made a number of recordings of uneven quality, though a few were popular hits. By 1930 Oliver's career as a soloist had ended. From 1930 to 1936 he led a succession of small orchestras across the country, though a severe dental condition prevented him from playing. After 1936 he lived in Savannah, with an ailing heart, and spent his last year there running a fruit stand and working as a janitor in a pool hall. He died on 8 April 1938.

One of the foremost first-generation New Orleans jazz cornetists, Oliver was a central figure in the transfer of ragtime and of the black blues and gospel song from nearby rural areas to the New Orleans urban band tradition. The recordings of his Creole Jazz Band are the best and most extensive documentation of how vocal blues and instrumental ragtime were fused by emerging jazz bands into a new music of distinctively black southern origins.

JOHN JOYCE
Tulane University

Ray Bisso, *Jelly Roll Morton and King Oliver* (2001); Lawrence Gushee, in *Jazz Panorama*, ed. Martin Williams (1962); Frederic Ramsey Jr., in *Jazzmen*, ed. Frederic Ramsey Jr. and Charles E. Smith (1939); Martin Williams, *King Oliver* (1960).

OutKast

RAP GROUP.

The Atlanta-based rap duo known as OutKast—composed of Andre Benjamin (known as "Dre" and, after 1999, "Andre 3000") and Antwan "Big Boi" Patton—is one of the most successful southern rap groups and has been instrumental in focusing national attention on the "Dirty South," the burgeoning rap music scenes and industry in Atlanta and other major southern cities. The duo has produced a series of singles and albums that have earned widespread critical acclaim, with each successive effort reaching wider audiences, and has built a reputation for eclectic and experimental rap and pop music, which nevertheless remains grounded in the environs, experiences, and cultural values of black, working-class urban southerners.

The two aspiring rappers began their collaboration while students at Tri-Cities High School in the East Point area of Southwest Atlanta, finding common ground in a preference for sharp dressing and New York rap groups like A Tribe Called Quest. Their recording career began in 1994, when they auditioned for producer Rico Wade, who worked out of his unfinished basement (called "the Dungeon") as part of a production team known as Organized Noize. After recording the 17-year-old rappers in the Dungeon, Wade soon secured a deal for them with LaFace Records, an Arista-backed company operated by Antonio "LA" Reid and Kenneth "Babyface" Edmonds, known primarily for R&B groups like TLC and Xscape.

Their first single, "Player's Ball," was a Christmas song set in the context of Atlanta's "player" culture and spent six weeks at the top of the *Billboard* rap charts in 1993. Their debut album, 1994's *Southernplayalisticadillacmusik*, featured richly textured production that was slower than most southern rap of the time and lyrics that, although still strongly oriented toward the spaces and culture of black Atlantans, rejected the hook-based approach of many southern bass rappers in favor of more complexly rendered themes and vocal performances. The album sold more than a million copies, reaching the Top 20 on the *Billboard* album charts and earning the group the "best new artist of the year award" from *Source* magazine in 1995.

In the 1996 release *ATLiens*, Patton and Benjamin ventured into production, efforts that resulted in the hit song "Elevators (Me and You)." The album met with widespread critical and commercial acclaim, selling more than a million and a half copies. The pair solidified their creative control by producing most of the songs on their next album, 1998's *Aquemini*, which reached

sales of 2.5 million copies. The album's hit song, "Rosa Parks," provoked a lawsuit by the song's namesake and civil rights–era legend, which was eventually settled in the group's favor.

The 2000 album *Stankonia* was a tour de force for OutKast and its label LaFace. The album sold five million copies and broke new ground as the first all-rap record to contend for the prestigious "Album of the Year" award at the Grammy awards. "Ms. Jackson" became the duo's first No. 1 pop single, and the album won two Grammy awards out of five nominations. Subsequently, they toured as the opening act for hip-hop singer Lauryn Hill, using a live backup band and cementing their position as representatives of hip-hop music's creative vanguard.

Following the release of *Stankonia*, the pair started their own record label, Aquemini Records, and in mid-2001 (a year that also saw the introduction of another venture, OutKast Clothing) Aquemini released its first record, by rapper Slimm Calhoun. OutKast released *Speakerboxxx/The Love Below* in 2003, which proved to be an enormous commercial, critical, and crossover success, earning the duo three Grammy awards, including "Album of the Year." The album produced two hit singles, "Hey Ya!" and "The Way You Move." Beginning in 2004, the pair further diversified by coproducing and starring in the $27 million film production *Idlewild*, which, along with an accompanying sound track album composed by the group, was released in 2006.

OutKast's career both contributed to and benefited from the emergence and subsequent development of Atlanta as the Southeast's rap music capital. Hailed in *Source* as "the country's newest and hottest hip-hop center" in 1994, by 2002 rap music was estimated to contribute half a billion dollars to Atlanta's economy. Over the course of the last decade, artists and labels from the city have increasingly dominated the "Dirty South" movement, which has helped the South move from a rap music backwater to a national center of rap music production. With a career that now has run for more than a decade, OutKast remains central to Atlanta's reputation as a center for innovative and compelling interpretations of the rap form.

MATT MILLER
Emory University

Chris Nickson, *Hey Ya! The Unauthorized Biography of Outkast* (2004); Roni Sarig, *Third Coast: Outkast, Timbaland, and How Hip-Hop Became a Southern Thing* (2007).

Parsons, Gram

(1946–1973) ROCK SINGER.
Born 5 November 1946 in Winterhaven, Fla., Gram Parsons was one of the most influential popular musicians of his generation. As a teenager, a devoted follower of Elvis Presley, Parsons performed with rock-and-roll bands from 1959 until 1963, when he joined an urban folk music group, the Shilos. After briefly attending Harvard in 1965, he joined the International Submarine Band and began drawing upon his southern background in an early attempt to synthesize country and rock. Beginning in the mid-1960s, Parsons devoted himself to what he called "cosmic American music"—essentially a dy-

namic combination of southern-derived styles with a solid country core.

The International Submarine Band dissolved in 1967, just prior to the release of *Safe at Home*, arguably the first complete country-rock album. In 1968 Parsons joined the popular folk-rock group the Byrds and, in tandem with longtime member Chris Hillman, led the band in the direction of country music. The Byrds' *Sweetheart of the Rodeo*, released in 1969, was a landmark in the evolution of country rock. It also featured one of Parsons's finest compositions, "Hickory Wind," an evocative tribute to his southern childhood. Parsons and Hillman went on to organize what became the definitive country-rock band, the Flying Burrito Brothers. As a Burrito, Parsons began to deepen his vision of the South, which had first emerged with "Hickory Wind." In his songs as well as his lifestyle, Parsons often portrayed himself as a southern country boy set adrift in the contemporary urban maelstrom. His finest song, "Sin City" (1969), was the classic statement of this theme.

After leaving the Burritos in 1970, Parsons produced little significant work until the release of his first solo album, *GP*, in 1973. The album featured Emmylou Harris on vocals and confirmed his mastery of the country-rock idiom. Throughout the album, the South was portrayed as an almost mythical land of stability and steadfastness.

On 19 September 1973, Gram Parsons died in Joshua Tree, Calif. An autopsy was inconclusive as to the cause of death. Several posthumous works, including *Grievous Angel* (1974), *Sleepless*

Nights (1976), and *Gram Parsons and the Fallen Angels—Live 1973* (1982), attest to his exceptional gifts as a singer and songwriter. Much of his work continues to inform contemporary popular music, especially in the country field. The principal carrier of his legacy since his death has been his former partner, Emmylou Harris.

STEPHEN R. TUCKER
Tulane University

Richard Cusick, *Goldmine* (September 1982); Ben Fong-Torres, *Hickory Wind: The Life and Times of Gram Parsons* (1998); Sid Griffin, *Nashville Gazette* (April–June 1980); Judson Klinger and Greg Mitchell, *Crawdaddy* (October 1976); Jason Walker, *God's Own Singer: A Life of Gram Parsons* (2002).

Parton, Dolly

(b. 1946) ENTERTAINER.
Dolly Parton is often described as a contemporary "Cinderella," a fairy tale princess, or a country gypsy—a platinum blonde heroine who escapes poverty in the foothills of the Great Smoky Mountains, achieves fame and fortune in Nashville and later Hollywood, and lives happily ever after. More realistically, she is a talented and creative artist and businesswoman.

Dolly Parton was born in Locust Ridge in Sevier County, Tenn., the fourth of twelve children, to Avie Lee Owens and Randy Parton. Her grandfather Owens was a minister, and her early life with family and community centered around religion and the church. She learned to love storytelling, music, and singing, as well as to adhere to a rigid Christian moral code. Her mother sang the traditional folk songs she had learned from a harmonica-playing Grandmother Owens. By the time she was five years old Parton was imagining lyrics and tunes, and by the time she was seven she had written her first song. An exceptionally intelligent child, Dolly Parton used the rich southern folk environment surrounding her to create poetry and music.

She began her singing career as a child on the *Cas Walker Radio Show*, broadcast from Knoxville, and she released her first record, "Puppy Love," in her early teens. At 18, after she graduated from high school, she moved to Nashville, and, despite a difficult beginning, which she describes in her song "Down on Music Row" (1973), she became a popular recording and television partner for country artist Porter Wagoner. Together, they recorded 13 albums and won awards for Vocal Duo of the Year in 1968, 1970, and 1971. In 1967 Dolly Parton released her first solo album. She has recorded over 30 albums for Monument and RCA. She has written and recorded hundreds of her own compositions, which are usually autobiographical songs, work songs, or sentimental, moralistic ballads, often sung in a traditional country style reminiscent of the Carter Family, an authentic southern folk group that was among the first to record country music during the early 20th century.

Based upon *Billboard*'s year-end hit charts, among her most successful singles have been "Mule Skinner Blues" (1970), "Joshua" (1971), "Jolene" (1974), "I Will Always Love You" (1974), "The Seeker" (1975), "All I Can Do" (1976), "Here You Come Again" (1978), "Heart-

Dolly Parton, country music singer and actress, 1987 (Columbia Records, New York)

breaker" (1978), "Two Doors Down" (1978), "You're the Only One" (1979), "Baby, I'm Burning" (1979), "Starting Over Again" (1980), "But You Know I Love You" (1981), and "Islands in the Stream," a duet with Kenny Rogers (1983). She was Female Vocalist of the Year in 1975 and 1976 and was the Country Music Association's Entertainer of the Year in 1978. In 1980 *Billboard* listed her among the top female artists in country music and *Dolly, Dolly, Dolly* and *9 to 5* among the top albums.

Dolly Parton achieved celebrity status by appealing to both country and pop music audiences and by entering the fields of television, film, and freelance writing. She has been featured in numerous periodicals and has appeared on the cover of *Playboy* (1978), the *Saturday Evening Post* (1979), *Parade* (1980), and *Rolling Stone* (1980). In 1976 she became the first woman in country music history to acquire her own syndicated television show, and she has since

starred in several films, *9 to 5* (1981), *The Best Little Whorehouse in Texas* (1982), *Rhinestone* (1984), *Steel Magnolias* (1989), and *Miss Congeniality 2: Armed and Fabulous* (2005). She published a book of poems titled *Just the Way I Am* (edited by Susan P. Shultz, 1979), wrote a novel, *Wild Flowers*, and published an autobiography, *Dolly: My Life and Other Unfinished Business* (1994). Parton and Herchend Enterprises in 1986 opened Dollywood, a theme park based on Parton's life and located at Pigeon Forge, Tenn. It remains among the most popular vacation destinations in the South. She has also donated more than one million books to preschool children across the United States, and she provides scholarships to high school students in Sevier County, Tenn. In return, the county honored her with a life-size statue in front of the courthouse.

Parton has received numerous awards. She has received seven Grammy awards—and garnered 42 nominations—and 10 awards from the Country Music Association—with 42 nominations. She received a star on the Hollywood Walk of Fame in 1984. Parton was inducted into the Nashville Songwriters Hall of Fame in 1996 and the Country Music Hall of Fame in 1999. That same year she joined with independent label Sugar Hill Records to create the acoustic album *The Grass Is Blue*. An instant favorite among critics and longtime fans, it won the International Bluegrass Music Association's album of the year and a Grammy for best bluegrass album. She followed it with *Little Sparrow* in 2001 and *Halos & Horns* in 2002. The patriotic *For God and Country* appeared in 2003 and was followed by the CD and DVD *Live and Well* a year later. *Those Were the Days* from 2005 found Parton covering her favorite pop songs from the 1960s and 1970s. She has received two Academy Award nominations, first for "9 to 5," which appeared in the film by the same name in 1982, and then in 2006 for her song "Travelin' Thru," which she wrote specifically for the film *Transamerica.* Parton was awarded the Living Legend medal by the U.S. Library of Congress on 14 April 2004 for her contributions to the cultural heritage of the United States. This was followed in 2005 with the National Medal of Arts, the highest honor given by the U.S. government for excellence in the arts.

Dolly Parton has demonstrated the strength of a southern cultural and musical background, and she retains a loyalty to her home place and her people. The lyrics she writes in songs like "Jolene," "My Tennessee Mountain Home," and "Coat of Many Colors" portray strong women who hail from the working-class South. Moreover, in film, television, and music, Parton herself is a country woman with stamina, intelligence, independence, and a sense of humor. She has popularized the idea that mountain women in particular are not the stereotypical hillbillies viewed in comic strips or popular situation comedies, but rather are complex, intelligent, articulate, and loving. Dolly Parton's music and personality will have a lasting impact upon popular images of women in the South.

RUTH A. BANES
University of South Florida

Chet Flippo, *Rolling Stone* (December 1980); Alanna Nash, *Dolly* (1978); Dolly Parton, *Dolly: My Life and Other Unfinished Business* (1994); *Playboy* (October 1978); Cecelia Tichi, ed., *Reading Country Music: Steel Guitars, Opry Stars, and Honky-Tonk Bars* (1998); Vertical files on "Dolly Parton," Country Music Foundation Library and Media Center, Nashville, Tenn.

Patton, Charley

(c. 1891–1934) BLUES SINGER.
Few people have had as great an impact on American music as has Charley Patton. Not only was Patton the first superstar of the blues, but many other forms of music today, such as gospel, R&B, soul, and, most particularly, rock and roll, were directly influenced by his work.

Charley was born to Bill and Annie Patton around 1891 near the central Mississippi towns of Bolton and Edwards. At an early age he had a predilection for making music, and he learned to play the guitar when still very young. But Charley grew up in a hard-working and religious farming family, and his father considered playing the guitar a sin tantamount to selling one's soul to the devil. His father often disciplined him for playing music, but Charley continued performing ragtime, folk songs, and spirituals at picnics and parties in Henderson Chatmon's string band, most likely for all-black audiences at first and then for whites who could afford to pay better.

In 1897, seeking to capitalize on the economic opportunities that the Mississippi Delta had begun to offer planters and day laborers, Bill Patton packed up his family and relocated north to Will Dockery's farm. It was at Dockery Farms that Charley invested his musical ability in the burgeoning blues. A number of guitar players already lived there, and Charley began to study the raw and rhythmic blues-playing technique of Henry Sloan, eventually crafting an extraordinarily inventive style of his own, which incorporated hitting heavy bass notes and playing slide guitar with a knife.

In the 22 years that followed his arrival at Dockery Farms, Charley never completely disavowed his religious upbringing. He continually vacillated between the roles of hard-drinking, womanizing rambler and god-fearing preacher. The rambling bluesman in him won out most often, but even then he stayed relatively close to home, never traveling farther than western Tennessee, eastern Arkansas, or northeastern Louisiana to play gigs. While in Jackson, Miss., in the summer of 1927, Henry C. Spier, a white music-store owner, arranged for Charley to go to Richmond, Ind., to record. Charley spent June 14 in a Gennett Records recording studio recording 14 songs. That recording session produced some of his most celebrated work, including "Pea Vine Blues," "Tom Rushen Blues," and "Pony Blues," the latter becoming an immediate "race record" hit. Later in that year, Charley traveled to Grafton, Wis., to record again, this time with fellow Delta-resident bluesman and fiddler Henry "Son" Sims. He recorded several more times, and his last recording session took place in New York City in January 1934.

Ever the Delta performer, Charley sang and recorded songs that included people, places, and events in his community. "Tom Rushen Blues" bemoans the possibility of a friendly sheriff losing his office to one not so amenable to public drunkenness: "Laid down last night, hopin' I would have my peace / I laid down last night, hopin' I would have my peace / But when I woke up Tom Rushen was shakin' me." In "Green River Blues" he sings "I'm goin' where the Southern cross the Dog," the junction of the Southern (Yazoo) and the Dog (Mississippi Valley) railroad lines, which lay just a few miles south of Dockery Farms, and in "Pea Vine Blues" he sings about a lover leaving on a train that ran to and from Dockery: "I think I heard the Pea Vine when it blowed. / I think I heard the Pea Vine when it blowed. / It blow just like my *rider* gettin' on board." In "High Water Everywhere (Pts. 1 & 2)" Charley sings about the Great Mississippi Flood of 1927, a flood that devastated much of the region: "Look-a here the water now, Lordy, / Levee broke, rose most everywhere / The water at Greenville and Leland, / Lord, it done rose everywhere / Boy, you can't never stay here / I would go down to Rosedale, / but, they tell me there's water there."

Over his short yet illustrious recording career, Charley recorded a variety of songs, including blues, which he sang in a loud, rough voice (much of which was nearly incomprehensible), and religious songs such as "You Gonna Need Somebody When You Die" (recorded under the pseudonym Elder J. J. Hadley), "Oh Death," and "I Shall Not Be Moved." His recordings earned him much widespread recognition, but his impact on American music stems primarily from those with whom he played, like Tommy Johnson, Son House, Big Joe Williams, Howlin' Wolf, and Muddy Waters. Bukka White once said his ambition in life was "to be a great man—like Charley Patton." Other blues musicians copied his style, and it can be reasonably argued that every rock and roller has been influenced by his style and music, whether consciously or not. His influence extends further than blues and rock and roll, though. Gospel patriarch Roebuck Staples, who also grew up on Dockery Farms, once said of Charley, "He was one of my great persons that inspired me to play guitar. He was a really great man."

Known today as the "Father of Delta Blues," Charley Patton died at 350 Heathman Street, in Indianola, Miss., on 28 April 1934, shortly after returning from his final recording session.

JAMES G. THOMAS JR.
University of Mississippi

Francis Davis, *The History of the Blues* (1995); David Evans, *Big Road Blues: Tradition and Creativity in Folk Blues* (1982), *Blues World* (August 1970); Gérard Herzhaft, *Encyclopedia of the Blues* (1997); Giles Oakley, *The Devil's Music* (1977); Robert Palmer, *Deep Blues* (1981); Gayle Dean Wardlow, *Blues Unlimited* (February 1966); Gayle Dean Wardlow and Edward M. Komara, *Chasin' That Devil Music: Searching for the Blues* (1998).

Pearl, Minnie

(1912–1996) COMIC FIGURE.
Minnie Pearl, the stage character created and performed by Sarah Colley, was one of the most popular and beloved performers in country music. Born on 25 October 1912 to a prominent family in Centerville, Tenn., Colley graduated from one of the South's premier women's schools, Nashville's Ward-Belmont, and aspired afterward to a theatrical career. In 1934 she began work for the Sewell Production Company, which organized dramatic and musical shows in small towns across the South. Colley became director of the company, and while promoting a play in Sand Mountain, Ala., she met a woman who became the model for her later comic creation. The hill country woman told her wry stories that reflected a humorous outlook on life, which appealed to Colley, who was soon repeating the stories and emulating the woman's temperament in creating the character of Minnie Pearl.

Minnie Pearl impressed audiences with her look. She wore a checked gingham dress, with cotton stockings, simple shoes, and most notably a straw hat with silk feathers and a dangling $1.98 price tag. "Howdeeee! I'm jest so proud to be here," Pearl screamed as she came on stage, and audiences soon learned to deliver the friendly greeting "Howdeee" back at her. She told stories and gossip of the fictional Grinder's Switch, which Colley based on the small-town doings of Centerville. Her routines revolved around her relatives and the townspeople, such as Uncle Nabob, Brother, Aunt Ambrosia, Doc Payne, Lizzie

Tinkum, and Hezzie—Minnie's somewhat slow-witted yet marriage-evasive "feller."

Minnie Pearl first appeared on the *Grand Ole Opry* in 1940 and would be a fixture on the show for 50 years. She was a regular on the television series *Hee Haw* from 1969 to 1991 and later appeared often on the cable television talk show, *Nashville Now*, with Ralph Emery. In 1975 she was inducted into the Country Music Hall of Fame.

Colley, who married pilot and businessman Henry Cannon in 1947, was a far cry from the simple country girl of her alter ego. She was a gracious embodiment of Nashville's gentrified society and active in numerous humanitarian causes. Diagnosed with breast cancer, she became a public spokeswoman in the 1990s for prevention and treatment of the disease, and the Sarah Cannon Cancer Center, the Sarah Cannon Research Institute, and the Minnie Pearl Cancer Foundation all honor her philanthropic work.

Colley died on 3 March 1996 after suffering a stroke, but the memory of her character, Minnie Pearl, survives as one of the South's most memorable comic figures.

CHARLES REAGAN WILSON
University of Mississippi

Minnie Pearl, *Minnie Pearl: An Autobiography* (1980).

Peer, Ralph

(1892–1960) MUSIC PUBLISHER AND TALENT SCOUT.

Although he was born in Kansas City, Mo. (on 22 May 1892), and although he never expressed a great fondness for southern folk music, Ralph Sylvester Peer became the single most important entrepreneur for country and blues recordings. He discovered, or was instrumental in the careers of, dozens of southern artists, both black and white, including Louis Armstrong, the Memphis Jug Band, Jimmie Rodgers, the Carter Family, Mamie Smith, the Georgia Yellow Hammers, Fiddlin' John Carson, Ernest Stoneman, Grayson and Whitter (with their initial recording of the murder ballad "Tom Dooley"), the Rev. J. M. Gates (one of the first black preachers to record extensively), the Rev. Andrew Jenkins (a prolific "event song" composer of items like "The Death of Floyd Collins"), and Gene Autry (who began as an imitator of Jimmie Rodgers). He initiated the practice of bringing recording crews into the South to document black and white folk music; he created the idea of having "blues" and "hillbilly" numerical series on commercial phonograph records; he was one of the first to publish and copyright country and blues songs; and in the 1930s and 1940s he became an innovative and trend-setting publisher of international reputation.

Peer's father was a Columbia Record Company phonograph dealer in Independence, Mo., and by the time he was 20, Ralph Peer was working full time in the retail record business. By 1920 he was in New York working for the Okeh Record Company (actually the General Phonograph Corporation), then one of the smaller of the record companies and one looking for ways to get an edge on its bigger competitors. It found one, when on 10 August 1920 Peer recorded black Cincinnati vaudeville performer Mamie Smith singing "Crazy Blues," a composition by a Georgia native named Perry Bradford. The record sold 7,500 copies within a week after its release and became the first in a long line of commercial recordings of blues by black artists. Three years later, in June 1923, Peer stumbled into a similar discovery for white folk music; on a field trip to Atlanta he recorded a millhand and radio personality named Fiddlin' John Carson. Peer thought Carson's singing was "pluperfect awful" but agreed to release his rendition of "The Little Old Log Cabin in the Lane," an 1871 pop song by Will Hays. It duplicated the success of "Crazy Blues," and soon Peer had initiated an "old-time music" record series on Okeh to parallel its blues series.

From 1923 to 1932 Peer made dozens of trips into southern cities—Dallas, El Paso, Nashville, Memphis, Atlanta, New Orleans, Charlotte, and Bristol—seeking out and recording on the spot hundreds of blues, gospel, jazz, country, Cajun, and Tex-Mex performers. On one such trip, to the Virginia-Tennessee border town of Bristol in August 1927, he discovered two acts that were to become cornerstones for commercial country music—the Carter Family and "blue yodeler" Jimmie Rodgers.

Central to all of this, though, was Peer's unusual interest in both black and white music and his perception of ways in which the two could mutually influence each other. He theorized that both genres were just emerging from their vernacular regional base into the national limelight. He encouraged acts like the Allen Brothers, the Carolina Tar Heels, and Jimmie Rodgers to incorporate blues into their music and felt that this was one of the reasons that Rodgers enjoyed a wider national appeal than did the Carters.

In 1925 Peer left the Okeh Company and went to work for the Victor Company, trading his huge Okeh salary for more modest gains but an additional incentive: the right to control the copyrights on the new song materials recorded by his artists. Peer began to look for artists who could create original material, which he could copyright for them and place in his newly formed Southern Music Publishing Company (1928); such artists would get payment not only for records but for song performance rights as well. The increased emphasis on new material encouraged many blues and part-time country singers to become professionals and prompted the music as a whole to become more commercialized. And throughout the 1930s and 1940s he continued to build a publishing empire (which exists today as one of the country's largest, the Peer-Southern organization) and to excel even at casual hobbies, such as horticulture, for which he received a gold medal for his important work. Though in later years he expressed disdain for the country and blues artists he developed ("I've tried so hard to forget them," he told a reporter), and though some of his artists felt that he had exploited them, Peer laid the foundation for the commercialization of

American vernacular music and thrust the rich southern folk music tradition into the mainstream of American popular music.

CHARLES K. WOLFE
Middle Tennessee State University

Nolan Porterfield, *Journal of Country Music* (December 1978); Charles K. Wolfe, in *The Illustrated History of Country Music*, ed. Patrick Carr (1979).

Penniman, Richard (Little Richard)

(b. 1933) ROCK-AND-ROLL SINGER. Born into a large black family, in Macon, Ga., on 5 December 1933, Penniman adopted his nickname, Little Richard, at about age eight, when he began singing at church and school functions. By his early teens, Little Richard was performing on the road all across the South. He sang in minstrel shows, attracting audiences and selling snake oil. He sang the blues in bands following migrant workers as far afield as Lake Okeechobee in Florida, and he journeyed into cities to find gay clubs, where he played Princess Lavonne in the first of his several transvestite acts. Before he was 20 he had recorded, with little profit, for RCA twice and for Peacock Records once. These songs were conventional jump blues that made him sound like a melancholy Dinah Washington.

Success came in New Orleans in September 1955 when he joined Robert "Bumps" Blackwell on Specialty Records and made "Tutti Frutti," one of the first and most important rock records. "Tutti Frutti" was a sublimated version of a bawdy song he had performed in sideshows for years but had never considered recordable. He and Blackwell then followed with a series of influential rock-and-roll hits. "Miss Ann" was about loving a white woman and included a 500-year-old rhyming folk riddle from the English oral tradition. "Long Tall Sally," backed with "Slippin' and Slidin'," narrated the antics of standard black folk figures such as John and Aunt Mary, along with more contemporary ones like Sally, who was "built for speed." "Keep a-Knockin'" and "Good Golly Miss Molly" emerged from the randy lore of prostitutes, circuses, and after-hours clubs and was reshaped as pop and teen lore—as when he purred to Molly, "When you rock 'n' roll, can't hear your mother call."

By 1957, however, Little Richard was called away from rock and roll, entered Bible school, and began preaching. Since then he has made several attempts to return to the world of rock and roll that he helped create, and his performance as a rock-and-roll singer in the 1986 movie *Down and Out in Beverly Hills* brought good reviews and new attention. Nevertheless, he has not regained the power he had in the mid-1950s to mine the underground lore of the American South and fix it in an iconic style for the international youth culture.

When the Rock and Roll Hall of Fame opened in 1986, Little Richard was among the first inductees. His pioneering contribution to the genre has also been recognized by the Rockabilly Hall of Fame. In 2005 Little Richard starred in a popular commercial series and worked on a pop single with Michael Jackson benefiting victims of Hurricane Katrina. Although he has been called back to performing since the mid-1980s, Little Richard's popularity has not matched that of his early career.

W. T. LHAMON JR.
Florida State University

W. T. Lhamon Jr., *Studies in Popular Culture* (1985); Charles White, *The Life and Times of Little Richard: The Quasar of Rock* (1994); Langdon Winner, in *The Rolling Stone Illustrated History of Rock 'n' Roll*, ed. Jim Miller (1976).

Pickett, Wilson

(1941–2006) SOUL AND R&B SINGER. The "Wicked" Wilson Pickett had one of the most fiery and distinctive voices of 1960s soul music. Many historians and fans agree that few artists could match Pickett's deep, guttural intensity in the studio and onstage while he was in his prime during his years of recording for Atlantic Records. Born in rural Plattville, Ala., on 18 March 1941, Pickett was one of 11 children in a family of God-fearing sharecroppers. Here he got his first taste of music, singing in local Baptist church choirs as a child. But like many of his generation, Pickett tired of the hardships of the agrarian life and headed north in his late teens to find better opportunity.

Landing in Detroit, Pickett fell into singing with a local gospel group called the Violinaires, who in their brief career accompanied the likes of the Soul Stirrers and the Swan Silvertones at church gigs around the country. It was not long, though, before the pull of the secular music world of R&B became too strong for Pickett, and he joined an up-and-coming vocal group called the Falcons, which also featured Sir Mack Rice and Eddie Floyd. The union would prove successful as the Falcons found a Top 10 R&B hit in 1962 with the searing "I Found a Love," featuring none other than Pickett on lead vocals.

Realizing his own solo potential, Pickett soon left the Falcons and was eventually signed by Atlantic Records in 1964. After a few initial misfires, Pickett struck gold when Atlantic sent him down to Memphis to record with its then-partner, Stax Records, where he began to hit his stride. He teamed up with Stax golden-boy producer, songwriter, and guitarist Steve Cropper, and the duo's first effort, "In the Midnight Hour," resulted in a definitive hit on the R&B and pop charts in 1965. The flurry of hits to follow in the next six years would prove to be the most successful era of Pickett's career. Gritty workouts like "634-5789 (Soulsville, USA)," "Mustang Sally," "Funky Broadway," and "Land of 1,000 Dances" would set a benchmark in the Deep Soul movement of the late 1960s and early 1970s.

Pickett did not confine himself to recording at Stax during these years. Several of his albums were recorded at the legendary FAME studios, another partner of Atlantic, in Muscle Shoals, Ala., with such prolific studio musicians, producers, and songwriters as Chips Moman, Spooner Oldham, and Rick Hall. Pickett even teamed up with young FAME studio musician Duane Allman on a blistering cover of the

Beatles' "Hey Jude" while in Muscle Shoals in 1969. Also during the late 1960s, Pickett collaborated on many popular songs with famed soul singer and songwriter Bobby Womack.

Pickett returned north in 1970 to record one of his last popular albums on Atlantic, *Wilson Pickett in Philadelphia*. Pickett's commercial career soon started to wane, though, and after recording one more album for Atlantic in 1971 Pickett left the label. He would spend the 1970s at RCA struggling with mediocre material and new trends, such as disco, that did not always suit his gospel and soul past. During the 1980s Pickett all but dropped off the recording map, though he did occasionally perform.

After spending almost two decades battling drug addiction and having several run-ins with the law, Pickett reemerged in 1999 with the critically acclaimed *It's Harder Now* on Bullseye Blues. The album gave him a comeback career on blues and soul circuits, earning him three W. C. Handy Awards and a Grammy nomination.

In 2004 Pickett retired from touring because of declining health, and two years later, on 19 January 2006, he died of a heart attack in his Reston, Va., home, leaving behind two daughters and a musical legacy matched by few of his era or any other.

MARK COLTRAIN
Hillsborough, North Carolina

Gerri Hirshey, *Nowhere to Run: The Story of Soul Music* (1984); Peter Shapiro, *The Rough Guide to Soul and R&B* (2006).

Powell, John

(1882–1963) MUSICIAN AND COMPOSER.

Powell was born in Richmond, Va., where his father, a schoolteacher, and his mother, an amateur musician, provided his primary musical education at home. He then studied music with his sister and piano and harmony with F. C. Hahr, a onetime student of Liszt. After receiving his B.A. from the University of Virginia in 1901, he studied piano with Theodor Leschetizky in Vienna (1902–7). There he also studied composition with Carl Navratil (1904–7). Powell made his debut as a pianist in Berlin in 1907. After four years of giving concerts in Europe, he returned to the United States, touring the country as a pianist and playing some of his own works. He continued to perform for many years in leading cities of Europe and America.

Powell composed many orchestral works, arrangements of folk songs, and choral settings; he also wrote three piano sonatas, one violin concerto, two piano concertos, and an opera, *Judith and Holofernes*. His other works include *Rhapsodie Negre* (piano and orchestra), 1918; *Sonata Virginianesque* (violin and piano), 1919; *In Old Virginia* (overture), 1921; *At the Fair* (suite for piano, also for orchestra), 1925; *Natchez on the Hill* (three country dances for orchestra), 1932; *A Set of Three* (orchestra), 1935; and Symphony in A Major (orchestra), 1947.

One of Powell's most important achievements lies in the area of ethnomusicology. A methodical collector of the South's rural songs, he was the founder of the Virginia State Choral Festival and the moving spirit behind the annual White Top Mountain Folk Music Festival. A member of the National Institute of Arts and Letters, Powell was honored by his native state when Governor John S. Battle designated 5 November 1951 as John Powell Day. Powell died in Charlottesville, Va., in 1963.

For the most part southerners have contented themselves with inherited music, folk songs, and contemporary tunes. Apart from Powell, southern composers have remained virtually unknown except to other musicians. During the first half of the 20th century, however, Powell received national recognition and acclaim not only as a virtuoso performer of the classical repertoire at home and abroad but also as a composer of distinctively American music. Although Powell used African American elements in his *Rhapsodie Negre* and *Sonata Virginianesque*, his abiding concern was with the cultivation of Anglo-American folk music, of which there existed a rich heritage in the South. His Virginian antecedents and environment had given him a profound sense of intimacy with the founders of the American nation.

Powell felt strongly about the value of those Anglo-Saxon cultural and ethical forces that he believed had motivated the molders of the American past; he wished to preserve them for future generations and ensure the persistence of those Anglo-Saxon ideals that he regarded as characteristically American. By the early 1920s patient research and study had convinced Powell that American folk music derived from Anglo-Saxon sources was of fundamental importance to the cultural life of the United States and to the development of a truly national school of American music.

L. MOODY SIMMS JR.
Illinois State University

Daniel Gregory Mason, *Music in My Time, and Other Reminiscences* (1983); L. Moody Simms Jr., *Journal of Popular Culture* (Winter 1973).

Preservation Hall

Preservation Hall, a New Orleans institution, celebrates the emergence of jazz as a popular musical innovation in the South. Philadelphians Allan and Sandra Jaffe founded the hall in the early 1960s at the suggestion of (and on property owned by) artist Larry Borenstein. Endeavoring to revitalize the roots of jazz, it has supported a resurgence of interest and activity in classic New Orleans jazz.

At its outset, Preservation Hall provided a stage for fine old black jazz musicians who were unemployed. It also resuscitated a nearly extinct institution of musical life in the Crescent City—the community hall. Figures of the New Orleans revival, such as George Lewis, Jim Robinson, and Alvin Alcorn, took up musical residence there. Repeatedly throughout the past four decades, classic jazz musicians of the city have looked to Preservation Hall to renew the old idiom.

Like Perseverance Hall and San Jacinto Hall before it, Preservation Hall serves a total community. It addresses social and economic problems as well as cultural needs of the city's jazz people.

The preservationist impulse itself accounts for the fundamental contribution of Preservation Hall. In an effort to preserve jazz, the Jaffes and their associates have recycled it, establishing the classic jazz aesthetic for a new era. The hall has in fact reinvented and revitalized its community for the future by reaching decisively into the past.

Preservation Hall has succeeded by combining imported, updated marketing techniques with an abiding appreciation for local, traditional lifeways. Its success rests in large part upon the generous life support it has provided to old jazz greats. Preservation Hall emerged as part of a national folk revival in the 1950s and 1960s, and its activities have sought from the beginning to underscore the primal claim to jazz of black Americans.

Hurricane Katrina devastated the musical culture of New Orleans, including affecting Preservation Hall. The institution closed in August 2005 for several months after the building flooded. The first post-Katrina performance by the Preservation Hall Jazz Band was on 27–28 April 2006. Benjamin Jaffe, son of the owners, salvaged from the flood historic master tracks, which became the basis for *Made in New Orleans: The Hurricane Sessions*, a compilation of rare recordings, photographs, and text about Preservation Hall, which was released in July 2007.

CURTIS D. JERDE
W. R. Hogan Jazz Archive
Tulane University

Jason Berry, Jonathan Foose, and Tad Jones, *Up from the Cradle of Jazz: New Orleans*

Music since World War II (1987); Al Rose and Edmond Souchon, *New Orleans Jazz: A Family Album* (1967; rev. ed., 1978).

Presley, Elvis

(1935–1977) ROCK-AND-ROLL SINGER.

Presley is probably the most famous southerner of the 20th century. Born in Tupelo, Miss., and reared in Memphis in near poverty, he became an international celebrity and one of the wealthiest entertainers in history. He has sold a billion record units worldwide, more than any other entertainer. Elvis had 149 singles on *Billboard*'s popular music charts, with 114 in the Top 40, 40 in the Top 10, and 18 singles reaching No. 1.

In 1954 Presley made his first recordings for Sam Phillips's Memphis-based Sun Records in a style that drew from diverse sources—gospel (black and white), blues (rural and urban), and country. In effect, he and his band forged a dynamic new musical synthesis, which later became known as "rockabilly." In 1955, after joining the *Louisiana Hayride*, a popular country show broadcast from Shreveport, Presley toured extensively throughout the South and acquired a vast and fervent following. National recognition came in 1956 with the success of his first RCA Victor release, "Heartbreak Hotel," a series of network television appearances, and a movie, *Love Me Tender*. He was often the subject of controversy, for his frenetic performances and his conspicuous adoption of black-derived material and musical styles.

From 1956 to 1966, including his celebrated stint in the army (1958–60),

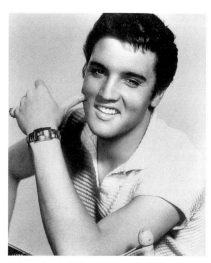

Elvis Presley, the "King of Rock and Roll," age 22, 1957 (Graceland, Inc., Memphis)

Presley dominated popular music. He also starred in 31 feature films. After a brief decline in popularity during the mid-1960s, he began a sustained comeback in 1968 and 1969 with an acclaimed television special, and his television specials in 1973 and 1977 remain among the highest-rated musical specials. During this period Presley returned to live performances for the first time since 1961.

In the 1970s Presley again became a major figure in American popular culture. He broke attendance records for his Las Vegas shows, and from 1969 to 1977 he performed 1,100 concerts across the nation. As the decade progressed, he often returned to the southern-rooted material and styles of his youth. Songs like "Amazing Grace" (1971), "Promised Land" (1973), and especially "American Trilogy" (1972) dramatized and reiterated Presley's affinity for the South.

His death in 1977 and the subsequent outpouring of public interest in his life and music served to expose the many tensions and contradictions in southern culture, which he had so vividly symbolized. He was insolent yet courteous; narcissistic yet humble; pious (reflecting the Pentecostalism of his childhood) yet often hedonistic, especially in his final years; extremely wealthy yet ever conscious of his poor origins. His diet, accent, name, and, most of all, his music, remained indelibly southern. His Memphis home, Graceland (open to the public since 1982), one of the most popular tourist attractions in the South, is an enduring reminder of the quintessentially southern character of Elvis Presley. It attracts over 600,000 annual visitors, and in 2006 Graceland was designated a National Historic Landmark. In 1992 the U.S. Postal Service honored Presley with a postage stamp, which became the best-selling commemorative stamp in history.

STEPHEN R. TUCKER
Tulane University

Peter Guralnick, *Careless Love: The Unmaking of Elvis Presley* (2000), *Last Train to Memphis: The Rise of Elvis Presley* (1994); Peter Guralnick and Ernst Jorgensen, *Elvis Day by Day* (1999); Valerie Harms, *Tryin' to Get to You: The Story of Elvis Presley* (2000); Greil Marcus, *Mystery Train: Images of America in Rock 'n' Roll Music* (rev. ed., 1982); Dave Marsh, *Elvis* (1982); Alanna Nash, *The Colonel: The Extraordinary Story of Colonel Tom Parker and Elvis Presley* (2003); Stanley Oberst and Lori Torrance, *Elvis in Texas: The Undiscovered King, 1954–1958* (2001); Jac Tharpe, ed., *Elvis: Images and Fancies* (1979).

Price, Leontyne

(b. 1927) GRAND OPERA AND CONCERT SINGER.

Leontyne Price was born in Laurel, Miss., where she grew up playing the piano and singing in the church choir. She graduated from Oak Park High School in 1944 and Wilberforce College in Ohio four years later. She then attended Juilliard School of Music on a scholarship, with financial aid from the Alexander F. Chisholm family of Laurel. Virgil Thomson selected her to sing the role of Saint Cecilia in a revival of his *Four Saints in Three Acts* on Broadway and at the 1952 International Arts Festival in Paris. After an audition with Ira Gershwin, she won the female lead in an important revival of *Porgy and Bess* opposite William Warfield, playing to packed houses from June 1952 until June 1954 on Broadway and in a world tour. In 1953 composer Samuel Barber asked her to sing the premiere of his *Hermit Songs* at the Library of Congress, and in 1954 she gave a Town Hall recital to enthusiastic reviews.

The NBC Opera Theater's production of *Tosca* in January 1955 marked her professional debut in grand opera, although her first performance in a major opera house came two years later in San Francisco, as Madame Lidoine in Poulenc's *Dialogues of the Carmelites*. In succeeding seasons she returned to San Francisco to interpret the title role of Verdi's *Aïda*, Donna Elvira in *Don Giovanni*, Leonora in *Il Trovatore*, the lead in the American premiere of Carl Orff's *The Wise Maiden*, Cio-Cio-San in *Madama Butterfly*, Amelia in *Un Ballo in Maschera*, Leonora in *La Forza del Destino*, Giorgetta in *Il Tabarro*, and the title role in Richard Strauss's *Ariadne auf Naxos*. With the Lyric Opera of Chicago she first sang Massenet's *Thaïs*, one of her few failures, and the role of Liù in Puccini's *Turandot*. She also appeared in Handel's *Julius Caesar* and Monteverdi's *Coronation of Poppea* in concert form with the American Opera Society.

Her Metropolitan Opera debut came on 27 January 1961, as Leonora in Verdi's *Il Trovatore*. In October of that year she became the first black to open a Metropolitan Opera season, appearing as Minnie in Puccini's *La Fanciulla del West*. She later sang Tatyana in *Eugene Onegin*, Pamina in *The Magic Flute*, and Fiordiligi in *Così Fan Tutte* at the Metropolitan. She opened the new house at Lincoln Center as Cleopatra in Samuel Barber's *Antony and Cleopatra*. She has performed with the Vienna State Opera, the Royal Opera House in London, the Paris Opera, La Scala, the Verona Arena, the Berlin Opera, the Hamburg Opera, and Teatro Colon. In 1961 she sang recitals at the World's Fair in Brussels and has given concerts throughout the world. She has recorded extensively, including American popular songs and black spirituals. She received 19 Grammy awards, more than any other classical singer, and was awarded a Grammy Lifetime Achievement Award in 1989. She often returns to Laurel, Miss., and gave one of the first nonsegregated recitals there. She retired after a final performance on 3 January 1985.

Price performed recitals in the United States and Europe after her retirement, and she gave a memorable concert at Carnegie Hall in October 2001 honoring the victims of the September 11 terrorist attack. In 1997 she wrote a children's book, *Aida*, which became the basis for a Broadway musical.

RONALD L. DAVIS
Southern Methodist University

Sir Rudolf Bing, *5000 Nights at the Opera* (1972); Arthur J. Bloomfield, *50 Years of the San Francisco Opera* (1972); Peter G. Davis, *The American Opera Singer: The Lives and Achievements of America's Great Singers in Opera and Concert from 1825 to the Present* (1999); Hugh Lee Lyon, *Leontyne Price: Highlights of a Prima Donna* (1973); Helena Matheopoulos, *Diva: Great Sopranos and Mezzos Discuss Their Art* (1992).

Price, Ray

(b. 1926) COUNTRY MUSIC SINGER. Ray Price, in a music career that has lasted more than 55 years, helped country music survive the death of Hank Williams and the introduction of rock and roll by creating a more forceful, rhythm-driven form of honky-tonk music. Later, in the 1960s, he broadened country music's audience by moving toward a lush, sophisticated sound.

He was born Noble Ray Price on 12 January 1926 in the east Texas farming community of Peach in rural Wood County. His parents split up when he was a young boy. He grew up spending summers working on his father's farm in Perryville, Tex., and attending school in Dallas while living with his mother. He also took classical voice lessons for several years, encouraged by his stepfather, an Italian immigrant who loved opera. The vocal control and power he learned would later set him apart

as a singer who could soar above his arrangements with a clarity and power that many other country singers lacked.

After serving as a U.S. Marine in World War II, Price began singing in Dallas-area nightclubs and, before long, on the city's *Big D Jamboree* radio show. He recorded his first songs for Bullet Records in 1951 and the following year signed with Columbia Records. Moving to Nashville, he briefly roomed with Hank Williams.

Price had several Top 10 hits early in his career, including "I'll Be There (If You Ever Want Me)" and "Release Me," but it wasn't until 1956 that he scored a No. 1 hit, with "Crazy Arms." The latter established Price's signature sound, a 4/4 shuffle beat spiced by single-note fiddle and a stinging steel guitar. Other country dance floor hits followed, including "I've Got a New Heartache," "My Shoes Keep Walking Back to You," "City Lights," "Invitation to the Blues," and "Heartaches by the Number."

In the 1960s Price shifted from traditional country music to a smoother style featuring sweet violins rather than raw fiddles. Although songs like "Make the World Go Away," "The Other Woman," and his emotion-drenched version of "Danny Boy" all did well, it was not until 1970, when he recorded a Kris Kristofferson song, "For the Good Times," that he returned to the No. 1 spot.

Price also has been known for identifying significant songwriters early in their careers. He cut the first major hits of Kristofferson, Bill Anderson, and Roger Miller, and he recorded early hits by writers Harlan Howard, Willie

Nelson, Hank Cochran, Danny Dill, and Mel Tillis. He also was known for hiring top musicians for his Cherokee Cowboys band, including steel guitarists Jimmy Day and Buddy Emmons, fiddlers Tommy Jackson and Buddy Spicher, and guitarist Pete Wade. Future country stars Willie Nelson, Roger Miller, Johnny Paycheck, and Johnny Bush were all members of his band before going on to launch their own singing careers.

Price has continued to perform into his eighties, his voice still rich and resonant. In March 2007, he released an album, *Last of the Breed*, with old friends Willie Nelson and Merle Haggard, both of whom consider Price a primary influence and, as Nelson put it, "the best country singer I've ever heard."

MICHAEL MCCALL
Country Music Hall of Fame

Pride, Charley

(b. 1938) COUNTRY MUSIC SINGER.
A little over a decade after Jackie Robinson broke the color barrier in baseball, Charley Pride accomplished a similar feat in country music. Born in Sledge, Miss., in the depths of the Great Depression to a family of poor cotton laborers, Pride not only opened new avenues of acceptance to minorities but set high standards of excellence in the field of country music.

Many blacks in the Mississippi Delta were drawn to the blues, but Pride was more interested in country music, especially the songs of Hank Williams. At night he would listen to country music radio programs, memorizing the words of their songs. The only member of his family with any musical inclination, Pride scraped up enough money when he was 14 to buy his first guitar, which he learned to play by listening to different picking styles. (Pride received only $3 per 100 pounds of cotton he picked with his 10 brothers and sisters.) When Pride left Mississippi three years later, he departed not to pursue a career in music but to try for athletic success through baseball.

Pride's luck with baseball was short lived. After stints with the Memphis Red Sox and Birmingham Black Barons, teams in the Negro American League, and two years in the army in the late 1950s, Pride eventually made it to the minor leagues, playing in 1960 for a team in Helena, Mont. Pride often sang between innings; the response he received from the venture encouraged him to sing more. Through his landlady in Helena he got his first musical break, singing in a local country bar. Still hungry to play major league baseball, Pride earned a tryout in 1961 from the California Angels. He did not make the team, and he returned to Helena, where he worked for a refining plant and sang in area nightclubs. The nightclub performances led to an invitation from Red Sovine in 1963 to do a recording audition in Nashville. Pride auditioned in Nashville for Chet Atkins the following year and signed with RCA Victor after the session.

Since 1965, when he recorded his first hit single, "Snakes Crawl at Night," he has accumulated numerous gold records and country music awards. His first album, *Country Charley Pride* (1966), garnered the 1967 Most Promising Male

Highway sign seen leaving Tutwiler, Miss.
(Highway 3), honoring black Mississippi country
singer Charley Pride (James G. Thomas Jr.,
photographer, University of Mississippi)

Artist Award from the Country Song
Roundup. (Fearing the album would not
sell well in the racially torn South, RCA
released *Country Charley Pride* without
Pride's picture on the cover.) In 1971 and
1972 he was named Male Vocalist of the
Year by the Country Music Association.
During the same period he released six
albums that became gold and received
three Grammy awards, the first for Best
Sacred Performance ("Did You Think to
Pray"), the second for Best Gospel Performance ("Let Me Live"), and a third
for Best Country Vocal, Male (*Charley
Pride Sings Heart Songs*). Billboard gave
its Trendsetter Award to Pride in 1970.
In 1976 he received Photoplay's Gold
Medal Award, and in 1980 Cash Box
named him its Top Male Country Artist
of the Decade.

Pride's gold albums include *Coun-
try Charley Pride* (1966), *The Country
Way* (1968), *Just Plain Charley* (1970),
Charley Pride 10th Album (1970),
Charley Pride Sings Heart Songs (1971),
Did You Think to Pray (1971), and *The
Best of Charley Pride*, vol. 2 (1972).
Other top albums recorded by Pride are

Charley (1975), *I'm Just Me* (1977), *You're
My Jamaica* (1979), and *There's a Little
Bit of Hank in Me* (1980). Among his
recent albums are *Comfort of Her Wings*
(2003) and *Pride and Joy: A Gospel
Music Collection* (2006). He released
gold and Top 10 singles such as "I Know
One" (1967), "Does My Ring Hurt Your
Finger" (1967), "Let Me Live" (1971),
"Did You Think to Pray" (1971), "Amaz-
ing Love" (1973), "We Could" (1974), "I
Got a Lot of Hank in Me" (1980), "Roll
on Mississippi" (1981), and "Never Been
So Loved" (1981).

Pride declined an initial invitation
in 1968 to become a cast member of the
Grand Ole Opry, but he joined the cast
in May 1993. He was inducted into the
Country Music Hall of Fame in 2000.

ELIZABETH MCGEHEE
Salem College

Charley Pride, *Pride: The Charley Pride
Story* (1994); Michael Streissguth, *Voices of
the Country: Interviews with Classic Country
Performers* (2004).

Rainey, Gertrude Malissa Nix Pridgett (Ma Rainey)

(1886?–1939) BLUES SINGER.
Acknowledged as the "Mother of the
Blues," Ma Rainey brought rural blues
to American musical life. Rainey was
one of the first popular stage entertainers to incorporate blues into her
repertoire, and in so doing, she brought
blues from folk culture to the American
mainstream through her touring performances and recordings. During an
era when smooth, female blues singers
dominated the urban scene, she played
an important role in connecting the
work of these women to that of less-

polished, male country blues artists. Rainey emerged as a cultural icon, particularly representing rural southern black life and early expressions of black feminism.

Ma Rainey was born Gertrude Pridgett, probably on 26 April 1886, in Columbus, Ga. Columbus was a stop on the minstrel circuit, and Rainey's family, although poor, abounded with singers, including her grandmother and both parents, Thomas Pridgett Sr. and Ella Allen-Pridgett. Rainey exhibited musical talent from a young age, beginning her career at the age of 14 in a local talent show, "Bunch of Blackberries," at the Springer Opera House in Columbus in 1900. Soon after, she began traveling in vaudeville and minstrel shows, and in 1904 she met and married William "Pa" Rainey, a minstrel show manager. Together, she and Pa Rainey toured with the Rabbit Foot Minstrels, Tolliver's Circus, Musical Extravaganza, and other tent shows across the United States and Mexico.

Although Rainey had not encountered the blues in Columbus, extensive traveling brought her into contact with the form by 1905, and she began to incorporate it into her repertoire. In 1912 Rainey met Bessie Smith, who joined the Rabbit Foot Minstrels in Tennessee. Rainey befriended Smith, helping her to develop her vocal talents, but the two performers remained distinctive stylistically. Although they sang together for only a short time, the two would become known as the most important figures in the development of classical blues.

After separating from Pa Rainey in 1916, Ma Rainey toured with her own band, Madam Gertrude Ma Rainey and Her Smart Sets. Rainey recorded her first work for Paramount in 1923, becoming one of the first women to record the blues professionally (several years after the first recordings by Mamie Smith). Her first session featured the number "Bi-Weevil Blues," and later sessions included collaborations with Louis Armstrong and the original release of "See See Rider," one of the most famous and most recorded blues songs of all time, with more than 100 versions. The success of her early albums led to Rainey's being part of the 1924 Paramount promotional tour, and her popularity continued to spread. She was known for her professional attitude and shrewd business sense, as well as her raw, "moaning" voice. As a stage presence she made a strong impression, with her large, gold-capped teeth, thick, straightened hair, sparkling jewelry, and sequined ensembles and with an ostrich plume in her hand. Her songs and vocal style evinced her deep personal connection to poverty, jealousy, sexual abuse, and the harsh existence of sharecropping. Her ability to capture the essence of southern black life endeared her to a wide southern black audience. She was outspoken on women's issues and acted as a role model for female entertainers to take charge of their own careers. Rainey was also bisexual, and the lyrics of her song "Prove It on Me" suggest her love for women and her privileging of female culture and female sexual agency. For these reasons, she is proudly reclaimed from the abuses of history by contemporary black feminist thinkers.

Rainey continued to record and tour throughout the 1920s, performing with a wide variety of blues artists of the day. She recorded her last session in 1928 in Chicago with pianist Tommy Dorsey and guitarist Tampa Red. Despite the declining popularity of her style of blues in the 1930s, she continued to tour, often appearing in tent show performances. She retired from music in the mid-1930s and spent her remaining years in Columbus operating two venues that she owned. Ma Rainey died of heart disease at age 53 in 1939.

Ma Rainey influenced generations of artists in many genres and mediums and became a symbol of strength and spirit in African American culture. Allusions to Ma Rainey and her impact span African American literature in the 20th century, as well as popular music, such as Bob Dylan's 1965 track "Tombstone Blues." In his 1932 collection, *Southern Road*, poet Sterling Allen Brown pays tribute to her in a poem titled "Ma Rainey," and she also strongly influenced the creation of the Shug Avery character in Alice Walker's 1983 Pulitzer Prize–winning novel, *The Color Purple*. Playwright August Wilson wrote *Ma Rainey's Black Bottom* in 1982, a play based on her career in Chicago in the 1920s. Dealing with issues of race, art, religion, and the historic exploitation of black recording artists by white producers, the play pays tribute to the impact of Rainey's early professional success as a black woman and the power of the music that she brought to the American mainstream.

FRANCES ABBOTT
Emory University

Angela Y. Davis, *Blues Legacies and Black Feminism: Gertrude "Ma" Rainey, Bessie Smith, and Billie Holiday* (1998); Daphne D. Harrison, *Black Pearls: Blues Queens of the 1920s* (1988); Sandra Lieb, *Mother of the Blues: A Study of Ma Rainey* (1981); Eileen Southern, *The Music of Black Americans: A History* (1997).

Redding, Otis

(1941–1967) SOUL SINGER.

Otis Redding epitomized the sound of soul music in the South in the 1960s. The "Big O," as he came to be known, was born in 1941 in Dawson, Ga., and was raised in nearby Macon, one of six children of a Baptist minister. Singing in church throughout his youth, Redding became increasingly fascinated by the rhythm-and-blues and rock-and-roll sounds to be heard on Macon radio, especially those of local luminary Little Richard, the Georgia Peach.

By 1956 Redding was playing locally with Johnny Jenkins and the Pinetoppers; by 1957 he was managed by Phil Walden (later of Allman Brothers and Capricorn Records fame); by 1958 he was married; and by 1960 he had cut his first single, "Shout Bamalama," for Bethlehem Records. The single revealed an exciting singer who had yet to grow beyond Little Richard imitation.

Deciding to try his luck elsewhere, Redding moved to California. He spent six months washing cars and recording two more singles, one for Finer Arts, the other for Alshire, both of which flopped. Back in Macon, Redding hooked up with guitarist Jenkins once again. The latter attracted the attention of Atlantic Records through a local hit entitled "Love Twist." Atlantic arranged for Jenkins to record at the still largely unknown Stax Studio in Memphis in 1962, and Redding was able to record "These Arms of Mine" and "Hey, Hey Baby" at the end of the session. Jenkins's material remains unissued; Redding's recording became his first single and launched a career that was to end on 10 December 1967 when his plane, en route from Cleveland to Madison, Wis., plunged into Lake Monona. All the original members of his band, the Bar-Kays, died in the crash with Redding, except for Ben Cauley and James Alexander. His funeral, held nine days later in Macon, was attended by 6,000 fans and a who's who of soul musicians and singers. He was survived by his wife, Zelma, and their three children.

Otis Redding, soul singer (Courtesy Stax Museum of American Soul Music, Memphis)

Between 1962 and 1967 Redding recorded prolifically. He was able to adapt to almost any material, recording songs as diverse as Bing Crosby's "Try a Little Tenderness" and the Rolling Stones' "Satisfaction," as well as a host of originals that are now standards such as "Respect" and "I've Been Loving You Too Long." In contrast with many of the soul singers of the period, Redding was equally at home with ballads and with up-tempo dance numbers. Many of the original compositions were cowritten with Steve Cropper, the guitarist for the Stax house band Booker T. & the MG's. Cropper also produced Redding's records and, on most of these, the MG's, coupled with the Bar-Kays' horns, provided the backup. Cropper was white, as were half of the Stax session musicians. This relatively rare musical integration was a large factor in making southern soul from Memphis and Muscle Shoals, Ala., so distinctive in the 1960s.

Redding's single style was immediately recognizable. His voice had a "catch" to it, and he was a master of timbral and dynamic variation and of rhythmic subtlety. In contrast to most soul performers, Redding never employed backup vocalists on his recordings. A typical record, such as "Try a Little Tenderness," continually adds instruments as it progresses, with everyone gradually playing louder while the rate of activity increases, Redding's voice becomes strained, the plane of sound gradually shifts upward, and the amount of call and response increases; finally, the tension is released through a syncopated drum break, over which Redding is so emotionally charged that he is reduced to singing vocables.

Live, Redding was the classic soul performer. He was always in action, continually sweating and discarding superfluous clothes as the performance went on. He generally used Booker T. & the MG's or the Bar-Kays as a backup band, but, as with the material, the type or quality of band did not really affect him.

He toured extensively from 1964 to 1967, achieving 17 hits on the rhythm-and-blues charts in the process (seven more Otis Redding records hit after his death). He had formed his own label, Jotis, recording Billy Young, Loretta Williams, and Arthur Conley, and he had also developed his own publishing company, Redwal Music. Redding was successful in Europe and was just starting to break through to the American white audience at the time of his death. Six months prior to that he had had a widely successful performance at the Monterey Pop Festival, and the song he was working on at the time of his death, "(Sittin' on) The Dock of the Bay," ironically became his first No. 1 hit. It reflected a somewhat softer sound and, perhaps, indicated a new direction.

ROBERT BOWMAN
Memphis, Tennessee

Clive Anderson, in *The Soul Book*, ed. Ian Hoare (1975); Geoff Brown, *Otis Redding: Try a Little Tenderness* (2003); Scott Freeman, *Otis! The Otis Redding Story* (2002); Gerri Hirshey, *Nowhere to Run: The Story of Soul Music* (1984); Jane Schiesel, *The Otis Redding Story* (1973).

Reece, Florence

(1907–1986) WRITER AND SOCIAL ACTIVIST.

Florence Reece is the author of several poems, short stories, and songs. A coal miner's daughter from Sharp's Chapel, Tenn., she is best known for her struggle song "Which Side Are You On?," written to rally support for the 1930 United Mine Workers' strike in Harlan County, Ky. No political ideologue, Reece wrote her song out of a sense of desperation when her husband, Sam, was blacklisted, beaten, and driven from their home because of his activities as a union organizer among his fellow miners. As she watched her children and others in the community suffer hunger and deprivation, Reece attempted to deal with her anger by writing these lyrics on the back of a calendar, reflecting the centuries-old southern folk tradition of articulating and simplifying complex personal and social problems through songs and storytelling. Along the picket lines across the South, her simple statement, rising out of a great frustration with the unfair exploitation of laborers and identifying the need for solidarity among all workers, quickly became a familiar chant sung to the tune of the old hymn, "I Am Going to Land on That Shore":

> If you go to Harlan County
> There is no neutral there.
> You will either be a union man,
> Or a thug for J. H. Blair.
> Which side are you on?

Reece's militant assertion that the poor and the powerless "had to be for themselves, or against themselves" is the message that made "Which Side Are You On?" as meaningful to civil rights workers in Harlem during the 1960s as to the miners of Harlan County during the 1930s.

Reece, who came from the same impoverished section of Tennessee as

Roy Acuff, continued to write prose and verse, finding her voice in the traditional themes of country and western music—motherhood, home, and country. In 1981 she published a collection of her work, *Against the Current*, which shows her abiding concern with social commentary and the problems of her people:

> If you take away their food stamps,
> And all their other means,
> What're you going to feed them on?
> They can't live on jelly beans.

BARBARA L. BELLOWS
Middlebury College

John W. Hevener, *A New Deal for Harlan: The Roosevelt Policies in a Kentucky Coal Field, 1931–1939* (1978), *Which Side Are You On? The Harlan County Miners, 1931–39* (1978); Loyal Jones, *Appalachian Journal* (Fall 1984).

Reed, Jimmy

(1925–1976) BLUES SINGER.
Jimmy Reed was born Mathis James Reed on 6 September 1925, the youngest of 10 children. His parents, Joseph Reed and Virginia Ross, were sharecroppers on a Delta plantation near the small hamlet of Dunleith, Miss. Reed attended public schools briefly, but after he finished third grade he began working in the fields full time. When he was about 10, a family member gave him his first acoustic guitar, and Reed also started playing harmonica.

In the late 1930s, after his family moved to Shaw, Miss., Reed joined a gospel quartet. Although it was doing well, he eventually decided to leave the group and move in with his brother and work on plantations near Duncan, Miss. He would often slip out of the fields and go up to the house to listen to bluesman, such as Sonny Boy Williamson I, Sonny Boy Williamson II, and Robert Jr. Lockwood, who were performing on the *King Biscuit Time* radio show. Jimmy also met Eddie Taylor, a young guitarist who was trying to make a living by traveling the Mississippi Delta and playing the blues. The two musicians would form a rocky musical relationship, which would last until Reed's death.

There is still some discussion about Taylor's influence on Jimmy Reed's musical style. "The Jimmy Reed style is MY style," Taylor himself often stated. "He don't have no style. And I got the style from Charley Patton and Robert Johnson." Reed did not agree with his partner, however. "[Eddie Taylor] ain't had nothing to with it, no more than just durin' the time when we was down South," he said. In any case, Taylor and Reed would often play together after a day of work in the fields. After a falling out with a white overseer, Reed decided to leave Mississippi and head for the big city. He was 18 years old.

In Chicago, Reed briefly worked as janitor at the YMCA and as coal hiker at the Hefter Coal Company, before he was drafted into the navy in 1943. After the war Reed started playing his harmonica and guitar in blues clubs around Gary, Ind., and in Chicago. In 1949 Taylor also moved north, and together the two boyhood friends performed in the bars on Chicago's South Side. Four years later they began recording for the Vee-Jay label, and in 1955 Reed scored his first hit with "You Don't Have to Go."

During the 1950s and early 1960s, Jimmy Reed was one of the most popular blues artists in the United States. His music appealed to a broad audience and cut across the color line, although Reed primarily played for white people at the height of his career. Numbers like "Ain't That Lovin' You Baby," "Honest I Do," "Baby, What You Want Me to Do," "Big Boss Man," and "Bright Lights, Big City" all became instant classics. Reed had 11 songs on the *Billboard* Hot 100 pop charts and over a dozen on the R&B charts. His music was popular among British bands, including the Rolling Stones and the Beatles. Elvis Presley, Ike and Tina Turner, Muddy Waters, and Chuck Berry were some of the artists who recorded versions of his songs. Reed's songs not only became blues standards but also crossed over into other music styles, such as rock and roll, soul, and country and western.

But Jimmy Reed's thriving career also had its darker sides. Like so many other blues singers, he saw most of the profits that were made on his records disappear into the bank accounts of various record corporations. The strenuous life on the road took a heavy toll on his health. Moreover, Reed suffered from epilepsy and chronic alcoholism, which proved to be a deadly combination. By the late 1960s his popularity had waned considerably. The Big Boss Man, as he was known, tried to make a comeback during the 1970s, but by that time his days as a successful bluesman were over. He died on 29 August 1976 after a show at the Savoy in San Francisco.

MAARTEN ZWIERS
University of Mississippi

Jim O'Neal, *Living Blues* (May/June 1975); Will Romano, *Big Boss Man: The Life & Music of Jimmy Reed* (2006).

R.E.M.

ROCK BAND.

R.E.M. was formed in 1980 by University of Georgia students Bill Berry, Peter Buck, Mike Mills, and Michael Stipe in Athens, Ga., and is known as a pioneering college rock band that bridged the gap between the post-punk era of the late 1970s and early 1980s and the alternative-rock era of the late 1980s and early 1990s. Stipe and Buck met at Wuxtry Records in downtown Athens and soon joined Mills and Berry (who had played music together while in high school in Macon, Ga.) to write songs and play at parties in the college town. The name "R.E.M." was chosen randomly from a dictionary by Stipe. The band was known for a unique sound, which was created by Stipe's low, mumbling vocals, Buck's oft-labeled "jangly," chord-driven lead guitar, Mill's progressive, melodic bass playing, and Berry's adept drumming, which combined a variety of genres and styles. Their first full-length album, *Murmur*, was chosen by *Rolling Stone* magazine as the album of the year in 1983, an acknowledgment that jump-started five years of constant touring and recording under the I.R.S. label. In 1988 R.E.M. signed with Warner Brothers and released some of its most critically acclaimed albums, including *Out of Time* (1990) and *Automatic for the People* (1992). In 1997 Bill Berry left the band to pursue farming, and R.E.M. continued as a trio. Although forced to reassess its songwriting process, the band has adapted and subsequently released albums that have been praised for their depth, tone, and quality of songwriting.

The many R.E.M. albums reflect a sense of the South, primarily through Stipe's lyrics, which, while considered a bit enigmatic, integrate southern sayings. *Murmur* features the song "Sitting Still" in which Stipe sings "Up to par, Katie bars the kitchen signs but not me in," using the phrase "Katie bar," meaning that one should prepare for coming trouble. The album *Fables of the Reconstruction* (1985) demonstrates some of the most overt references among the band's early music. "Can't Get There from Here" uses the common saying when asking for directions south of the Mason-Dixon Line as the title of the song, while the tune "Life and How to Live It" is about the late, mentally disturbed, Athens, Ga., writer Brivs Mekis. "Maps and Legends" is dedicated to the late Georgia folk artist Howard Finster, who designed the cover of the band's second album, *Reckoning* (1984). The final song on the record, "Wendell Gee," was named for a used car salesman who lived in Pendergrass, Ga. "Swan Swan H," from *Lifes Rich Pageant* (1986), is about the period of Reconstruction in the South and references Johnny Reb and the making of items from bones (presumably from casualties of war). The signature hit from *Out of Time*, "Losing My Religion," echoes earlier songs by using a common southern phrase describing how an individual can be driven almost to distraction, in the case of the song, by a simple crush. R.E.M.'s later music still retains references to the South, as in *Reveal*'s (2001) "Chorus and the Ring," when Stipe sings, "It's the knowing with the wink that we expect in southern women."

Visually, R.E.M. uses the work of southern artists and institutions in its music videos, album art work, and album titles. Rev. Howard Finster's Paradise Gardens, in Pennville, Ga., served as the setting for the video to "Radio Free Europe" (*Murmur*), as did folk artist R. A. Miller's whirligig farm outside of Gainesville, Ga., for the video for "Pretty Persuasion" (*Reckoning*). The video for "Low" (*Out of Time*) uses pieces of art from the Georgia Museum of Art's collection, featuring the painting *La Confidence* (c. 1883) by Elizabeth Jane Gardner Bouguereau. Most notable is the band's use of "Automatic for the People," the motto of Weaver D's, a soul food restaurant owned by Dexter Weaver in Athens.

R.E.M.'s impact on Athens is multi-faceted. Its influence on the music scene in the city continues and has resulted in constant national attention for local up-and-coming bands. The band members have shifted their focus to local issues by supporting many local charities and historic preservation efforts as well as lending their support to local politicians.

In 2006 R.E.M. was inducted into both the Rock and Roll Hall of Fame and the Georgia Music Hall of Fame.

RENNA TUTEN
University of Georgia

Marcus Gray, *It Crawled from the South: An R.E.M. Companion* (1993); Rodger Lyle Brown, *Party out of Bounds: The B-52's,*

R.E.M., and the Kids Who Rocked Athens, Georgia (1991); R.E.M.: The Rolling Stone Files: The Ultimate Compendium of Interviews, Articles, Facts, and Opinions from the Files of Rolling Stone (1995).

Revival Songs

The poetry and music of revivalism has been a major influence in American popular culture, especially in the South. In the first camp meetings, around 1800, preachers found the psalms and hymns of congregational worship inadequate: traditional hymns did not sufficiently emphasize the individual's quest for salvation through specific stages (conviction, conversion, assurance) recognized by revival preachers; moreover, hymnbooks were of little use in largely illiterate gatherings often held at night. In response to the camp-meeting environment, Americans created two major forms of popular religious song during the period from 1810 to 1860.

"Camp-meeting songs," or "spiritual songs," were strophic poems, often in narrative form, stressing the stages of conversion and often referring to various groups at camp meetings: preachers, exhorters, mourners, backsliders, and young converts, as in the following stanza from George Atkin's "Holy Manna":

Is there here a trembling jailer,
Seeking grace, and fill'd with fears?
Is there here a weeping Mary,
Pouring forth a flood of tears?
Brethren, join your cries to help
  them;
Sisters, let your prayers abound;
Pray, O pray that holy manna
May be scatter'd all around.

Written in a great variety of poetic meters, these songs were often set to secular tunes, including those of folk songs, traditional dances, military marches, and popular theater airs.

"Revival spiritual songs," or "choruses," consisted of couplets or quatrains, often taken from British evangelical hymnody, alternating with refrains:

On Jordan's stormy banks I stand,
And cast a wishful eye,
To Canaan's fair and happy land,
Where my possessions lie. [Samuel
  Stennant]
CHORUS: I am bound for the
  promised land,
  I'm bound for the promised land,
  Oh, who will come and go with
  me?
  I am bound for the promised land.

Often elements of the revival chorus appear between the lines of the original hymn:

I know that my redeemer lives,
Glory, hallelujah.
What comfort that sweet sentence
  gives, [Samuel Medley]
Glory, hallelujah,
CHORUS: Shout on, pray on, we're
  getting ground,
  Glory, hallelujah,
  The dead's alive, and the lost is
  found.
  Glory, hallelujah.

Revival spiritual songs, with their call-and-response patterns, met the need for a flexible format in which new songs could be created and learned immediately by a large gathering.

Camp-meeting songsters, books containing revival poetry, were first published around 1810. The first southern collection of music for camp-meeting songs was Ananias Davisson's *Supplement to the Kentucky Harmony* (Harrisonburg, Va., 1820). Davisson's book, designed for "his Methodist friends," contained many camp-meeting songs and a few revival choruses. During the 1840s the music of many more revival spiritual songs was printed in southern tunebooks, including B. F. White and E. J. King's *The Sacred Harp* (1844) and William Houser's *The Hesperian Harp* (1848). After the Civil War, the black spiritual emerged, essentially the same as the revival spiritual, despite differences in the date and circumstances of its notation. Indeed, the prevalence of call-and-response forms in African American music and the presence of blacks at early camp meetings suggest that mutual influences may have played a role in the spiritual song traditions of both races.

The revival movements of the late 19th century favored a new style of music based on urban models, especially the sentimental parlor song. "Gospel hymns" like "Sweet By and By" (S. F. Bennett and J. P. Webster) and "Leaning on the Everlasting Arms" (E. A. Hoffman and A. J. Showalter) have reached beyond the revival context. Many have entered the Sunday worship of southern denominations, where they are considered "old standard" hymns, to the virtual exclusion of the camp-meeting genres that preceded them. Late 19th-century gospel hymns were also the model for the flourishing repertoire of shape-note gospel convention and quartet music.

DAVID WARREN STEEL
University of Mississippi

Dickson D. Bruce Jr., *And They All Sang Hallelujah: Plain-Folk Camp-Meeting Religion, 1800–1845* (1974); George Pullen Jackson, *White Spirituals in the Southern Uplands* (1933); Ellen Jane Lorenz, *Glory, Hallelujah! The Story of the Camp-Meeting Spiritual* (1978).

Ring Shouters

Ring shouting is the oldest African American song form still practiced in America. It combines worship song and distinctive dance. Separate from spirituals, ring shouts were often performed at important religious holidays by rice- and cotton-plantation slaves in the South Carolina and Georgia Lowcountry, where a high percentage of slaves were African-born and maintained much of their native heritage.

A ring shout begins in a church meetinghouse when a lead singer, or "songster," begins the song while seated next to a "sticker," who sets the rhythm by beating the wooden floor with a broom handle or other stick. Behind them a cluster of singers, called "basers," clap hands or stomp feet and answer the leader's lines in a call-and-response fashion. Gender roles are strictly followed. The songster, sticker, and basers are always male. Slowly the women, dressed in the attire of their ancestors, including floor-length dresses and head-rags, move in to form a ring. Moving counterclockwise, they shuffle their feet, making sure not to cross them. Crossing one's feet is considered dancing and deemed inappropriate. Women join the basers in singing answers to the songster. Those in the ring sway, raise hands, and swoop down low to the ground to reinforce the message being sung.

During slavery, ring shouts were often conducted in secret. Observances of the tradition date back to 1845. During and after the Civil War, ring shouts were frowned upon by northern white missionaries, one writing that it was "too African, [too] dangerously extravagant."

In her landmark book, *Slave Songs of the Georgia Sea Islands* (1942), Lydia Parish recorded ring shout songs from McIntosh County, Ga. By then ring shouts were only practiced by the remote Gullah populations of the Lowcountry.

By 1980 the tradition was thought to have died out, until folklorist Fred Fussell and Frankie and Doug Quimby heard rumors that "Watch Night," or New Year's Eve, was still celebrated with all-night shouts at Mt. Calvary Baptist Church in the Bolden community of McIntosh County.

With the encouragement of the Quimbys and others, outsiders have witnessed the normally private form of worship by the McIntosh Ring Shouters in local festivals on St. Simons and Sapelo Islands. Occasionally the Shouters perform outside the region as well.

WILLIAM S. BURDELL III
St. Simons Island, Georgia

The McIntosh County Shouters: Slave Shout Songs from the Coast of Georgia (Smith-

sonian/Folkways, cassette or CD, 1984); Lydia Parrish, *Slave Songs of the Georgia Sea Islands* (1942; reprint, 1992); Art Rosenbaum, *Shout Because You're Free: The African American Ring Shout Tradition in Coastal Georgia* (1998); Clate Sanders, producer, *Down Yonder: The McIntosh County Shouters*, Georgia Public Television, video.

Ritchie, Jean

(b. 1922) FOLK SINGER.

Although she grew up a traditional musician in the Cumberland Mountains of eastern Kentucky, having sung an extensive repertoire of folk ballads and songs taught to her by other family members during her childhood, Jean Ritchie has also been a commercially successful singer and songwriter who was nationally influential during the urban folk music revival of the mid- to late 20th century.

Born on 8 December 1922, in the small community of Viper, in Perry County, Ky., Jean Ritchie was the youngest of the 14 children born to Balis and Abigail Ritchie (both parents were of Scots-Irish descent). The Ritchie family was locally renowned for keeping alive the older regional music traditions that had originated in the British Isles and been transported to (and transformed within) Appalachia by settlers during the 18th and early 19th centuries. When in the late 1940s Jean Ritchie began performing and recording those ballads and songs outside her home community, many folklorists and folk music revivalists saw her as a living embodiment of an otherwise dying culture—those people shared the perception of English scholars Cecil Sharp and Maud Karpeles, who, in their classic study, *English Folk Songs from the Southern Appalachians* (originally published in 1917 and considerably revised in 1932), lamented the dramatic decline of traditional balladry among the people of Appalachia after the World War I era.

Upon graduating from high school, Ritchie left Viper to attend college. In 1946, after receiving the B.A. degree in social work from the University of Kentucky, Ritchie moved to New York City to work at the Henry Street Settlement, a social service and community arts organization. There, she incorporated her family's ballads and songs into her educational programs for urban children, an experience that helped Ritchie realize the value of her Appalachian cultural heritage. Her reputation as an authentically traditional singer spread across New York City, which then was the epicenter of the burgeoning national urban folk music revival, and by the late 1940s she was appearing in folk music clubs in other cities. In 1949 Ritchie recorded ballads and stories for folklorist Alan Lomax and the Archive of American Folk Song at the Library of Congress. Ritchie's first commercial recordings were released in 1952 on an album issued by the Elektra label; later that year, she received a Fulbright award to study traditional music in the British Isles. In 1954 Ritchie released the album *Field Trip* on her own label, Greenhays Recordings. That album juxtaposed field recordings of traditional ballads and songs she had made in England, Scotland, and Ireland with recordings of her

own performances of those same ballads and songs from her family's repertoire. Among Ritchie's other important recordings were her 1961 two-album set on the Folkways label, *British Traditional Ballads in the Southern Mountains*; the 1963 live album for Folkways, *Jean Ritchie and Doc Watson at Folk City*; Ritchie's 1977 album on Greenhays, *None but One*, which combined her recordings of traditional material with several performances of her own song compositions (more extensively produced than her earlier recordings to appeal to a new audience, this album received a critics' award from *Rolling Stone* magazine); and her 1992 Greenhays album *The Most Dulcimer*, which showcased her playing on the instrument known as the Appalachian dulcimer. Ritchie is generally credited with having popularized that instrument during the urban folk music revival of the late 20th century.

Much of Ritchie's performance repertoire has long consisted of her family's beloved traditional ballads and songs; yet she has also sung Old Regular Baptist hymns as well as commercial songs she learned from listening to records or the radio. Although she did not have extensive formal musical training, Ritchie was always a sophisticated performer who was quite influential. (Bob Dylan was alleged to have based the melody of his protest song "Masters of War" on Ritchie's rendition of the traditional British mummer's song "Nottamun Town.") Additionally, Ritchie has been widely respected for her songwriting. Her best-known songs—"Now Is the Cool of the Day," "The L&N Don't Stop Here Anymore," "Black Waters," "Blue Diamond Mines," and "My Dear Companion"—have been recorded by numerous musicians working in such popular music genres as revivalist folk, bluegrass, country rock, and Americana.

Finally, Ritchie is a noted author of books. Her classic memoir, *Singing Family of the Cumberlands* (1955), memorably conveyed her experience of growing up within a highly musical culture in rural, pre–World War II eastern Kentucky. The book featured transcriptions of many of the traditional ballads and songs sung by members of her family. Other books by Ritchie include a popular instrument instruction manual, *The Dulcimer Book* (1963), and her collection of transcribed folk music from Appalachia, *The Swapping Song Book* (1965).

For her life's work, Ritchie has received several prestigious awards, including, in 2002, the National Endowment for the Arts' Heritage Fellowship and, in 2003, the University of Kentucky Associates Medallion for Intellectual Achievement. Also in 2003, Ritchie was inducted into the Kentucky Music Hall of Fame.

TED OLSON
East Tennessee State University

Karen L. Carter-Schwendler, "Traditional Background, Contemporary Context: The Music and Activities of Jean Ritchie to 1977" (Ph.D. diss., University of Kentucky, 1995); H. Russell Farmer and Guy Mendes, producers, *Mountain Born: The Jean Ritchie Story*, Kentucky Educational Television, 1996.

Rodgers, Jimmie

(1897–1933) COUNTRY MUSIC SINGER.

Generally acknowledged as "the Father of Country Music," James Charles "Jimmie" Rodgers, who was born 8 September 1897 in Meridian, Miss., was a major influence on the emerging hillbilly recording industry almost from the time of his first records in 1927. Although Rodgers initially conceived of himself in broader terms, singing Tin Pan Alley hits and popular standards, his intrinsic musical talent was deeply rooted in the rural southern environment out of which he came, as seen in the titles of many of his songs: "My Carolina Sunshine Girl," "My Little Old Home Down in New Orleans," "Dear Old Sunny South by the Sea," "Mississippi River Blues," "Peach Pickin' Time Down in Georgia," "Memphis Yodel," "In the Hills of Tennessee," the original "Blue Yodel" ("T for Texas"), and others.

In adapting the black country blues of his native South to the nascent patterns of commercial hillbilly music of the day, Rodgers created a unique new form—the famous "blue yodel"—which led the way to further innovations in style and subject matter and exerted a lasting influence on country music as both art form and industry. Through the force of his magnetic personality and showmanship, Rodgers almost single-handedly established the role of the singing star, influencing such later performers as Gene Autry, Hank Williams, Ernest Tubb, George Jones, and Willie Nelson.

The son of a track foreman for the Mobile & Ohio Railroad, Rodgers in

Jimmie Rodgers, the "Father of Country Music," 1929 (Jimmie Rodgers Museum, Meridian, Miss.)

his twenties worked as a brakeman for many railroads in the South and the West. Stricken by tuberculosis in 1924, he left the rails soon after to pursue his childhood dream of becoming a professional entertainer. After several years of hard knocks and failure, he gained an audition with Ralph Peer, an independent producer who had set up a temporary recording studio in Bristol, Tenn., for the Victor Talking Machine Company (later RCA Victor). There, on 4 August 1927, Rodgers made his first recordings. Within a year he reached national popularity and received billing as "The Singing Brakeman" and "America's Blue Yodeler." In 1929 he built a home in the resort town of Kerrville, Tex., and moved there in an effort to restore his failing health. The onset of the Depression and increasing illness further slowed the progress of his career, but

throughout the early 1930s he continued to record and perform with touring stage shows. By the time of his death in New York City at 35, in May 1933, he had recorded 110 titles, representing a diverse repertoire that included almost every type of song now identified with country music: love ballads, honky-tonk tunes, railroad and hobo songs, cowboy songs, novelty numbers, and the series of 13 blue yodels. In November 1961 Rodgers became the first performer elected to Nashville's Country Music Hall of Fame, immortalized as "the man who started it all." The Jimmie Rodgers Memorial Museum, in Meridian, Miss., hosts the annual Jimmie Rodgers Memorial Festival, which began in May 1953.

NOLAN PORTERFIELD
Cape Girardeau, Missouri

Bill C. Malone, *Country Music, U.S.A.: A Fifty-Year History* (1968); Nolan Porterfield, *Jimmie Rodgers: The Life and Times of America's Blue Yodeler* (1979); Mrs. Jimmie Rodgers, *My Husband, Jimmie Rodgers* (1975).

Scruggs, Earl

(b. 1924) BLUEGRASS MUSICIAN.
Earl Eugene Scruggs was born on 6 January 1924, in Cleveland County, N.C., on a farm near the small community of Flint Hill. He was the youngest of five children. His father, who played the banjo, died when Scruggs was four; his mother, brothers, and sisters all played music. By the time he was six he was playing string band music with his brothers. Scruggs learned fiddle and guitar but specialized in the five-string banjo. Before he was a teenager he de-

veloped a distinctive three-finger picking style based on that of older men in his neighborhood. In his teens Scruggs played locally with professional bands, but World War II put a temporary end to this; he worked in a textile mill until 1945. In December 1945 he became a member of Bill Monroe's Blue Grass Boys on wsm's *Grand Ole Opry*. In personal appearances and recordings with Monroe, Scruggs created a sensation with his banjo playing, and he quickly became one of the most emulated instrumentalists in country music.

In 1948 Scruggs left Monroe and teamed up with his partner in the Blue Grass Boys, guitarist-singer Lester Flatt, to form the Foggy Mountain Boys. In 1953, after modest beginnings on small radio stations, their broadcast career was given a considerable boost by the sponsorship of a flour manufacturer, Martha White Mills. In 1955 they joined the cast of the *Grand Ole Opry*, where they became one of its most popular and widely traveled acts. During the late 1950s they were responsible for popularizing bluegrass with folk music audiences outside the South. Their greatest exposure came through their association in 1962 with the popular CBS television series *The Beverly Hillbillies*, for which they recorded the theme and incidental music. Many of their Mercury (1948–50) and Columbia (1951–69) recordings are still available. A key figure in the success of Flatt and Scruggs was Earl's wife, Louise Certain Scruggs, who acted as the band's booking agent and publicist, a role she performed for her husband until her death in 2006. In

1969 Flatt and Scruggs won a Grammy award for Scruggs's instrumental "Foggy Mountain Breakdown." That same year they separated.

Earl began performing with sons Gary and Randy, and by 1972 they had organized as the Earl Scruggs Revue. With his banjo amplified, Earl fronted a band that featured country-rock repertoire and sound. The Revue (which eventually included another son, Steve) toured successfully throughout the 1970s, playing to younger, more urban audiences than those for which he and Flatt had performed. They recorded 16 albums for Columbia. By 1980 Scruggs was working as a single act, recording and appearing with various musicians, including the Dillards, Tom T. Hall, and Ricky Skaggs.

In 1971 Scruggs was closely involved with the conception and production of the award-winning album *Will the Circle Be Unbroken*, which brought together members of the California rock group the Nitty Gritty Dirt Band with pioneer Nashville musicians. In this and other activities he has shown an interest in bridging the social and musical gaps between the rural South of his youth and the urbanized world of his sons.

Scruggs was an inaugural inductee into the Bluegrass Hall of Fame in 1991. In 2002 he won a Grammy award for a new 2001 recording of "Foggy Mountain Breakdown," the same song that garnered him the award in 1969. The 2001 song came from a collaborative album entitled *Earl Scruggs and Friends*, which featured performances from a diverse array of artists, including Elton

John, Sting, and Johnny Cash. On 13 February 2003, Scruggs received a star on the Hollywood Walk of Fame.

NEIL V. ROSENBERG
Memorial University
St. Johns, Newfoundland

Neil V. Rosenberg, *Bluegrass: A History* (1985), in *Stars of Country Music*, ed. Bill C. Malone and Judith McCullough (1975); Earl Scruggs, *Earl Scruggs and the Five-String Banjo* (1968).

Seeger, Mike

(b. 1933) FOLK REVIVAL MUSICIAN AND FOLKLORIST.

Mike Seeger has arguably been the single figure most responsible for bringing traditional music of the American South to urban audiences around the world. Although other members of his illustrious family, especially his parents, Charles and Ruth Crawford Seeger, and his half brother, Pete, have earned equal or greater renown for the varied aspects of their careers in American music, Mike's undivided attention to championing authentic southern traditional music, and specifically its musical aspects rather than sociopolitical potential, secures his position as its premier ambassador.

Born on 15 August 1933 into one of America's most important musical families, Mike Seeger was surrounded by music from his early childhood. His parents were among the most important early figures in the American art music world to develop a deep interest in American vernacular music. Charles Seeger started as a composer and conductor but went on to earn the title

"Father of American Musicology." Ruth Crawford was a preeminent woman composer of the early 20th century. Both became involved with the Library of Congress's efforts to document traditional southern music, which was deemed threatened by the forces of modernization and commercialization. This music sounded throughout the Seeger household, and although Mike did not seriously approach learning to play a musical instrument until his teens, all the Seeger children participated in Saturday singings. Once he did get interested in learning the southern instrumental styles, starting with the autoharp, Mike soon mastered a number of instruments in a wide variety of playing styles, and he has continued to expand his instrumental arsenal over the ensuing decades. This includes banjo, fiddle, guitar, mandolin, jaw harp, and quills.

By his early twenties, Mike Seeger had become a major force in bringing to the attention of urban audiences undiscovered or forgotten southern music greats. Some of the seminal albums of authentic southern music in the early stages of the 1950s and 1960s folk boom were produced by Seeger for Moses Asch's Washington, D.C.–based Folkways records. These included *American Banjo: Three-Finger and Scruggs Style* (1957) and *Mountain Music Bluegrass Style* (1959)—two albums that augured the popular acceptance of bluegrass as a distinctive genre of southern acoustic string band music. *Negro Folk Songs and Tunes* (1957) introduced the highly influential Piedmont finger-style guitarist

Elizabeth Cotton, who had been working as a domestic in the Seeger household. *The Stoneman Family and Old Time Southern Music* (1957) and *McGee Brothers and Arthur Smith: Oldtimers of the Grand Ole Opry* brought stalwarts of early hillbilly music to the attention of the nascent urban folk revival scene. And *The Country Gentlemen* (1959) and *The Lilly Brothers and Don Stover* (1961) documented the migration of bluegrass to northern cities. Through the peak years of the folk revival, Seeger organized concerts and tours that featured many forgotten southern legends. Among others, this list includes Eck Robertson, Dock Boggs, Roscoe Holcomb, Wade Ward, Kilby Snow, Maybelle Carter, and Tommy Jarrell.

Meanwhile, having mastered a number of southern traditional musical styles, Mike Seeger also launched his performing and recording career. With Mike Cohen and Tom Paley, he formed the New Lost City Ramblers, likely that era's most important urban folk revival string band and one that influenced countless urban youngsters to follow suit. The Ramblers countered the major trend in popular music circles—that of performing diluted, often sing-along, versions of southern traditional music as popularized by artists such as the Weavers, the Kingston Trio, and Peter, Paul, and Mary. Equally important, and increasingly so after Tracy Schwarz replaced Paley in 1963, the Ramblers seamlessly integrated bluegrass with older musical styles, earning for bluegrass a sense of folk authenticity that many fastidious old-time and folk music enthusiasts were wary of according this

commercial form. By the latter half of the 1960s, as folk music became integrated with electrified rock, it became difficult for a traditional musician to sustain a professional career as part of an acoustic string band, and Seeger increasingly concentrated on a solo career, which continues today. Along the way, there have been a number of collaborations, including reunion concerts with the Ramblers and one album with the Strange Creek Singers featuring Seeger, Schwarz, Hazel Dickens, Lamar Grier, and Seeger's wife, Alice Gerrard.

Among many honors, Seeger has received four grants from the National Endowment for the Arts, six Grammy award nominations, a Guggenheim Fellowship, and the Rex Foundation's Ralph J. Gleason Award. For his extensive knowledge of southern music and culture, Seeger has been called upon to act as adviser to a number of agencies concerned with preserving southern traditional heritages, including the National Endowment for the Arts, the Department of State, and the Smithsonian Institution. He has served on the board of directors for the Newport Folk Festival, the National Folk Festival, and the American Old Time Music Festival.

AJAY KALRA
University of Texas at Austin

Mark Greenberg, *Sing Out!* 38, no. 4 (1994); Dick Spottswood, *Bluegrass Unlimited* (May 1985).

Shape-Note Singing Schools

The singing school was early America's most important musical institution. It offered a brief course in musical sight reading and choral singing, was taught by a singing master according to traditional methods, and used tunebooks, which were printed manuals containing instructions, exercises, and sacred choral music. Singing schools arose from British antecedents around 1700 as part of an effort to reform congregational singing in colonial churches. In New England the movement grew quickly and culminated in the first school of American composers and in the publication of hundreds of sacred tunebooks (1770–1810). Singing schools existed in the South as early as 1710, when they are mentioned in the diary of William Byrd II of Virginia. The movement spread during the 18th century as a pious diversion among affluent planters along the Atlantic Seaboard. After the Revolutionary War, itinerant Yankee singing masters established singing schools in the inland and rural South. Both Andrew Law (1749–1821) of Connecticut and Lucius Chapin (1760–1842) of Massachusetts were teaching in Virginia by the 1780s; in 1794 Chapin moved to Kentucky, where he taught for 40 years. Singing schools offered young southerners a rare chance to socialize. Even today, many older southerners associate singing schools with their courting days.

The spread of singing schools through the South was aided by the invention of shape or patent notes. This system, first published by William Little and William Smith in *The Easy Instructor* (Philadelphia, 1801), used four distinctive note heads to indicate the four syllables denoting tones of a musical scale (*fa*, *sol*, *la*, and *mi*) then employed in vocal instruction, making unnecessary the pupil's need to learn and memorize key signatures. Denounced by critics as uncouth, the simplified notation caught on in the South and West, where it became standard for sacred music publication. In 1816 Ananias Davisson (1780–1857) and Joseph Funk (1777–1862), both of Rockingham County, Va., became the first southern singing masters to compile and publish their own tunebooks. By 1860 more than 30 sacred tunebooks, all in shape notes, had been compiled by southerners, although many of these were printed outside the South, at Cincinnati or Philadelphia. One of the most popular of these was *The Southern Harmony*, by William Walker, of Spartanburg, S.C.: 600,000 copies were sold between 1835 and the beginning of the Civil War. *The Sacred Harp* (1844), by Georgia singing masters B. F. White and E. J. King, is still in print and is the basis of a flourishing musical tradition in six southern states.

Southern singing masters continued to teach the music of their Yankee predecessors but also introduced "folk hymns," melodies from oral tradition, which they harmonized in a native idiom and set to sacred words. Many, including tunes for "Amazing Grace" and "How Firm a Foundation," have remained popular and have become symbols of rural southern religion. Camp-meeting and revival songs with new refrains also formed part of the southern tunebook repertoire, especially after 1840. Southern singing masters established organizations such as the Southern Musical Association (1845) and the Chattahoochie Musical Association (1852, still active). These and other state and local conventions provided a forum where established teachers met to sing together, to examine and certify new teachers, and to demonstrate the accomplishments of their classes.

After the Civil War, singing schools and shape notes became increasingly identified with the South, while declining in popularity in other regions. Most teachers switched from the four-shape system to a seven-shape system to keep pace with new teaching methods. Leading singing masters established "normal schools" for the training of teachers. Periodicals such as *The Musical Million* (Dayton, Va., 1870–1915) helped to link teachers in many areas of the South. Small, cheap collections of music published every year began to supplant the large tunebooks, with their fixed repertoire. Although folk hymns and revival songs continued to be published, gospel hymns derived from urban models entered the southern tradition.

In the 20th century, singing schools have declined over most of the region but have survived in a few areas. They seldom last more than two weeks of evening classes, and may be as brief as one week. Pupils pay at least a token fee, but few teachers, if any, attempt to make a living as singing masters. Contemporary singing schools fall into three categories: (1) "Tunebook" schools are associated with surviving 19th-century books such as *The Sacred Harp* or *The Christian Harmony*. These schools preserve much of the 18th-century American repertoire and performance practice. (2) Denominational schools are sponsored by churches, especially by those (Primitive Baptist, Church of Christ) that prohibit instrumental music in their worship. These schools use denominational hymnals and, like their 18th-century predecessors, attempt to train skilled sight readers for congregational singing. (3) Shape-note gospel singing schools are associated with the "little-book" seven-shape gospel repertoire. These schools, often sponsored by local singing conventions or by publishing companies, have declined since mid-century as community "sings" have been replaced by quartet performances. All three types of singing schools are regarded by their adherents as important means of transmitting musical knowledge, skills, and traditions to future generations.

DAVID WARREN STEEL
University of Mississippi

Buell E. Cobb Jr., *The Sacred Harp: A Tradition and Its Music* (1978); Harry Eskew, "Shape-Note Hymnody in the Shenandoah Valley, 1816–1860" (Ph.D. diss., Tulane University, 1966); George Pullen Jackson, *White Spirituals in the Southern Uplands* (1933).

Shore, Dinah

(1917–1994) ENTERTAINER.
Francis Rose Shore was born on 29 February 1917 in Winchester, Tenn., to Solomon and Anna Stein Shore, Jewish Russian immigrants who owned a dry goods store in the town. At the age of two, Shore was stricken with polio. Although her family managed to obtain excellent care for the child, she was left with a somewhat deformed foot and a limp. The Shore family moved to Nashville in 1925, and Francis Rose became active in school and in extracurricular activities, including cheerleading,

sports, and music. The young woman's activities became more focused on music, and by the time she graduated from Vanderbilt University in 1938 she had made her radio debut on WSM. Pursuing a career in music led Shore to New York City, where she auditioned frequently for radio shows, singing the song "Dinah." Disc jockey Martin Block labeled her "the Dinah girl," resulting in Shore's stage name.

Shore became a singer on WNEW in New York, as well as on NBC in 1938, and signed a contract with RCA Victor in 1940. Her first starring show was the *Chamber Music Society of Lower Basin Street*, produced by NBC radio, and she joined Eddie Cantor's radio program *Time to Smile* in 1941. As the decade progressed, Shore starred in her own radio programs for General Foods and Proctor & Gamble and entertained American troops in the European Theater of Operations. She also starred in many films, including *Thank Your Lucky Stars* (1943), *Belle of the Yukon* (1944), *Till the Clouds Roll By* (1946), and *Fun and Fancy Free* (1947). She starred in *The Dinah Shore Show* from 1951 to 1956 and *The Dinah Shore Chevy Show* from 1956 to 1963, becoming a rare entity in the entertainment industry, a woman with a variety show—and a successful one at that. In the 1970s Shore shifted her focus to numerous variety and talk shows, which she continued into the early 1990s. She was the recipient of Emmy awards in 1956, 1957, 1973, 1974, and 1976.

Dinah Shore was associated with the South throughout her career, due to her down-home, girl-next-door image and her accent. Her early recording of "Blues in the Night" established this image, and later recordings such as "Buttons and Bows" and "Pass the Jam, Sam" used it to create hits and a large following. Playing upon her southern identity also produced a laugh for *The Carol Burnett Show* in the skit "Went with the Wind," when Shore portrayed the character Melanie from *Gone with the Wind*.

In the 1980s and 1990s, Shore came full circle back to Nashville when her final television shows were shown on TNN, the last being "Dinah Comes Home" (1991), in which she returned to the *Grand Ole Opry*. Shore died in Beverly Hills, Calif., on 24 February 1994.

RENNA TUTEN
University of Georgia

Bruce Cassidy, *Dinah! A Biography* (1979).

Silas Green Show

Silas Green from New Orleans was a traveling minstrel show that was owned, written, managed, and performed by black people. For over a half century (1907–58) the Silas Green Company toured urban and rural communities exclusively in the South and established itself as an institution among its black and white segregated audiences. Approximately ten months a year, six nights a week, the show traveled throughout Florida, Georgia, North and South Carolina, Virginia and West Virginia, Tennessee, Kentucky, Mississippi, Arkansas, Louisiana, and Alabama.

The family-oriented comedy and musical show combined the theatrical traditions of minstrelsy and black musical comedy. White minstrelsy created the "blackface," and the writers of *Silas Green* retained the use of the burnt cork makeup for the main characters of their show. The comedy, however, was acted out in the context of a loosely woven plot that had continuity—a break with minstrelsy that was pioneered by Cole and Johnson in 1898 with *A Trip to Coontown*, the first black musical comedy. The comic story of the *Silas Green Show* was interspersed with several chorus line numbers, one or two blues singers, and specialty acts that displayed a wide range of versatile talents. The musical sounds of *Silas Green from New Orleans* echoed the creative and innovative talents of black Americans. The band played ragtime, jazz, and swing tunes composed by southern and northern blacks, heralding and disseminating the music of its people throughout the South.

During the show's most successful years, in the 1930s and 1940s, the troupe numbered up to 75, and the tent in which the production was performed nightly had the capacity to accommodate an audience of more than 2,500 people. Buses, automobiles, and a Pullman car were used to transport the troupe, for it was important in the hostile racial environment of the South that the show travel as a unit. Furthermore, most of the local black communities could not provide all of the sleeping and eating facilities for the members of the company. The Pullman car and trailers provided these necessities.

Throughout its existence, *Silas Green from New Orleans* was black owned and controlled. The first owner of the company was "Professor" Eph Williams, a former circus performer and owner. Eph Williams acquired the show known as the *Jolly Ethiopians* from S. H. Dudley Sr. and Salem Tutt Whitney and renamed it the *Silas Green Company*. After Williams's death in 1921, Charles Collier, a protégé of Williams, bought the show and is credited with reorganizing and rejuvenating it. Collier died in 1942; his wife, Hortense, maintained the company until 1944 when she sold it to a partnership of Rodney Harris, Charles Morton, and Wilbur Jones. Jones soon bought out his partners and was the sole owner until he took it off the road in 1958. According to Jones, the three main factors contributing to the show's demise were increased overhead expenses, the popularity of television, and heightened racial tensions in the South brought on by the 1954 Supreme Court decision in *Brown v. Board of Education* declaring segregation in public schools unconstitutional.

Silas Green from New Orleans was probably the longest-running black-owned minstrel show in the United States. Noted personalities such as Ma Rainey, Bessie Smith, Dewey "Pigmeat" Markham, Mamie Smith, Nipsey Russell, Johnny Huggins, and the comedy team of Butterbeans and Susie were members of the cast for varying lengths of time.

ELEANOR J. BAKER
Bloomington, Indiana

Chicago Defender (2 July 1921, 24 June 1922, 16 April 1932); James W. Johnson, *Black Manhattan* (1968); John Johnson, *Ebony* (September 1954); Major Robinson, *Our World* (April 1949).

Smith, Bessie

(1894–1937) BLUES SINGER.
When Bessie Smith made her first
recordings, in 1923, she carved out for
herself a permanent niche in blues and
jazz history. By that time, her magnificent voice, captured by the relatively
primitive acoustical equipment of the
day, was already well known and greatly
admired throughout the South.

Born in Chattanooga, Tenn., on 15
April 1894, Smith had her first show
business experience when she was about
eight: accompanied by her brother
Andrew with his guitar, she danced and
sang for small change on a Ninth Street
corner. It was another brother, Clarence,
who in 1912 arranged for her to join a
traveling troupe led by Moses Stokes.
With this company, which also included
Gertrude "Ma" Rainey, Bessie Smith
launched her professional career.

Within a year Bessie Smith had left
the Stokes troupe and started to build
a faithful following among southern
theater audiences, especially in Atlanta,
where she became a regular attraction
at the 81 Theater. In the 1920s, she rose
to the pinnacle of her profession and
became the highest-paid black entertainer of her day. So great was her
popularity that her appearances caused
serious traffic jams around theaters
from Detroit to New Orleans. During
eight years as an exclusive Columbia
Records artist, she made 156 sides, some
of which saved that company from
bankruptcy, and all of which, over a
half century later, are still in catalogs
throughout the world.

Promotional hype dubbed her "Empress of the Blues," and the title remains
unchallenged, but Bessie Smith was not
restricted to that idiom. She was, along
with Louis Armstrong, the consummate
jazz singer, and her majestic delivery
became a major inspiration to such
successful and diverse singers as Billie
Holiday, Mahalia Jackson, and Janis
Joplin.

A victim of the Great Depression,
new musical trends, and a changing
entertainment scene, Bessie Smith saw
her career plummet in the early 1930s,
but it was on the upswing as the decade
went into its last lap. Sadly, the great
singer was not to enjoy the comeback
that seemed inevitable in 1937, nor
would she ever know the enormous impact of her artistry on American music.
On 26 September 1937, as she traveled
from Memphis for an appearance in
Clarksdale, Miss., a car accident took
her life. Her tragic death inspired contemporary playwright Edward Albee's
drama, *The Death of Bessie Smith*.

CHRIS ALBERTSON
New York, New York

Chris Albertson, *Bessie* (1972); Angela Y.
Davis, *Blues Legacies and Black Feminism:
Gertrude "Ma" Rainey, Bessie Smith, and
Billie Holiday* (1998); Will Friedwald, *Jazz
Singing: America's Great Voices from Bessie
Smith to Bebop and Beyond* (1996); Alexan-
dria Manera, *Bessie Smith* (2003).

Southern Culture on the Skids

ROCK BAND.
A little bit silly, a little bit raunchy, and
a whole lot of fun, Southern Culture on
the Skids, or SCOTS, as it is known to its
fans, has been a popular and influential
band since the mid-1980s. Guitarist and
singer Rick Miller cofounded the group

in Chapel Hill, N.C., in 1985, partly as a protest against the alternative southern rock of R.E.M. and others, as well as the heavily commercialized pop and country then dominating the airwaves. By 1988 the group had re-formed as a trio when Miller, the principal songwriter, joined up with singer and bassist Mary Huff and drummer Dave Hartman. In this configuration, SCOTS has released numerous extended-play albums and singles and at least 10 full-length albums, including the 1996 commercial success *Dirt Track Date*. Though still based in Chapel Hill, the band has made its living mostly by touring, and it is primarily through its wacky, high-energy concerts that SCOTS has built its strong and loyal fan base in the South, and across North America.

Growing up in North Carolina, Miller was exposed to country singers like Roger Miller and Tammy Wynette by his father, who had a business building mobile homes. Miller also spent time with his mother in southern California, where he discovered punk, surf, and rockabilly. Huff and Hartman both hail from Virginia, where they each played in a number of different bands, ranging from country to hard rock to punk and rockabilly. These influences inform the group's unique combination of roots rock, swamp rock, rockabilly, surf, traditional country, and 1960s "countrypolitan" musical styles.

The band's philosophy has always been to create music that is fun and that gets people on their feet, and its live shows have become legendary for their fast pace and audience participation. During the song "Eight Piece Box"—

which is ostensibly about fried chicken but is riddled with double entendres—the band members throw fried chicken into the crowd and invite people onto the stage to eat and dance. For dessert, they sometimes toss moon pies or pass around a big bowl of banana pudding. And they often stage limbo contests or get audience members to wrestle each other while wearing Mexican wrestler masks.

As its name suggests, the band typically sings about the seedier parts of southern life, including trailer parks, cheap motels, honky-tonks, muscle cars, and drive-ins (in 2002 it provided the music for the gore film *Blood Feast 2: All U Can Eat*). In addition to singing about sex (as in "Ditch Diggin'" and "Camel Walk," which is about a fetish for snack crackers), the band celebrates the pleasures of dancing ("Soul City" and "I Learned to Dance in Mississippi"), drunkenness ("Liquored Up and Lacquered Down"), moonshine ("Corn Liquor"), southern food ("Too Much Pork for Just One Fork"), and mobile homes ("Doublewide" and "My House Has Wheels"). It also incorporates southern kitsch into its image, with Miller usually dressing in bib overalls or white loafers and Bermuda shorts, Hartman wearing skinny-brim straw hats, and Huff sporting a beehive hairdo and Capri pants or a vinyl miniskirt.

The group has inspired numerous bands across the country to exploit the stereotypes of white-trash culture for shock value and comedy. Yet SCOTS owes its widespread appeal and staying power to its distinctive blend of satire and affection, for it celebrates what it also laughs at. As captured in the chorus "white trash—don't call me that," it identifies with all aspects of southern culture, even as it cultivates a certain detachment, making it impossible to tell where parody becomes homage and vice versa. Miller calls this brand of humor "sur-ruralism," and on top of bringing musical success to SCOTS, it also places it squarely within the literary traditions of important southern writers like Flannery O'Connor, whom it often cites as a major influence.

MICHAEL P. BIBLER
University of Manchester

Michael Canning, *St. Petersburg Times* (16 January 1998); Roger Catlin, *Chicago Sun-Times* (31 May 1996); Randy Harward, *Salt Lake City Weekly* (4 October 2001); Eddie Huffman, *Option* (February 1996); Jason MacNeil, *Country Standard Time* (February 2007); Chris Morris, *Billboard* (8 July 1995); Nick Rogers, *State Journal-Register* (Springfield, Ill.) (7 July 2005).

Spears, Britney

(b. 1981) POP SINGER.

It is unlikely that those holding the keys to the Valhalla of Southern Music are ever going to let Britney Spears do more than loiter in the lobby. In part, this reflects conflicts over the definition and boundaries of "southern music," particularly whether the pop style Spears has ridden to fame can count in any meaningful way as southern. But her fans and critics at the vernacular level settled the matter in the affirmative long ago. For them it is the arc of her life and the constellation of her values, rather than the qualities of her music, that reveal the outline of an enduring South.

Born in 1981 in Kentwood, La., Spears pursued a performing career from an early age. Local beauty pageants and talent shows and later appearances off-Broadway and on *The New Mickey Mouse Show* all moved her slowly up the career ladder. But it was not until 1998 that she hit pay dirt of staggering proportions. In her debut single ". . . Baby One More Time" and in the accompanying music video, Spears struck the same cultural nerve Elvis had twanged generations earlier, combining an intriguing and volatile mix of come-on sexuality and charming southern innocence. Critics and fans arrived at wildly different plots for her along the southern belle curve, but both sides were convinced that wriggling before them was the latest manifestation of that perpetually beguiling creature, the Southern Woman. For a time, fans savored the sweet country girl image she cultivated, and Spears melted skeptical journalists with a down-home personality softened by a Dixie accent, impeccable manners, and frequent references to her Southern Baptist faith. "Pop's reigning queen," cooed *Teen People* in the summer of 1999, "is first and foremost a nice Southern girl."

Over the next few years, however, critics served giant feasts of crow. From the debut of her controversial first music video, in which she made naughty with the camera wearing a cinched-up schoolgirl uniform, they had insisted that her cute southern style was all flummery concealing a white-trash sensibility. Subsequent albums, videos, and events provided skeptics increasing satisfaction, diving as Spears did into everraunchier territory. Indeed, the red latex catsuit for "Oops! . . . I Did It Again" in 2000 formed only a mild prelude to her strutting around in a bodysuit intended to make her look naked, French-kissing Madonna on national television, and, in a kind of coup de grâce, ending a Las Vegas evening in 2004 with a 55-hour wedding to an old Kentwood pal. Numerous marital, parenting, and fashion gaffes, vicious public fights with Mama, periodic rumors of substance abuse, unflattering paparazzi photos, and an escalating tempo of bizarre behavior have rocketed her into the firmament of a popular culture studded with celebrities derided as wealthy white trash.

Yet what sets Britney Spears apart from her dubious companions, aside from the astonishing figure of 31 million albums sold in the United States alone, is a Louisiana childhood that surfaces regularly among Britney-watchers as an explanation for almost everything good and bad about her life. Thus, though her music is perhaps in no recognizable way southern, she still has earned her place as one of the most widely recognized southerners in contemporary popular culture.

GAVIN JAMES CAMPBELL
Doshisha University

Gavin James Campbell, in *Pop Perspectives: Readings to Critique Contemporary Culture*, ed. Laura Gray-Rosendale (2008), *Southern Cultures* (Winter 2001).

Stax Records

From a meager and tentative start in 1959 as Satellite Records, by the mid-1960s Stax had become the record label most responsible for defining the commercially successful and widely influential "Memphis Sound." Although Memphis, as one of the most significant cultural crossroads in the South, had supported a number of vibrant live music scenes throughout the foregoing part of the 20th century and the city's hybrid sounds had received their first major national exposure when artists initially recorded by Sam Phillips left Memphis for greener pastures, it was Stax and its alumnus Chips Moman's American Sound Studio that sent Memphis-recorded music to the top of the national pop charts. Stax, with its gritty, muscular "southern soul" or "deep soul" sound, provided an uncompromised rootsy counterpoint to northern-urban black-pop crossover attempts by Motown and soul crooners such as Sam Cooke and Ben E. King. Its sound and success also shaped the trajectory of the Muscle Shoals–area recorded music, an equally successful and influential southern sound. Booker T. & the MG's, Sam & Dave, Otis Redding, and Wilson Pickett became and have remained household names, and Stax's 1960s sound was famously commemorated for successive generations in the 1981 movie *The Blues Brothers* and its sequel *Blues Brothers 2000*.

Although Stax struggled to stay afloat in racially torn Memphis after Martin Luther King's assassination and finally folded in 1976, it was not before hitting a second stylistic and commercial peak with psychedelic soul and funk. The premier exponent of that sound, Isaac Hayes, won multiple Grammy awards and an Oscar in 1972 for his score for the classic blaxploita-

Booker T. & the MG's (Courtesy Stax Museum of American Soul Music, Memphis)

tion movie *Shaft* and set the tone for black popular music for at least the next decade.

In 1957 Jim Stewart, a banker and an erstwhile country fiddler, started the Satellite record label in his wife's uncle's garage in Memphis. Next, convincing his older sister, Estelle Axton, to invest in a recording venture by mortgaging her house, he bought an Ampex monaural recorder and moved to a deserted grocery store in Brunswick, 30 miles east of Memphis. Finding little talent in the small community, Satellite rented the erstwhile Capitol movie theater at 924 East McLemore Avenue in Memphis and rechristened it Soulsville U.S.A. LaGrange, Ga.–born white guitarist, songwriter, and producer Lincoln Wayne "Chips" Moman helped in secur-

ing that deal and proved integral to the fledgling operation before leaving to work at FAME studios in Muscle Shoals and later his own American Studios back in Memphis.

Satellite did not have a focus on black music until the company's first break came, with WDIA dj Rufus Thomas recording "Cause I Love You" with his daughter Carla. The regional popularity of the record led New York's Atlantic Records head Jerry Wexler to offer Satellite a purportedly distribution-only deal. Carla Thomas next scored the studio's first national hit with her self-composed "Gee Whiz." Wexler signed the teenaged Thomas to his own Atlantic label on which he also released the song, thus starting an arrangement through which important

Atlantic-signed artists, many from the North, would record at Stax and later also at Muscle Shoals area studios and at Chips Moman's Memphis-based American Sound Studio. Such arrangements became a significant route for southern sounds to enter the popular mainstream.

Satellite's next hit came in July 1961 with the Mar-Keys' instrumental "Last Night." Released initially on Satellite, the record shot to No. 2 on the national pop charts. Threats of litigation by another company with the same name prompted the new name "Stax," from the initial letters of Stewart's and Axton's last names. Controversy surrounds the details of which musicians were featured on the spliced-together record, but the band that toured in the wake of its popularity was all white and featured seven members, two of whom, guitarist Steve Cropper and bassist Donald "Duck" Dunn, would soon constitute half of the most famous studio house band in American popular music, Booker T. & the MG's. Booker T. Washington and Al Jackson Jr., organist and drummer, respectively, were the earliest African American musicians to play sessions at Stax and formed the other half of that legendary combo. The Mar-Keys' Wayne Jackson partnered with Andrew Love to form the Memphis Horns. Over the next six years, both in the studio and on the road, Booker T. & the MG's and the Memphis Horns, and often the reconstituted Mar-Keys and the Bar-Kays, backed numerous Stax and Atlantic acts that appeared on regional and national pop charts with increasing frequency. Among these were Carla Thomas, Rufus

Thomas, William Bell, Otis Redding, Wilson Pickett, Sam & Dave, Eddie Floyd, Johnnie Taylor, and Albert King. Additionally, the exceptional success of the MG's as an individual recording act inspired many studio backup bands, including the Bar-Kays, War, and MFSB, to launch individual careers and encouraged studio musicians to form "supergroups" such as Stuff and Fourplay. Keyboardist, composer, and arranger Isaac Hayes and lyricist David Porter constituted a major songwriting and production team at Stax during this period, especially for Sam & Dave.

The year 1968 proved a landmark in Stax's history. In February, Otis Redding's "Sittin' on the Dock of the Bay," overdubbed and released posthumously after Redding's plane crash in December 1967, became Stax's first pop chart topper. The racial tensions resulting from the April assassination of Martin Luther King Jr. in Memphis and Atlantic Records' decision to end its partnership with Stax, taking with it all the recorded masters, sent the company into a tailspin. Stax was eventually sold for over two million dollars to the Paramount Pictures subsidiary Gulf-Western. Estelle Axton exited the picture, and African American executive vice president Al Bell, who had been hired in 1965, took increasing charge of the company.

Bell and Stewart borrowed money from Deutsche Grammophon to buy back Stax in 1970 and negotiated a distribution deal with Columbia. Although the 1964–67 period is remembered as Stax's creative zenith, Isaac Hayes and the Staple Singers found artistic and exceptional commercial success with their updated sounds during the post-1968 period. It must be noted, however, that Stax often sent its artists down to Muscle Shoals to record, and, among others, the Staples' hit "I'll Take You There" was recorded at the Muscle Shoals Sound studio for Stax. Other successful Stax acts from this period include Mel and Tim, Little Milton, the Soul Children, the Emotions, the reconstituted Bar-Kays, the Dramatics, Shirley Brown, and gospel singer Rance Allen. In 1972 Al Bell bought Stewart's share in the company; Stewart continued as chief executive, however. Under Bell, Stax attempted to diversify, investing in a Broadway play, signing black comedian Richard Pryor to the new Partee subsidiary, and even recording an album by the Rev. Jesse Jackson on the Respect subsidiary. One of the company's most ambitious projects was August 1972's WattStax concert at the Los Angeles Memorial Coliseum during the Watts Summer Festival. The multiagency benefit event featured all the main artists on Stax's roster and was attended by an audience of over 100,000—and comparisons to Woodstock were made.

Al Bell and Johnny Baylor, a black New York record executive Bell had hired in 1968, had drastically different approaches—and not always aboveboard—to running the now-multimillion-dollar empire, contrasting with the amicable family-business environment of the early years. Through increasing legal problems and multiple federal investigations starting in 1973, the label continued recording, albeit

with decreasing commercial success; only the Staple Singers charted in the Top 20 in its last three years. Based on petitions filed by creditors, a bankruptcy court shut down the Stax operation in January 1976. Although an environment of rapidly changing musical tastes precluded any subsequent historic landmarks for its remaining alumni—save perhaps actor Richard Pryor, Steve Cropper, and later Isaac Hayes—Stax's place in American popular music had long been secured.

AJAY KALRA
University of Texas at Austin

Rob Bowman, *Soulsville U.S.A.: The Story of Stax Records* (1997); James Dickerson, *Goin' Back to Memphis: A Century of Blues, Rock 'n' Roll, and Glorious Soul* (1996); Peter Guralnick, *Sweet Soul Music: Rhythm and Blues and the Southern Dream of Freedom* (1986; rev. ed., 1999).

Still, William Grant

(1895–1978) MUSICIAN AND COMPOSER.
Known as the "dean of Afro-American composers," William Grant Still spent more than 50 years composing, conducting, and playing music that reflected a fusion of his spiritual and musical imagination, his diverse ethnic ancestry, and 20th-century American culture.

His mother came from black, Spanish, Indian, and Irish stock and his father from black, Indian, and Scotch stock. Still was born on 11 May 1895, on a Woodville, Miss., plantation near the Mississippi River. He lived there only nine months before his father, a teacher and bandleader, died. His mother moved the family to Little Rock, Ark., where she began teaching. When Still was nine, his mother married a postal clerk, who entered Still's life with a Victrola and opera records. The voice of Still's maternal grandmother filled their home with spirituals. He later wrote, "I knew neither wealth nor poverty, for I lived in a comfortable middle class home."

Still left home to study at Wilberforce University. His mother wanted him to be a physician, but Still had already taught himself to play the violin and wanted to be a musician. He left Wilberforce for the navy during World War I, eventually returning, against his mother's wishes, to study music at Oberlin College. He worked as a young musician with W. C. Handy in Memphis and New York, played the oboe in Eubie Blake's band, and orchestrated for Paul Whiteman and Artie Shaw. In the 1920s he studied composition with George W. Chadwick at the New England Conservatory and in New York with the French ultramodernist Edgard Varèse, who led Still into a dissonant, melodic, and traditional style, reflecting his black heritage. "I made an effort to elevate the folk idiom into symphonic form," Still said. Two Guggenheim Fellowships in the 1930s allowed him to concentrate on composition.

As a black man, Still achieved many "firsts." He wrote the theme for the 1939 New York World's Fair. He conducted WOR's all-white radio orchestra in New York. In 1931, when composer Howard Hanson conducted Still's *Afro-American Symphony* in Rochester, N.Y., Still became the first African American to have written a symphony performed by a major orchestra. In 1936 he was the first black to conduct a major orchestra, the Los Angeles Philharmonic, and two decades later, leading the New Orleans Symphony, he became the first black to conduct a major orchestra in the Deep South.

During the 1940s, when he wrote "And They Lynched Him on a Tree" and "In Memoriam: The Colored Soldiers Who Died for Democracy," his works sounded a social conscience theme. For violin and piano, he wrote Peruvian and Mexican ballads. His operas, with librettos often written by his wife, Verna Arvey, told of Haiti, Spanish colonial America, Africa, and roadside, gas-station life in America. Poet Langston Hughes wrote the libretto for Still's *Troubled Island*. Still lived in Los Angeles, and Hollywood benefited from his presence. He arranged for Columbia and Warner Brothers and wrote the scores for the *Perry Mason* and *Gunsmoke* television series and for the films *Lost Horizons* and *Pennies from Heaven*.

In addition to the Guggenheim Fellowships, Still received honorary degrees and many awards. In 1974 Still's opera *A Bayou Legend* premiered in Jackson, Miss., and Governor Bill Waller named Still a "distinguished Mississippian." Though not a churchgoer, on every composition he wrote, "With humble thanks to God, the Source of inspiration." At age 83, on 3 December 1978, Still died in Los Angeles from a heart ailment.

BERKLEY HUDSON
Providence, Rhode Island

Catherine Reef, *William Grant Still: African-American Composer* (2003); Catherine Parsons Smith, *William Grant Still: A Study in Contradictions* (2000); Judith Anne Still, ed., *William Grant Still and the Fusion of Cultures in American Music* (2d ed., 1995); Judith Anne Still, Michael J. Dabrishus, and Carolyn L. Quin, *William Grant Still: A Bio-Bibliography* (1996).

String Band Tradition

Primarily a mid-19th- and 20th-century phenomenon, string bands have been, and continue to be, one of the South's major folk music ensemble forms. They derive from both Anglo- and African American musical cultures, although they are more frequently associated with whites than with blacks. String bands consist of a number of musicians, generally from three to six, most of whom play acoustic stringed instruments. The fiddle, present in the South from the earliest days of colonization, and the banjo, an instrument that developed in the 19th century from African roots, are typically the core instruments, usually joined by at least one guitar, an instrument that grew in popularity during the early years of the 20th century. These are the major instruments, but it is not uncommon to find others, including the mandolin, string bass, and piano. If there are vocalists—and there usually are—they are inevitably also instrumentalists.

A string band usually has in its repertoire a large number of tunes for square dancing, songs generally representative of the broad corpus of southern folk song, and recent country hit songs. The music is infectious, with fiddles speeding through the melody, propelled by a banjo played in various old-time "rapping" or "knocking" or up-picking styles and a guitar or two accentuating the beat with chords and, perhaps, connecting runs. Instrumental styles tend to be regionally defined. Singing is generally solo, although more modern harmonic vocal techniques are used increasingly.

String bands dominated the first decade of country music recordings, indicating the music's deep-seated ties to and familiarity within local communities. Groups had such colorful names as the Skillet Lickers, Dr. Smith's Champion Hoss Hair Pullers, Fisher Hendley and his Aristocratic Pigs, and Seven Foot Dilly and his Dill Pickles. By the mid- and late 1930s, though, the form had become less profitable for the record companies. Bands continued to be part of their communities, playing for such occasions as dances, picnics, and house parties. Their influence continues, providing a substantial foundation for string-based musical styles such as bluegrass and western swing. Many of the old "hillbilly" records from the 1920s and 1930s have been reissued and are available on releases by independent record companies, as well as a few major-label compilations.

Starting in the 1950s, revivalist musicians, generally from outside the South, began first re-creating the music and then, later, in some cases, using the music as inspiration for more contemporary performance styles. This interest spread across the nation and abroad, and, although modest in size, it has proven tenacious. Ironically, the string band revival was at first slow to come to the South, but that is no longer the case. Visit any of the major fiddlers competitions, and you are likely to see musicians from many parts of the nation, including younger southern players who are drawn to a music that once seemed in danger of vanishing.

BURT FEINTUCH
University of New Hampshire

Bob Carlin, *String Bands in the North Carolina Piedmont* (2004); Bill C. Malone, *Country Music, U.S.A.* (2d rev. ed., 2002), *Singing Cowboys and Musical Mountaineers: Southern Culture and the Roots of Country Music* (1994), *Southern Music—American Music* (1979); Charles K. Wolfe, *Tennessee Strings: The Story of Country Music in Tennessee* (1977).

Stuart, Marty

(b. 1958) COUNTRY SINGER.
Musical prodigy, singer, songwriter, record producer, writer, photographer, raconteur, artifact collector, and archivist, Marty Stuart is among the most versatile figures in modern country music. He was born John Marty Stuart in Philadelphia, Miss., on 30 September 1958. Drawn to gospel, bluegrass, and country music almost from infancy, Stuart was already a skillful mandolin and guitar player by the age of 12, at which time bluegrass music icon Lester Flatt hired him for his band. After the ailing Flatt disbanded his group in 1978, Stuart toured with fiddler Vassar Clements and guitarists Doc and Merle Watson. Next he joined Johnny Cash's band, where he remained until starting his own solo career in 1985. He also

married Cash's daughter, Cindy, a marriage that lasted only until 1988.

From his boyhood, Stuart had squirreled away country music memorabilia in his room. As his income grew and his contact with his musical heroes intensified, he became a more systematic collector of costumes, instruments, letters, song manuscripts, photos, and related material. He acquired a trove of Hank Williams artifacts so imposing that the Country Music Hall of Fame and Museum borrowed it for an exhibition. Later, Stuart's array, which he labeled Sparkle & Twang, was displayed at the Tennessee State Museum. Stuart also developed a passion for wearing and collecting the ornately decorated Nudie and Manuel stage costumes long favored by such traditional country acts as Porter Wagoner and Little Jimmy Dickens. The flashy dress and tall "rooster comb" hair became Stuart trademarks.

Stuart released his first album, *Marty, with a Little Help from His Friends*, in 1977. It did not gain him much critical attention, but the follow-up collection, *Busy Bee Café*, in 1982, did. Critics loved it. Stuart signed with Columbia Records in the mid-1980s but failed to chart any substantial hits there. He had better luck with his next label, MCA, where he scored five Top 10s, including "Hillbilly Rock," "Tempted," and "Burn Me Down." His 1991 duet with Travis Tritt, "The Whiskey Ain't Workin'," won them both a Grammy for best country vocal collaboration.

In 1992 Stuart became a member of the *Grand Ole Opry*. Five years later, he married fellow *Opry* star Connie

Smith. Rutledge Hill Press published his annotated book of photographs, *Pilgrims: Sinners, Saints, and Prophets*, in 1999. The next year Stuart produced the sound track album for the Matt Damon and Penelope Cruz movie *All the Pretty Horses*.

Stuart became increasingly busy as a producer after the turn of the century, masterminding records for Billy Bob Thornton, Jerry and Tammy Sullivan, Andy Griffith, Kathy Mattea, and Porter Wagoner, among others. In 2007 he published his second photo book, *Country Music: The Masters*.

EDWARD MORRIS
Former country music editor of
Billboard

Marty Stuart, *Country Music: The Masters* (2007), *Pilgrims: Sinners, Saints, and Prophets* (1999).

Sun Records

Sun Records was established in 1952 by Sam Phillips as the primary record label for commercial releases from that pioneering producer's Memphis Recording Service (founded in 1949). By the mid-1950s, Sun Records, based in Memphis, had emerged as arguably the most significant recording company of that era—and indeed it stands as among the most influential independent recording companies in the history of American popular music. Sun Records played a major role in the evolution of four genres of American music: blues, rhythm and blues, country (through the label's invention of the country music subgenre known as "rockabilly"), and, perhaps most crucially, rock and roll.

Elvis Presley's version of "Mystery Train," recorded at Sun Records and released on 20 August 1955 as the B-side of "I Forgot to Remember to Forget" (Charles Reagan Wilson Collection, Center for the Study of Southern Culture, University of Mississippi)

Best known as the label that issued the initial recordings of Elvis Presley, Sun Records also released the earliest recordings of such legendary musicians as Jerry Lee Lewis, Johnny Cash, Carl Perkins, Roy Orbison, and Charlie Rich. Other noteworthy musicians who recorded for Sun (and for Phillips International, an affiliated label) included bluesmen Little Walter, Little Milton, and James Cotton; rhythm-and-blues acts Little Junior Parker, Rufus Thomas, and Roscoe Gordon; country performers Harmonica Frank, Charlie Feathers, and Jack Clement; rockabilly pioneers Billy Riley, Sonny Burgess, and Warren Smith; and rock-and-roll instrumentalist Bill Justis.

Born 5 January 1923, Samuel Cornelius Phillips grew up outside Florence, Ala., the youngest of eight children. His parents lost virtually all their savings after the 1929 Wall Street crash, and the family remained poor through the Great

Depression. During his teenage years, Phillips played music and dreamed of becoming a lawyer. In the early 1940s his father died, and he was compelled to quit high school to earn money for the family. Choosing radio as his profession, Phillips studied audio engineering at Alabama Polytechnical Institute in Auburn and was later hired as a radio announcer by station WLAY in Muscle Shoals, Ala. In 1942 he married Rebecca Burns from the nearby city of Sheffield. Over the next few years, Phillips worked for a succession of radio stations: WMSL (Decatur, Ala.), WLAC (Nashville), and WREC (Memphis). At WREC, he prerecorded his shows, which led him to develop strong radio production skills and an extensive knowledge of commercial recordings, particularly those featuring music by African American musicians.

In 1949, excited by the music he heard performed in and near Memphis, Phillips decided to establish the Memphis Recording Service (the first successful recording studio in that city). Renting a small building in Memphis at 706 Union Avenue and borrowing money for the purchase of equipment, Phillips printed a business card that proclaimed "WE RECORD ANYTHING—ANYWHERE—ANYTIME." Many of the initial recordings from Phillips's studio were 16-inch acetate discs cut at 78 rpm, though by 1952 he was using magnetic tape during recording sessions. Phillips leased most of the earliest recordings he produced in his studio—mostly of black musicians—to various labels. For instance, he sold the master recording of Jackie Brenston's influential 1951 hit "Rocket 88," as well as recordings by

Chester Burnett (aka Howlin' Wolf), to the Chicago-based label Chess Records. By early 1952, Phillips decided to release his recordings on his own label. (He named this label Sun Records because, as he was quoted as saying, "the sun . . . was a universal kind of thing. A new day, a new opportunity.")

Through experimentation in his studio, Phillips, by the mid-1950s, had discovered Sun Records' signature production sound, achieved in part through employing a duo recording machine system to produce an echo known as "slapback" and in part through using sound transformers to generate distinctively warm tones.

Phillips had established the Memphis Recording Service in order to record black as well as white musicians from the Memphis area. "My aim was to try and record the blues and other music I liked," he once stated. He endeavored to preserve the music he liked, but Phillips also hoped to find new listeners for that music, stating that "I knew, or I felt I knew, that there was a bigger audience for blues than just the black man of the mid-South." This hunch led Phillips—who was alleged to have said, "If I could only find a white boy who could sing like a Negro I could make me a million dollars"—to attempt to produce a newly blended music that combined elements of both black and white musical tradition. Catching the producer's attention as possibly that "white boy" was a young singer who came to Phillips's studio during the summer of 1953 to make a vanity recording. Elvis Presley, born in Tupelo, Miss., but living in Memphis, was still a teenager when he first patronized the Memphis Recording Service, and Phillips nurtured Presley's rapid artistic development, encouraging the singer to record diverse songs from several musical genres—ranging from blues (Arthur "Big Boy" Crudup's "That's All Right"), to rhythm and blues (Little Junior Parker's "Mystery Train"), to bluegrass (Bill Monroe's "Blue Moon of Kentucky"), to mainstream pop ("I Don't Care If the Sun Don't Shine," originally recorded by Patti Page and Dean Martin). Five Presley singles were issued by Sun Records through the summer of 1955, after which time Phillips sold Presley's contract to RCA Records for $35,000. The singer's Sun releases (along with Presley's early RCA singles)—featuring Presley's exciting and keenly interpretive vocals set against a background of propulsive yet spare instrumental accompaniment composed of electric lead guitar, acoustic rhythm guitar, upright bass, and, sometimes, drums—revolutionized American popular music. A number of Phillips's subsequent 1950s-era productions for Sun—including such national hits as Carl Perkins's "Blue Suede Shoes" (1955), Johnny Cash's "I Walk the Line" (1956), and Jerry Lee Lewis's "Whole Lot of Shakin' Going On" (1957)—likewise inspired a generation of musicians (whether American or British or from other parts of the world) to embrace rock-and-roll music—and, inevitably, rock-and-roll attitude, which encompassed such qualities as individuality and emotional freedom.

All of Sun Records' best-known "stars" had left the label by 1963 for more lucrative contracts with major recording companies, and Phillips struggled to keep the small, independent label alive. The final Sun recording—a single by the group Load of Mischief—was released in January 1968, and in July 1969 Phillips sold Sun Records to Shelby Singleton, a Louisiana-based businessman. In the 1970s, Singleton reissued the Sun recordings produced by Phillips on an offshoot label called Sun International; that label also released new recordings by such revivalist acts as Sleepy LaBeef and Jimmy Ellis (aka Orion). After selling Sun Records, Sam Phillips essentially retired from the music industry. Over the next three decades, Phillips managed other business interests, yet he was increasingly recognized for his achievements with Sun Records during the 1950s. For example, Phillips was inducted into the Rock and Roll Hall of Fame (in 1986) and into the Country Music Hall of Fame (in 2001). He died of respiratory failure in Memphis on 30 July 2003.

TED OLSON
East Tennessee State University

Colin Escott, with Martin Hawkins, *Good Rockin' Tonight: Sun Records and the Birth of Rock 'n' Roll* (1991); Peter Guralnick, *Last Train to Memphis: The Rise of Elvis Presley* (1994).

Swamp Pop

A distinct rock-and-roll subgenre, swamp pop music combines New Orleans–style rhythm and blues, country-and-western music, and Cajun and black Creole music; it is indigenous to south Louisiana and a small part of east Texas. Swamp pop appeared during the mid- to late 1950s when teenage Cajun and black Creole musicians experimented with modern pop music elements. In doing so they unwittingly fused the sounds of artists like Fats Domino, Elvis Presley, and Little Richard with south Louisiana's ethnic music traditions.

The swamp pop sound is typified by highly emotional vocals, simple, unaffected, and occasionally bilingual (English and Cajun French) lyrics, honky-tonk pianos, bellowing sax sections, and a strong rhythm-and-blues backbeat. Upbeat compositions often possess the bouncy rhythms of Cajun and black Creole two-steps, and their lyrics frequently convey the local color and joie de vivre spirit that pervades south Louisiana. Slow, melancholic swamp pop ballads, however—with their tripleting keyboards, undulating bass lines, climactic turnarounds, and dramatic breaks—exhibit a despondency common to many traditional Cajun and black Creole compositions, born generations ago of widespread poverty, hard living, and the loneliness of rural existence.

Classics of the swamp pop genre include Dale and Grace's "I'm Leaving It Up to You," Johnny Preston's "Running Bear," Freddy Fender's "Before the Next Teardrop Falls," Phil Phillips's "Sea of Love," and Jimmy Clanton's "Just a Dream," all national Top 10 hits. Of these, the first three reached No. 1 on national charts. Over 20 swamp pop recordings have broken into the *Billboard* Hot 100 since 1958. In swamp pop's birthplace, however, fans and artists regard many obscure songs as essential to the genre's repertoire. These standards include such regional favorites as Clint West's "Big Blue Diamonds," Tommy McLain's "Sweet Dreams," Randy and the Rockets' "Let's Do the Cajun Twist," Johnnie Allan's "South to Louisiana," Rod Bernard's "This Should Go on Forever," and Cookie and the Cupcakes' "Mathilda," the latter of which is considered the unofficial anthem of swamp pop.

From its rural south Louisiana origins, swamp pop went on to exert an influence on popular music both in the United States and abroad. (The term "swamp pop" was actually coined by British music writer Bill Millar around 1970 and was popularized in the genre's homeland by his compatriot and fellow music writer John Broven.) Notable swamp pop–influenced tunes include Bill Haley and the Comets' rerecording of Bobby Charles's "Later Alligator," the Rolling Stones' version of Barbara Lynn's "You'll Lose a Good Thing," the Honeydrippers' rendition of "Sea of Love," and the Beatles' original composition "Oh! Darling," which exudes the swamp pop ballad sound. (Contrary to popular belief, artists like Dale Hawkins, Tony Joe White, and Creedence Clearwater Revival did not perform swamp pop music, nor do they appear to have been influenced by the sound.)

Although live swamp pop music can still be heard in south Louisiana and east Texas nightclubs and sometimes at regional festivals, the sound tends to be overshadowed today by its Cajun and zydeco sister genres, and it is often ignored by preservationists.

SHANE K. BERNARD
Avery Island, Louisiana

Shane K. Bernard, *Southern Cultures* (Fall/Winter 1996), *Swamp Pop: Cajun and Creole Rhythm and Blues* (1996); John Broven, *South to Louisiana: The Music of the Cajun Bayous* (1993).

Sweeney, Joel Walker

(c. 1810–1860) MUSICIAN.

Until recently "Joe" Sweeney enjoyed legendary status as the "inventor" of the five-string banjo. As a boy Sweeney learned to play the banjo from slaves on his father's farm, where he was born, near present-day Appomattox, Va. According to the legend, he improved their African-derived instrument by fashioning a wooden hoop to replace the original gourd body and, more important, by adding (around 1831) a short, high-pitched fifth (or thumb) string to the original four. The long-held claim that he thus invented the five-string banjo is supported by little documentary evidence, and recent informed opinion challenges it, primarily on the basis of illustrations clearly showing that some slave banjos had short thumb strings well before Sweeney was born. Slave banjos were undoubtedly quite variable in form, so Sweeney's real claim to fame is that he so popularized the particular form he grew up with that it became the standard. He was certainly the first documented white banjo player.

In the 1830s he traveled widely in the South, performing, in blackface, the music of his black mentors; and he became a mentor himself, apparently teaching a number of the early, influential minstrel banjo players. In the 1840s he became a national celebrity, performing first with circuses and then with minstrel shows in northern cities. Between 1843 and 1845 he toured and performed in England, reputedly including a performance for Queen Victoria. His brother, Sam, also an accomplished banjo player, was Jeb Stuart's personal minstrel during the Civil War. Joel Sweeney played a critical role in making the banjo an important and permanent part of southern music, especially in initiating and encouraging its widespread use by whites.

ROBERT B. WINANS
Wayne State University

Gene Bluestein, *Western Folklore* (Winter 1964); Burke Davis, *Iron Worker* (Autumn 1969); Scott Odell, in *New Grove Dictionary of Music and Musicians*, vol. 2, ed. Stanley Sadie (1980); Arthur Woodward, *Los Angeles County Museum Quarterly* (Spring 1949).

Taylor, Koko

(b. 1935) BLUES SINGER.

Koko Taylor, born Cora Walton on a farm near Memphis, Tenn., to sharecropping parents, developed an early love for music, particularly for what she heard in church and on B. B. King's Memphis radio show. Although her parents preferred her interest in gospel music, Taylor and her five siblings covertly made instruments and played blues music together. The young Taylor was especially influenced by and favored earlier blues queens, such as Bessie Smith and Big Mama Thornton.

In the early 1950s Taylor moved to Chicago and began working as a domestic, but at night she regularly went to blues clubs and often was invited to sit in with well-established bands. It was in just such circumstances that blues songwriter Willie Dixon discovered Taylor in 1962, and within just a few years Taylor signed a contract with Chess Records and recorded several albums, which included singles written by both herself and Dixon.

Taylor emerged as a blues powerhouse in the 1970s, touring and playing at festivals, at which she shared the stage with the likes of B. B. King, Buddy Guy, and Muddy Waters. In 1975 she signed with Alligator Records and remains with the company today. The albums Taylor has recorded with Alligator include *I Got What It Takes* (1975), *The Earthshaker* (1978), *From the Heart of a Woman* (1981), *Queen of the Blues* (1985), *Live from Chicago* (1987), *Jump for Joy* (1990), *Force of Nature* (1993), *Royal Blue* (2000), and *Deluxe Edition* (2002), six of which have been nominated for a Grammy.

Taylor has been featured in numerous newspapers and magazines, including *Living Blues*, as well as on television programs, and has appeared in several films, including *Blues Brothers 2000*. Additionally, the blues community has repeatedly and consistently honored Taylor and her work. Taylor has been awarded the W. C. Handy Award (renamed the Blues Music Award in 2006) 25 times, more than any other female artist, for the categories of Contemporary Blues Female Artist, Entertainer of the Year, Female Artist, Traditional Blues Female Artist, and Vocalist of the Year. Taylor has also received a Grammy award and a Blues Foundation Lifetime Achievement Award, as well as numerous other awards, and she was inducted into the Blues Hall of Fame in 1997.

Taylor's overwhelming success in a male-dominated industry has earned her the praise of blues critics, who hail her as the currently reigning "Queen of the Blues," placing her in a long tradition of blues queens with the likes of Bessie Smith and Ma Rainey. Additionally, Taylor's empowering lyrics and strong vocal style have influenced many younger female blues artists, including Shemekia Copeland and Bonnie Raitt.

AMY SCHMIDT
University of Mississippi

Barbara O'Dair, ed., *Trouble Girls: The Rolling Stone Book of Women in Rock* (1997).

Tharpe, Sister Rosetta

(1921–1973) GOSPEL SINGER.
Born Rosetta Nubin on 20 March 1921, in Cotton Plant, Ark., Sister Rosetta Tharpe is considered one of the greatest gospel singers of her generation. She was a flamboyant stage performer whose music also flirted with the blues and jazz genres. Billed as "Little Rosetta Nubin, the pint-sized singing and guitar playing miracle," Tharpe began performing at age four. She accompanied her mother, Church of God in Christ evangelist Katie Bell Nubin, who played mandolin and preached at tent revivals throughout the South. The elder Nubin was a traveling missionary and shouter in the classic tradition. She was known on the gospel circuit as "Mother Bell."

Tharpe was a prodigy and mastered the guitar by age six. She attended Holiness conventions and performed renditions of songs including "The Day Is Past and Gone" and "I Looked down the Line." Tharpe truly honed her unique style, though, when her family relocated to Chicago in the late 1920s and she was exposed to blues and jazz music. Although she performed gospel music in public, she often played blues in private settings. Consequently her unique style reflected secular influences. She bent notes on her acoustic guitar like jazz artists, and her vocal phrasing and vibrato-tinged style drew heavy inspiration from the blues.

During the 1930s Tharpe moved to New York and began playing at Café Society Downtown, the city's first major racially integrated nightspot. She also appeared at the Cotton Club on Broadway with Cab Calloway and His Orchestra. Eventually she signed a recording contract, a first for a gospel performer, and cut four sides for Decca Records in 1938. Tharpe's first records were big hits and included Thomas A. Dorsey's "Rock Me" and "This Train," but she held her core audience by recording material like "Precious Lord" and "End of My Journey" and appealed to her growing white audience by performing rearranged, uptempo spirituals such as "Down by the Riverside."

Tharpe loved her audience and enjoyed sharing her musical gifts. Significantly, Tharpe aligned herself with the secular music world with a sense of showmanship and glamour unique among gospel performers of her era. However, her forays into the secular music market proved controversial and shocked gospel purists. Switching to an electric guitar, Tharpe's fingerpicking style added a resonance to her guitar sound. By playing in nightclubs, she pushed spiritual music into the mainstream and pioneered pop gospel, bridging musical worlds and attracting a varied fan base of both black and white southerners and gospel and blues fans.

During World War II Tharpe was one of only two black gospel acts that recorded V-Discs for American soldiers overseas. She toured the United States with the Dixie Hummingbirds, and in 1944 she recorded with boogie-woogie pianist Sammy Price. Their first collaboration, "Strange Things Happening Every Day," cracked *Billboard*'s race records Top 10. In 1946 she teamed with the Newark-based Sanctified singer Madame Marie Knight, and their first single, "Up Above My Head," was a huge hit. Over the next few years they played to large crowds across the church circuit. In the early 1950s Tharpe and Knight cut some straight blues sides, and Knight then left religious music entirely. Tharpe, however, remained a gospel artist, but her record sales and live performances dropped, as purists took offense at her foray into the musical mainstream.

By defying categories Tharpe lost much of her U.S. audience by the mid-1950s. Her comeback was slow, but by 1960 she had resurged enough to appear at the Apollo Theater with the Caravans and James Cleveland. She continued touring even after suffering a stroke in 1970 and died in Philadelphia on 9 October 1973. A number of musicians have identified Tharpe's guitar playing and showmanship as an influence, including Elvis Presley, Jerry Lee Lewis, and Keith Richards.

MARK CAMARIGG
Living Blues *magazine*

Horace Clarence Boyer, *How Sweet the Sound: The Golden Age of Gospel* (1995); Tony Heilbut, *The Gospel Sound: Good News and Bad Times* (1997); Gayle Wald, *American Quarterly* (September 2003), *Shout, Sister, Shout! The Untold Story of Rock-and-Roll Trailblazer Sister Rosetta Tharpe* (2007).

Thornton, Willie Mae "Big Mama"

(1926–1984) BLUES SINGER.
Born Willie Mae Thornton on 11 December 1926 in Montgomery, Ala., to a religious family—her father was a preacher and her mother sang lead in the church choir—"Big Mama" Thornton left home at age 14 to pursue a career in show business. She toured with Sammy Green's Hot Harlem Revue during the 1940s, where she honed her skills not only as a blistering vocalist but as a harp blower and drummer. She was a staple on the Houston, Tex., circuit when Duke/Peacock Records boss Don Robey signed her in 1951. She debuted on Peacock Records with "Partnership Blues" that year, backed by influential Duke/Peacock trumpeter and producer Joe Scott and his band.

It was her third Peacock session with Johnny Otis's band that struck gold—Big Mama shouted "Hound Dog" (penned by songwriting royalty Leiber and Stoller) and soon hit the road as a newfound star. "Hound Dog" held down the No. 1 position on *Billboard*'s R&B charts for seven weeks in 1953. Sadly for Thornton, however, Elvis Presley's 1956 cover was even bigger, obscuring Thornton's legacy.

Though Thornton did cut some fine Peacock follow-ups through 1957, such as "I Smell a Rat," "Stop Hoppin' on Me," "The Fish," and "Just like a Dog," she never again reached the hit parade. She recorded several quality 45s in the early 1960s for a handful of small labels, but they did little to revive her career. As a result of her tour of Europe with the American Folk Blues Festival Package, Thornton recorded a number of sides for Arhoolie Records, including her first rendition of "Ball and Chain" in 1968, putting Big Mama back in circulation. Janis Joplin covered "Ball and Chain" at the 1968 Monterey Pop Festival, and after Joplin's band, Big Brother and the Holding Company, released the song on their album "Cheap Thrills," Big Mama got a two-album deal with Mercury Records in 1969.

Thornton recorded for Vanguard and Buddah into the 1970s and maintained a healthy performance schedule in addition to many gigs. She appeared on the *Dick Cavett Show* and on the sound track for the film *Vanishing Point*.

In the early 1980s, after years of hard living, Thornton's health fell into steady decline, resulting in her death on 25 July 1984, the year she was inducted into the Blues Foundation's Hall of Fame.

MARK COLTRAIN
Hillsborough, North Carolina

Lonnie Brooks, Cub Koda, and Wayne Baker Brooks, *Blues for Dummies* (1998); Gerhard Herzhaft, *Encyclopedia of the Blues* (1997).

Tubb, Ernest

(1914–1984) COUNTRY SINGER.
Ernest Tubb was a major personality in country music from the early 1940s to

his death on 6 September 1984. He was a much-admired and -imitated vocal stylist, a pioneer in the popularization of the electric guitar, a patron of young talent, and one of the leading architects of the popular honky-tonk style of country music.

Tubb was born on 9 February 1914 in the tiny community of Crisp, Tex., about 40 miles south of Dallas. Like many young musicians of his era, Tubb fell in love with the music of Jimmie Rodgers, and for many years he affected a singing-and-yodeling style that was quite similar to that of the Mississippi Blue Yodeler. He never met his hero, but in 1936 Carrie Rodgers, Jimmie's widow, became Tubb's champion. She loaned him one of Rodgers's guitars, helped him obtain bookings in south Texas, and persuaded the Victor Company to sign Tubb to a contract. The Victor affiliation resulted in eight recordings but brought Tubb little money or fame.

Success did not really come to Tubb until the early 1940s. In 1940 he made the first of his recordings with Decca (an association that lasted until 1975); he began performing on KGKO in Fort Worth and touring for Universal Mills as the Texas Troubadour; and in 1941 he recorded the enduringly popular "Walking the Floor over You." On the strength of the song's popularity, Tubb was invited to join the cast of the *Grand Ole Opry*, becoming a permanent member of the show in January 1943. Tubb's move to Nashville was symbolic and representative of the growing influence of "western" styles in country music. He was one of the first musicians to bring an electric guitar to the stage of the *Grand Ole Opry*, an innovation that had already been heard on his records and in his Texas personal appearances. Tubb was a leading record seller and popular concert attraction in country music until the mid-1950s (when rock-and-roll and country-pop music emerged); and long after that period he continued to be one of the most active in-person performers in country music, averaging close to 300 personal appearances a year until the late 1970s.

Because of his evident commercial viability, Tubb was able to exert great influence in the country music field. He played a prime role in persuading his industry to replace the word "hillbilly" with "country"; he was one of the first country singers to make records with other established performers (such as the Andrews Sisters, Red Foley, and Loretta Lynn); he and his band of musicians, the Texas Troubadours, made crucial contributions to the development of the honky-tonk style of performance; and he provided encouragement and support to many younger entertainers such as Hank Williams, Johnny Cash, Loretta Lynn, Jack Greene, Willie Nelson, and Cal Smith. Tubb's admission to the Country Music Hall of Fame in 1965 was warmly endorsed.

BILL C. MALONE
Madison, Wisconsin

Ronnie Floyd Pugh, *Ernest Tubb: The Texas Troubadour* (1998), *Journal of Country Music* (December 1978, December 1981), "The Texas Troubadours: Selected Aspects of the Career of Ernest Tubb" (M.A. thesis, Stephen F. Austin State University, 1978).

Turner, Ike and Tina

(1931–2007; b. 1939) R&B, ROCK-
AND-ROLL, SOUL, AND FUNK DUO.
Ike Turner in his early career and Ike
and Tina Turner as part of one of the
most exciting soul music revues in the
1960s and 1970s were significant contributors to the history of R&B, rock-
and-roll, soul, and funk music. Born on
5 November 1931 in Clarksdale, Miss.,
Ike Wister Turner was witness to acts of
unspeakable racist violence, including
one that led to his father Iziah Turner's
slow death. Around the age of seven
he started teaching himself the piano,
initially practicing on one owned by a
woman for whom he chopped wood. By
the time he exited high school, he was
heading his own band, Ike Turner and
the Kings of Rhythm, a group central
to the transition of rhythm and blues to
rock and roll. In 1951 the group traveled
to Sam Phillips's studio in Memphis to
record "Rocket 88," a single now often
acknowledged as "the first rock and roll
record."

For the next three years, Ike was
an active contributor to the Memphis
rhythm-and-blues scene as a backup
musician, bandleader, producer, talent scout, and entrepreneur. He soon
started backing and recording on his
own major artists in the area, including
B. B. King, Bobby Bland, and Howlin'
Wolf. By 1954 Ike Turner had relocated
to East St. Louis to participate in the
thriving rhythm-and-blues scene in that
city.

Tina Turner was born Anna Mae
Bullock on 26 November 1939 in
Brownsville, Tenn., near Memphis and
the small town of Nutbush, where her
father was an overseer on a farm. In
1956, after her parents had separated,
Anna Mae moved to live with her
mother and sister Alline in St. Louis,
where, hoping to break into showbiz,
she frequented nightclubs, including
ones where Ike Turner's band played.
The two became romantically involved
in 1959, and in 1960 they released their
first recording, "A Fool in Love," when a
singer Ike was supposed to record failed
to show up and Anna, then pregnant
with Ike's child, stepped in. Ike renamed
his act the Ike & Tina Turner Revue and
expanded it to include backup female
singers and dancers and an expanded
horn section.

Over the next three years, the couple,
who wed in 1962, placed "It's Gonna
Work Out Fine," "I Idolize You," "Poor
Fool," and other singles on the R&B
charts, yet they were largely relegated
to small labels and the chitlin' circuit
in the South. Their potential, however,
did not go unnoticed, and Phil Spector
recorded Tina Turner on "River Deep,
Mountain High." Ike was paid not to
interfere with the product. Following an
invitation to open for the 1969 Rolling
Stones U.S. tour, Ike and Tina crossed
over to rock audiences with fervent
reworkings of such songs as Creedence
Clearwater Revival's "Proud Mary,"
the Beatles' "Come Together," and Sly
and the Family Stone's "I Want to Take
You Higher." While the duo captivated
audiences worldwide, trouble had been
brewing on the home front, and Tina
divorced Ike in 1976. Ike's career took
a downward spiral, and trouble with
chemical abuse led to his incarceration,
resulting in his missing the ceremony

wherein the duo was inducted into the Rock and Roll Hall of Fame in 1991.

Tina meanwhile continued to attempt a solo comeback. In 1984 she released her fifth solo album, *Private Dancer*. The album produced the hit singles "Private Dancer," "Better Be Good to Me," and the No. 1 and Grammy-winning "What's Love Got to Do with It?" The album sold over five million copies. In 1985 Tina appeared in the movie *Mad Max: Beyond Thunderdome*, which featured two of her tracks: the Grammy-nominated "We Don't Need Another Hero" and the Grammy-winning "One of the Living." In 1986 she wrote her best-selling autobiography, *I, Tina*. In 2000 Tina dropped the Turner last name but secured her best showing in a decade with the album *Twenty Four Seven*.

Just as Tina, after two hectic decades of international solo stardom began to move into retirement, Ike, at age 70, picked up the threads of his career. With the autobiography *Takin' Back My Name* (1999), the Grammy-nominated and W. C. Handy Award–winning album *Here and Now* (2001), and the Grammy-winning album *Risin' Up with the Blues* (2006), Ike Turner finally emerged from his wife's and his past's sizable shadows.

AJAY KALRA

University of Texas at Austin

Mark Bego, *Tina Turner: Break Every Rule* (2005); John Collis, *Ike Turner: King of Rhythm* (2003); Ike Turner and Nigel Cawthorne, *Takin' Back My Name* (1999); Tina Turner and Kurt Loder, *I, Tina: My Life Story* (1986).

Vaughan, James D.

(1864–1941) GOSPEL MUSIC PROMOTER.

James D. Vaughan played a major role in the popularization of gospel music in America during the first half of the 20th century. His promotion company, the James D. Vaughan Company, was founded in 1912 in the middle Tennessee community of Lawrenceburg and remained in operation until 1964. Vaughan's enterprise began as a singing school and then was expanded to include sales of records, songbooks, and magazines. His first songbook, *Gospel Chimes*, was published under his own name in 1900. His company eventually published 105 songbooks, which enjoyed successful nationwide sales. Vaughan was a creative businessman who sent male vocal quartets to churches around the country to promote his music and books. He started one of the first commercial radio stations in Tennessee, WOAN, to play his music and plug his songbooks. In 1922 one of the Vaughan quartets made a recording of its music, and, although it was not made in the South, the record was one of the first specifically designed for a southern audience.

A devout member of the Church of the Nazarene, Vaughan was influential in the development and spread of gospel music from the 1920s through the 1960s. Vaughan helped preserve the shape-note singing tradition, and his gospel music helped lay the foundation for American country music. The gospel songbooks that Vaughan distributed had a profound impact on southern cultural life. Singing schools and conventions and gospel singing at church-related functions were immensely popular through the 1960s and involved thousands of southerners. Vaughan's books were affordably priced, and each sold an average of 117,000 copies.

KAREN M. MCDEARMAN
University of Mississippi

J. L. Fleming, "James D. Vaughan: Music Publisher, Lawrenceburg, Tennessee, 1912–1964" (Ph.D. diss., Union Theological Seminary, 1971); Bill C. Malone, *Southern Music—American Music* (1979); Charles K. Wolfe, *Tennessee Strings: The Story of Country Music in Tennessee* (1977).

Washington, Dinah

(1924–1963) BLUES AND JAZZ SINGER.

In his 2001 biography, *Q*, Quincy Jones describes Dinah Washington's vocal style, saying she "could take the melody in her hand, hold it like an egg, crack it open, fry it, let it sizzle, reconstruct it, put the egg back in the box and back in the refrigerator and you would've still understood every single syllable."

Born Ruth Lee Jones in Tuscaloosa, Ala., on 29 August 1924, Dinah Washington and her family sought opportunity in the North, moving to Chicago in 1927. Her mother played piano at St. Luke's Baptist Church, which proved important to her young daughter, as it was an instrument she soon learned in addition to her vocal pursuits. As with many R&B pioneers, spirituals made up much of Jones's focus in her early years as a performer. In 1940 she found a place as gospel legend Sallie Martin's accompanist on the road. Yet the world

of secular music was already starting to take hold. Before she hooked up with Martin, the budding vocalist won first prize at a Regal Theater amateur contest.

According to music writer Bill Dahl, "Whether it was bandleader Lionel Hampton, booking agent Joe Glaser, or Garrick Stage Bar boss Joe Sherman" who supposedly gave Ruth the memorable stage name of Dinah Washington, "it was obvious that Jones was headed for stardom. A featured billing at the Garrick led Hampton to hire her to sing with his big band in 1943."

Renowned jazz critic Leonard Feather happened to catch Washington with the Hampton band in December of 1943 at Harlem's Apollo Theater and persuaded Keynote Records to sponsor her debut recording session, but recording opportunities proved scarce while she was working for Hampton. It was only a matter of months before Washington left Hampton's band, recording three Los Angeles sessions for the Apollo label under her own name before signing with the then-fledgling Mercury. She cut her first album for Mercury in January 1946, and by the summer of 1948 her solo star was in rapid ascension.

During this time and throughout the 1950s, Washington ran with some jazz heavyweights. She recorded sessions with trumpeters Clifford Brown and Clark Terry, drummer Max Roach, and saxophonists Eddie "Lockjaw" Davis and Cannonball Adderley. Washington cleverly used Quincy Jones's talents as an up-and-coming arranger and employed pianist Wynton Kelly, drummer Jimmy Cobb, and tenor saxophonist

Eddie Chamblee in her combo for a number of gigs. Chamblee was also one of Washington's many husbands.

Finally, in 1959, much to the chagrin of many critics, Dinah Washington made the full-fledged leap to pop stardom, with the old Dorsey Brothers hit "What a Diff'rence a Day Makes." With the help of talent scout Clyde Otis, she mined more pop gold with "Unforgettable" and "This Bitter Earth." It was also Otis's idea to pair Washington with label mate Brook Benton for their seemingly playful duet "Baby, You Got What It Takes," which hid serious tension between the two, with the end result a huge hit in 1960.

In Detroit, on 14 December 1963, at age 39, Dinah Washington died from an unintentional but lethal combination of alcohol and diet pills.

MARK COLTRAIN
Hillsborough, North Carolina

Nadine Cohodas, *Queen: The Life and Music of Dinah Washington* (2006).

Watson, Doc

(b. 1923) FOLK MUSICIAN.
Arthel "Doc" Watson is a unique song stylist, an influential guitarist, and the repository of a vast range of American music originating in the South. Born 2 March 1923 in Deep Gap, N.C., Watson has been blind from birth. He grew up in a farm family oriented toward religion and music. His father was a song leader in the Baptist church, and the Watson family read the Bible and sang hymns most evenings. Watson learned traditional folk songs from his grandparents and his father, and the first instrument he played was the harmonica. He remembers at age six hearing a cousin play the banjo, and a brother-in-law gave him one several years after that.

Throughout Watson's youth, his father guided his musical education. Doc Watson's father gave him a harmonica each Christmas for years when he was a child, helped his young son learn the banjo, and then in 1934 made him a better banjo of hickory, maple, and cat skin. His father gave him money to buy his first guitar after the young boy learned to play the Carter Family's "When the Roses Bloom in Dixie." From his father's windup gramophone and the radio, Doc Watson remembers hearing songs by the Carter Family, the Skillet Lickers, Mississippi John Hurt, and Barbecue Bob. He still performs and records the songs he listened to growing up. In addition to his early education in traditional music, commercial country, and the blues, he learned jazz, big band, popular songs, and classical music while attending the North Carolina School for the Blind in Raleigh.

Doc Watson's first stage performance was at age 17 during a fiddlers' convention in Boone, N.C., where he played the "Mule Skinner's Blues." In 1941 he became a member of a group singing for local radio stations, and a woman at a local station gave him his nickname in this period. She suggested calling him "Doc" because "Arthel" was too formal.

Watson worked for nine years in the 1950s playing mostly electric guitar with Jack Williams and the Country

Gentlemen, a five-piece dance band, and he continued playing traditional music at home with friends and family. Folklorist Ralph Rinzler came from the Smithsonian Institution in 1960 to record a friend of Watson's, Clarence Ashley, and after Rinzler heard Watson, he encouraged him to seek a solo identity nationally. The Folkways album *Old Time Music at Clarence Ashley's* became Watson's first recording, and he was soon popular on the folk club and college campus circuit. Watson began recording for Vanguard Records in 1964, and the following year his 15-year-old son, Merle, began recording and touring with his father.

Doc Watson is an influential exponent of guitar flat-picking, which involves the use of a simple flat pick rather than a thumb pick or finger-picking. He is also an engaging storyteller, who explains the background to the songs he performs. Above all, his cultural significance is as an eclectic synthesizer of southern music. Watson absorbed the music of his time and place as a mid-20th-century rural southerner. He performs Jimmie Rodgers ("Miss the Mississippi and You"), the Delmore Brothers ("Blues Stay Away from Me"), Gaither Carleton fiddle tunes, A. P. Carter ("Keep on the Sunny Side"), Mississippi John Hurt ("Spikedriver Blues"), Barbecue Bob ("You Don't Know My Mind Blues"), Bob Wills ("Hang Your Head in Shame"), and Carl Perkins ("Blue Suede Shoes"). In concert he can draw from Ira Gershwin and Bob Dylan if requested. He has recorded over 30 albums.

Watson's son traveled, performed, and recorded with his father and earned praise for his bottleneck slide guitar playing. He died in a tractor accident in 1986. MerleFest, one of the nation's most important acoustic venues, has been held annually since 1988 on the grounds of Wilkes Community College in Wilkesboro, N.C. Doc Watson still lives with his wife, Rosa Lee, a few miles from his birthplace in North Carolina.

CHARLES REAGAN WILSON
University of Mississippi

Nicholas Dawidoff, *In the Country of Country: People and Places in American Music* (1997); Irwin Stambler and Grellin Landon, *The Encyclopedia of Folk, Country and Western Music* (2d ed., 1983).

WDIA

RADIO STATION.
In the fall of 1948, WDIA, in Memphis, Tenn., became the first radio station in the South to adopt an all-black programming format. The station was owned by two white businessmen, but the man most responsible for the format change at WDIA was Nat D. Williams, a local black high school history teacher. Williams was brought into the station to do his own show on an experimental basis, and it proved to be an overnight sensation. He was the first black radio announcer in the South to play the popular rhythm-and-blues records of the day over the airwaves. His show was so successful that within six months of its debut WDIA had changed its format from a classical music station to one appealing solely to black listeners and advertisers.

In addition to initiating an entirely new music format, Williams launched a wide variety of programming innovations at WDIA and recruited other talented blacks onto the airways. His first recruits were fellow high school teachers A. C. Williams and Maurice Hulbert. Both men went on to have long and distinguished careers in black radio. Nat Williams's most famous recruit was a youthful B. B. King, who used the exposure on WDIA to initiate his career as the country's premier urban blues artist. Rufus Thomas became one of the station's most popular on-air disc jockeys. In addition to these black males, Nat D. Williams also recruited the South's first black female announcers to WDIA's airways; two of the best known were Willa Monroe and Starr McKinney, both of whom did programs oriented toward black women.

Gospel music, religious programs, and black news and public affairs shows were also prominent on WDIA. The most acclaimed public affairs program was called *Brown America Speaks*; it was also created and hosted by Nat D. Williams. The program addressed race issues from a black perspective and won an award for excellence from the prestigious Ohio State Institute for Education in radio in 1949. With the success of WDIA, other radio stations around the country also began to adopt black-oriented formats, and black radio became a fixture in commercial broadcasting nationwide. WDIA still programs for a black audience in Memphis, making it the oldest black-oriented radio station in the country.

BILL BARLOW
Howard University

Bill Barlow, *Voice Over: The Making of Black Radio* (1999); Louis Cantor, *Wheelin' on Beale: How WDIA-Memphis Became the Nation's First All-Black Radio Station and Created the Sound That Changed America* (1992); Robert Gordon, *It Came from Memphis* (1995); Margaret McKee and Fred Chisenhall, *Beale Black and Blue: Life and Music on Black America's Main Street* (1981); Charles Sawyer, *The Arrival of B. B. King: The Authorized Biography* (1980).

Wells, Kitty

(b. 1919) COUNTRY SINGER.
Kitty Wells was born Muriel Ellen Deason in Nashville on 30 August 1919 to Myrtle and Charles Deason, both musicians. She sang and learned to play the guitar as a child and as a teenager sang with the Deason Sisters, consisting of herself, two sisters, and a cousin. After making her radio debut on WSIX, Nashville, Deason met singer Johnnie Wright, whom she married in 1937. They performed together with Wright's sister Louise, and later Jack Anglin, forming the Tennessee Hillbillies and the Tennessee Mountain Boys. The group separated at the onset of World War II when Anglin was drafted, but the Wrights continued to perform.

In 1943 Johnnie Wright gave his wife her stage name, Kitty Wells, after "Sweet Kitty Wells," the folk ballad recorded by the Pickard Family. In the late 1940s Wells established a recording career with RCA but continued to focus on her growing family. Paul Cohen, a music scout for Decca, contacted the singer in 1952 to see if she would be interested in recording a response to Hank Thompson's song "The Wild Side of Life," a tune that describes a woman lured away from her husband by "the glamour of the gay nightlife." Primarily interested in the paycheck, Wells countered with "It Wasn't God Who Made Honky Tonk Angels," explaining the point of view of the woman chastised in Thompson's song. Thompson sang that God must have made honky-tonk angels, but Wells refuted this, singing that philandering men were to blame for this angel's downfall. The controversial song immediately became No. 1 on the country music charts and remained there for six weeks, resulting in Kitty Wells becoming the first woman to have a No. 1 song.

Wells became a member of the *Grand Ole Opry* in 1953 but was banned from performing her "feminist" signature song on the air. Wells's career continued to grow in the 1950s with 23 Top 10 hits, including "One by One," a duet with Red Foley, the popularity of which set the stage for some of the great country duets of the 1960s through the present. Continuing to produce material explicitly expressing feminine feelings, such as "Paying for That Back Street Affair," Wells opened the door for other artists such as Loretta Lynn, Tammy Wynette, and Dolly Parton to accurately portray a woman's feelings before and during the sexual revolution of the 1960s and 1970s.

Wells continued to produce hits into the 1960s and 1970s and had her own television show, *The Kitty Wells Show*, in 1968. In 1976 she was inducted into the Country Music Hall of Fame and was awarded a Grammy award for Lifetime Achievement in 1991. Although Wells has ceased touring, she continues to make public appearances.

RENNA TUTEN
University of Georgia

Mary A. Bufwack and Robert K. Oermann, *Finding Her Voice: Women in Country Music, 1800–2000* (2003); A. C. Dunkelberger, *Queen of Country Music: The Life Story of Kitty Wells* (1977).

Whittaker, Hudson (Tampa Red)
(1904?–1981) BLUES SINGER.

Blues musician Tampa Red, known as "the Guitar Wizard," was prominently featured on southern performance circuits in the 1920s, followed by a successful career as a staple of the Chicago blues scene in the 1930s and 1940s. He was known as a master of slide or bottleneck guitar, playing with a distinctive and often-imitated style. One of the first black instrumentalists to make a recording, he enjoyed more than three decades in the studio, from 1928 to 1960.

Tampa Red was born Hudson Woodbridge in Smithville, Ga., probably in 1904. Shortly thereafter he moved to Tampa, Fla., to live with his grandparents, the Whittakers, whose last name he adopted. Little is known about his childhood or the development of his musical talents. He performed for some time on the southern theater circuit before traveling to Chicago in the mid-1920s, bringing with him the name Tampa Red—a combination of his hometown and the color of his hair. Upon arriving in Chicago, he began to work day jobs while playing guitar on street corners and in clubs, waiting for opportunities to further his music career. He was eventually hired to accompany popular blues performer Ma Rainey and through her teamed up with pianist Georgia Tom Dorsey. In 1928 the two recorded "It's Tight Like That," a new, upbeat-blues, ragtime-influenced number with suggestive lyrics, which was a national hit. They recorded several more songs as the "Hokum Boys," and consequently "hokum" style—characterized by analogies used to make sexual innuendoes—became popular briefly during the Depression. These early recordings showcase his unique sound and already-sophisticated approach to guitar technique.

Tampa Red played a National Resonator Guitar, one of the loudest, flashiest guitars available before amplification, which he bought the first year they were sold. His was a gold-plated tricone, and it earned him the nickname "The Man with the Golden Guitar." He slid a bottleneck along the strings of this famous guitar to create a crisp, pure sound, especially evident in his single-string solos. His performances also included expressive vocals and kazoo solos. He recorded in sessions with Memphis Minnie, Sonny Boy Williamson, and other major blues artists of the day. After the repeal of Prohibition in 1933 Chicago developed an enthusiastic blues audience and a number of popular blues venues, and Tampa Red (often backed by his band, the Chicago Five) became one of the central players on this scene. With his wife, Frances, as his business manager and Big Bill Broonzy and producer Lester Melrose as his close friends, Tampa Red became mentor to new blues musicians, with whom he shared his home and resources upon their arrival in Chicago. He was also known for his heavy drinking and escapades, which, together with his music, earned him a reputation as an iconic blues entertainer. He played frequently in a diverse array of Chicago's most popular and infamous venues—in the vaudeville circuit, on the streets, in down-home jukes, and behind the doors of Chicago clubs.

In the 1940s Tampa Red transitioned to the electric guitar and continued to record, creating hits that scored on R&B charts. These songs included a number of seminal records that would be covered by legendary blues artists of future generations, such as 1949's "When Things Go Wrong with You (It Hurts Me Too)." Artists like Elmore James, Fats Domino, and B. B. King later recorded chart-topping hits with covers of the song. In 1953 the death of his wife seemed to intensify his dependency on alcohol—a problem that would plague Tampa Red for the rest of his life. Although he experienced "rediscovery" in the late 1950s during a period of blues revival, he was never able to regain the success of his career in the preceding decades. He died destitute in Chicago in 1981 and was inducted into the Blues Hall of Fame later that same year.

With his upbeat blues and bottleneck technique, Tampa influenced many important blues figures, such as Muddy Waters, Mose Allison, and Elmore James. He has also emerged as an important cultural icon, particularly in southern African American literature. References to his music and legacy can be found in blues music, as well as in Ernest Gaines's novel *A Lesson before*

Dying. Writer Raymond Andrews discusses the cultural impact of Tampa Red on his own rural Georgia childhood, implicating Tampa Red as the archetypal bad bluesman of legendary status in southern black communities. Andrews's uncle, a hedonistic daredevil, adopted both Tampa Red's image and his nickname. The title character of Andrews's first novel, *Appalachee Red*, evinces the influence of this same rebellious, empowered image.

FRANCES ABBOTT
Emory University

Bruce Bastin, *Red River Blues: The Blues Tradition in the Southeast* (1995); Lawrence Cohn, ed., *Nothing but the Blues* (1993).

Wild Magnolias

MARDI GRAS INDIAN MUSICIANS. The Wild Magnolias are a Mardi Gras Indian group from New Orleans led by Theodore Emile "Bo" Dollis (b. 1944). Founded in 1957 as one of the city's many Indian "tribes" or "gangs," the Wild Magnolias gained distinction in 1970 as the first group to make studio recordings of the distinctive music of these black Carnival societies and continued to record in subsequent decades.

The Mardi Gras Indian phenomenon dates back to the late 19th century, when working-class blacks in New Orleans used a visual aesthetic inspired by Wild West shows as a means of expressing admiration for the resistance of Native Americans to white domination and of celebrating the concrete social and blood ties that existed between the two groups for centuries in the Gulf South. Composed of neighborhood-based groups, Indians spend all year meticulously preparing their outfits, which are never the same from one year to another. The physical violence that sometimes characterized meetings of groups of Indians earlier in the 20th century has been replaced with an intense culture of aesthetic competition. Groups and individuals strive to outdo one another in terms of the elaborateness or stylish qualities of their costumes and the expressive dancing and cryptic chanting performed while wearing them.

The music of the Indians, performed during rehearsals in neighborhood bars and during their appearances during Mardi Gras and on St. Joseph's Day, features chanted lyrics in a call-and-response form, with exclusively percussive backing on tambourines, cowbells, glass bottles, and a variety of other instruments. Lyrics of Indian songs may be sung in English, or may take the form of "Indian talk," a highly imaginative form of jargon that forms something of a secret language among these groups.

Bo Dollis began "masking Indian" while he was still in high school in the Central City area of New Orleans. He made costumes and masked with the White Eagles and the Golden Arrows before forming his own group, the Wild Magnolias, in 1957. In the 1960s, he formed a close bond with Joseph Pierre "Monk" Boudreaux (b. 1941), chief of the Golden Eagles, who would become his main collaborator in later musical endeavors. Other group members who also participated in recordings include June Johnson Jr., Crip Adams,

Tobias Johnson, Bubba Scott, and James Smothers.

The group performed at the 1970 New Orleans Jazz and Heritage Festival and, at the urging of JazzFest organizer Quint Davis, went into the studio and recorded their music with the help of local keyboardist and arranger Wilson "Willie Tee" Turbinton. The resulting release, a single of the traditional Indian song "Handa Wanda," was released on the Crescent City label in 1970. In 1974 the group released the album *Wild Magnolias* on Barclay/Polydor. In addition to the contributions of keyboardist and producer Willie Tee, the album featured the blind guitarist Snooks Eaglin, as well as Earl Turbinton and other talented New Orleans musicians. The song "Smoke My Peace Pipe (Smoke It Right)" scored a minor hit for the group, and they recorded a follow-up album for Polydor, *They Call Us Wild*, in 1975. In subsequent years the group recorded three albums for Rounder Records, and in 1999 released *Life Is a Carnival* on Blue Note. Monk Boudreaux left the group in 2001, but the Wild Magnolias and Bo Dollis remain some of the most acclaimed interpreters of the Mardi Gras Indian musical form.

MATT MILLER
Emory University

Michael P. Smith, *Mardi Gras Indians* (1994).

Williams, Hank

(1923–1953) COUNTRY MUSIC SINGER.
Widely acclaimed as country music's greatest singer and composer, Hiram Hank Williams was born on 17 October 1923 at Olive Hill, near Georgiana, Ala., the son of a sawmill and railroad worker. He was introduced to music in the Baptist church where he was faithfully taken by his mother, and, according to popular legend, he learned both songs and guitar chords from a black street singer in Georgiana, Rufus Payne ("Teetot").

Williams's evolution as a professional performer and composer began at the age of 14 when he won a talent show in a Montgomery theater singing his own composition, "WPA Blues." He obtained his first radio job in the same year, 1937, at WSFA in Montgomery. When World War II—a crucible that integrated country music's disparate regional styles and ultimately nationalized it—came, Williams worked in the Mobile shipyards and sang regularly in the honky-tonks of south Alabama. By the time the war ended, Williams had compiled eight hard years of performing experience and had built a style that reflected the composite musical influences of his youth: gospel, blues, and old-time country. Professionally, he acknowledged a debt to the Texas honky-tonk singer Ernest Tubb and to the Tennessee mountain singer Roy Acuff, whose styles Williams fused in a way that reflected a similar synthesis in the larger country field during the war and immediate postwar years.

Williams's climb to fame began shortly after the war when he became associated with Fred Rose, the famous Nashville songwriter and publisher. Rose encouraged Williams's natural songwriting abilities and published

Hank Williams, country music star, c. 1950
(Country Music Foundation, Library and Media
Center, Nashville)

his songs; helped him obtain recording contracts with Sterling and MGM
Records; persuaded Molly O'Day, one
of the greatest singers of the time, to
record some of Williams's compositions; and helped him get a position on
KWKH's *Louisiana Hayride* in Shreveport. The *Hayride*, which was then
second only to the *Grand Ole Opry* as a
successful country radio show, was the
vehicle that launched Williams on the
road to performing fame.

Hank Williams's national ascen-
dancy came in 1949 when he recorded
an old pop tune, "Lovesick Blues,"
which featured the yodeling he had
learned from another Alabama singer,
Rex Griffin. Williams soon moved to
the *Grand Ole Opry*, where he became
the most popular country singer since
Jimmie Rodgers. In the brief span from
1949 to 1953, Williams dominated the

country charts with songs that are still
considered classics of country music:
"I'm So Lonesome I Could Cry," "Cold
Cold Heart," "Your Cheating Heart,"
"Honky Tonk Blues," "Jambalaya," and
many others. With his band, the Drift-
ing Cowboys, Williams played a major
role in making country music a national
phenomenon. With a remarkably expressive voice that moved with equal
facility from the strident yodeling of
"Long Gone Lonesome Blues" to the
gentle lyricism of "I Just Told Mama
Goodbye," Williams communicated
with his listeners in a fashion that has
only rarely been equaled by other country singers. The word "sincerity" has no
doubt been overused in describing the
styles of country musicians, but in the
case of Williams it means simply that he
as a singer convincingly articulated in
song a feeling that he and his listeners
shared.

As a songwriter—not as a singer—
Williams played a most important
role in breaking down the fragile barriers between country and pop music.
Williams's singing was quintessentially rural, and his own records never
"crossed over" into the lucrative pop
market. His songs, though, moved into
the larger sphere of American popular
music and from there, perhaps, into
the permanent consciousness of the
American people. Like no earlier country songwriter's works, Williams's songs
appeared with great frequency in the
repertoires of such pop musicians as
Tony Bennett, Frankie Laine, and Mitch
Miller. For good or ill, this popularization into pop music continues.

Commercial and professional success did not bring peace of mind to the Alabama country boy. A chronic back ailment, a troubled marriage, and a subsequent divorce and remarriage accentuated a penchant for alcohol that he had acquired when only a small boy. After being fired by the *Grand Ole Opry* for drunkenness and erratic behavior, he returned to the scene of his first triumphs—the *Louisiana Hayride*. He died of a heart attack on 1 January 1953, but his legacy lives on in his songs and in the scores of singers, including his immensely talented son, Hank Jr., who still carry his influence.

BILL C. MALONE
Madison, Wisconsin

Colin Escott, *Hank Williams: The Biography* (1995); Chet Flippo, *Your Cheatin' Heart: A Biography of Hank Williams* (1981); Paul Hemphill, *Lovesick Blues: The Life of Hank Williams* (2005); George William Koon and Bill Koon, *Hank Williams, So Lonesome* (2002); Bill C. Malone, *Country Music, U.S.A.: A Fifty-Year History* (1968; rev. eds., 1985, 2002); Roger M. Williams, *Sing a Sad Song: The Life of Hank Williams* (1981).

Williams, Hank, Jr.

(b. 1949) COUNTRY MUSIC SINGER. Legendary for his hard-living lifestyle and beer-drinking ballads, Hank Williams Jr. is an established figure in the American country and southern rock genres. Born Randall Hank in Shreveport, La., on 26 May 1949 to country music legend Hank Williams and his wife, Audrey, this artist is most often referred to as "Hank Jr." or "Bocephus," a nickname given by his father after a

popular country comedian's ventriloquist dummy.

Nearly a month after his son's birth, Hank Sr. made a monumental debut on the *Grand Ole Opry*, which sent his career soaring for nearly three years until his untimely death in 1952. Urged by his mother, Hank Jr. followed in his father's footsteps, making his own *Opry* debut at the age of 11. Hank Jr. sang his father's songs for years to come, making his first record of his father's music at age 14 and garnering a hit with "Long Gone Lonesome Blues." Critics and fans alike found comfort in the melancholy honesty of the son's voice singing the father's songs.

Hank Jr. learned piano from rocker Jerry Lee Lewis in the 1960s and teamed up with Johnny Cash at Detroit's Cobo Hall in 1969 to perform the largest-grossing country concert to date. In 1970 he made an appearance on the *Ed Sullivan Show* and signed the biggest recording contract in MGM history. Yet the 21-year-old artist had lost the zest for living in the shadow of a father he hardly knew. He soon cut ties with the traditional country sound and began searching for a voice of his own.

The road to that voice would prove rocky but ultimately successful. The early 1970s found Hank Jr. conflicted internally, and in 1974 he attempted suicide while on a drug and alcohol binge. He later moved to Alabama to recuperate and further search for a unique sound. While in Alabama, he began playing with southern-rock pioneers Charlie Daniels, Marshall Tucker, and Toy Caldwell. Hank Jr.'s new voice quickly emerged as a mix of blues, rock, and country with a renegade attitude. In 1975 he released the signature album *Hank Williams, Jr. and Friends*, which included the hit "Stoned at the Jukebox."

In August 1975, he suffered a mountain-climbing accident in Montana that left him with severe head injuries. The artist endured a two-year recovery period in which he had to relearn speaking and singing. He made a full recovery, though, and his comeback album *The New South* (produced by Waylon Jennings in 1977) helped bring him into a new group of outlaw country musicians. Two of Hank Jr.'s signature songs, "Whiskey Bent and Hell Bound" and "All My Rowdy Friends," were released in late 1979, igniting a decade of Top 10 hits and an original rocking country sound.

In the 1980s he reemerged onto the music scene as a pop-culture icon and a successful crossover artist. In 1981 alone, he had three No. 1 hits, "Texas Women," "Dixie on My Mind," and "All My Rowdy Friends (Have Settled Down)." His boisterous stage show and blue-collar anthems proved appealing to both country and rock audiences, while his trademark dark beard and sunglasses made him one of the most recognizable figures of the 1980s. Much like on his telltale 1987 single, "Born to Boogie," Hank Jr. fans were always rowdy and ready to party. The Country Music Association named him Entertainer of the Year in both 1987 and 1988, as did the Academy of Country Music in 1986, 1987, and 1988. In 1990 he received a Grammy for Best Country Collaboration with Vocals, for an electronic duet performed with his father of "There's a Tear in My Beer." Both the recording and the video garnered acclaim for the use of electronic dubbing.

Although Hank Jr.'s singles began to slide down the charts in the 1990s, he managed to pick up one very important gig, with ABC's *Monday Night Football*. Tweaking one of his original tunes into a *Monday Night Football* theme song, he won three Emmys for the "Are You Ready for Some Football?" jingle. He rerecorded the theme song alongside Little Richard, Joe Perry, Clarence Clemons, Rick Nielsen, Bootsy Collins, Charlie Daniels, Steven Van Zandt, and other entertainers for the 2006 debut of *Monday Night Football* on ESPN.

Hank Jr. still performs regularly today and is considered an icon of bad-boy country style. He is often seen on stage and in music videos with country rockers like Gretchen Wilson and Kid Rock, both of whom are considered to have followed in his footsteps.

MARY MARGARET MILLER
University of Mississippi

Williams, Lucinda

(b. 1953) SINGER AND SONGWRITER. Lucinda Williams is one of the most respected singer-songwriters of the Americana roots-music movement, which began in the early 1980s. Her evocative lyrics and music command die-hard fan loyalty, and her perfectionist streak both on stage and in the recording studio are epic.

Born in 1953 in Lake Charles, La., to a musician mother and a poet father, Lucinda has used both parental disciplines in her music and performances.

Her poet father, Miller Williams, moved the family from one southern university town to another, exposing Lucinda to various writers and intellectuals during her formative years. Additionally, diverse musical influences such as Bob Dylan, Neil Young, Hank Williams, and Robert Johnson contributed to a style that transcends commercial musical definition.

Beyond her literary and musical influences, the physical southern landscape is infused into her songwriting, and her Grammy-winning album *Car Wheels on a Gravel Road* is a virtual map of the Mississippi River Delta basin. The album's songs reflect life in Mississippi (Macon, Greenville, Jackson, Vicksburg, Rosedale) and Louisiana (Lafayette, Lake Charles, Lake Pontchartrain, Slidell, Baton Rouge, Algiers, Opelousas). Sung with a gravelly voice and a southern drawl, Williams's songs have the descriptive force and brevity of a poet.

Lucinda first recorded an album of cover songs (Smithsonian/Folkways Records) called *Ramblin'* in 1979 to moderate success. She released *Happy Woman Blues*, her first collection of original material, the following year. Eight years later, in 1988, she released *Lucinda Williams*. With her second album of original music, Williams's reputation, already well established in Nashville and Austin, found a wider market. Coproduced with her guitarist, Gurf Morlix, the record sold 100,000 copies. Williams's skill as a songwriter and a gutsy, passionate singer won her a legion of fans and the respect of musicians. She became known as a musician

with a fierce drive to perfect her songs not only on vinyl but in concert as well. Her perfection at all costs, personal and professional, is legendary.

In 1989, on the force of *Lucinda Williams*, RCA Records signed Williams to her first major recording contract, one that she later sued to get out of because of a disagreement over artistic control. She rerecorded the songs originally recorded for RCA, again coproducing with Morlix. Another three years passed. In 1992 she released her third original effort, *Sweet Old World*. The album's single "Passionate Kisses" won the 1994 Grammy award for Best Country Song when it was covered by Mary Chapin Carpenter.

Lucinda teamed with Gurf Morlix a third time to record and produce her next album, *Car Wheels on a Gravel Road*, but before the record was released Williams guest-recorded on a Steve Earle record. Impressed by Earle and by his producer Ray Kennedy's producing ability, Lucinda shelved the original *Car Wheels* recordings to, again, remake the entire record, this time with Earle and Kennedy.

Throughout 1997 rumors circulated that the release of *Car Wheels on a Gravel Road* was imminent. The September *New York Times Magazine* portrayed Williams as a tantrum-prone, unrealistic artist who got lost in the minutia and could not bring a project to completion.

When she released *Car Wheels* in 1998, though, it was instantly hailed by those same critics as a classic—powerful, ageless, a rare accomplishment. It elevated Williams to the zenith of

Americana roots music and earned the 1998 Grammy for Best Contemporary Folk Album.

The demands and expectations to build on the success of *Car Wheels* were thus ironically lessened. By 1998 Williams had released only four records of original material in 19 years. Her next four records took nine years to release.

In 2001 Williams released *Essence*, followed by *World without Tears* in 2003. Critics considered them less accessible than *Car Wheels*, though she was awarded her third Grammy in 2002 for Best Female Rock Performance. In 2005 she released a DVD, *Lucinda Williams: Live from Austin, TX*, and a concert recording, *Live @ the Fillmore*. Williams's last record to date, *West*, arrived in 2007, again to wide praise.

WILLIAM S. BURDELL III
St. Simons Island, Georgia

Elizabeth Bukowski, www.salon.com (11 January 2000); Bill Friskics-Warren, *No Depression* (January/February, 2007), *No Depression* (July/August 1998).

Wills, Bob

(1905–1975) WESTERN SWING MUSICIAN.

James Robert Wills was born near the town of Kosse in the Black Belt of east Texas on 6 March 1905. From his family he learned to play fiddle music, which had been part of frontier cultural life from the East Coast to west Texas. From the blacks in the Black Belt he learned blues and jazz. At age 10, Wills played his first dance at a ranch in west Texas; by then he had begun to add blues and jazz idioms to traditional fiddle music. This combination was eventually called "western swing" and became one of the most distinctive sounds in all of American music. There is probably no better example of cultural cross-fertilization than Bob Wills's music, which brought together two strains of culture in the American South, one white, one black.

Wills performed his music at country ranch dances in west Texas years before introducing it to the general public on radio stations in Fort Worth. In the early 1930s he organized the Light Crust Doughboys, broadcast over the Texas Quality Network, and soon revolutionized music in Texas. His greatest success was with his Texas Playboys, in Tulsa, Okla., between 1934 and 1942. During those years he added brass, reeds, and drums, developing a band that by 1940 numbered 18 members. His recordings sold in the hundreds of thousands and his "San Antonio Rose" in the millions.

After the war he gave up most of the brass and reeds in his band and used more fiddles, guitars, steel guitars, and mandolins. This emphasis on strings helped Wills maintain his popularity even after the end of the age of the big bands. Because of his use of stringed instruments, Wills influenced two musical forces in the South that have dominated American music to the present—rock and roll and country and western. Western swing left a marked impression on early rockabillies such as Bill Haley and the Comets, Buddy Holly and the Crickets, and Elvis Presley. But Wills's greatest influence was on country and western. The Country Music Association awarded him its highest honor in 1968, naming Wills to the Country Music Hall of Fame.

What was it that made Wills's music appeal to the American people for more than 50 years? His music and style had many good qualities, but one quality stood out above all others—his music made people happy. At his dances, during his radio broadcasts, and through his recordings, Bob Wills helped find times of escape during the Depression and World War II. This was the secret to his success and one of his most direct contributions to humanity.

When Wills died in 1975, he left a rich cultural heritage. His compositions, including "Faded Love," "Maiden's Prayer," and "San Antonio Rose," are part of the repertoire of American country and pop artists. He also helped bridge the gap between the black and white musical cultures when he began combining them as a boy. Out of that cultural mix came Bob Wills's richest legacy, the happy, swinging rhythms called "western swing."

CHARLES R. TOWNSEND
West Texas State University

H. Ed Hurt, *Bob Wills: His Life—Times—and Music* (2000); Ruth Sheldon, *Hubbin' It: The Life of Bob Wills* (1995); Al Stricklin, with Jon McConal, *My Years with Bob Wills* (1996); Charles R. Townsend, *San Antonio Rose: The Life and Music of Bob Wills* (1976); Rosetta Wills, *The King of Western Swing: Bob Wills Remembered* (1998).

Wilson, Cassandra

(b. 1951) BLUES AND JAZZ SINGER. With a long and varied recording career, singer Cassandra Wilson has become one of the most popular contemporary jazz singers of the late 20th and early 21st centuries. She is known for her unique, multifaceted voice and her perpetual drive to explore a multitude of musical genres and styles, while infusing them with her own distinctive jazz sensibility. With 17 solo albums and a number of diverse collaborations to her name, Cassandra Wilson is a powerful and influential force in the world of jazz.

Born in Jackson, Miss., on 4 December 1951, Wilson was the third and youngest child of music teacher, guitarist, and bassist Herman Fowlkes Jr. and elementary schoolteacher Mary McDaniel. Both parents were music enthusiasts, bringing the sounds of Motown and jazz into their daughter's life at an early age and encouraging her love of music and her desire to perform. Although she was classically trained on the piano and played clarinet in middle school bands, Wilson wanted to play the guitar and learned to play through method books from her father. She began penning her own folk-style songs and participated in a folk trio and in musical theater productions at her recently desegregated high school in Jackson. After high school she attended Millsaps College and Jackson State University, graduating with a degree in mass communications. During her college years, Wilson spent her free time rehearsing and performing with a variety of cover bands that played pop, funk, and R&B, and she performed bebop for the first time with the Black Arts Music Society. In 1981 Wilson lived briefly in New Orleans, where mentors Earl Turbinton, Alvin Batiste, and Ellis Marsalis encouraged her to pursue performance in New York City, where she moved in 1982.

Wilson's focus then shifted toward improvisation. She honed her vocal skills while meeting and jamming with important jazz figures, including saxophonist Steve Coleman, who pushed Wilson to develop original material beyond the traditional jazz tunes. Coleman organized the M-Base collective, of which she was the lead vocalist and a founding member. Stylistically, this group married the grooves of funk and soul music with both traditional and avant-garde jazz, and Wilson worked seamlessly with the complex arrangements and heavy instrumentals. She sang on several of Coleman's albums in the mid-1980s, while also recording and touring as a member of the avant-garde trio New Air. Wilson recorded her first solo album for JMT, *Point of View*, in 1986. The album included many of Wilson's compositions, as well as collaborations and standards, and the album showcased her husky contralto voice and her unique manipulations of pitch and tone.

Wilson had established herself as a serious musician with her early albums but found critical acclaim with her first album of standards, 1988's *Blue Skies*, which was bookended by albums of primarily original work. She reached a turning point in her career in 1993 when she signed with Blue Note Records and broke through to audiences beyond the world of jazz. Her first album for Blue Note, *Blue Light 'til Dawn* (1993), illustrated her new signature sound, best described as a fusion of pop, jazz, blues, country, and world music, and included covers of songs by Robert Johnson, Joni Mitchell, and Hank Williams. Wilson's

music reconnected jazz with its blues roots and drew on pop production techniques for a rich, accessible sound.

Her 1996 album, *New Moon Daughter*, won a Grammy for Best Jazz Vocal Performance, and she recorded and toured with Wynton Marsalis in 1997, performing his Pulitzer Prize–winning composition *Blood on the Fields*. Paying tribute to Miles Davis, one of her greatest influences, Wilson performed as his opening act in 1989 at the JVC Jazz Festival in Chicago and produced the live concert album *Traveling Miles* in his honor in 1999. Wilson's 2006 album *Thunderbird* shows that her attention to multigenre projects still thrives. Produced by T-Bone Burnett, the album works with a live sound, including a lone slide guitar evoking the blues performers of earlier generations. Her style continues to evolve as she explores the intersections between musical traditions and pushes the boundaries of jazz.

FRANCES ABBOTT
Emory University

Will Friedwald, *Jazz Singing: America's Great Voices from Bessie Smith to Bebop and Beyond* (1996); Gary Giddins, *Visions of Jazz: The First Century* (2000); Alyn Shipton, *A New History of Jazz* (2007).

WLAC

RADIO STATION.
Founded in 1926, Nashville radio station WLAC is one of the top-ranked AM stations in its home city and among the best known in the South. Clear Channel Broadcasting is its owner, having purchased it from Billboard Broadcasting Corporation, which bought the station from the Life and Casualty Insurance

Company in 1978. The station serves a population of over 600,000 and is on the air 24 hours every day. A network affiliate of Fox News Radio, WLAC-AM today primarily broadcasts all-talk programming, airing popular conservative talk shows such as those of Glenn Beck, Rush Limbaugh, and Sean Hannity.

From the mid-1940s through the early 1970s, however, WLAC was known widely for its rhythm-and-blues programming. It became known as "Blues Radio," as its nighttime disc jockeys almost exclusively played black music—blues, rhythm and blues, and soul. Although the station's 50,000 watts of power brought listeners from most parts of the country, the majority of the audience listened from the South. Many were African Americans, and the disc jockeys catered to their preferences, at the same time influencing the musical tastes of the region, the nation, and both white and black artists, whose music—rock and roll—would eventually dominate the popular music world.

In the mid-1940s Gene Nobles began playing black music when requested by students at Tennessee State and Fisk universities. Randy Wood, who owned an appliance store in Gallatin, Tenn., then decided to try selling by radio the records he had tried unsuccessfully to sell to his store customers. On 17 February 1947 Nobles advertised records by Eddy Arnold, Nat King Cole, Johnny Mercer, and Ella Mae Morse, and Randy's Record Mart soon became the largest mail-order record store in the world. WLAC flourished, luring advertisers as well as listeners.

The station's most popular feature during this era was disc jockey John Richbourg and his 1:00 to 3:00 A.M. blues show. He became known as "John R." and the "granddaddy of soul." Because he promoted their music and often was the first to play their records or to prerelease a record to test the market, he became a favorite of black artists. If he liked a record that was not immediately popular, he played it persistently until it became a hit. Such was the case with Otis Redding's "These Arms of Mine," an example of Richbourg's assertion that he and his WLAC colleagues did not just play hits—"we made hits." Richbourg broadcast his last show on WLAC on 1 August 1973 and died in 1986.

Of WLAC's blues disc jockeys, Bill "Hoss" Allen was the only one still with the station after rock and roll pushed rhythm and blues out of the programming. He broadcast a late-night, black gospel show in the mid-1980s, when the station had turned otherwise to an all-talk format.

Remembered for its music, its disc jockeys, and its advertisements for sponsors such as Red Top Baby Chicks ("50 percent guaranteed to be alive at the time of delivery"), White Rose Petroleum Jelly, and Royal Crown Hair Dressing, the blues era at WLAC entertained a generation of listeners, who probably numbered between 8 and 12 million at its peak. Although programs like *Garden Gate*, featuring "The Old Dirt Dobber" Tom Williams, and a talk show conducted by Nashville media personality Ruth Ann Leach have been very successful, WLAC made its biggest impact during the years when the catch-phrase "This is John R. comin' at ya from way down in Dixie" could regularly be heard.

JESSICA FOY
*Cooperstown Graduate Programs
Cooperstown, New York*

Walter Carter, *Tennessee Showcase* (29 November 1981, 20 December 1981); Ron Courtney, *Goldmine* (February 1984); Nelson George, *Billboard* (19 April 1986); Gerry Wood, *Billboard* (18 June 1983); *The Working Press of the Nation*, vol. 3 (1985).

Wynette, Tammy

(1942–1998) COUNTRY SINGER.
Tammy Wynette was born Virginia Wynette Pugh on 5 May 1942 on a cotton farm in Itawamba County, Miss. Her father, a musician, died when she was eight months old. Tammy's mother left her in the care of her grandparents while she worked in a defense plant in Memphis during World War II. As a young girl Tammy had music lessons, played her father's instruments, and sang in a trio on a local gospel radio show. A month before her high school graduation, Tammy married Eurple Byrd, who proved an unreliable husband. She went to beautician school and worked as a barmaid and singer in Memphis. Tammy left Byrd when she was pregnant with her third child. She made trips to Nashville in pursuit of a country music career and hoped to get her break when she toured briefly with Porter Wagoner. Her failure to do so disappointed her but also made her more determined than ever to succeed.

In 1966 Tammy moved to Nashville with no job, no place to live, and three young daughters dependent on her. She met producer-songwriter Billy Sherrill of Epic records, who signed her and changed her name to Tammy Wynette. Her first single, "Apartment #9," got airplay, and her next song, "Your Good Girl's Going to Go Bad," reached the Top 10. "I Don't Want to Play House" and "D-I-V-O-R-C-E" topped the charts. In 1968, Sherrill and Wynette cowrote the signature song of her career, "Stand By Your Man," which reached No. 1 on country charts and No. 19 on the pop chart. Her next 11 albums went to No. 1, and within four years Wynette had won two Grammy awards and three Country Music Awards as Female Vocalist of the Year.

After a failed second marriage, Wynette married George Jones and had a fourth daughter, Georgette. The extraordinarily popular couple recorded a series of duets, including "Two Story House," "Golden Ring," and "(We're Not) the Jet Set." The couple divorced in 1975. Wynette had one more short, failed marriage before she married her fifth husband, George Richey. In 1979 Wynette published her autobiography *Stand By Your Man*, and two years later ABC broadcast a popular movie adapted from her book.

Wynette's troubled life seemed the stuff of her music. She experienced heartache and divorce, was abducted and beaten, had a death threat, and went through a public bankruptcy. She suffered several serious illnesses. In her successful career, she garnered a total of 20 No. 1 songs and sold over three million records. She continued to be popular throughout her career and continually recorded, earning the title

"First Lady of Country Music." In 1995 she and Jones reunited and recorded an album of duets. Wynette's soulful ballads are powerful and raw, and her lyrics are often complex, with ambiguous meanings revealed by parallel conflicts within the verses and the chorus. She sang of the difficulties of and the inequality within marriage, of the heartache of divorce and the effect on children, of uncaring spouses, and of the struggles of motherhood. Wynette died on 6 April 1998 at age 55. Her nationally televised funeral was held in the Ryman Auditorium in Nashville.

MINOA UFFLEMAN
Austin Peay State University

Jackie Daly, *Tammy Wynette: A Daughter Recalls Her Mother's Tragic Life and Death* (2000); Kenneth E. Morris, in *Popular Music and Society* (1992); Tammy Wynette, *Stand by Your Man* (1979).

Young, Lester

(1909–1959) JAZZ MUSICIAN.
Lester Willis "Pres" Young was an African American tenor saxophonist whose influential style was viewed as revolutionary when first recorded during the late 1930s. He was a primary influence in the development of modern jazz.

Born in Woodville, Miss., Young was the oldest of three children raised in the vicinity of New Orleans. His parents divorced in 1910, and his father remarried and took his children with him to Minneapolis by 1920. Willis "Billy" Handy Young, Lester's father, was a talented musician who taught his children various instruments and later toured the South with his family in a band that played carnivals. Lester studied violin,

trumpet, and drums but turned seriously to the saxophone by age 13. Young left the family band in 1927. He played in the next few years with Art Bronson's Bostonians, Eli Rice's Cotton Pickers, Walter Page's Blue Devils, and Eugene Schuck's Orchestra and with Eddie Barefield at the West Club in Minneapolis.

In the fall of 1933 Young moved to Kansas City, where he played with numerous musicians, including Fletcher Henderson's orchestra and its star saxophonist, Coleman Hawkins. Early in 1934 Young joined William "Count" Basie, beginning an association that was to lead eventually to national recognition. During the mid- to late 1930s Young was prominently featured on recordings and broadcasts with the Basie band. Although Young gained mixed reviews from critics, younger musicians were wildly enthusiastic. Important recordings include "Lester Leans In" (1939) and many accompanying Billie Holiday.

Young left the Basie band in December 1940 to start his own group, which performed in New York in early 1941. He was involved with his own bands after that, in Los Angeles and New York, before freelancing and then rejoining Basie in late 1943. During this second period with Basie, Young garnered the attention of the general public. In 1944 he won first place in the *Down Beat* magazine poll for best tenor saxophonist. He won many awards thereafter and became popular with a new generation of musicians, among them John Coltrane, Sonny Rollins, and Stan Getz. In 1956 Young was voted Greatest Tenor

Saxophonist Ever in a list of prominent jazz musicians.

Young's style changed after 1940. His tone became heavier and his vibrato wider. He was more clearly emotional, using wails, honks, and blue notes in his solos. He was inducted into the army in 1944, beginning a nightmarish experience, which included time spent at a detention barracks in Georgia. After the war he toured with his own small groups. He continued to develop and modify his style and was generally successful, except when his drinking, which was habitual by the early 1950s, weakened him physically. He died in New York in 1959.

Young is a leading example of many great jazz performers who were born and reared in the South but gained fame outside the region. His impact on jazz was profound. His melodic gift and logical phrasing influenced musicians on many instruments, and his personal formulas turned up in countless jazz compositions and improvisations.

LEWIS PORTER
Rutgers University

Frank Buchmann-Moller, *You Got to Be Original, Man! The Music of Lester Young* (1990); Douglas Henry Daniels, *Lester Leaps In: The Life and Times of Lester "Pres" Young* (2003); Luc Delannoy, *Pres: The Story of Lester Young* (1993); Nat Hentoff, in *The Jazz Makers*, ed. Nat Shapiro and Nat Hentoff (1975); J. G. Jensen, *A Discography of Lester Young* (1968); J. M. McDonough, *Lester Young* (1980); David Meltzer, *No Eyes: Lester Young* (2000); Lewis Porter, *The Black Perspective in Music* (Spring 1981), *Lester Young* (1985).

Page numbers in boldface refer to articles.

Fitzgerald, F. Scott, 87
Five Keys, 110
"Five Guys Named Moe," 268
Five Royales, 110
Fiyo on the Bayou, 308
Flatpick Guitar, 26
Flatt, Lester, 25, 28, 346, 362
Fleck, Bela, 28, 29, 30
Flora; Or, Hob in the Well, 43
Florence, Ala., 66
Florida, 21, 35, 60, 131, 165, 226, 230
Florida Folklife Center, 185
Floyd, Carlisle, 47
Floyd, Eddie, 136, 324, 358
Floyd, King, 287
Fly, 215
Flying Burrito Brothers, 315
Flying Fish, 30
Foggy Mountain Boys, 25, 29, 346
Foley, Red, 120, 187, 223, 378
Folk blues, 35, 36, 38
Folk Country, 258
Folklife festival, 66
Folk music, 9–10, 104–5, 224, 278, 342–43
Folkways (recording label), 275, 343, 347, 376
"Folsom Prison Blues," 201
Fontenot, Fremont, 154
Forbes (magazine), 186
Ford, Frankie, 218
Ford, Henry, 65, 228
Ford, Robert "Peg," 233
Ford, Tennessee Ernie, 120, 123
For God and Country, 317
"Forgotten Soldier Boy, The," 102
Forrest, Earl, 271
Fort Lauderdale, Fla., 75
Fortune (magazine), 192
Fort Worth, Tex., 11, 148, 149
Fort Worth Opera, 47
Foster, Leroy, 297
Foster, Stephen, 1, 84, 89, **229–30**, 247
Fountain, Pete, **230–31**
Four Saints in Three Acts, 329
Fowler, Wally, 72

Fox, Oscar, 10
France, 60, 63, 179, 235
Franklin, Aretha, 134, 135, 139, 165, 218, **231–32**, 256, 301
Franklin, Rev. C. L., 181
FreakMaster, 77
Frederick, O. W., 212
French Opera House, 44
Fresh, Mannie, 75, 76
Fresno, Calif., 96
Fried, Walter, 45
Frizzell, Lefty, 54, 82, 264
From the Plantation to the Penitentiary, 290
Fruit Jar Drinkers, 50
Fulbright, J. R., 204
Full Moon, 210
Full Tilt Boogie, 265
Fulson, Lowell, 269
Funk, 110, 135, 291
Funk, Joseph, 70, 128, 349
"Funky Chicken," 59
"Furry Plays the Blues," 276
Furtado, Tony, 29
Fussell, Fred, 342

Gaines, Cassie, 140, 284
Gaines, Ernest, 379
Gaines, Steve, 140, 284
Gaither, William, 69, 73
Galax, Va., 65
Gangsta Boo, 77
Gangsta Pat, 77
Gangsta Grillz, 78
Gant, Cecil, 108
Garcia, Jerry, 28
Garland, Jim, 103
Garlow, Clarence, 204
Garrard, Alice, 185
Garrick Gaieties of 1930, 290
Garrison, Lucy McKim, 144
Garth Brooks, 187
Gastonia, N.C., 101, 102
Gates of Glory, 190
Gaylord Entertainment Company, 237

House, Son, 193
Houseman, John, 225
House of Flowers, 162
Houser, William, 341
Houston, Cisco, 103
Houston, Tex., 13, 106, 149, 253; rap in, 76, 77; R&B in, 111; zydeco in, 152, 154
Houston Grand Opera, 46
Houston Symphony, 45
Howard, Harlan, 305, 330
Howard University, 59
Howell, Peg Leg, 36, **254**
Howlin' Wolf. *See* Burnett, Chester Arthur
Huff, Mary, 354
Hughes, Jimmy, 136
Hughes, Langston, 294, 360
Hulbert, Maurice, 377
Hunter, Charles H., 267
Hunter, Ivory Joe, 108
Hunter, Ma, 183
Hurricane Katrina, 76, 218, 220, 290, 312, 324, 327
Hurt, Mississippi John, **254–55**
Husky, Ferlin, 303
Hustle & Flow, 77, 78, 79

"I Am a Union Woman," 103
I Am What I Am, 265
"I Can Hear Them Singing over There," 190
I Can't Stop, 240
Iceberg Slim, 74
Idlewild, 79, 314
Idlewild South, 165
"I Don't Want Your Millions Mister," 103
I Get Joy, 240
"I Got a Woman," 135, 202
I Got Them Ol' Kozmic Blues Again, Mama, 265
"I Got You (I Feel Good)," 135
"I Hate the Communist System," 103
"I'll Be All Smiles Tonight," 3
"I'll Fly Away," 190
"I Love Beach Music," 176
"I'm a Honky Tonk Girl," 281

I'm 'Bout It, 76
Imitation of Life, 256
Imperial, 109, 219, 311
Impulse! (recording label), 207
Indianapolis, Ind., 36, 85
Indianola, Miss., 272
Industrial Workers of the World, 101
"I Never Loved a Man (The Way I Love You)," 136
Ink Spots, 110
In Old Virginia, 47, 325
Inspirations, 73
Instant (recording label), 307
"Instrumental Music of the Southern Appalachians," 172
International Bluegrass Music Hall of Fame, 297, 317, 346
International Latin Music Hall of Fame, 260
International Submarine Band, 315
Internet, 100, 113
In the Beginning, 233
Iraq, 210, 216
"Irene, Good Night," 274
I.R.S. (recording label), 338
I, Tina (Turner), 373
"It Makes No Difference Now," 81
It's Harder Now, 325
"It's Tight Like That," 379
"It's Your Love," 250
"It Wasn't God Who Made Honky Tonk Angels," 378
"I Walk the Line," 201

Jackson, Al, 138, 358
Jackson, Alan, 15, 54, 55, 192
Jackson, Anthony, 20
Jackson, Aunt Molly, 103
Jackson, Bruce, 74
Jackson, George, 287
Jackson, George Pullen, 130
Jackson, Judge, 131
Jackson, Mahalia, 1, 12, 20, 68, 222, 223, 231, **255–56**
Jackson, Michael, 59, 110, 324

Lone Star Brewing Company, 169

"Long Tall Sally," 323

Look-Ka Py Py, 291

Lord Infamous, 77

Los Angeles, Calif., 12, 103, 106, 209, 218

"Losing My Religion," 339

Lost Horizons, 360

Louisiana, 3, 21, 44, 56, 262, 279, 309, 356, 385; Cajun music in, 39–42, 173–74; French language in, 40, 41; honky-tonk music in, 80; zydeco in, 152–56; swamp pop in, 365–66

Louisiana Blues and Zydeco, 204

Louisiana Folk Foundation, 41

Louisiana Hayride, 53, 112, 264, **279–80**, 327, 382, 383

Louisiana Hot Band, 204

Louisiana Purchase, 63

Louisville Courier-Journal, 246

Louisville Democrat, 246

Louvin Brothers, 73

"Love in Vain," 261

Loveless, Patty, 15, 24, 31, 55

Love Me Tender, 327

"Lovesick Blues," 382

Love Supreme, A, 207

Lovett, Lyle, 240

Loyola University, 111

Luandrew, Andrew, 297

Lubbock, Tex., 251, 257

Lucinda Williams, 385

Ludlow, Noah, 63

Luman, Bob, 119

Lumbee Indians, 66

Lunceford, Jimmie, 87, 177

Lunsford, Bascom Lamar, 66, **280–81**

Luray, Va., 66

Luxury Liner, 244

Lyles, Bill, 180

Lynch, Laura, 215

Lynn, Loretta, 185, 205, **281–82**

Lynyrd Skynyrd, 125, 140, 141, 165, **283–85**

Mac E, 77

Macon, Ga., 13, 124, 136, 139, 165, 188

Macon, Uncle Dave, 51, **285–86**

Macon Ed, 254

Macy, Robin, 215

Maddox Brothers and Rose, 118

Made in New Orleans: The Hurricane Sessions, 327

Mad Max: Beyond Thunderdome, 373

Maguire, Martha "Martie" Erwin, 215

Mahara, W. A., 90

"Mahogany Hall Stomp," 84

Mainer's Mountaineers, 52

Maines, Lloyd, 215

Malaco Records, 182, **286–88**, 302

"Mal Hombre," 93

Malone, Bill C., 183, 204

Malone, David, 270

Malone, Kinney, 270

Malouf, Mitchell, 286

Man amongst Men, A, 214

Mandolin, 25, 29, **288–89**

Man in Black (Cash), 201

"Maple Leaf Rag," 6, 85, 114, 116, 117, 266, 267

"Maps and Legends," 339

Marable, Fate, 87

Ma Rainey's Black Bottom, 334

March on Washington, 256

Mardi Gras, 57, 63, 85, 155, 231. *See also* Carnival

Mardi Gras Indians, 292, 311, 312, 380–81

Mardi Gras in New Orleans, 198

"Margaritaville," 192

Mariachis, 94

Marion, N.C., 101

"Marion Massacre, The," 102

Mar-Keys, 358

Marsalis, Branford, 289

Marsalis, Wynton, 88, **289–90**, 388

Marshall, Arthur, 114

Marshall Tucker Band, 125, 140, 141

Martin, Edsel, 224

Martin, Grady, 304

Martin, Janis, 120

Martin, Mary, 1

Martin, Roberta, 222, 223

Mingus, Charles, 221
Minit (recording label), 307
Minstrel shows, 3, 4, 57–58, 63, **89–91**, 99, 114, 214, 230
"Miss Ann," 323
Mississippi, 21, 31, 37, 262, 263, 385; sacred harp singing in, 128, 131; blues in, 193, 196–97, 269. *See also* Mississippi Delta
Mississippi Blues Commission, 262
Mississippi Delta, 5, 32, 84, 110, 112, 163, 177, 193–94, 208, 255, 256, 261, 262, 271, 318, 337
Mississippi Delta Blues, Volume 2, 196
Mississippi John Hurt: Folk Songs and Blues, 255
Mississippi Public Broadcasting, 113
"Mississippi Rag," 114
Mississippi River, 246, 319
Missouri, 32, 87, 114
Missourians, 87
Mr. Wizard, 197
Mitchell, George, 196
Mitchell, Joni, 276
Mitchell, Lu, 104
Mitchell, Willie, 136, 239, 240
Mi Tierra, 226
Mobile, Ala., 20, 65
Modeliste, Joseph "Zigaboo," 291, 292
Modern Sounds in Country and Western Music, 203
"Molly Darling," 50
Moman, Chips, 136, 301, 324, 356, 357, 358
Monday Night Football, 384
Monk, Thelonious, 88, 207, 221, **294–96**
"Monkey on a Stick," 75
Monroe, Bill, 24, 25, 26, 27, 40, 54, 120, 288, **296–97**, 346
Monroe, Charlie, 24, 288, 296
Monroe, Willa, 377
Monroe Brothers, 24, 52
Monterey Pop Festival, 137, 265, 370
Montgomery, Ala., 104
Montgomery, Bob, 251
Montgomery, Carl, 300
Montgomery, Eurreal "Little Brother," 87

Montgomery, Melba, 264
Montgomery Bus Boycott, 103
Monument Records, 124, 215, 316
Mooche, 58
Moody, Dwight L., 65, 70
Moore, Dorothy, 287
Moore, Gatemouth, 112
Moore, Johnnie, 109
Moore, Oscar, 109
Moore, Scotty, 118, 119
Moore, Wild Bill, 108
Morgan, Sam, 87
Morganfield, McKinley (Muddy Waters), 37, 193, 194, 195, 196, 294, **297–98**
Morlix, Gurf, 385
Morris, Gary, 249
Morton, Charles, 352
Morton, Ferdinand "Jelly Roll," 6, 20, 83, 84, 86, 116, **298–99**, 310
Mose Chronicles, Live in London, Vol. 1, 164
Mosier, Jeff, 141
Most Dulcimer, The, 343
Moten, Bennie, 87
Motown Records, 238
Mountain Dance and Folk Festival, 66
Mountain music, 9, 10
Mountain Music Bluegrass Style, 347
Mountain Soul, 24
Mountain View, Ark., 67
"Move on up a Little Higher," 68
Mt. Olive, Ala., 66
Muddy Waters. *See* Morganfield, McKinley
Mugge, Robert, 197, 270
Muleskinner News, 26
Mullican, Moon, 81, 120
Murder in the Cathedral, 224
Murfreesboro, Tenn., 210, 286
Murmur, 338, 339
Murphey, Michael, 105
Muscle Shoals, Ala., 13, 124, 139, 165, 299–300, 301
Muscle Shoals Rhythm Section, 137
Muscle Shoals Sound, 124, 136, 137, 287, **299–302**, 359